Your All-in-One Resource

On the CD that accompanies this book, you'll find additional resources to extend your learning.

The reference library includes the following fully searchable titles:

- *Microsoft Computer Dictionary*, 5th ed.
- *First Look 2007 Microsoft Office System* by Katherine Murray
- Windows Vista Product Guide

Also provided are a sample chapter and poster from *Look Both Ways: Help Protect Your Family on the Internet* by Linda Criddle.

The CD interface has a new look. You can use the tabs for an assortment of tasks:

- Check for book updates (if you have Internet access)
- Find links to helpful tools and resources
- Go online for product support or CD support
- Send us feedback

The following screen shot gives you a glimpse of the new interface.

Microsoft

Microsoft® Office
Word 2007 Inside Out

Katherine Murray
Mary Millhollon
Beth Melton

PUBLISHED BY
Microsoft Press
A Division of Microsoft Corporation
One Microsoft Way
Redmond, Washington 98052-6399

Library of Congress Control Number: 2007926330

Printed and bound in the United States of America.

2 3 4 5 6 7 8 9   QWT   2 1 0 9 8

Distributed in Canada by H.B. Fenn and Company Ltd.

A CIP catalogue record for this book is available from the British Library.

Microsoft Press books are available through booksellers and distributors worldwide. For further information about international editions, contact your local Microsoft Corporation office or contact Microsoft Press International directly at fax (425) 936-7329. Visit our Web site at www.microsoft.com/mspress. Send comments to mspinput@microsoft.com.

Acquisitions Editor: Juliana Aldous Atkinson
Project Editor: Lynn Finnel
Editorial Production: Custom Editorial Productions, Inc.
Cover Design: Tom Draper Design

Body Part No. X13-24204

Contents at a Glance

Table of Contents

Part 1: Word 2007: Starting Your Document with Latest and Greatest

What do you think of this book? We want to hear from you!

Microsoft is interested in hearing your feedback so we can continually improve our books and learning resources for you. To participate in a brief online survey, please visit:

www.microsoft.com/learning/booksurvey/

Part 3: Visual Elements: Tables, Charts, Diagrams, Pictures

Part 4: Professional Polish: Lists, Styles, Backgrounds, and Borders

Part 5: Collaborative Projects: Shared Documents, Revisions, Security

Part 6: Complex Documents: Sections, Master Documents, and References

Part 7: Publishing: Word to the World

What do you think of this book? We want to hear from you!

Microsoft is interested in hearing your feedback so we can continually improve our books and learning resources for you. To participate in a brief online survey, please visit:

www.microsoft.com/learning/booksurvey/

About the CD

The companion CD that ships with this book contains many tools and resources to help you get the most out of your Inside Out book.

Your Inside Out CD includes the following:

- **Welcome** In this section you'll find the following:
     ❑ Electronic, searchable PDF version of Microsoft Office Word 2007 Inside Out
    ❑ Sample files
    ❑ Quick links to product support, CD support, and other frequently used resources

- **Additional eBooks** In this section you'll find the following eBooks:
    ❑ Microsoft Computer Dictionary, Fifth Edition
    ❑ First Look 2007 Microsoft Office System (Katherine Murray, 2006)
    ❑ Sample chapter and poster from Look Both Ways: Help Protect Your Family on the Internet (Linda Criddle, 2007)
    ❑ Windows Vista Product Guide

- **Extending Office** In this section you'll find third-party tools and Microsoft resources for extending the features of Microsoft Office 2007.

- **Resources** In this section you'll find troubleshooting articles, background documents, blogs, and other resources for using Word 2007.

- **Bonus Content** In this section you'll find additional appendixes for Microsoft Office Word 2007 Inside Out.

System Requirements

The following are the minimum system requirements necessary to run the CD:

- Microsoft Windows Vista, Windows XP with Service Pack (SP) 2, Windows Server 2003 with SP1, or newer operating system

- 500 megahertz (MHz) processor or higher

- 2 gigabyte (GB) storage space (a portion of this disk space will be freed after installation if the original download package is removed from the hard drive)

- 256 megabytes (MB) RAM

- CD-ROM or DVD-ROM drive

- 1024×768 or higher resolution monitor

- Microsoft Windows or Windows Vista–compatible sound card and speakers

- Microsoft Internet Explorer 6 or newer

- Microsoft Mouse or compatible pointing device

> **Note**
>
> An Internet connection is necessary to access the hyperlinks on the companion CD. Connect time charges may apply.

Support Information

Every effort has been made to ensure the accuracy of the contents of the book and of this CD. As corrections or changes are collected, they will be added to a Microsoft Knowledge Base article. Microsoft Press provides support for books and companion CDs at the following Web site:

http://www.microsoft.com/learning/support/books/

If you have comments, questions, or ideas regarding the book or this CD, or questions that are not answered by visiting the site above, please send them via e-mail to:

mspinput@microsoft.com

You can also click the Feedback or CD Support links on the Welcome page. Please note that Microsoft software product support is not offered through the above addresses.

If your question is about the software, and not about the content of this book, please visit the Microsoft Help and Support page or the Microsoft Knowledge Base at:

http://support.microsoft.com

In the United States, Microsoft software product support issues not covered by the Microsoft Knowledge Base are addressed by Microsoft Product Support Services. Location-specific software support options are available from:

http://support.microsoft.com/gp/selfoverview/

Microsoft Press provides corrections for books through the World Wide Web at *www.microsoft.com/mspress/support/*. To connect directly to the Microsoft Press Knowledge Base and enter a query regarding a question or issue that you may have, go to *www.microsoft.com/mspress/support/search.htm*.

Conventions and Features Used in This Book

This book uses special text and design conventions to make it easer for you to find the information you need.

Text Conventions

Convention	Feature
Abbreviated menu commands	For your convenience, this book uses abbreviated menu commands. For example, "Choose Tools, Forms, Design A Form" means that you should click the Tools menu, point to Forms, and select the Design A Form command.
Boldface type	**Boldface type** is used to indicate text that you enter or type.
Initial Capital Letters	The first letters of the names of menus, dialog boxes, dialog box elements, and commands are capitalized. Example: The Save As dialog box.
Italicized type	*Italicized type* is used to indicate new terms.
Plus sign (+) in text	Keyboard shortcuts are indicated by a plus sign (+) separating two key names. For example, Shift+F9 means that you press the Shift and F9 keys at the same time.

Design Conventions

This icon indicates a reference to the book's companion CD.

> **Note**
> Notes offer additional information related to the task being discussed.

Cross-references point you to other locations in the book that offer additional information on the topic being discussed.

> **CAUTION**
> Cautions identify potential problems that you should look out for when you're completing a task, or problems that you must address before you can complete a task.

INSIDE OUT

This statement illustrates an example of an "Inside Out" problem statement

These are the book's signature tips. In these tips, you'll get the straight scoop on what's going on with the software—inside information on why a feature works the way it does. You'll also find handy workarounds to different software problems.

TROUBLESHOOTING

This statement illustrates an example of a "Troubleshooting" problem statement

Look for these sidebars to find solutions to common problems you might encounter. Troubleshooting sidebars appear next to related information in the chapters. You can also use the Troubleshooting Topics index at the back of the book to look up problems by topic.

Sidebar

The sidebars sprinkled throughout these chapters provide ancillary information on the topic being discussed. Go to sidebars to learn more about the technology or a feature.

Introduction

Welcome to Microsoft Office Word 2007 Inside Out—your guide to the next generation of content authoring. Whether you create newsletters, blogs, annual reports, journal articles, or any number of interactive and imaginative documents, Microsoft Office Word 2007 enables you to create, edit, enhance, and share content in just about any print or electronic form you can imagine.

For many people, Microsoft Word is a familiar friend, a regular part of their daily business routine. Office Word 2007 includes the new Microsoft Office Fluent interface, which brings you the tools you need, depending on the task you are performing and the object you have selected. (Chapter 1 introduces you to all the components in the Word 2007 window—that's where you'll learn how to work with the new Microsoft Office Ribbon.) New and experienced Word users will be pleased to discover how easy it is to change the entire format of a document by simply choosing a new theme; dramatically enhance pictures by applying Quick Styles with shadows, frames, and more; create professional, interactive diagrams using SmartArt, and much more. And because Word 2007 is based on the Office Open XML file format, the content you create in Word can be reused in a virtually unlimited number of ways, extending the use of your content to all sorts of print and electronic documents, free from platform restrictions.

The bottom line in Word 2007 is that no matter what your experience level may be, you will be able to create, enhance, and share high-quality, professional, reusable content easier than ever before.

Getting Familiar with Word 2007

If you've been using Word for a long time, you may wonder whether going through the effort of learning the new interface and finding your favorite commands all over again is worth the trouble. We can answer this one easily for you: It is. Word 2007 is not just an incremental release offering feature improvements—it is as close to an entirely new product as you can get. After reviewing years' worth of feedback from thousands of users like you, Microsoft went back to the drawing board and designed a state-of-the-art document authoring program that enables you to quickly create sophisticated, high-quality content that meets the needs of a global, continually connected, and increasingly mobile workforce.

What does this mean to you, as an individual Word 2007 user? Here are just a few of the things you can do:

- Create professionally designed documents easier than ever before

- Compose, format, and save your own building blocks of information so you can insert reusable content as needed

- Choose from among a huge array of formatting possibilities for text, pictures, diagrams, and more

- Change the look of your entire document by selecting a different theme

- Easily include content controls that enable you to integrate your business processes with the documents you create (no programming required)

- Simplify the mailings you do using the enhanced mail merge features

- Post to a blog from directly within Word

The various parts and chapters in this book walk you through the process of using Word 2007 in various aspects of document creation. Along the way, you'll discover tips, tricks, and troubleshooting ideas that will help you get the most out of the new program.

> **Note**
>
> We want to send out a big "Thank you!" to Stuart Stuple and Tristan Davis for reviewing key chapters, answering our questions, and recommending additional tips and techniques.

About This Book

Microsoft Office Word 2007 Inside Out is divided into eight major parts, each of which focuses on a specific aspect of document creation:

Part 1 provides an introduction to Word 2007 (including a detailed tour of the new user interface) and walks you through tasks you'll use to create your first documents quickly.

- Chapter 1 explores the way our working world has evolved since the early days of Microsoft Word, and shows how the new changes in Word 2007 are uniquely designed to meet the global demands of an always-on workforce.

- Chapter 2 provides you with all the basics for document creation and includes content on sharing documents with those using previous versions of Word.

- Chapter 3 describes the importance of setting up your page and controlling pagination.

- Chapter 4 shows you how to use professionally designed templates as the basis for documents of all kinds.

- Chapter 5 introduces you to themes, a great time-saving and format-enhancing feature that enables you to change the font, color, and effects of your document with a single click of the mouse.

Part 2 focuses on developing the skills you'll use as you create and work with content in your documents.

- Chapter 6 covers all the fundamental concepts for editing documents in Word 2007, the new Equation builder , and another technological advancement to document creation, bound Document Property fields.

- Chapter 7 shows you the ins and outs of navigating through your document using a variety of different methods.

- Chapter 8 explains how to use various text tools that are designed to help you speed up typing repetitive text, such as utilizing Building Blocks, AutoCorrect, and Math AutoCorrect, which brings the new Equation Builder functionality to your fingertips.

- Chapter 9 shows you how to use translation, research, and reference tools; proofread your document, set language options for proofing, and set proofing exceptions.

- Chapter 10 discusses how to use the outlining features to organize your thoughts and create a roadmap for your content so that you can work with it easily.

Part 3 takes a look at all things visual—in this part of the book you learn how to work with pictures, diagrams, charts, WordArt, and more.

- Chapter 11 introduces you to ways you can create tables to display your information in a structured way. Using the Table Styles gallery, you can choose a professional look for your table, create new table templates you use repeatedly, or customize the look of your tables.

- Chapters 12 and 13 teach you everything you need to know about creating, enhancing, and working with art objects of all kinds in your documents. You'll find out how to add SmartArt diagrams and charts to your pages, and insert drawings, photos, WordArt, and clip art to your document as well.

Part 4 shows you how to make the most of formatting features in Word 2007.

- Chapter 14 shows you how to create and control the format of paragraphs and lists in your document.

- Chapter 15 introduces you to styles and shows you how to customize the format of various items by creating, modifying, and saving styles you can use repeatedly in your documents.

- Chapter 16 explores ways you can change the format of page backgrounds, text boxes, and frames.

- Chapter 17 shows you how to make sections or pages of your document stand out by adding borders and shading to selected areas.

Part 5 is all about sharing your documents with others.

- Chapter 18 provides an overview of how you can share your documents with others. In this chapter you learn to work with shared workspaces, save files to the network server, use shared templates, and more.

- Chapter 19 discusses specific ways to collaborate with others who will be revising your document. Learn to track, evaluate, and merge changes in your document.

- Chapter 20 covers the security features in Word that enable you to remove sensitive data before sharing files, add protection to selected areas and tasks, and work with IRM (available only with selected Office 2007 suites).

Part 6 covers the tasks you are likely to need when you are working with long or complex documents.

- Chapter 21 teaches you how add and control columns in your document; additionally, you'll learn how to create and work with sections.

- Chapter 22 shows you how to work with master documents and subdocuments in your long document.

- Chapter 23 introduces you to the process of adding citations—including footnotes and endnotes--to your document.

- Chapter 24 shows you how to create a table of contents and add other reference tables to make features in your document easier to find.

- Chapter 25 walks you through the steps for creating and formatting an index for your long document.

Part 7 shows you how to publish your content in a variety of ways.

- Chapter 26 provides all the ins and outs of printing in Word.

- Chapter 27 covers how to write and post content to a blog from within Word.

- Chapter 28 shows you how to use Word's mail merge feature to create mailings you can distribute in a variety of ways.

- Chapter 29 introduces content controls in Word and shows you how you can easily incorporate your business processes directly into your documents.

- Chapter 30 covers Open XML in Word, spotlighting the big changes in the native file format and introducing the ways you can work with XML in your documents.

- Chapter 31 shows you how to create, manage, and use macros in Word and explores using Visual Basic to add functionality to your documents.

Appendixes A through E are included on the CD.

- Appendix A explains how to install Word 2007, as well as upgrade and repair Word installations.

- Appendix B introduces the various ways you can customize Word to fit your needs. Additionally, you'll learn about the accessibility features in this appendix.

- Appendix C is all about Multilanguage support in Word 2007.

- Appendix D provides the MOS Word 2007 Standards.

- Appendix E introduces you to some of the popular Word 2007 add-ins and shows you how to add them to Word.

Room to Create with Office Word 2007

Welcome to a whole new way of creating, editing, enhancing, and sharing the documents you create. Take those file folders full of dot-matrix text-only printed reports and pitch them. Throw away the whiteout. Leave behind those boring, routine, ho-hum marketing plans; file the black-and-white mugshot personnel photos; and forget that you ever had to learn how to use a three-hole punch.

This is all said a bit tongue-in-cheek, but we want you to be ready for something new. Perhaps you've been using Microsoft Office Word for a long time and you love it—that's great. Office Word 2007 has something new for you. Maybe you've never really spent a lot of time creating documents, and you're about to learn the art of creating complex documents for your new job. Word 2007 offers you a powerful, but uncomplicated way to find just what you need to accomplish the tasks specific to your project.

Whether you're a new or experienced Word user, you are about to enter a creative new world that enables you to produce the high-energy, colorful, professional documents you envision—all in a fraction of the time it previously took—using a single, multifaceted and intuitive tool: Microsoft Office Word 2007.

Word 2007 includes many features that make creating professional documents as easy as possible. You can start your document based on professionally designed templates; you can apply quick styles to the text, charts, and images in your document to ensure a high-quality look. Another feature enables you to create and save blocks of text you use repeatedly in your documents, which cuts down on the time you spend typing or copying and pasting—and reduces the margin for error created when you have to rekey information multiple times. These features are just the tip of the iceberg! Before we get into the new features of Word, though, let's take a quick look at how far Word has come.

A Quick Look Back: The Origins of Word

Those of us who have been using Word since its beginning in 1983 have a certain fondness for the program. It's like watching a favorite family member grow...and grow...and grow.

The earliest version of Word was revolutionary in that it enabled us to significantly re-duce much of the repetitive work involved in the tedious tasks we had to perform—for example, typing the minutes of a board meeting or writing a school essay. With Word, we could save our files and cut, copy, and paste information we'd already entered; there were menus and they could be used with shortcut keys and a mouse, greatly speeding up numerous tasks. Typing a report no longer required correction tape; and you could make headings stand out (what did we ever do without boldface?) and be sure your page numbers would print in the same spot on every page.

When the first version of Word for Windows was released in 1989, it had only two toolbars. That was plenty for us at the time. We were thrilled to have that much func-tionality. When the next version of Word arrived three years later, it had the same two toolbars, but new nested dialog boxes provided an expanded range of choices for the documents we created.

Then came a period of enormous growth in functionality and features (see Table 1-1). Between 1989 and 2003, Word exploded, feature-wise. Users loved having a huge range of choices for their documents, and having a word processing program that could "do it all" was a definite plus when you were responsible for producing many kinds of documents. But all this power and flexibility came at a price. The previous version of Word, Word 2003, has 31 toolbars, 19 task panes, context menus, dockable menus, hierarchical menus, and expanding menus. How in the world will you find the commands you need in order to accomplish what you set out to do today? If the docu-ment you're creating is something you've done a dozen times before, you already know where the commands you need are located—but what if you're trying something new? How will you find just what you need? Better leave yourself plenty of time for explora-tion.

Table 1-1 **The Growth of Word**

Release	Screen resolution	Toolbars	Added Features
Word for Windows 1.0 (1989)	640 × 480	2	
Word for Windows 2.0 (1992)	640 × 480	2	Nested dialog boxes
Microsoft Word 6.0 (1994)	800 x 600	8	Right-click contextual menus, ScreenTips, tabbed dialog boxes, toolbars on bottom of screen, wizards
Microsoft Word 95 (1995)	800 x 600	9	Auto spell-check, Auto features (such as AutoCorrect)
Microsoft Word 97 (1996)	1024 x 768	18	Toolbars all around screen and floating, redockable menu bar, multilevel context menus, icons on menus, grammar check-ing, hierarchical pull-down menus, Office assistant

Release	Screen resolution	Toolbars	Added Features
Microsoft Word 2000 (1999)	1024 x 768	23	Expanding menus, default toolbars on a single row, help pane
Microsoft Word 2002 (2001)	1024 x 768	30	Task panes, Type A Question For Help box, Smart Tags, Paste options
Microsoft Word 2003 (2003)	1024 x 768	31	11 new task panes, Research features

As you will see in this chapter and throughout the book, the 2007 release of Word makes it easier for us to access what's really important in a first-class word processing program. Great features have been there all along, and some were easier to find than others. By simplifying the entire user interface, bringing just the right tools to you when you're working on specific tasks, and offering a large collection of professionally designed themes, color palettes, and galleries of predefined styles, table formats, headers and footers, and more, this latest version of Word helps you create high-quality, effective documents files you can share easily with others—in less time than it would take you to wade through all the menus in Word 2003.

> **Note**
>
> For an interesting behind-the-scenes look at the design choices that went into the dramatic user interface changes in MIcrosoft Office 2007, see Office program manager Julie Larson-Green's video on Channel 9: *http://channel9.msdn.com/Showpost.aspx?postid=114720*.

A Whole New Way of Working: Word 2007 Changes

To say that the world has changed since the early days of Word for DOS would be a huge understatement. Going to work in the early 1980s meant getting in the car (or on the train) and traveling the half-hour to the office, where you would open your diary and run your finger down the page, scanning the appointments you had made for first thing in the morning. Meetings were always face-to-face or on the phone; appointments with clients required driving; and reports, newsletters, and marketing materials took weeks—if not months—and big budgets to produce.

Now fast-forward to 2007. The latest statistics we have on the world of work tell us that, for example, in the United States, 20.8 million people do some amount of work at home as part of their primary job. This includes almost 30 percent of workers in management, professional, and related roles. Additionally, approximately 1 in 5 sales professionals report working from home.

In addition to this flexible workplace, we have a global workforce. Companies may have work teams or vendors all over the globe; you can draft a document in Seattle in the morning and others may be reviewing it in Ireland, China, and New York by lunchtime. Worldwide cooperative creative writing is possible with Word used in conjunction with Microsoft Office Groove or Microsoft Office SharePoint. We need to be able to contact each other instantly and share files easily and securely.

Not only have the walls of our offices come down, but the obstacles that used to make it difficult (and expensive!) to create high-color, professional-quality documents have all but been erased. Now many of us have the capacity for color printing on our desktops (or at least down the hall). We can print our own reports, design and produce newsletters, and customize our own mass mailings by using our own know-how and the software on our computers. The tasks that used to require a whole team of people—writer, designer, photographer, layout artist, proofreader—are now often being completed by a single person (although the graphic art may not be as good!). This enables us to create really fine documents at a fraction of the cost, in far less time, while retaining control of the project by keeping it in-house.

What the Work World Needs Today

One of the huge challenges this kind of flexibility and power brings is that we can do so much and do it so quickly that we need to be able to make quick decisions about what we want and need to focus on right away. What task is really at hand, right now? Which document should you work on this morning, knowing you need to do something completely different this afternoon? We need to be able to make choices about our priorities and then act on them without a lot of clutter on our desktops or distractions in our minds.

If you're like most of us, you know that's not always an easy thing to do.

No matter what our roles at work, to be successful today, we need to somehow be able to balance the following critical needs:

- To gather and process information accurately and efficiently to make sound business decisions (and weed out the irrelevant data we receive)

- To connect with others (customers, vendors, employees, peers, managers, and stakeholders) in a timely and effective way

- To learn about and use tools that help us complete tasks, manage relationships, track business processes, and demonstrate professional results

- To produce quality materials that help move our company or department toward its established goals (for example, increased awareness, improved client satisfaction, enhanced partnerships)

Enter Word 2007

The teams responsible for the design of Office have been listening and learning from Office users for years. Their research involves conducting detailed observation, data records, studies and focus groups; going out into the field and talking with users; and gathering, reading, and analyzing the data they receive from those users who chose to participate in the Office 2003 Customer Experience Improvement Program. The huge changes you see in Office 2007 are a direct result of what users have said they need. Here's a quick list of the design goals for the 2007 release as they specifically relate to Word:

- **Make the product easier to use** The first thing you'll notice about Word is that the new design does away with the over-abundance of text-heavy toolbars and the layers of nested dialog boxes. Word now brings you the tools you need to complete the task you're working on. The tabs on the Ribbon (we'll cover this in more detail in the next section) offer groups that are related to the next step in the natural process of creating a document, so finding the command you need next is simple and intuitive.

  Because the tools you see are related to the context in which you're working, you're likely to discover tools you didn't know about before. If you're adding a header, for example, you will see how easy it is to create a different header for the first page of a document, because the Ribbon displays all options related to headers in one easy-to-see area (see Figure 1-1).

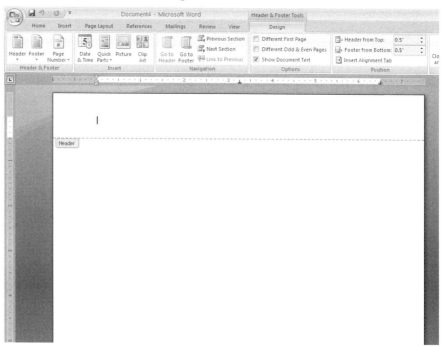

Figure 1-1 The Ribbon displays the contextual Header & Footer Tools, which contains all options related to headers so that you can find what you need easily when you add a header to your document.

- **Help you become more efficient** The redesign saves you time by making the options you need easier to find; the flexibility in the way you can now work with Word (choosing primary mouse-based or keyboard-based techniques) enables you to choose the work style you like best. Choosing templates is now easier and more intuitive (and the selection is greatly expanded), and the addition of many predesigned elements—cover pages, pull quotes, equations, sidebars, and more—enables you to add professional elements to your page with a click of the mouse button. Document Themes and Quick Parts (content you can customize to fit your own document needs) make it easy to ensure that your document looks professional quickly. File sizes are smaller, and expanded support for Windows SharePoint Services makes it easier than ever to share files with others. If you enjoy blogging, you'll be pleased to know that you don't have to leave Word to add a post to your favorite blog.

- **Make it easier to find what you need** Enhanced ScreenTips help you understand how a feature can be used and provide a link for more detailed help. Live Preview lets you see the effect of a change (such as a style, font, or color) before you select it. Galleries display a range of choices you can select quickly without digging through multilayered menus. Additionally, Help is another feature that received a facelift as result of user feedback. The new interface enables you to search online and offline content with a click of the mouse, and the Table of Contents is synchronized with the displayed Help topic, making it easier than ever to find the answer to your query.

- **Make it easier to create great professional-quality documents** In addition to the expanded template collection that is available when you create a new document in Word, you can now share your templates with others or display user-reviewed templates as part of the selection process. Galleries and Live Preview show you instantly what the predesigned content items—headers and footers, pull quotes, sidebars, and more—will look like when you add them to your page. Choose from among dozens of professionally designed color and font schemes, and add special touches—such as shadows, rotation, and glow—to your pictures.

This list provides just a quick glimpse of some of the ways in which Word 2007 improves and streamlines the way we can work today. As you begin to use the program, however, the dramatic changes begin to sink in. Let's start off by taking a closer look at the Word 2007 window.

Getting Familiar with the Word 2007 User Interface

The new design of the user interface throughout the primary Office 2007 applications has received a lot of press. Early reactions were generally positive—people were intrigued by the idea that Office designers went "back to the drawing board" when they began brainstorming about the new look and feel of the user interface.

Office 2007 Beta 2 was downloaded more than 3 million times in its first two months of availability—that's a lot of people, worldwide, testing out the new user interface! Experienced users were wary—why fix what's not broken?—and power users wondered whether the simplified design would make it impossible to use the shortcuts, macros, and more they had come to rely on to expedite their document tasks.

John Obeto, editor of SmallBizVista.com and an experienced Office user, put it this way when he was asked what he thought of the new Office 2007 design: "Liked it, then hated it, now starting to really like it. Like the fact that I could do more without think-ing initially, then started to hate the fact that a lot of my now conditioned (Pavlovian?) responses/shortcuts were no longer effective. Furthermore, while a lot more commands and functions are exposed, customization is now hidden several levels deep, prompting me to scream several times! However, more time spent on it, and breaking in new users on it re-started the love affair, as training seems to be shorter, with more accomplished."

At the end of the day, the positive response carried. New users were able to find what they needed easily; and expert users—particularly those who are involved in training other users—seemed happy with the level of flexibility and customization (and the fact that they could continue using all their favorite shortcuts from Word 2003 in their Word 2007 documents).

Find What You Need, Intuitively

When you open Word 2007 for the first time, you will immediately notice that the screen looks more open and inviting. Figure 1-2 shows the Word 2007 window.

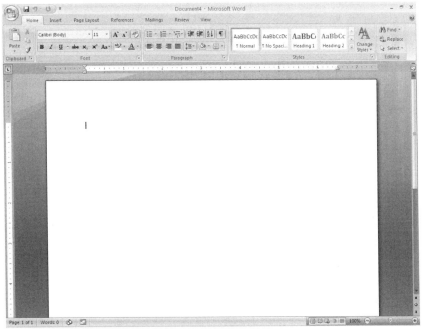

Figure 1-2 The Word 2007 window.

Exploring the Ribbon

You'll see the word *Ribbon* used to describe the new tool area stretching across the top of the Word window. This is the place you'll find the commands you need when you are working with your document in different ways. For example, when you create the document, the Home tab provides the commands you are likely to use as you start out. When you're ready to share your document with others, the Review tab offers a variety of tools for preparing the file for review and working with the review copies when you receive them. The Ribbon actually is made up of several important elements:

- Tabs (Home, Insert, Page Layout, References, Mailings, Review, and View) stretch across the screen just below the window's title bar.

- Groups are collections of commands available on the Ribbon when a specific tab is selected. For example, when the Insert tab is selected, the groups displayed include Pages, Tables, Illustrations, Links, Header & Footer, Text, and Symbols.

- Contextual tabs help keep the window uncluttered by displaying task-related commands only when an object is selected in the document. When you select a picture, for example, the contextual Picture Tools appears along the top of the Ribbon. The commands displayed when the tab is selected all relate to the object you've selected (see Figure 1-3).

Figure 1-3 Contextual tabs appear above the Ribbon when an object is selected in the document.

> **Note**
>
> The Ribbon is fully displayed by default when you begin working with Word. If you want to minimize the Ribbon to get maximum room on the screen, press Ctrl+F1. The Ribbon reduces to the tabs only. To redisplay the Ribbon, press Ctrl+F1 again. If you want to reduce the display of the Ribbon to only the tabs, you can double-click any tab to minimize it. Then, to redisplay the full Ribbon, simply double-click any tab.

A Major Redesign for the File Menu

The File menu has been given a makeover as well. Now, instead of the word *File* appearing on the far left side of the window, you see the Microsoft Office 2007 logo. This is called the Microsoft Office Button, and changes from the old File menu aren't simply cosmetic—the new design includes two panels that add a whole new level of functionality. On the left, you see the major file tasks, such as New, Open, Save, and Print; on the right, you see subchoices of those major tasks. For example, when you position the mouse over Print, the choices shown in Figure 1-4 appear.

Figure 1-4 The Microsoft Office Button provides you with additional choices when you select the major commands.

> **Tip**
> One of the first things you'll see when you click the Microsoft Office Button is the new expanded Recent Documents list. This is a great way to get to your favorite documents directly, without using the Open dialog box.

The order of the options on the Microsoft Office Button follows the basic progression of the life cycle of your document. Two great new additions include the Prepare command, which provides you with options for completing the document, and the Publish command, which includes commands that enable you to post to a blog, publish the document to a document server, or share the document on a shared document workspace.

Choose File Tasks Quickly with the Quick Access Toolbar

Just to the right of the Microsoft Office Button is a new feature called the Quick Access Toolbar. On this three familiar tools appear: Save, Undo, and Redo. You can customize the Quick Access Toolbar to include other tools you use regularly. For example, if you blog, you can add the Blog tool to the Quick Access Toolbar by clicking the Microsoft Office Button, pointing to the Publish command, and right-clicking the Blog subcommand. Finally, select Add To Quick Access Toolbar (see Figure 1-5).

Figure 1-5 Add your favorite tools to the Quick Access Toolbar.

> **Note**
>
> If you add a number of tools to the Quick Access Toolbar, you may want to give it more room by displaying the toolbar in its own row below the Ribbon. Right-click anywhere on the Ribbon and choose Show Quick Access Toolbar Below The Ribbon. To return the display of the toolbar to its original state, right-click the Quick Access Toolbar and choose Show Quick Access Toolbar Above The Ribbon.

Using Dialog Launchers

The Ribbon is great for providing you with groups of commands that are related to the task at hand, but at times you need to be able to choose from among a large selection of options. In those cases, having a traditional-style dialog box comes in handy. Dialog boxes are available for some groups on the Ribbon. You can tell which ones have a dialog box by looking for the small boxed arrow symbol, called a dialog launcher, in the lower right corner of a group. For example, the Font group on the Home tab has a dialog launcher in the lower right corner. When you click the launcher, the dialog box appears (Figure 1-6).

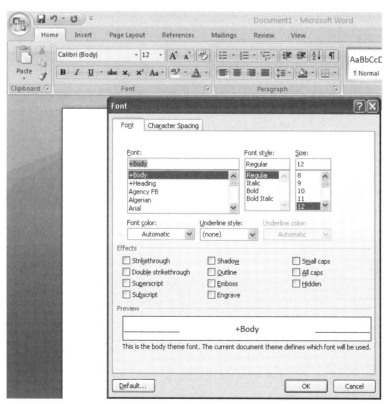

Figure 1-6 Dialog launchers display dialog boxes.

Options for displaying dialog boxes are also available at the bottom of any gallery that offers additional options. For example, when you click Columns in Page Layout group, a gallery of column settings appears. Click the More Columns option at the bottom of the gallery to launch the Columns dialog box (see Figure 1-7).

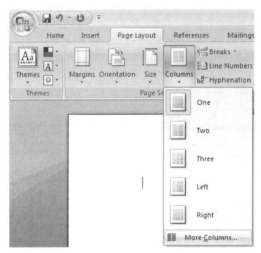

Figure 1-7 Click the More command at the bottom of a gallery to display additional options.

Applying and Using Themes

One of the great additions to Word 2007 is the far-reaching themes feature. When you apply a theme to your Word document, the theme applies a set of coordinated formatting choices—including fonts, colors, table styles, chart styles, special effects, and more—throughout your document. The beauty here is that you can apply and change themes with literally a click of the mouse button, and the choices displayed in the various galleries in Word are all coordinated to match the theme you have chosen for the document.

You apply a theme to your document by clicking Themes on the Page Layout tab (see Figure 1-8). The palette of themes appears so that you can click your choice. If you want to change the theme later, you can simply return to the Themes gallery and click the new theme you want to apply.

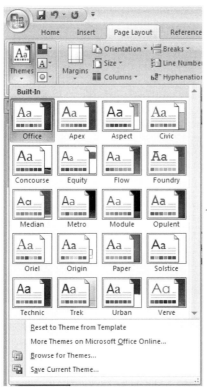

Figure 1-8 The theme you choose for your document helps you make formatting choices for all the elements in your document with a single click.

Working with Galleries

Word now includes all sorts of galleries—themes, styles, WordArt, and more—that graphically display your range of choices so that you can click the design, color, layout, and style you want. You will see galleries displayed in different ways, depending on your screen resolution and the size of the Word window. The Ribbon was designed to adjust to the size of the screen, so in some cases you may see galleries appear as selections on the Ribbon, while other galleries appear as drop-down items.

Basically you'll see galleries represented two ways in Word. Some galleries are shown as part of a group on the Ribbon (similar to the Picture Styles gallery shown in Figure 1-9); you can click the More button in the lower right corner of the gallery to display the full collection of choices. Other galleries (such as those available for Themes, Margins, and Position commands) display as drop-down galleries so that you can make your selection.

More button

Figure 1-9 Some galleries display a few choices in the tab of a selected tab.

Other galleries open as a palette of choices, like the WordArt gallery shown in Figure 1-10. Using galleries, you can easily see at a glance which color combination, format, color scheme, transition, or chart type you want. The choices you see in the galleries are connected with the theme you've selected for your document, which helps you be sure that when you're choosing a chart type, for example, it reflects the colors, fonts, and effects used in other parts of your document.

To choose an option in a gallery, simply click your choice, and the setting is applied to the current document or selected object.

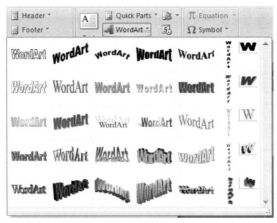

Figure 1-10 Some galleries open as palettes, enabling you to easily see which choice fits your project.

Using Live Preview

Live Preview is a great new feature that lets you see how a change will look before you make it. When you point to an option in a list or gallery (such as the Quick Styles gallery shown in Figure 1-11), the effect is applied temporarily to your document so that you can see how it will look. If you want to keep the change, click the option. If you want to keep looking, point to a different option.

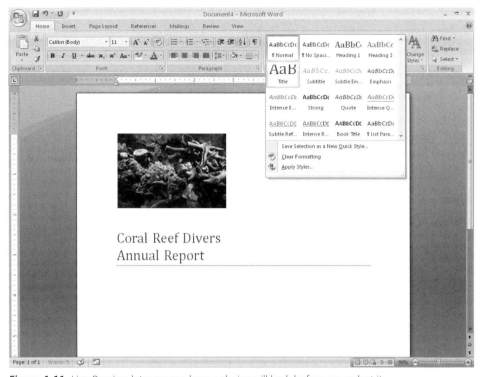

Figure 1-11 Live Preview lets you see how a choice will look before you select it.

> **Note**
>
> Live Preview is especially helpful when you are trying to get just the right look for a specific item. Use Live Preview to quickly test out different styles, select chart options, add shadow or glow to a picture, or choose another document theme, color, or background.

Making Quick Formatting Changes with the Mini Toolbar

If you're like other Word users, many of the choices you make while you're working on a document have to do with formatting. Another new feature in Word 2007 brings the most common formatting options to you so that you don't have to leave your creative zone to choose the options you want. Whenever you select text, the new Mini Toolbar appears above the text you selected (see Figure 1-12). If you want to use the Mini Toolbar, move the mouse toward it and select the option you want; otherwise, move the mouse pointer away so that it fades out.

Figure 1-12 The Mini Toolbar displays quick formatting choices whenever you select text.

> **Note**
>
> If you find the Mini Toolbar distracting or don't think you'll use it, you can turn off the feature by clicking the Microsoft Office Button and choosing Word Options (in the lower right corner of the menu). In the Popular section, click the Show Mini Toolbar On Selection check box to clear it. Then click OK. Now the Mini Toolbar is disabled and will not appear the next time you select text. (It will appear, however, when you right-click selected text.) To reactivate the MiniToolbar, display the Options dialog box again and reselect the check box.

Viewing Documents in Different Lights

While you're working on your document, you can easily change to a different view by clicking one of the view tools in the bottom right corner of the Word window or by clicking the View tab and choosing a view in the Document Views group. You can also use the new Zoom slider (in the lower right corner of the Word window) to enlarge or reduce the display of the document. Word offers you many different ways to view your work, depending on the type of document you're creating and the task at hand:

- Print Layout view seems to be the view most people use as they create and edit their documents. This view, which is used by default when you create a new document, shows how the document will look when printed. In this view, you can see headers and footers, as well as footnotes and endnotes. The edges of the page and the space between pages are also visible as you type and edit.

> **Tip**
>
> You can alternately suppress and display the top and bottom margins of your document in Page Layout view by double-clicking the space between the pages. By default, Page Layout view shows a gap between pages. Position the pointer over the page break, and the pointer changes to two arrows. A tooltip prompts you to double-click the space to remove it. Double-click at that point, and the space between the pages is removed, enabling you to view text before and after the break in a continuous paragraph. To return the page display to the default setting, position the pointer over the page break line and double-click.

- Full Screen Reading view gives you the maximum amount of space on the screen so that you can review and comment on the file. Note, however, that Full Screen Reading view does not display the document as it will look in print—that's the job of Page Layout view. By default, when you first begin using Full Screen Reading view, the functionality is limited to only reviewing and commenting. If you want to be able to type and edit in Full Screen Reading view, click View Options in the upper right corner of Full Screen Reading view and choose Allow Typing (see Figure 1-13).

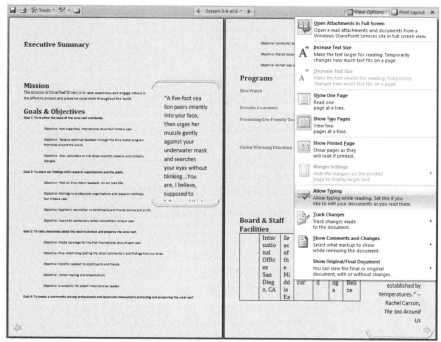

Figure 1-13 Full Screen Reading view enables you to view, comment on, and edit your document with a maximum amount of room on the screen.

- Web Layout view displays the page as though it were a Web page. The first thing you will notice when you select the Web Layout view tool is that the page margins are not used, and depending on the content of your document, the format of your document may seem skewed (see Figure 1-14).

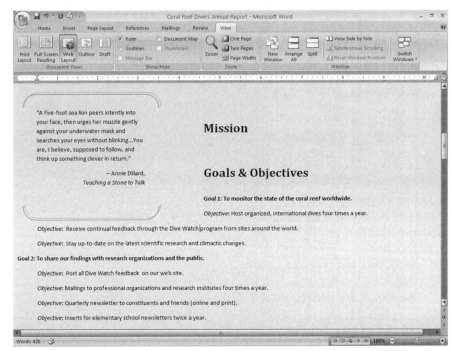

Figure 1-14 Web Layout view shows you what your document will look like as a Web page.

- Outline view enables you to see the document in outline form, with headings and subordinate text indented so that you can easily identify and work with sections in a long document.

- Draft view (formerly known as Normal view) is a fast, no-frills mode that many people prefer to use when they need to write or edit something quickly. Note that some elements—such as headers and footers—are not visible while you're working in Draft view.

Using Special Views: Document Map and Thumbnails

In addition to these five primary working views, Word 2007 enables you to use other views to navigate through longer documents. The Document Map is a panel along the left side of the work area that provides you with clickable headings you can use to navigate to different sections in your document (see Figure 1-15). This feature is really useful when you are moving back and forth among sections.

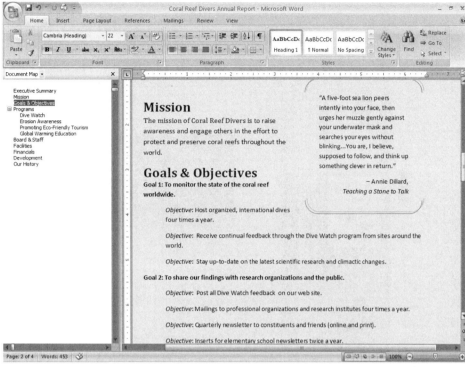

Figure 1-15 The Document Map gives you a panel of clickable headings you can use to navigate among sections in a long or complex document.

Thumbnails view also enables you to easily see how your document is shaping up. When you click Thumbnails in the Show/Hide group of the View tab, the left panel opens, displaying your document with the pages represented graphically. This is a great view when layout is important, and you want to create a sense of flow and variety in your document (see Figure 1-16).

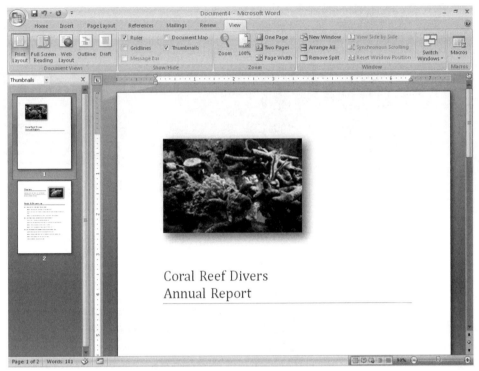

Figure 1-16 Thumbnails view enables you to see miniature graphical representations of the pages in your document.

A New View for Headers and Footers

Word 2007 provides expanded support for working with headers and footers. When you create a header or footer (by clicking the Insert tab, choosing Header or Footer from the Header & Footer group, and choosing the design you want by selecting it from the gallery), the header and footer area opens. The cursor is positioned in the header or footer, and a full array of contextual Header & Footer Tools are displayed in a tab along the top of the Ribbon.

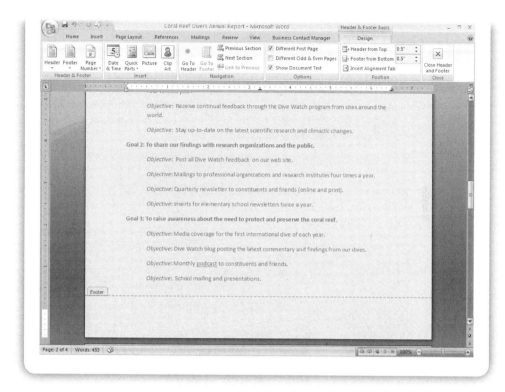

Chapter 1

Displaying Rulers and Gridlines

When you are working on a document in which the alignment and sizing of elements is important, you will want to turn on rulers and gridlines to make sure items line up on the page and meet the measurements you need. The controls for both items are found in the Show/Hide group in the View tab.

There's a new tool located at the top of the vertical scrollbar that enables you to display and hide rulers quickly. The rulers are displayed by default, so to hide the rulers, click the View Ruler button. The rulers are removed. To redisplay the rulers, click the tool a second time.

Alternatively, you can display vertical and horizontal rulers by clicking the View tab and then clicking the Ruler check box. To hide the rulers, click the Ruler check box to clear it.

> **Note**
>
> If you don't like rulers cluttering up your work area and you want to remove the vertical ruler in Print Layout view, you can turn it off using Word Options. Click the Microsoft Office Button and choose Word Options. Choose Advanced and scroll down to the Display options. Click the last option in the group, Show Vertical Ruler In Page Layout View, to clear the option's check box. Now click OK to save your changes. When you return to Print Layout view, the vertical ruler will be gone.

Adding gridlines is a similar process. Choose View and click the Gridlines check box. Gridlines appear on your document so that you can easily align pictures, quotes, or other elements on your page (see Figure 1-17).

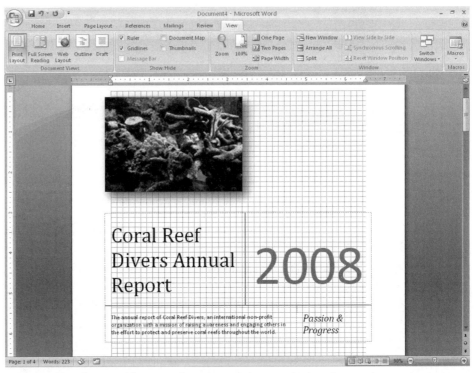

Figure 1-17 Gridlines enable you to align pictures, charts, and other elements in your document.

Viewing More Than One Page at a Time

The Zoom group in the View tab includes five different tools that enable you to change the size and number of pages you view on the screen at any one time. Page Width view is selected by default, but you can easily change the view to match your own comfort level.

To change the size of the text, click the Zoom tool. The Zoom dialog box opens so that you can choose one of the preset sizes or specify your own by clicking in the Percent box and typing a new value (see Figure 1-18). You can also change the number of pages displayed by clicking the Many Pages button and dragging to select the number of pages you want to display on the screen. The Preview window shows you how your document will look, and the sample text area shows how readable (or not!) your text will be. When you've made changes you are happy with, click OK to save them.

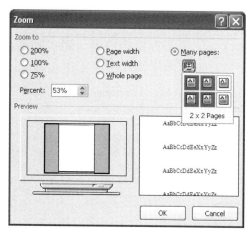

Figure 1-18 Use the Zoom dialog box to change the way your document is displayed.

Back on the View tab, you can switch among multipage views easily by clicking the One Page, Two Pages, or Page Width tools. Each of these tools behaves the way you would expect—One Page shows you the whole page at the cursor position; Two Pages displays the page on which the cursor is active and the next full page in the document; and Page Width magnifies or reduces the size of the document so that it fits the width of the Word window.

Working with Multiple Documents

When you are working on a big project, chances are that you will have more than one document open at the same time. If you're copying and pasting your research notes into a new journal article you're writing, or if you're incorporating the latest fundraising figures in the annual report, you'll need an easy way of moving among open documents while you work. The View tab includes the Window group to give you the means to do just that.

When you want to easily move among open Word documents, use the Switch Windows tool. When you click Switch Windows, a list shows you the various open windows; just click the one you want to see.

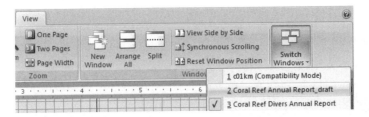

Use the New Windows command when you want to open a new copy of the current document in a new window. You might use this command so you can edit different portions of a large document at the same time instead of endlessly scrolling back and forth. When you're ready to close the copy, click the close button.

For more about reviewing, comparing, and merging documents, see Chapter 19, "Sharing Documents and Collaborating Online"

The Arrange All, Split, and View Side By Side commands all enable you to choose how you want to view the open documents. View Side By Side displays the Compare Side By Side dialog box so that you can choose the other open document you want to compare with the current one. Select your choice and click OK to display the document.

> **Note**
> Depending on the number of open document windows and your screen resolution when you use the Arrange All command, the Ribbon may disappear. This happens due to the auto scale feature of the Ribbon. To return the full view of the Ribbon, simply resize the height of the document window.

When you use the View Side By Side command, Word sets the default to Synchronous Scrolling, which means that as you scroll through one document, the other document scrolls automatically. This is helpful for comparing documents in which you're looking for paragraphs, sections, or even phrases that might be slightly different (see Figure 1-19).

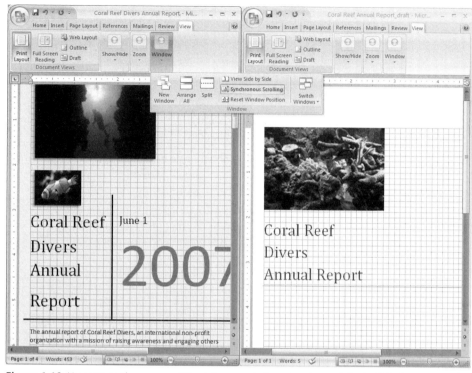

Figure 1-19 You can easily compare Word documents by using the tools in the Window group of the View tab.

> **Note**
>
> If you also like open documents to appear as a single task on your Windows Taskbar, you can use Word Options to display them that way. Click the Microsoft Office Button, choose Word Options, and then click Advanced. Scroll down to the Display options and click "Show All Windows In The Taskbar" to select it. Click OK to save your changes.

Understanding Status Bar Data and Tools

In previous versions of Word, the status bar was basically underutilized space. There were a few controls housed there, and the status bar was not customizable, even though it provided some helpful functions—you could view the page number, switch from Overtype to Insert mode, and turn tracking on and off. The customizable status bar in Word 2007 goes beyond providing a quick glimpse of your document's key information—each option displayed can be used to open dialog boxes or toggle various settings:

Page: 23 of 28 | Words: 6,510

- The Page area shows the number of the current page and the length of your document. You can also click this area to display the Go To tab in the Find and Replace dialog box.

- Word displays a continually updating word count on the status bar as well. Click this area to see the Word Count dialog box and get additional statistics on number of characters, paragraphs, and more.

- To detect errors, an ongoing spelling and grammar checker continuously reviews your document content. Click this icon to go to the error and see options for correcting it.

In addition to the controls that show in the status bar by default, you can add or remove options by right-clicking anywhere on the bar. The Customize Status Bar list appears, giving you statistics about your document and showing you which features are currently enabled (see Figure 1-20).

Customize Status Bar

	Formatted Page Number	1
	Section	1
√	Page Number	1 of 1
	Vertical Page Position	1"
	Line Number	1
	Column	1
√	Word Count	0
√	Spelling and Grammar Check	No Errors
√	Language	
√	Signatures	Off
√	Information Management Policy	Off
√	Permissions	Off
	Track Changes	Off
	Caps Lock	Off
	Overtype	Insert
	Selection Mode	
	Macro Recording	Not Recording
√	View Shortcuts	
√	Zoom	100%
√	Zoom Slider	

Figure 1-20 The Customize Status Bar list enables you to add or remove additional options.

Controlling Word 2007 Options

You've already seen a few tips in this chapter that take you into the Word Options area. Word Options has benefited from a major redesign and reorganization in this latest version of the program. Now you access Word Options by clicking the Microsoft Office Button and choosing Word Options in the bottom right corner of the menu.

The Word Options window offers you a collection of settings to change (see Figure 1-21). The Popular options are displayed by default, but you can choose from the following categories, depending on what you'd like to change: Display, Proofing, Save, Advanced, Customize, Add-Ins, Trust Center, and Resources. We cover Trust Center and Resources in detail in the last two sections of this chapter, so we'll focus on the other options now.

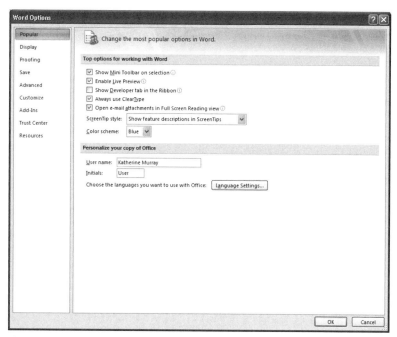

Figure 1-21 Display the Word Options dialog box by clicking the Microsoft Office Button and clicking Word Options in the bottom right corner of the menu.

Here's a quick rundown of what you'll find in each of the Word Options categories:

- Popular includes options for setting up Word the way you like it—choosing whether to turn off Live Preview and the Mini Toolbar, use ClearType, and display attachments opened from e-mail in Full Screen Reading view. It also allows you to personalize Word with your user name, initials, and language choices.

- Display options include controlling the way the page appears (do you want white space to appear between pages in Page Layout view?), choosing whether you want formatting marks to show up on the screen, and specifying a number of print options.

- Proofing controls the options for working with AutoCorrect and setting up your choices for the spelling checker and the grammar checker. Additionally, you can indicate exceptions you want to apply to specific files.

- Save enables you to specify where you want to save your Word documents by default. Additionally, you can indicate how you want documents you share with others—or post to a document management server—to be saved and updated. The Save category also enables you to choose whether you want to embed fonts in your document so that others viewing your file will have access to the same fonts whether or not these fonts are installed on their system.

> **Note**
>
> Embedding fonts in your Word document increases the size of the file.

- Advanced covers many options related to a variety of tasks in Word. You'll find options for editing; cut, copy, and paste; display; saving (these are different options from the ones shown in the Save category); printing; XML; and compatibility. You can also choose the number of documents that are listed in the Recent Documents list.

- Customize provides you with options for customizing the Quick Access Toolbar and setting up your own keyboard shortcuts.

- Add-Ins enables you to manage add-in programs that come with Word 2007 and that you have added to Word.

Setting Up the Microsoft Word Trust Center

The Microsoft Word Trust Center is a new feature in Word 2007 that provides enhanced privacy and security options when you are working with files from other sources or sharing the files you create

To display the Trust Center, click the Microsoft Office Button and choose Word Options. Click Trust Center.

The opening screen of the Trust Center provides you with a series of links concerning privacy and security. Click the Trust Center Settings button on this first screen to see the full range of choices available to you (see Figure 1-22). The following list describes the types of items you can set up in each of the Trust Center categories:

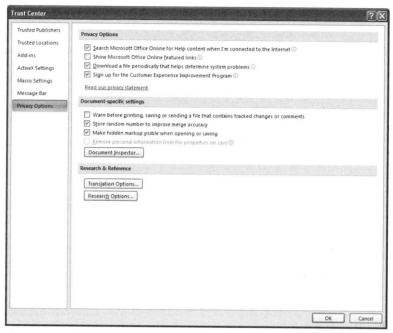

Figure 1-22 The Trust Center provides you with a number of categories you can use to protect your files and your computer system.

- Trusted Publishers enables you to specify which publishers of information, add-ins, and more you deem to be trustworthy. Only add people and organizations you know to be secure (it's better to be prompted each time you open a file if there's any chance that a file might be corrupt or have a virus attached). When you specify a publisher as a Trusted Publisher, Word automatically trusts macros in any files from that source.

- Trusted Locations is a list of acceptable locations and sites you trust. The locations may store documents or templates that include macros. You can add new locations, modify existing locations, and remove locations by using this setting. When you open a document or template from a trusted location, the macros will be enabled automatically, and you won't be prompted to enable or disable them.

- Add-Ins controls the way in which Word treats all third-party add-in utilities. There are three options in this setting: You can insist that all add-ins be digitally signed by the publisher, be prompted when an add-in is unsigned (the code will be blocked), or disallow all add-ins

- ActiveX Settings lets you control how you want Word to handle all Microsoft ActiveX controls that are not recognized as being from a trusted source. Options range from disallowing the ActiveX controls to running in Safe Mode with restrictions.

- Macro Settings gives you options to control whether the macros you run in a document must be from a trusted source and digitally signed. You also have the option of enabling all macros (which isn't recommended) or disabling all macros.

- Message Bar settings enable you to specify when you want the Trust Center to display alerts in the Message Bar that appears just below the Ribbon. When you are opening a file from a questionable source, the Message Bar tells you that the source is not trusted and gives you options for proceeding. The Message Bar settings in the Trust Center give you the option of turning this notification off (it is turned on by default). Additionally, the Allow Trust Center Logging check box at the bottom of this screen gives you the choice of logging all notifications you receive in the Message Bar.

- Privacy Options provides you with settings that enable you to choose whether Word connects to the Internet when you search for help, whether files can be periodically downloaded to log problems with the software, and whether you are signed up for the Customer Experience Improvement Program. Additionally, you can choose document-specific settings (such as whether you are alerted before you send or print a document that has comments and tracking turned on) and translation and research options.

> **Note**
>
> If you're interested in setting up parental controls for Word, go to the Trust Center and click Privacy And Research Options. Parental Control is available in the lower right corner of the Research Options dialog box.

Using Your Word Resources

The last option in the Word Options dialog box is Resources. This is where you'll find links to enhance, improve, and—if necessary—fix the way Word operates. The Resources window is shown in Figure 1-23. As you can see, this is where you go when you want to get the latest update for your version of Office 2007, repair a problem you're having with Word, get contact information for tech support, activate your version of the program (the button will still say Activate even after your software has been activated), register for online classes, and more.

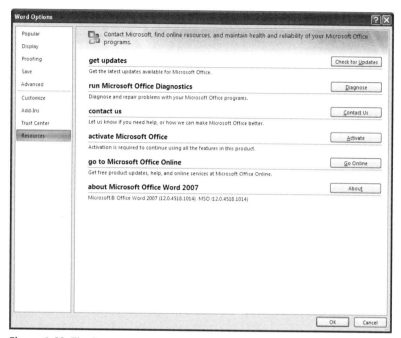

Figure 1-23 The Resources category in the Word Options dialog box enables you to get program updates, diagnose problems, and more.

And if you were wondering where in the world the About box went (formerly it was in the Help menu of all applications), here it is, tucked away at the bottom of the Resources list.

What's Next?

This chapter introduced you to the way in which the working world has changed since the earliest versions of Word and brought you up-to-date by introducing the major new features in the Word 2007 release. The next chapter shows you how Word 2007 fits naturally into the life cycle of your documents—large and small—and gives you ideas for ways to streamline your creative process, whether you're working on your own or as part of a team.

Document Creation with Word 2007

A fter spending a few minutes in Microsoft Office Word 2007, you can see that Office Word 2007 ratchets up your formatting power well beyond traditional word processing basics. In this version, numerous new features have been added—such as Quick Style galleries, Live Preview, Themes, Building Blocks, and Content Controls—that bring you a whole new way of creating, editing, enhancing, and sharing the documents you create. You no longer have to take those cumbersome steps to add a header, footer, or cover page; spend hours manually modifying formatting throughout a document; or hire a graphics designer to create professional-looking, impactful illustrations. But before we get too far into all the exciting new features Word 2007 offers, first we need to get to the root of the power behind Word—what remains its fundamental legacy—*document creation.*

INSIDE OUT   Word 2003 commands at your fingertips

If you're a Microsoft Office Word 2003 veteran, the new Microsoft Office Fluent interface may be a bit of a shock at first. The comforting menu that's been a part of Word since its inception is missing, the familiar toolbars have been replaced with a Ribbon, and you may feel as though you're a complete novice even though you've been using Word for years. Rest assured, your knowledge of Word 2003 commands is still beneficial. Many of the shortcuts you used in Microsoft Office 2003 are still available, such as Alt+O+T to open the Tabs dialog box. But if you can't find a feature previously available on a toolbar, menu, or task pane, this book's companion CD has two resources: (1) a Microsoft Office Excel workbook, Word2003_to_Word 2007commands.xls that contains the locations of Word 2003 commands in Word 2007, and (2) a link to an Interactive Word 2003 to Word 2007 command reference guide you can use to navigate to the command by using the Word 2003 interface. The interactive command reference guide will provide information to the command's new location in a ScreenTip, and if you need more help, clicking the command animates the location in Word 2007. Another valuable resource is the Get Started tab, available as an add-in for the Ribbon, which provides links to the interactive command reference guide, training courses, and other Microsoft Office Online content. For download details on adding the Get Started tab to the Ribbon, see Appendix E, "Working with Word 2007 Add-Ins."

If you're one who's uncertain about making the transition, from one veteran to another, there's far more to Word 2007 than a new look—the added functionality and enhancements take document creation to an amazing new level of technology that simplifies and streamlines processes so you can more easily create professional-looking documents.

Creating and Working with Content in Word

In Word 2007, you'll find word processing features are abundant and more powerful than ever and you'll be pleased to see standard tried-and-true word processing features and tools are on hand as expected. Whether you're a new user, a Word power user, or somewhere in-between, this chapter shows you how to master the fundamental yet oh-so-important document creation and management tasks Word enables you to perform.

Creating New Documents from Templates

Frequently, the first step you take when working with Word is opening a blank document. This procedure sounds pretty straightforward, but just to warm up a little, let's start with a look at the New Document dialog box. To open the New Document dialog box, shown in Figure 2-1, click the Microsoft Office Button and then click New.

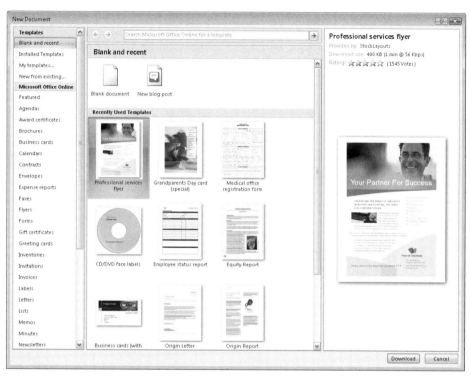

Figure 2-1 The New Document dialog box enables you to create new documents based on your existing templates, access Microsoft Office Online resources, search Microsoft Online templates, open recently used templates, and preview selected templates.

In Word 2007, the New Document dialog box is your passport to the world of templates. The New Document dialog box in Word 2007 replaces the New Document task pane in Word 2003. This new, resizable dialog box provides quick access to your templates, the built-in templates, and the Microsoft Office Online templates along with a large preview area to help you choose the templates you need. The following describes the two primary components in the New Documents dialog box you can use to access templates.

- **Templates list** Provides links to templates stored on your computer or network and templates available from Microsoft Office Online. You can access the following templates: blank Normal, new Blog Post, recently used, currently installed, and Microsoft Office. In addition, you can use the New From Existing link to create a new document or template based on a file that already exists on your computer or network.

- **Search text box** Enables you to enter keywords in the text box to search the extensive collection of templates stored on Microsoft Office Online.

Note that Microsoft now enables their customers to submit templates in the Template Gallery, on Microsoft Office Online, and as you browse templates from Office Online, you may see customer submitted templates. When viewing templates from Microsoft Office Online, a small toolbar is displayed that enables you to sort your search results by the most relevant, by a 5 star–based customer rating system, or in alphabetical order (by name). It also enables you to show or hide templates submitted by customers. A view of templates from Microsoft Office Online in the New Document dialog box is shown below.

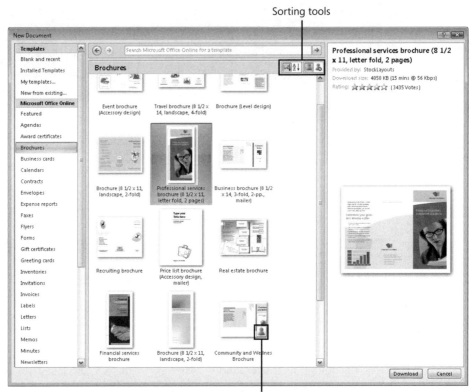

Sorting tools

Customer Template

> **Note**
>
> To remove a template from the Recently Used Templates view, right-click the template and choose Remove Template. To clear the Recently Used Templates view, right-click in the area and choose Remove All Recent Templates. Keep in mind that when you remove templates from the Recently Used Templates area, you are only removing their appearance from that section of the dialog box; you are not permanently removing any templates stored on your computer.

To open a new document based on any template shown in the New Document dialog box, simply double-click a template icon in the center area or select a template icon and click Create. Alternatively, right-click a template icon and click Create on the shortcut menu.

Note

Only customers running genuine, and properly licensed, Microsoft Office applications can download templates from Microsoft Office Online. For more information about the Microsoft Genuine Advantage, see the Inside Out tip titled "The Microsoft Office Genuine Advantage" in Chapter 4, "Formatting Documents Using Templates."

Note

To bypass the New Documents dialog box and create a new, blank document based on your Normal template, you can add the New command to your Quick Access Toolbar. Simply click the More button at the end of the Quick Access Toolbar, and you'll find New in the Popular commands.

For information about working with templates, including the Normal template, see Chapter 4.

Accessing Recently Opened Documents

The Recent Documents list resides in the right pane when you click the Microsoft Office Button. Up to 50 recent documents can be listed, and you can keep a document from being removed by *pinning* it to the list. To do so, simply click the pushpin to the right of the document listed. Figure 2-2 shows a Recent Documents list containing 17 file names, which is the default setting, and one pinned document. File names will slowly make their way to the bottom of the list as you open additional documents, but a file name will not be removed from the list if it is pinned. To control how many file names appear in your Recent Documents list, click the Microsoft Office Button, click Word Options, and then click Advanced. The Show This Number Of Recent Documents option is located in the Display section. Note that although up to 50 recently used documents can be displayed in the Recent Documents list, your screen size and display resolution may limit the actual number of documents that can be displayed.

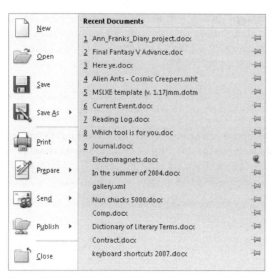

Figure 2-2 By default, the Recent Documents list shows the last 17 files that were opened. It can display up to 50 documents in the list.

INSIDE OUT   Clearing your document history list

You might think that clearing your document history from the Windows Start menu (by right-clicking Start, pointing to Properties, clicking the Start Menu tab, clicking the Customize button, clicking Clear List, and then clicking OK) would automatically clear the Recently Used Documents list in Word 2007—but it doesn't. Instead, this feature clears the history from the Recent Items (Windows Vista) or My Recent Documents (Windows XP) feature found in the Windows operating systems. To clear the Recent Document list in Word, you must type **0** in the Show This Number Of Recent Documents text box.

Inputting Data

Along with typing text and pasting content from other documents or applications, you have a few options when it comes to inserting information into Word 2007 documents:

- **Insert the contents of another Word document or text file.** You can insert the contents of another document into the current document without copying and pasting by clicking the Object drop down arrow in the Text group on the Insert tab and using the Text From File command. The contents of the selected document are inserted into the currently displayed document (and the originating document remains unchanged).

- **Use speech recognition.** You can use speech recognition to dictate text in your Word documents. Talking into a high-quality microphone, usually part of a headset designed for such purposes, and using a combination of your voice and the mouse, or keyboard, will obtain the best results.

> **Note**
>
> Speech Recognition is now provided by Windows Vista or Windows XP and is no longer part of the Microsoft Office installation. Windows XP users may need to download and install Microsoft Speech to use this feature.

- **Handwrite content using the mouse or a stylus.** If you have handwriting recognition software installed, or if you are using a TabletPC, Word can recognize handwritten marks you make with your mouse or a stylus. When you use handwriting recognition, you can retain your written marks, create drawings, or configure Word to interpret your handwriting and display the information as typed text.

Performing Basic Editing Tasks

As you know, merely entering information into a Word document doesn't usually create a finished product. Instead, your documents are the result of entering information and then editing and formatting the entered text, images, and objects. This section provides information about selecting, copying, cutting, and pasting text; using the Clipboard; and undoing, redoing, and repeating changes—in other words, some of the common tasks you'll perform in Word.

All Word users, regardless of skill level, can refer to this section as a quick guide or as a way to discover faster or more convenient methods to complete common editing tasks.

Selecting Text

Generally speaking, you can streamline many editing tasks by first selecting the text you want to edit. In fact, you can speed up most text modification tasks by mastering precise selection techniques. You can select text in a variety of ways. Usually (and not too surprisingly), you will select text by using the mouse or keyboard commands. (You can also select text that contains similar formatting by using the Styles And Formatting task pane, but because that topic is slightly more advanced and is related to creating and using styles, that technique is addressed in Chapter 15, "Using Styles to Increase Your Formatting Power.") Regardless of how you select text, you can cancel a selection, or *deselect*, by clicking any area outside the selected text or by pressing an arrow key.

> **Note**
>
> You can access a couple of key text selection options in Word Options in the Advanced
> section under Editing Options. You can specify whether to automatically select para-
> graph marks when you select paragraphs (the Use Smart Paragraph Selection check box)
> and whether to select entire words when you select part of one word and then part of
> the next word (the When Selecting, Automatically Select Entire Word check box). Both
> text selection settings are activated by default.

Selecting Information with Your Mouse

Though clicking and dragging with the mouse is the most common way to select text
and other elements (such as graphics, tables, objects, and so forth) in Word documents,
Table 2-1 provides some alternate methods you can use for selecting text using the
mouse.

Table 2-1 Common Methods of Selecting Text by Using the Mouse

Selection	Method
Word or single element	Double-click the word
Sentence	Press Ctrl and click in the sentence
Paragraph	Triple-click within the paragraph or place your mouse to the far left of the paragraph, (this unmarked area is called the *Selection Bar*) and double-click
Entire line	In the Selection Bar, point at a line and click once; drag in the Selection Bar to select multiple lines or paragraphs
Noncontiguous selection	Select the first item (as described above), hold Ctrl, and then select additional text elsewhere within your document
Large block of text	Click at the start of the selection, scroll to the end of the selection, and then hold down Shift as you click at the end of the selection
Vertical block of text	Press Alt and then drag over the text (Note that this method does not work in Word tables and it may require practice since using Alt+click will trigger the Research task pane)
Entire document	Triple-click in the Selection Bar or hold Ctrl and click once in the Selection Bar (Note if using the Ctrl+click method you must first deselect any selected text)

Selecting Text by Using Keyboard Commands

As you become more proficient in Word, you might find using both the mouse and the keyboard to select text will increase productivity. Such as when you are using the mouse, use the mouse to select text and when you are using the keyboard, use the keyboard to select text. Doing so limits how frequently you move your hand from your keyboard to your mouse and back again. For the most part, selecting text by using keyboard commands requires you to press Shift while you press the keyboard combination that moves the insertion point in the direction of the text you want to select. For example, Ctrl+Right Arrow moves the insertion point to the next word, and Shift+Ctrl+Right Arrow selects the text from the insertion point to the beginning of the next word. Table 2-2 lists the text selection keyboard commands that might be most useful for you.

 For an exhaustive list of keyboard commands, see this book's companion CD or search for **keyboard shortcuts** in Help.

Table 2-2 Keyboard Commands for Selecting Text

Keyboard command	Selects
F8	Turns on Extend Selection Mode; press twice to select a word, three times to select a sentence, and four times to select the document; press F8 once and then the Enter key to select by paragraph, or press F8 once and then the period (dot) to select by sentence
Ctrl+Shift+F8+arrow keys or mouse button	Vertical or horizontal blocks of text beginning at the insertion point
Esc	Turns off Extend Selection Mode (text will remain selected)
Ctrl+Shift+Left Arrow or Ctrl+Shift+Right Arrow	From the insertion point to the beginning of a word or end of a word, respectively
Shift+Home or Shift+End	From the insertion point to the beginning or end of the current line, respectively
Shift+Page Up or Shift+Page Down	One screen up or down, respectively, beginning from the insertion point
Ctrl+Shift+Home or Ctrl+Shift+End	From the insertion point to the beginning of the document or end of the document, respectively
Ctrl+A	Entire document

Copying, Cutting, and Pasting

Thanks to those who opted into the Customer Experience Improvement Program (CEIP), Microsoft found copying, cutting, and pasting were among the top features used and greatly expanded these functions in Word 2007. You'll find the Paste Options button selections have been improved, the arrow below the Paste command on the Home tab provides quick access to the Paste Special and Paste Hyperlink commands, and Word 2007 users now have the ability to set default paste options as described in the Inside Out tip titled "Setting Default Paste Options."

To use the Copy and Cut functions, select the text you want to manipulate and then choose one of the commands listed in Table 2-3. To paste information, position the insertion point where you want to insert the information and then choose one of the Paste commands, also listed in Table 2-3. Alternatively, you can right-click selected text and choose Cut, Copy, or Paste from the shortcut menu. In addition to cutting and pasting, you can reposition text by using the drag-and-drop feature, which essentially enables you to use the mouse to cut or copy (using Ctrl+drag) and paste text without using the Cut and Paste commands.

Table 2-3 Copy, Cut, and Paste Features

Keyboard shortcut	Button	Action
Ctrl+C or Ctrl+Insert	Copy	Copy
Ctrl+Shift+C to Paste use Ctrl+Shift+V	Format Painter	Copy Format (Format Painter)
Ctrl+X or Shift+Del	Cut	Cut
Ctrl+V or Shift+Insert	Paste	Paste
Ctrl+Alt+V Alt+H+V+H	Paste / Paste / Paste Special... / Paste as Hyperlink	Paste Special and Paste As Hyperlink

Note

The Paste As Hyperlink command is enabled when content from an external source, such as another Word document or an Office Excel workbook, that has been previously saved, is present on the Clipboard.

Paste Options Buttons

Copying and pasting data has always been an easy way to reuse previously created data, but one drawback in previous versions of Word is the added steps for reformatting the pasted data. Newly added commands for the Paste Options button provide more control over the formatting of the pasted content. Additionally, the commands change according to the source of the copied content, the destination, and whether you are pasting from another program. Figure 2-3 provides a graphic with a few of the variations you may encounter.

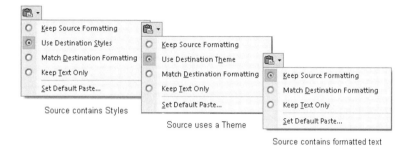

Figure 2-3 By default, the Paste Options button appears whenever you paste an element in your Word document.

> **Note**
>
> To ignore Paste Options after pasting, simply continue to work within your document or press Esc—the Paste Options button will quietly disappear until the next time you paste an object.
>
> To turn off the Paste Options button, click the Microsoft Office Button, click Word Options, and then click Advanced, In the Cut, Copy, And Paste options, clear the Show Paste Options Buttons check box.

INSIDE OUT   Setting Default Paste Options

Long-awaited options for setting default paste actions have been added to Word 2007. You can specify whether to keep the source formatting (the default setting), match the destination formatting, or keep the text only when you paste data originating from another document, the same document, and from other programs. For example, if you want to always paste as plain text, then set each option to Keep Text Only. You can set the default Paste commands in Word Options in the Advanced section, or from the Paste Options button by clicking Set Paste Defaults.

Using the Office Clipboard

There are actually two Clipboards used by Word, the system Clipboard and the Office Clipboard. (For a distinction between the two, see the Inside Out tip entitled, "The Office Clipboard and the system Clipboard" later in the chapter.) The Office Clipboard enables you to store up to 24 items—including text, objects, and graphics—which means you can copy or cut 24 elements from various applications without losing data in the digital abyss. (Of course, as soon as you copy item 25, the first item you copied to your Office Clipboard is removed.) Further, the Office Clipboard task pane provides an easy way to see which Clipboard item contains the information you want to access, as shown in Figure 2-4. In this example, 4 items are stored on the Office Clipboard, including some text copied from a Word document, a Microsoft Expression image, a clip art image, and some Excel data. Each Clipboard item's parent application is identified by an associated icon.

Figure 2-4 The Clipboard holds up to 24 items and displays some of the copied and cut items' contents to help you identify which item you want to paste into a document.

Opening the Office Clipboard

To open the Office Clipboard manually, on the Home tab, in the Clipboard group, click the Clipboard Dialog Box Launcher. After the Office Clipboard is open, you can click the Options button to select or deselect any of the following options:

- Show Office Clipboard Automatically

- Show Office Clipboard When Ctrl+C Pressed Twice

- Collect Without Showing Office Clipboard

- Show Office Clipboard Icon On Taskbar (selected by default)

- Show Status Near Taskbar When Copying (selected by default)

You can also open the Office Clipboard by using the Office Clipboard icon that appears in the Windows taskbar by default whenever the Office Clipboard appears in any Microsoft Office program. Double-click the icon to display the Office Clipboard in the current window. For example, if the Office Clipboard is open in Word, you can start Excel and then double-click the Office Clipboard icon on the taskbar to display the Office Clipboard in Excel.

Pasting Office Clipboard Content

After information is stored on the Office Clipboard, you can paste the information into a document by positioning the insertion point where you want to insert the information, displaying the Office Clipboard, and then clicking the item you want to paste. If you want to paste everything stored on the Office Clipboard into your document, click the Paste All button in the task pane.

Deleting Office Clipboard Content

To delete items from the Office Clipboard, you can either click the arrow that appears when you hover your pointer over a Office Clipboard item or right-click an item and click Delete. If you want to clear the entire Office Clipboard, click the Clear All button in the task pane.

INSIDE OUT   **The Office Clipboard and the system Clipboard**

You might be wondering how the Office Clipboard relates to the system Clipboard. Here's a quick rundown of how the two Clipboards relate to one another:

- The last item you copy to the Office Clipboard is stored on the system Clipboard.
- Clearing the Office Clipboard also clears the system Clipboard.

When you click the Paste command on the Home tab, or press Ctrl+V (or any other Paste keyboard command) to paste information, you paste the contents of the system Clipboard (which by default is the last item you added to the Office Clipboard).

Undoing, Redoing, and Repeating

Fortunately, changes you make to documents are not set in stone. You have ample opportunity to change your mind when it comes to editing text—not only can you undo edits you've recently made, but you can also redo undone edits and even repeat an action if you need to. Most likely, you'll use the Undo command more frequently than the Redo and Repeat commands, so let's look at that feature first.

Using Undo

The Undo feature enables you to undo one or many changes made to a document during the current session. In previous versions of Word, Undo is limited by resources and document size (maximum document size of 32 MB without graphics), which can work to your advantage or disadvantage. Now, in Word 2007, up to 1,000 actions are stored, so you have plenty of time during the current session to discard your edits. To Undo one or more actions, use any of the following methods:

- Click the Undo button on the Quick Access Toolbar or click the arrow and display the Undo list and click the action you want to undo. (If you don't see the action you're looking for, scroll through the list.) Note when you undo an action in the list, you also undo all the actions that appear above it in the list.

- Press Ctrl+Z or Alt+Backspace to undo the last action.

> **Note**
>
> Though the past 1,000 actions are retained, there may be still be times you encounter a message that you aren't able to undo a current action. If you're a little apprehensive about moving ahead without the Undo safety net, you can take precautionary action. One easy approach is to simply perform the "risky" action last so that you won't lose your current Undo list until you're sure you'll no longer need it. Another workaround is to copy the element you want to perform the action on, paste the information into a blank document, perform the desired action on the copied version of your information, and then copy and paste the modified information into the original document. Using this method, you can ensure that if the action doesn't go as planned, your original document remains intact.

Redo

Repeat

Using Redo Or Repeat

The default Redo button on the Quick Access Toolbar is a combination of two commands, Redo and Repeat. Both icons used by the default Redo command are displayed next to this paragraph. When you create a new document you will see the Repeat command but as soon as you undo an action, you automatically activate the Redo command. The main role of the Redo command is to enable you to redo an undone action before you make any further changes. The Repeat feature is fairly self-explanatory—clicking this command repeats the last action you performed. For example, if you applied color or a border to text, you could use the Repeat command to apply the same formatting. To use the Redo or Repeat command you can perform any of the following actions:

- Click Redo on the Quick Access Toolbar immediately after you've undone an action—before you've made any other changes.

- Press Ctrl+Y or Alt+Enter to redo the last undone change.

INSIDE OUT   Where is the Redo list?

If you miss the Redo button that includes a Redo list, rest assured, it's still available. To add the Redo button that includes a list of Redo actions to your Quick Access Toolbar, click the More button at the end of the Quick Access Toolbar, and then click More Commands. From the Choose Commands from list, select Commands Not In The Ribbon and locate the Redo command (the first Redo command with the icon) that provides a list of Redo actions. Click the command to select it and then click Add to add it to your Quick Access Toolbar.

You can keep the default Redo button and the Redo button you just added on your Quick Access Toolbar, however if you are tempted to leave the default Redo button on the Quick Access Toolbar because the Repeat functionality is handy, an alternative option is to remove the default Redo button and use the keyboard shortcut for Repeat (F4) to repeat your last action. For more information on customizing the Quick Access Toolbar, see Appendix B, "Customizing Word and Enhancing Accessibility."

Creating Theme-Enabled Documents

At the core of document creation in Word 2007 is Themes. As discussed in the previous chapter, a Theme includes colors, fonts, and effects. Every document saved in the new file format comes pre-equipped with a document Theme, and new, blank documents use the Office Theme by default. You can turn any Microsoft Office document into a Theme-ready document by incorporating various Theme elements as you begin creating your documents and later, as you format the document. This section covers the concepts of Theme elements, found on the Page Layout tab in the Themes group, and how they are integrated into Word 2007.

See Themes in Action

The best way to understand the concept of Theme-enabled documents is to see Themes in action. From the Microsoft Office Button, click New to create a new document based on one of the Installed Templates. Navigate to the Page Layout tab, open the Themes gallery, hover your mouse over the various Themes, and note how Live Preview instantly displays how the document will look if the Theme is applied.

Theme Colors

The new color palettes have a Theme Colors section and a Standard Colors section. Figure 2-5 shows the same color palette, for two Themes. The Office Theme is shown on the left and the Origin Theme is shown on the right. The colors in the Theme Color section are identified by its element, as opposed to the actual color displayed. In Figure 2-5, both color palettes are shown with the Background 2 element selected. For the Office Theme, the color for Background 2 is Tan and for the Origin Theme, the color for Background 2 is Ice Blue.

If you want to enable a color to change when the Theme Colors change, use colors from the Theme Colors section. If you want a color to remain the same regardless of the Theme, select a color from the Standard Colors section or use More Colors.

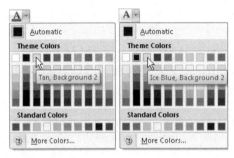

Figure 2-5 As you hover your mouse over the colors in the color palette, a ScreenTip provides more information about the Theme element.

Each color palette has 10 columns of coordinating colors. The first four colors are for text and backgrounds (two dark colors and two light colors), and the additional six colors are for accents. The first row provides the main colors for the Theme; the additional rows provide five variations of the color, starting with the lightest tint and ending with the darkest shade.

> **Note**
> *Tint* is a color mixed with white and *shade* is a color that is mixed with black.

Theme Fonts

Each Theme incorporates two fonts: one for use in headings and another for body text. The fonts used in the Theme are identified in the Theme Fonts section, as shown in Figure 2-6.

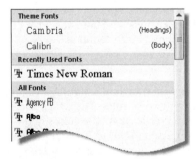

Figure 2-6 The Office Theme uses Cambria for headings and Calibri for body text.

Like the color palettes, if you want the font to change when the Theme Fonts change, use the Theme fonts found in the Theme Fonts section of a Font list. Otherwise, the fonts will not change if your Theme Fonts change.

Theme Effects

Theme effects are a combination of formats such as line style, fill, and shadow or three-dimensional effects. They are used for various graphic elements, as shown in Figure 2-7.

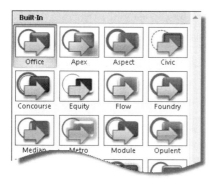

Figure 2-7 Theme effects provide a set of graphical effects for objects such as charts and Smart-Art.

You'll find various tips throughout this book on how to continue to integrate Theme elements in your documents. For more in-depth information on Themes, along with how to create and customize document Themes, see Chapter 5, "Applying Themes for a Professional Look."

Opening Word 97-2003 Documents in Compatibility Mode

When you open documents created or saved in previous version of Word, the document is automatically opened in Compatibility Mode. Word 2007 indicates when you are working in Compatibility Mode by displaying [Compatibility Mode] in the title bar. You can also specify that you want your Word 2007 documents to conform to Compatibility Mode specifications so that your document will appear properly in earlier versions of Word.

The purpose of Compatibility Mode is to ensure that no new or enhanced Word 2007 features are available while you work so that others who access the document using previous versions of Word can continue to have full editing capabilities. Table 2-4 contains a list of the various behaviors you will encounter when working in Compatibility Mode.

Chapter 2

Table 2-4 Compatibility Mode Behaviors

Element	Behavior in Compatibility Mode
Charts	Reverts to Microsoft Graph, used in previous versions of Word
Content Controls	Unavailable; however, legacy controls are available
Equations	Unavailable
Pictures and Clipart	Contextual Picture Tools display formatting commands that are compatible with previous versions of Word rather than the new enhanced graphic functionality
SmartArt	Reverts to the Diagram Gallery, used in previous versions of Word
Themes	Unavailable

Documents can still be exchanged with those who use Word 2000 through Word 2003, provided they have the Microsoft Office Compatibility Pack for Word, Excel, and PowerPoint 2007 File Formats installed. The Compatibility Pack can be downloaded from the Microsoft Office Online Web site (*www.office.microsoft.com*). If you have an Internet connection, you can access Office Online by clicking the Microsoft Office button, clicking Word Options, clicking Resources, and then clicking the Go Online button. Additionally, your colleagues can be automatically prompted to install the Microsoft Office Compatibility Pack, if necessary, when opening a Word 2007 document in a previous version if they use Microsoft Update to install all needed updates. In previous versions of Word, the ability to check for updates on Microsoft Office Online is found on the Help menu.

Converting Existing Word Documents to the Word 2007 File Format

When you open a document saved in a previous version of Word, you will need to convert it to the new file format to take advantage of functionality that is new to Word 2007. To convert an existing Word document to the Word 2007 file format, use the built-in Convert tool, as described here:

1. Open the document you want to convert in Word 2007.

2. Click the Microsoft Office Button and then click Convert.

> **Note**
>
> The Convert command will only be available when using Compatibility Mode.

3. Read the text in the Microsoft Office Word message box, which explains that you are converting the current document to the newest file format and that though you will be able to use the latest features of Word, the layout of the document may change.

4. Click OK.

CAUTION

The document will be converted to the new file format, given the new file extension (.dotx for macro free documents or .dotm for macro enabled documents), and a copy of the original will not be preserved. Though you can save a converted document back to the Word 97-2003 file format, if you have any conversion concerns, you should make a backup copy of your document prior to using the Convert tool or use Save As to save your document in the new file format instead. For more information about saving documents, see the section titled "Saving Documents," later in this chapter.

Running the Compatibility Checker

When you are working in Word 2007, you can use the Compatibility Checker to find out which elements in your document are not fully supported by Word 97-2003. You may want to check for compatibility if you know the document you are working on will be viewed or edited in earlier versions of Word, or if you plan to save your document as a Word 97-2003 document. Using the Compatibility Checker, you can review a summary of the elements in your document that will behave differently in earlier versions of Word (see Figure 2-8). If you are not sure what a summary item means, you can click the Help link below the number of occurrences in the Summary area to get additional information. After you review changes, click OK and then either save the document in Word 97-2003 format knowing what changes will take place or make changes in your document and run the Compatibility Checker again. The following list briefly describes the types of changes that most frequently take place when you save Word 2007 documents in a file format compatible with earlier versions of Word:

- Alignment tabs are converted to traditional tabs.

- Building Blocks may lose some information.

- Citations and bibliographies become static and are no longer automatically updated.

- Content Controls become static text.

- Embedded objects can no longer be edited.

- Equations are converted to images.

- SmartArt graphics are converted to single objects that cannot be edited.

- Text box positioning may change.

- Tracked moves are shown as deletions and insertions.

To run the Compatibility Checker, open the document in Word 2007 and click the Microsoft Office Button, point at Prepare, and click Run Compatibility Checker. After the Compatibility Checker runs, a dialog box appears that lists any compatibility issues, as shown in Figure 2-8.

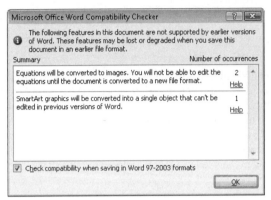

Figure 2-8 The Compatibility Checker is a built-in tool that you can use to check the contents of the current document. After the checker runs, it lists all elements that will be affected if the current document is saved in a file format that is compatible with earlier versions of Word.

Saving Documents

Whenever you create and edit documents, you need to save your work—an obvious statement, but one well worth emphasizing. You should save your work as frequently as possible, not just when you're closing a document. In this section, we'll take a quick look at techniques that make saving documents as effortless as possible.

Saving Changes to Existing Documents

Saving your document in the same location with the same name is easy. Simply follow any of these procedures:

- Click the Microsoft Office Button and then click Save.
- Click the Save button on the Quick Access Toolbar.
- Press Ctrl+S.

Take advantage of the simplicity of the Save procedure. Whenever you're about to take a break, press Ctrl+S as you start to roll your chair away from your desk. When your phone rings, click the Save button as you reach for the receiver. Saving your work regularly helps you avoid major data loss headaches when you least expect them (because, as everyone knows, system crashes or disasters usually strike at the most inopportune times).

TROUBLESHOOTING

Pressing Shift and clicking the Microsoft Office Button doesn't change the Save and Close commands to Save All and Close All

In earlier versions of Word, you can press Shift and open the File menu, and the Save and Close commands would change to Save All and Close All. In Word 2007, this capability has been removed. However, it is easily resolved by adding the Save All and Close All commands to your Quick Access Toolbar (using the More Commands option). Alternatively, you can use the Customize Keyboard dialog box to assign keyboard shortcuts to the FileSaveAll and FileCloseAll commands.

Saving Files by Using the Save As Dialog Box

The Save As dialog box appears every time you save a new document or opt to save an existing document as a new file or in a new location by clicking the Microsoft Office Button and then clicking Save As (or by pressing F12). Figure 2-9 shows the new Save As dialog box when using Windows Vista. Notice the Save As dialog box provides the ability to add or modify document properties. You can add tags and title text as well as specify whether to maintain Word 97-2003 compatibility (if you are saving a .doc file in a Word 2007 format). You can also specify whether to save a thumbnail with the file.

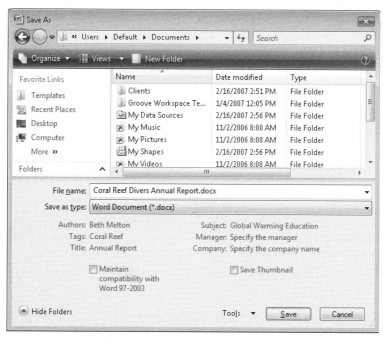

Figure 2-9 The new Save As dialog box includes the standard Save As functions as well as provides quick access to some document property settings.

As you save documents, you'll notice that the various icons accompanying saved Word documents can give clues to how documents are saved. Figure 2-10 shows three examples of Word icons. The file shown on the left is saved in the Word 97-2003 (.doc) format, the middle file is saved as a Word 2007 (.docx) document with a thumbnail image, and the right file is saved as a Word 2007 (.docx) document without a thumbnail image. Note that the three files shown are the same file saved in different ways, and the left file is 31 KB (largest), the middle file is 23 KB (medium), and the right file is only 13 KB (smallest).

CAUTION!

Keep in mind that including a thumbnail image when you save a document in Word 97-2003 format increases the file size and has been known to cause instabilities in a document. You'll still see a slight increase in file size when using the new Word 2007 file formats; however, the new Office Open XML Format handles images differently than the binary format and is therefore more stable.

Which tool is for you.doc

Which tool is for you.docx

Which tool is for you update.docx

Figure 2-10 The icons accompanying Word files on the screen vary depending on file format and Save options. Here, you can see icons for the .doc (Word 97-2003) format, .dotx (Word 2007) format with a thumbnail image, and .dotx format.

Note

At times, you'll want to create a folder to contain a newly created file. You can easily create a new folder during the Save procedure by clicking the Create New Folder button on the toolbar of the Save As dialog box, or right-clicking an empty area of the file list and using the New, Folder command.

You can save Word documents in a variety of file types, which can be convenient if you're saving a file for someone who is using an application other than Word or if you're creating HTML, Portable Document Format (PDF), XML Paper Specification (XPS), or XML documents.

A complete list and description of file format types available in the Save As dialog box can be found on this book's companion CD.

Obtaining Additional File Format Converters

At some point, you might face the task of converting a document for which Word has not supplied a converter, and no converter for the file type is available on the Microsoft Office CD-ROM. When this situation arises, you'll have to install another converter. In some cases, you can easily obtain a converter from Microsoft Office Online or in the Office Resource Kit. If neither the Web site nor the Office Resource Kit provides what you're looking for, your next step should be to find a third-party solution. One well-known third party file-conversion solution is Dataviz's Conversions Plus software. In addition, you can search for shareware sites, using your favorite search engine, for file conversion programs.

Specifying a Default Save Format

The default setting when you save Word documents saves documents using the Word Document (.docx) format. If you frequently save your documents in a format other than the default .docx format (for example, you might frequently save files that use macros, so you prefer to use the .docm format), you can change the default setting to another file format by displaying Word Options. Then in the Save section, shown in Figure 2-11, select a new default format.

Figure 2-11 The Save options in Word enable you to configure default Save settings.

Retrieving Local and Shared Documents

The poet William Wordsworth once claimed that he wrote his best works in a single sitting. But most of us usually don't work that way—instead, we return to documents time and again for one reason or another, including to collaborate and review information with others while we work. As with other files in Windows, you can use the Windows interface to retrieve documents in a variety of ways. For example, you can open a document using the Documents or My Recent Documents option from the Start menu, or opening My Computer, navigating to a document and double-clicking the file to open it. In Word, the best source for retrieving Word documents is the Open dialog box. To display the Open dialog box, perform either of the following actions:

- Click the Microsoft Office Button and then click Open.
- Click the Open button in your Quick Access Toolbar. (To add the Open button, click the More button at the end of the Quick Access Toolbar and then click Open.)
- Press Ctrl+O.

To use the Open dialog box, navigate to the file you want to open and double-click the file name.

> **Note**
>
> To open multiple files from within the Open dialog box, select files while pressing Shift (for a continuous selection) or Ctrl (for a noncontiguous selection) and then click the Open.
>
> You may also want to take note of the options available when you click the arrow on the Open button, such as Open And Repair, which can be used to attempt to open a file that's been damaged or corrupted.

Taking Advantage of AutoRecover and Background Saves

As all computer users know, you always run the risk of losing data when you least expect it. To help reduce the risk of losing data, Word is installed with the AutoRecover and Background Saves features activated by default. These two features work together to help save your information without interrupting your workflow too much. These features can be summarized as follows:

- **AutoRecover** Creates temporary files of open documents. These files are used if your system crashes or if there's a power failure. These files are considered temporary because they are deleted when you either close the open documents or exit Word.
- **Background Saves** Enables you to continue working in Word while you save a document. A pulsing disk icon appears on the status bar when a background save is taking place. You can toggle background saves off and on using the Allow Background Saves option found in Word Options in the Advanced section under the Save options.

> **Note**
>
> If you attempt to save a long document while Word is still performing a background save, you might get a Same Name error because Word uses the same name to complete both save operations. If this occurs, simply wait a moment while the background save completes and then save the document normally. You can tell when a document is being saved by looking for the Save message and Save Progress bar on the status bar.

> **Changing the AutoRecover Save Interval**
>
> By default, the AutoRecover feature in Word stores unsaved changes made to an active file every 10 minutes. You can turn off the AutoRecover feature or change the frequency of AutoRecover saves by displaying Word Options. Then in the Save section, you'll find the Save AutoRecover Information Every __ Minutes option.

Keep in mind that the AutoRecover feature isn't a replacement for saving your files. AutoRecover only temporarily saves changes made to active documents. It is specifically a tool designed to help you recover a file after a system crash. You need to continue to save and back up your documents regularly.

> **Note**
>
> By default, Word does not automatically create backup files. To turn on the automatic backup feature, check the Always Create Backup Copy check box in the Save section on the Advanced tab in Word Options. The backup copy will have Backup Of appended to the beginning of the file name and will have a .wbk file extension. Note the backup copy is a version of the document that you saved prior to the most recent save.

If you experience a system crash while working in Word, Word displays a Document Recovery task pane along the left side of the Word window after you restart your system and reopen Word. The Document Recovery task pane shows up to three versions (recovered, AutoSaved, and original) of each Word file that was open at the time of the crash. The most current version (usually the recovered version) is shown at the top of the group of related files. You can select which files you want to save from among the recovered versions of documents that appear in the Document Recovery task pane.

To open a recovered document, click the entry in the Document Recovery task pane, as shown in Figure 2-12, or click the arrow next to the item and click Open. In addition, you can save or delete a recovered file or view repairs made to a recovered file by clicking the item's arrow and then selecting the desired command.

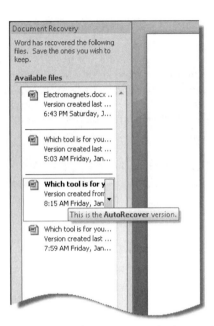

Figure 2-12 After a system crash, the AutoRecover feature enables you to choose which version of a document you want to use.

> ## Recover the Most Recent Versions of Files
>
> When you see two or three versions of the same file listed in the Document Recovery task pane's Available Files list box, keep in mind that an AutoRecover file is usually in better shape than an original file. Be sure to check the Last Saved time listed with each recovered document to verify that you're recovering the most recent version. If later during the same session you determine that you would rather use a different version, click the Recovered button on the status bar to reopen the Document Recovery task pane.

After you've made your recovery decisions, click Close in the lower right corner of the Document Recovery task pane to close the pane. If you determine that you want to use a different recovered document after you've closed the Document Recover task pane, click the Recovered button on the status bar to reopen the task pane.

When you close a recovery file without saving it, the recovery file is deleted—you can't recover a deleted recovery file. Furthermore, when you close Word after recovering documents, you will not be able to re-access the various saved versions whether you deleted them or not. If you are not sure which file to save, consider saving all of the recovered files with different names so you can compare and review the files without losing any of them. After you are sure which file you want to keep, you can delete the files you don't need in the same manner you delete other Word files.

Word 2007 and Microsoft Office 2007 Integration

The 2007 Microsoft Office system was designed to save time, and its newly added features, such as shared Themes, make reusing data across Office programs easier than ever. Perform your number crunching tasks in Excel, use the results in a Word document, and then use the main topics of the document in a Microsoft Office PowerPoint 2007 presentation—all without recreating the data or painstakingly reformatting the shared content. And you can maintain a set of coordinated individual Microsoft Office documents simply by using the same shared customized or built in Theme, such as the Flow Theme shown below.

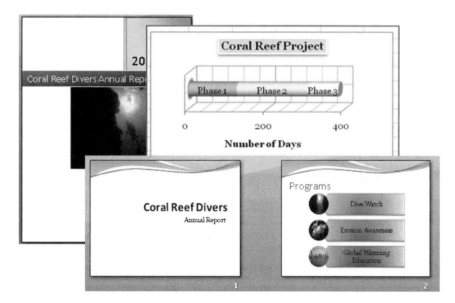

This section covers a few of the new time-saving additions, along with some longstanding favorites, for using Word with Excel and Office PowerPoint 2007.

Turn Word Documents into PowerPoint Presentations

As previously mentioned, content in a Word document can be transformed into a PowerPoint presentation without retyping or even copying any of the document content. To set up a Word document for PowerPoint slides, format your document by using the Heading styles found in the Quick Style gallery on the Home tab, as shown below.

For each new slide, apply the Heading 1 style to the paragraph you want to use as a slide title. Then apply Heading 2 to the paragraph containing the first level of text for the slide, and so on. Note that text not formatted with a heading style will be omitted in the presentation.

Then, in PowerPoint, on the Home tab, in the Slides group, click the arrow below New Slide. Then at the bottom, click Slides From Outline to select your saved Word document.

> **Note**
>
> If you want the inserted slides to follow the PowerPoint Theme rather than the Theme used in the Word document, right-click each slide and select Reset Layout.

Edit PowerPoint Notes or Handouts in Word

The ability to use Word to edit notes or handouts for PowerPoint presentations has been available since PowerPoint 4, but it is such a timesaver that it's worth reviewing here. Create Handouts In Microsoft Office Word (formerly called Send To Word or ReportIt) can be found in PowerPoint by clicking the Microsoft Office Button and viewing the Publish options.

Sharing Excel Data with Word

When pasting Excel data in a Word document, you can take advantage of Word Table Styles and new Paste options to paste perfectly formatted Excel data in one simple click. Just click Match Destination Table Style in the Paste Options button choices, as shown below.

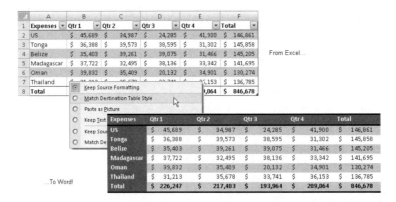

> **Note**
>
> To set a default table style in Word 2007, place your insertion point in a table to display the contextual Table Tools and click the Design tab. Then, in the Table Styles gallery, select a table style you would like to use as the default table style. Right-click the table style and click Set As Default. Learn more about Table Styles in Chapter 11, "Organizing Concepts in Tables."

This section covers only a handful of the methods you can use to integrate and reuse data in the Microsoft Office 2007 system programs. After you've mastered the new Word 2007 functionality found in this book, see *Advanced Microsoft Office Documents 2007 Edition Inside Out*, by Stephanie Krieger (Microsoft Press, 2007), to learn more about Microsoft Office 2007 document integration.

What's Next?

This chapter reviewed the basics of document creation and introduced enhancements and new functionality that have been added to essential document creation tasks in Word 2007. It also contained an overview of working with Word documents in a mixed version environment and provided several methods for sharing data between the Microsoft Office applications. The next chapter takes you through another phase of document creation—page layout, the function that is responsible for how the overall content of your document is displayed on a printed page or on the screen.

Documents take planning. But even after the most thoughtful planning, document designs sometimes travel down unplanned paths, seemingly on their own. Maybe a single-column publication suddenly becomes a multiple-column document, or a piece that wasn't supposed to be a booklet turns out to work perfectly in a booklet format. In those types of cases, everything changes—margins, orientation, column specifications, headers, and footers. While these kinds of changes might seem daunting—especially when you are working under a tight deadline—Microsoft Office Word 2007 can help you efficiently adapt to all sorts of changes with a little know-how.

Whether you successfully plan your work in advance or change strategies midstream, the page setup features of Office Word 2007 help you control page layout basics. Specifically, when you plan or redesign your pages, you can make choices about the following page setup specifications and options:

- Headers, footers, and page number settings

- Top, bottom, left, and right margin sizes

- Document orientation

- Paper size and tray or cartridge to use when printing

- Whether to print one or two pages per sheet

- Page and text breaks

- Header and footer content and positioning

- Text flow and spacing for languages that use vertical orientation

This chapter covers the preceding topics as well as related page setup features provided in Word.

INSIDE OUT   Planning Page Setup

Although you can select your page settings at any point during the creation or editing of your document, taking time up front to plan basic document settings can save you time, trouble, and corrections later. In addition, if you're creating a standard document for others in your department to use or that you will use repeatedly, setting the basics early can ensure that you don't have to open multiple documents to readjust margin settings, page size, and more. In those cases, you can use an existing document as a guide or create a template with your settings to simplify applying current settings and making future changes.

Planning up front is usually best; however, Word enables you to change direction whenever you want. Keep in mind that when you make drastic changes to an existing document's setup—such as changing the page from portrait to landscape orientation—the content of your page will be dramatically affected. For instance, if you switch to landscape orientation after you've entered text and graphics, set headers and footers, and created section divisions in portrait orientation, you'll most likely have to adjust a few settings to display your information properly on the shorter, wider page.

For additional information on formatting complex documents and planning strategies, see Chapter 22, "Formatting Columns and Sections for Advanced Text Control."

Basic Page Setup Options

In many cases, you'll use the Page Setup options on the Page Layout tab shown in Figure 3-1. The options in the Page Layout tab include Themes, Text Direction (if you have support for Chinese, Japanese, or Korean enabled), Margins, Page Orientation, Page Size, Columns, Breaks, Line Numbers, and Hyphenation.

Dialog launcher

Figure 3-1 The Page Setup options on the Page Layout tab streamline access to common page layout features including text direction, margins, page orientation, and breaks.

Changing Margins and Orientation

The page setup items that you'll adjust most often are likely to be margins and page orientation. Word makes accessing these settings a snap by including the Margins and Orientation galleries on the Page Layout tab. The margins of your document control the amount of white space at the top, bottom, right, and left edges of the document. You can also control the amount of space used for the gutter, which is the space reserved on the inside edges of facing pages to save room for binding. You can customize the gutter setting along the left or top margin of the page.

Changing Margin Settings

When you begin working with a new Word document, the left, right, top, and bottom margins are set to 1 inch, or 2.54 centimeters, depending on your specified unit of measure. Note that this default setting is different than the default margin settings in previous versions of Word. In Microsoft Office Word 2007, you can change margin settings in three basic ways.

> **Tip**
>
> To change the default setting for measurement units shown in Word, click the Microsoft Office Button and then click Word Options. In the Advanced area, scroll to the Display options, and select a measurement unit from the Show Measurements In Units Of list box. You can choose to work with Inches, Centimeters, Millimeters, Points, or Picas.

- Choose a margin setting from the Margins gallery on the Page Layout tab, as shown in Figure 3-2.

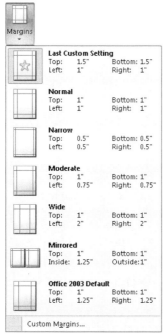

Figure 3-2 The Margins gallery highlights current margin settings and provides a variety of other common settings along with the Microsoft Office 2003 Default margin settings at the bottom of the gallery.

- At the bottom of the Margins gallery, click Custom Margins to open the Page Setup dialog box and enter your desired settings in the text boxes provided for the top, bottom, left, and right margins.

Tip

The next time you open the Margins gallery, your custom settings will be listed at the top as Last Custom Settings. If you want new documents to default to your custom settings, see the section titled "Saving Page Setup Defaults to the Current Template" later in this chapter.

- In Print Layout view, drag the edge of the shaded area on the horizontal or vertical ruler to the margin setting you want, as shown in the following image.

Tip

Press the Alt key or hold down both the left and right mouse buttons while dragging the margin indicators to display exact measurements on the Ruler.

Binding Documents

If you'll be binding the document you create, be sure to specify a gutter margin large enough to accommodate the binding. If your document is to be printed single-sided, every gutter margin will show the spacing you enter along the left margin. If your document is to be printed double-sided, on the Page Layout tab, click the Page Setup dialog launcher. On the Margins tab, click the Multiple Pages arrow, and then choose Mirror Margins to make sure that the margin settings are applied to the left and right interior margins. If you select any option other than Normal on the Multiple Pages list in the Pages area of the Page Setup dialog box, Word disables the Gutter Position option and adds the gutter setting to the appropriate margin, such as applying the gutter setting to the inside margins for book fold documents.

For more information about printing, see Chapter 26, "Printing with Precision."

Choosing Orientation

A document's orientation affects the way content is printed on a page. Typically, letters, invoices, reports, and newsletters use portrait orientation and charts, calendars, and brochures use landscape orientation.

To change the orientation of a document, navigate to the Page Layout tab on the Ribbon. Select the Orientation option in the Page Setup group. Click Landscape to change the orientation so that the document is printed with the long edge of the paper serving as the top of the page, or click Portrait to print the document with the short edge of the paper serving as the top of the page. Note that page orientation can also be found in the Page Setup dialog box, which can be accessed by clicking the Page Setup dialog launcher.

Selecting Paper Size and Source

Another page setup task involves preparing your document for final printing. Specifically, you need to specify a paper size and paper source. Word offers a range of paper sizes. The standards are readily available in the Size gallery on the Page Layout tab. You can quickly access paper sizes ranging from letter, legal, and A4 to standard business envelopes. In addition to the usual paper sizes, Word also supports numerous envelope, executive, index card, photo, panorama, banner, and custom sizes.

Choosing a Paper Size

To select a standard paper size, click the Size button on the Page Layout tab and select a paper size option in the Size gallery, as shown in Figure 3-3.

Chapter 3

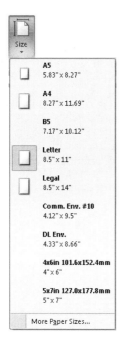

Figure 3-3 Choose from standard paper sizes from the Size gallery.

> **Note**
>
> To select a paper size beyond the standard fare, click More Paper Sizes in the Size gallery to open the Page Setup dialog box, and then click the Paper tab. You can access additional paper sizes from the Paper Size list or use the Height and Width text boxes to enter custom settings.

Selecting the Paper Source

Paper source refers to the source of the paper, envelopes, or other medium that you'll use when you print a document. If you're working with a printer that supports multiple trays, you can customize the settings for the documents you print. For example, you can print one page on letterhead from one tray and print subsequent pages on blank stock.

To select a paper source, click the Page Setup dialog launcher on the Page Layout tab, and then click the Paper tab, as shown in Figure 3-4. In the Paper Source area, click the paper tray you want to use as the source for your document's first page and then click the tray you want to use as the source for all other pages.

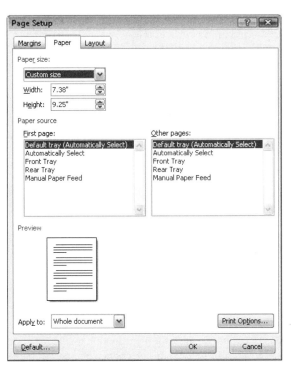

Figure 3-4 Use the Paper Source area in the Page Setup dialog box to select a paper source.

Because so many Page Setup options overlap the Print Options settings, Word makes it easy to access Print Options on the Paper tab in the Page Setup dialog box. When you're working with Page Setup options, take a moment to check your print options by clicking the Print Options button in the lower right corner of the Paper tab. The Print Options button opens the Word Options dialog box, which includes Print options on both the Display and Advanced screens. Coordinating print and page setup options might come in handy, for instance, if you want to use A4 or legal paper sizes or you plan to use duplex printing. In those cases, you can set your print and page setup options at the same time, thereby avoiding having to remember to set appropriate print options when you print the document.

For more information about printing in Word, see Chapter 26.

Saving Page Setup Defaults to the Current Template

After establishing the page settings the way you want them in your document, you can save the specifications as your default settings in the document's template (for a more in-depth look at working with templates, see Chapter 4, "Formatting Documents Using Templates"). When you save page setup settings as your default, Word saves the settings to the current template. If your document isn't based on a custom template, the changes are applied to the Normal template (by default, all new Word documents use the Normal template if they aren't based on another template). When you create default page setup settings, they will be applied to all new documents that are created based on the template.

> **Note**
>
> Templates in Word 2007 can have a .dotx or .dotm file extension and are equivalent to the .doc extension in previous versions of Word. The main difference between the .dotx and .dotm formats is that the .dotm extension indicates that the template has macro capabilities enabled.

To save your settings as the default, follow these steps:

1. Place the insertion point where you wish to configure the settings you want to use as the default.

> **CAUTION !**
>
> If changing the default settings for your Normal template, make those changes sparingly because your Normal template takes on all settings found in the Page Setup dialog box. Determine which settings the majority of your documents use and set them accordingly. If you need particular specifications for certain documents, consider creating a new template for those settings rather than modifying your Normal template.
>
> **For more information on creating your own templates see Chapter 4.**

2. Open the Page Setup dialog box.

3. Enter the page setup choices you want to apply to the document's template.

   The section titled "Working with Varying Page Settings" later in this chapter describes each available setting in detail.

4. In the lower left corner of the Page Setup dialog box, click Default.

   A message box, as shown in Figure 3-5, asks whether you'd like to change the default settings in the current template and indicates which template you are updating. In Figure 3-5, the Memo.dotm file will be modified. To apply the page settings to the current template, click Yes. If you decide not to alter the template settings, click No.

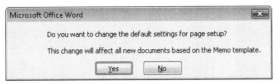

Figure 3-5 Making the current page setup settings the new default settings alters the template attached to the current document.

Backing Up Your Customizations

For best results when backing up templates and restoring the default Normal template, always keep a clean backup copy of your standard template in a directory other than the Template directory on your hard disk or server. In that way, if you need to return to earlier default specifications, you can do so by simply copying your backup file into the Template directory.

If you are using the Windows Vista operating system, you can restore templates to earlier versions by replacing an existing template with a shadow copy. A shadow copy of a file is a backup file that Windows Vista saves when you use the Back Up Files Wizard or have System Protection turned on, which is scheduled to run once a day by default. To access a list of shadow copies, right-click the template you want to restore and choose Restore Previous Versions.

Finally, to restore your Normal template to the default settings, you can have Word rebuild the Normal template the next time you start the software. To do this, simply exit Word, rename the Normal template file (choose an easy-to-recognize name, such as Normal_old), and then restart Word. Word automatically builds a new Normal template based on the default settings.

For more information about working with templates and the default location of your Normal template, see Chapter 4.

Controlling Page and Section Breaks

As you know if you've created documents of any length, Word automatically adds page breaks at appropriate points to indicate page divisions and show you how printed pages will look. In Print Layout and Full Screen Reading views, an automatic page break looks truly like an actual space between pages—you can see where one page ends and another begins. In Draft view, page breaks appear as dotted lines. Often, instances arise when you might want to add page breaks manually. In Word, you can easily add manual breaks to control pages, sections, and columns. Note that some Word features automatically add sections breaks for you when you insert particular elements, such as Cover Page Building Blocks.

> **Note**
> If you see a solid line instead of the white space allocated to the page margins in Print Layout view, place your mouse pointer on the solid line and double-click the left mouse button to show the white space. Note that the Show White Space Between Pages In Print Layout View option can also be found in Word Options in the Display area.

Adding Manual Page Breaks

In some cases, you might want to add your own page break to control where data is positioned on the page. For example, you might want to insert a manual page break in the following instances:

- To create a page containing minimal information, such as a cover page or acknowledgements page

- To separate document content

- To ensure that a figure or table and its caption begin on a new page

- To begin a new section with a heading at the top of a page

- To end a section when you don't want anything else printed on the current page

To create a manual page break, place the insertion point where you want to insert the break and then do one of the following:

- On the Page Layout tab, click Breaks in the Page Setup group, and then click Page in the Breaks gallery, as shown in Figure 3-6.

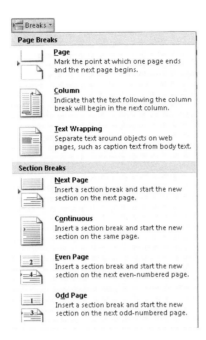

Figure 3-6 The Page Breaks gallery enables you to view the type of break you are creating before you create it.

- Click Page Break in the Pages group on the Insert tab.

- Press Ctrl+Enter.

Tip

If you want to insert a page break and a blank page simultaneously, on the Insert tab in the Pages group, click Blank Page.

Creating Additional Sections

Page Setup options are applied to a section of a document as opposed to the pages themselves. By default, new documents based on your Normal template contain a single section. If your document requires a change to the page layout, such as varying page margins, orientation, or headers and footers (other than a different first page or different odd and even pages), then you need to create additional sections to make these changes.

> **Note**
>
> Keep in mind that you can also use styles or text boxes to handle many formatting situations instead of adding sections within your pages.
>
> ● **For more information about using styles and text boxes, see Chapter 15, "Using Styles to Increase Your Formatting Power" and Chapter 16, "Formatting Layouts Using Backgrounds, Watermarks, and Text Boxes."**

The Breaks gallery shown in Figure 3-6 provides a much needed visual improvement to the process of creating and modifying section breaks. Now, the type of break you set can be clearly evident before you "experiment" with a dialog box option.

> **Tip**
>
> To view the section number in the new customizable status bar, right-click the status bar and click Section.

To use the Breaks gallery, position your cursor where you want to begin a new section and then select an option in the Breaks gallery. The Breaks gallery includes the following page break and section break options.

Table 3-1 Breaks Gallery Options

Type of Break	Break Characteristics
Page	Ends the current page and starts a new page.
Column	Starts a new column when using multiple-column formatting.
Text Wrapping	Separates text around objects from the body text.
Next Page	Ends the current page and starts a new section.
Continuous	Begins the new section at the insertion point.
Even Page	Ends the current page and starts a new section. The new page will always print on an even page.
Odd Page	Ends the current page and starts a new section. The new page will always print on an odd page.

> **Tip**
>
> To change page layout settings and insert a section break at the same time, either place your insertion point at the location you wish to start the new settings or select the portion of the document that will contain the settings, and then display the Page Setup dialog box. From the Apply To list at the bottom of any tab in the dialog box, select This Point Forward or Selected Text, respectively. After you make your modifications and click OK, section breaks will be inserted into your document as needed and your page layout settings will be applied to that section.

Inserting Text Wrapping Breaks

When you add a text-wrapping break, Word forces a text break for layout reasons without starting a new paragraph. For instance, you might want to break text at a particular position to appear before and after an inline table, graphic, or object, or you might want to present lines of poetry without applying the document's paragraph style (including paragraph spacing) to each line of text. The Text Wrapping Break option is similar to inserting a manual line break in your document, which you can add by pressing Shift+Enter. Frequently, text-wrapping breaks are used to separate text from Web page objects or other text and are the equivalent of inserting a `<br/>` tag in XHTML code.

Chapter 3

TROUBLESHOOTING

My document includes unwanted breaks

You finish your document and print a draft, or you open a document that was created by another individual for editing or review. What's this? The document is breaking at odd places or including unwanted blank pages.

The underlying problem is that no two printers are the same and each paginates a document differently. What may look perfect on one computer may not look the same when viewed on another computer or if you print the document using a printer other than the one you normally use. The primary issue is that manual page breaks were used in an effort to control document pagination, such as inserting a manual page break to keep paragraphs together on the same page or keep a table or figure together with its caption. If you've ever used this method, then chances are you've encountered the ongoing battle of deleting and reinserting manual page breaks.

Instead of using manual page breaks, you can use pagination formatting instead. Pagination formatting allows you to specify which paragraphs need to stay together on the same page or whether all lines of a paragraph need to remain on the same page. By using pagination formatting, you turn the hassle of continuously deleting and reinserting manual page breaks over to Word.

To resolve this problem, first locate and delete the unwanted manual page or section breaks. You may need to turn on the formatting marks view to see where these breaks are located. To do so, on the Home tab in the Paragraph group, click Show/Hide (the button with the paragraph symbol).

Place your insertion point in the paragraph that needs to be formatted with a pagination option. Then, on either the Page Layout or Home tab, in the Paragraph group, click the dialog launcher to open the Paragraph dialog box. On the Line And Page Breaks tab, use the Keep Lines Together option to keep all lines of a paragraph on the same page. Use the Keep With Next option to force a paragraph to stay on the same page as the following paragraph.

For additional details on pagination formatting options, see Chapter 14, "Aligning Information and Formatting Paragraphs and Lists."

Working with Varying Page Settings

Depending on a document's complexity, you might want to vary the margins. For instance, a standard report might have equal margins on the right and left sides, a format that makes setting margins simple. In contrast, a document you want to bind or fold, or a publication that's designed so that the left and right pages complement each other, might require more finely tuned adjustments to page settings.

When you want to set up a document that requires varying page settings, you can simplify your task by using the Page Setup dialog box and setting several settings at the same time.

Along with using the Page Setup dialog launcher and various galleries to display the Page Setup dialog box, use any of the following techniques:

- Double-click anywhere in the vertical or horizontal ruler and, in Print Layout view, double-click outside of any page.

Note

To display rulers, click the View Ruler command above the vertical scroll bar or, on the View tab in the Show/Hide group, click Ruler.

- Press Alt+P, S, P.

The Page Setup dialog box in Word 2007 (shown in Figure 3-7) looks similar to the Page Setup dialog box found in previous versions of Word. If you have support for

Chinese, Japanese, or Korean enabled through Microsoft Office Language Settings 2007, you'll also see the Document Grid tab in your Page Setup dialog box.

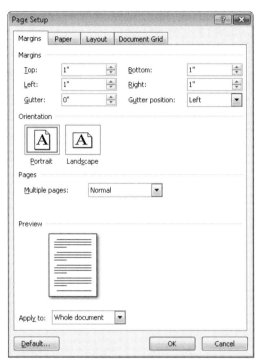

Figure 3-7 The Page Setup dialog box enables you to vary the page settings within a document.

The Page Setup dialog box enables you to choose the settings that affect the margins, paper type, layout, and spacing of your document.

> **Note**
>
> To configure language settings for the 2007 Microsoft Office system while working in Word, click the Microsoft Office Button in the upper left corner of the window. Click Word Options, ensure that Popular is selected, click Language Settings, add or remove language support, click OK, and then restart Word if prompted.

To summarize, the tabs in the Page Setup dialog box enable you to enter basic page settings, such as the following:

- **Margins** You can specify settings for the top, bottom, left, right, and gutter margins; choose page orientation; and select formatting for multiple pages. See the

Sidebar tip titled "Binding Documents" earlier in this chapter for more on using gutter margins.

- **Paper** You can make choices about paper size as well as the source for the paper and envelopes on which you'll print your information. In addition, you can access the Print dialog box from this tab by clicking Print Options.

- **Layout** This tab enables you to set options for sections, headers and footers, and overall content alignment. In addition, you can access the Line Numbers dialog box by clicking Line Numbers as well as the Borders And Shading dialog box by clicking Borders. See the section titled "Including Headers and Footers" later in this chapter for additional information on the Layout tab.

- **Document Grid** The Document Grid is available with some Language Settings configurations. This tab enables you to control the horizontal and vertical text flow as well as line and character spacing in documents that use East Asian languages. By using this tab, you can also specify Drawing Grid settings (click Drawing Grid), which give you control over grid display and other grid settings, and access the Font dialog box by clicking Set Font.

Multiple Page Settings

The Multiple Pages setting, found on the Margins tab of the Page Setup dialog box, enables you to specify whether your document should include mirror margins, two pages per sheet, book fold, or reverse book fold. To change the page settings for a multiple-page document, follow these steps:

1. Open your document. On the Page Layout tab, click the Page Setup dialog launcher to display the Page Setup dialog box.

2. Enter the Margins, Paper, and Layout settings on their respective tabs.

3. On the Margins tab in the Pages area, click the Multiple Pages arrow. Table 3-2 explains the effects of the Multiple Pages choices.

4. Click your Multiple Pages choice and then specify the Apply To option if you selected Mirror Margins or 2 Pages Per Sheet. If you selected Book Fold or Reverse Book Fold, you can specify how many sheets are contained in each booklet.

> **Note**
> If your document has more pages than the number of pages you selected for a booklet, Word prints the document as multiple booklets.

Table 3-2 **Choosing Page Settings for Multiple Pages**

Setting	Preview	Description
Normal		Used for single-sided printing. Each page has a specific left and right margin.
Mirror Margins		Used for duplex printing in which the margins mirror each other. The left and right margins become the inside and outside margins, respectively.
2 Pages Per Sheet		Divides the current page into two pages.
Book Fold		Treats each left and right page as a spread, using a gutter and mirroring margins as applicable.
Reverse Book Fold		Enables you to create a booklet written in a right-to-left text orientation, such as one written in Arabic or Hebrew, or in an East Asian language that has vertical text (this option is available only when a relevant language is enabled in the Microsoft Office 2007 Language Settings).

Aligning Content Vertically Between Margins

Word gives you the option of indicating how you want the content between the top and bottom margins of your page to be aligned. To control vertical alignment, display the Page Setup dialog box, click the Layout tab, click the Vertical Alignment arrow, and then select an alignment option. By default, the vertical alignment is set to Top. You can choose among Top, Center, Justified, or Bottom. Word aligns the page content based on your selection. For example, if you click Center, Word centers the contents of the page between the top and bottom margins. If you choose Bottom, Word aligns the page contents with the bottom margin and places any extra space at the top of the page, above the content.

Creating a Page or Section Border

If you want to set up page and section borders for your document while taking care of the rest of your page settings, you can do so by using the Page Setup dialog box or Page Layout tab. To access border settings, on the Page Layout tab in the Page Background group, click the Page Borders option, or open the Page Setup dialog box, click the Layout tab, and then click Borders. The Borders And Shading dialog box appears. Similar to the Page Setup dialog box, the Borders And Shading dialog box includes an Apply To list box. Using the Apply To options, you can add borders to selected pages, text and paragraphs, sections, first page of a section, every page except the first page of a section, and the entire document.

For full coverage of adding page borders, see Chapter 17, "Commanding Attention with Borders and Shading."

Including Headers and Footers

Adding text to the header (top) and footer (bottom) areas in a Word document serves a number of purposes, but headers and footers are used primarily to repeat information at the top or bottom of each page. You can easily insert page numbers, text, Building Blocks, pictures, and clip art in document headers and footers.

> Note
>
> You can see a document's headers and footers only in printed documents, Print Layout view (if white space between pages is not suppressed), Print Preview, and Full Screen Reading view (if the Show Printed Page option is selected). Headers and footers are hidden in the Web Layout, Outline, and Draft views.

Adding Page Numbers

Word enables you to add page numbers in two principal ways. You can add basic page numbers by using the Page Number gallery on the Insert tab, or you can add page numbers along with additional content by using the built-in or custom Header and Footer galleries. When you use the Page Number gallery, you can add a page number to the Top Of Page, Bottom Of Page, Page Margins, or Current Position. After you select a position, choose a page-numbering design from the gallery of designs, as shown in the following image.

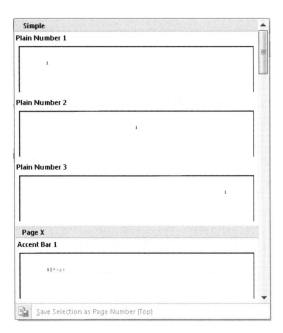

When you insert a page number by using the Page Number gallery, Word automatically inserts the selected page number and opens the header and footer layer in your document for additional editing. If you want to add more complex page numbering as well as additional information, you can add headers and footers as described in the next section.

Creating Headers and Footers

Headers and footers are special sections on each page that often provide the sort of useful information that many people take for granted—such as page numbers and chapter titles. Headers present information at the tops of pages, while footers provide information at the bottoms of pages. For example, in a book, the chapter names and book title often appear in the header, while the page numbers appear in the footer. You'll often use headers and footers to provide readers with important information about the publication, which could include the title, author, page number, creation date, last modified date, confidentiality statements, graphics, and other items. Word provides an array of header and footer options, as discussed later in this chapter.

You can control whether headers and footers differ on odd and even pages, whether the first page has a different header or footer, and where headers and footers are placed relative to the edge of a printed page.

To create a header or footer, on the Insert tab in the Header & Footer group, select a Building Block from the respective gallery.

Chapter 3

> **Note**
>
> If the desired Header or Footer selection doesn't use your preferred fonts or colors, then modify or change your document Theme, found on the Page Layout tab in the Themes group, before manually making formatting changes. The fonts and colors shown in the Header and Footer galleries are linked to the document Theme and update if the document Theme is changed.
>
> **For more information on customizing a document Theme, see Chapter 15, "Applying Themes for a Professional Look".**

When the Header and Footer sections are active, you can add text, numbers, field codes, graphics, Building Blocks, and objects to customize your document's headers and footers. The next section of this chapter describes how you can edit and customize headers and footers.

When you insert a header or footer, the Header and Footer areas become accessible, the content area of the document becomes temporarily unavailable, and the Header & Footer Tools display along with the contextual Design tab, as shown in Figure 3-8.

Figure 3-8 To create headers and footers in documents, you enter and format numbers, text, Building Blocks, and graphics in the header and footer areas.

The Design tab includes the following:

- **Header Gallery** Enables you to edit or remove a header. Also enables you to select a header's contents and save the selection to the Header gallery so you can use the header in other documents.

- **Footer Gallery** Enables you to edit or remove a footer. Also enables you to select a footer's contents and save the selection to the Footer gallery so you can use the footer in other documents.

- **Page Number Gallery** Inserts a page number field, such as {PAGE}. You can use this option to add a page number to the top of the page, bottom of the page, in the page's margins, or at the current position. This button also includes the Remove Page Numbers option and the Format Page Numbers option, which opens the Page Number Format dialog box and enables you to apply number formatting such add chapter numbers, continue numbering from prior pages, or start numbering at a specified page number.

- **Date & Time** Opens the Date And Time dialog box, which enables you to insert the current date and time or update the information automatically, insert date fields such as {DATE \@ "M/d/yyyy"}, and insert time fields such as {TIME \@ "h:mm"ss am/pm"}.

- **Picture** Opens the Insert Picture dialog box and displays the images in your Pictures folder by default.

- **Clip Art** Opens and closes the Clip Art task pane and enables you to search and insert clip art items into your header or footer.

- **Go To Header** Jumps to the header section if you are working in the footer section, thereby enabling you to jump quickly from the footer to the header.

- **Go To Footer** Jumps to the footer section if you are working in the header section, thereby enabling you to jump quickly from the header to the footer.

- **Previous Section** Displays the header or footer used in the previous section based on the current location of your cursor. If you click Previous Section while in the footer area, the cursor jumps to the footer area in the preceding section of your document. Note that you must have section breaks, different first page, or different odd and even headers and footers in your document to use this feature.

- **Next Section** Displays the header or footer used in the next section based on the current location of your cursor. If you click Next Section while in the header area, the cursor jumps to the header area in the next section of your document. Note that you must have section breaks, different first page, or different odd and even headers and footers in your document to use this feature.

Chapter 3

- **Link To Previous** Links the headers and footers in the current section to the preceding section, thus enabling you to create a continuous flow from section to section. You can also click in the header or footer area and click Ctrl+Shift+R to link the header or footer area to the preceding section. Note that you must have additional sections in your document to use this feature.

- **Different First Page** Specifies that you want to format the first page's headers and footers differently. For example, you might prefer to omit the page number on a cover page. This option is also available in the Page Setup dialog box.

- **Different Odd & Even Pages** Enables you to format headers and footers separately for odd and even pages. For example, you might choose to have the left page headers display the book's title while the right page headers display the chapter title. This option is also available in the Page Setup dialog box.

- **Show Document Text** Toggles the display of the document's contents. You can hide document text to simplify your view as you create and edit headers and footers.

- **Header From Top** Enables you to control where the header is positioned from the top edge of the page. This option is also available in the Page Setup dialog box.

- **Footer From Bottom** Enables you to control where the footer is positioned from the bottom edge of the page. This option is also available in the Page Setup dialog box.

- **Insert Alignment Tab** Opens the Alignment Tab dialog box to insert a tab relative to the margin or indent. See the following Inside Out tip titled "Alignment Tabs: The 'Relative' Scoop" for more information on this new feature.

- **Close Header And Footer** Closes the header and footer areas as well as the Header & Footer Tools.

> **Tip**
>
> To manually add or edit a document's header and footer, right-click the header or footer area and select Edit Header or Edit Footer, respectively.

INSIDE OUT   Alignment Tabs: The 'Relative' Scoop

When aligning content in the header or footer on the same line, such as a left-aligned company name and right-aligned date, a common method used for mixed alignment is manual tabs. The problem with using manual tabs is that, if the left or right margins change, the alignment of the content will not change and the manual tabs need to be adjusted. More often than not, adjusting the tabs is often overlooked, and the header or footer content does not line up with the rest of the document.

The answer to this problem is the new Alignment Tab functionality. An Alignment Tab aligns data relative to the margin or indent, whereas a manual tab is set in a fixed position and does not automatically change position if the margins change. To view the Alignment Tab settings, right-click a header or footer in the document and click Edit Header or Edit Footer, respectively, to view the Header & Footer Tools. On the Design tab, click Insert Alignment Tab to open the Alignment Tab dialog box, as shown in the following image.

There is a small caveat to using an Alignment Tab—there is no visual indication that an Alignment Tab is present, such as the manual tab indicators that you see in the Ruler. When using an Alignment Tab to align data in the header or footer, it's recommended that any unused manual tabs be removed from the Ruler to help clarify the formatting. To remove a manual tab, simply drag it off of the Ruler.

The Alignment Tab dialog box is only accessible when viewing the Header & Footer Tools, but they can be utilized anywhere in your document by adding Insert Alignment Tab to your Quick Access Toolbar. To do so, right-click Insert Alignment Tab and then click Add To Quick Access Toolbar.

Chapter 3

Working with Field Codes in Headers and Footers

When you use the Header & Footer Tools and the Design tab to add elements—such as page numbers, dates, and times—to headers and footers, Word often accomplishes the task by inserting field codes. You can control field codes in a number of ways, including the following:

- You can edit a field code by right-clicking the field code and then choosing Edit Field. The Field dialog box appears, which enables you to select from various formats that you can use to display the field's data.

- You can toggle the display between field data and field codes by right-clicking a field and choosing Toggle Field Codes.

- To update a field, select the field and press F9. Alternatively, right-click the field and choose Update Field. You can also click a field, such as a date that updates automatically, and choose the Update command that appears above the field in a new type of container called a Content Control.

- To control whether fields appear with or without gray backgrounds online, click the Microsoft Office Button in the upper left corner of the window, click Advanced, scroll to the Show Document Content area, and select an option in the Field Shading list. Available options include Never, Always, or When Selected.

To create different headers and footers for part of a document, you must divide the document into sections and then create headers and footers for each section. If you are working in a document divided into sections but want to continue using the same headers and footers from section to section, click in a section and then, on the Design tab in the Navigation group, make sure Link To Previous is selected.

Deleting Headers and Footers

To delete a header or footer from a document or section, simply open the header and footer areas (double-click in a header or footer area, or right-click a header or footer area and choose Edit Header or Edit Footer) to display the Header & Footer Tools. Or, on the Design tab, click Remove Header or Remove Footer from the respective Header or Footer gallery. You can also select and delete header and footer content in the same way you select and delete any other content.

CAUTION

If your document contains multiple sections, before you remove or edit headers and footers in your document, remember to turn off the Link To Previous option in following sections to avoid inadvertently changing or deleting headers and footers in the those following sections.

Working with the Document Grid

If support for Chinese, Japanese, or Korean is enabled through Microsoft Office Language Settings 2007, you can use Word's Document Grid to help you control line and character placement in your documents. To choose grid settings, use the Document Grid tab in the Page Setup dialog box, as shown in Figure 3-9.

Figure 3-9 The Document Grid enables you to precisely control line and character spacing in documents that contain East Asian text.

Specifying Document Grid Settings

By using the Document Grid tab, you can control the text flow, number of columns, number of characters per line, character **pitch** (spacing between characters), number of lines per page, and line pitch. To use the Document Grid features, follow these steps:

1. On the Page Layout tab, click the Page Setup dialog launcher to open the Page Setup dialog box, and then click the Document Grid tab.

2. If you want the text to be shown vertically, appearing top to bottom as you type, in the Text Flow area, click Vertical. Otherwise, for traditional right-to-left text display, leave Horizontal selected.

If desired, specify a number of columns in the Columns box. Notice that the Preview image adjusts to display your page setup settings while you work.

3. To turn on the Grid feature, select one of the following options:

    - Specify Line Grid Only Makes only the settings in the Lines area on the Document Grid tab available so that you can choose the amount of space between lines (by selecting the number of lines you want to appear on the page) and the pitch, or spacing, between lines.

    - Specify Line And Character Grid Makes all settings in both Character and Lines areas available. This setting enables you to choose both the number of characters per line and the number of lines per page. You can also choose the pitch of both characters and lines.

    - Text Snaps To Character Grid Disables the Pitch settings and gives you the means to choose the number of characters per line and lines per page.

4. Click the Apply To arrow, choose the option that specifies the portion of the document to which you want to apply the grid, and then click OK.

If you changed the text direction in the Document Grid tab for the entire document, Word automatically updates any existing content after you click OK. If you retained the original text direction prior to the cursor and applied the This Point Forward setting, Word applies the grid effects for existing and new content after the cursor's location. If necessary, Word begins a new page to separate content with different formats.

Displaying the Drawing Grid

You can display the Drawing Grid on your page to help you align objects and text, regardless of your language settings. To toggle the display of gridlines, simply navigate to the View tab and, in the Show/Hide group, click Gridlines.

Or, if you installed support for East Asian languages, click the Drawing Grid button on the Document Grid tab in the Page Setup dialog box to access the Drawing Grid settings. Or on the Page Layout tab, in the Arrange group, click Align, and then click Grid Settings. Figure 3-10 displays the Drawing Grid dialog box.

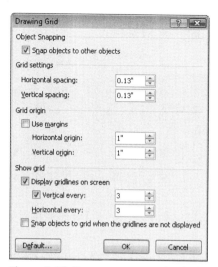

Figure 3-10 You can customize the display of the Document Grid by modifying the Drawing Grid dialog box settings.

You can see the Document Grid while you work only when you're working in Print Layout view.

Adding and Controlling Line Numbers

If you're working on a document that requires line numbering, such as a legal document or formal literature piece, line numbers can serve as useful references. Line numbers are placed in the margin next to each line in a document and enable quick references to specific lines in a document.

To add line numbers, you can select an option from Line Numbers on the Page Layout tab or choose settings from the Line Numbers dialog box, which can be accessed from the Layout tab in the Page Setup dialog box. Figure 3-11 shows both the Line Number options and the Line Numbers dialog box. By using these tools, you can choose whether to number an entire document continuously, restart numbering on each page, restart numbering in each section, or stop numbering for specific paragraphs. In addition, you can use the Page Setup dialog box to apply numbering to selected parts of a document in the same way that you control margins and other page setup options.

Chapter 3

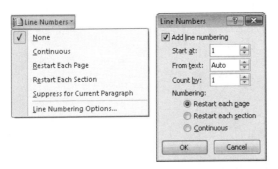

Figure 3-11 The Line Numbers feature enables you to add and control line numbering for a section, selected text, or the entire document.

To use the Line Numbers on the Page Layout tab to control line numbering, follow these steps:

1. Position your cursor in the document or section in which you want to add line numbers.

2. On the Page Layout tab, click the Line Numbers button and choose an option.

To use the Line Numbers dialog box (accessible from the Layout tab in the Page Layout dialog box) to control line numbering, follow these steps:

1. Click anywhere in a document you want to number, or click in a section that you want to number.

2. On the Page Layout tab, click Line Numbers and choose Line Numbering Options, or on the Page Layout tab, click the Page Setup dialog launcher.

3. In the Page Setup dialog box, click the Layout tab, if necessary.

4. On the Layout tab, click Line Numbers. The Line Numbers dialog box appears, as shown in Figure 3-11.

5. Select the Add Line Numbering check box. In the Start At box, type the number with which you want numbering to begin.

6. In the From Text box, specify number placement by using the up or down arrows, typing a number (by default, the From Text spacing is measured in inches), or accept Auto (the default setting).

7. In the Count By box, enter a value to specify which lines should be accompanied by numbers. For instance, if you want to show a number next to every other line, you would enter **2** in the Count By box. To display a number next to each line, retain the default Count By setting of **1**.

8. In the Numbering area, click Restart Each Page if you want each page to be individually numbered, click Restart Each Section if you want the numbering to begin again with each subsequent section, or click Continuous if you want numbers to increase throughout the document.

9. Click OK to close the Line Numbers dialog box and return to the Page Setup dialog box. Click OK to close the Page Setup dialog box.

TROUBLESHOOTING

I don't have enough room for line numbers

If you've created heading styles that extend all the way to the left margin of your page, you might find them truncated when you add line numbering. You can fix this by displaying the Line Numbers dialog box and changing the From Text setting. By default, From Text is set to Auto, but by decreasing the amount of space between numbering and text, you can usually make room for both line numbering and headings.

What's Next?

This chapter covered page setup features related to Word and looked at various methods that you can use to master document layout and pagination. The next chapter shows you how to take a frequently used document layout, along with content that is specific to that document, and turn it into a template to quickly create new documents based on your previous specified settings—functionality that will save you time in new document creation.

Formatting Documents Using Templates

In 1983, Microsoft Word for MS-DOS 1.0 made big news on the document creation front—finally, users could actually see italics, boldfacing, and underlining on the screen! Now, more than 20 years later, Microsoft Office Word 2007 provides far greater document formatting and building features, well beyond those first baby steps into the world of WYSIWYG. As you can see throughout this book, Office Word 2007 lets you build documents by using graphics, links, Building Blocks, Content Controls, and XML-based document parts in addition to applying formatting such as boldfacing, italics, and underlining. But one commonality has persisted through the years—computers still need to be told what to do, no matter how automated a task might seem. Therefore, to best control your documents in Word, you need to understand document formatting basics. In that way, you can tell Word exactly what you want it to do when you format your documents.

Nature of Document Formatting Tools

The 2007 release of Word sports some dynamic new document formatting pieces such as Building Blocks, Content Controls, and the various Quick Style galleries found throughout the application. But amidst the exciting advances, templates still serve as the glue holding together document formatting tools. Because Word documents now use XML technology, templates offer more control and flexibility than ever before. Two notable additions to Word 2007 are new formatting templates, such as Themes and Quick Style Sets. While document templates supply content, layout, and formatting, Themes and Quick Style Sets supply formatting to a document.

Prior to creating a document template, which is described in this chapter, you may want to consider your formatting needs. If your new documents do not need preset layout or content and all they need is preset formatting capabilities, then consider utilizing one of the new formatting templates instead. Learn more about creating and customizing Themes in Chapter 5, "Applying Themes for a Professional Look," as well as creating and customizing Quick Style Sets in Chapter 15, "Using Styles to Increase Your Formatting Power." To determine which type of template you need, you must first understand the basics of document templates.

Whenever you create a new document in Word, your document is based on a template that provides default document creation settings. Every Word document uses a template, whether users realize it or not. Templates are available locally on your computer as well as online, and they serve as patterns for documents. They can contain standard (or boilerplate) text, Content Controls for placeholder text or form fields, Building Blocks for insertion of frequently used content, styles for uniform formatting, page layout for preset margins and orientation, macros for automating tasks, key assignments for quick access to frequent commands, and a predefined selection of headers, footers, and cover pages—all of the tools needed to produce new documents quickly and efficiently. For information about creating specific elements in your template, see the Sidebar "Designer's Toolbox" later in this chapter.

Fundamentally, a template creates a copy of itself by default when you open it, thereby allowing you to use preconfigured settings to create a document. In Word 2007, document templates are available in two file formats:

- **.dotx** New template format that uses the Office Open XML Format and does not contain macros

- **.dotm** New template format that uses the Office Open XML Format and contains macros

INSIDE OUT   Creating Documents Prgrammatically

Word 2007 documents are merely a collection of various parts contained in a ZIP file, or package. The ZIP package contains document parts such as individual XML files, graphics, charts, and embedded objects. Viewing the internal components of the ZIP package is simply a matter of renaming the file with a .zip file extension and opening it in any tool that functions on ZIP technology. The following figure is a view of a macro-enabled template opened in Windows Explorer along with the contents of the word folder.

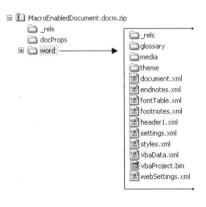

A document is now stored in individual document parts such as headers, footers, end-notes, styles, and media. This new functionality enables developers to create new Word documents as well as access and alter data without going through the Word application. For example, if an address or logo stored in the header of several documents changes, the headers can be updated without the need to open each document in Word to make the modification.

For more information on XML in Word, see Chapter 30, "Working with XML." If you want a more in-depth look at creating and editing documents in the Office Open XML Format, see Advanced Microsoft Office Documents 2007 Edition Inside Out by Stephanie Krieger (Microsoft Press, 2007).

Beyond the new file formats, Word 2007 templates work similarly to the binary templates used in earlier versions of Word. You can control how documents and templates interact in a number of ways. For example, you can base documents on existing templates, create custom templates for new and existing documents, attach templates to documents, load global templates, and edit templates.

Note

Word 2007 also supports creating and using templates saved in the Word 97–2003 Document file format (.dot) in Compatibility Mode. If you create a template in Office Word 2007 that you want to use in earlier versions of Word, you can use the Save As dialog box to save your template as a binary template (.dot) using the Word 97–2003 Document file format.

In this chapter, you'll learn how to create, use, and control document templates to enhance and automate document creation, editing, and formatting.

Understanding How Templates Work

As mentioned previously, every Word document is based on a template. In Word 2007, a template contains the structure and tools for shaping the style, formatting, content, and page layout of finished files. Most templates on Microsoft Office Online (www.office.microsoft.com) include visual elements such as graphics, Content Controls, and custom Building Blocks that are associated with the template. In contrast, Word bases new, blank documents on the Normal template which, by default, contains no visual elements. The Normal template is discussed in more detail later in this chapter in the section titled "Getting the Scoop on the Normal Template."

visual elements

The main purpose of templates is to make formatting and inserting information into documents as efficient, error-free, and automatic as possible. The fewer formatting and typing tasks you have to perform, the better. In addition to speeding up document creation, templates enable you to provide custom editing environments for particular projects and clients because templates can also include interface tools (such as a customized Quick Access Toolbar or a customized Ribbon) as well as the previous list of content and layout settings.

Regardless of the information included in templates or whether your template includes macros, you can use two main types of templates when you work in Word: global templates and document templates. Global templates (most notably the Normal and Building Blocks templates) contain settings that are available to all documents regardless of the template used to create the document. In contrast, document templates, such as letterhead and those from Microsoft Office Online, contain settings that are available only to documents based on that template. When a document is based on a template, the template is attached, or linked, to the document, and the settings stored in the document template are made available to the document through the link. (For more information about attaching templates, see the section titled "Attaching Templates to Documents" later in this chapter.) If this difference between global and document templates seems a little cloudy at the moment, don't despair. Once you have reviewed the information in this chapter and experiment with templates for a while, you'll see the value of knowing how to use and customize global and document templates as you work.

Getting the Scoop on the Normal Template

No matter what template you use to format a specific document, the Normal template, or Normal.dotm, is always open, which is why it's considered a global template. Whenever you start Word, it automatically looks for the Normal template in the User Template location specified in the File Locations dialog box. The default location of the User Templates, or Templates, folder is:

- **On Windows Vista:** C:\Users*user name*\AppData\Roaming\Microsoft\Templates

- **On Windows XP:** C:\Documents and Settings*user name*\Application Data\Microsoft\Templates

To access the File Locations dialog box, click the Microsoft Office Button, click Word Options, click Advanced, scroll to the bottom of the Advanced options window, and click File Locations to display the File Locations dialog box, as shown in Figure 4-1.

Figure 4-1 The File Locations dialog box, accessible from the Advanced options area in the Word Options dialog box, lets you view and control the location of Word references to find templates.

TROUBLESHOOTING

I don't see the AppData or Application Data folder

By design, the AppData folder in Windows Vista and the Application Data folder in Windows XP are hidden folders. If you do not see the AppData or Application Data folder in your User Profile folder, you need to configure Windows to display hidden files and folders. To do this, open an Exploring window, such as My Computer, and from the Tools menu click Folder Options. In the Folder Options dialog box, click the View tab, select the Show Hidden Files And Folders option in the Advanced Settings area, and click OK.

The Normal template uses the Office Theme and contains default styles (but no boilerplate text) that are automatically available whenever you create new, blank documents. As you work in a document, any styles, macros, or other customizations that you save are stored in the Normal template unless you specify otherwise. In addition, you can modify the Normal template to change the default document formatting in Word. As you can imagine, the longer you work with Word, the more customized your Normal. dotm file can become.

If the Normal template is damaged, moved, missing, or renamed, Word creates a new Normal template the next time you start Word. The new template is based on the default settings. This automatically generated Normal template won't include any customizations that you've made to a previous version of Normal.dotm. Of course, you can intentionally rename your Normal template to force Word to create a new Normal template. If you do this, Word creates a fresh Normal template, and then you can copy selected components from the renamed template into the newly generated Normal template by using the Organizer, as described in "Using the Organizer to Rename, Delete, and Copy Styles" later in this chapter. To rename the Normal template, close Word and then display Normal.dotm in your Templates folder, as previously noted in this section. Right-click the Normal template, click Rename, and enter a new name for the template. The next time you open a new, blank document in Word, the document will be based on the standard Normal template without any custom settings.

TROUBLESHOOTING

Word crashes during startup—could the Normal template be corrupt?

If Word crashes during startup, you can quickly determine whether the problem is due to a damaged Registry entry, an add-in, or a corrupt Normal.dotm file. To get to the root of the problem, try starting Word in Safe Mode. When you start Word in Safe Mode, Word opens but prevents add-ins and global templates (including Normal.dotm) from loading automatically. To start Word in Safe Mode, simply hold the Ctrl key while starting Word. Note that you need to continue holding the Ctrl key until you are prompted to start Word in Safe Mode.

If Word opens properly when this method is used but crashes when you try to open it normally, you can deduce that the error doesn't lie in the Word installation. Instead, the error is caused by a damaged Normal template, third-party add-in, or Registry corruption.

To test whether the Normal.dotm file is the culprit, rename the Normal.dotm file and then attempt to start Word normally. If Word starts, a new Normal.dotm file will be created, and you can use the Organizer to copy any components you need from the renamed file into the newly created Normal.dotm file.

If Word still doesn't start properly after you rename your existing Normal.dotm file, the next likely culprit is a third-party add-in followed by Registry corruption.

For additional information on troubleshooting third-party add-ins and Registry corruption, see the Troubleshooting guide on this book's companion CD.

CAUTION

Because the Normal template is so necessary and so widely used, it's often the first target of macro virus creators. Third-party add-ins that aren't developed properly can display virus-like qualities that can lead to the corruption of your Normal template. Since Word automatically saves changes made to your Normal template during the current session upon exiting, a method you can use to help protect yourself against viruses and corruption is to change the automatic behavior to instead prompt you before Word automatically saves changes to your Normal template. After all, changes to your documents aren't automatically saved, and you should have the same control over determining which changes should be saved to your Normal template. To do so, click the Microsoft Office Button and then click Word Options. In the Advanced area under the Save options, turn on Prompt Before Saving Normal Template.

Additionally, if you work with a highly customized Normal template, it's recommended that you back up your system's Normal.dotm file every few weeks.

If you find that you are prompted to save changes to Normal.dotm each time you exit Word, then this should be investigated. See the Troubleshooting guide on this book's companion CD for the steps you need to take to rectify this issue.

Starting with a Template

When you install Word, the setup program installs 32 templates and provides easy access to over 80 categories of professionally designed templates available from Microsoft Office Online. With all of these prebuilt templates at your disposal, you can easily create new documents based on templates without having to create a custom template. In this part of the chapter, you'll learn how to create new documents based on templates that you have on hand or can access easily. Building templates from scratch or previously created documents or templates is discussed later in this chapter.

Using Templates from the New Documents Dialog Box

As mentioned, Word provides easy access to a number of built-in templates that you can use to create new documents. To access Word templates, click the Microsoft Office Button and then click New. Figure 4-2 displays the New Document dialog box.

Chapter 4

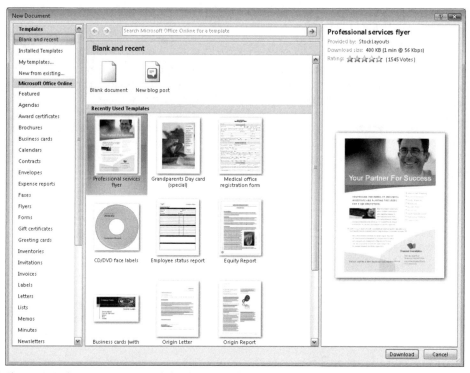

Figure 4-2 The New Document dialog box provides easy access to installed templates, recently used templates, and professionally designed Microsoft Office Online templates.

The New Document dialog box lets you access all installed and recently used Word templates, in addition to Microsoft Office Online templates and any templates you have saved to your Templates or Workgroup Templates folders.

> **Note**
>
> The location for Workgroup Templates is not set by default. Typically, this location is a shared folder on your network. The Workgroup Templates location can be set in the File Locations dialog box located in Word Options in the Advanced area.
>
> Once you set a location for Workgroup Templates in the File Locations dialog box, you will no longer be able to remove the Workgroup Templates location without editing the Registry. If you find that you prefer not to map Workgroup Templates to a folder after you've added a location, simply map the Workgroup Templates option to the Templates folder. By doing this, you basically instruct Word to show the templates in your Templates folder for both User Templates and Workgroup Templates. If you map the Workgroup Templates option to any other location, your My Templates tab in the New dialog box will contain files that you would probably prefer not to include.

The following list is a summary of the template options found in the New Document dialog box:

- **Blank and Recent** Provides the standard blank document template (based on Normal.dotm), along with the New Blog Post and recently used templates.

- **Installed Templates** Displays a list of built-in templates that were installed with Word 2007.

- **My Templates** Opens the New dialog box and displays templates that you have saved to your computer. Each tab in the New dialog box indicates a subfolder within the Templates folder (see the section titled "Creating Custom Templates" later in this chapter).

- **New From Existing** Opens the New From Existing Document dialog box and enables you to create a new document based on another document (regardless of whether the document is a template).

- **Microsoft Office Online** Grants access to an enormous collection of templates that you can download from Microsoft Office Online. You should spend some time investigating the extensive selection of templates from Microsoft Office Online—ranging from marketing and business forms, letters, and contracts to stationery, calendars, certificates, and flyers. At the time of this writing, there were about 2,000 templates available for Word (not including customer-submitted templates), and they fluctuate nearly every day.

The Microsoft Office Genuine Advantage

The Microsoft Office Genuine Advantage program was designed to provide additional value to those who own a genuine licensed copy of Microsoft Office and to help protect those who have unknowingly purchased a counterfeit copy of Microsoft Office. Counterfeit software may contain spyware or malware, not to mention that those who purchased the software may have also unknowingly given their credit card information to counterfeiters.

Each time you download a template from Microsoft Office Online, your copy of Microsoft Office is authenticated as noted in the Microsoft Office Genuine Advantage dialog box, shown below.

Chapter 4

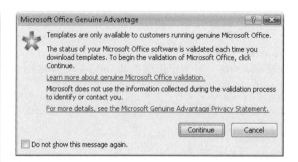

When you validate your copy of Microsoft Office, a match between your PC's hardware profile and your 25-character Product Key is created and no personal information is collected.

To use a template available in the New Document dialog box to create a new document, follow these steps:

1. Click the Microsoft Office Button, and then click New to display the New Document dialog box.

2. In the Templates area, choose the type of template you want to use.

3. If you are using a template from the Installed Templates or My Templates categories, verify the Create New options in the New dialog box. Make sure that Document is selected to create a new document based on a selected template, and then double-click the template (or select the template and click OK).

If you're opening a template that's installed on your computer, Word immediately creates a new document based on the selected template. If the template isn't installed on your computer, then the Microsoft Office Genuine Advantage dialog box displays as described earlier in this chapter in the Sidebar titled "The Microsoft Office Genuine Advantage."

When you open an online template, a new document based on the template is downloaded to your system and displayed in Word. You can then type the contents of the new document and save the document locally or store it on the server, just as with any other document.

Note

If you prefer to browse the extensive Template Gallery in your Web browser, display Word Options, click Resources, and then click Go Online. When your Web browser opens, in the Navigation bar at the top of the page, click Templates to navigate to the Template Gallery.

Templates with Text You Can Use

Do you have an idea about what you want to say but aren't sure where to find the right template? In Word 2007, you can easily find templates with text you can use by using the Search Microsoft Office Online For A Template text box located at the top of the New Document dialog box. For example, you might want to send a thank you note and find that you are struggling with those perfect words to properly convey your thanks. If you type thank you in the Search text box and then click the Start Searching arrow, the search results will include templates prepopulated with text relating to content commonly found in thank you notes. All you have to do is fill in the names and addresses, and you're good to go.

Along with searching, you can browse templates from Microsoft Office Online by category. Need help with a letter? The Letters category offers a wide range of letters such as business, academic, and employment. The following image shows a sampling of letters found in the Community category.

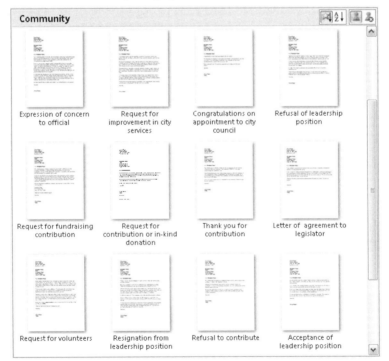

You can even find a letter to help you express your concerns about getting bumped from an overbooked flight. From greeting cards and personal letters to business, employee, legal, and healthcare forms, you're bound to find a template with text you can use!

In addition to retrieving templates from your own computer and Microsoft Office Online, you can access templates stored on a network, FTP site, document server, or Microsoft SharePoint Technologies site. Workgroups frequently need to share templates, so storing templates online provides an ideal way to share templates and ensure that the most up-to-date templates are readily available to team members. In Word, you can easily create new documents based on templates that are stored on networks or the Internet. For more information about sharing documents and using workgroup templates, see Chapter 18, "Sharing Documents and Collaborating Online."

Creating Custom Templates

When you're familiar with how templates work and how to use existing templates, you're ready to start creating your own templates. In Word, you can create templates in three ways. You can base a template on an existing document, base a new template on an existing template, or create a template from scratch. The method that you use depends on the resources you have on hand, as follows:

- **Create a template based on an existing document** You have a document that contains most or all of the settings you want to use in your template. When you base a template on an existing document, you create a template that contains the same document Theme as well as all of the styles, macros, and other settings in the document. Most likely, you'll want to modify the document's settings slightly to fine-tune your template.

- **Create a template based on an existing template** You have a template that contains many of the settings you want to use in your new template, but you want to add or change a few settings without affecting the existing template. The main procedural difference is that you open a template (.dot, .dotx, or .dotm) file instead of a document (.doc) file.

- **Create a template from scratch** You have no model to use as a starting point for your template. Building a template from scratch is similar to creating a document from scratch.

When you create custom templates, you should save your templates in the Templates folder as previously described in this chapter. Saving your templates in the Templates folder makes them easily accessible via the New dialog box. Otherwise, you need to either locate the template in Windows Explorer and double-click the template to create a new document based on the template, or locate the template in the New dialog box by using the New From Existing command and navigate to the location of your template.

> **Note**
>
> You should save your template with the .dot, .dotx, or .dotm extension, but any document file that you save in the Templates folder will also act as a template by default. To ensure that your files are saved as template files, you might want to display file extensions in the Windows Explorer. In Windows, known file extensions are hidden by default. To show extensions, open an Exploring window, such as My Computer, and from the Tools menu, click Folder Options. On the View tab, clear the Hide Extensions For Known File Types check box and then click OK.

Now that we have a few details out of the way, let's look more closely at creating templates. Regardless of what you use to start your template creation, the steps you need to use are fundamentally the same. The following sections provide the actions you must take depending on the method you are using to create your template and how to save your template after it has been created.

Creating a Template Based on an Existing Document

1. Click the Microsoft Office Button and then click Open.

2. In the Open dialog box, open the document that contains the formatting and/or text that you want to include in your template.

Creating a Template Based on an Existing Template

1. Click the Microsoft Office Button and then click New.

2. In the New Document task pane, click My Templates to display the New dialog box.

3. Select a template similar to the one you want to create. In the Create New options, click the Template option and then click OK.

Creating a Template Based on a New, Blank Template

- Click the Microsoft Office Button, click New, and double-click the Blank Document thumbnail.

Saving Your Template

Once your template has been created, perform the following steps:

1. Click the Microsoft Office Button, point to Save As, and then click Word Template.

2. In the Save As dialog box, perform one of the following steps to open the Templates folder, as shown for Windows Vista or Windows XP in Figure 4-3.
   - If using Windows Vista, in the Favorites Links area, click Templates.
   - If using Windows XP, in the My Places bar, click Trusted Templates.

Figure 4-3 For Windows Vista, use Templates in the Favorite Links area. For Windows XP, use Trusted Templates in the My Places bar.

3. In the File Name box, type a name for the new template.

4. In the Save As Type text box, ensure that Word Template (*.dotx) is shown or, if you intend to include macros in your template, click the Save As Type list and then click Word Macro-Enabled Template (*.dotm).

5. If using Windows Vista, you can also take the following actions:

   ❏ Edit information in the Authors, Tags, and Properties fields, if desired, by clicking the placeholder text and replacing it.

   ❏ Click the Save Thumbnail check box if you want to save a thumbnail image of your new template. Saving a thumbnail image (a small image of the first page of a document and its contents) is a good idea because the thumbnail will display in the New Document dialog box as well as the Preview pane in the New dialog box, thereby aiding you in quickly finding the correct template.

Note

As noted in Chapter 2, "Document Creation with Word 2007," the new Open Office XML Format handles graphics differently than the old binary format and is therefore more stable.

---

6. Click Save.

By default, a template saved in the Templates folder appears on the My Templates tab in the Templates dialog box or on a custom tab if the template is placed in a subfolder as noted in the following Inside Out tip titled "Adding and Removing Word Templates and Tabs in the New Dialog Box."

INSIDE OUT   Adding and Removing Word Templates and Tabs in the New Dialog Box

You can control which templates and tabs appear in the New dialog box. To do so, you simply add templates and folders to the User Templates or Workgroup Templates folders. Each folder that you create in either of the template folders creates a tab with the same name in the New dialog box once a document or template is placed in the folder. The following image shows two folders stored in the Templates folder named Coral Reef Divers and Custom Paper Sizes that appear as tabs in the New dialog box.

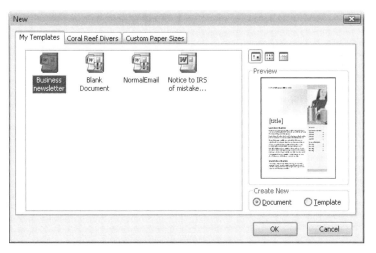

To create a new folder, in the Save As dialog box, click the Create New Folder button on the toolbar in the Save As dialog box or right-click an empty area of the file list and use the New/Folder command.

Once you have added templates and folders, the next time you click My Templates in the New Document dialog box, the tabs and templates you added will be available in the New dialog box. If you want to restore the original tabs and templates, simply delete the templates and folders from the Templates folder. You can right-click and delete templates from within the New dialog box, but you will need to access the contents of the Templates folder to delete the subfolders and remove the tabs from the New dialog box.

You can now modify or add content, styles, boilerplate text, Content Controls, Building Blocks, macros, and any other elements you want to include in your template. For information about creating specific elements in your template, see the following Sidebar titled "Designer's Toolbox."

Designer's Toolbox

Word provides a packed toolbox for you when you create templates. You can design your templates by using built-in or custom Themes, Quick Style Sets, Building Blocks, Content Controls, or macros along with Quick Tables and Table Styles, as described in the following list:

- **Provide an overall format that you can utilize throughout your document** A *Theme* is a set of colors, fonts, and graphics elements (such as gradients and 3D effects) that work together to provide a unified look for your document. Newly added content is automatically formatted to match the document Theme. For more information about creating and customizing Themes, see Chapter 5.

- **Include Building Blocks** Templates can save you from repeatedly typing information that recurs in related documents by including relevant custom Building Blocks such as fax cover pages, Table of Contents, text boxes, headers, and footers. For more information about Building Blocks, see Chapter 8, "Working with Building Blocks and Other Text Tools."

- **Automatically insert graphics, charts, tables, logos, and other special formatting** Templates can contain logos, graphics, backgrounds, and other visual elements so that you don't have to create them. You'll often find these types of items in templates designed for letterhead, recurring newsletters, invoices, labels, timesheets, and business reports—all types of documents that are created regularly. For more information about creating and adding visual elements, see the chapters in Part III, "Visual Elements: Tables, Charts, Diagrams, Pictures."

- **Include predesigned tables and Table Styles** Quick Tables and Table Styles enable you to offer quick table-building and formatting capabilities in any document based on your template. For more information about Quick Tables and Table Styles, see Chapter 11, "Organizing Concepts in Tables."

- **Provide all relevant styles for a particular document** As described in Chapter 15, you can create and use a series of styles to generate a particular look for a document. By creating a template that contains a set of styles or by creating new Quick Style Sets, you can easily access and consistently apply the styles throughout similar and related documents.

- **Include placeholder text, Content Controls, and protection** Word 2007 enables you to include a variety of Content Controls that you can use as placeholder text to help you create form-like templates, along with drop-down lists, combo boxes, rich text, plain text, date pickers, pictures, and Building Blocks galleries. For example, you could insert a Picture Content Control in a template, such as a newsletter or monthly certificate. Then, when you create a document based on your template, you simply click the Picture Content Control, which serves as a placeholder, and insert the image. You can also protect part or all of a template so that data entry is limited to only Content Controls. For more information about adding, controlling, and working with Content Controls, see Chapter 29, "Customizing Documents with Content Controls."

- **Include macros for automation** To help streamline tasks in certain types of documents, you can include macros in a template that can be assigned to a button on the Ribbon, the Quick Access Toolbar, or to a keyboard shortcut. For more information about macros, see Chapter 31, "Working with Macros and VBA."

- **Display a customized Ribbon or Quick Access Toolbar** If a particular type of document always uses specific Word tools, you can create a template that displays a Word interface that caters to the tasks associated with the document type. To learn about customizing the Quick Access Toolbar or the Ribbon, see Appendix B.

All of these formatting features can help you provide a high level of reusable document formatting through a single template. Furthermore, a convenient aspect of using templates with defined styles and Themes is that you aren't forever committed to using particular formatting. You can change a document's formatting at any time by adjusting the properties of the styles and Themes.

Once you have created a new template, you should test the template to verify whether it works as intended by using the template to create a document. To do so, click My Templates in the New Document task pane, click the tab on which the template is located (if necessary), make sure that the Document option is selected in the Create New area in the Templates dialog box, and then double-click the new template.

INSIDE OUT   **Providing Single-Click Access to Templates**

If you create a custom document template that you'll access frequently to create new documents, you might consider adding a custom button to the Quick Access Toolbar or creating a desktop shortcut that enables you to quickly open a new, blank document based on a particular template. To add a custom button, you first create or record a macro. You then add a button to your Quick Access Toolbar that runs the macro. To learn how to record a macro and add the macro to your Quick Access Toolbar, see Chapter 31. For more information about customizing the Quick Access Toolbar, see Appendix B.

To create a desktop shortcut, right-click your desktop, click New, and click Shortcut. Enter the path to the template or use the Browse button to locate the template. Click Next, enter a shortcut name (or use the default name, which is the same as the file name), and then click Finish.

Attaching Templates to Documents

Every document has a template linked, or attached to it, that controls the basic layout and settings used in the document by default. If you create a new, blank document, the Normal template is attached to the document. When you create a document from an existing template, that document template is automatically attached to the document. You can specify which document template you want to attach to a document regardless of which template is currently attached. When you replace the existing document template with a new one, you can choose to automatically update the document's text with the new styles, which makes short work of modifying the formatting throughout the document.

Note

Another method you can use to quickly update a document's styles is to use Quick Style Sets, a new type of formatting template, instead of attaching a new template to your document. For more on creating Quick Style Sets, see Chapter 15.

Chapter 4

To attach a document template to a document and update the document's styles based on the newly attached template, follow these steps:

1. Open your document.

2. Verify that the Developer tab is available on the Ribbon. If you do not see the Developer tab, click the Microsoft Office Button, click Word Options, and in the Popular area, click Show Developer Tab In The Ribbon.

3. Click the Developer tab and then click Document Template in the Templates group. The Templates And Add-Ins dialog box appears, as shown in Figure 4-4.

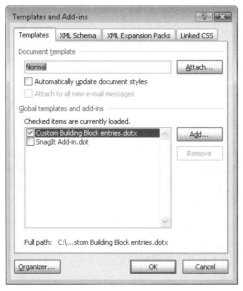

Figure 4-4 The Templates And Add-Ins dialog box helps you attach a different template to a document, automatically update styles, and control global templates and add-ins.

4. Click Attach to display the Attach Template dialog box, which looks very similar to the Open dialog box. The contents of the Templates folder are displayed by default.

5. Select the template you want to attach to the current document and then click Open (or simply double-click the desired template).

   If you want to attach a template that's not stored in the Templates folder, you'll need to navigate to the template's location in the Attach Template dialog box.

6. To automatically apply the newly attached template's styles to the current document, select the Automatically Update Document Styles check box in the Templates And Add-Ins dialog box.

7. Click OK to attach the selected template to the current document.

If you direct Word to automatically update styles, keep in mind that the document text must be formatted with styles that have the same style names as those included in the newly attached template. If the style names are the same, Word will update the text formatting to match the newly attached template's style formats. If the document's style names are different from the attached template's style names, you'll have to select and replace instances of each style. If you find that you're faced with changing styles manually, consider using the Select All Instances feature in the Styles And Formatting task pane to choose all instances of an "old" style and then click the new style name in the Styles task pane to replace the styles.

For more information about changing all instances of a style, see Chapter 15.

Modify Attached Templates

Instead of replacing an attached template with a different one, you might occasionally want to modify an attached template and perform some minor tweaking or add a new component. Modifying an attached template has the following effects:

- Macros, Building Blocks, Styles, and a customized Quick Access Toolbar in the modified template are available for use in any document based on the template, including existing documents.

- If the Automatically Update Document Styles option is selected in the Templates And Add-Ins dialog box as previously discussed in this section, then modified styles are updated and new styles are made available in previously created documents.

- Added or modified boilerplate text, graphics, and format settings (such as page margins, orientation, and column settings) are subsequently applied to new documents based on the modified template. Existing documents aren't affected.

For more information about how to modify existing templates, see "Modifying Existing Templates" later in this chapter.

Working with Global Templates

As mentioned, Word uses two types of templates—global and document. All documents have access to the Normal and Building Blocks global templates, and many documents have attached document templates that provide formatting instructions. In addition, you can load other templates as needed to serve as global templates to enable you to use the template's features without modifying the Normal.dotm file or replacing the attached document template. Keeping all of these template possibilities in mind, you can see that the interface features available in a current document can be influenced by the following templates:

- **Normal template (Normal.dotm)** Global template that can contain features such as macros, custom Building Blocks, and keyboard shortcuts.

- **Building Blocks template (Building Blocks.dotx)** Global template that contains built-in Building Blocks and can contain custom Building Blocks entries. Additional information on Building Blocks.dotx can be found in Chapter 8.

> **Note**
>
> The Normal and Building Blocks templates do not display in the Templates And Add-ins dialog box because they are automatically loaded by Word.

- **Document template** Can provide macros, a customized interface, and custom Building Blocks to documents based on the template along with custom formatting and style settings.

- **Additional installed global templates** Can contain features such as macros and additional Building Blocks that can benefit any open Word document.

Note that styles are only provided to the document through the document template because the purpose of document templates is to apply formatting. Global templates generally provide productivity tools such as stored macros, Building Blocks, and Ribbon and Quick Access Toolbar customizations, along with keyboard shortcut settings that you can use while you work with any document (not just documents based on a particular document template). By design, templates should be used as global templates when they contain features that benefit any open document. Once you have loaded a global template, items stored in the template are available to any document during the remainder of the Word session.

Manually Loading Global Templates

When you load global templates, they are listed in the Templates And Add-Ins dialog box. You can specify whether you want to use them on a per document or per session basis. To manually load a global template, follow these steps:

1. On the Ribbon, click the Developer tab.

   If you need instructions on how to show the Developer tab, see step 2 earlier in this chapter in the section titled "Attaching Templates to Documents."

2. In the Templates group, click Document Template.

3. On the Templates tab in the Global Templates And Add-Ins area, click Add to display the Add Template dialog box, which displays the contents of the Templates folder by default.

4. Double-click the name of a template that you want to include in the global template list as previously shown in Figure 4-4.

5. Click OK to complete the setup.

> **Note**
>
> Another type of add-in that may appear in the Global Templates And Add-Ins list is a Word add-in that uses a .wll file extension. This older type of add-in was at one time the only type supported by Word. It is now known to cause a delay when Word starts due to the older file type and because, when scanning a file for macros, it uses the virus-scanning engine utilized by third-party virus scanners, such as Norton AntiVirus. In this scenario, you may see Running virus scan in the status bar. However, if your virus scanner doesn't explicitly scan Microsoft Office documents as they are opening, then Word is checking the add-in for macros and is not performing a virus scan.
>
> The only way to prevent the delay when Word starts is to remove the add-in from the Startup folder by using the steps provided in "Unloading Global Templates" found later in this section.

Automatically Loading Global Templates

If you often load the same global template, you can configure Word to load the global template automatically whenever you start Word. The easiest way to accomplish this task is to copy the template into the Word Startup folder. The default location of the Word Startup folder can be found in one of the following default locations:

- **On Windows Vista** C:\Users\user name\AppData\Roaming\Microsoft\Word\Startup

- **On Windows XP** C:\Documents and Settings\user name\Application Data\Microsoft\Word\Startup

> **Note**
>
> The location of the Word Startup folder can be changed in the File Locations dialog box found in Word Options in the Advanced area.

Be careful when choosing to load global templates automatically. Configuring your system to load global templates each time Word starts uses up system memory and can slow Word startup.

Unloading Global Templates

By default, global templates are unloaded (but not removed from the list of global templates) when you exit Word. If you prefer, you can unload global templates before exiting Word. When you are finished with a global template, you can unload it or remove a manually loaded global template from the global template list. Note that neither action deletes the template file; unloading and removing a global template from the global template list merely stops the template from serving as a global template. To unload a global template, open the Templates And Add-Ins dialog box (located on the Developer tab), and perform one of the following actions:

- Clear the check box next to the template's name in the Global Templates And Add-Ins list to stop using the global template.

- Select the manually loaded global template in the Global Templates And Add-Ins list and then click Remove to stop using the loaded global template and remove the template from the list.

- If the global template is stored in your Word Startup folder or the Startup folder located in the Office installation path, exit Word and move the template from the respective startup folder to another location. If you have another copy of the template, simply delete the template from the respective Startup folder. Note that the Remove button in the Templates And Add-Ins dialog box will be disabled if the template is located in a Startup folder.

TROUBLESHOOTING

A previously removed global template reappears the next time Word starts

Some third-party add-ins designed for previous versions of Word—such as a popular screen capture program called SnagIt created by TechSmith or the Word Redaction add-in created by Microsoft—programmatically load a global template manually each time that Word starts so as to integrate additional functionality in Word. These templates can be unloaded and removed from the Global Templates And Add-Ins list. However, they will return because they are loaded each time Word starts by a Component Object Model (COM) add-in, which isn't listed in the Templates And Add-Ins dialog box. To resolve this issue, uninstall the add-in using Add Or Remove Programs found in Control Panel.

For more information and troubleshooting procedures related to COM add-ins, see the Troubleshooting guide found on this book's companion CD.

Modifying Existing Templates

You can modify existing templates by opening and manually changing the template file; modifying a document that has the template attached and saving changes to the template; or by copying, deleting, and renaming template components by using the Organizer. Regardless of how you make changes to a template, when you modify a template, the modifications affect new documents based on the template. Changes to the content and layout of the template do not affect existing documents based on the template.

Modifying an Existing Document Template File

To modify an existing document by working directly in the template, you must first open the file as a template from the Open dialog box, as follows:

1. Click the Microsoft Office Button and click Open.

2. Display the contents of the Templates folder (or the folder containing the template you want to modify), and then locate and open the template you want to modify.

3. Change any of the template's text and graphics, styles, formatting, Content Controls, macros, Building Blocks, Quick Access Toolbar, and keyboard shortcuts.

4. On the Quick Access toolbar, click Save.

Remember that whenever you make changes to a document template, you should test the changes by creating a new sample document based on the template. To apply any style changes to an existing document to which the template is attached, ensure that the Automatically Update Document Styles check box in the Templates And Add-Ins dialog box is selected after you open the document.

Modifying an Existing Document Template While Working in a Document

You can modify a template while you work in a Word document. For instance, you can change the default Page Setup options as discussed in Chapter 3, "Mastering Page Setup and Pagination," or you can change or add a style to the attached document template by modifying a style or creating a new style (as described in Chapter 15). In the Create New Style dialog box (or in the Modify Style dialog box), select the New Documents Based On This Template option. When you save the document, Word displays a message box that asks whether you want to update the attached document template, as shown in Figure 4-5.

Figure 4-5 You can modify and save changes to an attached document template while you work in a document.

Using the Organizer to Rename, Delete, and Copy Styles

In addition to modifying templates by making changes in template and document files, you can use the Organizer to manage template components. The Organizer dialog box contains tabs for Styles and Macro Project Items, as shown in Figure 4-6.

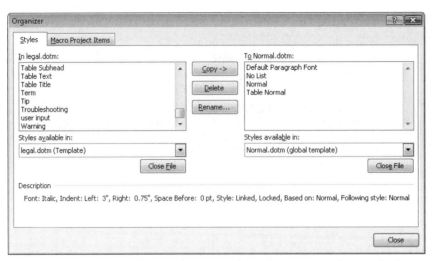

Figure 4-6 You can copy, delete, and rename styles and macros stored in specific documents and templates by using the Organizer.

To use the Organizer to copy and manage styles and macros in documents and templates, follow these steps:

1. On the Developer tab in the Templates group, click Document Template.

2. In the Templates And Add-Ins dialog box, click Organizer.

3. In the Organizer dialog box, click the Styles or Macro Project Items tab, depending on the element you want to copy, delete, or rename.

4. To copy items to or from templates or files other than the current file's template and the Normal.dotm template, click Close File to close the active document and its attached template or to close the Normal template. Then click Open File and select the template or file you want to open by double-clicking it in the Open dialog box.

5. Select the items you want to copy, delete, or rename. Click Copy, Delete, or Rename as appropriate.

6. Click Close when finished with the Organizer.

TROUBLESHOOTING

I can't copy items to a particular template

If you try to copy styles or macros to a template that's protected in some way, you might not be able to open the template, accept or reject tracked changes in the template, or save changes to the template. This problem might be due to any of the following reasons:

- The template is protected for tracked changes, comments, or forms.

- The template is encrypted and requires you to enter a password.

- The template is protected by a password. If you don't know the password, you can only open the template as a read-only file.

- The file attributes are set to read-only.

- You don't have access to the server on which the template is stored.

- The template might be open on another computer on your network.

To save changes to a template, the protection settings must be removed from the template, you must gain the proper access permissions, or you must wait until the template is no longer open on another computer on the network.

In some instances, you might want to protect templates. To learn more about protecting documents, see the following section titled "Protecting Templates," as well as Chapter 20, "Addressing Document Protection and Security Issues."

Protecting Templates

Protecting your templates can ensure that templates remain intact, without unintentional alterations. Protecting your templates can be especially important if you're sharing them with other people on a network or online. However, if you protect your template in the same way you protect standard Word documents, those settings will be in effect when you create a new document based on your template because essentially the template is also being opened. For example, if you add a password to open the template to create a new document based on the template, the password must be entered. If the content in the template is sensitive, then a password is recommended. However, if the password is an effort to protect modifications to your template, then you should utilize network security rather than the security options found in Word. With that in mind, you can protect your templates in the following ways:

- **Suggest that they be opened as read-only** Click the Microsoft Office Button and click Save As. Click Tools at the bottom of the Save As dialog box and click General Options. In the General Options dialog box, select the Read-Only Recommended check box and then click OK. Note that the recommendation to open the template as read-only will be presented each time a new document based on the template is created.

- **Encrypt the document or template** Click the Microsoft Office Button and click Save As. Click Tools at the bottom of the Save As dialog box and click General Options. In the General Options dialog box, enter a password in the File Encryption Options For This Document text box and then click OK. Note that the password must be entered to create new documents based on the template.

Chapter 4

- **Create a file-sharing password** Click the Microsoft Office Button and click Save As. Click Tools at the bottom of the Save As dialog box and click General Options. In the General Options dialog box, enter a password in the File Sharing Options For This Document text box and then click OK. Note that a dialog box requesting the password to modify or open as read-only will be presented each time a new document based on the template is created.

- **Protect formatting and editing changes** Click Protect Document on the Review tab or Developer tab. The Restrict Formatting And Editing Task Pane opens, which enables you to specify detailed formatting and editing restrictions. Note that new documents based on the template will contain the same restrictions.

- **Prevent the template from being forwarded, edited, or copied by unauthorized people** Apply Windows rights management by clicking Permission on the Review tab or Developer tab and then clicking Restrict Access. By using this feature, you can restrict permission to the document to specific people, thereby preventing copying and printing of the document, and you can designate a date for the document permission to expire.

> **Note**
>
> Information Rights Management tools are only available when using Microsoft Office Ultimate 2007, Microsoft Office Professional Plus 2007, and Microsoft Office Enterprise 2007.

For more information about tracking changes and adding comments, see Chapter 20, "Revising Documents Using Markup Tools." For more information about Windows Rights Management and security in Word, see Chapter 21.

What's Next

This chapter explained how to take frequently used document layout, along with content specific to that document, and turn it into a template to quickly create new documents based on previously defined settings, as well as how to use global templates to provide shared functionality to all open documents. The next chapter provides an in-depth look at one of the most exciting new technological advances of Word 2007 and one you've read about in every chapter so far—document Themes.

Applying Themes for a Professional Look

If you've ever spent any amount of time painstakingly selecting fonts, coordinating colors, or wishing you had a graphic artist on hand to handle all of the choices you need to make in creating high-impact and persuasive documents, you will love using the Theme in Microsoft Office Word 2007. If you've used styles in previous versions of Word, you will be excited to learn how to apply Themes in your document. Themes enable you to choose—with a single click of the mouse—a consistent, professional look for your documents. What's more, you can use the same Theme for all sorts of collateral materials so that your annual report has a similar design to your brochures, your organization's stationery, your newsletter, and your Web page.

Office Word 2007 includes a gallery of 20 Themes right out of the box. You can also modify Themes to create new ones or design Themes from scratch. In addition, you can download new Themes from Microsoft Office Online so that your Themes gallery is continually expanding.

> **Note**
>
> Because Themes are new in Word 2007, they will not be available when you save your Word document in previous Word formats. The settings used to create the Theme (fonts, colors, and effects) are converted to styles in previous versions of Word. To obtain the full benefit of Themes—being able to change the Theme font, color, and effects with a single click of the mouse button—create and save the document in Word 2007 format.

Themes in Word 2007

As you learned in Chapter 1, "Room to Create with Office Word 2007," one of the key design objectives in the new look and feel of Word 2007 is to provide users with easy-to-use tools for creating professional, high-quality documents. Themes constitute a big step toward this design goal by enabling you to apply the work of professional designers to the documents you create with a click of the mouse. In addition, you can create your own Themes that include the fonts, colors, and styles used in your existing materials.

To create the best possible effect for professional documents, most people invest some time in finding and choosing formatting options for headings, body text, captions, borders, and so on. Choosing fonts that seem to go together well by using colors and styles that complement each other typically takes at least a little trial and error. And when you're working under a deadline, that trial and error period uses up precious time.

Word 2007 attempts to cut out much of the time you spend selecting options to control the format of your document. By choosing a Theme, you can create professional documents with a coordinated set of colors, fonts, and backgrounds. You'll never again have to wonder about what looks good together. When you create a new document, you can simply choose the same Theme you used for previous documents, thereby ensuring that everything you create has the same look and feel, and thus adding to the consistent way you present your department or company (which helps build recognition).

Themes represent a huge addition to Microsoft Office 2007 and not simply to Word alone. When you create a document using the Opulent Theme in Word, you can also craft a presentation in Microsoft Office PowerPoint 2007 that uses the same Opulent Theme. And let's not leave out Microsoft Office Excel 2007—the same Themes are available for your worksheets and reports in Office Excel 2007 as well. This means you can put together a complete package—your monthly newsletter and program literature, your year-end financials and fundraising reports, and a professional presentation for your board—all by using the same Theme that can literally be applied with a single click of the mouse.

> **Note**
> A few things must be in order before you can change Themes with a click of the mouse, however. First, you need to work with a document in Word 2007 format (Themes are not available in Compatibility Mode). Next, you need to assign styles to the elements in your document (such as Heading 1 or Heading 2 from the Styles group of the Home tab). Themes look for and replace the formats of each of the styles applied to the document elements.

What's in a Theme?

Document Themes enable you to change the way that text, tables, and special elements are formatted throughout your document. A Theme includes the following elements:

- The font used for headings and body text (including the color, style, and spacing)
- Theme effects including 3-D effects, shadowing, lighting, and more

Figure 5-1 displays an annual report that uses the Verve Theme. The Theme settings influence the format of the document in the following ways:

- The font style and color used for the "Facilities" heading

- The font type, style, and color used for the paragraph text

- The fonts used in the table headings and row values

- The table style (alternating banded rows) applied to the table

- The color used in the shape symbol to the left of the heading if it has been added with Insert, Shapes.

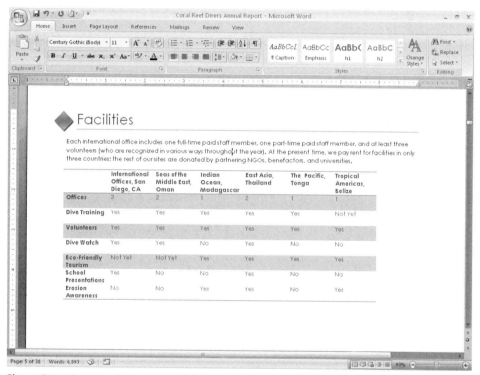

Figure 5-1 When you choose a new Theme, styled elements in your document change automatically.

When you choose a Theme, the settings are instantly applied to styled elements in your document. You can change Themes as often as you like, trying on different looks until you get just the right effect for your document.

Chapter 5

Themes, Quick Styles, and Templates

Every document already has an applied Theme. When you first create a blank document by clicking the Microsoft Office Button and choosing New (or pressing Ctrl+N), the Office Theme is applied automatically. This Theme coordinates many of the formatting choices that you make throughout the document. For example, suppose that you choose the Equity Theme for your current document. A specific set of fonts, colors, and Theme effects are applied to the document.

Additionally, the Quick Styles available in the Styles area of the Home tab are orchestrated to fit, design-wise, with the Equity Theme. The fonts represented in the Quick Styles are those determined by your Theme selection. If you choose a different Theme, different styles will appear in the Styles gallery to reflect your selection. You can further fine-tune your selection by choosing a particular Quick Style set for your document. When you click the Change Styles arrow (in the Styles group of the Home tab) and choose Style Set, a list of design categories appears (see Figure 5-2). You can choose the category that reflects the style you want to create, and all items—fonts, colors, and effects—consistent with the Theme choices are applied to your document.

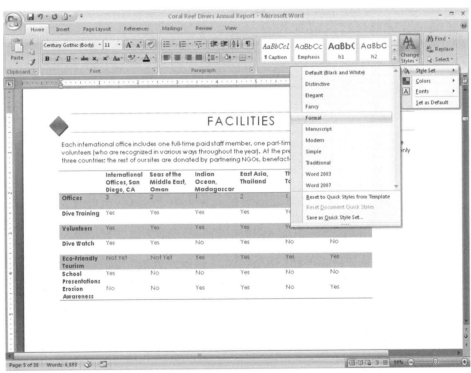

Figure 5-2 The Quick Style set helps you target the style of your document in relation to the selected Theme.

Other galleries offer choices related to the Equity template selection as well. For example, when you create a table and choose a style in the Table Styles gallery (available on the Design tab of the contextual Table Tools tools), the table styles in that gallery are orchestrated to match the Equity Theme, as shown in Figure 5-3.

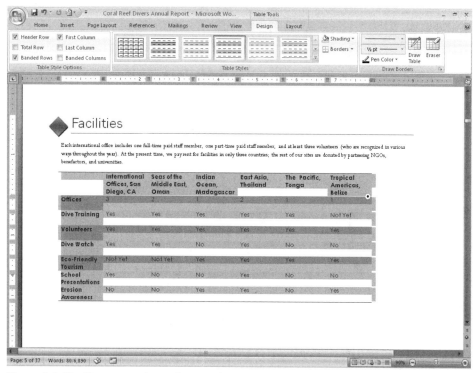

Figure 5-3 The Theme you choose for your document takes care of all the formatting choices for you.

Trying Themes with Live Preview

Word includes a new Live Preview feature that enables you to experiment with changes before selecting them. To preview different Themes in your document, select the Page Layout tab and click Themes. The Themes gallery opens, displaying a number of different Theme choices.

When you point to a Theme that you want to preview, the name of the Theme appears in a ScreenTip above the Theme thumbnail and the changes appear in the document window, as shown in Figure 5-4. The current Theme remains highlighted in the Themes gallery so that you can clearly see both the selected Theme and the previewed Theme. When you find a Theme that you want to use, simply click it to apply it to your document.

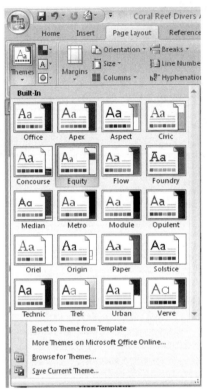

Figure 5-4 Use Live Preview to observe how a new Theme will look before you select it.

Downloading Themes from Microsoft Office Online

Microsoft Office Online offers an additional and continually expanding supply of Themes and templates to use with the 2007 Microsoft Office products. To find out what's new on Microsoft Office Online, click the Page Layout tab and choose Themes in the Themes group. Scroll down to the bottom of the gallery and choose More Themes On Microsoft Office Online. Scroll through the available Themes and click one that you want to try. When you click Download Now, the Theme is downloaded to your computer and saved in the Custom area of the Themes gallery.

Changing a Theme

When you discover a Theme that you like, simply click it to apply it to the selected document. If you are creating a new document, the Office Theme is applied automatically.

The fonts, colors, and effects that are part of the Theme are automatically applied to the current document.

A Theme choice doesn't mean that you give up your right to change your mind. You can further fine-tune your document by changing the fonts, colors, and Theme effects applied when you selected the Theme. The next section instructs you how to work with these settings in your documents.

Changing Theme Colors

Chances are that you selected a specific Theme because it offers either the font selections or the colors that you want. If you want to change the colors of the selected Theme (this does not change the built-in Theme itself, but instead modifies the colors already applied to your current document), follow these steps:

1. Click the Page Layout tab.

2. In the Themes group, click the Theme Colors button. A palette of Theme colors appears, as shown in Figure 5-5.

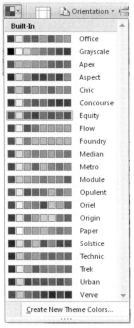

Figure 5-5 Use the Theme Colors button to choose a new color scheme for your document.

3. Position the mouse pointer over a color selection that you'd like to see previewed in your document. (Notice that, even though the colors of your document change, the fonts and formats remain the same.)

Chapter 5

4. Click the color scheme that you want to apply to your document and press Ctrl+S to save your file.

Further possible changes to your document might include applying Quick Styles to your work, creating new styles, or working with style sets. To find out more about creating and working with styles in your documents, see Chapter 15, "Using Styles to Increase Your Formatting Power."

Choosing a New Font Selection

Each Theme that you select contains a set of coordinated fonts that work well together for the various types of content that you might include in your document. Font sets include one font type in two sizes (one for headings and one for body text) or two fonts that complement each other for headings and text.

You can choose a different font set for the Theme applied to your document by following these steps:

1. Click the Page Layout tab.

2. Click the Theme Fonts button in the Themes group. The Theme Fonts gallery appears.

3. Position the pointer on a font set selection to preview the effect in your document, as shown in Figure 5-6.

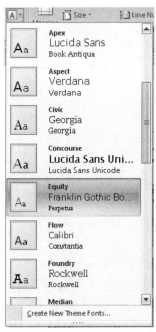

Figure 5-6 Choose a different font set for your document by clicking the Theme Fonts button.

4. Click the font selection that you want to apply to the Theme. The fonts are instantly changed.

5. Save your document.

Overriding Theme Settings

The Theme settings that you choose for your document change all of the formatting used throughout your document. But you don't have to settle for those selections all the way through the document—you can change sections, headers, or special items (such as captions, quotations, or other elements) by applying different settings. Be aware, however, that when you change a font, color, or effect directly (such as changing a heading in your document to Times Roman when the Theme used Calibri), that element will no longer change automatically when you choose a different style.

To override the Theme font settings that are currently applied in your document, simply select the text that you want to change, click the Home tab, and then click the Font arrow. At the top of the Font list, Word shows you which fonts are used in the current Theme. You can click any font in the list to apply it to selected text.

If you want to ensure that all elements in your document can be changed easily when you choose a different Theme, consider changing the styles used in individual Themes. For more information about working with styles in Word 2007, see Chapter 15.

Selecting Theme Effects

You can use Theme effects to add an extra touch to your charts, SmartArt graphics, shapes, and pictures. Theme effects control the line thickness, fill color or shade, and lighting of the selected object. To change the effects selected for your current Theme, click the Effects button in the Themes group of the Page Layout tab. The Effects gallery opens, as shown in Figure 5-7.

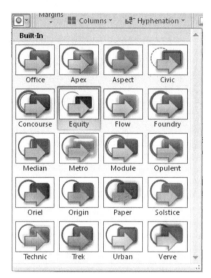

Figure 5-7 Theme effects control the lighting, shadow, and edging of objects in your document.

INSIDE OUT

I can't tell which settings are in effect in my Theme

When you first begin creating a new document, you probably don't have a great deal of content to work with. Therefore, you may not be sure which settings are in effect for your particular Theme. You can see the shadow, lighting, and edging effects that are being used in your document by clicking the Page Layout tab and clicking the Effects button in the Themes group. The Effects gallery opens, and the current effect is highlighted. From the thumbnail of the selected effect, you can view the shadow, lighting, and edging effects that are in use. If you want to change the effects, click a different thumbnail in the gallery and those settings are applied to your document.

Creating a Custom Theme

The Themes provided by Word take the guesswork out of designing professional documents and just generally make life easier. But having Themes to choose from doesn't mean that you should ignore your own creative urges. Word makes it easy for you to put together your own Themes, a feature that comes in handy if you want to design a Theme that reflects a specific set of styles and colors that you are using in your organization's materials.

Creating Your Own Color Scheme

How hard is it to choose a set of colors that really work together? If you're in touch with your creative side, you may feel confident about your ability to mix and match colors. If colors aren't your thing (or you rely on others to tell you whether your clothing choices match), choosing compatible colors may seem like a big chore. Either way, Word helps you put together a Theme color set to give your document a professional look. Here's how to do it:

1. Click the Page Layout tab and click Theme Colors in the Themes group to display the Theme Colors gallery.

2. Scroll to the bottom of the list and click Create New Theme Colors. The Create New Theme Colors dialog box appears, as shown in Figure 5-8.

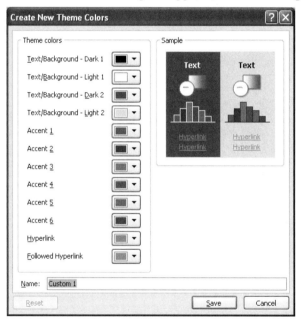

Figure 5-8 Select the colors for a new color scheme in the Create New Theme Colors dialog box.

3. Click the arrow of any element that you want to change. A color palette appears so that you can select the color for that item.

Continue changing colors until you've made all of the desired changes for the new Theme colors. The Sample area displays changes as you make them.

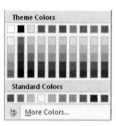

4. When you're satisfied with the colors you've selected, click the Name box and type a name for the new color scheme.

5. Click Save to save your new color scheme.

Apply the new Theme Colors to your document by clicking the Theme Colors button in the Themes group and choosing the customized Theme from the Custom area at the top of the list.

> **Note**
>
> If you add a custom Theme element—a font set or color scheme—and then decide that you don't like it after all, you can easily delete it from the list by displaying the gallery (click Theme Colors or Theme Fonts) and right-clicking the item in the Custom area at the top. A list appears, offering three options: Edit, Delete, and Add Gallery To Quick Access Toolbar. Click Delete to remove the custom item.

Customizing Theme Font Sets

You can create your own Theme font set by displaying the Theme Fonts gallery (click Theme Fonts in the Themes group on the Page Layout tab), scrolling to the bottom of the list, and clicking Create New Theme Fonts. The Create New Theme Fonts dialog box appears, as shown in Figure 5-9.

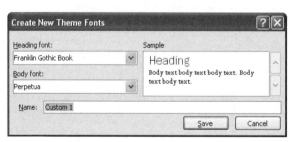

Figure 5-9 Choose a new font for your headings and body text in the Create New Theme Fonts dialog box.

Click the Heading Font arrow to display a list of all fonts available on your system. When you select the font that you want to use for the headings in your document, the Sample area displays the effect of your selection; choose the Body Font in the same way. Enter a name for your new Theme font by typing it in the Name box, and click Save to save the selection to the Fonts list. The new set appears at the top of the list in the Custom category.

Saving Your Custom Theme

After you've finished tailoring the Theme settings to reflect your particular style, you can save the Theme so it is accessible through the Themes gallery in the Themes group of the Page Layout tab.

Begin by displaying a document that contains all of the settings that you want to use in your new Theme. Click the Page Layout tab and select the Themes button in the Themes group. Scroll down to the bottom of the Themes gallery and choose Save Current Theme. The Save Current Theme dialog box appears.

Type a descriptive name for the Theme and click Save. The new Theme is now available when you click Themes in the Themes group.

CAUTION

Because the 2007 Microsoft Office applications look in a specific folder to find the Themes for your documents, it's important that you leave the default folder (Document Themes) selected when you save your Theme. Otherwise, the Theme will not be displayed in the Themes list by default, and you will have to use Browse For Themes (also in the Themes list) to find your customized Theme.

What's Next?

This chapter explored the Themes available in Word 2007 and demonstrated how to apply and customize them. Additionally, this chapter included ideas for creating and saving your own personal Themes that you can use in future documents. The next chapter introduces techniques for aligning and formatting paragraphs, lists, and special text items.

PART 2

Working with Content: From Research to Review

Mastering Document Fundamentals

After you create a new document—whether it's blank or based on an existing document or template—the next process is to insert information into the document and format it. Granted, that's a fairly obvious observation, but the steps necessary to perform standard editing and formatting tasks are well worth discussing. And if you want to take advantage of the new features introduced in Microsoft Office Word 2007, then learning more about these essential concepts will help you streamline your working style.

Along with the fundamental concepts, this chapter also covers inserting Symbols, Special Characters, and the new Equation builder; inserting and controlling Dates and Times; and another technological advancement to document creation, bound *Document Property* fields, a discussion which includes a first look at the power of Content Controls.

Formatting Text and Paragraphs Efficiently

An important aspect to consider before you jump in and start formatting a document is the flexibility of your formatting. For example, if you find you need to change an indent throughout your document, do you want to painstakingly select every instance of the indent and change it? Or would you rather specify your preferred indent setting in a single change and have the indents update automatically throughout the document? If the latter sounds more appealing, then for primary formats, such as the main font used throughout your document or main formatting of individual paragraphs, consider using Styles. Styles not only provide flexibility by enabling you to modify document formats simply by modifying the Style (covered in Chapter 15, "Using Styles to Increase Your Formatting Power"), but they also enable you to format content more efficiently by applying many formats to text with a single click of the mouse. Whether your formatting plan is to create or modify Styles for your formatting needs—which can be accomplished by picking up formats already in use in your document—or apply direct formatting throughout your document without implementing Styles, fundamentally, text formats, enhancements, and paragraph formats will be the same.

Formatting document content is one of the principal tasks in Office Word 2007, and you'll find formatting commands readily available on the Home tab, shown in Figure 6-1.

Figure 6-1 The Home tab contains many of the formatting options available on the Formatting toolbar in previous versions of Word.

> **Note**
>
> Word 2007 comes with a number of preconfigured Quick Style Sets, which use the Theme Fonts to help you speed up the formatting process in your documents. Quick Style Sets include font families, sizes, and color settings that can be automatically applied to document components. You can modify Theme Fonts, create custom Quick Style Sets, and make them readily accessible from the Home tab. For more information about Theme Fonts, see Chapter 5, "Applying Themes for a Professional Look." For more information about Quick Style Sets, see Chapter 15.

Along with the Home tab, the Mini Toolbar provides easy and efficient access to the most frequently used text-formatting commands. Instead of selecting text and navigating to the Home tab, you can use the Mini Toolbar, shown in Figure 6-2, which appears next to selected text. As you move the mouse pointer closer, the Mini Toolbar fades in, and becomes a functioning formatting toolbar. It then fades away as you move the mouse pointer away.

The option to Show Mini Toolbar On Selection can be found by clicking the Microsoft Office Button, clicking Word Options, and then clicking Popular.

Figure 6-2 The Mini Toolbar displays next to selected text and when you right-click text in a document.

To add the entire Font group to your Quick Access Toolbar, right-click the group, rather than a specific command, and click Add To Quick Access Toolbar.

Specifying Fonts and Sizes

 As you know, the world of documents embraces numerous fonts. Thus, it should come as no surprise that Word can handle thousands of fonts that are compatible with the Windows operating systems, including Adobe PostScript fonts (if the Adobe Type Manager is installed) and TrueType fonts. In general, Word supports the following types of fonts:

- **Outline fonts** TrueType and OpenType fonts are outline fonts. Outline fonts are created from line and curve commands. OpenType is an extension of TrueType, and both types of font can be scaled and rotated. These fonts look good in all sizes and on all output devices supported by Microsoft Windows. Most fonts installed with Microsoft Office are TrueType or OpenType fonts.

> **Note**
>
> Word 2007 added correct recognition of OpenType fonts, although it does not yet support any of the advanced OpenType features. The new default fonts, Cambria and Calibri, along with the rest of the font family—Candara, Consolas, Constantia, and Corbel—are OpenType fonts designed specifically for optimum display with ClearType enabled.

- **Printer fonts** Printer fonts are found in most programs that support printing and are used most often with laser and dot-matrix printers. Printer fonts can be internal (they do not display in the Fonts folder), cartridge (such as a font expansion pack), or downloadable. For more information about printer fonts, see your printer's documentation.

TROUBLESHOOTING

Why aren't all of my fonts available?

The Fonts displayed in the font list are those that are supported by the current printer driver to produce WYSIWYG (What You See Is What You Get) output, so the Font list may not include all of the fonts found in the Fonts folder in Control Panel. For example, if an inkjet printer is your current printer, the list may only display TrueType or OpenType fonts. A laser printer may also include printer fonts, and a Generic/Text Only printer will display only a few printer fonts.

Note that some vector fonts—Modern, Roman and Script—along with screen fonts—such as Fixedsys, MS Sans Serif, MS Serif, System, and Terminal—have not been displayed on the Font list since Word 97.

Chapter 6

You can force Word to use a font that is not in the list by typing the name of the font, exactly as it is named in Windows, into the font list and pressing Enter. If a document contains fonts that are not on the font list, these fonts will still be used. However, the quality of the printed output may be poor, as in the case of the vector fonts listed previously, or font substitution may be used, as in the case of missing fonts or screen fonts (which are intended for display only).

To check for font substitution in a document, or to change substituted fonts, click the Microsoft Office Button, click Word Options, and in the Advanced section, click the Font Substitution button found in the Show Document Content options.

In Word, the quickest way to specify a font is to select the text you want to format and then select a font in the Font list box on the Home tab, as shown in Figure 6-1. The Font list contains all the currently available fonts, and you can temporarily increase or decrease the height of the font list using the sizing handle found at the bottom. You can also press Ctrl+D to open the Font dialog box.

Note

As mentioned in Chapter 2, "Document Creation with Word 2007", if you want the font to follow the Theme, use the Theme fonts found in the Theme Fonts section of a Font list. Otherwise, the fonts will not change if your Theme Fonts change. If viewing the Font dialog box, the Theme fonts are identified as +Body and +Headings. In the Font list on the Home tab, they are identified as (Body) and (Headings).

To view fonts installed on your computer, display Control Panel and open the Fonts folder. To use a macro to print a list of available fonts in Word, go to the Microsoft Knowledge Base and search for Article 209205, "Macros to Generate Lists of Available Fonts in Word" (*support.microsoft.com/kb/209205*).

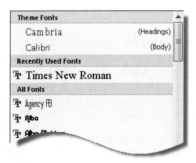

Figure 6-3 The Font list displays font names in their respective fonts; the first two fonts are from the current Theme.

For comprehensive information about fonts, visit the Microsoft Typography Web site at *www.microsoft.com/typography*.

INSIDE OUT   Serif vs. Sans Serif fonts

All fonts can be classified as *serif* or *sans serif.* You can easily differentiate between the two font types. Serif fonts add "hooks" to their letters, similar to the font used in this book's main body text. Examples of serif fonts are Cambria and Times New Roman. In contrast, sans serif fonts have plain-edged letters, like the font used in the headings throughout this book and in this paragraph. Examples of sans serif fonts are Calibri, Arial, and Verdana.

Using sans serif fonts for headings and serif fonts for body text is common practice in the print community because most readers find this combination easiest to read in hard copy. For online documents, the print setup is often switched for easier reading on the screen; serif fonts are used for headings, and sans serif fonts are used for body text. You'll find most of the built-in Theme Font sets follow these practices and use both a serif font and a sans serif font.

Once you select a font for your text, you'll probably want to specify a size. The quickest way to size text is by using the Font Size list, located to the right of the Font list on the Home tab (shown previously in Figure 6-1). As you probably know, font sizes are measured in points, and 72 points equals an inch. By default, the Font Size list provides a variety of common point sizes, and like the Font list, the Font Size list is now temporarily resizable. To apply a font size, select the text you want to resize or position your cursor at the point where you want the size specification to apply to newly entered text, click the Size arrow, and select a size from the list.

If you want to use a font size not found in the Font Size list, use the following steps:

1. Select the text you want to resize or position your cursor at the point where you want the size specification to apply to newly entered text.

2. On the Home tab, in the Font group, click in the Font Size text box. Select the currently displayed font size, if necessary, type a new value, and then press Enter.

Note

You can enter half-point sizes in the Font Size text box by using decimal notation (for example, 10.5), and you can specify sizes as tiny as 1 point and as large as 1,638 points (which is approximately two feet high). When you type large numbers in the Size text box, don't include a comma separator—use numbers only.

Word 2007 users can also resize text using the Grow Font and Shrink Font commands, which are available on the Home tab, as well as the keyboard shortcuts listed in Table 6-1 to change the font size. When you use the Grow Font or Shrink Font commands on text that contains mixed font sizes, the font size will grow or shrink relative to its original size.

Table 6-1 Keyboard Shortcuts for Sizing Text

Keyboard shortcut	Sizing effect
Ctrl+]	Enlarges font by 1 point
Ctrl+[	Reduces font by 1 point
Ctrl+Shift+>	Increases font to the next larger size in the Size list
Ctrl+Shift+<	Decreases font to the next smaller size in the Size list

INSIDE OUT   Specifying a default font

You might find changing the default font settings especially useful if you frequently modify the font in documents that use either the Normal template or another specified template. This modification can be made without opening the template. For the Normal template, create a new, blank document. To use another specified template, simply open a document that uses the template. Then, on the Home tab, click the dialog launcher in the Font group, or press Ctrl+D, to display the Font dialog box. Select the settings you want to configure for the template's default font and then click Default. A message box, similar to the one shown below, will display confirming the change.

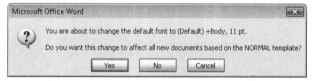

If you click Yes, all new documents created using the template will be based on the new default font settings. Previously created documents will not inherit the change unless it affects styles used in the document and the option to Automatically Update Document Styles is selected, as discussed in Chapter 4, "Formatting Documents Using Templates."

Applying Text Attributes and Effects

In addition to selecting fonts and resizing text, you can apply formatting attributes, including boldfacing, italics, and underlining. A notable addition to Word 2007 is quick access to various Underline styles and Underline color, which are made available by clicking the arrow next to the Underline button, as shown in Figure 6-4.

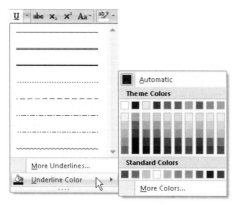

Figure 6-4 Word provides a variety of Underline styles and colors that you can now easily access from the Underline button on the Home tab.

Other notable additions to Word 2007 are the text effects, such as strikethrough, superscript, and subscript, which are now included on the Ribbon.

To apply text attributes or effects, simply select your text or position your cursor. Then, click the appropriate Ribbon command or use the appropriate keyboard command, as listed in Table 6-2.

Table 6-2 Text Attributes and Effects Commands

Format	Home Tab Command	Keyboard shortcut
Bold	**B**	Ctrl+B
Italic	*I*	Ctrl+I
Underline	U ▾	Ctrl+U Underline Words Only: Ctrl+Shift+W Double Underline: Ctrl+Shift+D
Strikethrough	abc	(No built-in keyboard shortcut)
Subscript	x_2	Ctrl+=
Superscript	x^2	Ctrl+Shift+=

> **Note**
> The majority of keyboard shortcuts for text attributes and effects as well as Ribbon commands are *toggle commands*, which means that you perform the same action both to apply and to remove a formatting attribute. The exception is the keyboard shortcut for the Underline command, Ctrl+U. If an underline style other than the single underline is applied, then press Ctrl+U once to change the underline to a single underline or twice to remove all underlining. Note the Underline command on the Ribbon will remove all underlining in one action.

Additional Text Formats

In addition to basic formatting, Word provides a number of other text formats that can be found in the Font dialog box. To access the Font dialog box, click the dialog launcher in the Font group or press Ctrl+D. Here is a list of additional text effects you'll find in the dialog box:

- Double Strikethrough
- Shadow
- Outline
- Emboss
- Engrave
- Small Caps (Ctrl+Shift+K)
- All Caps (Ctrl+Shift+A)
- Hidden (Ctrl+Shift+H)

Changing Case

Occasionally, you might want to change lowercase text to all caps, all caps to lowercase, mixed-case text to title case, and so forth. Fortunately, you can perform these potentially tedious maneuvers without retyping text. In fact, all you need to do is use the Change Case command on the Home tab. The Change Case command provides the following options:

- Sentence case.
- lowercase
- UPPERCASE
- Capitalize Each Word (Title Case)
- tOGGLE cASE

You can also use Shift+F3 to change the case of text. This keyboard shortcut will cycle through the Change Case options, and the outcome depends on what you have selected in your document. If you select a paragraph or sentence, provided the period is selected, Shift+F3 will cycle through UPPERCASE, lowercase, and Sentence case., as opposed to UPPERCASE, lowercase, and Capitalize Each Word.

INSIDE OUT   **All Caps vs. Change Case**

Though there isn't a visual difference between using the All Caps Font effect (Ctrl+Shift+A) and the UPPERCASE option of Change Case, there is a distinct difference between the two. All Caps is a format that is stored with the text, similar to Bold or Underline, and the Change Case function simply changes the case of the text as if it were originally typed that way in the document. For example, if you use the Clear Formats command, discussed later in this section, text that you format using the All Caps format will revert to the case you originally used when you typed it; whereas, with Change Case the case of the text is maintained when you use the Clear Formats command.

Using the Highlight Tool

The main idea behind highlighting is to call attention to important or questionable text in documents. When reviewing documents, highlight colors can be used to indicate a particular issue (for example, turquoise highlight specifies that a page reference needs to be completed, bright green highlight draws attention to repeated information, and so forth). Highlighting parts of a document works best when the document is viewed on the screen, although you can use highlighting in printed documents if necessary. To apply a single instance of highlight, select the text or object and then click the Text Highlight Color command in the Font group on the Home tab. For multiple highlights, click the Text Highlight Color command without selecting any text or objects. The mouse pointer will display as Highlighter with an I-beam, which you can use to drag through text to highlight it. To quickly turn off highlighting, click the Text Highlight Color button again, or press Esc.

To change the Highlight color, click the arrow next to the Text Highlight Color command to display the Highlight color palette. To remove the Highlight format, use the No Color option.

Note

You can display or hide highlighting (but not the text itself) on the screen and in the printed document without permanently removing the highlighting. To do so, display Word Options and in the Display section, clear the Show Highlighter Marks check box (the option is selected by default) and then click OK.

Changing Text Color

Applying color provides another avenue for customizing text attributes. For example, the font color for headings might match a specific color in a logo, or you might add color to text when you're creating a brochure, a newsletter, or any other document. The most straightforward way to apply color to text is to follow these steps:

1. Select the text you want to color. Alternatively, position your cursor where you want the text color to begin when you type.

2. Click the Font Color arrow on the Home tab.

3. Select a color from the color palette, shown in Figure 6-5.

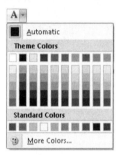

Figure 6-5 Use the color palette to specify the color you want to apply to selected text.

After you've applied color to some text, the Font Color button retains that color setting for the rest of your current session (or until you select another color in the color palette). The thick underline under the *A* on the Font Color button reflects the most recently selected color. You can select other text and simply click the Font Color button to apply the same color to the text; you don't have to repeatedly select the same color in the color palette each time you want to apply the color. By default, the Font Color button is set to Automatic (which generally equates to black).

> **Note**
>
> As described in Chapter 2, "Document Creation with Word 2007," if you want the Font Color to swap if the Theme is changed, use the colors found in the Theme Colors section of the color palette. If you want the color to remain the same regardless of the Theme, select a color from the Standard Colors section or use More Colors.

Working with Hidden Text

Hidden text is used by several Word features, such as index fields and table of contents fields, and it can be used for a variety of document tasks. For example, you may want to exclude portions of a document from printing or remove portions of a document from view on the screen.

To display hidden text on the screen, click the Show/Hide button in the Paragraph section on the Home tab or press Ctrl+Shift+8 to toggle your display. When hidden text is displayed, the hidden text is identified with a dotted underline.

Hidden text does not print by default, regardless of whether it displayed on your screen. If you want to include hidden text, you need to configure your Print options. To do so, display Word Options. In the Display section under Printing Options, select Print Hidden Text. Note that this option is an application option as opposed to an option that is stored with the document. It will remain in effect for all documents.

> **Note**
>
> Prior to sharing a document, make sure it does not contain hidden text by clicking the Microsoft Office Button, pointing at Prepare, and clicking Inspect Document. The Document Inspector can check for hidden text, revisions, personal information, and other types of metadata not immediately visible in a document. For more information about the Document Inspector and preparing documents for sharing, see Chapter 20, "Addressing Document Protection and Security Issues."

Controlling Character Spacing

Another key font formatting enhancement is character spacing. Word provides space-tweaking features that were once available only to professional typesetters. Depending on the font and font effects you are using, you might need to use the character spacing features to improve the look and readability of your documents. For example, you may determine you need more space between text characters when using the Small Caps font effect.

Other potential uses of the character spacing features are to stretch a heading across a column of text, raise or lower a small inline graphic so it appears as part of the surrounding text, or condense the space between characters by as little as 0.1 point to fit text in an specific amount of space. To view the primary character spacing options, click the Font dialog launcher on the Home tab and then click the Character Spacing tab, or press Ctrl+D. Figure 6-6 shows the Character Spacing tab in the Font dialog box.

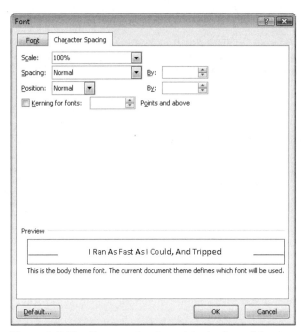

Figure 6-6 The Character Spacing tab in the Font dialog box enables you to rescale selected text, adjust spacing between characters, and reposition text.

You can control the following spacing parameters:

- **Scale** Lets you stretch or compress selected text characters horizontally as a percentage of the text's current size. You can choose a scaling option from the list box, or you can manually enter a scaling value from 1% to 600%. The Scale option is set to 100% for normal text.

- **Spacing** Enables you to expand or condense the spacing between text characters by the amount you enter in the By text box. If you decide you don't like the expanded or condensed spacing settings, you can choose Normal in the Spacing list box to revert to standard letter spacing.

- **Position** Enables you to raise or lower selected text relative to the text's baseline by the amount you enter in the By text box. To reset the text on the baseline, choose Normal in the list box.

- **Kerning For Fonts** Enables Word to automatically adjust the amount of space between specific character combinations so that words and letters look evenly spaced. In the Points And Above text box, you can specify the minimum font size that should be automatically kerned. Generally, kerning is used for headings and larger fonts sizes (12 to 14 points and larger). In Word, kerning works only with TrueType or Adobe Type Manager fonts. Be aware that turning on the Kerning For Fonts feature can slow processing. If you want to manually kern characters, select the characters and use the Spacing option to tighten or loosen the characters' positions.

To recap, the Scale option narrows and widens the actual characters, whereas the Spacing option adjusts the space between characters.

Clearing Formatting Attributes

Up to now, we've been looking at adding font formatting attributes, but at times you might want to remove all formatting attributes in a paragraph or selected text. Word provides the Clear Formatting command on the Home tab (Alt+H+E). To clear all formatting from a selected text or a paragraph, select the text or click in the paragraph and then click the Clear Formatting command. Note that the Clear Formatting command does not clear formatting from text highlighted using the Text Highlight Color.

> **Note**
>
> To reset font formats to only font formatting defined in the Style, press Ctrl+Spacebar. Alternatively, to reset paragraph formats to only paragraph formatting defined in the Style, press Ctrl+Q.

Positioning Content Effectively

Whenever you create documents (reports, brochures, newsletters, and so forth), regardless of their purpose, you'll need to position (and reposition) text, graphics, and other elements within the documents. You can easily align and move content within a Word document by using the alignment commands found in the Paragraph group on the Home tab and by using the Click And Type feature, discussed in the Inside Out tip titled "When Should I Use Click and Type?" later in this section.

Text Alignment Commands

Word offers four quick and easy paragraph and element alignment options—Left, Center, Right, and Justified—as described in Table 6-3. To apply an alignment setting, select multiple elements within the document or click anywhere within the paragraph or element you want to align. Then use one of the options shown in the following table.

Chapter 6

Table 6-3 Text Alignment Options

Setting	Home Tab Command	Keyboard shortcut	Description
Left	≣	Ctrl+L	Aligns text and other elements (such as graphics and tables) along the left margin, or paragraph indent, leaving a ragged right edge. Left alignment is the default setting.
Center	≣	Ctrl+E	Aligns the midpoint of the selected element with the center point between the page's margins or paragraph indents.
Right	≣	Ctrl+R	Aligns text and other elements along the document's right margin, or paragraph indent, leaving the left margin ragged.
Justified	≣	Ctrl+J	Creates straight (or flush) left and right edges by adding white space between words to force the text to align with the left and right margins or paragraph indents.

For tighter justification, use the Do Full Justification The Way WordPerfect 6.x For Windows Does option. This is found in Word Options at the bottom of the Advanced section under Compatibility Options. Click the plus (+) next to Layout Options to expand the list. Note that Compatibility options are stored with the document as opposed to being an application option, which affects all open documents.

For a full discussion on aligning information in Word documents, see Chapter 14, "Aligning information and Formatting Paragraphs and Lists."

INSIDE OUT   When should I use Click And Type?

The Click And Type feature, which was introduced in Word 2000, continues to be available in Word 2007. This feature enables you to double-click anywhere in an empty area of a page to position the insertion point and add text, graphics, tables, or other items. The results are similar to inserting empty paragraphs (pressing Enter), tabs, and spaces to position text, which is not an ideal practice—Word is not a typewriter, and the more you attempt to use it as a glorified typewriter the more you will find what should be simple tasks end up becoming more complex than necessary.

For short documents that need to be created, printed, and saved for future reference, Click And Type can help get a small task accomplished quickly, for example, double-clicking at the bottom center of a letter to insert a signature block. However, for documents that will undergo complex formatting, multiple editing sessions by one or more authors, or evolve through the years, Click And Type may be inefficient over time, and there's no substitute for using proper layout methods. For more complex documents, consider using other layout choices such as tables, which are covered in Chapter 11, "Organizing Concepts in Tables," and text boxes, covered in Chapter 16, "Formatting Layouts Using Backgrounds, Watermarks, and Text Boxes."

By default, the Click And Type feature is enabled in Word 2007. You can verify whether the feature is currently activated by going to Word Options, clicking Advanced, and locating the Enable Click And Type option near the bottom of the Editing Options.

Inserting Symbols and Special Characters

Sometimes your text will require symbols and special characters that aren't readily available on your keyboard. For example, you might want to show a copyright symbol, insert words containing accent marks, include small "dingbat" graphics, insert a nonbreaking space, and so forth. Quite a few symbols and special characters are available in Word if you know where to look. Nicely enough, when you find what you're looking for, Word makes it easy to insert and reuse symbols and special characters in the future.

Inserting Symbols

The Symbol list and the Symbol dialog box, both found on the Insert tab in the Symbols group, work together to take care of your symbol and special character needs. The dynamic Symbol list updates as you use symbols in the list or from the Symbol dialog box, and the last symbol you insert is first in the list. That way, symbols you use frequently will be readily available.

To access the Symbol list, click the Symbol button on the Insert tab. To access the Symbol dialog box, click the More Symbols option at the bottom of the Symbol list. Figure 6-7 shows both the Symbols tab in the Symbol dialog box and the Symbol list.

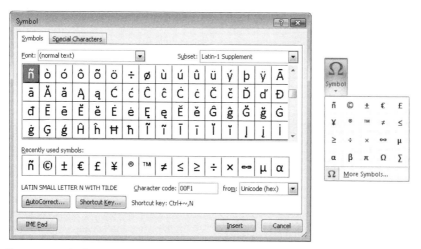

Figure 6-7 In this figure, the ñ and © symbols have been used recently, so they appear in the Recently Used Symbols row near the bottom of the Symbol dialog box and as the first two symbols in the Symbol list.

Chapter 6

INSIDE OUT   Using the keyboard to insert symbols

Symbols can also be inserted using the keyboard. You can use built-in keyboard commands, assign your own keyboard shortcuts, or create AutoCorrect entries. To find the keyboard command for a symbol, display the Symbol dialog box, click a symbol, and then view the associated keyboard command in the lower portion of the dialog box.

Using the keyboard to insert symbols is a little different from other keyboard shortcuts. You may need to hold Alt and press the numbers provided (ASCII character code) on the numeric keypad; other symbols may use two consecutive keyboard commands, which are identified with a comma separation. For example, you may need to type the number and letter combination provided (Unicode hexadecimal value) in the document followed by Alt+X, or press two separate keyboard shortcuts consecutively.

To assign your own keyboard shortcut or create an AutoCorrect entry for symbols you commonly use, select the symbol and then click the respective button at the bottom of the Symbol dialog box. For more on creating AutoCorrect entries, see Chapter 8, "Working with Building Blocks and Other Text Tools." For keyboard shortcuts, see Appendix B, "Customizing Word and Enhancing Accessibility."

When you're inserting symbols from within the Symbol dialog box, keep in mind that you can insert multiple symbols during a single visit. Unlike most dialog boxes, the Symbol dialog box is modeless, which means you can leave the dialog box open and click back into the document to reposition your cursor for the next insertion.

Inserting Symbols Automatically

In addition to inserting symbols manually and using keyboard shortcuts, Word enables you to automatically create symbols as you're typing, without displaying the Symbol dialog box. The magic behind this trick is the AutoCorrect feature. When the AutoCorrect feature is turned on, you can automatically insert symbols that are included in the built-in list of AutoCorrect entries. Table 6-4 lists the symbols you can create using the AutoCorrect feature.

When symbols are inserted automatically, Word 2007 accompanies the symbol with an AutoCorrect Options button. (If the button doesn't appear immediately, position the pointer over the symbol until it appears.) Figure 6-8 shows the AutoCorrect Options available after typing ==> to insert a bold right arrow symbol.

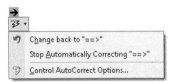

Figure 6-8 The AutoCorrect Options button enables you to control whether automatically generated symbols should replace typed text.

Table 6-4 AutoCorrect Symbols

Symbol	Typed characters
©	(c)
®	(r)
™	(tm)
...	...
☺	:) or :-)
☺	:| or :-|
☹	:(or :-(
→	-->
←	<--
➔	==>
⬅	<==
⇔	<=>

If an AutoCorrect symbol is inserted but you would prefer to display the typed text, simply press the Backspace key once after you type the text. For example, if you want to display (c) instead of ©, type an opening parenthesis, c, and then a closing parenthesis (at which point the text changes to the copyright symbol automatically). Then, press the Backspace key (which removes the copyright symbol and redisplays the (c) text).

In some cases, you might find yourself removing a symbol repeatedly. Instead of driving yourself crazy, hover the pointer over the inserted symbol to display the AutoCorrect Options button, click the button, and then click Stop Automatically Correcting. This action will delete the AutoCorrect entry, and the typed combination will no longer be converted. For more information on AutoCorrect, see Chapter 8.

Inserting Special Characters

Inserting special characters is similar to inserting symbols. Logically enough, special characters can be found on the Special Characters tab in the Symbol dialog box, as shown in Figure 6-9. Most of the special characters are typesetting characters that you use when refining document text. For example, when you want to prevent the text from breaking if it wraps to the next line, you might insert a nonbreaking hyphen in a telephone number or a nonbreaking space between a first and last name.

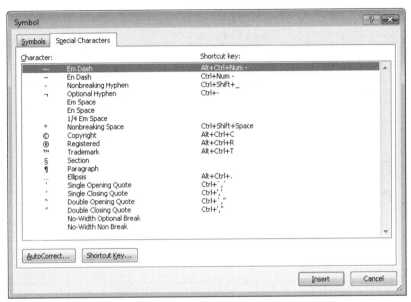

Figure 6-9 The Special Characters tab in the Symbol dialog box provides quick access to special characters.

You can insert special characters by using the Special Characters tab in the Symbol dialog box or pressing keyboard shortcuts. Note that special characters are not added to the Symbol list after you add them to your document.

> **Tip**
>
> If you find that the special characters do not meet your needs, a suitable substitute may be found amongst the symbol characters. For example, the em dash (about the width of an uppercase *M*) allows text to break if it wraps to the next line. If you need to insert a nonbreaking em dash, a horizontal bar (2015, Alt+X) can be used instead of the em dash found on the Special Characters tab of the Symbol dialog box.

Inserting Mathematical Equations

Word 2007 vastly improved capabilities for inserting mathematical equations. In previous versions of Word, equations are created using a separate utility, the Microsoft Equation Editor, which isn't part of the standard installation. For Word 2007, a new set of tools was created to build equations and this is part of the standard installation. Here are some of the notable improvements over the old functionality:

- Regular Word text (not objects): can be integrated with regular Word formatting

- High-quality display and typography: uses TeX standards and a brand-new math font

- Linear Format: keyboard-based syntax; uses notation similar to TeX

- MathML support: equations can be pasted in calculating or graphing applications

- Custom Equations: can be saved as Building Blocks for quick insertion

The Equation Gallery, as shown in Figure 6-10, can be found on the Insert tab in the Symbols group.

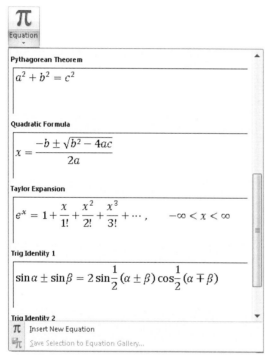

Figure 6-10 The Equation Gallery includes a built-in collection of common equations that you can insert into your documents and modify to meet your needs.

> **Note**
>
> The new Equations functionality is not available in Compatibility Mode and documents containing Equations opened in previous versions of Word or saved in the Word 97-2003 file format will be converted to images.

To insert a new equation, click the Equation button, click the arrow below the Equation button and click an equation in the Equation gallery, or press Alt+=. Once an equation is inserted, the contextual Equation Tools will display, as shown in Figure 6-11. The Design tab contains a large collection of tools, symbols, and mathematical structures you can use to insert and control equations.

Figure 6-11 The contextual Equation Tools provide the tools, options, symbols, and structures necessary to meet most of your equation building needs.

When you insert an equation, it is placed in a Content Control, a new container in Word 2007 that contains the equation and provides additional functionality beyond the commands found on the Design tab, such as those in the Tools group. For example, you can convert the equation to an inline display or change the placement of the equation (by default, equations are centered as a group) by using the Equation Options (the arrow in the lower right corner of the Content Control), as shown in Figure 6-12.

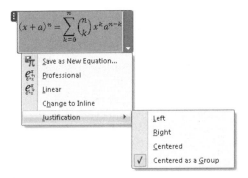

Figure 6-12 Equation options enable you to save an equation as a new Building Block, specify whether to show the equation in professional layout (the default) or on a single line (linear), align the equation in line with text, or align the equation left, right, or center.

> **Note**
>
> While editing the equation, you can find additional functionality in the context sensitive shortcut menus, which means the commands will change depending on the selected group of equations. For example, if you want to place an equation on multiple lines centered around the equal sign, right-click before or after the equal sign and click Insert Manual Break.

Accessing Equation Tools and Options

In addition to the equation options provided by the Content Control and the shortcut menus, you can manage equations by using the contextual Equation Tools that display when you insert an equation. Specifically, the Tools group includes the following:

- **Equation command** Opens the Equations Gallery, similar to clicking the arrow below the Equation button on the Insert tab

- **Professional** Shows equations using typical math notation and layout, such as superscripts and subscripts (default)

- **Linear** Shows equations on a single line and uses linear notation

- **Normal Text** Toggles the font used in equations between regular text and math text

- **Equation Dialog Box Launcher** Opens the Equation Options dialog box, as shown in Figure 6-13; among other options, you can use the Equation Options dialog box to specify whether you want to automatically show equations in Professional format as well as specify the default alignment setting

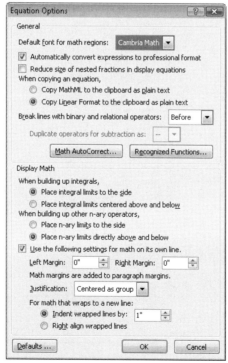

Figure 6-13 The Equation Options dialog box enables you to control how equations display by default and provides quick access to the Math AutoCorrect rules (which are contained on the Math AutoCorrect tab in the AutoCorrect dialog box).

Chapter 6

For more information about working with the Math AutoCorrect feature, see Chapter 8.

> **Note**
>
> If you create equations that look fine in Word 2007 on the screen but do not print as expected, make sure you have downloaded the most up-to-date drivers from your printer manufacturer's Web site.

Accessing Equation Symbol Sets and Structures

Though Word 2007 provides a few common built-in equations, you will probably want to build many of your own equations. To help you build your equations, the Design tab offers a large collection of math-related symbols and structures. To access the symbol sets, click the More arrow in the Symbols gallery. To access additional symbol sets, click the arrow next to Symbol Set, as shown in Figure 6-14. For a list of symbol sets and their descriptions, see Table 6-5.

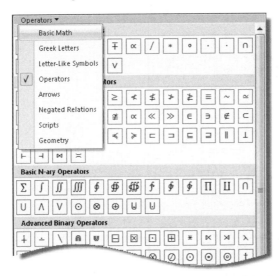

Figure 6-14 You can click the More arrow expand the Symbols gallery and access additional symbol sets, or you can scroll through the currently active Symbols menu by clicking the row up and row down arrows.

Table 6-5 Symbol Sets and Descriptions

Symbol Set	Description
Basic Math	Commonly used mathematical symbols, such as > and <
Greek Letters	Uppercase and lowercase letters from the Greek alphabet

Symbol Set	Description
Letter-Like Symbols	Symbols that resemble letters
Operators	• **Common Binary Operators** Symbols that act on two quantities, such as + and ÷
	• **Common Relational Operators** Symbols that express a relationship between two expressions, such as = and ~
	• **Basic N-ary Operators** Operators that act across a range of variables or terms
	• **Advanced Binary Operators** Additional symbols that act on two quantities
	• **Advanced Relational Operators** Additional symbols that express a relationship between two expressions
Arrows	Symbols that indicate direction
Negated Relations	Symbols that express a negated relationship
Scripts	The mathematical Script, Fraktur, and Double-Struck typefaces
Geometry	Commonly used geometric symbols

In addition to numbers, letters, and symbols, most equations also require mathematical structures. The Structures group on the Design tab provides structures you can insert and then customize if necessary by filling placeholders (small dotted boxes) with values. Available structures are categorized into the following groups: Fraction, Script, Radical, Integral, Large Operator, Bracket, Function, Accent, Limit And Log, Operator, and Matrix. Figure 6-15 shows the Radical category.

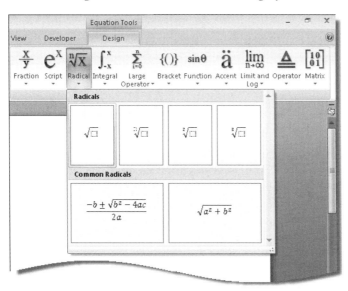

Figure 6-15 Word provides a large collection of mathematical structures that you can use to build equations. In this figure, the active control shows the Radical category and the square root is selected.

Equation placeholders do not appear in Full Screen Reading view, Print Preview, or printed documents.

Inserting Date and Time Elements

Word offers a variety of elements that you can use to insert dates and times—those that automatically update as well as static dates—into documents. The Date And Time dialog box, found on the Insert tab in the Text group, provides a quick and easy method of inserting dates and times in your documents. When you click Date & Time, the Date And Time dialog box appears, as shown in Figure 6-16.

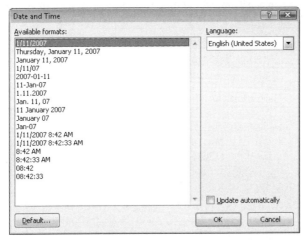

Figure 6-16 The Date And Time dialog box enables you to insert either static dates and times or those that will update automatically.

> **Note**
>
> The Default button in the Date And Time dialog box sets the default format for dates and times used in Word fields (those that update automatically), such as the *Date* field, which can be inserted by pressing Alt+Shift+D, or the *Time* field, which can be inserted by pressing Alt+Shift+T. The last default that is set will also be selected by default the first time you access the dialog box during your current Word session.

INSIDE OUT   Uncovered: Date and Time AutoComplete Inconsistency

Dates can also be inserted in a document by using AutoComplete, which has been available in Word since Word 97, by typing the first few characters of the current date and then pressing Enter, or Tab, when the ScreenTip for AutoComplete displays. However, depending on your language settings, such as English (United Kingdom) or English (Australia), effectively using AutoComplete to insert dates can be a bit tricky if not next to impossible. For example, if a date format such as 11 January 2007 is desired, after typing *11 J*, AutoComplete offers 11 Jan. 2007 in the ScreenTip instead of 11 January 2007.

The underlying issue is that AutoComplete uses the list of date formats found in the Date And Time dialog box, (which changes according to the selected language), for AutoComplete suggestions – it doesn't use the Default Date format. If using a language such as English (United Kingdom) or English (Australia), then a date format such as 11 Jan. 2007 is listed in the Date And Time dialog box.

A few workarounds can be used, such as ignoring the first AutoComplete suggestion, typing the first four characters of the name of the month, accepting the AutoComplete suggestion for the month, or pressing the Spacebar and then accepting the AutoComplete suggestion for the year. But all of these tend to require a bit of thought and a watchful eye.

Other workarounds include using the Date And Time dialog box, creating a macro to insert the current date in the preferred format as static text (a macro to accomplish this is covered in Chapter 31, "Working with Macros and VBA"), or using two keyboard shortcuts: one to insert the *Date* field, using the Default Date format, and then another keyboard shortcut to convert the field to static text. If you are interested in the latter method, first set your desired date format as the default in the Date And Time dialog box. Then press Alt+Shift+D to insert the *Date* field, move the cursor back into the field, then press Ctrl+Shift+F9 to convert the field to static text.

When you use the Date And Time dialog box to insert a date and select the Update Automatically option, the *Date* field will be used. This causes an automatic update to the current system date each time you open the document or update the fields. Should the date fail to update, for example if the document is left open overnight, then place your cursor in the date, and click the Update option found above the *Date* field in the Content Control to update the date. If you do not want a date in a document to update automatically, see the following Troubleshooting tip entitled "Dates in My Document Keep Updating Automatically."

TROUBLESHOOTING

Dates in my document keep updating automatically

The *Date* field may be used in a document template as a method to automatically insert the current system date in new documents based on the template. The problem with using this method is that more often than not, the date the document was created—not the current system date—is the desired date.

To resolve this issue, you can select the date and press Ctrl+Shift+F9 to convert it to static text or use the *CreateDate* field in the template instead of the *Date* field. When a new document based on the template is created, the *CreateDate* field in the document will update to the current system date, rather than inheriting the creation date of the template, because the document is newly created.

Making this correction in either the template or documents based on the template is a fairly simple process. First, open the document or template, press Alt+F9 to toggle on the view of Field Codes. The date will look something like:

```
{ DATE \@ "d MMMM yyyy" }
```

Place the cursor in front of *Date* and type **CREATE**. The date field should now look something like:

```
{ CREATEDATE \@ "d MMMM yyyy" }
```

Press Alt+F9 to toggle off the view of Field Codes and if necessary, place the cursor in the field and then press F9 to update the field. The date the document was created should now be displayed.

If you prefer to use the Field dialog box to insert the *CreateDate* field or other date and time fields, it can be accessed on the Insert tab, near the bottom of the Quick Parts gallery.

Inserting Document Property Fields

Additional data stored with a document, such as document properties, has been a part of computer files for as long as most of us can remember. It's actually quite useful—similar to including additional information on the outside of a manila file folder to help identify its contents. As handy as document properties may appear to be, they haven't necessarily been used by many users, mainly due to the extra steps it takes to add and modify the data.

In Word 2007, document properties have undertaken a new role in document creation. You can now insert bound document property fields in your document and if the property is updated in the document, it will also be updated in the file properties and vice-versa. This enhanced functionality is brought to us by the new Office Open XML Formats and another exciting new feature, Content Controls.

> **Note**
>
> Bound document property fields are not available if working in Compatibility Mode, and document property fields will be converted to static content if opened in previous versions of Word or saved in the Word 97-2003 file format.

To access the bound document property fields, navigate to the Insert tab and display the Quick Parts gallery. If you have custom Building Blocks in the Quick Parts gallery, Document Property will be listed below the custom Building Blocks as shown in Figure 6-17.

Figure 6-17 You can insert and modify document properties while you work by using new bound document property fields.

> **Note**
>
> The Document Property list may also contain document properties used in a SharePoint Document Library.

You can also access a document's properties by clicking the Microsoft Office Button, pointing to Prepare, and clicking Properties. The Document Properties panel will open above the workspace, as shown below.

To display the Properties dialog box, which contains additional properties, click Document Properties in the top left corner of the panel and then click Advanced Properties.

> **Note**
>
> If you're using Windows Vista, document properties can also be updated and modified in the new Save As dialog box. To display more document properties, simply resize the dialog box.

When you insert a bound document property field, it is placed in a Content Control, as shown below, using the Title document property field. When the field is active, you'll see the title of the field above the data.

Deleting a Content Control that contains a document property field does not delete the information stored in the document. To delete the data stored in the document property, you need to delete the data in the Content Control, the Document Properties panel, or the Save As dialog box (if using Windows Vista).

Additionally, if you use the Document Inspector to remove document properties and personal information, the bound document property fields will be converted to static text in the document.

Content Controls: First Look

Content Controls are XML-based and offer technology that opens the doors to streamlining document creation in Word 2007. Content Controls aren't just text placeholders or the new form controls for Word 2007, they play a far greater role—they enable data to be bound, or *mapped*, to elements in an XML file, such as a Word document, provided it's saved in the new Open XML Format. It's the XML Mapping technology that enables you to update a document's properties within the document or to insert a cover page, containing bound document property fields, from the Cover Page gallery on the Insert tab. It also enables you to swap a cover page with another inserted cover page without losing any data that was previously typed in the document property fields. They are so flexible you'll see Content Controls used in several built-in features, and you can take advantage of the same functionality by adding bound Content Controls in your Word 2007 documents. Without a doubt, Content Controls are an exciting advance in document creation! If you are interested in learning more about Content Controls see Chapter 29, "Customizing Documents with Content Controls," and Chapter 30, "Working with XML."

What's Next?

This chapter covered some of the essential concepts related to formatting text and paragraphs; inserting symbols and special characters; using the new Equation builder; inserting and controlling dates and times; and using bound document property fields. The next chapter will delve into more fundamental, yet worthwhile topics: document navigation, document views, and that ever-so-useful utility that turns what could be repetitive, mundane editing into an effortless task—Find And Replace.

Honing Document Navigation Skills

As an experienced Microsoft Office Word 2007 user, you've undoubtedly grown accustomed to using a few standard techniques for finding files and winding your way through documents. This chapter shows you what's new in navigation in Office Word 2007 and takes a look at the variety of ways you can move through your Word documents beyond the basics of clicking, scrolling, and paging up or down.

Navigating Easily in Word 2007

By now you already know that the big news in Word 2007 is the major redesign, resulting in the Microsoft Office Fluent Interface. The tabs on the Ribbon, the groups of commands, and the contextual tools all help you move easily from one task to another while you're working on your documents. Two primary changes in the navigation features in Word 2007 make getting around in documents easier:

- Now you can press Alt to display KeyTips, which show you what to press to navigate through the program by using the keyboard.

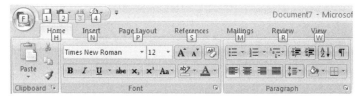

- You can click Page in the status bar to display the Go To tab of the Find And Replace dialog box quickly, enabling you to move directly to the page you want without using shortcut keys or clicking tabs or commands. Type the number of the page you want to jump to, and click OK.

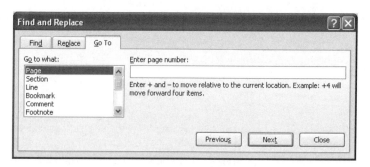

Other ways to navigate quickly in your documents include

- Using the Document Map and thumbnails
- Use shortcut and function keys
- Click Browse Object to move through the document
- Use Find to locate specific items
- Add bookmarks to return to specific areas easily

Being able to navigate your documents easily helps you get things done faster and more easily in Word. The most important thing is not the technique you use but the fact that you are comfortable with it and it gets you where you want to go. This chapter walks you through these various navigating techniques.

Accessing Document Areas Using the Document Map and Thumbnails

The Document Map and Thumbnails navigation features have been around for a few versions of Word, but they are often overlooked, even by many veteran Word users. In Word 2007, both features get a higher profile on the View tab in the Word 2007 Ribbon. You'll find them in the Show/Hide group, as you see in Figure 7-1.

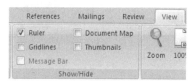

Figure 7-1 Choose Document Map or Thumbnails in the Show/Hide group and your choice appears along the left side of the Word window.

Each of these features provides you with both a unique view of your document and a different way of moving to different pages.

- Document map lists the headings in your document and enables you to move to a different section by clicking the heading you want to move to.

- Thumbnails view displays clickable images of individual pages so that you can see the various pages in your document and move to the page you want by clicking it.

To use the Document Map most effectively, your document should be formatted with built-in or defined heading styles or outline-level paragraph formats. If your document doesn't use designated styles, Word attempts to identify paragraphs that seem to be headings and displays them in the Document Map.

For more information about working with styles, see Chapter 15, "Using Styles to Increase Your Formatting Power."

Note that you can view either the Document Map or Thumbnails, but you cannot view both panes simultaneously in the same window. To shift from Document Map view to Thumbnails view, click the arrow in the new drop-down list located at the top left corner of the pane, and choose Thumbnails. To use Thumbnails view to navigate through your document, scroll through the Thumbnails and click the one you want to move to. That page is displayed in the Word window (see Figure 7-2).

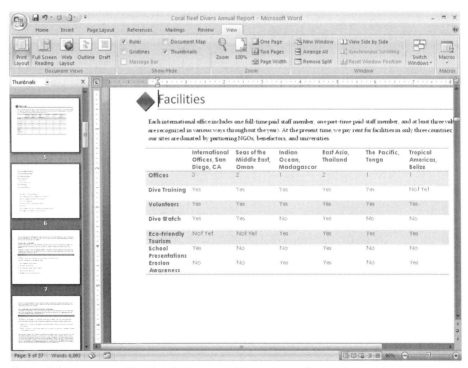

Figure 7-2 You can use Thumbnails view to navigate to a specific page in your document.

By default, all levels of headings are visible when you open the Document Map. To change the default setting, right-click the Document Map, and choose a heading level, as shown in Figure 7-3. You can also click the plus (+) and minus (-) signs next to individual headings with subheadings to expand and collapse sections. To jump to a section in your document, click the section's heading. The heading of the section currently shown in your workspace is highlighted in the Document Map so you can quickly see the current position of the insertion point within the document.

Figure 7-3 You can expand and collapse heading levels for individual sections.

Moving in the Document Using Shortcut and Function Keys

If you have used Word for a while, you probably have a set of shortcut keys you use to move through documents quickly. Word 2007 preserves all the shortcut keys from Word 2003, enabling you to navigate your documents in a manner you're accustomed to. Table 7-1 provides you with the most common keyboard shortcuts and function key combinations.

Table 7-1 Keyboard Shortcuts and Function Keys for Navigating within Documents

Keyboard shortcut	Action
Alt+Down Arrow	Moves to the next object
Alt+End	Moves to the end of the row
Alt+F1 (or F11)	Moves to the next field
Alt+F4 (or Ctrl+ F4 or Ctrl+W)	Closes the active document
Alt+F6 (or Ctrl+F6)	Moves to the next window
Alt+Home	Moves to the start of a row
Alt+Page Down	Moves to the end of the current column
Alt+Page Up	Moves to the top of the current column
Alt+Right Arrow	Goes forward to the next page in Web view
Alt+Shift+C	Closes the open pane
Alt+Shift+F6 (or Ctrl+Shift+F6)	Displays the previous window
Alt+Up Arrow	Moves to the previous object
Arrow keys	Move the insertion point left, right, up, or down
Ctrl+Alt+Page Down	Moves the insertion point to the bottom of the window
Ctrl+Alt+Page Up	Moves the cursor to the top of the window
Ctrl+Alt+S	Splits the window view
Ctrl+Alt+Y (or Shift+F4)	Finds the next instance of a search term
Ctrl+Alt+Z (or Shift+F5)	Moves to the previous location of the insertion point (even if the insertion point was in a different Word document)
Ctrl+Down Arrow	Moves to the next paragraph or next table cell
Ctrl+End	Moves to the end of the document
Ctrl+F	Displays the Find tab in the Find And Replace dialog box
Ctrl+F4 (or Alt+F4 or Ctrl+W)	Closes the active document
Ctrl+F5	Restores a document's window from maximized to the previous window size
Ctrl+F6 (or Alt+F6)	Displays the next window
Ctrl+F7	Activates the window so you can move it using the arrow keys
Ctrl+F8	Activates the window so you can resize the window height and width using the arrow keys
Ctrl+F10	Maximizes the document window
Ctrl+G (or F5)	Displays the Go To tab in the Find And Replace dialog box

Keyboard shortcut	Action
Ctrl+Home	Moves to the beginning of the document
Ctrl+Left Arrow	Moves one word to the left
Ctrl+O (or Ctrl+Alt+F2 or Ctrl+F12)	Displays the Open dialog box
Ctrl+Page Down	Browses to the next item (based on the current Browse Object setting)
Ctrl+Page Up	Browses to the previous item (based on the current Browse Object setting)
Ctrl+Right Arrow	Moves one word to the right
Ctrl+Shift+F6 (or Alt+Shift+F6)	Displays the previous window
Ctrl+Up Arrow	Moves to the previous paragraph
Ctrl+W (or Ctrl+F4)	Closes the active document
End	Moves to the end of the current line
Esc	Closes an open gallery or cancels the current action
F6	Moves to the next pane or frame
F11 (or Alt+F1)	Moves to the next field
Home	Moves to the beginning of the current line
PageDown	Displays the next screen
PageUp	Displays the previous screen

Navigating with Browse Object

Another way to move through documents is to use the Select Browse Object menu and its associated buttons. You can find the three browse buttons—Previous Find/Go To, Select Browse Object, and Next Find/Go To— at the bottom of the vertical scroll bar in the lower right corner of the editing window. When you click Select Browse Object, a gallery of browse tools appears.

To use the Browse Object to move through your document, follow these steps.

1. Display the Select Browse Object menu by pressing Ctrl+Alt+Home or by clicking the Select Browse Object button (it has a round small round icon) toward the bottom of the vertical scroll bar.

2. Select the type of object you want to browse for (for example, Browse By Heading). See Table 7-2 for available options.

3. Click the Previous and Next buttons (above and below the Select Browse Object button in the vertical scroll bar) to navigate from one browse object to the next. Alternately, you can press Ctrl+Page Up to move to the previous object or Ctrl+Page Down to move to the next browse object.

Table 7-2 Tools

Button	Description
	Browses by using the Go To tab in the Find And Replace dialog box
	Browses by using the Find tab in the Find And Replace dialog box
	Browses by moving between the last three edits
	Browses by moving from heading to heading
	Browses by moving from graphic to graphic
	Browses by moving from table to table
	Browses by moving from field to field
	Browses by moving from endnote to endnote
	Browses by moving from footnote to footnote
	Browses by moving from comment to comment
	Browses by moving from section to section
	Browses by moving from page to page

Chapter 7

Finding Text and Elements Within the Current Document

You probably already know that you can find characters, words, phrases, and text elements by typing a search string in the Find And Replace dialog box and then clicking Find Next to move from one instance of the search string to the next. Display the Find And Replace dialog box by clicking the Home tab and choosing Find in the Editing group.

In many cases, conducting a simple text search using the Find tab may get you where you want to go. But sometimes you'll want to further refine your search parameters. Click the More button to see additional options. The following list gives you a quick look at the search parameters you can use in the Find And Replace dialog box, and Table 7-3 provides you with a list of wildcard characters you can use to streamline your search as you move through your documents:

- **Search** Enables you to specify whether to search Down, Up, or through All of the document. Note that Word does not search headers, footers, footnotes, or comments.

- **Match case** Searches for text in upper- or lowercase, exactly as you've entered it. This option is unavailable when you select the Use wildcards, Sounds like, or Find all word forms check box.

- **Find Whole Words Only** Searches only for whole words, not parts of longer words. This option also is unavailable when you select the Use wildcards, Sounds like, or Find all word forms check box.

- **Use wildcards** Enables you to use wildcard characters in place of text to expand and refine your searches. If you enter wildcard characters in the Find What box without selecting the Use Wildcards option, Word will treat the wildcards as plain text. When the Use Wildcards check box is selected and you want to search for a character that is also a wildcard, precede the character with a backslash (\). For example, to search for an asterisk, you must enter *****.

- **Sounds like (English)** Searches for terms that sound like the word or words entered in the Find What box. For example, if you enter **eight** in the Find What box, and then select the Sounds Like check box, Word will find all instances of *eight* as well as *ate*. This feature works only with legitimate words—entering the number **8** and selecting the Sounds Like check box won't return *eight*, *ate*, or *8*, and entering **u r** won't return *you are*.

- **Find all word forms (English)** Searches for all forms of the word entered in the Find What box. For example, if you enter **speak** in the Find What box, Word will find *speak, speaking, spoke, spoken, speaks,* and so forth.

- **Match prefix** Searches for all words that being with the text entered in the Find What box. For example, if you enter **ed** in the Find What box and select the Match Prefix check box, Word will find and select the prefix ed in words such as educate, edition, editing, and so forth.

- **Match suffix** Searches for all words that end with the text entered in the Find what box. For example, if you enter **ed** in the Find What box and select the Match Suffix check box, Word will find and select the suffix ed in words such as mentioned, moved, named, happened, and so forth.

> **Note**
>
> Word does not find words that match both the prefix and suffix to text in the Find What box when you use the check box options. For example, if you enter **ed** in the Find What box and select both the Match Prefix and Match Suffix text boxes, Word does not find words such as educated or edited. To conduct a search that specifies both the prefix and suffix of the words included in your search results, you would have to use wildcards, such as <(ed)*(ed)>, as described in Table 7-3.

- **Ignore punctuation characters** Searches for matching text regardless of punctuation. Keep in mind that this option ignores added punctuation shown in the text, not punction included in the Find What box.

- **Ignore white-space characters** Searches for matching text regardless of the number of spaces between search string letters or words.

> **Tip**
>
> Look for text directly below the Find What box to see whether any search options are being applied to the current search. For example, if Down is selected in the Search List box and the Match Case check box is select, the text Search Down, Match Case will appear below the Find What text box and the options will be applied to the current search.

Table 7-3 Using Wildcards in the Find And Replace Dialog Box

Wildcard	Specifies	Example
?	Any single character	**p?t** finds *pet, pat, pit*
*	Any string of characters	**p*t** finds *pest, parrot, pit*
<	Finds the text at the beginning of a word	**<mark** finds *market* but not *demark*
>	Finds the text at the end of a word	**ter>** finds *winter* but not *terrain*
[ ]	Finds one of the enclosed characters	**t[oa]n** finds *ton* and *tan*
[-]	Finds any character within the specified range	**[r-t]ight** finds *right, sight,* and *tight*
[!x-z]	Finds any single character except characters in the range inside the brackets	**cl[!a]ck** finds *clock* and *cluck* but not *clack* or *click*
{n}	Finds exactly *n* occurrences of the preceding character or expression	**ble{2}d** finds *bleed* but not *bled.*
{n,}	Finds at least *n* occurrences of the preceding character or expression	**fe{1,}d** finds *fed* and *feed*
{n,m}	Finds from *n* to *m* occurrences of the preceding character or expression	**10{1,3}** finds *10, 100,* and *1000*
@	Finds one or more occurrences of the preceding character or expression	**mo@d** finds *mod* and *mood*

Finding Instances of Formatting

In addition to finding text strings, you can find (and replace, if you'd like) various formatting settings. To view the available formatting parameters in the expanded Find tab of the Find And Replace dialog box, click the Format button in the lower left corner. Choosing Font, Paragraph, Tabs, Language, Frame, or Style from the Format menu displays the corresponding formatting dialog box. For example, choosing Font displays a dialog box named Find Font, which looks very similar to the Font dialog box. Choosing the Highlight option lets you specify highlighted or unhighlighted text in the Find What box. For example, choose Highlight once to find highlighted text, choose Highlight again to indicate that you want to find text that is not highlighted, and choose Highlight a third time to find all instances of the search text regardless of highlighting.

Tip
You can also control basic character formatting by using keyboard shortcuts. To do so, click in the Find What box and press keyboard shortcuts such as Ctrl+B (bold), Ctrl+I (italic), and Ctrl+U (underline) to toggle among applied, not applied, and neither (which equates to no formatting) settings.

You can find instances of formatting without entering text in the Find What box. For example, you could search for highlighted text that isn't italic in the current document by clicking in the Find What text box and applying the Format settings without typing any text. You can, of course, specify text in combination with formatting settings if that's what you need to find.

To clear all formatting commands in the Find What box, click the No Formatting button (if no formatting commands are applied, the Formatting button appears dim). Generally, you'll want to clear formatting when you complete one Find operation and are ready to conduct another.

Finding Special Characters Using Codes

Word further expands your search capabilities by providing special codes you can use to find document elements, such as paragraph marks, tab characters, endnote marks, and so forth. To view the available special characters, click the Special button in the bottom of the Find And Replace dialog box. The Special list includes the same options available in Word 2003.

When you choose an option from the Special menu, a code is inserted in the Find What box. If you'd prefer, you can enter a code directly in the Find What box. Table 7-4 lists some commonly used special character codes. Notice that some codes can be used only in the Find What or Replace With box, and that the Use Wildcards option must be turned on or off in certain instances.

Note
Word can't find floating objects, WordArt, watermarks, or drawing objects. However, if you change a floating object into an inline object, Word can find the object.

Table 7-4 Using Special Character Codes in the Find And Replace Dialog Box

Special character	Code	Find And Replace Box
ANSI characters	^0*nnn* (where *0* is zero and *nnn* is the character code)	Find what, Replace with
ASCII characters	^*nnn* (where *nnn* is the character code)	Find what, Replace with
Any Character	^?	Find what (with the Use wildcards check box cleared)
Any Digit	^#	Find what (with the Use wildcards check box cleared)
Any Letter	^$	Find what (with the Use wildcards check box cleared)
Caret Character	^^	Find what, Replace with
Clipboard Contents	^c	Replace with
Closing Field Brace (when field codes are visible)	^21	Find what (with the Use wildcards check box cleared)
Column Break	^n or ^14	Find what, Replace with
Comment	^a or ^5	Find what (with the Use wildcards check box cleared)
Em Dash	^+	Find what, Replace with
Em Space (Unicode)	^8195	Find what (with the Use wildcards check box cleared)
En Dash	^=	Find what, Replace with
En Space (Unicode)	^8194	Find what (with the Use wildcards check box cleared)
Endnote Mark	^e	Find what (with the Use wildcards check box cleared)
Field	^d	Find what (with the Use wildcards check box cleared)
Find What Text	^&	Replace with
Footnote Mark	^f or ^2	Find what (with the Use wildcards check box cleared)
Graphic or Picture (in-line only)	^g	Find what (with the Use wildcards check box selected)
Graphic or Picture (in-line only)	^1	Find what (with the Use wildcards ceck box cleared)
Manual Line Break	^| or ^11	Find what, Replace with
Manual Page Break	^m	Replace with
Nonbreaking Hyphen	^~	Find what, Replace with

Special character	Code	Find And Replace Box
Nonbreaking Space	^s	Find what, Replace with
Opening Field Brace (when field codes are visible)	^19	Find what (with Use wildcards check box cleared)
Optional Hyphen	^-	Find what, Replace with
Page or Section Break	^12	Fine what, Replace with
Paragraph Character	^v	Find what, Replace with
Paragraph Mark	^p or ^13	Find what (with the Use Wildcards check box cleared), Replace with
Section Break	^b	Find what (with the Use wildcards check box cleared)
Section Character	^%	Find what, Replace with
Tab Character	^t or ^9	Find what, Replace with
Unicode Character	^Unnnn (were *nnnn* is the character code)	Find what (with the Use wildcards check box cleared)
White Space	^w	Find what (with the Use wildcards check box cleared)

Jumping to Document Areas Using Go To

We started this chapter by mentioning the fast way to display the Go To tab of the Find And Replace dialog box (click the Page box in the left side of the status bar). You can use the Go To tab to move quickly through a document, and go just about anywhere you'd like. For example, you can go directly to a page, section, line, bookmark, comment, footnote, endnote, field, table, graphic, equation, object, or heading.

You can display the Go To tab in the Find And Replace dialog box several different ways:

- Press F5 or Ctrl+G.

- Click the Find arrow in the Editing group on the Home tab, and click Go To.

- Click the Go To button in the Select Browse Object menu. (To display the Select Browse Object menu, click the Select Browse Object button toward the bottom of the vertical scroll bar.)

To use the Go To tab, select a component in the Go To What list box, enter the appropriate value or parameter in the box to the right, and then click Go To (or click Previous or Next if no value or parameter is specified). Here are two examples of uses for the Go To feature:

- To display a particular page in the document, select Page in the Go To What list box, type the page number in the Enter Page Number box, and then click Go To.

- To display the next bookmark in the document, select Bookmark in the Go To What list box, select the bookmark name in the list box, and then click Go To.

Creating Bookmarks for Document Navigation

Bookmarks are a great feature if you find that you often need to return to a particular area in a document. They work in just the way you'd imagine they would—similar to a bookmark you place between pages in a novel. You can set multiple bookmarks in Word and give each bookmark a unique name so that you can return to your place (and remember the topic at hand) easily. Here are the steps for inserting and naming a bookmark:

1. Position the insertion point where you want to insert a bookmark, and then, click Bookmark in the Links group on the Insert tab. The Bookmark dialog box appears, as you see in Figure 7-4.

2. In the Bookmark dialog box, type a name for the bookmark, and then click Add.

Figure 7-4 Use the Bookmarks dialog box to create a bookmark in your document.

After you insert a bookmark, you can use the Go To tab to find the bookmarked area as described in the preceding section, or you can click Bookmark on the Insert tab to open the Bookmark dialog box, select the bookmark's name, and then click Go To to move to that point in your document.

Working with Document WindowsIn Chapter 1, "Room to Create with Office Word 2007," you learned about the different views you can use in Word as you work on your documents. You can do the line-by-line work in Page Layout view or Draft view; you can prepare your document for the Web in Web Layout view; you can get a sense of the overall structure (and work with sections in your document) by using Outline view. You can also review the document in an unencumbered window by using Full Screen Reading view, and you can see how your document will look in print by using Print Preview.

In addition to these main views, you can further alter the way your document windows are displayed by changing the size and format of the display. This section shows you how to use commands on the View tab to change the way your documents appear so that you can navigate through (and between) them as easily as possible.

Changing the View

Part of finding what you need quickly in a document involves displaying the file in a way that helps you do just that. The Zoom group of the View tab provides you with a set of tools that enable you to change the display of your current document.

- Use Zoom to display the Zoom dialog box and choose from among preset zoom percentages (or select your own in the Percent box). Additionally, you can choose whether you want to display multiple pages and determine the width of the page as it is displayed.

- 100% shows the document at 100 percent size, no matter which previous view was used. This means that if you have enlarged the document to 125%, clicking this tool will take the document display down to 100%; but if you were viewing the document at 50%, clicking it will increase the magnification to 100%.

- One Page displays the current page of the current document as one complete page in the display (depending on whether the document is in portrait or landscape orientation, this results in 62% and 68% zoom, respectively).

- Two Pages displays two pages side by side in the display. This view is helpful if you are checking the continuity of items in your document and want to be able to scan more than one page at a time.

- Page Width displays the page according to the width of the text margins on the page. This view won't give you a sense of the full layout of the page (use One Page or Two Pages for that), but it does give you a quick way to display your content in a way that's easy to read.

Displaying and Arranging Windows

In addition to being able to select from among a variety of views in Word 2007, you can also work with multiple windows. You'll find the commands for working with document windows in the Window group of the View tab. This section introduces you to the most common window tasks you'll use as you navigate through documents in Word.

Split Window View

Word 2007 includes a simple tool for splitting the current document window into two parts. This enables you to compare portions of your document easily, without having to open two different copies and switch back and forth between them. For example, suppose that you are working on a lengthy annual report for your organization and, as you write the conclusion of the report, you want to be sure to use wording similar to what you used at the beginning of the report.

You can split the window view by clicking the View tab and choosing Split in the Window group. A gray line appears across the center of your document. You can then drag the line to the position on the screen where you want the split to be made and click the mouse. The split is added and the horizontal ruler appears at that point in the document (see Figure 7-5). To select the pane of the window you want to navigate, simply click in the document in that portion of the window.

> **Tip**
>
> You can also split the window easily by using the splitter, the dash symbol located just above the View Ruler button at the top of the vertical scroll bar. When you position the pointer over the tool, the cursor changes to a double-headed arrow. Click and drag the tool downward; the current window splits and you can navigate through each pane independently.

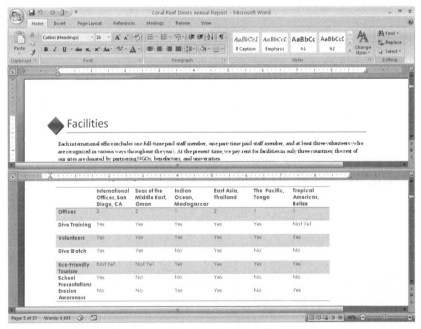

Figure 7-5 Split a window into two by dragging the splitter in the top of the vertical scroll bar.

To return the split window to a single display use one of the following methods: click the View tab and choosing Unsplit in the Window group, double click the splitter bar, or drag the splitter back to it's "home" position, .

Viewing Pages Side by Side

Being able to display pages side by side is very helpful when you are working with multiple documents. Suppose, for example, that you're referencing a larger document in a short report you're writing. You can easily find the text you want to use and insert it at the right point in your document when you can see both documents open on the screen at the same time.

Begin by opening both documents in Word. Then click the View tab and chooses View Side By Side in the Window group. The Compare Side By Side dialog box appears, providing a list of open documents. Click the document you want to display beside the current one, and click OK. By default, Synchronous Scrolling is turned on, which means that when you press PgDn or PgUp (or use any other navigation technique) to move through the document, both documents scroll simultaneously. To turn off Synchronous Scrolling, simply click that choice in the Window group.

When you are ready to return to single document display, click the Window group in one of the documents and select View Side By Side again (see Figure 7-6). The original document is returned to your display.

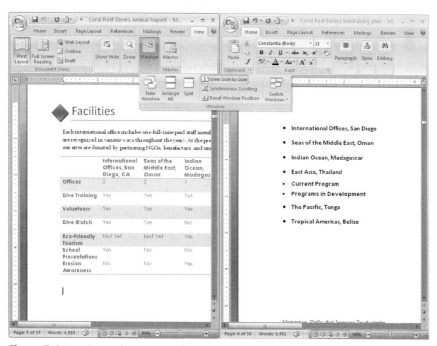

Figure 7-6 Viewing and navigating documents side by side enables you to find what you need in reference documents easily.

For more about working with multiple versions of a document and comparing documents side by side, see Chapter 19, "Revising Documents Using Markup Tools."

Switching among Multiple Windows

If you tend to work with multiple Word documents open at any one time, you will like the Switch Windows command in the Window group. This command existed in previous versions of Word, but its placement in the View tab along with other window controls makes it easier to find and use.

To move to another document while working in Word, click the View tab and click Switch Windows in the Window group. A list of open windows appears. Simply click the one you want to display. This is easier than minimizing and then looking for the documents you need as you need them—and it's more direct than cycling through open documents using Alt+Tab. Try it—simplicity is good.

What's Next?

This chapter highlighted some of the quickest ways you can navigate through your Word 2007 documents. The next chapter introduces you to the collection of Word text tools you can use to make sure that your document is as professional, accurate, and effective as possible.

Working with Building Blocks and Other Text Tools

Microsoft Office Word 2007 includes a number of tools designed to help you speed up typing repetitive text and those monotonous tasks you might face daily or deal with those infrequent tasks that you rarely carry out that usually take a few moments to refresh your memory. These tasks might range from typing the name of your company or department hundreds of times a day (or at least it feels like it) or recalling how to spell what must be one of the longest words in the dictionary to reusing frequently used document content, such as adding a fax cover page to a document, inserting a logo or certain graphic, adding headers or footers in a specific format; creating standardized tables, and inserting certain equations—most of which you can easily perform but are time consuming.

One of the tools that will assist you with your productivity is a long-standing, favorite time-saving feature that has been completely redesigned from the ground up and is now more powerful and more visible than ever before—an improvement so far-reaching that its old name could no longer adequately describe its new functionality. What was formerly known as AutoText has been reborn in Office Word 2007 as Building Blocks and is the primary focus of this chapter. You'll also find other time-saving text tools, such as AutoCorrect, AutoFormat, and Smart Tags, all of which have been around for several versions, along with a new member of the AutoCorrect family, Math AutoCorrect, which brings the new Equation Builder functionality to your fingertips and facilitates creating equations by using a keyboard-based syntax.

Tools at Your Fingertips

All of the tools in this chapter play key roles in speeding up productivity and, in many instances, more than one can be used to accomplish the same result. To determine the best tool for your needs, the following list is a summary of the role that each tool plays in document creation.

- **Building Blocks** Reusable pieces of content that can be inserted into a document from various built-in or custom galleries and can be used in combination with Content Controls. Can store any type of document content such as text, tables, illustrations, headers, footers, text boxes, equations, and more. Best tool for large amounts of data. Uses visual and mouse-based insertion, but can also be inserted by using the keyboard. For more information on Building Blocks, see the next section titled "Building with Building Blocks."

- **AutoCorrect** Designed to aid in error correction by automatically correcting typographical errors as you type. Can also be used as a shorthand method for typing repetitive phrases and complex spelling. The latter is the best tool for heavy keyboarding, albeit it does require a bit of memorization. See the section titled "Maximizing AutoCorrect" later in this chapter to learn more about putting this tool to work and how to control those unexpected automatic changes.

- **Math AutoCorrect** Works in combination with the new Equation Builder and enables the creation of equations by using Linear Format, a keyboard-based syntax, that uses TeX-like notation and converts strings to symbols or groups of characters. Best for creating equations by using the keyboard. Like AutoCorrect, it does require some memorization to take advantage of its full potential. For more information, see the section titled "Linear Format: Math AutoCorrect" later in this chapter.

- **AutoFormat** Enables quick insertion of common symbols, such as an en or em dash and common fractions. Converts straight quotes to smart quotes as well as URLs and e-mail addresses into hyperlinks. Automatically creates tables, numbered and bulleted lists, and aids in other formatting tasks, such as adding indents and defining styles. Get in-depth coverage in the section titled "Using AutoFormat Effectively" later in this chapter.

- **Smart Tags** Recognizes specific types of text and allows you to perform actions related to the type of data, such as measurement conversions, getting the latest information on your favorite stock, obtaining a map or driving directions from an address, and more. For additional information, see the section titled "Getting 'Smarter' with Smart Tags" later in this chapter.

Building with Building Blocks

After spending a short amount of time using Word 2007, you'll quickly spot the many Building Block galleries available to you while you work. Headers, Footers, Page Numbers, Text Boxes, Cover Pages, Watermarks, Quick Tables, Tables of Contents, Bibliographies, and Equations were created to help you build professional-looking documents quickly and efficiently. The built-in Building Blocks are Theme enabled, which means that if you modify the document Theme, the formats automatically update—even in the Building Block galleries.

You can customize Building Block entries to fit your needs, import new Building Blocks from Microsoft Office Online (www.office.microsoft.com), create custom Building Blocks and add them to their relevant galleries, or use custom galleries that can be added easily to your Quick Access Toolbar. You can view the many Building Blocks by browsing the various galleries, or you can check out the entire collection at once by opening the Building Blocks Organizer, found on the Insert tab under the Quick Parts options, as shown in Figure 8-1.

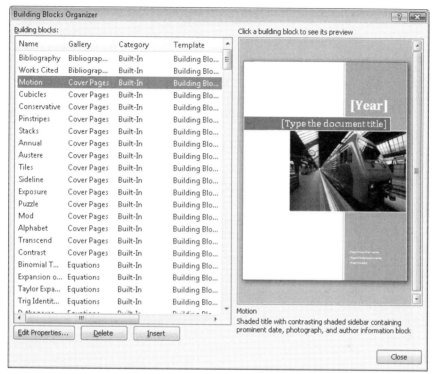

Figure 8-1 The Building Blocks Organizer provides quick access to built-in and custom Building Blocks.

Unlike its predecessor, built-in Building Blocks are not stored in the Normal template, but rather in a specific template named Building Blocks.dotx. This template is loaded as a global template the first time you access a Building Block gallery or the Building Blocks Organizer in your current Word session, so it's not uncommon to initially experience a slight delay while the Building Blocks load.

TROUBLESHOOTING

My Building Block galleries are missing or Building Blocks.dotx is corrupt

If you encounter a message stating that Building Blocks.dotx is corrupt or if the Building Block galleries are missing, then this issue can be resolved by using one of the following methods:

- If you use Symantec's Norton AntiVirus or if it has ever been installed on your computer, its Office Plug-in option is known to cause an error message stating that Building Blocks.dotx is corrupt. To rectify this issue, take the following steps:

  1. Exit Word and open Norton AntiVirus.

  2. Click Options, click Miscellaneous, and clear the Enable Office Plug-in check box.

For more information go to the Microsoft Knowledge base and search for Article ID 329820, "How to use Office programs with the Norton AntiVirus Office plug-in" (*http://support.microsoft.com/kb/329820*).

- If you do not use Norton AntiVirus or if the Office Plug-in is disabled, then re-create your personal copy of Building Blocks.dotx by using the following steps:

  1. Exit Word and navigate to Building Blocks.dotx by using one of the following locations.

     ❑ For Windows Vista: C:\Users*user name*\AppData\Roaming\Microsoft\ Document Building Blocks\1033

     ❑ For Windows XP: C:\Documents and Settings*user name*\Application Data\Microsoft\Document Building Blocks\1033

> **Note**
>
> The numbered folder is specific to your language version of Word. For example, 1033 is an English language folder.

  2. Move or delete Building Blocks.dotx, and a new one is created the next time you access a Building Block gallery or the Building Blocks Organizer.

Note that Building Blocks .dotx cannot be renamed. It must be moved out of the Document Building Blocks folder or deleted; otherwise, it will continue to load.

Finally, there are two Building Blocks.dotx files used by Word. There is also a master Building Blocks.dotx file, located in the Office installation path, that is used to create your personal copy of Building Blocks.dotx and should not be deleted.

To familiarize yourself with the various built-in Building Blocks, scroll through the Building Blocks Organizer to view them. You can click any entry to preview the Building Block in the organizer's preview pane. Note that, unlike the Building Block galleries, the preview does not automatically update to the current document Theme. The list of Building Blocks in the organizer is sorted by the name of the gallery by default. You can sort Building Blocks by Name, Gallery, Category, Template, Behavior, or Description by clicking a column heading in the organizer. If you are unable to see all of the columns, use the scroll bar at the bottom to view them.

> **Tip**
>
> While viewing a Building Block gallery, you can quickly locate a Building Blocks entry in the Building Blocks Organizer by right-clicking a Building Block, such as a Cover Page or a Header, and then clicking Organize And Delete. The Building Blocks Organizer opens with the entry selected automatically.

Inserting Existing Building Blocks

You can insert a Building Block in a document simply by clicking the Building Block on its corresponding gallery (such as the Text Box gallery available on the Insert tab). A few of the various Building Block galleries that you'll find in Word 2007 are shown in Figure 8-2. Alternatively, use the Building Blocks Organizer to preview and insert a Building Block in your document. Note that you cannot double-click a Building Block name to insert it from the organizer—you must click the Insert button.

> **Tip**
>
> Former Word users may be familiar with an AutoComplete tip that displays after typing the first few characters of the AutoText entry. The increased number of built-in Building Blocks also increased the likelihood of inadvertently inserting them into your document, and this capability is now removed. However, AutoComplete is still available for the current system date, months, and days of the week.
>
> If you want to insert Building Blocks by using the keyboard, type the Building Block name and then press F3.

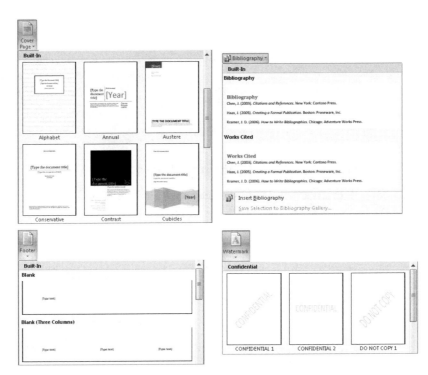

Figure 8-2 Building Block galleries provide a quick visual method for inserting reusable content in your documents.

A Building Block gallery can be added to your Quick Access Toolbar by right-clicking the gallery button on the Ribbon and then clicking Add To Quick Access Toolbar. Some Building Block galleries, such as the Cover Page, Table of Contents, and Quick Table galleries, contain additional commands on the shortcut menu. For example, if you right-click a Building Block in the Cover Pages gallery (a Building Block entry rather than the button on the Ribbon), you'll find Insert At Beginning Of Document, Insert At Current Document Position, Insert At Beginning Of Section, Insert At End Of Section, or Insert At End Of Document. If you right-click a Building Block in the Quick Tables gallery that is found on the Insert Tab under Table options, you'll also find Insert At Page Header (beginning of the current page) and Insert At Page Footer (end of the current page), as shown in Figure 8-3.

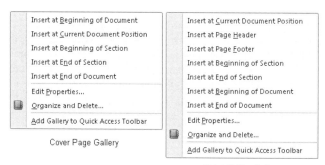

Cover Page Gallery

Quick Tables Gallery

Figure 8-3 Right-click a Building Block entry to obtain additional options.

After you insert a Building Block, you can freely customize the Building Block's formatting and properties without affecting the Building Block stored in the template.

TROUBLESHOOTING

What happened to my AutoText entries?

If you upgraded Word from a previous version, then you might find that previously created AutoText entries stored in your Normal template are missing and do not appear in the Building Blocks Organizer. This is typically due to Word using a new Normal.dotm file instead of your old Normal.dot file from the previous version. To resolve this issue, take the following steps:

1. Exit Word and locate Normal.dotm. (If you do not know where Normal.dotm is located, use Windows Search or refer back to Chapter 4, "Formatting Documents Using Templates," and the section titled "Getting the Scoop on the Normal Template".)

2. Locate your Normal.dot file and, if necessary, place it in the same location as Normal.dotm.

3. Rename Normal.dotm to OldNormal.dotm.

4. Right-click Normal.dot and click Open (do not double-click the file). Word should start and Normal.dot should open in Word.

5. Click the Microsoft Office Button and then click Convert to convert Normal.dot to the new file format. Save Normal.dot as Normal.dotx. (Word will convert it to Normal.dotm automatically.)

6. Close Normal.dotx, navigate to the Insert tab, click Quick Parts, and then click Building Blocks Organizer.

   Your old AutoText entries should now be listed in the organizer in the AutoText gallery.

Chapter 8

If you prefer to keep your Building Blocks in one location, such as Building Blocks.dotx, you can move your old AutoText entries to Building Blocks.dotx by using the Edit Properties button at the bottom of the organizer and changing the Save In template to Building Blocks.dotx. For more information on moving, modifying, and redefining Building Block entries, see the section titled "Modifying Building Block Properties" later in this chapter.

Creating Building Blocks

Quick Parts ▾

Frequently used document content, such as a paragraph or several paragraphs of data, logos, graphics, specifically formatted headers or footers, standard tables, or equations—any type of content—can be easily turned into a Building Block. You can create Building Blocks from newly created content or even data from documents that were created in previous versions of Word. Simply select the data that you want to turn into a reusable Building Block. On the Insert tab, click Quick Parts, and then click Save Selection To Quick Part Gallery, or press Alt+F3. The Create New Building Block dialog box displays as shown in Figure 8-4.

Tip

If you want to include all paragraph formatting, such as style, line spacing, indentation, alignment, and so forth, select the paragraph mark (¶) along with your content. If you aren't already viewing formatting marks, navigate to the Home tab and, in the Paragraph group, click the Show/Hide ¶ button to toggle the formatting marks so you can verify that you included the paragraph mark in your selection. If you do not include the paragraph mark, the inserted Building Block will match the formatting of the current paragraph.

If you want your Building Blocks to be Theme enabled so that the formats update automatically, then use Theme fonts and colors from the Theme Color section of the color palettes.

Figure 8-4 The Create New Building Block dialog box enables you to name, classify, describe, and control the placement of Building Blocks that you create.

The Create New Building Block dialog box contains the following options:

- **Name** Enter a unique name for the Building Block. If you have a set of related Building Blocks, consider starting all of the names with the same first word to group the pieces together when necessary, such as Annual Report Cover, Annual Report Header, and Annual Report Table.

- **Gallery** Add your new Building Block to a specific gallery, such as Cover Pages, Page Numbers, Headers, Footers, Quick Tables, Watermarks, and so on. If your Building Block is a general Building Block and isn't related to an existing gallery, use Quick Parts so that they will appear under the Quick Parts gallery. To use the Custom galleries or the AutoText gallery, see the Inside Out tip titled "Using Custom Galleries and the AutoText Gallery" later in this chapter.

> **Tip**
>
> Some Building Block galleries perform additional actions when you insert a Building Block from the gallery. For example, a Cover Page is added as the first page or is swapped with another previously inserted Cover Page. Headers, Footers, and Page Numbers are inserted in the Header and Footer layer in the document. To view other actions, right-click the Building Block entry and use an alternate command, shown previously in Figure 8-3.

- **Category** Place the Building Block in a category, shown on the Building Block galleries and in the Building Blocks Organizer. Consider creating a new category for your company or department so that all of the associated Building Blocks are placed in the same category throughout the Building Block galleries and to quickly sort them in the Building Blocks Organizer.

Chapter 8

> **Tip**
>
> To display your Building Blocks at the top of the Building Block galleries, create a Category name that starts with a symbol, such as an asterisk, or place the name in parentheses.

- **Description** Provide a brief description to help remind you and inform others about the main purpose of the Building Block. Descriptions appear as enhanced ScreenTips in the Building Block gallery (provided that Show Feature Descriptions In Screen Tip is turned on in Word Options) and also appear below the preview pane when you select a Building Block in the Building Blocks Organizer.

- **Save In** Building Blocks can only be saved in templates. You can save Building Blocks in Building Blocks.dotx (selected by default), Normal.dotm, or a global template so that they are available to all open documents. They can also be saved in a document template that makes the Building Blocks available only to documents using that template. The Save In list contains Building Blocks.dotx, Normal.dotm, loaded global templates, the attached document template for the active document if it's a template other than Normal.dotm, and any saved template provided that it is open and the current file. If you are creating Building Blocks to share with others, you want to save your Building Blocks in a separate template so you can distribute them. For more information on templates, see Chapter 4. For more information on sharing Building Blocks, see the Inside Out tip titled "Sharing Custom Building Blocks" later in this chapter.

> **Note**
>
> If you save or modify a Building Block in Building Blocks.dotx, Normal.dotx (provided that the Prompt Before Saving Normal Template option is turned on in the Advanced area of Word Options), or a global template, you are prompted to save changes to the template when you exit Word. For attached document templates, you are prompted to save changes to the template on closing the document.

- **Options** Specify whether the Building Block should be Inserted As Content only at the location of the cursor (such as an equation), Inserted In Its Own Paragraph (such as a heading), or Inserted In Its Own Page (inserts a page break before and after the Building Block).

> **Tip**
>
> Use the Save Selection To *Gallery Name* gallery found at the bottom of the Building Block galleries to quickly access the Create New Building Block dialog box and automatically select the corresponding gallery in the dialog box.

The following image displays a few custom Building Blocks assigned to different Building Block galleries by using a custom Category name (Coral Reef Divers) to place them at the tops of the galleries so that they can be easily found for quick insertion.

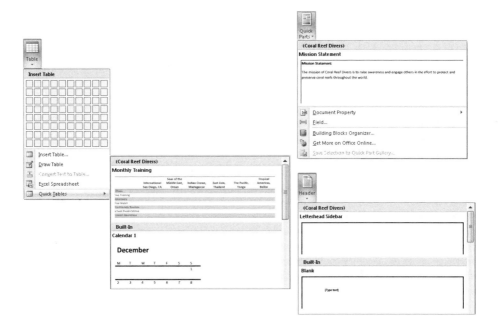

 For a template containing several examples of custom Building Blocks, see "Sample Building Blocks.dotx" on this book's companion CD.

INSIDE OUT   Sharing Custom Building Blocks

To share custom Building Blocks, they should be saved in a template other than Building Blocks.dotx or Normal.dotm so that they can be easily distributed. If you have a set of company or department Building Blocks that need to be shared with multiple individuals, you'll be pleased to know that each person does not need their own personal copy. Two primary locations are recognized by Word, and each location can be used for a specific purpose, such as sharing Building Blocks in a single template with a workgroup. The following list describes each location:

- **Document Building Blocks folder** Used for personal Building Blocks and available to all documents. Depending on your operating system, the location of the Document Building Blocks folder is one of the following locations:

    ❑ Windows Vista: C:\Users*user name*\AppData\Roaming\Microsoft\Document Building Blocks\1033

❑ Windows XP: C:\Documents and Settings*user name*\Application Data\Microsoft\Document Building Blocks\1033

> **Note**
>
> The numbered folder is specific to your language version of Word. For example, 1033 is an English language folder.

- **Word Startup folder** Used for company or workgroup Building Blocks. Templates placed in the Word Startup folder automatically load as a global template when Word starts, and the Building Blocks are available to all documents. The location of the Word Startup folder can be determined—or modified and pointed to in a shared network location—in Word Options at the bottom of the Advanced area by clicking the File Locations button. The location of the Word Startup folder can also be set during an administrative installation by using the Office Customization Tool (OCT) found in the Office Resource Kit 2007.

> **Note**
>
> If Building Blocks are specific to a certain type of document, then they should be placed in a document template instead of the Document Building Blocks or Word Startup folder.

After the template is placed in the respective folder, you need to exit and restart Word for the templates to load and make the Building Blocks available. If you prefer to use the Building Blocks immediately, then you can manually load the template as a global template as described in Chapter 4 in the section titled "Working with Global Templates."

> **Note**
>
> If you add a number of custom Building Blocks to the Building Blocks template, remember to back up the template and store your backup copy in a separate location. Like the Normal.dotm template, the Building Blocks.dotx template could potentially become corrupt and you could lose your custom Building Blocks.

Modifying Building Block Properties

You can modify the properties of a Building Block—including changing the Save In template —by changing the information in the Modify Building Block dialog box, which looks very similar to the Create New Building Block dialog box (shown earlier in Figure 8-4). To modify Building Block properties, access the Modify Building Block dialog box by taking either of the following actions:

- Right-click a gallery item and choose Edit Properties.

- Click Quick Parts on the Insert tab, click Building Blocks Organizer, select the name of the Building Block in the organizer list, and click the Edit Properties button.

After you open the Modify Building Block dialog box, make any desired changes and click OK to close the dialog box. A message box displays asking whether you want to redefine the Building Block entry as shown in Figure 8-5. If you click Yes, the changes are effective immediately.

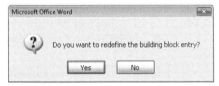

Figure 8-5 When you modify a Building Block entry, you are asked to confirm your modifications.

You can also redefine a Building Block, such as changing the content or formatting. Simply make your modifications and select the content. On the Insert tab, click Quick Parts, and then click Save Selection To Quick Parts Gallery, or press Alt+F3. In the Create New Building Block dialog box, type the same name as the Building Block that you want to redefine and make any other necessary changes, such as changing the gallery or category. When you click OK, you are prompted with a message asking whether you want to redefine your entry shown previously in Figure 8-5.

> **Tip**
>
> If you download Building Blocks from Microsoft Office Online, a template containing the Building Blocks is placed in your Document Building Blocks folder. It's recommended that you move the downloaded Building Blocks to Building Blocks.dotx by editing the properties and changing the Save In location. Otherwise, several templates will load the first time you access a Building Block gallery or the Building Blocks Organizer, and you might see an increase in the initial delay. After the Building Blocks are moved, you might want to periodically delete the downloaded templates from the Document Building Blocks folder because they no longer serve a useful purpose. The location of the Document Building Blocks folder can be found in the Inside Out tip titled "Sharing Custom Building Blocks" earlier in this chapter.

Deleting Building Blocks

To delete content created by inserting a Building Block, simply delete the content as you would any other content. To delete a Building Block entry, select the Building Block in the Building Blocks Organizer and then click Delete. A message box displays that asks you to confirm the deletion. If you are sure, click Yes. As with new Building Blocks and modifications, you are prompted to save changes to the template accordingly, so you have one last chance to change your mind before permanently deleting a Building Block from a template.

INSIDE OUT   Using Custom galleries and the AutoText gallery

When creating or modifying a Building Block, you can select a Custom gallery or the AutoText gallery for your entries; however, by default, they only display in the Building Blocks Organizer. These galleries can be added to your Quick Access Toolbar for quick insertion by using the following steps.

1. Right-click the Quick Access Toolbar and then click Customize Quick Access Toolbar.

2. In the Choose Commands From list, select Commands Not In The Ribbon.

3. Locate AutoText or Custom *Gallery Name*, select the AutoText gallery or your desired custom gallery, and then click Add to add it to your Quick Access Toolbar.

4. Click OK to accept your changes and close Word Options.

Custom galleries can also be added to the Ribbon; however, doing so requires some XML knowledge, and this capability isn't found within the Word application. For more information on customizing the Quick Access Toolbar and the Ribbon, see Appendix B, "Customizing Word and Enhancing Accessibility."

Maximizing AutoCorrect

AutoCorrect is a terrific Word feature that corrects your errors —almost before you know you've made them. AutoCorrect comes with a library of more than one thousand different items that is shared across the 2007 Microsoft Office applications, and you can train it to learn new corrections as you work. For example, if you type **yuor** when you mean to type **your**, AutoCorrect automatically reverses the characters in words that it recognizes without any further action from you. You can also use the AutoCorrect functionality as a shorthand method to quickly insert common text and phrases.

AutoCorrect options can be found in Word Options in the Proofing section by clicking the AutoCorrect Options button or by pressing Alt+T+A. The AutoCorrect tab of the AutoCorrect dialog box is shown in Figure 8-6, and Table 8-1 contains a description of the options. All AutoCorrect options are turned on by default, so you should turn off any unwanted options to prevent the correction from occurring while you work.

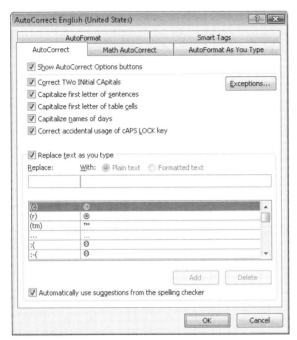

Figure 8-6 Use the AutoCorrect Options dialog box to specify which items you want corrected automatically.

Table 8-1 Setting Autocorrect Options

AutoCorrect Option	Description
Show AutoCorrect Options Buttons	Displays an AutoCorrect Options button when a change is automatically made in your document
Correct TWo INitial CApitals	Converts the second uppercase character to lowercase
Capitalize First Letter Of Sentences	Capitalizes the first letter of the first word in a new sentence; also applies to the first letter you type after pressing Enter
Capitalize First Letter Of Table Cells	Capitalizes the first letter of the first word entered in the cell of a table
Capitalize Names Of Days	Capitalizes the first letter of days of the week
Correct Accidental Usage Of cAPS LOCK Key	Catches the accidental pressing of the Caps Lock key, releases it, and toggles the case of typed characters
Replace Text As You Type	Enables AutoCorrect to make changes to text as you type; if you disable this option then common misspelled words will not be automatically corrected

Chapter 8

AutoCorrect Option	Description
Replace and With text boxes	Enables you to add your own AutoCorrect entries to the AutoCorrect library
Automatically Use Suggestions From The Spelling Checker	Automatically corrects misspelled words that are similar to words in the main dictionary used by Spell Check
Exceptions	Enables you to specify which items **not** to correct automatically; for more information, see the section titled "Entering Exceptions" later in this section

Controlling AutoCorrect While Working in Your Document

When the AutoCorrect utility makes a change in your document, an AutoCorrect Options button provides you with options for controlling the change if it is unwanted. To view the AutoCorrect Options button, position the mouse pointer over the change that was made. A blue line displays below the change, and the AutoCorrect Options button appears as shown in the following figure. If you see only the blue line, place your mouse pointer below the change on the blue line.

Click the AutoCorrect Options button, and then click the Undo or Change option to revert to the previously typed data in the single instance only (you can also press Ctrl+Z or Undo to obtain the same result). Use the Stop option to always prevent the change, or click Control AutoCorrect Options to display the AutoCorrect dialog box. Note that the text of the Undo and Stop options varies depending on the correction made. Variations of some of the Undo or Change and Stop options that you might encounter are shown in the following figure.

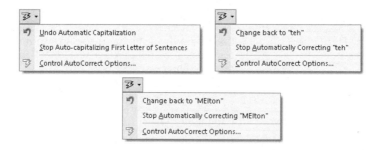

Adding AutoCorrect Entries

You can add new AutoCorrect entries by using a few different methods. If you find a misspelled word that is not automatically corrected and Word provides a list of suggestions for the spelling error, you can easily add the misspelled word as an AutoCorrect entry at the same time that you correct the misspelled word in your document. If you are using the Check Spelling As You Type feature, then after you right-click the misspelled word to view suggestions, use the AutoCorrect menu and select the correct word to both add the entry to AutoCorrect and correct the spelling error in your document. If you are using the Spelling And Grammar dialog box, then select the correct suggestion on the Suggestion list and then click the AutoCorrect button that displays for spelling errors.

> **Note**
>
> AutoCorrect entries are case sensitive. For example, if your misspelled word starts with a capital letter, then the only time that AutoCorrect makes the correction is when it is typed in the exact same case as the AutoCorrect entry. To avoid this situation, use the AutoCorrect dialog box to add your entry as described in the following section.

You can also use the AutoCorrect dialog box to add new AutoCorrect entries. This method is useful if you have several entries to add, if you need to control the case of the AutoCorrect entry as described in the previous cautionary note, or if you want to use AutoCorrect to replace lengthy words or phrases. For example, if you include your organization's detailed legal copyright statement on everything you print, you can create an AutoCorrect entry that inserts the entire mission statement when you type the letters **lgco.**

> **Note**
>
> AutoCorrect entries are stored in .acl files and are language specific. If you work with multiple languages, verify your current proofing language before creating new AutoCorrect entries.
>
> Additionally, AutoCorrect entries cannot exceed 255 characters. If your AutoCorrect replacement text exceeds the limitation, then create a Building Block instead.

To add new entries by using the AutoCorrect dialog box, use the following steps:

1. Click the Microsoft Office Button, click Word Options, navigate to the Proofing area, and then click the AutoCorrect Options button or press Alt+T+A.

2. In the Replace text box, type the characters that you want to use for your AutoCorrect entry. To make the entry case insensitive, use lowercase letters.

Chapter 8

CAUTION

Do not use characters that form a word or acronym that you need to use in your Word documents or other 2007 Microsoft Office applications, for they will always be corrected automatically.

Furthermore, playing tricks on your co-workers, such as changing 2007 to 2006, is strongly discouraged.

3. In the With text box, type the word or phrase that you want replaced automatically in your document as you type. Include any desired capitalization and punctuation.

4. Click Add. Word then adds the new AutoCorrect entry to the list.

Tip

To use the Formatted Text option, you need to select the formatted data in a document and then display the AutoCorrect dialog box. However, depending on the formatting, you might want to create a Building Block instead.

Formatted AutoCorrect entries (rich text entries) are not shared with other 2007 Microsoft Office applications and are stored in your Normal template.

Replacing and Deleting AutoCorrect Entries

You can edit AutoCorrect entries in the AutoCorrect dialog box by modifying the text in the With text box. The button beneath the list then changes from Add to Replace. When you use the Replace button, Word displays a message box asking you to confirm the action.

You can delete entries in a similar way. Display the AutoCorrect dialog box and, on the AutoCorrect tab, scroll or type the first few characters of the entry in the Replace text box to quickly navigate to the entry. Select the desired entry and click the Delete button. Unlike replacing entries, Word does not display a confirmation for deleting AutoCorrect entries. If the deletion is accidental, you can immediately click the Add button to add the entry back.

Entering Exceptions

Although AutoCorrect is extremely helpful, there are times when you might not want it interfering with what you're trying to do. For example, you might be typing a document full of chemical compounds or creating a list of access codes for the new server. You don't want AutoCorrect to get in there and change the capitalization while you type.

In this case, you have two options: You can disable AutoCorrect while you're working on the document, or you can create an exception to specify what you don't want Auto-Correct to change. To add an exception, display the AutoCorrect dialog box, click the Exception button, and add your exception to the respective tab in the AutoCorrect Exceptions dialog box, as shown in Figure 8-7.

Figure 8-7 You can use exceptions to prevent AutoCorrect from making specific corrections.

The Automatically Add Words To List option in the AutoCorrect Exceptions dialog box enables you to add exceptions as you work by clicking Undo or pressing Ctrl+Z immediately after an undesired correction is made. Note that this only applies to case changes and not to the Replace Text As You Type option.

To enter AutoCorrect exceptions, click Exceptions on the AutoCorrect tab in the Auto-Correct dialog box, and you can add the following three types of exceptions:

- **First Letter** This form of capitalization controls the words immediately following abbreviations. (For example, you might have a phrase such as after the merging of Lake Ltd. and Smith Co., in which the word and should not be capitalized.)

- **INitial CAps** Enables you to enter words and phrases with unusual capitalization that you don't want changed. This might include company names or abbreviations or terms peculiar to your business or industry.

- **Other Corrections** Enables you to add additional items that you don't want AutoCorrect to change. This might include names, locations, unusual spellings, and phrases that reflect terminology particular to your work.

Linear Format: Math AutoCorrect

Linear Format is used for creating equations by using a keyboard-based syntax notation, similar to TeX, that converts strings to symbols or groups of characters to Professional Format. For example, a caret (^) converts the next typed character to superscript and an underscore (_) converts the next typed character to subscript. The advantage to Linear Format is that you can create an equation by using notation such as (a^2+b^2) + (c^2+d^2), and it is converted to Professional Format while you type, as shown in the following image.

$$\frac{a^2 + b^2}{c^2 + d^2}$$

The newest member of the AutoCorrect family, Math AutoCorrect is very similar to AutoCorrect but is used for Linear Format. For example, Math AutoCorrect changes \pi to π or \int to∫.

> **Note**
>
> Math AutoCorrect entries are case sensitive. An entry such as \Sigma changes to Σ (the uppercase Greek character) and \sigma changes to σ (the lowercase Greek character).

Math AutoCorrect options can be found in the AutoCorrect dialog box (Alt+T+A) as shown in Figure 8-8.

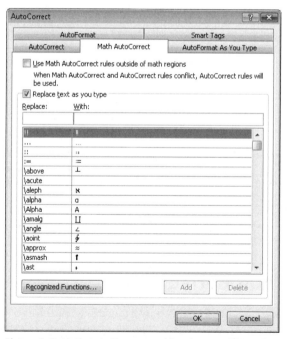

Figure 8-8 Math AutoCorrect enables the use of Liner Format to create equations.

> **Note**
>
> The Recognized Functions button provides a list of expressions that are not automatically italicized when creating equations. You can add additional expressions to the list.

If you want to use Math AutoCorrect anywhere in your document, select the Use Math AutoCorrect Rules Outside Of Math Regions option. Otherwise, you can only use Math AutoCorrect in an Equation Content Control by inserting a new equation from the Equation gallery on the Insert tab or by pressing Alt+=.

> **Note**
>
> The Equation gallery and the ability to insert new equations are disabled if using Word in Compatibility Mode; however, Math AutoCorrect can still be used.

To create new Math AutoCorrect entries, first select the desired symbol or group of symbols in a document and display the AutoCorrect dialog box (Alt+T+A). On the Math AutoCorrect tab, type your replace characters in the Replace text box. Your replace characters do not need to start with a backslash (\), but this syntax is recommended to maintain consistency.

> **Note**
>
> If you have standard equations, consider turning them into Building Blocks and associate them with the Equations gallery to ease insertion.

INSIDE OUT   Call attention to your equations

You can add emphasis to an equation by adding a rectangle (\rect) around the equation so it stands out. For example, create a new equation (Alt+=) and type \rect (\quadratic) (note the spaces). Your equation should look like the following image:

$$\boxed{x = \frac{-b \pm \sqrt{b^2 - 4ac}}{2a}}$$

Note that spaces are important because they trigger Math AutoCorrect so that the equation is converted as you type. In the example equation, once you type the space after \rect, you see a small rectangle. The space after (\quadratic) converts to a quadratic formula. After you type the closing parentheses and the space, the rectangle is placed around the equation.

Math AutoCorrect entries can be modified and deleted by using the same steps provided in the section titled, "Replacing and Deleting AutoCorrect Entries" earlier in this chapter.

If you're unfamiliar with the new Equation Builder in Word 2007, refer to Chapter 6, "Mastering Document Fundamentals," for more information.

Using AutoFormat Effectively

If you granted three wishes to Word users, at the top of the list would be improved control over automatic features. Until you understand what's going on behind the scenes with the various tools, you often don't know where to go when Word begins indenting lists that you don't want indented, adding numbers that you don't want added, or adding formatting, symbols, or lines that span the entire width of the page against your will. Such is the downside of automated functionality.

But the good news is that you have control over these automatic features. You can turn each feature on and off and control the items you want Word to change on the fly. This section takes a look at another automatic feature, AutoFormat As You Type. A description of each option is provided, along with instructions on how to implement the options so that you can obtain the most effective use and control over this automatic functionality.

> **Note**
>
> Like AutoCorrect, when Word automatically makes a formatting change, an AutoCorrect Options button displays and provides the Undo and Stop options. If the AutoCorrect Options button does not disappear, press Esc to dismiss it.

The AutoFormat As You Type options can also be found in the AutoCorrect dialog box (Alt+T+A). Table 8-2 provides a description of each option and instructions on how to utilize the option in a document.

Table 8-2 AutoFormat As You Type Options

AutoFormat Option	Description and Use
"Straight Quotes" With "Smart Quotes"	Converts typed quotes and apostrophes to smart, or *curly*, quotes
Fractions (1/2) With Fraction Character (½)	Replaces full-sized typed fractions, such as 1/2, with the fraction symbol; only works for common fractions such as ¼, ½, and ¾
Bold And _Italic_ With Real Formatting	A word surrounded by asterisks or underscores is formatted as bold and italic, respectively; the asterisks and underscores are removed
Internet And Network Paths With Hyperlinks	Automatically converts recognized URLs, network paths, and e-mail addresses to hyperlinks
Ordinals (1st) With Superscript	Inserts ordinals (such as 1st, 2nd, 3rd) when you type full-sized ordinals
Hyphens (--) With Dash (—)	Replaces two consecutive hyphens (--) with an em dash (—); for an en dash (–), type a space before and after two consecutive hyphens (--)
Automatic Bulleted Lists	An asterisk (*) followed by a tab at the beginning of a line is converted to a bulleted list
Border Lines	Three consecutive symbols, such as ~,#,*, -,_,= at the beginning of a line are converted to borders
Built-In Heading Styles	Automatically formats short paragraphs (without a period) with Heading styles after pressing Enter twice; a short paragraph at the beginning of the line is formatted with Heading 1, a tab preceding a short paragraph is formatted with Heading 2, two tabs followed by a short paragraph is formatted with Heading 3, and so on
Automatic Numbered Lists	A number followed by a period and a tab or space at the beginning of a line is converted to a numbered list; numbers not followed by a period, along with a tab or at least two spaces, can be converted to a numbered list after pressing Enter
Tables	A series of vertical bars (|) and underscores (_) are converted to tables after pressing Enter; entry must start and end with a vertical bar
Format Beginning Of List Item Like The One Before It	Applies identical formatting to the second and consecutive items in a list; formatting of last character, even a space, determines format
Set Left And First Indent With Tabs And Backspace	Pressing Tab at the beginning of a previously typed paragraph formats the paragraph with a First Line Indent; pressing Backspace after Tab formats the paragraph with a Left Indent
Define Styles Based On Your Formatting	Applies built-in styles that match paragraph formatting; recommended that this option be left turned off because it doesn't always function and, when it does, you have no control over which style is applied

Chapter 8

> **Where is the AutoFormat command?**
>
> The AutoFormat command enables you to apply many of the AutoFormat As You Type options to previously typed documents, along with a few others. Although it does not display in the Ribbon by default, its options (also found in the AutoCorrect dialog box) and command are still available. To add the AutoFormat command to your Quick Access Toolbar, right-click the Quick Access Toolbar and then click Customize Quick Access Toolbar. Display the commands for Commands Not In The Ribbon, select AutoFormat, and then click Add to add it to your Quick Access Toolbar.

Getting 'Smarter' with Smart Tags

The new release of Word continues to support Smart Tags. Smart Tags deliver what their name suggests—tagged data includes additional actions that make you "smarter" by giving you wider access to the data in your applications. A Smart Tag displays with a purple dotted underline below the tagged data. When you hover your mouse over the data, a Smart Tag Actions button appears as shown in the following figure.

123·Main·Street

A Smart Tag is meant to be an intuitive link, an easy connection to more information about the tagged item. For example, suppose that you're writing a report that summarizes new research that your department has recently completed. When you type the list of contributing writers, you see the name of a person you recognize, but you can't recall her department. In theory, if the information about the employee has been entered, you should be able to position the pointer over the employee's name and view additional information about her such as her name, phone, office status (in a meeting or out of office), online status, and e-mail address as well as the ability to create a new e-mail message addressed to her, call her on the telephone, or send an Instant Message. If you like this theory, then you'll like Smart Tags.

Using Smart Tags

If you are unfamiliar with how Smart Tags work in Word (or Microsoft Office) documents, then the best way to understand their capability is to see them in action by following these steps:

1. Display the AutoCorrect dialog box (Alt+T+A).

2. Click the Smart Tags tab, and select the Label Text With Smart Tags option as shown in Figure 8-9.

Figure 8-9 Turn Smart Tags on and off and select the options you want in the AutoCorrect dialog box on the Smart Tags tab.

Note

Smart Tags are turned off by default in Word 2007.

3. Select Financial Symbol, click OK to accept the changes, and close the dialog box.

4. Create a new document and type your favorite stock symbol, such as MSFT. Press the spacebar, and you should see a purple dotted underline appear below the stock symbol.

5. Click the Smart Tag Actions button (hover your mouse over the stock symbol if you do not see it).

6. Click Stock Quote On MSN Money Central.

Word opens your default browser (such as Internet Explorer), takes you to MSN Money Central, and displays a stock quote.

The actions that appear when you click the Smart Tag action button vary depending on the type of data that is tagged. Figure 8-10 contains a sample of several options that you might encounter.

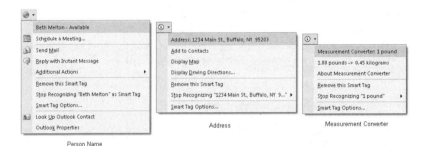

Figure 8-10   Smart Tags expand the ways that you can use data among applications, enabling you to create mail, schedule meetings, look up phone numbers, or place a phone call as you work.

Turning Off Smart Tags

If you don't want to use Smart Tags, simply display the Smart Tags tab in the AutoCorrect dialog box (as shown in Figure 8-9), clear the Label Text With Smart Tags check box, and then click OK. Smart Tags are now disabled.

> **Note**
>
> Turning off Smart Tags does not remove existing Smart Tags from your documents. To remove Smart Tags from a document, display the AutoCorrect dialog box, navigate to the Smart Tags tab, and click the Remove Smart Tags button. If you want to remove a single Smart Tag, use the Remove This Smart Tag command found in the Smart Tags Action button options.

Rechecking Your Document

After you make a change to Smart Tags, you should recheck your document by clicking the Recheck Document button on the Smart Tags tab in the AutoCorrect dialog box. Word warns you that changes made by the grammar checker might be reversed as you recheck Smart Tags. If you want to continue, click Yes; otherwise, click No.

Obtaining Additional Smart Tags

New Smart Tags are created by developers, and you can obtain additional Smart Tags from the Microsoft Web site. Start by establishing your Internet connection, and then display the Smart Tags tab in the AutoCorrect dialog box. When you click More Smart Tags, Word starts your default browser (such as Internet Explorer) and takes you to Microsoft Office Marketplace to find more information. Follow the prompts on the screen to navigate to and download Smart Tags that you can use to extend the functionality of Word.

> **Note**
>
> Office Marketplace hosts third-party downloads, services, and solutions, and not all of these items are free.

Understanding Smart Tags

Smart Tags do more, reach further, and are more flexible than ever before. Those who develop Smart Tags find that they have more control over the Smart Tags they create and are able to develop and deploy Smart Tags easily. Support for XML throughout the 2007 Microsoft Office system adds an extra boost by enabling developers to use XML to extend the Microsoft Office Smart Tag List Tool (MOSTL), the Smart Tag recognizer and action handler, without going back into the code.

How does your organization use Smart Tags? In terms of corporate possibilities, companies that want their employees to be able to link to critical resources inside the company use Smart Tags. Smart Tags are ideal for documents that must be processed, such as invoices or expense reports. For example, suppose that a user enters a tracking number in a document. A Smart Tag recognizes the item and, when the user clicks the Smart Tag, the options offer the user the ability to view—right from the current document—that particular order in the inventory system. Another option might fill in the details from that invoice automatically, thereby saving the user keystrokes, time, and error checking. The Smart Tag possibilities are endless.

What's Next?

This chapter took a look at how you can effectively implement Building Blocks and other text tools to help turn repetitive tasks into a few clicks of the mouse or strokes on the keyboard. The next chapter takes a look at proofing, research, and reference tools. Learn more about the new contextual spell check feature and improved automatic word count, along with how to translate text, look up definitions in a dictionary, and use an encyclopedia—all without leaving Word.

Refining with Research Services and Reference Tools

Microsoft Office Word 2007 adds resources to your reference library without taking up an inch of shelf space. By default, when you install Office Word 2007, you also install several standard reference tools, including research resources, a dictionary, a grammar guide, a thesaurus, a translation tool, and a document statistics tool. These tools can be found in a central location, on the Review tab, in the Proofing group, as shown here.

The greatest advantage that reference tools in Word have over traditional reference books is that you can access and customize the Word tools while you work—without stopping midsentence; digging out your trusty encyclopedia, dictionary, or grammar guide; flipping through pages; and then modifying your text after you find the answer to your question. In fact, you don't even have to leave your Word window. Furthermore, Word reference tools enable you to apply information you find—such as spelling and grammatical changes—automatically, thereby speeding up your word processing tasks even more. Once you learn how to use Word reference tools properly, you'll find that they can be extremely handy. In this chapter, we focus on getting the most out of the electronic research and reference tools that are readily available every time you work in Word.

Translation Tools

A notable new addition to the research tools is the Translation ScreenTip that provides a translation for words in a ScreenTip when you hover your mouse over a word in a selected language, as shown here.

The Translation ScreenTip is a new feature in Word 2007

To display a Translation ScreenTip, on the Review tab, click Translation ScreenTip and select your desired translation language. (The available languages depend on the specific Proofing Languages you have installed.)

For more Translation options, you can use click Translate in the Proofing group on the Review tab. This will display Translation options in the Research pane, which is described in more detail in the next section.

Using the Research Task Pane to Research Information

The Research task pane, or pane, provides access to a number of free and fee-based reference tools, including reference books, research sites, business and financial sites, and other services. Some of the offerings available in the Research pane includes the following:

- **Encarta Dictionary** Provides definitions of words or phrases. You can choose from a variety of Encarta dictionaries.

- **Thesaurus** Provides word choices in selected languages.

- **Translation** Translates words, sentences, or an entire document from one selected language into another and offers links to online fee-based translation services that can provide professional translations.

- **Factiva iWorks™** Provides news about companies, industries, and business topics.

- **Encarta Encyclopedia** Links you to articles found in the online Encarta encyclopedia.

- **MSN Search** Serves as a typical search engine and presents links to World Wide Web sites related to specified research keywords.

- **MSN Money Stock Quotes** Provides stock information from the MSN Money Web site.

Figure 9-1 shows the Research pane. You can display the Research pane in any of the following ways:

- On the Review tab, click Research, Thesaurus, or Translate.

- Press Alt and then click a word or selected text, or press Ctrl+Shift+O.

- Right-click a word or selected text and click Look Up.

Figure 9-1 The Research pane enables you to look up facts, figures, and words without leaving the Word window.

Generally, you'll quickly refer to the Research pane while you work and then move on. In addition to using research services, you can also customize the task pane by adding and removing services as well as applying filters by turning on the parental control feature. The next few sections describe how to use the Research pane.

Looking Up Words, Dictionary Style

Another added benefit of the Research pane is that you can quickly look up definitions and spelling while working in Word. To research a word's definition or origin, right-click the word and then click Look Up. The Research pane appears and displays potentially relevant information. You can conduct further research on the term by choosing another research service in the list below the Search For box. To track down a word's spelling, you can type your best guess in the Search For box (just as you might open a dictionary to a page near your best guess) and then click Start Searching. If you guessed correctly, the Research pane displays definitions and other relative links. If you guessed incorrectly, the Research pane lists some possible spelling alternatives, with links to definitions of the suggested words.

Using Research Services

When you use research services in the 2007 Microsoft Office system, you can access information that's stored online and on your computer without leaving your Microsoft Office application. The fundamental process is to specify your research keyword or keywords, using one of the methods listed in the previous section.

By default, the Research pane is configured to look in All Reference Books and with the exception of clicking the Research button on the Review tab, the search will be preformed automatically. If you click the Research button, you'll need to type the text you are searching for in the Search For text box and click the Start Searching arrow next to the Search For text box.

To select a specific Research Service, click the arrow next to the list of services as shown here.

Depending on your research selection, your results might look similar to any of the examples shown in Figure 9-2. After research results appear, click any item to expand the listing or click associated links to view additional information.

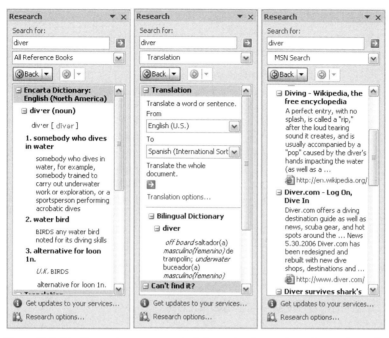

Figure 9-2 The Research pane presents information in a variety of ways depending on the research service you choose.

If you don't find what you're looking for when you conduct your research, expand the Can't Find It? section, if necessary, in the Research pane (which appears at the bottom of your research results list) and click a link to another research service, such as All Reference Books or All Research Sites.

> **Tip**
>
> To use only the Thesaurus, click Thesaurus on the Review tab, press Shift+F7, or right-click a word or selected phrase you want to look up and then in the Synonyms options click Thesaurus.

INSIDE OUT **Some tips on translation**

If you are having trouble finding appropriate translations, try looking up the singular forms of nouns (for example, *child* instead of *children*) and search using the infinitive forms of verbs (for example, *swim* instead of *swam*). Searching for root words generally results in greater success during translation.

Also, keep in mind you are using a machine translation service. Machine translation services can help you determine the main ideas in documents, but they shouldn't be used for important or sensitive documents because computers cannot preserve your text's full meaning, detail, or tone. To translate critical documents, you should use a professional human translator. The translation tool serves approximately the same function as a language dictionary, and it doesn't correct for accuracy of vocabulary and sentence structure. The Translation feature is not a full-service translation utility, but it's a nice way to interpret a few words or phrases.

Controlling Research Services

Although some research services are free, a number of research services available in the Research pane are fee-based. Therefore, you can pick and choose which services (if any) you'd like to use and configure your pane accordingly by activating, deactivating, adding, updating, and removing research service options available in the pane.

Notice that you can activate and deactivate services as well as add and remove services. When you activate or deactivate a service, you control whether an installed service is used for searching. In contrast, adding or removing a service controls the list of services that you can activate or deactivate. Let's look at activating and deactivating services first.

Activating and Deactivating Research Services

The key to controlling installed research services lies in the Research Options dialog box. To display the Research Options dialog box, click Research Options in the Research pane. Activated services appear selected in the Research Options dialog box, as shown in Figure 9-3. You can activate and deactivate installed research services by selecting and clearing the check boxes.

Figure 9-3 The Research Options dialog box enables you to set up the research options that will be available when you conduct searches that involve research.

Adding Research Services

You can install additional research services on your system if they are available. To do so, follow these steps:

1. Display the Research pane and then click the Research Options link.

2. In the Research Options dialog box, click Add Services to display the Add Services dialog box, which is shown in Figure 9-4.

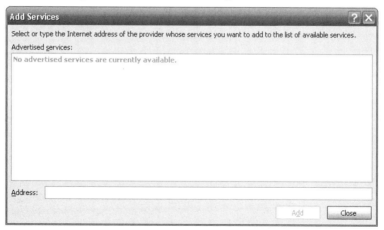

Figure 9-4 Adding research services enables you to expand the available research services on your computer.

3. Select an advertised service in the Advertised Services list (if any are available) or, in the Address box, type the address of the service you want to add and then click Add.

After you add a service, it is automatically enabled for searching. Further, it will appear in the Search For list in the Research pane the next time you display the list. You can control whether the service is included in your searches by activating or deactivating the service in the Research Options dialog box.

Updating and Removing Research Services

When you use research services and subscribe to research service providers, you might find that you want to update or remove existing services. In both cases, you'll use the Update Or Remove Services dialog box, as shown in Figure 9-5.

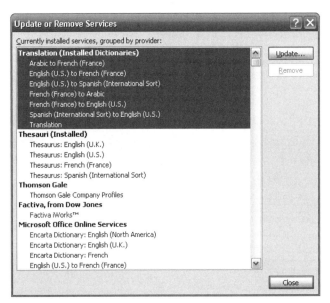

Figure 9-5 To update or remove a research service, select the service in the Update Or Remove Services dialog box and then click Update or Remove.

To update a research service, display the Research pane and then perform either of the following procedures:

- If updates are available, the Get Updates To Your Services link appears at the bottom of the Research pane. Click this link, select the service you want to update (if necessary), and click Update.

- Click Research Options, click Update/Remove, select the service you want to update, and click Update.

To remove a research service provider from your system, follow these steps:

1. Display the Research pane and click Research Options.

2. Click Update/Remove, select the research service provider you want to remove, click Remove, and click Close.

Remember, you can deactivate a research service instead of removing a research provider. You might opt to deactivate a service instead of removing it if you think you might want to use the service in the future.

Using Parental Control to Block Offensive Content

To some extent, you can apply a filter that blocks questionable content to control the type of content that can be included in research results that appear in the Research pane. The parental control feature for the Research pane is similar to parental controls available in some Web browsers. To block content, you turn on the Parental Control feature and provide a password, as follows:

1. Display the Research pane and click Research Options.

2. Click Parental Control, select Turn On Content Filtering To Make Services Block Offensive Results, select Allow Users To Search Only The Services That Can Block Offensive Results (if desired), enter a password, and click OK. Figure 9-6 shows the Parental Control dialog box with both filtering options selected and a password entered.

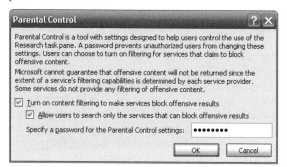

Figure 9-6 You can filter research results as well as limit research activities to services that can block offensive content.

3. In the Confirm Password dialog box, reenter your password and click OK.

4. After you turn on the Parental Control feature, the Research Options dialog box displays a statement that the feature is turned on and that some services might be unavailable or produce limited results. Figure 9-7 shows the modified Research Options dialog box with the Parental Control message. Click OK to close the Research Options dialog box.

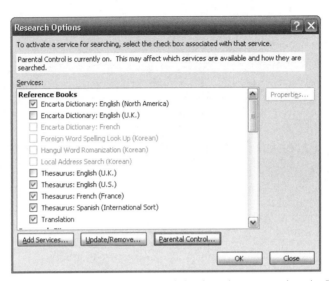

Figure 9-7 The Research Options dialog box alerts users when the Parental Control feature is turned on.

Building a Document's Credibility by Using Spelling and Grammar Tools

Two frequently used reference tools in Word are the spelling and grammar tools. The popularity of these tools is understandable—most people know that nothing detracts from a document's credibility more than spelling and grammatical errors. This section of the chapter covers spelling and grammar tools and takes you beyond a standard spelling and grammar check that might be familiar to those who have used proofing tools in previous versions of Word or other word processing applications. (After all, isn't how to check spelling and grammar one of the first things we learn?) It also provides information on how to set language options for proofing, set proofing exceptions, control spelling options, and control grammar options—starting with a notable new addition, the ability to check documents for contextual spelling errors.

Contextual Spelling Errors

A long awaited addition has been added to the proofing tools family, and Word 2007 now has the ability to check for contextual spelling errors, or to be more specific, words that are spelled correctly but are used in the wrong context. Here are a few examples of contextual spelling errors:

- Seven is greater then five. (Seven is greater *than* five.)

- John is dependant on Bill. (John is *dependent* on Bill.)

- The policy is now in affect. (The policy is now in *effect*.)

The Use Contextual Spelling option can be found in Word Options in the Proofing section and is turned on by default. Note that you do not need to check for potential contextual spelling errors separately; they are included when you use the proofing tools, which are described in the next section.

Benefiting from Automated Proofing

By default, Word checks for proofing errors whenever you open a document or type information in a document. With automatic proofing, Word flags potential spelling errors with a red wavy underline, potential grammatical errors with a green wavy underline, and potential contextual spelling errors with a blue wavy underline, as shown in Figure 9-8 (although you won't be able to differentiate between green, red, and blue here).

Here is an example of at splling error.

Here are an example of a grammar error.

Hear is an example of a contextual spelling error.

Figure 9-8 By default, Word automatically checks your document for spelling, grammar, and contextual spelling errors, and it flags the errors with wavy underlines.

> **Note**
>
> A blue wavy line is also used for the Mark Formatting Inconsistencies option, found in the Advanced section of Word Options and turned off by default. If both options are enabled, a quick way to way to distinguish which type of error is being identified is to right-click the word, or words, and note the offered suggestion.
>
> Suggestions for contextual spelling errors will be alternate word choices, and suggestions for formatting inconsistencies will offer to replace the direct formatting with a defined style.

Word also displays Proofing Status in the Status Bar. The icon indicates whether your document contains any potential errors. If errors are detected, the icon contains an X mark; if no errors are found, the icon contains a check mark.

> **Tip**
>
> If you do not see Proofing Status, right-click the customizable Status Bar and click Spelling And Grammar Check.

Chapter 9

Fixing Marked Text Quickly Case by Case

After Word marks potential proofing errors, you can resolve each issue on a case-by-case basis. To access options for fixing a potential error, you can right-click text that has a wavy underline or click Proofing Status in the Status Bar to select the next instance of a potential error. Both techniques display a shortcut menu containing error-fixing options. Different options are available depending on whether the potential error is a spelling issue, a grammar issue, or a contextual spelling issue. The shortcut menu for a contextual spelling issue is shown in Figure 9-9.

Figure 9-9 Word provides a selection of relevant error correction options when you right-click text flagged as a potential error.

The possible remedies are listed in Table 9-1

Table 9-1 Error-Fixing Proofing Options

Proofing option	Description
List of Suggestions	For potential spelling or contextual spelling errors, provides one or more words that might represent the correctly spelled version of the word in your text. For potential grammar errors, provides a brief description of the problem or possible replacement text.
Ignore	Instructs Word to ignore only the flagged proofing error.
Ignore All	Instructs Word to ignore all instances of the flagged proofing error in the current document.
Add To Dictionary (Spelling only)	Adds the word as it's spelled in your document to your custom dictionary, which ensures that the term won't be flagged as a potential error in the future. (Custom dictionaries are discussed in detail in the section titled "Managing Custom Dictionaries" later in this chapter on page 235.)

Proofing option	Description
AutoCorrect (Spelling only)	Enables you to add an AutoCorrect entry for the misspelled word. You can have the misspelled word automatically replaced with the correctly spelled word by clicking the correctly spelled word in the AutoCorrect menu, as shown in Figure 9-10. Alternatively, you can manually add an AutoCorrect entry. For more information on AutoCorrect, see Chapter 8, "Working with Building Blocks and Other Text Tools."
Language	Enables you to specify that a particular word or phrase is written in another language. If proofreading tools are installed for that language, Word uses the appropriate language dictionary to check the text. If a corresponding language dictionary is not installed, Word will skip the specified words without marking them as potential errors
Spelling or Grammar	Displays the Spelling or Grammar dialog box, which provides access to additional proofing options. These dialog boxes are similar to the Spelling And Grammar dialog box, which you can access on the Review tab in the Proofing group or by pressing F7.
About This Sentence (Grammar only)	Provides additional information about the potential error flagged by Word.
Look Up	Displays the Research pane and presents information from reference sources about the flagged text. If your computer is online, you can find additional information about the term by using other research services and resources such as encyclopedias and Web sites. Note that this option provides information about the flagged text but doesn't necessarily present a grammatical fix.

Figure 9-10 You can select a correctly spelled word in the AutoCorrect menu so that future instances of the mistyped text you've selected are automatically replaced with the correctly spelled word.

> **CAUTION**!
>
> As noted in Chapter 8, to create a case-insensitive AutoCorrect entry, the replace characters must be lowercase. If the entry you wish to add contains uppercase characters, you must manually create the AutoCorrect entry. Otherwise, the case must be identical for it to be corrected.

You can also resolve spelling and grammar issues by correcting your text without accessing the shortcut menus. When you manually correct a proofing error, Word automatically removes the wavy underline.

> Tip
>
> To use the keyboard to jump to the next proofing error, press Alt+F7.

Specifying a Proofing Language

If you work with multiple languages, you might want to use a different proofing language for all or part of a document—you can even set a proofing language for a specific word. To change your proofing language, follow these steps:

1. Select all or a portion of the document for which you want to change the proofing language.

2. On the Review tab, click Set Language. The Language dialog box will display, as shown in Figure 9-11.

Figure 9-11 The Language dialog box enables you to specify a specific proofing language for a portion of a document or the entire document.

Note

You might want to consider setting the proofing language by using a style rather than direct formatting. Doing so will make it easier to apply the proofing language and to keep track of the text that uses an alternate language. For more information on styles, see Chapter 15, "Using Styles to Increase Your Formatting Power."

3. Select your desired proofing language in the list and click OK to close the dialog box and set your language. Note that the proofing tools for the selected language must be installed, or Word will disregard proofing errors.

4. Clear the Detect Language Automatically check box if you do not want Word to automatically switch proofing languages based on your typed text.

Tip

To keep track of the proofing language used in your document and for specific text, you can display the proofing language in your Status Bar. To do so, right-click the customizable Status Bar and click Language.

Another notable change to the 2007 release of Microsoft Office is that it is now possible to purchase a single language pack. You do not need to purchase and install the entire set of 37 languages to use just one.

For more information on single and multiple language packs, visit Office Online (*www.office.microsoft.com*) **and search for Microsoft Office Language Pack 2007.**

Chapter 9

Proofing an Entire Document

At times, you might prefer to check your spelling and grammar all at once instead of right-clicking every instance of a potential error. In those cases, you can use the Spelling And Grammar dialog box to work through your document or block of selected text. To access the Spelling And Grammar dialog box, on the Review tab, click Spelling & Grammar or press F7. The Spelling And Grammar dialog box will display as shown in Figure 9-12, Figure 9-13, and Figure 9-14.

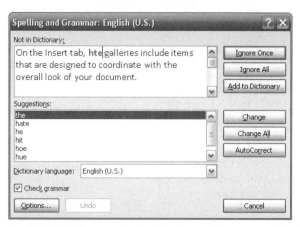

Figure 9-12 When you use the Spelling And Grammar dialog box to correct errors, you have a greater selection of suggestions and options to pick from than when you right-click potential errors. This version of the dialog box draws attention to the misspelled word, the, which is shown in red text when viewed in the dialog box.

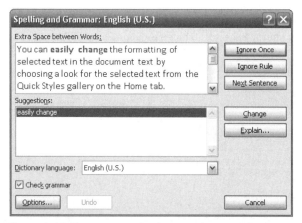

Figure 9-13 The grammar checker provides error-checking options similar to the options available in the spelling checker. This version of the dialog box draws attention to more than one space between two words, and the error is shown in green text when viewed in the dialog box.

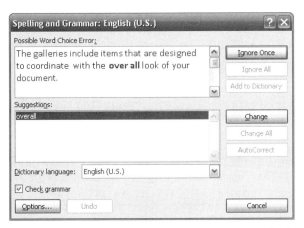

Figure 9-14 The contextual spell check provides error-checking options similar to the options available in the spelling checker. This version of the dialog box draws attention to the words over all, which are often used in the wrong context and are shown in blue text when viewed in the dialog box.

Along with using the options described in Table 9-1, you can click in the upper portion of the dialog box and make editing changes. This dialog box is also modeless, which means you can leave the dialog box open, click in the document, make modifications, and then resume the proofing check.

> **Tip**
>
> To check only a portion of your document, select the text you wish to check for proofing and then click the Spelling & Grammar button on the Review tab to display the Spelling And Grammar dialog box. When the end of the selected text is reached, Word displays a dialog box stating that Word has finished checking the selected text and asking whether you'd like to continue checking the remainder of the document.

INSIDE OUT   Activating the grammar checker

You can control whether the grammar checker is activated by selecting or clearing the Check Grammar check box in the Spelling And Grammar dialog box, but to access this particular check box only, click Spelling & Grammar on the Review tab or press F7. If you display the Spelling dialog box or the Grammar dialog box by right-clicking an underlined potential error, the Check Grammar check box will not be available.

Controlling Proofing Display and Exceptions

In general, while you are creating and editing a document, keeping an eye on spelling and grammatical errors is a must. And using the automated proofing tools is an efficient way to find your potential proofing errors quickly. However, certain types of documents, or portions of documents, might be difficult to read due to the red and green wavy lines that appear throughout the content. These documents might contain a lot of abbreviations, slang, and words that aren't in the standard dictionary; or in the case of technical documents, they might contain fragmented sentences, blocks of programming code, and words that aren't usually capitalized. In these situations, the content is correct and the proofing marks detract from the document's readability. The following provides a few options that you can use to suppress the display of proofing marks and that you can use to specify that perceived spelling and grammar errors should be ignored by all proofing tools. We also have recommendations for using each option:

- **Check Spelling As You Type and Check Grammar As You Type** These options are found in Word Options in the Proofing section. If you clear the Check Spelling As You Type option, the display of the red and blue wavy lines will be suppressed when viewing a document. If you clear the Check Grammar As You Type option, green wavy lines will be suppressed when you view a document. However, you can still use the Spelling & Grammar feature to check the document for proofing errors. These are application options, which means they are specific to your Word installation and apply to all documents. It's recommended that they be used for your personal use only because they will not change the way others view your documents.

- **Hide Spelling Errors In This Document Only and Hide Grammar Errors In This Document Only** These options are found in Word Options in the Proofing section. Their effect is similar to disabling the Check Spelling As You Type and Check Grammar As You Type; however, they are saved with the document, as opposed to being application options. Spelling errors or grammar errors are not completely ignored—you can still use the Spelling & Grammar feature—but all red and blue wavy lines (if you select the Hide Spelling Errors In This Document Only option) and green wavy lines (if you select the Hide Grammar Errors In This Document Only option) are suppressed when you view the document. If others will be viewing the document, it's recommend that these options be used only after a document has been finalized.

CAUTION

If the document is still in the editing stages and will be edited by others, selecting Hide Spelling Errors In This Document Only and Hide Grammar Errors In This Document Only could result in documents that contain legitimate proofing errors. Many Word users have grown accustomed to Word automatically proofing their documents as they type. If they are not familiar with the proofing options—and if they do not see the red, green, or blue wavy lines—then proofing errors can be inadvertently overlooked.

- **Mark As Final** This option is found by clicking the Microsoft Office Button and pointing to Prepare. When a document is marked as final, it cannot be edited, and proofing errors are suppressed from view. It's recommended that this option be used when working in a collaborative environment to let others know the document has been finalized. Note that Mark As Final is not intended to be used for document security because other users can turn off the Mark As Final option and edit the document. Additionally, proofing errors will return to view when Mark As Final is turned off.

- **Do Not Check Spelling Or Grammar** This option is considered a language option and is in the Set Language dialog box, found on the Review tab by clicking Set Language. You can set the Do Not Check Spelling Or Grammar option for specific words, paragraphs, or the entire document, and proofing errors are ignored by all proofing features. It's recommended that this option be used when proofing errors need to be suppressed in only portions of a document, as opposed to the entire document, such as for blocks of programming code or medical terminology.

> **Tip**
>
> When using the Do Not Check Spelling Or Grammar option, consider creating a Character type style, (discussed in Chapter 15), and using it for the text that should be ignored by the proofing tools. Doing so will enable you to quickly mark text that should be ignored. Then, during the final review of the document, you can check for any inadvertent proofing errors by temporarily enabling proofing for the text that's associated with the style.
>
> For example, some programming code blocks contain comments that should be proofed. To enable proofing, modify the style and clear Do Not Check Spelling Or Grammar and enable the option again after you are finished with your review.
>
> Note that you might need to use the Style option Select All # Instances to select all text associated with the style and reapply the style after making your modifications.
>
> Additionally, the Select All # Instances option can be used to quickly scan the document and view those areas that are ignored by the proofing tools. For additional information on how to create styles and the options described in this tip, see Chapter 15.

Using the spelling and grammar tools to check your documents shouldn't replace proofreading by a real person. These features are helpful, but they can't definitively correct your text in all instances. Instead of thinking of the spelling and grammar checking tools as a teacher correcting your work, visualize an assistant who taps you on the shoulder whenever your text seems to go astray and then offers advice on how to fix the problem. Ultimately, you'll need to read through your document carefully to ensure its accuracy.

Configuring Spelling Options

You can control a few spelling options by configuring Proofing settings in Word Options, as shown in Figure 9-15. (Click the Microsoft Office Button, click Word Options, then click Proofing.) Table 9-2 provides a description of each option under the heading When Correcting Spelling In Microsoft Office Programs. As the heading implies, these options are shared across the 2007 Microsoft Office system. By configuring these spelling checker options, you can customize spelling tasks to be as streamlined as possible for the particular types of documents you create.

Figure 9-15 The Proofing options enable you to specify how Word should proof your documents.

Table 9-2 Spelling Options for Microsoft Office

Spelling Option	Description
Ignore Words In UPPERCASE	Excludes words in all uppercase from spelling checks. The spelling checker would be hard pressed to understand all acronyms, so this check box is selected by default. If you use a number of acronyms—and you'd like to check them—you can add the acronyms to your custom dictionary and clear the Ignore Words In UPPERCASE check box.
Ignore Words With Numbers	By default, any words that contain numbers are ignored by the spelling checker. You'll especially appreciate this option if you're proofreading documents such as catalogs or price lists in which product codes are combinations of numbers and letters.
Ignore Internet And File Addresses	By default, the spelling checker ignores Internet addresses, file path names, and e-mail addresses. For example, text such as *C:\clients\microsoft* and *www.microsoft.com* is automatically ignored by the spelling checker. If you prefer to check these types of elements, clear the Ignore Internet And File Addresses check box.
Flag Repeated Words	Ignores repeated words. For example, if you select this option, the spelling checker does not flag *Walla Walla* as a mistake. (Interestingly, if you use *WallaWalla*, it is flagged as a spelling error and the proposed suggestion is *Walla Walla*. Keep in mind that you are your own best proofreader.)

Spelling Option	Description
Enforce Accented Uppercase In French	Used with the French (Canada) proofing language. French words that contain uppercase letters that are missing an accent mark are indentified.
Suggest From Main Dictionary Only	Word checks all open dictionaries during its spelling check, including the main dictionary and your custom dictionaries. Use this option if you prefer to use only the main dictionary.
French Mode	Used with the French language. Enables spelling rules that predate the French Academy of Language spelling reform of 1990 and those that are recommended by the spelling reform.

> **Tip**
>
> The Recheck Document button under the heading When Correcting Spelling And Grammar In Word enables you to recheck a document for words and grammar you previously chose to ignore. This feature is also useful for rechecking a document after you've modified your spelling options.

Configuring Grammar Options

Like the spelling checker, the grammar checker has options that you can configure in Word Options. As described earlier in this chapter, the options Check Grammar As You Type and Hide Grammatical Errors In This Document control whether the grammar checker is turned on or off and whether green wavy underlines appear in the document.

The Check Grammar With Spelling check box performs essentially the same function as the Check Grammar check box in the Spelling And Grammar dialog box: It enables you to turn off the grammar checker while you're using the spelling checker. When you clear this check box, you can check spelling without addressing grammar issues. (The green wavy underlines used to flag potential grammar problems will continue to appear in your document if the Check Grammar As You Type check box is selected.) Selecting this option usually speeds up document checking because Word skips the grammar issues and presents only the potential spelling errors. The Writing Style options and Grammar Settings (displayed when you click the Settings button) enables you to define grammar rules that Word should follow, as discussed next.

For more information about the Show Readability Statistics option, see the section titled "Judging a Document's Readability Level" on page 242.

Specifying Grammar Rules

The rules used when checking grammar in a document can be easily changed. For example, you might want to use passive voice or start a sentence with *And*. You might also want Word to check for punctuation errors, such as two spaces after a period, which according to the Chicago Manual of Style, typing two spaces between sentences when using a word processing program is no longer necessary.

In these cases, adding exceptions for proofing and controlling the display of proofing marks in a document—as discussed in the section titled "Controlling Proofing Display and Exceptions" earlier in this chapter on page 230—might be too aggressive for your needs, and adjusting the grammar settings for your desired writing style might be all it takes to prevent the display of unwanted green wavy lines throughout your document or having to continuously ignore the same grammar errors that are brought to your attention when using the Spelling & Grammar feature. You can specify your preferred settings in Word Options by using the following steps:

1. Click the Microsoft Office Button, click Word Options, click Proofing, and then specify whether you want the grammar checker to check grammar only or grammar and style by selecting the appropriate option in the Writing Style list.

2. Click Settings. The Grammar Settings dialog box appears, as shown in Figure 9-16.

Figure 9-16 You can choose which grammar and style rules you want Word to use when it searches for potential grammatical errors.

3. Select your preferred writing style, such as Grammar Only or Grammar & Style; punctuation rules; grammar rules; and style rules.

> **Note**
>
> Grammar Only is the default setting. Grammar Style—such as passive voice or starting a sentence with a conjunction, for example, starting a sentence with *And*—is not checked by default.

An important aspect to keep in mind is that the grammar settings are application specific, which means they are not stored in the document and the rules will apply to all documents. If you are sharing your documents with others, and if they do not use the same settings, they might see different grammatical errors when they view the document, If you want proofing errors suppressed, you need to use the methods described in the previous section, "Controlling Proofing Display and Exceptions."

> **Tip**
>
> When viewing the Grammar Settings dialog box, click the Help button (?) to quickly display Help content that provides brief descriptions of the grammar and writing style options found in the dialog box.

Managing Custom Dictionaries

When you install Word, you also install a main dictionary. The spelling checker uses the main dictionary whenever it checks your document for spelling errors. You can also add words to your custom dictionary or add existing dictionaries to the list of dictionaries Word uses to check documents.

When you click Add To Dictionary in the Spelling And Grammar dialog box, Word adds the selected term to your custom dictionary. After you add terms to your custom dictionary, Word checks both the main dictionary and your custom dictionary (named CUSTOM.DIC by default) whenever you run the spelling checker. You can also edit and delete terms in your custom dictionary as well as create additional custom dictionaries that you can use whenever necessary.

Modifying Custom Dictionaries

As mentioned, you can add terms to your default custom dictionary by clicking Add To Dictionary in the Spelling And Grammar dialog box. You can also add terms to your custom dictionary by right-clicking words that are flagged by a red wavy underline and choosing Add To Dictionary from the shortcut menu. Because adding terms to the custom dictionary is so easy, words that shouldn't be included, such as words or abbreviations that should be ignored in one document but might be incorrect in other documents, might need to be removed. For example, you might want to allow the word *lite* in a marketing piece but have Word catch the misspelling in other documents. If you regularly add terms to your custom dictionary, or if you suspect that incorrect terms have been added, you should review and manually correct your dictionary to ensure accuracy.

To access and modify your custom dictionary, follow these steps:

1. Click the Microsoft Office Button, click Word Options and then click Proofing. (Alternatively, click the Options button in the Spelling And Grammar dialog box.)

2. Click Custom Dictionaries. The Custom Dictionaries dialog box appears, as shown in Figure 9-17. Notice that the CUSTOM.DIC dictionary is selected by default.

Figure 9-17 The Custom Dictionaries dialog box provides options for creating and modifying custom dictionaries that Word uses in conjunction with the main dictionary.

3. Select a dictionary in the Dictionary List and then click Edit Word List to display a dictionary editing dialog box, as shown in Figure 9-18.

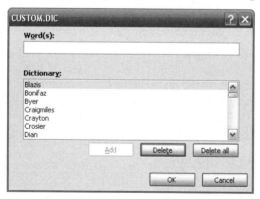

Figure 9-18 The dictionary editing dialog box provides an easy way to create and modify custom dictionaries.

4. Within this dialog box, you can perform the following actions:

❏ Manually add a term to a custom dictionary. Enter a term in the Word box and then click Add or press Enter. The terms are automatically arranged alphabetically.

❏ Delete a term included in a custom dictionary. Select a word in the Dictionary list and then click Delete.

4. Click OK twice when you have finished modifying your custom dictionary.

When you add terms to a custom dictionary, you should keep the following points in mind:

- Words cannot be more than 64 characters and cannot contain spaces.

- The custom dictionary is limited to 5,000 words and cannot be larger than 64 kilobytes (KB).

- Dictionaries are American National Standards Institute (ANSI) text files, which can only contain characters that conform to the ANSI encoding standard.

With careful maintenance of your custom dictionary, including adding frequently used terms, you can keep your spelling checker working at peak performance and increase your efficiency. With a well-maintained custom dictionary, you'll avoid having to continually dismiss terms that appear regularly in your documents but aren't included in the main dictionary.

Creating New Custom Dictionaries

At times, you might work on jargon-laden documents that use very specific terminology. For example, if you occasionally work on medical documents that contain terms such as *brachytherapy, echography,* and *osteotomy,* you could create a custom dictionary named Medical that you could activate whenever you're using medical terminology. To create a custom dictionary that you can use in addition to CUSTOM.DIC, follow these steps:

1. Display Word Options and the Proofing options. (Alternatively, click the Options button in the Spelling And Grammar dialog box.). Then click Custom Dictionaries.

2. In the Custom Dictionaries dialog box, click New. The Create Custom Dictionary dialog box appears. This dialog box displays a list of the custom dictionaries currently available to Word in the UProof folder.

3. Type a name for the new custom dictionary in the File Name box and then click Save. When you create a custom dictionary, the file is saved with the .dic extension in the UProof folder, along with the CUSTOM.DIC file and any other custom dictionaries you've created.

After you create a new dictionary, it is added to the Dictionary List in the Custom Dictionaries dialog box and its check box is selected. When the spelling checker runs, it refers to the main dictionary and all custom dictionaries that are selected in the Dictionary List.

Chapter 9

> **Tip**
>
> When you want to use your custom dictionaries, make sure that the Suggest From Main Dictionary Only option is cleared (the default setting) in the Proofing section of Word Options. If this check box is selected, Word won't refer to your custom dictionaries when the spelling checker is started.

To add terms to a new custom dictionary, select the dictionary in the Custom Dictionaries dialog box, click Modify, and then manually enter terms. You can also add terms to the dictionary as you work, as described in the section titled "Choosing a Default Dictionary" later in this chapter on page 239.

Adding Custom Dictionaries

Most of the time, you'll either use the CUSTOM.DIC dictionary or create a new custom dictionary. However, you can also add existing dictionaries to the Dictionary List in the Custom Dictionaries dialog box. For example, if you have *Stedman's Medical Dictionary* on your computer, you can add it to the list of custom dictionaries. Adding an existing dictionary is similar to creating a new custom dictionary. To do so, follow these steps:

1. Display Word Options and the Proofing options. (Alternatively, click the Options button in the Spelling And Grammar dialog box.) Then click Custom Dictionaries.

2. In the Custom Dictionaries dialog box, click Add to display the Add Custom Dictionary dialog box, which looks almost identical to the Create Custom Dictionaries dialog box.

3. Navigate to the desired dictionary file (you might need to consult your documentation for the custom dictionary to determine the location) and double-click the dictionary's file name. The dictionary will appear in the Dictionary List, and its check box will be selected.

By default, custom dictionaries are stored in one of the following locations:

- For Windows Vista: C:\Users*user name*\AppData\Roaming\Microsoft\ UProof

- For Windows XP: C:\Documents and Settings*user name*\Application Data\Microsoft\UProof

If you have a custom dictionary file (with a .dic extension), you can store the file in the UProof folder. It will then be easily accessible from the Custom Dictionaries dialog box.

Converting an Existing List of Terms to a Custom Dictionary

If you have an existing list of terms or a style sheet containing terms you frequently use, you can quickly create a custom dictionary without having to retype or copy all the terms in the dictionary editing dialog box. To convert a list to a custom dictionary, follow these steps:

1. Verify that each term appears on a separate line with no blank lines inserted between terms. Then save your document as a plain text (.txt) file and close the file.

2. Right-click the file name in Windows Explorer and rename the file by using the .dic extension. (You must be viewing file extensions when renaming the file.)

3. After you rename the file, store it in your UProof folder in the location provided in the section titled "Adding Custom Dictionaries" earlier in this chapter on page 238.

The next time you display the Add Custom Dictionary dialog box, you'll see your newly created dictionary listed among the available custom dictionaries. Double-click the newly added dictionary to add it to the Dictionary List in the Custom Dictionaries dialog box.

Choosing a Default Dictionary

By default, all terms you add to a dictionary while running a spelling check are added to the CUSTOM.DIC dictionary. You can change the custom dictionary in which added words are stored by changing the default custom dictionary. By reconfiguring your default dictionary, you can quickly build very specific custom dictionaries without having to enter terms manually. Let's return to the medical dictionary example. While you're working on a medical document, you could specify the medical dictionary as your default custom dictionary. Then whenever you click Add To Dictionary, the specified term would be added to the medical dictionary instead of CUSTOM.DIC. Configuring Word in this way would serve two purposes: It would avoid adding unnecessary terms to the CUSTOM.DIC dictionary, and it would save you from manually typing terms in the medical dictionary.

To specify which custom dictionary serves as the default file, perform the following actions:

1. Display Word Options, click Proofing, and then click Custom Dictionaries to display the Custom Dictionaries dialog box.

2. Select the custom dictionary you want to be the default in the Dictionary List.

3. Click Change Default.

The default custom dictionary will appear at the top of the list with *(Default)* after its name, as shown in Figure 9-19. Now when you add a word to your custom dictionary (by clicking Add To Dictionary in the Spelling And Grammar dialog box or right-clicking a word with a red wavy underline and then clicking Add To Dictionary in the shortcut menu), the term will be added to the new default custom dictionary.

Figure 9-19 The default custom dictionary appears at the top of the Dictionary List.

Disabling, Removing, and Deleting Dictionaries

Most of the time, you won't need to have Word check all your custom dictionaries every time you're working on a document. Therefore, you might want to disable some custom dictionaries until you need them. Other times, you might want to remove a custom dictionary from your Dictionary List altogether. Word enables you to do this without deleting the dictionary file. In some cases, you might want to delete a dictionary file because you no longer use it. You can perform all these tasks easily, from within the Custom Dictionaries dialog box, as follows:

- **Disable a dictionary** Clear the dictionary's check box in the Dictionary List. When a dictionary's check box is cleared, Word doesn't refer to the dictionary when it checks spelling.

- **Remove a dictionary** In the Dictionary List, select the name of the dictionary you want to remove and then click Remove. This action does not delete the file, it simply removes it from the Dictionary List.

- **Delete a dictionary** Click New or Add, select the dictionary file name in the Create Custom Dictionary or Add Custom Dictionary dialog box, and press Delete (or right-click the dictionary file name and choose Delete from the shortcut menu). Click Yes in the Confirm File Delete message box and click Cancel to close the dialog box. This operation sends the dictionary file to your Recycle Bin. Finally, you'll want to remove the reference to the dictionary in the Custom Dictionaries list, as described in the preceding bulleted item.

Creating an Exclusion Dictionary

You might encounter a situation where it is useful to be able to force the spelling checker to flag a word as misspelled, even though it is listed in the main dictionary as a correctly spelled word. The following are examples of when you might want to flag a word for closer inspection and use an exclusion dictionary:

- **Obscene or embarrassing words** Several words are spelled similarly to an obscene or embarrassing word, such as when one inadvertently leaves a letter out of the word shift, adds another t at the end of but, or uses pubic instead of public.

- **Style guidelines** Your company or department might require that certain words use a specific spelling. For example, *catalog* is a correctly spelled word, but style guidelines might require the word to be spelled *catalogue*.

To create an exclusion dictionary, follow these steps:

1. Locate your UProof folder in one of these locations.

   ❏ For Windows Vista: C:\Users*User Name*\AppData\Microsoft\UProof

   ❏ For Microsoft Windows XP: C:\Documents and Settings*User Name*\Application Data\Microsoft\UProof

2. Locate the exclusion dictionary for your preferred language. For example, the name of the English exclusion dictionary is ExcludeDictionaryEN0409.lex.

> **Note**
>
> The number, or numbers and letters, at the end of the file name is associated with a Language ID and uses the Hex value for the Locale Identification ID (LCID). To find the value for your desired exclusion dictionary, visit the Microsoft Knowledgebase (www.support.microsoft.com) and search for article 221435.
>
> The Hex value for the exclusion dictionary will be listed in parentheses after the LCID. You need the number, or numbers and letters, after *&H*. If the value contains only three characters after *&H*, then add a leading zero. For example, the Hex value for English Australia is (&HC09), and the exclusion dictionary is named *ExcludeDictionaryEN0c09.lex*.

3. Open the file in a text editor—such as Notepad—add each word using lowercase letters, and press Enter after each word.

4. Save and close the file.

> **Note**
>
> You might need to restart Word before words in the exclusion dictionary are identified as spelling errors.

Once words are added to your exclusion dictionary, the words will be flagged as proofing errors, and they will not be offered as suggestions for a potentially misspelled word.

Chapter 9

Scrutinizing Document Statistics

In addition to the standard reference book features included in Word, you have several other electronic reference tools that can analyze your documents. Namely, you can analyze a document's readability level by using Flesch Reading Ease and Flesch-Kincaid Grade Level scores, and you can display word count statistics to track the length of your text while you work.

Judging a Document's Readability Level

You can configure Word to display a readability level for a document after you finish checking spelling and grammar. Word determines readability levels by assigning Flesch Reading Ease scores and Flesch-Kincaid Grade Level scores to documents. These scores are obtained by rating the average number of syllables per word and average number of words per sentence. The Flesch Reading Ease score is based on a 100-point scale, in which a higher score means that a document is easier to read. You should aim for scores ranging from 60 to 70 in most cases. The Flesch-Kincaid Grade Level score rates text based on U.S. school grade level. For example, a score of 8.0 means that an eighth grader should be able to understand the text. Most documents intended for the general public should score near the 7.0 or 8.0 level.

To display reading statistics, select the Show Readability Statistics option and completely check your document's spelling and grammar as follows:

1. Display Word Options, click Proofing, select Show Readability Statistics, and click OK.

2. Run a complete spelling and grammar check by clicking Spelling & Grammar on the Review tab, or pressing F7. When the check is complete, Word automatically displays information about the reading level of the document, as shown in Figure 9-20.

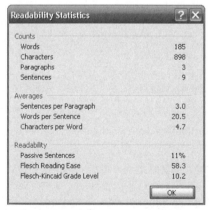

Figure 9-20 The Readability Statistics dialog box shows readability levels in addition to other details, such as word count and average words per sentence.

Displaying Word Count Statistics

At times, you might want to show word count statistics. For example, you might have been given a limit on how many words a document can have for a particular assignment—Web sites, magazines, and newspapers commonly set this type of limit. A notable addition to word count in Word 2007 is live word count ability, which keeps track of the number of words in your document as you type and which can be displayed in your Status Bar. You can easily count the words in your document by using one of the following methods:

- Note the number after *Words* in your Status Bar. (If you do not see Words, right-click the Status Bar and click Word Count.)

- Click Words: # (Number Of Words In Document) in the Status Bar.

- On the Review tab, click Word Count.

- Press Ctrl+Shift+G.

The last three methods will display the Word Count dialog box with word, character, paragraph, and line count information, as shown in Figure 9-21.

Figure 9-21 The Word Count dialog box gives you a quick summary of your document's statistics.

> **Note**
>
> Line count also includes empty paragraphs in the document. If you use empty paragraphs to separate paragraphs that have text, the line count might not be accurate.

The Word Count dialog box includes the Include Footnotes And Endnotes option so that you can choose whether to include those elements in your word count.

Finally, you can also perform a word count on selected text, including noncontiguous selections. To do so, select the text you want to count, note the count of Words in the Status Bar (as shown in Figure 9-22), or display the Word Count dialog box.

Words: 179/8,784

Figure 9-22 Live Word Count keeps count of words while you type. When text is selected, the count will display with the count of the selected words, and the total count of all words in the document.

What's Next?

This chapter looked at the Research and proofing tools in Word and how to configure them with your preferred settings. The next chapter looks at valuable tools for creating complex documents, outlining, and the ease of using Outline view to edit documents that have been outlined using the Heading styles.

Outlining Documents for Clarity and Structure

When you're tackling anything big, it helps to start with the end in mind. When it comes to creating long or complex documents, your outline is the foundation on which everything else is built. The outline represents the major ideas in your document and gives you a clear roadmap to follow as you're capturing the thoughts you want to share with others. It also helps you organize your presentation into manageable pieces that others can navigate, review, and respond to.

In this chapter, you'll learn about the outlining capabilities of Microsoft Office Word 2007. Whether you love outlining and want to make the best use of all available tools or you're only creating the blasted thing because your supervisor asked for it, you'll find the tools easy to understand and use. With practice and a few tips and techniques, you might find yourself actually enjoying it.

Outlining Enhancements in Word 2007

The biggest change in Office Word 2007 is also the change that makes creating, modifying, and managing your outlines much easier. Word 2007 brings all of the tools that you need to outline your document together in one convenient place: the Outlining Ribbon. To display the tools, click the View tab and then click Outline in the Document Views group.

The Outline Tools group on the Outlining tab provides you with the tools you need to create and set the various levels of your outline quickly. Simply point and click to set the level of display that you want to show in your outline, turn formatting on and off, and tweak the outline to your heart's content (see Figure 10-1).

Figure 10-1 The new Outlining tab includes all of the tools you need for working with outlines in Word 2007.

Presenting Creative Outlining with Word 2007

Although many of us learned about outlines for the first time in elementary school, working with outlines in the daily business world doesn't have to conform to any rigid rules that might be floating around in the back of your head. The idea of an outline is simply to get your ideas down in a way that provides you with a structure for your document and helps ensure that you're covering the major points necessary to include in your document. If you find yourself stuck in the planning stage of your document, try some of the following techniques to get the ideas flowing:

- **The process outline** Does your document lend itself to a series of steps? For example, if you're writing an article about managing an international project, plan out what you want to say as a series of steps. Perhaps the first thing you do in managing a global initiative is to determine the scope of the project. That's step 1. Next, you take a look at the resources you have available. There's your second heading. Third, who are the members of your team? Continue until you have completed the process and then review your major steps. Your outline headings can evolve directly from those steps that you've identified.

- **The question outline** You can also use a series of questions to help you identify the important sections of your outline. Basic questions might include the following: What is this document about? (This would be your "Overview" or "Introduction" section.) Who is this document for? What is the mission of our company? Who are our department managers? Where is our facility? What types of services and products do we offer? Who are our customers? How have we improved since last year? What's new and exciting about us? What will we focus on next year?

  Each of these questions gives you a different vantage point from which to consider the content for your document. Put yourself in your readers' shoes. What do they want to see? What do they want to know about you? Questions can help you make sure that you are providing the information that will best connect with the readers of your document.

- **The big-to-small outline** Another way to approach a writing task is to move from the big picture to the individual point of view. This works well in documents that you hope will influence others—for example, sales documents, annual reports, grant proposals, or fundraising materials. Your document starts with the big picture—the statement of a problem, concern, or desire that is common to most of us—and then moves toward the specific (how your company or organization uniquely meets the need you established in the big picture). For example, suppose that you are writing an annual report for Coral Reef Divers. Using the big perspective, you would talk about the environmental threats to the coral reef and the important role that the coral reef serves in balancing the ecosystem. You could then zoom in to talk about the specific factors that your organization identifies as most important and, finally, fully explore the services and options that your organization provides as a response.

Eleven Reasons to Outline Your Next Complex Document

Even if you're a stream-of-consciousness writer, you'll find some benefit in outlining your long or complex documents. Once you create an outline in Word 2007, you've got something to start with—something you can use to build your document, edit it, and organize (or reorganize) it. With that outline, you can even move seamlessly to and from a table of contents that's linked to the work in progress.

If you do not typically use outlining (and you're not alone), consider these reasons for outlining long documents in Word:

- **You're more likely to meet your goals.** If your job involves writing grant proposals, producing product evaluations, writing annual reports, or composing print publications, you know that your document must reach a particular goal. You need to know where you're going, why you're going there, and who you're trying to take with you. When you first type document headings in Word, you're defining the steps that take you to the goal of your document. Your headings reflect the major categories of information that your audience wants to know. As you create the outline, you can make sure you're covering all of the topics necessary to reach your goal.

- **You can create an organized, thoughtful document.** Your outline lists not only the major categories but also smaller subtopics within each category. The multi-level capabilities offered by Word outlines (up to nine levels) enable you to organize your thoughts to the smallest detail.

- **The headings remind you where you're going.** Once you've produced an outline that you're happy with, you're free to write the document as your muse strikes. If you tend to write as inspiration leads, you can simply go with the flow and let the words fly—in the appropriate sections, of course. (If you change your mind, you can always move the sections later if you choose.) If you're more of a left brain, analytical writer, you can craft your sentences within the structured topics, making sure you've got the requisite topic sentence, supporting sentences, and closing or transition sentence.

Chapter 10

- **You can easily reorganize your document at any time.** Word gives you the means to move parts of your document easily, even after your long document is filled with text. You can collapse topics to their headings and move them around as you like. And of course, Undo usually reverses your most recent action if you decide it was a bad move.

- **You can expand and collapse topics.** The expand and collapse outline features of Word enable you to change what you're viewing in the document. A fully expanded outline shows everything entered thus far—therefore, all of the text you've written, subheadings you've added, and notes you've inserted are visible in a fully expanded outline view. If you want to limit the display to only headings and sub-headings, you can collapse the outline to show only those items. This enables you to check that your organization is logical, you've covered everything you want to cover, and your topics are in the right order.

- **You can divide long documents into subdocuments or merge subdocuments into one long document.** The Master Document feature of Word enables you to divide long documents into smaller chunks so that you can work with them more easily. When you pull the document back together, all of the pieces can be merged into one coherent whole. Using the outlining feature enables you to see at a glance the most logical places for divisions.

  For more information about creating and working with Master Documents, see Chapter 22, "Creating and Controlling Master Documents."

- **You can see what doesn't fit.** Outlining also gives you a way to see what doesn't work in your document. If there's a topic that really needs to be a separate document or a heading that is begging for a rewrite, it stands out. Of course, you can edit, move, and enter text in Outline view, so making those changes is a simple matter.

- **You can easily change heading levels.** The outlining feature of Word comes with its own tab complete with commands, giving you the means to promote or demote headings and text. For example, if you want to change a level-1 heading to a level-2 heading, you can do so with the click of a button. This also works for text that you want to raise to a heading or headings that you want to drop to body text.

- **You can work seamlessly with the table of contents.** If you've created a table of contents (TOC) for your document, you can update it on the fly and move directly to it to make changes, if needed. This saves you the hassle—and potential error—of creating a document with a separate TOC that might not be updated when the document is updated.

- **You can easily divide your document by sections when you're working with a team.** If your company or organization is like many others, producing the annual report is a big deal. Many people—from a variety of departments—might be involved in the creation, editing, design, and review of the document. When you work from an outline, you can easily assign specific sections to people in various departments—the finance manager writes the financial narrative, the operations manager drafts the section about the building expansion. You get the idea. You can then put the document back together and use the outline to organize the document exactly the way you want it before beginning the final review stage.

- **You can print your outline for handouts, reviews, or talking points.** Word gives you the option of printing only the outline of your document, which is a nice feature when you want to show others the key points in a document or presentation but don't want them reading along word for word. Whether you do this in the review stage, as part of a collaborative effort, or to condense your finished document to a printable outline, you can display and print only the headings that you want your readers to see.

Viewing a Document in Outline View

Being able to view the outline of your document is helpful whether you're starting a document from scratch or working with an existing file with text and headings already entered and formatted. You can display Outline view in several different ways: by clicking the View tab and choosing Outline in the Document Views group, by pressing Ctrl+Alt+O, or by clicking Outline in the View tools in the bottom right corner of the Word window.

If you enter headings in your document and format them with one of heading styles (Heading 1, Heading 2, or Heading 3) provided by Word, they appear as headings in Outline view, as shown in Figure 10-2. The basic text styles applied to your document are reflected in the outline, but all paragraph formatting (indents, before and after spacing, and line spacing) is suppressed. When you return to Print Layout or Web Layout view, the paragraph formatting is visible again.

Chapter 10

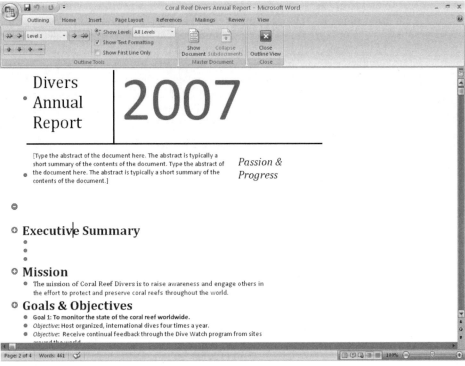

Figure 10-2 Outline view makes use of the headings styles you apply in your document. Paragraph text also appears by default when you first display the outline.

TROUBLESHOOTING

Headings don't show up in Outline view

When you switch to Outline view, why don't any of your headings appear? If you didn't use the built-in heading styles that Word offers—Heading 1, Heading 2, or Heading 3—Word won't automatically recognize the headings as outline levels. To correct the problem, click the headings in the outline one by one, click the Outline Level arrow in the Outline Tools group, and choose the heading level you want in the list. If you want to change all of the headings at once, select all of your headings (press and hold Ctrl while you click to the left of the headings you want to select), click the Outline Level arrow, and choose the level you want to apply to the headings.

Several different types of symbols appear in Outline view, as shown in Table 10-1. They provide clues as to what action to take while working in an outline.

Table 10-1 **Outline Symbols**

Symbol	Description
⊕	If double-clicked, alternately displays and hides subordinate headings and text paragraphs
⊖	Indicates that there are no subordinate headings or text paragraphs
⊕ **Goals & Objectives**	Shows that the topic includes body text or subheadings
• Goal 1: To monitor the state of the coral reef worldwide. • *Objective*: Host organized, international dives four times a year. • *Objective*: Receive continual feedback through the Dive Watch program from sites around the world. • *Objective*: Stay up-to-date on the latest scientific research and climactic changes.	Topic marker; indicates that the lowest-level outline entry is formatted as body text

Exploring the Outlining Tools

When you display your document in Outline view, the Outlining tools appear automatically in the Ribbon. The Outlining tab provides two different groups: Outline Tools and Master Document. The Outline Tools group includes everything you need to work with the various levels in your outline and tailor the display of the outline to show only what you want to see (see Figure 10-3). The Master Document group offers two tools that come in handy when you create and work with subdocuments. Table 10-2 lists and describes the Outlining Tools.

Figure 10-3 The Outlining tab in the Ribbon includes all of the tools you need to apply, change, and view outline levels in your document.

Table 10-2 **Outlining Tools**

Tool	Name	Description
	Promote To Heading 1	Raises the outline level of the selection to the highest outline level, Heading 1
	Promote	Raises the outline level of the selection by one level
Level 1	Outline Level	Enables you to view and change the outline level of the selection
	Demote	Lowers the outline level of the selection by one level
	Demote To Body Text	Lowers the outline level of the selection to the lowest outline level, body text
	Move Up	Moves the selection up one level in the outline
	Move Down	Moves the selection down one level in the outline
	Expand	Expands the outline heading to show subheadings and text
	Collapse	Reduces selection to top-level headings, hiding subordinate headings and text

Creating a New Outline

Creating a new outline in Word is simple. If you're just starting a document, simply click the Outline button in the View tools in the lower right corner of the Word window. Follow these steps to start the new outline:

1. Type the text for your heading. The heading is automatically formatted in the Heading 1 style.

2. Press Enter. The insertion point moves to the next line in the outline.

3. To create a sublevel, click Demote on the Outlining toolbar or press Tab.

   Word indents the insertion point and changes the first outline symbol (–) to a plus (+) symbol, indicating that the heading now has a subordinate entry.

4. Type the text for that entry.

5. Press Enter to move to the next line in your outline.

   By default, Word creates the next heading at the same level as the heading you last entered.

6. If you want to create another sublevel, click Demote or press Tab. To raise an entry one heading level, click the Promote button or press Shift +Tab. If you want to move all the way out to the left margin and create a Heading 1 outline level when you have created multiple sublevels, click the Promote To Heading 1 button.

7. Continue typing entries until your outline is completed. Figure 10-4 displays a sample outline with multiple outline levels.

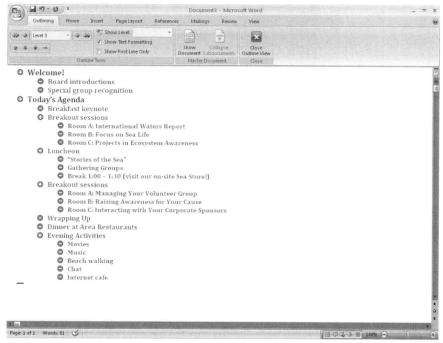

Figure 10-4 Outlining is a simple matter of identifying key topics in your document, naming them, and ordering them the way you want.

It's true that you must format your headings in the styles that Word will recognize—Heading 1, Heading 2, or Heading 3—for them to act and display properly in the Outline window, but you can create styles you like for those headings. You can use the Styles gallery to change the formatting choices for those styles and save the changes in the current document. Word can also make the changes to all similar heading styles in your document automatically. For more information on using Styles to format headings easily, see Chapter 15, "Using Styles to Increase Your Formatting Power."

> **Note**
>
> In some instances, you might want to use the Tab key to actually insert a Tab character between words and not to demote a heading level in your outline. When you want to insert an actual tab in your outline, press Ctrl+Tab instead of simply pressing the Tab key.

Choosing Outline Display

When working in Word's Outline view, you can customize the display so that you see only the heading levels you want to work with. For example, you might want to see only the first-level heads in your outline so you can ensure that all of your most important topics are covered. Or you might want to see every level to check the completeness of the subtopics. You can easily move back and forth between various outline displays by using the Outline Tools.

Displaying Different Levels of Text

To limit the display of your outline to only Heading 1 levels, for example, click the Show Level arrow to display the list of levels. Click Level 1 to display only the first level, as shown in Figure 10-5.

Figure 10-5 In the Show Level list box, control the levels displayed in Outline view by choosing what you want to see.

INSIDE OUT   Copy document headings without all of the text

Being able to collapse the outline display to headings only provides you with a quick look at the overall organization of your document. If only you could copy and paste only the headings of your outline as well. Unfortunately, when you highlight the entire outline, copy it, and paste it into another document, the whole thing—headings and subordinate text—goes along for the ride. One workaround is to create a table of contents (TOC) to the appropriate level (Chapter 24, "Generating First-Class Tables of Contents and Reference Tables," tells you how) and then convert the TOC to regular text. You can then copy the headings and paste them into a document.

> **Note**
>
> Other methods of changing which heading levels appear can be used. You can click the Expand or Collapse button on the Outlining toolbar, or you can double-click the Plus (+) symbol to the left of a heading to display subordinate items.

Showing the First Line of Text

When you want to see the paragraph text you enter, you can have Word display only the first line of text so that you can see the content of the paragraph without displaying the entire paragraph. Why might you want to display only the first line of text?

- To check the order in which you discuss topics

- To decide whether to move text to a different part of the document

- To review the primary points you've covered under subheadings

When all levels in your outline are displayed, you can reduce the outline to only the first line of text by clicking the Show First Line Only check box in the Outline Tools group. The display changes to show the first text lines, as shown in Figure 10-6. To display full paragraphs again, click the check box a second time to clear it.

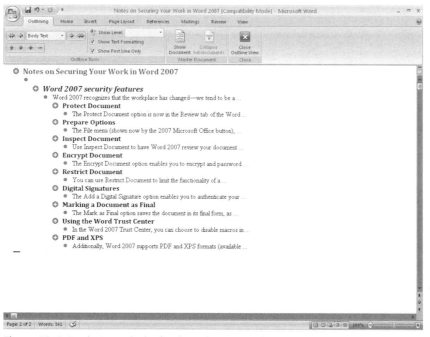

Figure 10-6 Displaying only the first line of a paragraph lets you see the general subject of your text so that you can make informed choices about reordering topics.

Removing and Showing Formatting

Another quick change that you might want to make is to suppress the display of formatting in your outline. As you know, when you change to Outline view, the headings are shown with whatever character formatting they're assigned in the other Word views. When you're working in the outline, however, you might find formatting differences distracting while you consider the content and organization of your topics.

To hide the formatting in your outline, click the Show Text Formatting check box in the Outline Tools group of the Outlining tab. This control actually functions as a toggle, meaning that the first click hides the formatting and the second displays it again. Figure 10-7 shows you what a simple outline looks like when all formatting has been suppressed.

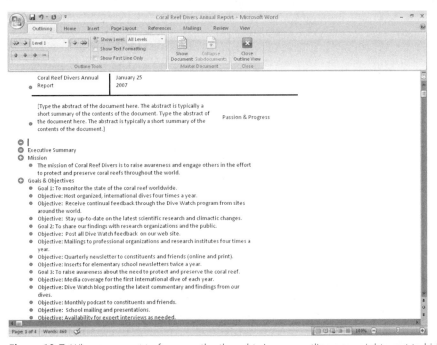

Figure 10-7 When you want to focus on the thoughts in your outline, you might want to hide the formatting.

Working with Headings in Outline View

Whether you create an outline from scratch or use the outline created as part of your existing document, you'll invariably want to change some headings and insert and delete others. Headings are easy to work with in Outline view—with a simple click of a tool, you can change heading levels, move headings in the outline, and even demote the heading to body text if you like.

Adding a Heading

When you want to insert a heading in an existing outline, in Outline view, find the heading that you want the new heading to follow. Then simply place the insertion point after that heading and press Enter. If you want the heading to be at the same level as the heading preceding it, simply type the new heading. If you want to promote or demote the heading level, click the appropriate button before typing your text.

Applying Outline Levels

You can choose the outline level for your heading by using the Outline Level list box on the Outlining toolbar. Simply click in the heading to which you want to apply the outline level and then click the Outline Level arrow to display the list, as shown in Figure 10-8. Click your choice, and the format is applied to the heading.

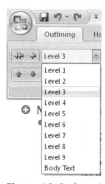

Figure 10-8 If you know which outline level you want to assign to the new heading, choose it directly from the Outline Level list box.

Promoting and Demoting Headings

Once you have text in your outline, you can easily change outline levels, such as moving a heading from level 1 to level 2 or from body text up to level 3. Put simply, promoting a heading takes it one level higher in the outline, and demoting a heading moves it one level down in the outline.

Each time you click the Demote button, Word moves the heading one level down the Outline Level scheme. Outline view shows the change by indenting the heading and changing the formatting. Conversely, the Promote button raises the heading level of the selected text until you reach Heading 1, which is the highest outline level available.

When you want to demote and promote in larger increments, such as moving a heading all the way to the topmost level or changing a heading to body text, use the Promote To Heading 1 or Demote To Body Text buttons.

Chapter 10

When might you want to promote or demote text? You could be working on a report and realize that a topic you've placed at a Heading 2 level is really part of another topic. You can first change the heading level to reflect the level that the heading should be so as to fit in the outline where you want it to go, and then you can move the selection to that point. You can also drag and drop the selection where you want it to appear in the outline; you may need to adjust the heading level depending on where you drop the section.

Displaying Outline and Print Layout View at the Same Time

You can easily view your document in both Outline view and Print Layout view at the same time. Simply drag the split bar (located at the top of the vertical scroll bar) down the screen to open another window displaying the current document.

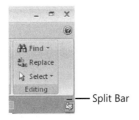 —— Split Bar

To change that area to another view, click in it to give it focus and then select the view you want, such as Outline view. Figure 10-9 demonstrates how the document appears when you are viewing a document in both Print Layout and Outline view.

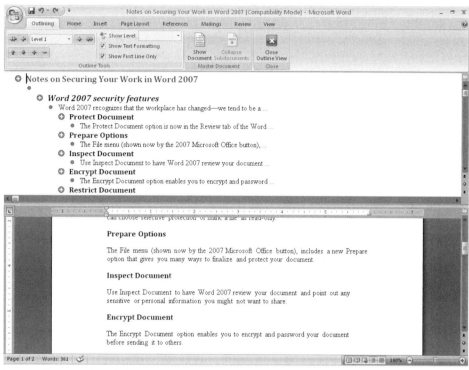

Figure 10-9 Use the split bar to open another window and display the current document using different views.

Changing Your Outline

Once you arrange all heading levels the way you want them, you might decide to move some of your outline topics around. That's one of the biggest benefits of using Outline view—you can easily see which topics fit, which do not fit, or which would work better somewhere else.

Expanding and Collapsing the Outline

The symbols in the Outline window give you clues about what, if anything, is subordinate to the level displayed in the outline. You can use these symbols (introduced in Table 10-1) to alternately display and hide sections and subsections in your document.

You'll find two easy methods for expanding and collapsing the topics in your outline. You can double-click the plus sign to the left of the heading you want to expand. Or, if you prefer, you can simply make sure the heading is selected and then click Expand.

Collapse works the same way. Simply click in the heading of the topic you want to hide and then double-click the plus sign, or click Collapse on the Outlining toolbar.

Moving Outline Topics

Another benefit to Outline view is that you can move entire topics easily. Whether you choose to use the Outlining tools, cut and paste text using the Office Clipboard, or drag what you've selected from place to place, you can easily move portions of your document around as needed.

Moving Topics Up and Down

When you want to move part of an outline to an earlier point in your document or closer to the end, you can use two of the Outlining tools—Move Up and Move Down—to do the trick. Start by selecting the entire part you want to move and then click Move Up to move the selection up one heading. If you want to move it more than one level up, click Move Up as many times as needed to position the selection in the right place.

Use Move Down in the same way. Select the part of your outline that you want to move and then click Move Down on the Outlining toolbar. If you want to move the selection more than one level down, continue to click Move Down.

If you want to move only a heading and not an entire topic, simply click in the heading before choosing Move Up or Move Down. Word moves only the selected heading and leaves any subordinate headings and text in place.

Cutting and Pasting Parts of the Outline

You can also cut and paste parts of your documents in Outline view. This procedure is helpful when you know you want to move a topic but are not exactly sure where you want to put it. You can cut and paste part of an outline by following these steps:

1. Select the portion of the outline you want to move.

2. Click the Home tab, and then click Cut in the Clipboard group. (Alternatively, you can click Ctrl+X if you prefer.)

   The selected portion is removed from the outline to the Office Clipboard.

3. Scroll through the outline until you find the place where you'd like to paste your selection. Click to place the insertion point there.

4. Click Paste in the Clipboard group on the Home tab (or use Ctrl+V). The selection is pasted at the new location.

> **Forget What's on the Clipboard?**
>
> The Clipboard keeps track of everything you copy, cut, or paste while you're working in a specific application. When you are moving sections around in your document, you can easily lose track of what you've clipped out of your file. To view the Clipboard, click the Home tab and click the dialog launcher in the Clipboard group.

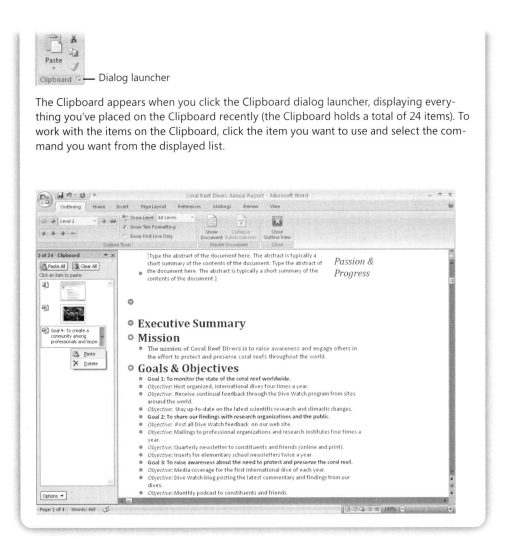

Dialog launcher

The Clipboard appears when you click the Clipboard dialog launcher, displaying every-thing you've placed on the Clipboard recently (the Clipboard holds a total of 24 items). To work with the items on the Clipboard, click the item you want to use and select the com-mand you want from the displayed list.

Dragging to a New Location

If the part of your outline you want to move is within dragging distance of the new loca-tion (meaning that you can highlight and drag the section to that point easily), you can simply highlight it and drag it to the new position. As you drag, the pointer changes, showing a small box beneath the arrow. A horizontal line moves from line to line, track-ing the point at which the selection will be inserted when you release the mouse button.

You may want to display only high-level headings before you move part of your outline. This enables you to see more of your outline on the screen, and you'll have a shorter dis-tance to drag what you're moving. Even if text is not displayed, subordinate headings and body text are moved with the heading.

Printing Your Outline

At various stages throughout the process of viewing, editing, arranging, reorganizing, and formatting the headings in your outline, you might want to print a copy to see how things are shaping up. Printing is the same basic process whether you're printing a long document or a simple outline. Here are the steps:

1. Switch to Outline view and then display your outline.

2. Display only those headings you want to print by using the Collapse and Expand buttons and selecting the outline levels you want to see.

3. Click the Microsoft Office Button and point to Print. Click Print to display the Print dialog box, select your options, and click OK to print as usual.

   The outline is printed as displayed on the screen.

TROUBLESHOOTING

I have too many page breaks in my printed outline

Suppose that you've finished working on the outline for the Coral Reef Divers report, and the development team is waiting to see what you've come up with. You've gone back over it several times to make sure you have all of the sections organized properly and the outline levels set correctly. Everything looks good.

But when you print the outline, there are big gaps in the center of the pages. In the file, the text looks fine—what's the problem? Chances are the blank spots are due to Word's treatment of manual page breaks. If you've inserted manual page breaks in your document, you need to remove them before printing the outline; otherwise, the blank spots will prevail.

To remove the manual page breaks, click the Home tab and click the Show/Hide tool in the Paragraph group to display all formatting marks in your outline. Then move to each page break symbol, double-click it, and press Delete. Save your document and print again. The unwanted breaks should be gone.

Using the Document Map vs. Using Outline View

If you've used previous versions of Word, you might already be familiar with the concept of the Document Map. The Document Map creates a listing of headings in your document and displays them in a panel along the left side of the document. The headings are linked to the document so that you can click any topic to move easily to that part of the document. To display the Document Map, click the View tab and then click the Document Map check·box in the Show/Hide group.

The great thing about the Document Map is that you can view your document in two ways at once—in the outline listed in the Document Map panel and in Print Layout view. You can move to the topic you want to see easily by clicking the heading in the left panel of the work area.

Why have a Document Map *and* an outlining feature? First, the Document Map is a handy tool when you want to do things such as check the wording of a topic, make sure the text you've added fits the heading, and see at a glance that you've covered all of the topics you intended to cover. But when you want to change the heading levels of text, reorganize parts, or affect the table of contents in any way, you need to use the Outlining feature of Word 2007. For major structuring changes, text reorganizations, heading modifications, and more, you want to work in Outline view. For simple, lay-of-the-land operations, the Document Map provides you with a clear picture of your document in a form that you can access and navigate quickly. However, for all other outline-related tasks, you can find what you need in Outline view.

What's Next?

Outlining your document gives you a game plan to follow as you proceed into the research and writing phase of your project. The next chapter moves you into new territory by illustrating techniques for adding and formatting tables.

Chapter 10

PART 3

Visual Elements: Tables, Charts, Diagrams, Pictures

CHAPTER 11

Organizing Concepts in Tables

A s a reader, you may like tables for many reasons: They give you information quickly, in bite-sized chunks (think USA Today); they enable you to see easily how pieces of information relate to one another; and they break up long passages of text and add visual interest to the page. Understanding a table is usually easier than laboring through pages of text.

As someone creating a document in Microsoft Office Word 2007, you will like tables because they enable you to add a professionally designed element to your document almost effortlessly; they add value by giving readers additional ways to understand your key points; and they enable you to organize and present what might otherwise be tedious data in a professional, colorful, and smart way.

This chapter introduces you to working with tables in Office Word 2007. We'll start with a look at the Quick Tables included in Word and then branch out into using the contextual Table Tools to customize tables by using various editing and formatting techniques.

Creating Well-Formed Tables

The secret to creating an effective table is in the planning. What do you want the table to show? What will your readers be looking for, and how can you best organize that data to help them find what they need? Here are some additional questions to ask as you're thinking about the table you're going to create:

- Do you need to create the table in a limited space in your document?
- How many rows and columns will you need?
- Will the table content include text, numbers, or both?
- Will you use functions for totaling and averaging columns?
- Will you have other, similar tables in your document?

Creating Tables in Word

Word provides you with a number of ways to create tables for your document, but by far the biggest star is Quick Tables, which enable you to add ready-made, professional tables to your document with the click of the mouse button. Each method of adding tables has its own merit, however. Here are your choices:

- Add a Quick Table to insert a predesigned table at the cursor position

- Choose the number of rows and columns you want in the Insert Table gallery and let Word create the table for you

- Use the Insert Table dialog box to AutoSize cell content and choose the number of rows and columns you want to create

- Draw a table freehand on the page

- Select text and then choose Convert Text To Table to turn it into a table quickly

- Embed a Microsoft Office Excel spreadsheet.

The method you choose will depend on your data—for example if you want to take advantage of formula creation in Excel use the Excel Spreadsheet method, or Convert Text to Table method if you are transforming a data list that already exists in your document into a table.

This section introduces you to each of these methods. However, we'll start with the fastest and easiest first: Quick Tables.

Adding a Quick Table

If you use tables regularly in your documents, Quick Tables will be a huge time-saving benefit for you and a nice treat for the people who read your documents. Quick Tables are really Building Blocks that Word stores and displays in a gallery. To add a Quick Table to your document, follow these steps:

1. Click to position the cursor where you want the table to appear.

2. Click the Insert tab and click Tables in the Tables group.

3. Point to Quick Tables. A gallery of Quick Tables appears (see Figure 11-1).

4. Scroll through the Quick Tables gallery until you find a table you want to use. Click it to add it to your document.

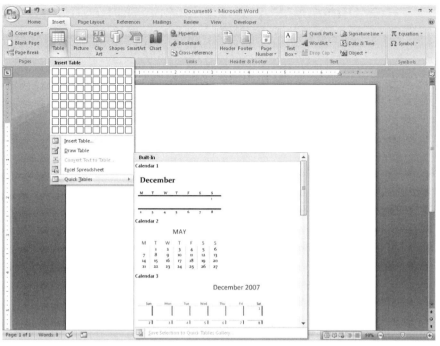

Figure 11-1 Choose from the Quick Tables gallery to add a preformatted table to your document.

Note

Chapter 5, "Applying Themes for a Professional Look," covers the way in which Themes influence formatting options available for various items in your document. A Theme includes specific fonts, colors, and effects that are then coordinated with charts, Quick Styles, and even Quick Tables and table styles (more about this later in the chapter). The content and overall design of the tables you see displayed in the Quick Tables gallery will remain the same no matter which Theme you have selected for your document. But if you change the Theme, you will notice that the colors, fonts, and shading effects used in the Quick Tables change to match the new Theme.

Using the Row and Column Grid to Create a Table

When you click Table in the Tables group on the Insert tab, a mixed list of options appears, as you saw in Figure 11-1. The grid of blank boxes at the top of the Table list is a clickable control that you can use to point and click your way to creating a new table. Here's how to do it:

1. Display the Table list by clicking the Insert tab and clicking Table.

2. Move the pointer down and to the right until the number of rows and columns you want to create in the table is selected (see Figure 11-2). Notice that the number of rows and columns is displayed at the top of the list. Additionally, Live Preview shows the table at the cursor position in your document.

3. When the table is the size you want, click the mouse. The table is added to the document.

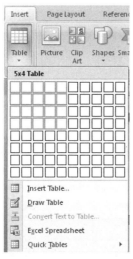

Figure 11-2 Create a table your way by dragging the pointer over the table grid.

Inserting a Table and Specifying AutoFit Options

When you know the number of rows and columns you want to create in a table, and you want to control the way the text fits in those cells, you can use the Insert Table dialog box to create the table in the dimensions you want. Click the Insert tab, choose Tables, and click Insert Table. The Insert Table dialog box appears, as you see in Figure 11-3.

Figure 11-3 Use the Insert Table dialog box when you know the number of rows and columns you want your table to have.

Enter the values you want by clicking and typing (or use the arrows to increase or decrease the numbers displayed in the fields). In the AutoFit Behavior area, choose whether you want the columns in the table to be set to a specific width (this is helpful if you are formatting a table to precise specifications so that it will fit in a particular spot in your document). Additionally, you can click AutoFit To Contents to have Word adjust the size of the table cell to fit the contents of that cell, or AutoFit To Window to resize the table to maximize the space available in the document window.

If you want Word to remember the settings you've entered in the Insert Table dialog box and apply them to other tables you create in the current document, click the Remember Dimensions For New tables check box and then click OK.

Drawing a Table

If you prefer to draw tables as you go along rather than relying on ready-made tables and tools, click Table on the Insert tab and choose Draw Table. The pointer changes to an electronic "pencil" that you can use—by clicking and dragging—to draw the table the way you want it. You can also add lines for rows and columns and make editing changes while you work.

The contextual Table Tools appear on the Ribbon, with Draw Table selected in the Draw Borders group of the Design tab. You can customize the line style, thickness, and color by using the tools in this group (more about this later in the chapter). If you add a line you want to remove, click the Eraser tool and click the line you want to remove.

Chapter 11

> **Tip**
>
> If you want to create a table in the middle of a text section and have the text automatically wrap around it, press Ctrl while you draw the table.

Converting Text to a Table

When you have lists of information that you think would look better—or make more sense—in a table, you can convert the text to a table easily. Select the text in your Word document and then click Table on the Insert tab. Then choose Convert Text To Table.

The Convert Text To Table dialog box asks for input similar to that requested in the Insert Table dialog box. You specify how many columns and rows you want to use, how you want to use AutoFit, and finally, which characters have been used to delineate the individual text entries. Click your choices and click OK. Word makes the text into a new table.

> **Converting Tables to Text**
>
> What happens when you don't want a table to be a table anymore? Suppose that you've created a great table for the annual report, but now someone wants it in text form—no tables allowed. How do you preserve the data and lose the grid? You can make the change easily. Click the table and, in the Table Tools, click the Layout tab. Choose Convert To Text in the Data group. In the Convert Table To Text dialog box, select the character you want Word to use to mark the beginning and end of individual text entries. You might have Word separate your table entries by inserting commas, paragraph marks, or another character between them. Click OK to convert the table to text.

Inserting an Excel Spreadsheet

Especially in situations when you're working with a lot of data, or you need to be able to perform calculations with that data, having Excel features available to you as you work in Word is a great idea. When you add an Excel spreadsheet as a table in your Word document, you have access to the conditional formatting features in Excel, cell styling, table formatting, and more. Here are the steps:

1. Position the pointer at the point in the document where you want to create the table.

2. Click the Insert tab and choose Table.

3. Click Excel Spreadsheet in the Table list. An Excel worksheet window pops up over your Word document. The Ribbon changes to reflect Excel features.

4. Enter your data, create formulas, and apply formats as needed (see Figure 11-4).

5. Return to the Word document by clicking outside the Excel worksheet area.

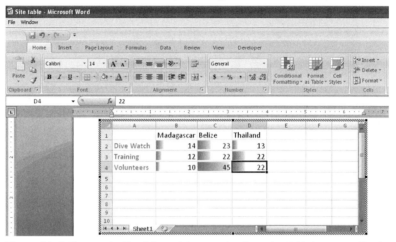

Figure 11-4 Choose the Excel Spreadsheet option from the Table list to use Excel spreadsheet features in your table.

Whenever you want to modify the table, simply double-click it in the Word document, and the Excel window will open. You can then edit the information as needed, apply formatting changes, and more. When you click outside the worksheet, the window closes, and the data in your table is updated to reflect your changes.

Creating Nested Tables

Now in Word 2007 you can easily create nested tables—tables within tables. A nested table enables you to show readers various elements that go into a particular data item in your table. Suppose, for example, that the Coral Reef Divers annual report includes a table that shows program participation at each of the international sites. One program in particular is more fully developed than the others, and in this case, inserting a table within a table can show readers what contributes to the data shown in the resulting cell (see Figure 11-5).

Chapter 11

Table 4: Program Participants by Site

	Madagascar	Belize		Thailand
Dive Watch	14		23	13
Training	12		22	22
Volunteers	10	Trainees	20	22
		Level 1	21	
		Level 2	4	
			45	

Figure 11-5 You can easily create a table within a table to help display your data as completely as possible.

To create a nested table, simply click in the cell in which you want to add the second table and repeat the table creation steps given previously. You can add a Quick Table or choose to draw the table freehand. Either way, you can then use Table Styles to format the table to achieve the look you want.

> **Tip**
>
> For more about formatting your table with Table Styles, see the section titled "Changing Table Format by Using Table Styles" later in this chapter on page 283.

Editing Tables

Creating the table is a start—but it's only a start. Once your data is entered, you'll no doubt want to reorganize it, edit it, add to it, and delete some of it. That means adding rows and columns—perhaps moving the rows you already have—and deleting others. You might decide to rearrange the order of columns, which means moving data from one side of the table to the other. To do that without any unexpected surprises ("Hey, why did Word paste my whole table in that single cell?!"), you need to understand some of the hidden features behind the table display you see on your screen.

Displaying Table Formatting Marks

One of the secrets in moving and editing table data successfully lies in seeing the unseen. Each cell, row, and column in a table is given a marker that delineates the end of the item. When you move, copy, or paste information, these unseen markers might go along, giving you unexpected results at best or overwriting your existing data at worst. To display the hidden marks in your current Word table, click Show/Hide in the Paragraph group of the Home tab. The various table formatting marks will appear, as shown in Figure 11-6.

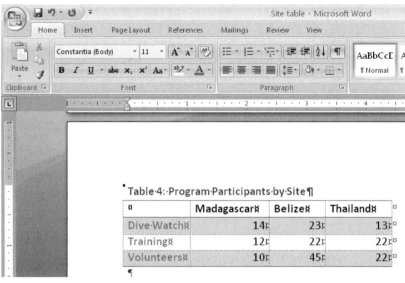

Figure 11-6 Table formatting marks identify the end of individual cells, rows, columns, and the table itself.

When you select table data for moving, copying, or deleting, be sure to turn formatting marks on so that you don't inadvertently include hidden formatting codes that can change the look or behavior of your table.

INSIDE OUT Control the way formatting marks are displayed in your document

If you don't see all the formatting marks you expect, someone may have set the View options to limit the ones that are displayed by default. You can turn all the formatting marks back on by clicking the Microsoft Office Button and choosing Word Options. Click the Display tab and click the Show All Formatting Marks check box. Then click OK to return to your document. Now all of your formatting marks will appear automatically whenever you click Show/Hide.

Selecting Table Cells

To move and copy rows, columns, and cells, start by selecting them to let Word know which data you want to work with. As you get comfortable working with tables, you'll discover the tricks to selecting just the data you want for various operations. Table 11-1 lists selection methods you'll use in working with tables.

INSIDE OUT   **Use multiple table selections**

You can select noncontiguous sections of a table by pressing and holding Ctrl while you click additional selections. In a product listing, for example, this capability enables you to choose only the products that will be included in the 2008 catalog and copy them to a new table, leaving behind all products you don't want to use.

Table 11-1 Selecting Table Segments

Selection	Method	Use
Entire table	Click the table and then click the table move handle that appears in the upper left corner of the table.	You want to move, copy, format, or delete an entire table.
Single row	Click outside the table to the left of the row.	You want to reorder, format, copy, move, insert, or delete a row.
Single column	Click outside the table just above the column.	You want to move, format, copy, insert, or delete a column.
Single cell	Click to the left of any data entered in the cell.	You want to move, copy, delete, or clear that cell.
Multiple cells, rows, or columns	Drag across the elements you want to select.	You want to move, format, copy, or delete sections of a table.

Copying and Pasting Table Data

Although copying is basically a simple operation, copying table data can be a bit tricky because the pasted data can sometimes go where you don't expect it to go. For example, if you want to copy all the information into one cell in the new table, the data might instead be spread over the entire row, replacing existing data. If you want to copy multiple cells to multiple cells in the new table, the incoming cells might all be lumped into the cell at the insertion point. Or now, with the easy method of inserting nested tables that Word 2007 provides, you can easily—and accidentally—create a nested table in your existing table when you really meant simply to copy a few cells. How do you avoid these kinds of copy surprises?

First, know what you're copying. The trick is to select cell data if you want to copy cell data. Likewise, select the cells themselves (or rows or columns) if that's what you want to copy. By capturing the table formatting marks when you highlight the section you want to copy, you can be sure you get the results you expect.

Next, know where you're copying to. If you are copying a row or a column, make sure you've allowed enough room for the incoming data so that important entries won't be overwritten and lost. The Paste Options button can help you with this. After you copy the table data you want, click in the table where you want to place the data and right-click. The context menu displays the options that are appropriate to the type of data you've copied—you may see a simple Paste option, or Paste Cells and Paste As Nested Table may be options that appear (see Figure 11-7).

Figure 11-7 Before you paste table data, right-click in the cell to see your Paste options.

Inserting Columns and Rows

It's not unusual for a table to grow beyond its original conception—some tables seem to take on a life of their own once you begin adding data in the columns and rows. When you want to add another column in your table, you can do it one of two ways:

- Click the column label of the column beside which you want to add the new column. Then click Layout in the contextual Table Tools and choose Insert Left or Insert Right in the Rows & Columns group (see Figure 11-8).

- Right-click the column label of the column, point to Insert, and click Insert Columns To The Left or Insert Columns To The Right.

Figure 11-8 The Layout tab of the contextual Table Tools has what you need to insert columns and rows.

When you manually add data to a table by typing the entry and pressing Tab, Word will continue creating new rows as long as you continue entering data. But when you want to add rows in the middle of a table, for example, or add many rows at once, you can follow the procedures given previously (but choose Insert Above or Below instead of Left or Right).

If you want to insert multiple columns or rows, simply highlight the number of columns (or rows) that you want to insert. For example, to add three columns to the left of an existing column, highlight three contiguous columns, beginning with the one beside which you want to insert the new columns. Then right-click the selected columns, point to Insert, and choose Insert Columns To The Left. The three columns are added as you specified.

Inserting Cells

In some circumstances, you might want to insert cells in a table without adding an entire row or column. You might need to do this, for example, when you have overlooked a product name and number in your listing and need to add it without changing the entire table. To insert cells in a table, simply select the cell (or cells) below which you want to insert new cells. Right-click the selected cell, point to Insert, and choose Insert Cells. In the Insert Cells dialog box, click the option you need and click OK. The cells in the table are changed accordingly.

Deleting Columns, Rows, and Cells

If you decide that you don't need certain rows or columns after all, or if you have empty rows you didn't use, you can easily delete them. Simply highlight the rows or columns and right-click. The context menu will display a choice for deletion that depends on what you've selected. If you selected a row, you'll see Delete Row in the context menu; if you selected a single cell, you'll see only Delete Cell.

You can also delete table elements by clicking the table handle in the upper left corner of the table and click Delete in the Rows & Columns group of the Layout tab. A list of deletion options appears so that you can choose the item you want to delete.

When you choose to delete cells in a table, Word displays the Delete Cells dialog box so that you can identify where you want remaining cells to be shifted. Click your selection and then click OK to return to the document.

Moving Rows and Columns

In some instances, you might want to select parts of your table and move them to other parts of your document, perhaps creating a new table, moving rows to another position in the table, or dividing one large table into two to make them easier to understand. (You can also use the Split Table command, on the Layout tab of Table Tools, to divide one table into two.)

When you want to move rows or columns, simply select the rows or columns you want to move and drag the selected block to the new location. Be sure to click Show/Hide in the Paragraph group of the Home tab before you select the columns or rows so that you can be sure you've included the end of row or column markers in your selection. The table rows or columns are relocated as you specified.

Merging Cells

Sometimes tables seem to grow out of proportion. If this has happened to your table, and you're looking for a way to consolidate data, you can use the Merge Cells command to take data from separate cells and combine it in one cell. To merge cells in your table, select the rows or columns you want to merge and click the Layout tab in Table Tools. Then click Merge Cells in the Merge group. The data is combined into a single cell.

> **Note**
>
> After a merge, you'll probably need to do some editing to get your data looking the way you want. Data takes on the format of the receiving cell, and you might wind up with extra lines and odd capitalization as a result.

Splitting Cells

As you might imagine, splitting cells is the opposite of merging them. When you have a collection of data that you want to divide into separate cells, rows, or columns, you can use Split Cells on the Layout tab of the contextual Table Tools. To split cells, begin by selecting the cell, row, or column you want to split. Click Split Cells in the Merge group of the Layout tab. In the Split Cells dialog box, enter the number of columns and rows over which you want to divide the data. If you have previously merged the data you are now splitting, Word "remembers" the number of columns and rows and suggests those values for the division. To retain the basic format and apply existing row and column formatting to the new columns and rows, leave the Merge Cells Before Split check box selected. Click OK to split the cells.

Adjust Column Sizes After Splits and Merges

After you split or merge cells in your table, you'll probably need to redistribute the space in the columns. To resize a column quickly, point to the column border in the top row of the column you want to change. When the pointer changes to a double-headed arrow, drag the column border in the direction you want to resize the column. When the column is the size you want it, release the mouse button.

If you need a more precise measurement for the width of the column, right-click in the column and choose Table Properties. Then click the Column tab in the Table Properties dialog box. Enter the appropriate column width in the Preferred Width box and click OK.

Resizing Tables

You won't always know how large a table is going to be when you first begin creating it. Word gives you options for controlling the size of the table and offers flexibility for resizing your table exactly the way you want. This section explains how you can work with Word to best handle table-sizing issues.

Understanding AutoFit

You may remember that when you create a table by using the Insert Table dialog box, you're given the option of choosing AutoFit for your table. AutoFit enables you to automatically resize your window as needed, and it is actually already working, by default, to create fixed column widths in your table. AutoFit offers three options:

- **Fixed Column Width** Enables you to choose a specific width for the columns you create.

- **AutoFit To Contents** Adjusts the width of columns to accommodate the data you enter.

- **AutoFit To Window** Sizes a table so that it fits within a Web browser window. This size changes depending on the size of the window, which means that the table will be automatically redrawn as many times as the user resizes his or her browser window.

INSIDE OUT   **Test AutoFit To Window**

If you want to see how resizing your table will affect the rest of the text displayed in your document, you can easily test AutoFit To Window by creating your table, choosing AutoFit To Window (you can do this before you create the table or afterward), and then displaying the table in Web Layout view. When the table is displayed, resize your document window. The table is automatically reformatted so that it always fits within the borders of the window.

Resizing an Entire Table

Although AutoFit does a good job of keeping on top of the way your table needs to grow (or shrink), there will be times when you want to make those changes yourself. The easiest way to resize a table is to drag a table corner. Here's the process in a nutshell: Click the table resize handle in the lower right corner of the table and drag it in the direction you want the table to be resized. The cells are redrawn to reflect the new size of the table.

Note

You can resize tables only in Print Layout and Web Layout views. Although you can see a table in Draft view, the table resize handle is not available.

Setting Preset and Percent Table Sizes

The Table Properties dialog box gives you two very different sizing options. To open this dialog box, right-click in your table and choose Table Properties. To create a table based on a fixed measurement, click the Table tab and in the Size section, select the Preferred Width check box and enter the width for the table you're going to create. Click the Measured In arrow and select Inches. Then click OK.

The best use of this feature, however, is in creating a table that reformats automatically based on the size of the browser window. In other words, if you're viewing your table as part of a Web page, and you reduce the size of your browser window, the table will reformat so that it will stay visible, even in the smaller window. This is a great feature if you're often switching back and forth between applications and want to keep your information open on the screen. To create a table whose dimensions are based on a percentage of screen display, click the Measure In arrow, select Percent, and then click OK. The table will be reformatted as needed to stay within the size of the Web browser window.

Changing Column Width and Row Height

The fastest way to change the width and height of columns and rows is also the easiest. You simply position the pointer over the dividing line of the column or row you want to change and, when the pointer changes to a double-headed arrow, drag the border in the desired direction. Be sure that you've "grabbed" the border for the entire column or row, however—it's possible to move the border for a single cell, which won't help if you want to adjust an entire column or row. (Make sure all cells are deselected if you want to resize the entire column.)

Distributing Data Evenly in Rows and Columns

Distributing your data refers to the process of spacing and aligning data within cells. By default, when you create a basic table and enter text, the text aligns along the left border of the cell, placed in the first line of the cell. To distribute your data evenly in the rows and columns of your table (spacing it evenly between the top and bottom margins of the row and in the center of the column), right-click in the column or row you want to change. Choose Cell Alignment and then select one of the Align Center commands. Or use the Alignment group on the Layout tab..

Changing Text Direction

While we're talking about distributing data, how about rotating the text in your table cells? You can turn your horizontal text on a vertical axis, which gives you the means to create interesting column headings for your tables.

To change the display of existing text, start by selecting it and then clicking Text Direction in the Layout tab's Alignment group. Here's what you can expect to happen:

- On the first click, the Text Direction tool displays the text vertically, with the start of the text at the top of the page and the text extending down toward the table.

- Click again, and the Text Direction tool displays the text vertically, with the start of the text at the top of the table, extending upward toward the top of the page.

- Click a third time, and the Text Direction tool puts your text back to normal.

Enhancing Your Tables with Formatting

Depending on the nature and complexity of your document, the tables you create may range from simple to complex. Word includes formatting features you can apply to your tables to give them just the look you want. You can change basically everything about a table—from the font to the shading to the line style and thickness and the display (or not) of the table grid.

By far, the easiest way to change the format of your table is to apply a table style. This section covers this method and also provides quick steps for customizing specific elements of your table.

TROUBLESHOOTING

Where is the Table AutoFormat feature?

If you are a Word 2003 user, you may wonder where the Table AutoFormat feature went in Word 2007. Table Styles enables you to choose and then change the format of tables you create quickly in your documents. In Word 2007, Table AutoFormat lives on in both of these features.

Changing Table Format by Using Table Styles

One of the greatest changes in Word 2007 is the simple and elegant way you can control a host of formatting options in your document. The Theme used in your document controls the formatting choices you'll see for all kinds of elements—your tables included.

When you add a table to your Word document, the contextual Table Tools appears above the Ribbon. Click the Design tab, and you'll see the Table Styles. These styles enable you to change the format of your table with a simple click of the mouse. A table style can add the following formatting elements to your table:

- A new font, size, style, and color for table text

- A different look for gridlines and the table border

- A new style of shading for columns and rows

- A different kind of alignment for table data

> **Tip**
>
> Use the Table Style options on the Design tab of the contextual Table Tools to control the types of styles you see in the Table Styles gallery and to apply quick changes to your selected table. For example, if you want to see styles that include shading behind alternate columns, click the Banded Columns check box.

To apply a table style to your table, follow these steps:

1. Click in the table.

2. Click the Design tab in the contextual Table Tools.

3. Click one of the designs in the Table Styles gallery on the Ribbon, or, if you don't see one you like, click the More button in the lower right corner of the gallery to display a larger selection. As soon as you click a style, it is applied instantly to your table (see Figure 11-9).

Chapter 11

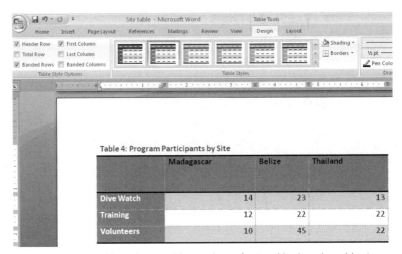

Figure 11-9 Use Table Styles to add a quick, professional look to the tables in your document.

Note

You can also use Live Preview to see how the change will look before you actually select it—just position the mouse pointer over a style you like, and the table will appear with that format. If you want to use that style, click it in the Table Styles gallery.

How Do Themes Affect Table Styles?

When you add a Quick Table to your Word document, the colors, fonts, and effects used in the tables displayed in the Quick Table gallery are preselected to match the document Theme in use. The table styles that appear on the Design tab of the contextual Table Tools are also coordinated so that their color schemes, fonts, and line styles all correspond to the design elements in that particular Theme.

This means that if at some point you choose a different Theme for your document (by clicking the Page Layout tab, choosing Themes, and making a new choice), the tables in your document will automatically change to reflect the colors, fonts, and line styles used in the new Theme.

If you modify some table style elements but do not save your changes as a new table style, those changes will not be updated when the new Theme specifications are applied. For example, suppose that you added a yellow highlight to the data in one column of your table. When you apply a new Theme, the colors, fonts, and line styles will change, but the yellow highlight remains.

Creating Your Own Table Styles

If you have adopted a particular type of table format that you want to use for all your organization's documents, you can easily create a table style and save it to the gallery for reuse later. To create a new table style, follow these steps:

1. Create the table as usual and apply any formatting you want to be reflected in the final style.

2. Click in the table to select it.

3. Click the Design tab of the contextual Table Tools and click the More button in the lower right corner of the Table Styles gallery.

4. At the bottom of the gallery, click New Table Style. The Create New Style From Formatting dialog box appears, as Figure 11-10 shows.

5. Make any additional formatting choices (for example, font color, size, and style; line width, style, and color) and enter a name for the style in the Name box.

6. Finally, select whether you want the table style to be available in all documents or only in the current document. Then click OK to save the new table style.

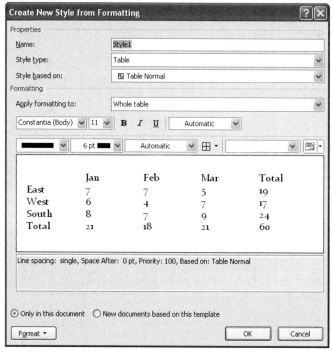

Figure 11-10 Create a new table style based on a table format you want to use regularly in your documents.

Now your new table style is available in the Table Styles gallery. If you decide that you'd like to further modify or delete the style, simply right-click it and choose Modify Table Style or Delete Table Style.

> **Tip**
>
> If you want to designate one of the table styles in the Table Styles gallery as the default table style used for all the tables you create, simply click it and choose Set As Default.

More Formatting Fun

As mentioned earlier in this chapter, the simplest and most convenient way to format your tables involves using tables styles, because they are predesigned to coordinate with the overall Theme selected for your document—so you know they're going to look good. But if you really want to break out of the mold and make some customizations of your own, you may want to use the following table formatting tools to do it:

- Experiment with custom borders on your table by selecting the table and choosing Borders on the Design tab of the contextual Table Tools. Use the Line Weight, Line Style, and Pen Color tools in the Draw Borders group to help get the style just right. And of course, if you don't like what you see, use the Eraser tool to remove it.

- Put your own shading behind table data by using the Shading tool on the Design tab of Table Tools. When you click Shading, a color palette appears, displaying choices that are in line with the selected Theme and also giving you the option of choosing custom colors. Again, have fun and experiment, but if things go horribly wrong, choose No Color or press Ctrl+Z to undo your creative catastrophe.

Positioning Tables in Your Document

You use the options on the Table tab of the Table Properties dialog box to control the way in which your table is positioned. Display the dialog box by right-clicking in your table and choosing Table Properties. Then click Table. Click Left, Center, or Right alignment to specify whether you want your table to be positioned on the left margin of the document, centered between the margins, or aligned on the right.

Flowing Text Around Tables

Text wrap becomes an important consideration when you're working with multiple tables in a long document. On the Table tab in the Table Properties dialog box, you have the option of choosing None—which means text will not wrap around the table at all but appear above and below it—or Around, which flows text up to and around the table.

When you click Around, the Positioning button becomes available. Click Positioning to display the Table Positioning dialog box (shown in Figure 11-11), which enables you to make choices that control where the table is positioned in your document by default.

Figure 11-11 The Table Positioning dialog box enables you to control the default table position for your document.

These choices include the following:

- The horizontal and vertical positioning of the table (choose Left, Right, Center, Inside, or Outside)

- The element to which the table position is relative (choose Margin, Page, Column for the horizontal position and Margin, Page, Paragraph for the vertical position)

- The space you want to leave between the table and surrounding text

- Whether you want to allow the text to overlap the table boundary and whether you want the table to stay fixed in place or move with text if it is reformatted

Chapter 11

> **Note**
>
> Different tables require different settings. Take the time to experiment with the best effects for your particular table.

> **Sorting Table Data**
>
> One of the great things about Word tables is that they provide more than a clear way of organizing data—they also give you a means of *reorganizing* data. Word includes a Sort function so that you can easily reorder the information in your table by searching and sorting on certain key words or phrases. You might, for example, want to organize a conference registration list by sorting first according to state and then alphabetically by last name.
>
> To use the Sort feature, select the table data you want to sort and click Sort in the Data group of the Layout tab. In the Sort dialog box, enter your preferences for the sort procedure and click OK to complete it.

Working with Functions in Tables

Although Word is happy to leave the truly complicated calculations to its sister, Excel, the program includes support for working with a number of functions in your tables. Some of the Word tables you create will no doubt include numbers—and some of those columns will require totals, averages, and more. You can create a number of calculations, depending on what you want the data in your tables to do. You can create your own formulas and work with other Word functions by using the Formula dialog box, shown in Figure 11-12.

Figure 11-12 You can create your own formulas in the Formula dialog box.

To create a formula in a table, follow these steps:

1. Click in the cell where you want to add the formula.

2. Choose the Layout tab in the contextual Table Tools. Click Formula in the Data Group and the Formula dialog box appears. Word may insert the function it expects you to use based on the cell you selected in the table.

3. You can use the displayed formula as is or highlight and erase the existing formula, type = in the Formula box, and click the Paste function arrow. Choose the function you want to use. The function is added to the Formula box, and parentheses are supplied.

4. Click OK to close the Formula dialog box. Word will then calculate the answer and display it in the table cell.

Controlling Table Breaks

If you are working on a large table and know that the table will be divided among several pages, you have some additional choices to make. If you want to make sure that your table breaks at a particular point, click in that row to position the cursor and then display the Table Properties dialog box (alternatively, right-click the table and choose Table Properties). Click the Row tab.

Click the Allow Row To Break Across Pages check box to tell Word to insert the page break at that point in the table. If you want that row to be repeated as the header row on subsequent pages, click Repeat As Header Row At Top Of Each Page.

What's Next?

This chapter showed you how to quickly add, edit, and format professional-looking tables in Word. The next chapter enables you to display your data in a different way, through the use of charts and diagrams.

Chapter 11

Showcasing Data with SmartArt and Charts

You've probably noticed that, in general, the days of the long, boring document are over (thank goodness!). Rarely do you receive an annual report, sales brochure, or even a departmental report that doesn't have some kind of illustration to spruce things up. Microsoft Office Word 2007 includes many new features that enable you to illustrate your documents easier than even. And not only can you add illustrations easily, but you can customize them and apply an almost unlimited number of formatting styles to really make the images and charts stand out.

This chapter begins the discussion of illustrations in Office Word 2007 by spotlighting two specific items you are likely to use often in your Word documents; SmartArt diagrams and charts.

Adding SmartArt Diagrams

SmartArt is a new addition to Word 2007 that dramatically simplifies the process of creating diagrams of all sorts. When you need to create any kind of diagram that illustrates a process, a workflow, a listing, or the way things work together, you can do it quickly—with just a few clicks of the mouse—by using SmartArt.

SmartArt is an interactive diagramming tool that is a dramatic improvement over the diagram feature available in previous versions of Word. With that tool, you were limited to only six diagram types, and your formatting options were also limited. With SmartArt, you can choose from a huge collection of diagram styles, customize them to your heart's content, and include your own photos within the body of the diagram. What's more, you can apply a variety of design styles to add depth, shadow, shine, and perspective to the diagrams you create.

Creating the SmartArt Diagram

When you're in the document, begin by positioning the cursor where you want the diagram to appear. Click the Insert tab and, in the Illustrations group, click SmartArt. The Choose A SmartArt Graphic dialog box appears, as shown in Figure 12-1.

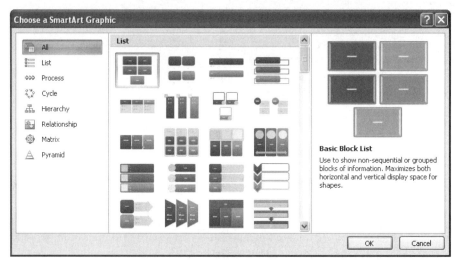

Figure 12-1　Start your SmartArt graphic by choosing the type of diagram you want to create.

> **Tip**
>
> SmartArt works only with documents saved in Word 2007 format. If you are working in Compatibility Mode, the Diagram Gallery that was available in Word 2003 will appear when you click SmartArt.

The Choose A SmartArt Graphic dialog box gives you the option of choosing several different types of diagrams, each used to convey a specific type of information:

- A list diagram displays a nonsequential series of items. You might use a list diagram to introduce a series of new products in your spring catalog.

- A process diagram can show a step-by-step process. For example, you might use a process diagram to show a new trainee how to log on to your computer system.

- A cycle diagram can show the workflow of a particular operation, typically something that is repeated in a cyclical process.

- A hierarchy diagram shows levels, so it is a logical candidate for organization charts.

- A relationship diagram shows how various items relate to each other. You might use a relationship diagram, for example, to show how different roles in a volunteer work group complement each other to provide specific services to the organization.

- A matrix diagram is helpful when you want to compare four items in a format that is easy for viewers to understand. You might use a matrix diagram to explain the research focus for each quarter of the next fiscal year.

- A pyramid diagram shows items in relationship that typically build from the bottom up. A good example of a pyramid diagram is a fundraising chart in which the bottom level represents the largest number of beginning level donors, and the top level represents the smaller percentage of major donors who contribute to the organization.

Begin the process of creating your SmartArt diagram by choosing the diagram type you want in the left panel of the Choose A SmartArt Graphic dialog box. Notice that when you click a diagram type, styles for that particular diagram appear in the center of the dialog box. Click the style you like and, on the right, you'll see an illustration and detailed description of the type of diagram you've selected (see Figure 12-2). Click OK to create the diagram.

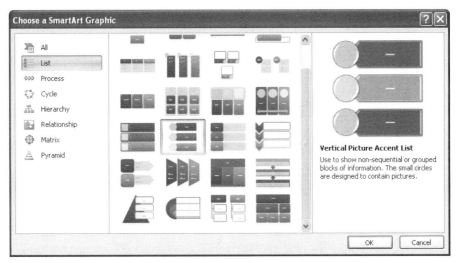

Figure 12-2 The SmartArt graphic style you select is displayed and described in the right side of the dialog box.

The diagram appears at the cursor position. Figure 12-3 shows a list diagram as it first appears. Notice that SmartArt Tools appear automatically in the Ribbon after you create the diagram.

Chapter 12

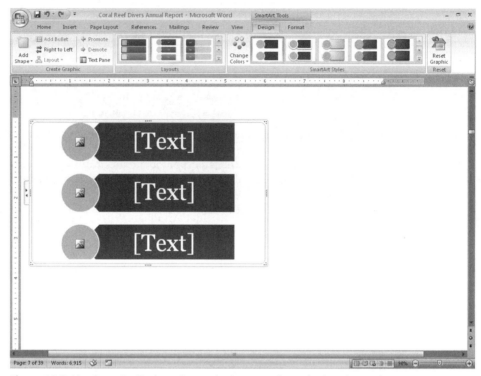

Figure 12-3 Use SmartArt Tools to choose the layout, style, and color of your diagram.

Adding and Formatting Diagram Text

Adding text to your diagram is simple: Just click in the first text box and type the text you want to display in the box. Press Tab to move to the next text box. Repeat as needed until the text boxes are filled. If you run out of text shapes and need to add a new one, click the Add Shape down arrow (in the Design tab of the SmartArt Tools contextual tab) and choose whether you want to add a shape after, before, above, or below the current shape.

You can format the text in the diagram by highlighting the text and choosing the text options from the Mini Toolbar that appears above the selected text. You can also apply WordArt styles to your text by highlighting the text, clicking the Format tab, and choosing the WordArt style you want from the gallery (see Figure 12-4).

Figure 12-4 Change the look of your diagram text by applying WordArt styles.

Making Formatting Changes in the Diagram

Similar to the chart options available in traditional charting in Word, SmartArt diagrams also offer you a variety of layouts and styles you can apply directly to the diagrams in your documents. To change the layout of the diagram, click it and select the Design tab on the SmartArt Tools contextual tab. Then click the More button in the Layouts gallery to display the full range of layout possibilities. Depending on the type of diagram you've created, you will see a variety of layout options. Click the one that best fits the data relationships you're trying to convey.

Like other objects in Word 2007, the formatting settings you can apply to your Smart-Art is influenced by the theme selected for the document. You can change the colors in your SmartArt diagram by selecting a preset color palette with the Change Colors tool. When you choose Change Colors, a palette of choices appears. The colors that correspond to the selected theme appear in the top portion of the palette. Point to the one you want to preview and click your final choice to apply it to the diagram in your document.

Chapter 12

SmartArt Quick Styles give you a gallery of ready-made styles (complete with 3-D settings, shadows, rotation, lighting, and more) that you can apply to your diagram with a click of the mouse. Click the More button to display all the choices and select the one you want (see Figure 12-5).

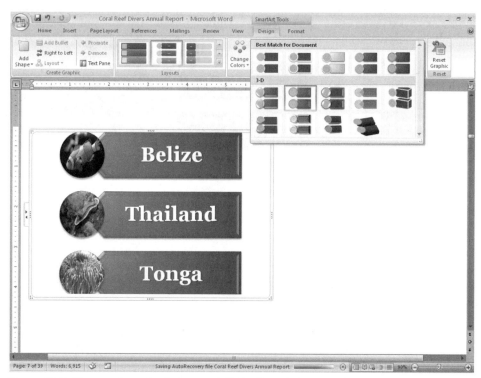

Figure 12-5 Choose a SmartArt Style to apply 3-D effects, lighting, and more.

> **Note**
>
> You may start out with rectangles in a list diagram or circles in a relationship diagram, but that doesn't mean you have to stick with those shapes. You can replace a traditional shape with a unique one by selecting the traditional shape and clicking the Format tab on the contextual SmartArt Tools tab. Click the Change Shape down arrow and select a shape from the displayed list. The shape in your diagram is replaced with the new shape. This can be done for any part of the graphic which can be selected as a separate shape (for example, one rectangle in a list).

Creative Charting

When will you use charts in your Word documents? Don't limit yourself to showing ho-hum data in colorless ways. You can use a chart for more than simply trying to keep readers' eyes from glazing over when they are looking at lists and tables of sales results of the third quarter of your fiscal year. Here are a few suggestions of ways you can use charts in your documents.

- Use a chart to announce a new sales competition for your staff (see Figure 12-6).

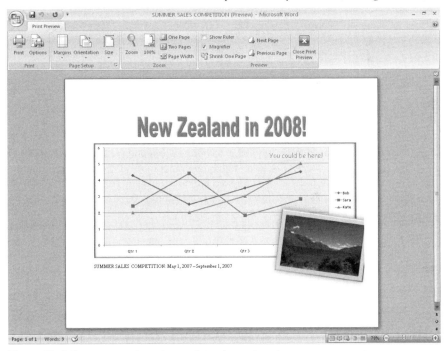

Figure 12-6 You can use charts in a variety of ways to get your message out.

- Create a pie chart to show the number of volunteers each of your regional sites has trained in the previous quarter.

- Use a bar chart over a photo of the new construction on your building to show the staff how it's coming along.

- Use textured columns to show which sites are recruiting the greatest number of divers (see Figure 12-7).

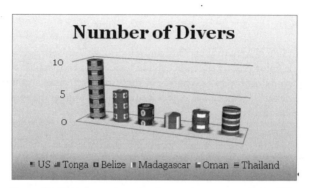

Figure 12-7 Use a variety of colors and textures to help differentiate the data your chart shows.

Note

What's the difference between a chart and a graph? Nothing, really. The terms are often used interchangeably to describe the graphical depiction of data—early on, the term *charting* referred to a type of mapmaking. *Graphing*, on the other hand, involved plotting data points and discerning trends and relationships. Today, the terms mean essentially the same thing; charts and graphs help you illustrate trends and relationships in your data. *Diagramming* usually refers to the process of using a specific model to generate flowcharts or diagrams. This chapter shows you how to use the charting capabilities of Office Word 2007 to illustrate concepts in your documents and also shows you how to use one of the exciting new additions in Microsoft Office 2007: SmartArt diagrams.

Introducing Word 2007 Chart Types

Charts are often used to illustrate relationships—how one item relates to another, how an item this year relates to the same item last year, how a product is selling over time. Eleven different types of charts are available as you create your Word documents:

- **Column charts** A column chart is used to show data comparisons. You might show, for example, how two data series "stack up" against each other for the first quarter.

- **Line charts** A line chart plots data points over time or by category. You might use a line chart to show a trend in product returns over a six-month period.

- **Pie charts** A pie chart shows the relationship of different data items to the whole. Each pie comprises 100 percent of the series being graphed, and each slice is shown as a percentage of the pie. You might use a pie chart to show the relative size of individual departments in the northeastern sales division of your company.

- **Bar charts** Word shows a bar chart as horizontal bars, graphing data items over time (or other categories). You might use a bar chart to compare the stages of different products in a production cycle.

- **Area charts** An area chart gives you the means to compare data two different ways: You can show the accumulated result of the data items, and you can show how the data (and their relationship to one another) change over time. For example, you might use an area chart to show how many students took each module of the exam at two different universities.

- **XY (Scatter) charts** An XY chart enables you to plot pairs of data points over time. You might use an XY chart to contrast the test scores from a battery of exams given at two different universities.

- **Stock charts** A stock chart displays four values for a single item—open, high, low, close—and is designed to show the variance in a particular item within a specific period of time.

- **Surface charts** A surface chart is a great way to compare the change of three data items over time. Through the use of colored levels, a surface chart shows in three-dimension form where the data in a particular series leads (see Figure 12-8).

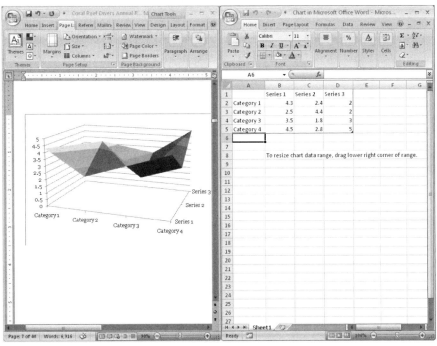

Figure 12-8 A surface chart enables you to illustrate series data in three dimensions.

- **Doughnut charts** A doughnut chart is similar to a pie chart in that it shows the relationship between data items. Doughnut charts enable you to compare two sets of data and the way in which they relate to the whole and to each other. You might use a doughnut chart to portray two different sales campaigns. The sections of the doughnut could represent the different sales channels, and you could compare and contrast the different effects of each channel.

- **Bubble charts** A bubble chart enables you to plot three different data series. Each item is plotted at a particular point in time and shows the data value as a bubble. This would enable you to see, for example, which accounts had the highest charges during the second quarter.

- **Radar charts** A radar chart plots multiple data points and shows their relation to a center point. You might use a radar chart to show how each regional sales division fared in a recent sales competition.

Charting Changes in Microsoft Office 2007

Each of the core 2007 Microsoft Office system applications includes a new chart engine that offers dramatically enhanced and expanded charting capabilities. Now you can choose from a gallery of chart styles; add drop shadow effects, glows, and more; and customize chart elements in many different ways.

When you first create a chart in Word, the chart opens a Microsoft Office Excel 2007 datasheet if Office Excel 2007 is installed on your computer. If Excel isn't installed or you are working in Compatibility Mode, Word will use Microsoft Graph to create the chart. (Microsoft Graph is a full-featured graphing utility available in previous versions of Word.)

Creating a Basic Chart

The process of creating a chart in Word is simple. First click to position the cursor wherever you want the chart to appear (you can move it later if you choose).

Then, to create the chart, follow these steps.

1. Click the Insert tab on the Ribbon.

2. Click Chart in the Illustrations group. The Insert Chart dialog box appears, as shown in Figure 12-9.

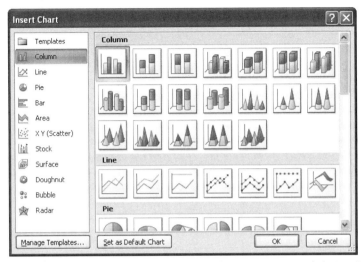

Figure 12-9 The Insert Chart dialog box enables you to view and choose the type of chart that meets your needs.

3. Choose the chart type you want to create by clicking it in the left pane of the Insert Chart dialog box. The gallery area on the right shows the various styles available for the chart type you select.

4. Click OK to create the chart.

5. The default chart in the type you selected appears in the document on the left side of the Word window, and Excel (or Graph, if you don't have Excel installed on your computer) displays a datasheet that includes your data in the right side of the window (see Figure 12-10). You can now modify the data in the datasheet to reflect the data relevant to your document. Click the close box to close the datasheet, and the chart in your document is updated accordingly.

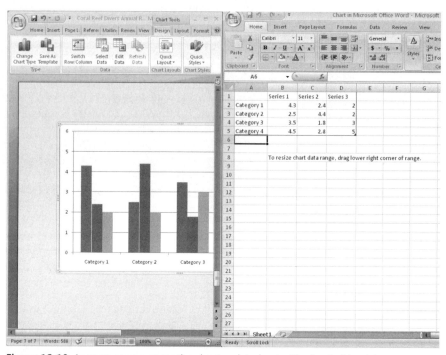

Figure 12-10 As soon as you create the chart, a datasheet with placeholder data appears. Replace the data with your own, and the chart is updated automatically.

That's all there is to adding your first chart to a Word document. But now comes the fun part—enhancing the chart by using the Word Chart Tools.

> **Note**
>
> The gallery area of the Insert Chart dialog box contains all the chart types available to you, so if you prefer, you can simply use the vertical scroll bar in the dialog box to view all the different chart styles. That way, if you really aren't sure what the type of chart you want to create is called—but you know it when you see it—you can look over all the styles quickly and make your selection by double-clicking it.

Changing the Chart Type

Making sure you've got the right chart for the data you're displaying is an important part of communicating your point most effectively. Some charts, such as bar and column charts, are best for comparing data items—for example, tracking the sales of apples compared to oranges. Other charts, such as pie charts, are better for showing the relation of individual items to a whole—such as the fundraising totals of your two top volunteer groups as they compare to total fundraising dollars in August 2007.

Word makes it simple for you to select and change chart types. Start by creating a new chart or by displaying the chart you've already created. Double-click the chart, if necessary, so that the contextual Chart Tools are displayed on the Ribbon. Click the Design tab and then click Change Chart Type in the Type group (on the far left side of the Ribbon). The Change Chart Type dialog box (which you saw earlier as the Insert Chart dialog box) opens, offering you the range of chart types that were available to you when you initially created the chart. Simply click the chart type you want, click OK, and Word changes the display of the chart in your document and modifies the datasheet if needed.

> **Note**
>
> If you really like the chart type you've selected, you can make it the default chart that is used automatically uses whenever you create a new chart. Simply click Set As Default Chart in the Insert Chart (or Change Chart Type) dialog box. Each time you create a new chart, the chart type you selected will be the chart created by default.

Creating a Chart Template

Word offers so many ways to enhance the design of your charts that you may want to create your own chart templates so the charts you create are consistent in all the documents you create. If you work for a company that standardizes its published materials, creating and using a custom chart template gives you the means to make your charts distinctive while keeping them professionally appealing and consistent with your overall brand.

After you've created, enhanced, and saved your chart (which you'll learn how to do in this chapter), you can save your chart as a template. The chart will then be available to you in the Templates folder that appears in the left pane of the Insert Chart dialog box.

To create a chart template based on an existing chart , simply select the chart and then click the Design tab in the contextual Chart Tools. In the Type group (farthest to the left on the Ribbon), click the Save As Template option. In the Save Chart Template dialog box, enter a name for the new chart and click Save (see Figure 12-11). Word saves the chart by default in the Templates folder, making it available to all your other Microsoft Office applications as well. The next time you open the Insert Chart dialog box, the template you saved will be available in the Chart Templates folder.

Chapter 12

Figure 12-11 Save a customized chart as a template so that you can use it in other documents you create.

Note

If you change the theme selected for your document, any charts you create using a chart template will not update to reflect the new theme. To update the format of your chart, click the edge of the chart frame to select it, and then click Reset To Match Style in the Current Selection group in the Format tab of the contextual Chart Tools.

Understanding the Chart Tools

As soon as you create a chart, Word adds the contextual Chart Tools to the Ribbon, offering you a collection of specialized tools you'll use to design, enhance, format, and save the chart you create (see Figure 12-12).

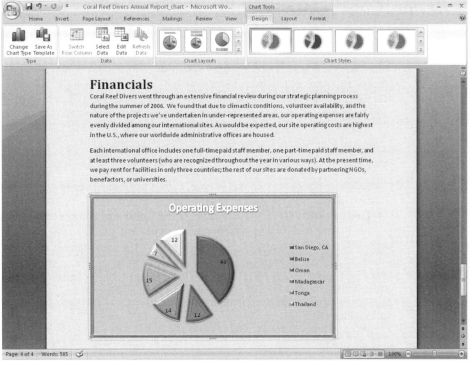

Figure 12-12 The contextual Chart Tools enable you to change the design, layout, and format of your chart.

The contextual Chart Tools offer three tabs with different sets of tools for different types of tasks.

- **Design tab** Enables you to change the type of your chart, work with chart data, select a chart layout, and choose the style and color of chart you want to create.

- **Layout tab** Lets you focus in on specific chart elements. With the Layout tools, you can add pictures, shapes, and more; add and format labels; modify the axes in the chart; add color, pictures, or 3-D effects to the background; and insert elements like trend lines, markers, and more that help readers analyze the data they are reviewing.

- **Format tab** Includes tools that let you enhance the look of your chart by choosing the size of shapes on the chart; adding shadows, fills, and outlines; changing the size of the chart; and selecting text wrapping and positioning options.

Throughout the rest of this chapter, you'll learn more about when to use each of the tabs in Chart Tools to change, enhance, and finalize the charts in your Word documents.

Chapter 12

Entering Chart Data

When you first create a new chart, Word inserts its own set of dummy data into the datasheet and displays the datasheet in either Excel or Graph (depending on whether you have Excel installed on your computer). You use the datasheet to enter, arrange, and select the data you want to include in your chart. Throughout the life of your Word document, you can add to and update the information in the datasheet as needed. This way your chart always stays fresh and relevant to your most current data.

> **Note**
>
> You can choose to link or embed chart data in a Word document. If you link a chart, the chart in your Word document will be updated whenever the source document changes. If you embed a chart in your document, you'll be able to edit the chart as you would normally, by double-clicking it in the hosting document.

You will use the Data group (available on the Design tab of the contextual Chart Tools) to work with your chart's datasheet (see Figure 12-13). Here's a quick look at the tools in that group.

Figure 12-13 Use the Data group in the Design tab of the contextual Chart Tools to work with the data in your chart's datasheet.

- Switch Row/Column enables you to swap rows and columns to create a different display of the data in your datasheet

- Select Data displays the Select Data Source dialog box so that you can choose the data range you want to use for the chart. Additionally, you can choose the series and category items you want to include or hide from display.

- Edit Data displays the datasheet so that you can change, add to, or delete information on the datasheet.

Working with the Datasheet

Figure 12-14 shows the datasheet that appears when you create a new pie chart in Word. As you can see, the series names (Series 1, Series 2, and Series 3) and the category names are all generic. The data in the datasheet doesn't mean anything at this point—it simply provides the chart engine with something to display in the sample chart.

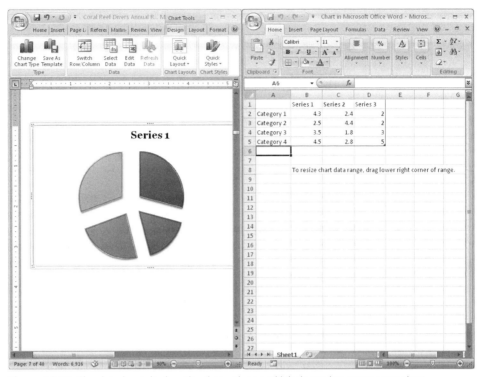

Figure 12-14 The datasheet displays the data values and labels used to create your chart.

The datasheet is actually an Excel worksheet, so the tools on the Ribbon may look familiar to you. Changing the data in the datasheet is a simple matter of clicking in the cell you want to change and typing the new information. You'll find the following items on the datasheet.

- **Categories** The items in the columns are the categories placed along the horizontal axis of the chart. Categories might include months, quarters, stages of a project, or some other unit by which value can be measured.

- **Data Series** The data series show the items that are being graphed, according to the categories selected.

- **Values** The data entered in the cells of the datasheet are scaled against the value axis, which is the vertical axis in the created chart.

> **Note**
>
> When you're adding your own information in the datasheet, be sure to reset the chart data range by dragging to select the rows and columns that contain your data. (Otherwise, the default chart data range will be used when you display the chart.)

Making Sense of Categories and Series

So what's the difference between a category and a series? You can set up the organization of your chart any way that will best portray the data comparisons you're trying to show, but generally a chart enables readers to easily compare two or more sets of data in a specific relationship. For example, consider the objectives here and see how the categories and series are designed to answer the question the objective poses.

- Objective Find out which volunteer recruitment methods are working best for in different locations
  - ❏ Categories Direct, online, event, and training
  - ❏ Locations Belize, Tonga, Thailand, Oman

The resulting bar chart shows each of the locations, side by side, compared by recruitment method (category).

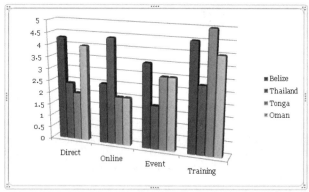

- Objective Evaluate volunteer interest in different age groups
  - ❏ Categories Definitely interested, Somewhat interested, Unsure, Not interested
  - ❏ Series Student, young professional, manager, retiree

This chart shows the various user groups and illustrates their level of interest in volunteering for Coral Reef Divers. Being able to analyze your information in this way helps you identify and plan the next steps in your recruitment program.

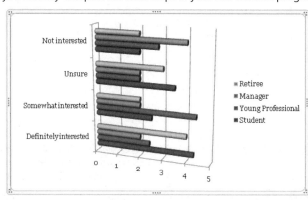

> **Note**
>
> If you close the datasheet by clicking the Excel close button, you can redisplay it while you edit the chart by clicking Edit Data in the Data group in the Design tab of the contextual Chart Tools.

Changing the Data Arrangement

By default, the new Word chart displays the categories along the horizontal axis and the values along the vertical axis, but if you choose, you can flip that arrangement to display your data differently.

To change the arrangement of the data in your chart, follow these steps.

1. Select the chart you want to change. The contextual Chart Tools appears.

2. Click the Design tab.

3. In the Data group, click Switch Row/Column. The chart is redrawn automatically.

> **Tip**
>
> Although you're creating a chart for use in your Word document, you might want to use data from other programs to create the chart. Because the chart datasheet is actually an Excel worksheet, you can link to external data sources supported by Excel. To display your choices for using external data in your Excel datasheet, click the Data tab in the datasheet and choose the option in the Get External Data group that best reflects the type of data you want to use. For more about working with Excel 2007, see *Microsoft Office Excel 2007 Inside Out*, by Mark Dodge and Craig Stinson (Microsoft Press, 2007).

Editing and Enhancing Chart Information

Creating your chart is only half the fun. Once you decide on the basic style you want, you can add to, edit, and enhance your chart in a variety of ways. Simply click the chart you want to change and the contextual Chart Tools appears automatically along the top of the Ribbon. You use the Chart Tools, shown in Figure 12-15, to change the chart layout, choose a chart style (including colors and shadow effects), add titles and labels, change the look of the background and axes, and much more. The sections that follow show you how to add specific items to your charts to make them easier for readers to understand.

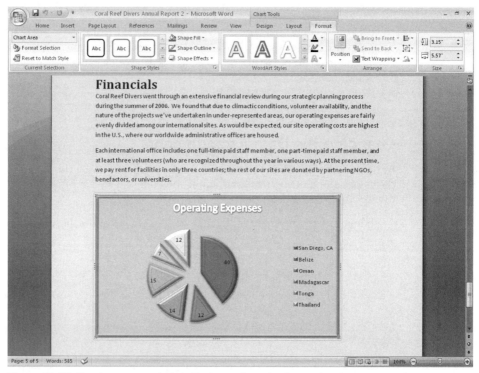

Figure 12-15 Use the contextual Chart Tools to edit and enhance the charts in your document.

> **Note**
> Although many of the elements you'll find on the Chart Tools tab apply to all the different chart types, some controls are disabled for certain charts. For example, the tools in the Axes group on the Layout tab are disabled when a pie chart is selected because they don't make sense with that type of chart.

Choosing a New Chart Layout

Now in Word 2007 you can apply a ready-made chart layout to the chart you've just created. A chart layout is like a template—complete with a legend style, data labels, and more—that you apply to the chart you've already created. You can choose a chart layout for your chart when you want to save yourself the time and trouble of choosing a number of chart options individually.

To apply a chart layout to your chart, click the chart to select it and then click the Design tab in the contextual Chart Tools. Click the More button in the lower right corner of the Chart Layouts gallery to display the whole collection of chart layouts (see Figure 12-16). Simply click the layout to apply it to your chart.

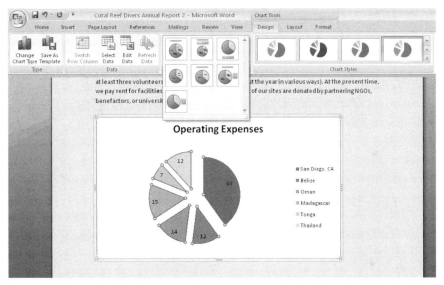

Figure 12-16 Use the Chart Layouts gallery to apply specific chart formats to the charts in your document.

Applying a Chart Style

Word includes another design feature that makes creating a professional chart much easier. The Chart Style gallery includes dozens of visual styles you can apply to a chart in your document. Chart Styles include:

- Color selection
- 3-D effects
- Shadow effects
- Outline style and color
- Background effects

To apply a chart style to your chart, select the chart and then click the Design tab on the Chart Tools contextual tab. Click the More button in the lower right corner of the Chart Styles gallery and then choose the style you want from the displayed collection (see Figure 12-17).

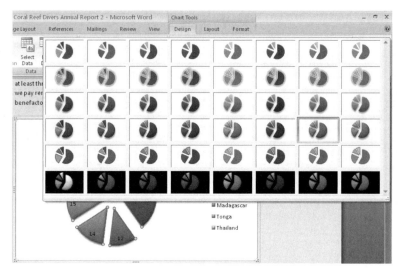

Figure 12-17 The Chart Styles gallery gives your chart a professional look at the click of a button.

Change Fonts with the Mini Toolbar

By now you've noticed that Word 2007 is all about context. Whatever project you're working on, Word offers you just the tools you need to complete it. When you want to change the font used in a chart, simply highlight the text you want to change. The Mini Toolbar appears over the text so that you can easily choose a new font, change the size, make the font larger or smaller, change the color, and more. Simply click your choice and the text is changed. All things should be so simple.

Adding a Chart Title

Not all charts need titles, but a chart title can help readers understand the "big picture" you're trying to communicate. To add a title to your chart, choose the Layout tab on the contextual Chart Tools and click Chart Title in the Labels group. In the gallery, choose whether you want the title to be centered on the chart or placed above the chart. (If you decide later that you want to move the title, you can simply drag it to the point on the chart you want it to appear.) Centered Overlay Title enables the chart to be displayed at maximum size (which is important if you have a fairly complex chart), while Above Chart reduces the chart size slightly to make room for the title. Experiment with each choice to find the one that's right for your chart.

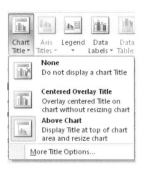

Working with Axes

The axes of your chart are important in that they set up the structure for the way in which data is displayed. You can use two different tools in the contextual Chart Tools to work with axes. Both are found in the Layout tab of the contextual Chart Tools.

If you want to tell Word to display the title of an axis, click Axis Titles in the Labels group. To add an axis to your chart, begin by clicking Axis Titles and pointing the axis you want to change (Primary Horizontal Axis or Primary Vertical Axis). When you point to the Horizontal Axis selection, choose Show Title Below Axis to add the title text box to the chart. (You can click and drag the title box anywhere on the chart you'd like it to appear—but be sure to keep it close to the axis so your readers will understand what it refers to.) If you select Primary Vertical Axis, you will see three choices: Rotated Title, Vertical Title, and Horizontal Title. Click the choice that reflects the way in which you want the vertical axis to be displayed on the chart. After you add the axis, simply click in the text box and type the text for your axis title.

If you want to change the way in which information is displayed along the axis, you can choose Axes in the Axes group. When you click the Axes tool, a list appears, offering Primary Horizontal Axis and Primary Vertical Axis as options. Choose the axis you want to change, and another set of choices appears (see Figure 12-18). For the horizontal axis, your choices involve whether the axis runs right to left (or vice versa) and where the data labels appear. For the vertical axis, you can choose the value increments you want to appear on the axis (thousands, millions, or billions).

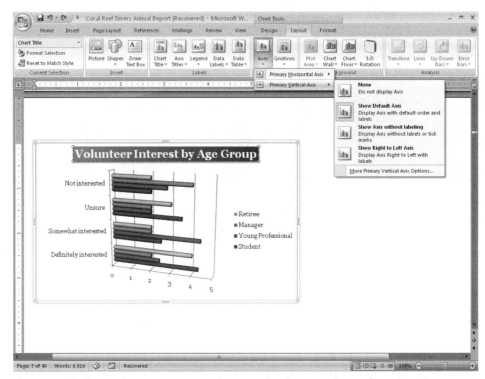

Figure 12-18 Choose the axis you want to change and make your selection from the gallery.

If you want to further control the axes in your chart, you can choose More Primary Vertical Axis Options or More Primary Horizontal Axis Options at the bottom of each of the respective galleries. Figure 12-19 shows the Format Axis dialog box. In this dialog box, you can choose the increments for the values on the vertical axis, set tick mark type, and determine the placement of the chart floor. In the Format Axis dialog box for the horizontal axis, you can also set axis type and tick mark settings, and choose where the vertical axis crosses the horizontal axis. Additionally, in both dialog boxes, you can choose line color and fill, shadow, and 3-D effects for the axes.

> **Note**
> You will be able to choose settings for the chart floor only when you are working with a 3-D chart.

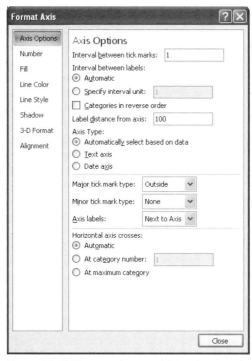

Figure 12-19 You can choose additional options for the axes in your chart by using the Format Axis dialog box.

> **Note**
>
> To hide or display axis tick marks, display the Format Axis dialog box and select the Major Tick Mark Type and Minor Tick Mark Type options that add or remove the tick marks from the chart. Click OK to save your settings.

Add Gridlines and Trendlines

If you're working with complicated charts that have multiple data series, gridlines can help clarify the comparisons and conclusions you want readers to draw from your chart. Select the Gridlines tool in the Axes group of the Chart Tools. Then click either Primary Horizontal Gridlines or Primary Vertical Gridlines. Both choices give you the option of selecting major gridlines, minor gridlines, or major and minor gridlines.

> **Note**
>
> You can get creative with the gridlines in your chart if you want to shake things up a little bit. The new enhancement features in Word 2007 enable you to choose new gradients for your gridlines, and add shadows and arrows. Simply right-click the gridline you want to change in the chart and select Format Gridlines. The dialog box that appears will be either Format Major Gridlines or Format Minor Gridlines, depending on which set of gridlines you selected.
>
> Choose Line Color, Line Style, or Shadow in the left panel and then select the options you want to apply to your chart. Click Close to save your settings and apply them to your chart.
>
> Be forewarned, however: With gridlines, a little goes a long way. Be sure to add only what your reader needs to understand your data—too many lines will clutter up your chart and make it more difficult for readers to decipher, they may even render the chart un-readable if there are too many too close together.

Displaying and Positioning a Legend

Word assumes that you want a legend for your chart when you first create it. If you don't feel the legend is needed and want to have more space for your chart, you can remove the legend by clicking Legend in the Labels group of the Layout tab (available in the Chart Tools). When you choose None, the first option on the list, the legend is hidden. The chart is enlarged to fill the space the legend previously occupied.

You can also control where the legend is placed in the chart by clicking the Legend tool in the Labels group. A list of options appears that gives you a range of options for the placement of the legend (see Figure 12-20)

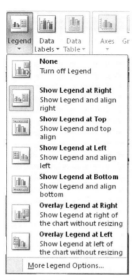

Figure 12-20 The Legend tool in the Labels group enables you to control the placement of your chart legend.

> **Tip**
>
> You can further change and enhance the legend you add to your chart by clicking More Legend Options at the bottom of the options list that appears when you click Legends in the Labels group.

Working with Data Labels

Data labels are helpful when you need to give the reader further clues about which data items go with which series or category. Word gives you the ability to add several different kinds of data labels to your charts. You might want to add percentages to pie slices, for example, or category labels to stacked bars. Click Data Labels in the Labels group to display a list of placement choices for the data labels on your chart.

By default, Word displays data values in the pie slices or bars of your chart. You can change the type of information displayed and add special features such as color, shadows, outlines, and 3-D options by choosing Data Labels in the Labels group and clicking More Data Label Options. In the Format Data Labels dialog box (see Figure 12-21), you can choose the label contents you want to display (series name, category name, value, or percentage).

Chapter 12

Figure 12-21 Display and enhance data labels on your chart using options in the Format Data Labels dialog box.

> **Note**
>
> You can choose to display more than one type of label. For example, you might want to display both percentages and category names on a pie chart. If you select more than one label type, use a separator to distinguish the labels. Click the Separator arrow to display a list of choices and then click the separator you want to use.

One more way to make sure that readers get the connection between your data trends and the categories being plotted: You can use the Legend Key feature to add small legend tags to the left of each data label. Readers will be able to see at a glance which items relate to the categories in your chart legend.

> **Note**
>
> The data labels Word uses are taken directly from your datasheet. If you want to change a data label on the chart, it's best to go back to the datasheet and make the change. Otherwise, the label change might not "stick," and you might see the same old label displayed the next time you display your chart.

TROUBLESHOOTING

I can't see axis titles in my chart

If you're having trouble seeing the axis titles along the Category and Values axes on your chart, the chart area might be too small to display all the chart information successfully. Try resizing the chart by clicking it and then dragging one of the resize handles outward, enlarging the chart. If that doesn't do the trick, right-click the axis title while editing the chart and then choose a smaller font size on the Mini Toolbar.

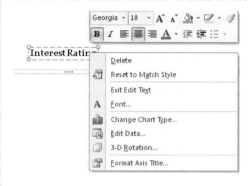

Formatting Charts

Word gives you the ability to format all the different elements included in your chart. You might want to change the font of a title, resize the labels, change the background color, change the line thickness, apply a pattern, or do any number of other things—including adding drop shadows, glow effects, or 3-D enhancements.

To choose the chart object you want to work with, click the chart, choose the Layout tab on the Chart Tools, and click the Chart Elements arrow in the Current Selection group. A list of possible objects appears, as shown in Figure 12-22. Click your choice, and Word selects that item in the chart. You can then right-click the item to display a format choice—for example, right-clicking a legend displays a shortcut menu including the Format Legend command. When you select that command, a formatting dialog box appears in which you can select the colors, styles, and placement for the legend.

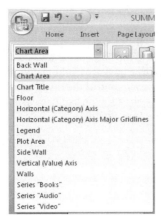

Figure 12-22 Use the Chart Elements list to select the chart element you want to change.

The formatting commands available change depending on the type of chart you're cre-ating and the chart element you've selected. You'll see a different set of options, for ex-ample, when you right-click a chart axis, than you will when you right-click the legend.

Changing the Format of Your Chart Elements

Word includes a Ribbon-full of formatting choices that enable you to add color and texture to the shapes of the elements in your chart. Additionally, you can use the For-mat options to apply special effects to your text by changing color, adding mirroring, shadowing, glow effects, and more. Here are a few possibilities to consider as you think about the ways you want to enhance your chart.

- Do you want a border around your chart? If so, what kind? You make those choic-es on the Format tab of the Chart Tools.

- Do you want to choose a different color or line thickness for the border of your chart? Look in the Shape Styles group of the Format tab for the choices you need.

- Would you like to add a drop shadow to the chart? Click the Shape Effects down arrow, point to Shadow, and choose the style you want.

- Do you want to apply a special text effect to your title or axes titles? Choose a WordArt style that reflects the way you want the text in your chart to appear.

You can change each of these items by first selecting the chart you want to change and then by clicking the Format tab on the Chart Tools. Figure 12-23 shows the commands that are available when the Format tab is selected.

Figure 12-23 The Format tab includes tools for changing colors, shapes, shadows, and more in your charts.

Formatting Shapes

Word provides you with an almost unlimited number of ways to enhance charts in your documents. One way you can make a big visual difference in your charts is by applying formats to the shapes that make up the chart. For example, consider the chart title in Figure 12-24. The 3-D style applied to the title is one of many available in the Shape Styles gallery (on the Format tab of the contextual Chart Tools).

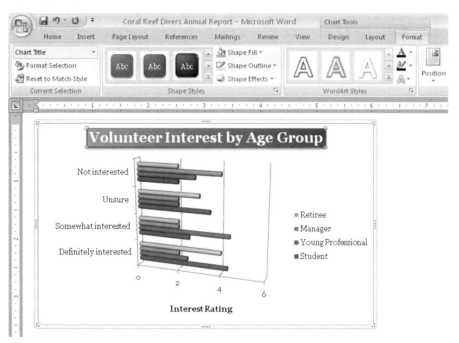

Figure 12-24 You can add special styles to the shapes in your chart by using the Shape Styles gallery.

Begin by selecting the object in your chart you want to change. Anything clickable qualifies—you can change the title, the label area, the individual data series, the axes, and more. When you select an element, Word automatically updates the Shape Styles to show the styles available for that chart element. You can click the More button to see the whole gallery of styles available for the selected element. Click your selection to apply it to the chart.

Adding Shadows, Glows, and More

Additional choices in the Shape Styles group of the Format tab enable you to make further changes to the shape you've selected.

- Shape Fill displays a palette so that you can change the color, gradient, pattern, or texture of the selected shape.

- Shape Outline includes color selections as well as line width and style choices that change the outline of the shape.

- Shape Effects displays a gallery of style choices that enable you to add shadows, make the shape glow, soften the edges, rotate the shape in 3-D, and much more (see Figure 12-25).

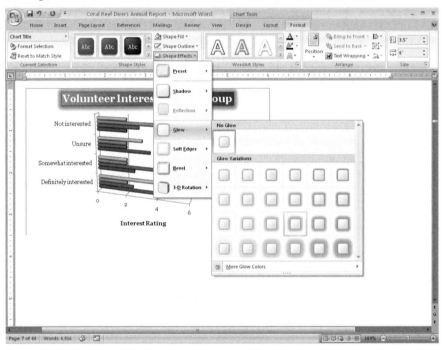

Figure 12-25 The Shape Effects gallery gives you options for dramatically changing the look of shapes in your chart.

What's Next?

This chapter showed you how the improved and expanded chart features in Word 2007 make it easy to create, modify, and enhance SmartArt diagrams and charts in your Word documents. The next chapter continues this creative focus by showing you how to make the most of Word's ability to add impact with pictures and objects. Additionally, you'll find out how to arrange art objects on the page—including your SmartArt diagrams and charts—to help give your document that finished, professional look.

CHAPTER 13

Adding Visual Impact with Pictures, Drawings, and WordArt

You've probably heard that pictures liven up your documents. That's true. You may also have heard that images help reinforce your message and give peoples' eyes a welcome rest. That's also true. But the real reason you'll want to enhance your Microsoft Office Word 2007 document by adding pictures, clip art, drawings, and more is that it's great fun and it adds life to your pages. No kidding—with literally a few clicks of the mouse, you can add, edit, and stylize images in your document in a huge variety of ways: adding shadows and frames, applying three-dimensional (3-D) styles, changing colors, angles, and much more. And once you get the picture looking just the way want you want it, it's an easy matter of flowing your text around it in such a way that your entire document looks great.

Of all the things you can do in Office Word 2007 to make your documents look inviting and professional, the features covered in this chapter are second only to the ability to add Themes (which, as you learned in Chapter 5, "Applying Themes for a Professional Look," enable you to stylize your entire document—heads, text, and more—with a single click of the mouse button). So have fun, experiment, and get creative!

Adding Art to Your Word Documents

Word 2007 simplifies the whole process of adding visual impact to your documents. When you click the Insert tab on the Ribbon, you'll find an Illustrations group containing all the tools you need to create various types of images. For example, you can add:

- Photos, logos, and more by using the Picture tool

- Clip art (including photos and media clips) by choosing Clip Art

- Shapes for quick drawings, simple diagrams, and more by clicking Shapes

This section shows you how to add illustrations to your document by using each of these Illustrations group tools. (To find out more about adding SmartArt diagrams to your document or creating custom charts to display data, see Chapter 12, "Showcasing Data with SmartArt and Charts.") Additionally, this section shows you how to put artistic touches on special text items by using WordArt (available in the Text group on the Insert tab).

Inserting Pictures

Perhaps the easiest way to add images to your document is to click the Picture tool in the Illustrations group of the Insert tab. The Insert Picture dialog box appears, enabling you to navigate to the folder storing the image you want to add. Select the picture and then click Insert to add it to your document.

INSIDE OUT   **Add multiple images**

You can add more than one picture at once by using the Insert Picture dialog box. Simply click the first image you want to add, and then press and hold Ctrl while you click additional images. When everything you want is selected, click Insert. Word then imports all selected images at once into the current document.

Using a Photo As a Page Background

You can turn a picture you like into a background for your Word document. Click the Page Layout tab. Then in the Background group, click Page Color. Choose Fill Effects from the list that appears.

In the Fill Effects dialog box, click the Picture tab. Then choose Select Picture and, in the Select Picture dialog box, choose the picture you want to use for your background. Click Insert to add the picture to the Fill Effects dialog box. Then click OK. The image is added to the background of your document. Note that if the image size is smaller than the length and width of your page, it will be repeated, or tiled, as needed to fill the space.

If you want to remove the picture, on the Page Layout tab, click Page Color, and then click No Color. The background picture is removed (because the new selection overrides any previous Page Color selection.

Adding Clip Art

You probably already know that Word includes a collection of clip art you can use in your own documents. You'll find all sorts of different topics represented, from animals to transportation to people and holidays. When you want to insert a piece of clip art in a document, click Clip Art in the Illustrations group. The Clip Art task pane appears along the right edge of the document window (see Figure 13-1).

Figure 13-1 Use the Clip Art task pane to find and add images that illustrate ideas in your document.

In the Clip Art task pane, type what you're looking for in the Search For box and then click Go. You don't need to know the name of a specific category—simply enter a word that describes the kinds of images you want to display; for example, sea. A selection of clips related to the word or phrase you entered appears in the task pane. Click the one you want, and Word adds it to your document.

Narrowing Your Art Search

By default, the Clip Art task pane searches for clip art—cartoon-like drawings that relate to the word or phrase you entered. You can find other types of art in the Clip Art task pane as well—photographs, movies, and even sounds. And Word makes it easy for you to search for a specific format if you need a particular file type for your document. For example, suppose that you need to find the best photographs you can locate in a JPEG format, to be used in an annual report. You can narrow your search so that only JPEG images related to sea are displayed, which makes finding what you need much easier. Here's how to do it:

1. Click Clip Art in the Illustrations group of the Insert tab. The Clip Art task pane appears.

2. In the Search For box, enter a word or phrase that describes the types of images you'd like to see.

3. Click the Results Should Be arrow to display the list of media types.

4. Click the expand button to the left of Photographs to see the available choices.

5. Click the check box to the left of JPEG File Interchange Format (see Figure 13-2).

Figure 13-2 Limit your search to a specific format or topic to maximize your results.

6. Click Go.

The Clip Art task pane displays only JPEG photos that reflect the topic you entered at the top of the pane.

Searching for Clips Online

Microsoft Office Online now offers more than 150,000 clips—including art, music, and video. The whole process of adding clip art to your Word documents has been streamlined so that now you can copy the clip directly to your Office Clipboard. (Previously, you needed to download the art to your Clip Art folder and then use it—now you can just copy it, plug it into your document, and go.)

Office Online includes a large, colorful, and varied collection of art for all kinds and styles of documents. Every day a new Clip Art of the Day is posted, and—to get a sense of what's popular—you can see what other people are downloading and adding to their documents .

You can go directly to Office Online in search of clip art whenever the Clip Art task pane is open on your screen. Just click the Clip Art On Office Online link, located at the bottom of the task pane. This takes you right to the Clip Art page of Office Online, where you can search for, select, and copy the images and media clips that are right for your document.

Manage Your Images and Media Clips

The Microsoft Clip Organizer enables you to keep all your image, sound, and motion files in one place, arranged according to category. To start the Microsoft Clip Organizer, click the Organize Clips link at the bottom of the Clip Art task pane. To choose a clip from the Microsoft Clip Organizer, simply navigate to the clip you want and select it in the view window. Here's a quick look at some of the tasks you may want to use the Clip Organizer to accomplish:

- Save your favorite images and media clips by dragging the item to your Favorites folder.

- Add your own images to the Clip Organizer by selecting Add Clips To Organizer from the File menu and clicking Automatically.

- Create a new collection in the Clip Organizer by choosing New Collection in the File menu. You can then name the collection and add your own clips.

- Review the properties of a specific image or media clip by selecting the item and then choosing Preview/Properties from the clip's context menu.

- Add or edit clip keywords by selecting the clip and choosing Edit Keywords. Use the Add, Modify, or Delete buttons to change the keywords as needed.

- Remove clips you no longer need by deleting them from the existing category or deleting them from the Clip Organizer. Select the clip and choose the Delete option that reflects the type of deletion you want.

Adding Shapes and Lines

If you are familiar with the drawing tools in Word 2003, you may wonder where they went in Word 2007. Now your favorite drawing tools are included with Shapes in the Illustrations group of the Insert tab. When you want to draw any configuration of shapes or lines, you'll begin with the Shapes tool. Click Shapes, and a gallery full of shapes and lines appears (see Figure 13-3).

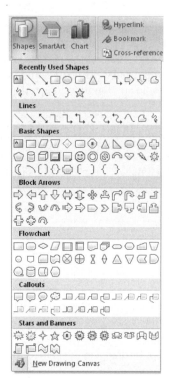

Figure 13-3 The Shapes gallery gives you a big selection of shapes and tools to use.

To draw a shape or line, simply click the tool you want and use the pointer to draw the object on the screen. If you plan to use multiple shapes and lines—perhaps to create a simple diagram or flowchart—working on the drawing canvas helps you keep all items together and work with them as a group. Using the drawing canvas is optional, however—you can choose to simply draw the shapes and lines directly on the document page. The next section gives you more detail on using the drawing canvas when you're working with shapes.

Working with the Drawing Canvas

You'll find the New Drawing Canvas option at the bottom of the Shapes gallery. Although it's not required that you use a drawing canvas to create all your drawings and shapes, the drawing canvas does make it easier when you need to draw and work with multiple shapes in one area. When a drawing's shapes are contained in a drawing canvas, you can move and resize the drawing as a unit as well as position the drawing relative to surrounding text and graphics.

When you choose New Drawing Canvas from the Shapes gallery, a new canvas appears, displaying a framelike boundary. You can drag the sides and corners to resize the canvas as needed. Although the drawing canvas doesn't have borders or background formatting, you can add formatting features to the drawing canvas just as you can customize any other drawing object. You might want to add color and shading, resize the frame, or add 3-D effects.

Using the Drawing Grid

When you're using shapes and lines, the drawing grid is another tool that can be helpful by enabling you to align items in the drawing as you create them. The drawing grid is available whether you're using the drawing canvas or not.

To display the drawing grid, click the View tab and click Gridlines in the Show/Hide group. A grid appears on the work area of your document, as Figure 13-4 shows. Notice that the margins of the document are left blank.

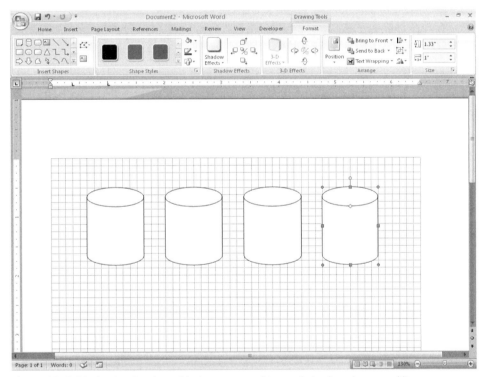

Figure 13-4 Display the drawing grid when you need to precisely align shapes and lines.

Now when you draw a shape or line, the object automatically snaps to a line on the grid. If you are displaying inches as your unit of measurement, the gridlines appear at intervals of 1/8 of an inch. If your unit of measurement is set to centimeters, the grid marks off 1/3 of a centimeter with each block. And if you are using picas, each grid block is equal to 1/8 of a pica.

To change the unit of measurement displayed in the grid, click the Microsoft Office button and choose Word Options. Click the Advanced tab and scroll down to the Display options. Click the Show Measurements in Units Of arrow and choose the measurement setting you prefer. You can choose from Inches, Centimeters, Millimeters, Points, and Picas.

> **Tip**
>
> If you want to position an object in such a way that it doesn't conform to the grid (even though the grid is still enabled), click the shape and hold the mouse button down for a moment; then press Alt and drag the shape or line to the position where you want it to appear. When you release the mouse button, the object will remain where you placed it, whether or not it is aligned with the grid.

Adding WordArt

When used inventively (and sparingly), WordArt can add a little life to your documents by providing color and depth to special text items. WordArt is available in the Text group of the Insert tab. When you click WordArt, a gallery of WordArt styles appears (see Figure 13-5).

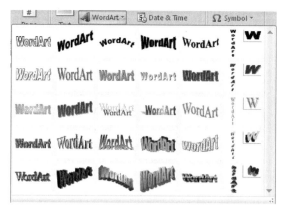

Figure 13-5 The WordArt gallery offers a number of ways to spruce up special text.

To add a WordArt object to your document, follow these steps:

1. Click in your document where you want the WordArt to appear.

2. Click WordArt in the Text group of the Insert tab. The WordArt gallery appears.

3. Click the WordArt style you want to use.

4. In the Edit WordArt dialog box, type the text you want to use. If you want to change the font and style attributes, you can also do that in this step (this is also something you can change easily later).

5. Click OK to save your settings. The WordArt object appears in your document.

> **Tip**
> If you want to convert existing text into a WordArt object, select the text before you click WordArt in the Text group. The selected text will appear automatically in the Text box in the Edit WordArt Text dialog box.

Enhancing Pictures

Now that you know how to add various visual elements to your document, this section shows you how to use the editing and enhancement tools in Word to put a professional polish on them. Whether you want to do simple tasks like correct lighting problems or crop out unnecessary elements--or stylize the images by adding shadows, frames, and more--this is where the fun of working with images in Word really begins. We'll start with the Picture Styles because they give you the most dramatic enhancements for the smallest amount of effort.

Applying Picture Styles to Your Images

Picture styles work similarly to the other quick styles you'll find in strategic places throughout Word. When you select a picture in your document, the contextual Picture Tools become available on the Ribbon. The Picture Styles have their own group in the middle of the Format tab.

The Picture Style gallery shows the various styles you can apply to the selected image. You can display the entire selection of styles by clicking the More button in the lower right corner of the gallery (see Figure 13-6). Preview the various styles by positioning the mouse pointer over an item in the gallery; when you find one you want to use, click the mouse to select the picture style.

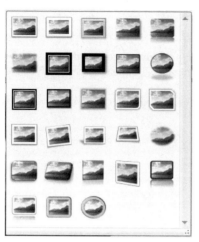

Figure 13-6 The Picture Styles gallery provides you with many different ways to display an image.

Adding a Picture Shape

If you want to create a unique effect, you can apply a shape to the picture so that the image appears within the body of the shape. You might do this, for example, when you want a picture to pop off the page and catch the reader's attention (see Figure 13-7). To add the shape to the selected image, click Picture Shape and choose the shape you want to apply from the palette that appears.

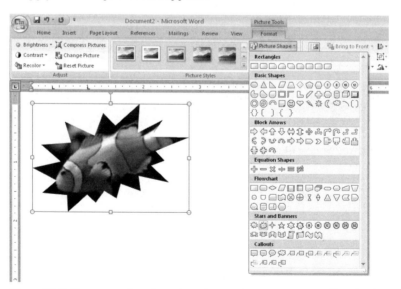

Figure 13-7 You can apply a shape to a picture to create a cut-out effect for the image.

Displaying a Picture Border

When you click Picture Border in the Picture Styles group, a color palette appears, enabling you to choose the color of the border you want to apply, as well as the weight and style of the line used to create the border. The top portion of the palette lists the colors that match the Theme that is currently applied to your document; the Standard Colors area of the palette provides primary colors. If you want to choose a color that does not appear in the palette, click More Outline Colors and then select the color from either the Standard or Custom tab. To apply it to the selected picture, click OK after you choose the color.

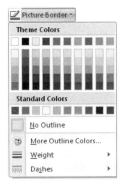

Adding a Picture Effect

Picture effects give you a huge range of special formats you can apply to the selected picture. You can choose from among a variety of shadow styles, apply a glow to the outer edges, display a reflection of the image, soften the edges, create a beveled effect, and apply 3-D effects and rotation.

To apply a picture effect, select the picture and then click Picture Effects in the Picture Styles group. A palette of choices appears. Point to the effects category you want to apply (Preset, Shadow, Reflection, Glow, Soft Edges, Bevel, and 3-D Rotation). A palette of effects opens to display your choice. Use Live Preview to see how the different effects will appear in your document (see Figure 13-8).

Figure 13-8 Use Picture Effects to enhance your pictures by adding shadows, bevel effects, 3-D effects, and more.

Editing and Adjusting Images

Word includes a number of image adjustment tools you can use to bring out the best in your images. You'll find the whole set located in the Adjustment group of the contextual Picture Tools. To display the tools, click on the picture you want to change. The Picture Tools appear on the Ribbon. The Format tab is automatically selected.

The Adjustment group is located on the far left. Depending on the type of change you want to make to your picture, click one of the following tools:

- **Brightness** Changes the amount of light included in an image. When you click Brightness, a palette of brightness options appears, with values ranging from +40% to -40%. You can use the Live Preview feature to point to a setting and see how it will affect the selected image. When you find a brightness level you like, click it to apply it to the image.

- **Contrast** Controls the way in which items in your picture are defined. When you click Contrast, a palette of contrast options appears. Experiment with the different settings until you find the one that looks right in your picture.

- **Recolor** Enables you to apply a color wash to your picture that may give it an old-fashioned feel (like a sepia-toned image) or enable it to blend naturally with the color scheme in the Theme applied your document. When you click Recolor, a palette appears offering you a number of different color possibilities (see Figure 13-9). Again, point to the ones you're considering, and Live Preview will show you the results. Click the one you decide on, and it is applied to the image in the document.

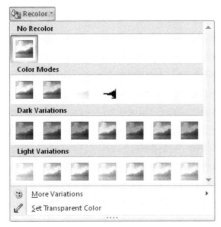

Figure 13-9 Use Recolor Picture in the Adjust group to add a color wash to the image in your document.

- **Compress Pictures** Reduces the file size of the image (not the actual size of the image in the document) so that when you save the file, it will be as compact as possible. When Word displays the Compress Pictures dialog box, click OK to compress all images in the document. If you want to compress only the selected images, click the Apply To Selected Pictures Only check box before you click OK.

> **Tip**
>
> Click Options in the Compress Pictures dialog box to display additional choices for compression. In the Compression Settings dialog box, you can choose to compress images on save, delete image areas that have been cropped, or specify the type of compression you want depending on the desired output for your document (screen, print, or e-mail).

- **Change Picture** Displays the Insert Picture dialog box so that you can replace the selected photo with a new one.

- **Reset Picture** Reverses any modifications you've made to the original photo and returns it to its original size, shape, and coloring.

Cropping Pictures

Cropping images is a simple process, but it can dramatically improve the look of your photo by enabling you to remove unnecessary elements from the image. For example, suppose that a diver's swim fin appears in the corner of an underwater photo you want to use for the Coral Reef Divers annual report. You can easily crop the photo to remove the unwanted fin and help your readers focus on the important part of the photo.

To crop your photo, follow these steps:

1. Insert the photo in your document and make sure it is selected. The Picture Tools appears.

2. Click Crop in the Size group. The pointer changes to a cropping tool.

3. Position the tool on the edge or corner of the image where you want to begin cropping. Drag the side or corner of the image inward until the portion of the picture you want to remove has been cropped out (see Figure 13-10).

Figure 13-10 Crop a photo to make sure only the best part of the image is displayed.

Tip

When you crop a photo, the rest of the image isn't gone; its display is merely suppressed. This means that if you decide to move the photo to another part of the document and redisplay the hidden part of the image, you can do that. Just select the Crop tool again and this time drag the corner or side outward to reveal the rest of the hidden image. Note, however, that if you have selected the Delete Cropped Areas Of Pictures check box in the Compression Settings dialog box, the cropped portions of the image will be deleted when you save the document.

Resizing Pictures

An operation that goes hand-in-hand with cropping is resizing the images you import. This is one technique you'll use all the time—pictures rarely come into your documents at just the right size.

Resizing a picture in Word is similar to resizing any object. To begin, click the image. Handles appear around the edges of the object. If you want to enlarge the image, click in one corner of the picture and drag the handle outward. When the image is the size you want, release the mouse button.

If resizing your picture to a precise measurement is important, use the Size command available in the picture's options. Here's how:

1. Right-click the image in your document.

2. Choose Size from the options that appear.

3. In the Size dialog box, enter the Height and Width settings (see Figure 13-11). Additionally, you can enter other positioning values, such as Rotation and Cropping.

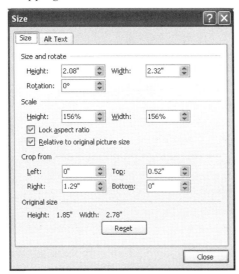

Figure 13-11 Use the Size dialog box when entering a specific size for an image is important.

4. Click OK to save your settings, and Word resizes the image according to your specifications.

Rotating Pictures

Some of your documents are likely to be fairly straightforward and won't require a lot of special picture techniques. But once in a while you will have a reason to do something fun like rotating pictures. The rotating control in Word enables you to simply drag a picture in the direction you want to rotate it—very simple and easy to use. Instead of moving the image in predesigned increments, the Rotate tool lets you be in control of how far you want the picture to rotate.

Start by clicking the picture in your document. You'll notice that a round green handle appears in the top center of your image. This is the rotate handle. Position the mouse on that handle. The pointer changes to a curved arrow, indicating that you can drag the handle in the direction you want to rotate the image.

> **Tip**
> When you apply shadows or frames or other special picture effects to the image, Word automatically takes the angle into account, with no calculating required. Nice.

Adding Captions to Pictures

Readers like to know what your images contain, so unless you're certain that readers will understand what your images are showing, you may want to consider adding figure captions. The process is simple, and you can control the look and placement of the text by following these steps:

1. Right-click the picture you want to add the caption to.

2. Click Insert Caption. The Caption dialog box appears, as Figure 13-12 shows.

Figure 13-12 You can easily add captions to the images in your document by right-clicking a picture and choosing Insert Caption.

3. In the top text box, type the caption you want to appear with the figure. You may want to customize the look of the caption by changing one of the following items:

   ❑ If you want to hide the label (for example, Figure), click the Exclude Label From Caption check box.

   ❑ If you want to change the way in which the captions are numbered, click the Numbering button and select your choice.

4. Click OK to save the caption settings and return to the document.

The caption is displayed in a color, font, size, and style that is controlled by the Theme selected for your document. If you change the Theme later (by clicking the Page Layout tab, selecting Themes, and choosing a new Theme from the gallery), the captions will be reformatted automatically.

If you prefer to change the format of the captions, you can do so by clicking the Home tab and choosing new settings from your choices in the Font group. Remember, however, that once you change the captions from a Theme-supported style, you'll have to reformat them automatically if you ever apply a new Theme.

Modifying Drawings

In the preceding section, you learned how to change and enhance the pictures you include in your document. This section focuses on drawings—the shapes and lines you add to help illustrate concepts in your text. Pictures and shapes share some similar techniques because they are both art objects. In that sense, anything you can do to a picture object—move, copy, resize, rotate, or delete—you can also do with a shape or line.

But shapes and lines have some peculiarities that pictures don't have. For example, although you can recolor a picture by changing the overall color wash or mode assigned to it, you cannot actually change the picture itself. When you create a shape, on the other hand, you can choose from a wide range of color options to fill the shape with color—you can blend colors, make them transparent, choose gradients, even fill them with textures. And what's more, you can add text directly into the shapes so that they are more than just a pretty, they are functional too.

Applying Shape Styles

When you first add a shape to your document, it may not look like much—perhaps just a simple black outline on a white page. You can change that dramatically with a click of the mouse.

Select the shape or shapes, and the contextual Drawing Tools appears on the Ribbon. Click one of the selections in the Shape Styles palette or click the More button in the lower right corner of the gallery to display the entire collection. Then click the style you want to apply to the shape. Suddenly it takes on depth, color, and in some cases, lighting qualities (see Figure 13-13).

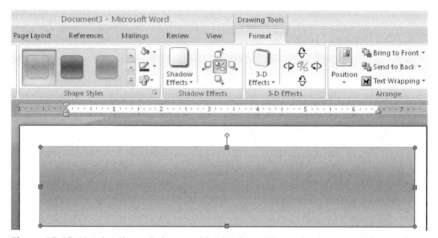

Figure 13-13 Use the Shape Styles to add color, line style, and perspective to your shapes.

> **Note**
>
> Similar to Picture Styles, some of the settings in the Shape Styles are controlled by the Theme currently selected for your document. For example, the colors shown in the Shape Styles gallery correspond to the overall colors used in the Theme currently in use.

Adding and Formatting Shape Text

Adding text to shapes is also simple to do. Right-click the shape you want to include the text and then choose Add Text (see Figure 13-14). The cursor is positioned in the shape. Type the text you want to appear in the shape. Notice that the text reformats automatically to accommodate the amount of room in the shape.

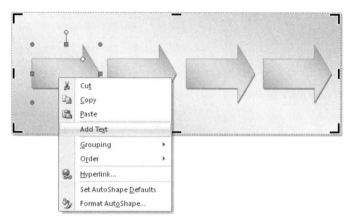

Figure 13-14 Choose Add Text to position the cursor inside the shape.

If you want to reformat the text inside the shape, simply highlight the text and choose the formatting you want from the Mini Toolbar that appears above the selected text (see Figure 13-15). For best results, keep the text items short and easy to understand.

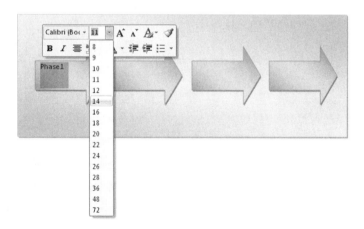

Figure 13-15 Change the format of shape text by using the Mini Ttoolbar that appears above the added text.

Modifying Lines and Fills

A shape you create in Word has two main areas: the borders (called the shape out*line*) and the interior (called the shape *fill*). The Shape Fill and Shape Outline tools in the Styles group of the Drawing Tools palette, just to the right of the Shape Styles gallery, enable you to choose different settings for the display of those items.

Changing the Shape Fill

You can be really creative with the interior of the shapes you add to Word, displaying them in wild colors (or better yet, colors that correspond to your logo or letterhead), adding special textures, even inserting pictures. Follow these steps to enhance the interior of your shapes:

1. Click the shape you want to change.

2. Click Shape Fill arrow in the Styles group of the Drawing Tools.

3. From the list that appears, choose the type of effect you'd like to apply. Figure 13-16 shows the gallery that appears when you choose Textures. Table 13-1 describes what each of the choices in the Shape Fill list enables you to do.

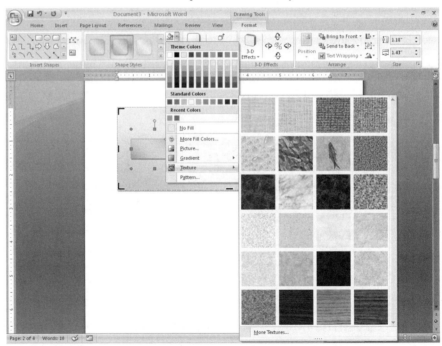

Figure 13-16 The Shape Fill gallery provides you with a wide range of choices for formatting the shapes in your document.

4. Click your choice, and the format is applied to the shape.

Table 13-1 Shape Fill Options

Choose	When you want to
A color	Fill the shape with a color you select
No Fill	Display no fill color or pattern in the shape
More Fill Colors	Choose a color other than the ones shown in the Theme Colors and Standard Colors areas of the palette
Picture	Fill the shape with a photo or other image
Gradient	Give the shape lighting effects and perspective
Texture	Add a textured appearance—such as sand, wood, metal, or fabric—to the selected shape
Pattern	Apply a pattern in the current color to the surface of the shape

Choosing a Custom Color

When you click More Colors, the Custom Colors dialog box appears, enabling you to choose a specific hue. You can choose a color either by using the crosshair or the slider bar to the right of the display area. Beneath the display area, you see Red, Green, and Blue value boxes that reflect the color values indicated by the crosshair and slider bar. The Red, Green, and Blue value boxes specify exact RGB color values for graphics. If you know the RGB values of a specific color you want to use, you can enter those values in the appropriate boxes, or you can click the up and down arrows to scroll through values. Click OK to save your choice.

Making Shapes Transparent

When you click More Fill Colors, the Custom tab of the Colors dialog box appears. At the bottom of the tab, you see a Transparency slider. You can use the Transparency option to enable another shape, text, image, chart, or page background to be visible through the shape.

By default, a shape is set to 0% transparency when it is created. To increase the transparency, simply drag the slider to the right. When transparency is set to 100%, the background object will be completely visible through the shape. For most purposes, using a setting of 50 to 60% enables you to see the image behind the shape without losing sight of the shape itself.

Formatting Shadows and 3-D Effects

In addition to adding textures and colors, you can apply shadow and three-dimensional (3-D) effects to your shapes and lines in Word 2007. Although some shadow and 3-D effects are available in the previous version of Word, these features have been dramatically improved in Word 2007. Now you have a whole collection of options at your disposal for tailoring your shapes and lines to get just the look you want.

Adding and Controlling Shadows

You can instantly add depth to your drawings in Word by adding a shadow to the edge of an object. The Shadow Effects group in Word enables you to add various shadow styles to objects, adjust shadow position, and change shadow color.

To add a shadow effect to a shape, begin by clicking the shape you want to add a shadow to and then click the Shadow Effects arrow. A gallery of shadow styles appears (see Figure 13-17). Click the style you want to apply.

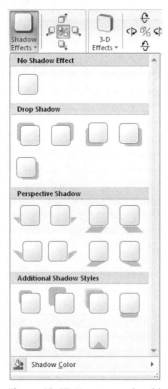

Figure 13-17 You can easily add depth to a shape in your document by adding a shadow effect.

If you later want to remove the shadow, click the shape and choose Shadow Effects again. This time click No Shadow Effect, at the top of the gallery.

Changing the Position of Shadows

After you apply a shadow, you can manually adjust the shadow's position relative to the object. Word includes a great tool in the Shadow Effects group that makes this simple to do.

The Shadow Effects control on the right side of the group enables you to fine-tune the way the shadow is positioned related to the shape. The item in the center works as a toggle: Click it once to turn off the shadow and click it a second time to redisplay the shadow. Each of the four tools—above, below, and to the left and right of the center tool—nudge the shadow in the direction of the tool (up, down, left, and right, respectively). If you have struggled with shadows that don't look quite right in previous versions of Word, you will love the flexibility this little item adds.

> **Tip**
>
> To nudge a shadow in larger increments, press and hold Shift while clicking the nudge tool you want to use.

Coloring Shadows

In addition to adjusting a shadow's position, you can also color a shadow. To do so, follow these steps:

1. Select the shape with the shadow you want to change.

2. Click the Shadow Effects arrow. The Shadow Effects list appears.

3. Point to Shadow Color. A color palette appears, showing Theme Colors, Standard Colors, and Recent Colors.

4. Click the color you want to use for the shadow, or click More Shadow Colors to display the Colors dialog box (then select the color and choose OK to apply it).

The Shadow Colors palette also includes a Semitransparent Shadow option. This option is selected by default so that the shadow added to shapes and objects is somewhat transparent, giving it a more realistic look than a solid color would provide. If you want a more dramatic shadow, you can remove the check mark by clicking Semitransparent Shadow.

INSIDE OUT **My document includes color images, but I want them to print in black and white**

You can accomplish print images in black and white two different ways: by recoloring the images or by changing your print settings. To recolor the images, select all images in the document that you want to change and click Recolor in the Adjust group. Click Grayscale in the Color Modes area of the Recolor gallery. To change print settings, display the Print dialog box and click Properties. On the Paper/Quality tab, choose Black & White in the Color area. Click OK twice to save your setting and return to the document. Now your entire document will be printed in black and white.

Applying and Customizing 3-D Effects

You might wonder what else is involved in making a shape appear three-dimensional. Shadows seem to be the most important characteristic, right? Word 2007 includes additional formatting choices you can use to make the shape appear even more realistic on the page. For example, you can set the depth and height of an object, apply a special surface covering like metal or plastic, and choose the way in which you want the light to reflect off the shape's surface.

Adding 3-D Effects

To add 3-D effects to the shapes in your document, you will use (not surprisingly) the 3-D Effects group in the Drawing Tools. When you click the 3-D Effects arrow, a gallery of 3-D styles appears, giving you choices related to the positioning and perspective of the shape (see Figure 13-18). Position the pointer over an item to preview how it will look in the document. When you find the one you like, click it to select it.

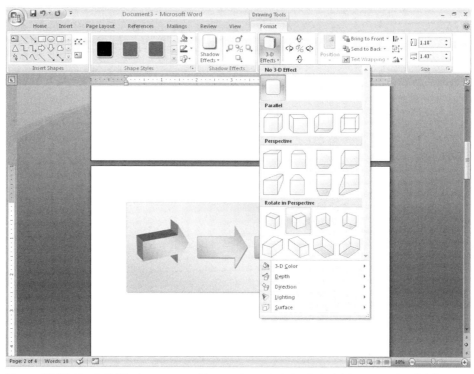

Figure 13-18 The 3-D Effects group enables you to control depth, height, perspective, lighting, and more.

Controlling Light, Color, Angle, and Other Settings

After you apply a 3-D style to an object, you can change the 3-D style's appearance, including its color, depth, direction, lighting, and surface. To modify an object's 3-D effects, you select the object, click the 3-D Effects arrow, and then choose the item that corresponds to the setting you want to change (see Figure 13-19). Table 13-2 presents the choices available in the 3-D Settings gallery.

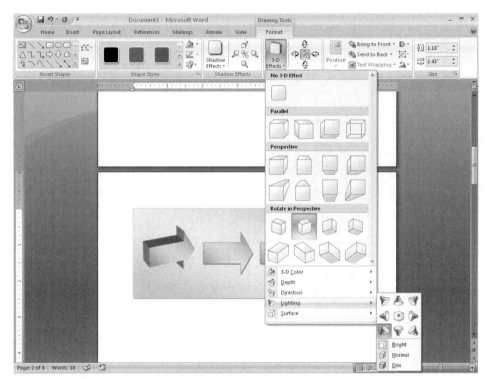

Figure 13-19 Control a shape's lighting, color, surface, and more by using 3-D Effects.

Table 13-2 Understanding 3-D Effects

Choose	When you want to
3-D Color	Change the color of the 3-D portion of the shape
Depth	Modify the depth of the 3-D shape
Direction	Change the perspective from which the shape is viewed
Lighting	Cause the lighting to come from a different direction
Surface	Display the surface of the shape to resemble metal, plastic, matte, or wire frame

Adjusting 3-D Angle

The 3-D Effects group includes a tilt tool that enables you to fine-tune the angle at which the 3-D shape is displayed. Similar to the nudge tool in the Shadow Effects group, this tool is actually a set of five tools. The item in the center is a toggle that turns the 3-D settings on and off. Each of the tools—above, below, left, and right—causes the shape to be tilted in the corresponding direction. Experiment with the tools to get just the right look for the position of 3-D shapes in your document.

INSIDE OUT   I want to add text to freehand drawings

When you create a freehand drawing, you can't right-click the drawing and choose Add Text. To work around this limitation, you can click Text Box in the Text group on the Insert tab and then draw a text box on top of your freehand drawing. Then type and format text in the text box. If you want to ensure that the text and drawing aren't separated or layered incorrectly in the future, choose the shape and the text box (by pressing Shift as you click the objects), and then click Group in the Arrange group on the Ribbon.

Arranging Art on the Page

Now that you know how to add and enhance pictures as well as how to create and modify drawings, the final step of working with art in your document involves arranging objects on the page so that everything flows together well. To accomplish this, you need know how to group and ungroup objects, handle object layering, and set up text flow the way you want it.

Aligning Objects

When you have a number of objects in your document, arranging them so that they fit together well is a big part of making sure your document looks as good as possible. If you've created a drawing that includes a number of shapes and lines, or you've added special elements to offset WordArt titles, or you want to ensure two photos line up on the page, you can use the Align tool in the Arrange group to put things in their proper order.

Here are the steps for aligning objects on your page:

1. Select the objects you want to align by pressing and holding Shift while clicking the objects.

2. Click Align in the Arrange group on the Ribbon. A list of Align choices appears (see Figure 13-20).

Figure 13-20 Choose Align to ensure that objects on your page line up.

3. Point to the choice you want to preview in your document and then click to select it. All selected items are aligned according to your choice.

TROUBLESHOOTING

I can't select multiple objects

If you press Shift and click items in your document and they don't select, most likely the Text Wrapping setting for the items you're trying to select is still set to In Line With Text. To make the object available for selection and alignment, choose Text Wrapping (in the Arrange group) and select In Front Of Text.

> **Note**
>
> You can't select pictures and shapes at the same time; and if the picture is a bitmap, you can't select it with other objects. The workaround for this problem is to place all of the objects in a drawing canvas.

Note

If you have the Snap Objects To Grid feature turned on while you work on the drawing grid, you can override the feature by pressing Alt while you drag an object.

Distributing vs. Aligning

When would you want to distribute, as opposed to align, the objects on your page? When you are working with multiple objects in a shared space, you can use Distribute to arrange the objects so that they are evenly spaced. Here are a few guidelines for using Distribute to arrange objects on your page:

- Distribute Horizontally and Distribute Vertically are available only when you have selected three or more objects.

- Distributing objects spaces them evenly between the top and bottom margins or the left and right margins. If you want to lessen the amount of space between objects, you can increase the size of the objects or increase the margins for the selected page.

- By default, the objects you select are distributed relative to each other. To distribute objects relative to the drawing canvas instead, select the items and then choose Align to Canvas.

Grouping and Ungrouping Objects

All art objects you add to your document—pictures, shapes, lines, and WordArt—are individual objects in their own right. If you create a drawing by using a variety of art elements (whether you use a drawing canvas or not), being able to combine those elements into a single group enables you to move, copy, and modify all items at once.

You may also group objects to ensure that certain objects stay together no matter what. Grouping also comes in handy when you want to make sure that layered objects don't inadvertently become incorrectly layered. You can ungroup grouped items at any time, which means that you can edit any part of a grouped object whenever necessary.

To group objects, begin by arranging the objects where you want them to appear in the document. Then select the objects you want to group (by pressing Shift and clicking each object you want to include). Next click Group in the Arrange group in the Drawing Tools. The multiple handles that surrounded each item now disappear, and one set of handles appears for the entire group. You can move, copy, and resize the group as needed.

If you want to make a change to any object in the group, you'll need to ungroup it before you can work with it. To ungroup objects, select the group and click Ungroup in the Arrange group on the Ribbon.

Controlling Object Layering

When you create a drawing that contains many objects, you'll need to control which objects are layered in front of and behind other objects. Paying attention to how objects are layered can save you from inadvertently hiding parts of your drawings that should be visible.

Put your objects in the right order on the page by selecting an object and clicking either Bring To Front or Send To Back in the Arrange group. Clicking the item itself performs the action—in other words, when you click Bring To Front, the selected object moves to the front of any other objects at that point on the page.

Both the Bring To Front and Send To Back tools have their own sets of options, however. Click the arrow to the left of each selection to see how you can further qualify the selection. Depending on the number of objects you have layered in your drawing, you may want to move the object in front of text, bring it forward one level, or send it backward behind another object. Experiment with these choices to get a feel for them. You will use these tools often if you do a lot of drawing in Word.

> **Tip**
>
> If you're having trouble selecting an object, it may be positioned behind another object on the page. Press Tab to cycle through the selected objects until the handles of the object you want are displayed, indicating that it is selected.

Choosing Art Position

Depending on how many pictures, drawings, and WordArt objects you will be using on your pages, you may want some kind of method of positioning your object that doesn't require clicking and dragging or aligning and distributing. The Position tool in the Arrange group enables you to select the position on the page where you want your images to appear, and then text automatically flows around it. Here's how to easily position an image in your document:

1. Select the image you want to position.

2. Click Position in the Arrange group. A gallery of position options appears.

3. Click the position you want to use for the current page.

Now as you add headlines, text, and other objects to the page, the image will be placed in the position you indicated. If you want to fine-tune your selection of the image position, click More Layout Options at the bottom of the Position gallery to display the Advanced Layout dialog box. There you can specify your choices related to the horizontal alignment, vertical alignment, and position of the object, as well as the way in which it relates to surrounding text.

Controlling Text Wrapping

If the Position tool helps you determine how the image relates to the entire page (and it does), the Text Wrapping tool enables you to determine the relationship between your art and your text. When you choose a Text Wrapping option, you are telling Word how you want the text to flow around (or through or behind) the image you have added. This is a simple and flexible feature that gives you a number of creative ways to create and enhance the layout of your page. Here's how to do it:

1. Click the image you want to use.

2. In the Arrange group on the Ribbon, click the Text Wrapping arrow. A list of Text Wrapping options appears. By default, In Line With Text is selected, which means that the image is treated like text and will move with the paragraph as you add text to the document.

3. Select the Text Wrapping choice that you want to apply to the selected image. The selection is applied to the image, and the text reflows accordingly. Table 13-3 describes each of the choices in more detail.

Table 13-3 Text Wrapping Choices

Choose	When you want to
In Line With Text	Keep the image in line with the text so that it moves along with the current paragraph (this is selected by default).
Square	Wrap the text to the left and right of the image.
Tight	Flow the text right up to the edge of the selected object with no outer margin of white space.
Behind Text	Flow the text over the image.
In Front Of Text	Display the text behind the image.
Top And Bottom	Flow the text above and below—but not through—the image. Text does not appear on the sides of the image; this is left blank
Through	Flow text up to the border of your picture (you can use this with Edit Wrap Points to create a special text flow for your pages).
Edit Wrap Points	Create a new boundary for your image that enables you to design the way the text wraps around it.

TROUBLESHOOTING

My images are only displaying halfway

If the image is not displaying completely, check your Text Wrapping settings. Display the Text Wrapping choices (in the Arrange group) and click Top And Bottom or In Front Of Text. If the image still doesn't display properly, check with the manufacturer of your graphics card to see whether an updated driver is available.

Adding and Editing Wrap Points

Most of the Text Wrapping choices are self-explanatory; you can see what they do by experimenting with them in your document. But one item is worth further exploration because it can enable you to create sophisticated layouts easily.

You can use the Edit Wrap Points choice in the Text Wrapping list to create your own boundary for text flow in your document. You do this by simply dragging one of the edit points into a position that shows the text where to flow. Here's how it's done:

1. Select the image you want to use.

2. Click Text Wrapping in the Arrange group and make sure either Tight or Through is the choice selected. (If you choose any other wrapping style, Edit Wrap Points will not be available.)

3. Choose Edit Wrap Points. A red dashed boundary with several black handles appears around your image.

4. Click one of the handles and drag it to create the boundary you want to set for the text flow (see Figure 13-21). The line stays where you put it.

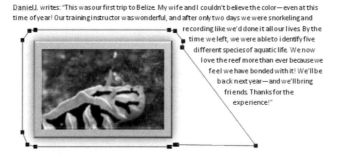

Figure 13-21 You can create your own Edit Wrap Points to customize the text flow on your page.

5. To create another handle (you aren't limited to following the shape of the image—you can stretch and add edit points any place you choose), simply click in the boundary line and drag it out to the point at which you want it. This creates another handle at that point and establishes the boundary where you put it.

What's Next?

This chapter introduced you to all things art—now you know how to add, enhance, and arrange pictures, clip art, shapes, and WordArt. The next chapter takes you into the realm of text formatting by showing you a variety of ways to create professional and effective paragraphs and lists.

PART 4

Professional Polish: Lists, Styles, Backgrounds, and Borders

Aligning Information and Formatting Paragraphs and Lists

Professional-looking documents rely on accurate content alignment and styling—no matter how avant-garde a document's layout happens to be. Typesetters and layout artists have long recognized that effectively aligning page elements plays a large role in increasing a document's readability and keeping the reader's eye on the page. Even people untrained in design can quickly see that "something's wrong" when they view a page that's been slapped together without regard to formatting and alignment. Therefore, when you work in Microsoft Office Word 2007, you should give serious thought to formatting and aligning document elements. If you learn to use Office Word 2007 formatting and alignment tools effectively—maybe even automatically—you'll be able to seamlessly integrate design tasks throughout the document creation process.

In this chapter, we look at formatting and alignment commands associated with a single type of element: *paragraphs*. And because a list falls into the category of paragraph formatting, we cover lists here as well. Now, paragraph formatting and alignment isn't as narrow a topic as it might sound at first. If you have used Word in the past, you probably know that Word addresses document formatting and layout on three levels: character, paragraph, and section. Character formatting includes applying font styles and attributes (as discussed in Chapter 6, "Mastering Document Fundamentals," and Chapter 15, "Using Styles to Increase Your Formatting Power"). At the other end of the formatting spectrum, section formatting options control margins, headers, footers, gutters, and other page setup configurations (as covered in Chapter 3, "Mastering Page Setup and Pagination"). Paragraph formatting represents the middle ground of document formatting and alignment. Clearly, paragraph formatting isn't as narrowly focused as character formatting tasks, and they aren't as encompassing as section setup commands. But don't let paragraph formatting's midlevel classification fool you—working with paragraphs is one of the most fundamental and essential skills you need to master to use Word effectively.

Paragraphs in Word Documents—More than Thematic Blocks of Text

When you think of the word *paragraph*, is a block of text the first thing that comes to mind? Actually, the paragraph mark at the end of a paragraph is the primary component of a paragraph—the text contained in the paragraph is secondary. It's the paragraph mark (¶) that holds paragraph formatting, such as the style, alignment, and indents. When it comes to formatting and editing documents, the more you understand the role of the paragraph mark the more control you will have over your Word documents.

Each time you press Enter after a character, heading, graphic, table, chart, list item, or any other element. If you press Enter to create a blank "line" between paragraphs, you insert a paragraph mark and create what is considered an empty paragraph because it does not contain text or another element. You can display paragraph marks (along with other hidden text) in your documents by clicking Show/ Hide on the Home tab, in the Paragraph group, shown here.

Figure 14-1 illustrates the concept of various paragraph elements in Word. Notice the paragraph mark after each bulleted list item, each paragraph of text (including the text box), each heading, and the empty paragraph.

·Executive Summary¶

While much progress remains to be made, we have had a stellar year! ¶

First and foremost, I once again commend the outstanding dedication of our volunteers, researchers, educators, business partners, and private entities for their work in helping to restore nature's balance in the world's coral reefs. As you know, coral reefs play a major role in the Earth's health, and all too often, they receive too little attention.¶

¶

·Programs¶

• → Dive Watch¶
• → Erosion Awareness¶
• → Promoting Eco-Friendly Tourism¶

"A five-foot sea lion peers intently into your face, then urges her muzzle gently against your underwater mask and searches your eyes without blinking...You are, I believe, supposed to follow, and think up something clever in return."¶

– Annie Dillard, ¶
Teaching a Stone to Talk¶

Figure 14-1 In Word, any content followed by a paragraph mark is considered a paragraph, even if it does not contain content.

INSIDE OUT   Showing specific formatting marks

The Show/Hide button in the Paragraph group provides a quick way to display all formatting marks, such as paragraph marks, spaces, tab characters, and other marks that indicate special formatting. In some cases, you might find you want to display only specific formatting marks. You can easily alter your display to show specific formatting marks as follows:

1. Click the Microsoft Office Button, click Word Options, and then click Display.

2. Under the heading titled Always Show These Formatting Marks On The Screen, select the formatting marks you want to display. For example, select only Paragraph Marks to show only paragraph marks.

3. Click OK to close Word Options.

After you specify which formatting marks you want to display, those marks will appear in your document, regardless of whether you click Show/ Hide. (Note that Show/ Hide continues to show all formatting marks when you toggle the button on, regardless of your Display settings.) To hide formatting marks activated using the Display settings, you'll need to revisit Word Options to reconfigure the formatting marks.

When you format a paragraph, the paragraph formatting information is stored in that paragraph's paragraph mark. The paragraph formatting that is stored in that paragraph mark applies to the text contained in the paragraph. If you want an example of this behavior, apply a paragraph format, such as an alignment, copy the paragraph mark at the end of the paragraph, select another paragraph mark, and then paste. The destination paragraph should have the same paragraph formatting as the source.

In Word, you can format paragraphs by setting the following paragraph formatting parameters:

- Paragraph alignment
- Indentation
- Spacing between lines
- Spacing before and after paragraphs
- Tabs
- Line and page breaks
- Hyphenation

In the following sections of the chapter, you'll learn how to manage these paragraph features. The final topic before we tackle the particulars of list-making describes how to create drop caps. Even though a drop cap might be viewed as more of a text format, they are most commonly used when formatting paragraphs.

Technically speaking, some tasks performed while you are in Outline view relate to paragraph formatting, but those topics aren't addressed in this chapter. Word offers a comprehensive collection of outlining tools and features. For an in-depth look at outlining, see Chapter 10, "Outlining Documents for Clarity and Structure."

Formatting Text and Paragraphs Efficiently

Before you dive in and start formatting a document, let's review an important aspect covered in Chapter 6—the flexibility of your formatting. For example, if you find you need to change an indent throughout your document, do you want to painstakingly select every instance of the indent and change it? Or would you rather specify your preferred indent setting in a single change and have the indents update automatically throughout the document? If the latter sounds more appealing, then for primary formats—such as the main formatting of individual paragraphs—consider using Styles. Styles provide flexibility not only by enabling you to modify document formats simply by modifying the Style (covered in Chapter 15), but they also enable you to format content more efficiently by applying many formats to text with a single click of the mouse. Whether your formatting plan is to create or modify Styles for your formatting needs (which can be accomplished by picking up formats already in use in your document), or to apply direct formatting throughout your document without implementing Styles, paragraph formatting will be fundamentally the same.

Formatting Paragraphs by Aligning and Indenting Text

One of the most common paragraph formatting tasks is aligning paragraphs within a document, as discussed in Chapter 6. But alignment matters don't stop with left, center, right, and justify alignment–you can also control alignment at the paragraph level by specifying text alignment and indentation.

To review which Ribbon buttons and keyboard shortcuts can help you align and indent paragraphs, see Table 14-1.

Table 14-1 Ribbon Buttons and Keyboard Shortcuts for Aligning and Formatting Paragraphs

Format	Button	Keyboard shortcut	Description
Align Left		Ctrl+L	Aligns information along the left margin of the page or specified area, with a ragged right edge.
Align Center		Ctrl+E	Aligns the midpoint of each line with the horizontal center of the page or area.

Format	Button	Keyboard shortcut	Description
Align Right	≣	Ctrl+R	Aligns information along the right margin of the page or specified area, with a ragged left edge.
Justify	≣	Ctrl+J	Aligns text flush with both the left and right margins of the page or specified area.
Decrease Indent	≣	Ctrl+Shift+M	Decreases a paragraph's indent by one tab stop. By default, automatic tab stops are set every 0.5 inch.
Increase Indent	≣	Ctrl+M	Increases a paragraph's indent by one tab stop. By default, automatic tab stops are set every 0.5 inch.

Using the Ruler to Align Paragraphs

Formatting buttons and keyboard shortcuts give you quick access to paragraph alignment and indents, but the Word ruler offers an intuitive and more precise method for controlling paragraph alignment. In addition, it provides a greater variety of alignment settings. The trick to using the ruler effectively is to become comfortable with the ruler. To get started, take a look at Figure 14-2, which shows the Word 2007 ruler (which looks extremely similar to the ruler in earlier versions of Word). The next few sections describe how to use the ruler to format paragraphs.

First line indent marker   Right indent marker

Left indent marker   Hanging indent marker

Figure 14-2 You can use the Word ruler to quickly and accurately align document content by using the Indent Markers.

Displaying and Configuring the Ruler

By default, Word displays the ruler in Normal, Web Layout, and Print Layout views and does not display the ruler in Outline and Reading Layout views. If you don't see the ruler in Normal, Web Layout, or Print Layout view, you can display it by navigating to the View tab and clicking Ruler. Alternatively, you can click the View Ruler button above the vertical scrollbar.

As you can see in Figure 14-2, the *0* (zero) mark on the ruler corresponds to the left margin setting. By default, the left and right margins are set to 1 inch, or 2.54 centimeters, for Letter paper size. Thus, the default setup provides 6.5 inches, or 16.51 centimeters, between the margins for content.

> **Note**
>
> To change the unit of measure displayed on your ruler, view Word Options and in the Advanced area, in the Display section, change the unit in the Show Measurements In Units Of list.

Adjusting Left and Right Indents

To use the ruler to adjust left and right indents, click within the paragraph or select the paragraphs you want to adjust. Then click and drag the Left Indent or Right Indent marker on the ruler. You can obtain more accuracy and view the actual measurements on the ruler, instead of the divisions on the ruler or tick marks, by holding Alt (or press and hold both mouse buttons) as you as drag the indent marks as shown here.

Note that when you drag the Left Indent marker, the First Line Indent and Hanging Indent marker will also move.

INSIDE OUT   Overriding the Drawing Grid

The Drawing Grid, if object snapping is enabled, is also in effect when you use the ruler. By default, the horizontal grid is 0.13 inches, or 0.33 centimeters, which means when you drag the indent markers or other elements, such as a manual tab, they will snap to these increments (note that this does not apply when you initially add a manual tab). When you hold the Alt key, you override the object snapping, which enables you to align content to a precise measurement. To view the Drawing Grid settings, on the Page Layout tab, in the Arrange group, click Align and then click Grid Settings.

Creating First Line and Hanging Indents

You can use the ruler to create a hanging indent or a first line indent, as illustrated in Figure 14-3. To do so, click in the paragraph you want to format (or select multiple paragraphs) and then drag the First Line Indent marker left or right to the desired location.

Figure 14-3 You can drag the First Line Indent marker to create a hanging indent or a first line indent.

> **Tip**
>
> You can press Ctrl+T to create a hanging indent that aligns body text with the first tab marker. (By default, tabs are set every 0.5 inch, or 1.27 centimeters.) You can press Ctrl+Shift+T to "unhang" an indent, regardless of how the hanging indent was created.
>
> If the paragraph contains a first line indent, pressing Ctrl+T will create a Left Indent.

Aligning Paragraphs by Using the Paragraph Dialog Box

Using Ribbon buttons, keyboard shortcuts, and the ruler to align paragraphs can be quick, but aligning paragraphs by using the Paragraph dialog box offers its own advantages. By configuring settings in the Paragraph dialog box, you can align paragraphs precisely as well as apply a number of paragraph formatting settings at one time.

To display the Paragraph dialog box, shown in Figure 14-4, on the Home tab, click the dialog launcher in the Paragraph group. Alternatively, right-click a paragraph (or selected paragraphs) and click Paragraph.

> **Tip**
>
> You can also display the Paragraph dialog box by using the dialog launcher found in the Paragraph group on the Page Layout tab.

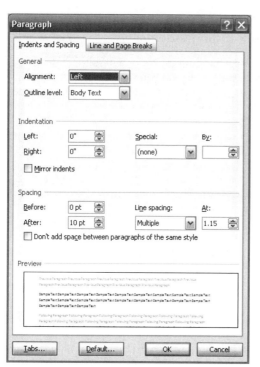

Figure 14-4 The Paragraph dialog box provides precise and complete control of paragraph formatting.

The Indents And Spacing tab offers the following paragraph alignment options:

- **Alignment**   Sets the position of paragraph contents relative to the margins. Available alignment options are Left, Centered, Right, and Justified. The options in this list correspond to the alignment buttons on the Ribbon.

- **Left Indentation**   Indents the paragraph from the left margin by the amount you specify. To display text or graphics within the left margin, enter a negative number in the Left text box.

- **Right Indentation**   Indents the paragraph from the right margin by the amount you specify. To display text or graphics within the right margin, enter a negative number in the Right text box.

- **Special and By**   Controls the paragraph's first line and hanging indentation. The Special list box has three options: (None), First Line, and Hanging. The (None) option is selected by default. To specify the first line indent, enter a value in the By text box. The Special list box changes to display First Line automatically. For a hanging indent, select Hanging from the Special list and enter a value in the By text box.

You can configure other paragraph settings in the Paragraph dialog box, including paragraph spacing parameters, as you'll see next.

Language-Specific Paragraph Options

If you have additional languages enabled for Microsoft Office (which is achieved by selecting Start, All Programs, Microsoft Office, Microsoft Office Tools, Microsoft Office 2007 Language Settings and adding another Editing Language), you might see an additional tab in the Paragraph dialog box that contains paragraph options relevant to the particular language. For example, the following graphic shows the Asian Typography tab, which appears when Japanese is enabled in an English (US) version of Microsoft Office:

For more information about working with language features in Word, see Appendix C, "Multilanguage Support in Word 2007."

Addressing Spacing Issues

If you used previous versions of Word, when you first started using Word 2007, you might have been a little surprised to discover the change in default spacing. The new default spacing uses 10 points of space after each paragraph and 1.15 lines of space between the lines of a paragraph. One of the primary reasons for the new defaults is that the new spacing makes documents easier to read online. Interestingly, if you are accustomed to using single spacing and adding an empty paragraph mark to create space between paragraphs, if you use the new defaults instead of single spacing and empty paragraphs, approximately 3 additional lines are added per page.

> **Note**
>
> If your documents aren't required to follow a specific standard, consider giving the new spacing defaults a few days prior to deciding if you prefer them or not. I disliked the 1.15 line spacing at first (I already used about 10 points of space between paragraphs), but after using this setting for several documents, single line spacing now makes the content appear a little squished when I view a document online.

Additionally, using empty paragraph to create empty lines can end up causing you more work in the end. Consider sorting, copying, and pasting functions, to name a few. When you sort multiple paragraphs, the empty paragraph marks are sorted to the top of your sorted paragraphs, and you need to delete them and manually add them back. And when you copy and paste paragraphs, you might need to manually add and remove the empty paragraph marks.

Long gone are the days when you had to press Enter twice at the end of each paragraph or use tricks such as selecting a paragraph mark and changing the font size to add or increase the space between paragraphs. Adding paragraph spacing is a simple matter of configuring paragraph settings before, during, or after you enter text. You can easily adjust paragraph spacing at any time in your documents to help improve readability. In particular, you can control line spacing within paragraphs as well as specify the amount of space above and below paragraphs.

Additionally, if you want to omit space between some paragraphs, such as for an address block, insert a manual line break by pressing Shift+Enter after each line in the address block instead of pressing Enter to begin a new paragraph.

Note

If you want to change the new default spacing for the entire document, or for all new documents based on the Normal template, see Chapter 15 and the section titled "Managing Styles" on page 431.

INSIDE OUT   Cleaning up empty paragraph marks

If you previously used empty paragraphs to create space between paragraphs and now prefer to use formatted space instead, you can easily clean up documents that have empty paragraph marks by using Find And Replace. When you press Enter twice, you create a pattern of two paragraph marks in sequence. Using Find And Replace, you can find each occurrence of two paragraph marks and replace each set with a single paragraph mark. To do so, follow these steps:

1. On the Home tab, click Replace in the Editing group and then click More.

2. Place your cursor in the Find What text box, click the Special button, and then click Paragraph Mark. You should see ^p in the Find What text box. Click the Special button again and click Paragraph Mark. You should now see ^p^p in the Find What text box.

3. Place your cursor in the Replace With text box, click the Special button, and then click Paragraph Mark. (Alternatively, type **^p**.)

4. Click Replace All and confirm the replacement. (You may need to click Replace All multiple times until you have replaced all occurrences of multiple paragraph marks.)

5. Click Close to close the Find And Replace dialog box.

After you have removed multiple paragraph marks, you can use formatted space between paragraphs to format your document.

Additionally, if you have several documents in which you need to clean up multiple paragraph marks, consider recording a macro using your Find And Replace steps. For more on how to record macros and add them to your Quick Access Toolbar or assign a keyboard shortcut, see Chapter 31, "Working with Macros and VBA." For more on using Find And Replace, see Chapter 7, "Honing Document Navigation Skills."

Specifying Line Spacing

In Word, you can adjust line spacing in several ways, including using the Ribbon, keyboard shortcuts, and the Paragraph dialog box.

 One quick way to configure a paragraph's line spacing is to click in the paragraph you want to configure—or select multiple paragraphs—and then click Line Spacing on the Home tab, in the Paragraph group. Line Spacing offers the following options: 1.0, 1.5, 2.0, 2.5, and 3.0. Selecting a number instantly adjusts the selected paragraphs' line spacing. If you select Line Spacing Options, the Paragraph dialog box displays.

The Paragraph dialog box enables you to adjust paragraph line spacing to a precise 1/10 of a point by using the Line Spacing option in conjunction with the At text box in the Indents And Spacing tab (shown previously in Figure 14-4). The Line Spacing list box provides the following options:

- **Single** Accommodates the largest font per line plus a small amount of extra space to create the appearance of a single-spaced paragraph.

- **1.5 Lines** Inserts 1.5 times the space allotted for a single line space to the selected paragraph(s).

- **Double** Inserts twice the space allotted for a single line space to the selected paragraph(s).

- **At Least** Sets a minimum amount of space for each line as specified in the At text box. When Word encounters a larger font size or a graphic that won't fit in the minimum space, Word increases that line's spacing to accommodate the text or graphic.

- **Exactly** Forces Word to apply an exact line spacing, as specified in the At text box, regardless of what size text or graphics Word encounters. (Otherwise, Word accommodates the largest text or graphic in a line by default.) If Word encounters text or graphics too large to fit in the allotted line space, the text or graphics will appear cut off in your document.

- **Multiple** Enables you to use the At text box to specify a line spacing setting from 0.06 through 132 lines, in increments of 1/100 of a line. This option provides extra-fine control over line spacing.

Last but not least, you can quickly adjust a paragraph's line spacing by clicking in a paragraph or selecting multiple paragraphs and then pressing any of the following keyboard shortcuts:

- Ctrl+1 applies single-line spacing to selected paragraphs.

- Ctrl+2 applies double-line spacing to selected paragraphs.

- Ctrl+5 applies 1.5-line spacing to selected paragraphs.

Adjusting Spacing Above and Below Paragraphs

In addition to adjusting spacing between lines within paragraphs, you can configure the space displayed above and below paragraphs, as opposed to adding an empty paragraph mark. By using this method to add space, you're not limited to separating paragraphs by one or two lines—you can separate paragraphs by 0.5 inch, 3 points, and so forth. In addition, if you use spacing consistently within your document, and you find that your document (or a section within your document) runs a little long or comes up a little short, you can select the entire document, a section, or a few paragraphs, and adjust the paragraph spacing options by using the Paragraph dialog box to tighten up or lengthen your document in just a few steps. For additional tips on fitting text see Chapter 26, "Printing with Precision."

To add spacing above and below selected paragraphs, follow these steps:

1. Click in the paragraph you want to configure, or select multiple paragraphs.

2. On the Home tab, in the Paragraph group, click the dialog launcher and then click Indents And Spacing.

3. Enter values in the Before and After text boxes in the Spacing section, and click OK. The Before and After spacing options require you to specify in points how much space to insert before and after paragraphs. Keep in mind that 72 points equals approximately 1 inch.

> **Note**
>
> You can also type other units of measure after the value, and they will be converted to points. Use *cm* for centimeters, *in* for inches, and *li* for line. For example, .6 *li* will be converted to 7.2 points.

If you create styles for your documents, you'll want to consider configuring the Before and After settings when you create paragraph styles. Adding before and after spacing to paragraph styles helps to ensure that spacing will be applied consistently and automatically throughout your document.

For more information about creating styles, see Chapter 15.

> **Tip**
>
> You can instantly add 12 points of space before a paragraph by selecting the paragraph(s) you want to format and pressing Ctrl+0 (zero). Press Ctrl+0 (zero) again to remove the space.

Chapter 14

Controlling Alignment by Using Tabs

Back in the days of the typewriter, tabs were used for all types of alignment such as tabbed tables, charts, and columns. Now Word offers a variety of text alignment tools, including specific features you can use to create columns, Word tables (instead of tabbed tables), and charts. But even with the advanced Word formatting features, tabs continue to play a key role in aligning text and performing other tab-related activities. For example, tabs frequently come into play when you want to create simple lists, a simple tabbed table that includes dotted leader lines between the tabbed entries, center-aligned or decimal-aligned text, and so forth. Figure 14-5 shows a variety of tab types in action. When viewing formatting marks, each tab character will appear as a right pointing arrow in the document.

> **Tip**
>
> Instead of using a tabbed table to separate data, use a borderless Word table instead. This will provide the appearance of a tabbed table but enable more control over the alignment of the data. For more on Word tables, see Chapter 11, "Organizing Concepts in Tables."

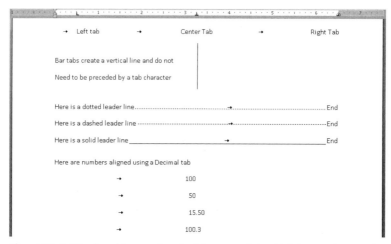

Figure 14-5 Word enables you to select from a variety of tab types when you're adding tab stops.

New documents based on the default Normal template include automatic tab stops every 0.5 inch, or 1.27 centimeters, and these tab stops don't appear in the ruler. You can adjust the default tab stop setting, add custom tabs, clear all tabs, and create tabs with leader lines. To adjust tabs, use the ruler or Tabs dialog box, as discussed in the following sections.

TROUBLESHOOTING

My text keeps shifting to the next tab stop

If you have used tabs to align text and have needed to add a few more text characters within the tabbed text, you might find that the text shifts to the next tab stop even though there appears to be ample room. The underlying issue is too many automatic tabs or a combination of spaces and tabs to align the text. An example of text aligned at the 3-inch mark on the ruler using automatic tabs is shown here.

Note the 6 tab characters preceding the text (spaces weren't added for this example). Each time the default automatic tabs are set and you press the Tab key, 0.5 inch of space will be reserved for each tab character. If you add text at the beginning of the line, and if it exceeds 0.5 inch, then the text following the tab, or tabs, will shift as shown here.

To resolve this issue, use a manual tab instead of multiple automatic tabs. In this example, a manual Left tab has been set at 3 inches on the ruler.

As a result, there is a total of 3 inches of space available for text between the left margin and the manual tab stop. This space can be used before the text will shift to the next tab stop. In addition, pressing Tab once is far easier than adding multiple tabs and multiple spaces to align text. For more on setting manual tabs, see the next section.

Chapter 14

Putting the Ruler to Work to Set Tabs

You can set manual tabs by using the horizontal ruler in Word. Using the ruler has a couple of advantages: You get visual feedback as soon as you set the tabs, and you can drag the ruler tabs to the left or right until you're satisfied with their positions. (You can even drag tabs off the ruler to delete them.) As soon as you set a manual tab on the ruler, selected text preceded by a tab character moves to reflect the setting. To use the ruler to add manual tabs, you need to complete the following steps:

1. Click in a paragraph or select multiple paragraphs in which you want to set tabs, or position the insertion point at the location where you want to create a new paragraph containing the tab settings.

2. Select the desired tab type by clicking the button at the left end of the horizontal ruler, called the *Tab Selector*, shown to the left of this paragraph. Each click of your mouse will cycle through the available tab types. Table 14-2 lists the tab types along with other available indent markers, and Figure 14-5, shown previously, shows the various tab types in action.

3. After you selecxt a tab type, click in the lower portion of the ruler (in the white space below the numbers) to insert a manual tab. If you position a manual tab incorrectly, you can drag it off the ruler to delete it or drag it left or right to reposition it.

Table 14-2 Tab and Indent Types

Button	Name	Description
Left Tab icon	Left Tab	Text begins at the tab stop and continues right. This is the most commonly used tab type.
Center Tab icon	Center Tab	Text is centered on the tab stop as you type.
Right Tab icon	Right Tab	Text begins at the tab stop and moves left as new text is typed.
Decimal Tab icon	Decimal Tab	Aligns a number on the decimal point, or where the decimal point would appear if the number does not show a decimal. When used in a Word table, numbers do not need to be preceded by a Tab character.
Bar Tab icon	Bar Tab	Creates a vertical line. This setting enables you to draw vertical lines that span any number of horizontal lines of text. This tab type is not used for aligning text in a document.
First Line Indent icon	First Line Indent	Activates the First Line Indent feature. Using this method, you can create a first line indent with a single click instead of dragging the indent marker.
Hanging Indent icon	Hanging Indent	Activates the Hanging Indent feature. Using this method, you can create a hanging indent with a single click instead of dragging the indent marker.

INSIDE OUT   Carrying tabs from one paragraph to the next

If you set tabs in a paragraph, the tab settings will automatically be included in the next paragraph if you press Enter at the end of the paragraph and continue typing to create a new paragraph. On the other hand, if you format tabs in a paragraph that's already embedded among other paragraphs, the tab settings will not automatically extend to the existing paragraphs that follow.

If you want to extend tab formatting to existing paragraphs, you need to select all the paragraphs you want to format before you set the tabs.

Note that if the paragraph contains multiple lines, you'll see the manual tab when your cursor is in any line of the paragraph. However, the manual tab belongs to the paragraph, rather than to each line. For example, deleting the manual tab will affect all lines of the paragraph.

Finally, if you want to set tabs throughout an entire document, press Ctrl+A to select the document and then set your tabs on the ruler. Be aware that setting tabs for an entire document might affect existing tabs, so be sure to review your document after you make wide-ranging changes. In addition, you might want to clear any existing tabs before inserting your new global tabs. The process of deleting tabs is described in the section titled "Clearing Manual Tabs" later in this chapter on page 375.

Creating Tabs by Using the Tabs Dialog Box

In addition to clicking the ruler to create tabs, you can use the Tabs dialog box to add tabs. The Tabs dialog box enables you to use precise measurements to set tabs. You can also create tabs that use leader lines. (*Leaders* insert formatting, such as dots or dashes, in the space leading to the tab stop, as shown in Figure 14-5.) Neither of these tasks can be accomplished using the ruler. The main drawback of creating tabs by using the Tabs dialog box is that you won't be able to see how your tabs affect your text until after you close the dialog box and view your document. To display the Tabs dialog box, perform any of the following actions:

- Press Alt+O+T.
- Double-click an existing tab in the horizontal ruler.
- Click Tabs in the Paragraph dialog box.

CAUTION

At the time of this writing, there is a known issue in accessing the Tabs dialog box from the Paragraph dialog box. In the Paragraph dialog box, when you click Tabs, the current Paragraph settings are set as the Document Defaults for not only the current document but also the Normal template. Until this problem is corrected, it is recommended you use an alternate method to access the Tabs dialog box, such as Alt+O+T. Or, add the Tabs command to your Quick Access Toolbar. (When customizing your Quick Access Toolbar, Tabs is found in Commands Not In The Ribbon.) For more on Document Defaults, see Chapter 15.

Figure 14-6 shows the Tabs dialog box. If the currently selected paragraph contains manual tabs, when you display the Tabs dialog box, the tab positions will be listed in the Tab Stop Position list box. Notice that the Default Tab Stops option is set to *0.5 inches* (or 1.27 if your preferred unit of measure is centimeters) by default.

Figure 14-6 The Tabs dialog box enables you to modify the default tab stop settings, insert tabs at precise positions, create leader lines, and clear existing tabs.

To use the Tabs dialog box to set manual tabs, follow these steps:

1. Click in the paragraph or select multiple paragraphs in which you want to set tabs, or position your insertion point at the location where you want to create a new paragraph containing the tab settings.

2. Display the Tabs dialog box (press Alt+O+T or double-click an existing manual tab on the ruler).

3. Type a tab location—such as *1.75 (inches)* or *4.45* (centimeters)—in the Tab Stop Position text box.

4. In the Alignment section, specify whether you want a left, center, right, decimal, or bar tab.

5. Select a leader line style, if desired, and then click Set. The manual tab will be listed in the Tab Stop Position list box.

6. Add more manual tabs, if necessary, by repeating steps 3–5. Then click OK to close the Tabs dialog box when you've finished setting manual tabs.

To change the default tab and indent setting (used when you click Increase Indent or Decrease Indent on the Home tab), you can type a new setting in the Default Tab Stops text box in the Tabs dialog box. For example, you could change the default 0.5-inch setting to 0.75 inch. The default setting is used if manual tabs aren't set when you press Tab or click the Increase Indent and Decrease Indent buttons.

Clearing Manual Tabs

Just as you can add manual tabs using the horizontal ruler and the Tabs dialog box, you can also clear manual tabs using these same tools. You can even clear all tabs at one time if you're really in "spring cleaning" mode. To remove tabs, select the paragraph(s) you want to modify, and then perform one of the following procedures:

- Drag the tab markers off the ruler. (Simply click a tab marker and drag it down into the document area.)

- Display the Tabs dialog box (press Alt+O+T or double-click an existing tab marker in the Ruler), select the tab you want to delete, and click Clear.

- Display the Tabs dialog box and click Clear All.

TROUBLESHOOTING

Ruler options are unavailable when multiple paragraphs are selected

In some instances, you might want to modify several paragraphs that have different tab settings so that they all have consistent tab settings. You can do so using both the horizontal ruler and the Tab dialog box. The easiest way to accomplish this task is by performing the following steps:

1. Select the paragraph(s) you want to format. If the tab markers in the horizontal ruler appear shaded or dimmed, the tab settings aren't currently applied to the entire selection. (You probably already know this, so the dimmed tab markers shouldn't faze you.)

2. Double-click a dimmed tab marker (or press Alt+O+T) to display the Tabs dialog box.

3. Click Clear All, click OK, and then click the horizontal ruler to define tab settings that will apply to the entire selection.

Controlling Line and Page Breaks

As mentioned in Chapter 3, you should use pagination formatting, instead of using manual page breaks, to specify which paragraphs need to stay together on the same page or if all lines of a paragraph need to remain on the same page. The main area to turn to for pagination formatting is the Line And Page Breaks tab in the Paragraph dialog box, shown in Figure 14-7.

Figure 14-7 The Line And Page Breaks tab contains pagination formatting options to prevent paragraphs from breaking across pages and to keep paragraphs together on the same page.

To apply the line and page break settings, select the text you want to format, display the Line And Page Breaks tab, and select the appropriate check boxes. The following line and page break options are available:

- **Widow/Orphan Control** Ensures that the last line of a paragraph doesn't appear by itself at the top of a new page (a widow) or that the first line of a paragraph doesn't appear by itself at the bottom of a page (an orphan). Widow/ Orphan Control is selected by default.

- **Keep Lines Together** Prevents page breaks from occurring within a paragraph. When a page break is needed, Word moves the entire paragraph to the next page.

- **Keep With Next** Prevents a page break from occurring between the selected paragraph and the following paragraph. This feature can be useful when you're using paragraphs that work together to create a single element, such as a table and a table caption or a heading and the following paragraph. (Note that the Heading styles use this format by default.)

> **Note**
>
> If you want to keep a group of paragraphs or rows in a Word table together, omit the last element in the group when using the Keep With Next pagination format.

- **Page Break Before** Inserts a page break before the selected paragraph. Typically this format is used in a Style, such as Heading 1, used for chapter headings so that each chapter will automatically start on a new page when the Heading 1 style is applied. For more on styles, see Chapter 15.

A new option in the Paragraph dialog box for Word 2007 is Tight Wrap which applies to how paragraphs wrap around text in text boxes. For more on this option see Chapter 16, "Formatting Layouts Using Backgrounds, Watermarks, and Text Boxes." The Line And Page Breaks tab also contains a Suppress Line Numbers option, which prevents line numbers from appearing if you're using the line numbering feature. For more information about line numbering, see Chapter 21, "Formatting Columns and Sections for Advanced Text Control." In addition, the Line And Page Breaks tab contains a Don't Hyphenate check box that can be used to suppress hyphenation for selected paragraphs when using automatic hyphenation. Hyphenation is covered next.

Taking Control of Hyphenation

When you work with paragraphs, you need to decide whether you're going to hyphenate words at the ends of lines to create more evenly aligned edges within ragged-edge paragraphs or control "rivers" of white space within justified paragraphs. By default, hyphenation is turned off in Word. This means that if a word is too long to fit on a line, the entire word is moved to the beginning of the next line. If you prefer, you can activate Word's built-in Hyphenation feature to eliminate white space and gaps along the edges of your text. When you use the Hyphenation feature, you can opt to apply hyphenation manually or automatically, as follows:

- **Automatic hyphenation** Word automatically hyphenates an entire document. If you later change the document's contents, Word rehyphenates the document as needed, while you work.

- **Manual hyphenation** Word searches for instances in which hyphenation is needed, and then you manually decide whether to add a hyphen at each instance. If you later modify the document, Word displays and prints only the hyphens that fall at the ends of lines. To rehyphenate the document, repeat the manual hyphenation process.

> **Note**
>
> If you want to apply hyphenation to text that's written in a language other than the Microsoft Office default language, you need to ensure that the language is enabled for editing (through the Microsoft Office 2007 Language Settings), and you need to install Microsoft Office 2007 Proofing Tools for the language.

Either way, the process of adding hyphenation begins with Hyphenation on the Page Layout tab, shown here.

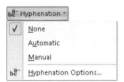

Hyphenate an Entire Document Automatically

To automatically hyphenate an entire document, on the Page Layout tab, in the Page Setup group, click Hyphenation and then click Automatic. To configure the automatic hyphenation settings, click Hyphenation Options to display the Hyphenation dialog box, shown in Figure 14-8.

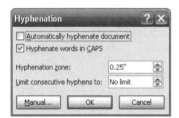

Figure 14-8 The Hyphenation dialog box enables you control hyphenation settings for automatic or manual hyphenation.

> **Tip**
>
> You can format nonbreaking hyphens to prevent a hyphenated word, number, or phrase from breaking if it falls at the end of a line. For example, you might not want to break a phone number at the end of a line. To insert a nonbreaking hyphen, on the Insert Tab, click Symbol, click More Symbols, and then click Special Characters. Alternatively, press Ctrl+Shift+Hyphen.

In the Hyphenation Zone text box, enter the amount of acceptable white space to leave between the end of the last word in a line and the right margin. If you want fewer hyphens, make the Hyphenation Zone value larger. If you want to reduce ragged edges, make the Hyphenation Zone value smaller.

In the Limit Consecutive Hyphens To text box, type the maximum number of consecutive lines that can end with a hyphen and then click OK.

If you want to turn off the automatic hyphenation feature as well as remove automatically inserted hyphens, on the Page Layout tab, click Hyphenation and then click None.

Hyphenating All or Part of a Document Manually

When you hyphenate a document manually, you can hyphenate the entire document, or you can select part of the document before you display the Hyphenation dialog box. To hyphenate text manually, either select the text you want to hyphenate or make sure that no text is selected if you want to hyphenate the entire document. On the Page Layout tab, click Hyphenation and then click Manual.

When Word identifies a word or phrase that should be hyphenated, the Manual Hyphenation dialog box appears, as shown in Figure 14-9. You can click Yes to insert the specified hyphen; use the arrow keys or mouse to reposition the hyphen location and then click Yes; click No to ignore the suggestion and move to the next word; or click Cancel to end the hyphenation process.

Figure 14-9 When you manually hyphenate a document, the Manual Hyphenation dialog box appears each time a word needs to be hyphenated. And Word suggests locations where you can hyphenate that word.

> Note
>
> If hyphenation is not required in the selected portion of the document, the Manual Hyphenation dialog box will not be displayed.

Creating Drop Caps in Existing Paragraphs

A popular format frequently associated with paragraphs is drop caps. *Drop caps* are the large letters that appear at the very beginning of chapters or sections, as shown in Figure 14-10 and at the beginning of each chapter of this book.

O n the Insert tab, the galleries include items that are designed to coordinate with the overall look of your document. You can use these galleries to insert tables, headers, footers, lists, cover pages, and other document building blocks. When you create pictures, charts, or diagrams, they also coordinate with your current document look.

Figure 14-10 Drop caps are large, stylized letters that are frequently used to identify the beginning of a prominent section in a document, such as a chapter.

Word provides an easy way for you to add drop caps to paragraphs. When you use the Drop Cap feature, Word increases the font size of the first letter of a paragraph and places it in a frame. After the drop cap is automatically created and situated, you can further modify it. To create a drop cap, follow these steps:

1. Click in the paragraph that you want to customize with a drop cap, or, if you want to enlarge more than just the first letter in the paragraph, select the letters or word(s) you want to format as drop caps.

2. On the Insert tab, in the Text group, click Drop Cap to display the Drop Cap gallery, as shown here.

3. Select Dropped or In Margin to add the drop cap to your paragraph. To control drop cap settings, click Drop Cap Options to display the Drop Cap dialog box, as shown in Figure 14-11.

Figure 14-11 The Drop Cap dialog box enables you to set parameters before the graphic for the first letter is created and inserted in your document.

If you decide not to display a drop cap in your paragraph, you can easily remove the formatting. To do so, click in the paragraph containing the drop cap, display the Drop Cap gallery, and then click None.

Finally, note that drop caps appear above your paragraph in Normal view and Outline view. To view drop caps properly on the screen, view documents that contain drop caps in Web Page Layout, Print Layout, or Reading Layout views.

Creating Effective Lists

Another way to align text is to create bulleted and numbered lists. Adding bulleted and numbered lists to your document can go a long way toward making your document more readable, which is an achievement your readers will be grateful for. Lists can also help you make your point clearly and succinctly, enabling the ideas to stand out instead of being lost inside a large paragraph.

Throughout this chapter, both bulleted and numbered lists are referred to simply as lists, because they behave the same way. When you choose a bullet, of course, you're using a special symbol, character, or graphic to start a text line. When you use a number, you're selecting the font, size, and color of the numeral you want to use. In addition, you can use roman numerals, letters, and other line identifiers in numbered lists. (This technique is covered later in this chapter in the section titled "Improving Numbered Lists" on page 390.)

The remainder of this chapter shows you how to create lists—both bulleted and numbered—in Word documents. You'll learn the recommended methods for list-making and discover how lists can make your work easier and more effective, whether you create short articles, long dissertations, or something in between.

When Bullets Work

Word gives you the capacity to create bulleted lists with a number of looks. For instance, you can select bullet characters, colors, and indents. Further, you can place bulleted lists side by side in a multicolumn format. Here are some guidelines to remember when you create bulleted lists:

- **Be concise.** Fewer words make a larger impact. Unless you *must* include paragraphs of text for each bullet item, pare your prose down to fewer than three sentences if you can.

- **Stick to the point.** A general rule is one point, one bullet. Don't try to cram more than one idea into each bullet item.

- **Be clear.** Flowery language isn't necessary—clear and simple is best.

- **Don't overdo it.** Bullets can be so much fun (and easier to write than big blocks of text) that you might be tempted to use them liberally throughout your document. Resist the temptation to overuse bullets in your work and use them only when they bring clarity to your content.

- **Choose a bullet that makes sense.** If your report is about a new drive train your company is manufacturing, would baby-bottle bullet characters really make sense? Probably not. Be sure to fit the bullet characters you choose to the style and expectations of your audience.

- **Don't use too many at once.** Don't make your lists burdensome for your readers. If possible, say what you need to say in five to seven bullet points and move back to paragraph style.

> Tip
>
> Bullets are ideal for those times when you want to convey short, to-the-point pieces of information. The fact that you use bullets instead of numbers implies to your reader that the points can be read and applied in any order; there's no necessary sequence in a bulleted list.

When Numbers Matter

The type of information you create determines whether you need numbered lists in your documents. If you're writing a how-to manual about fly-fishing, you might have quite a few numbered steps, explaining important procedures for preparing equipment, finding the right spot, and setting up for your first cast. If you're creating a marketing plan with a timeline and an action sequence, your steps will define a process that builds a bigger promotions system. Whatever the purpose of your numbered list, you can make sure it's most effective in these ways:

- **Use numbers that fit your tone** In an upbeat publication, you might want to use specialty numbers or a casual font with oversized numbers. In a more serious piece, you'll want the numbers you select to carry a more professional tone.

- **Keep steps clear.** Most often, numbered steps are used to describe a process. Conveniently enough, steps can add clarity to a complex procedure. Therefore, don't muddy the waters by overburdening a numbered step with too much information. Include one or two instructions per step and then move on to the next numbered step.

- **Remember the white space.** Whether you're working with bulleted or numbered lists, the white space in your document is as important as the text on the page—it might be a humbling statement, but it's true. White space gives your readers' eyes a rest, so space list items and avoid crowding steps too closely.

- **Align by design.** As with spacing for bulleted and numbered lists, the alignment of lists matters. Make sure the indents in the second line of the list item align with the first character of text, and make sure that lists present a consistent alignment pattern throughout your document.

Chapter 14

> Tip
>
> A numbered list communicates a sequence: First, we have the team meeting; next, we implement the plan; then, we write the report; and finally, we present our results. These items, in a list, would be numbered because they show a definite order and a logical process.

INSIDE OUT   Controlling Automatic Lists

If you want full control over your lists, you need to make sure that you have the AutoFormat options turned off for numbering and bullets. The rationale behind this is automatic formatting options for list feature can conflict with numbered and bulleted lists. If you want to manually add the number and bullet formatting, clear these options before you begin list-making. To do so, follow these steps:

1. Click the Microsoft Office Button, click Word Options, then click Proofing.

2. Click the AutoCorrect Options button and then click the AutoFormat As You Type tab option.

3. In the Apply As You Type section, make sure Automatic Bullet Lists and Automatic Numbered Lists are cleared. (Note that these options are selected by default.)

For more on the AutoFormat As You Type options, see Chapter 8, "Working with Building Blocks and Other Text Tools."

Creating a Quick List

 Word enables you to create both numbered and bulleted lists from existing text and as you type. To create a list from existing text, select the text and then click either Bullets or Numbering on the Home tab in the Paragraph group. Each selected paragraph will be formatted as a single numbered or bulleted list item. As mentioned, you can also create lists while you type. To create a quick list while you type, follow these steps:

1. Place the insertion point where you want to add the list.

2. Click the Numbering button if you want to create a numbered list, or click Bullets if you want to create a bulleted list. Both are shown in Figure 14-12.

3. The list item is added. Type your first item and press Enter. The next bullet or number is added.

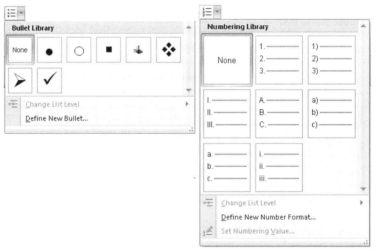

Figure 14-12 The Bullet and Numbering galleries contain recently used bullets and numbering, the bullet and numbering libraries, and bullets and numbering in the current document.

4. Continue entering your list items, pressing Enter after each item.

If you are using a numbered list, when you add or delete an item in the list, the list items will automatically renumber accordingly.

Tip

If you want to start a new paragraph within a bulleted or numbered list, but you're not yet ready for the next bullet or number, press Shift+Enter instead of just Enter. Pressing Shift+Enter ensures that the added information appears as a paragraph but will still be part of the current bulleted or numbered item. When you press Enter later to continue your list, a bullet or number will appear.

Creating Lists While You Type

You can also create lists while you type by using the AutoFormat As You Type features found in the AutoCorrect dialog box. These options are turned on by default, but to verify them, display Word Options, click Proofing, and then click the AutoCorrect Options button. (Alternatively, press Alt+T+A to display the AutoCorrect dialog box.) On the AutoFormat As You Type tab, verify Automatic Bullet Lists and Automatic Numbered Lists are selected.

If you are creating complex numbering schemes or using multiple numbered lists in a document, this method is not recommended due to the lack of control you have over lists automatically generated by Word. With this in mind, you can use the following to create bulleted or numbered lists as you type.

To create a bulleted list in Word, type an asterisk (*), press Tab, type a list entry, and then press Enter. By default, Word will change the asterisk to a bullet and the AutoCorrect Options button will appear and enable you to control the automatic bulleted list feature. If you want to create the bulleted list, simply continue to type, and the AutoCorrect Options button will disappear.

Similarly, if you have Automatic Numbered Lists selected in your AutoFormat options, to create a numbered list while you type, enter a number (you can enter any number, but generally, you'd probably want to start with the number 1), press Tab, enter text, and press Enter. Word will format the entry as a numbered list item and display the AutoCorrect Options button that enables you to control the creation of a numbered list. Again, to continue creating the numbered list, simply continue to type the next numbered list entry.

> **Tip**
>
> If you want space added between the list items, rather than pressing Enter twice to add an empty paragraph between the list items, use formatted space before or after each paragraph, as described in the section titled "Adjusting Spacing Above and Below Paragraphs" earlier in this chapter on page 369.

TROUBLESHOOTING

A number is bold or is not formatted like the other numbers in the list

If your numbers are formatted differently from other numbers in the list, the likely cause is the paragraph mark at the end contains the undesired format.

To resolve this issue, turn on the display of formatting marks (on the Home tab, in the Paragraph group, click Show/Hide), select the paragraph mark, and then clear the formatting. For example, if the number is bold, click Bold to remove the format.

Ending a List, the Way You Want

One of the challenges users often face with bulleted and numbered lists is that the lists seem to want to go on forever. After you press Enter on your last list entry, yet another bullet (or number) shows up. Get rid of the extra bullet or number by doing one of three things:

- Click the Bullets or Numbering button to turn off the feature.

- Press Backspace twice to delete the number or bullet and place your cursor at the left margin. The first time you press Backspace, the cursor will line up below the text of the previous list item, as opposed to lining up under the number in previous versions of Word. If your list is indented, continue to press Backspace until your cursor reaches the desired position.

- Press Enter twice, instead of once, after the last item.

See the section titled "Creating and Using Multilevel Lists" later in this chapter on page 395 for new ways Word 2007 works when you use Enter and Backspace in a multilevel list.

Enhancing Bulleted Lists

The default Word settings for bulleted and numbered lists are fine when you're creating a quick, simple document that will be passed around the office and eventually end up in the dumpster. But what about those special reports you create or the procedure manuals that others rely on? Those need to have a more professional look and feel, and the treatment of the lists in your document suddenly become more important.

You can improve a basic bulleted list in several ways. You might want to customize your list by choosing your bullet from the Bullet gallery, selecting a picture bullet, creating your own bullets, or changing indents and spacing for your bullet items.

Choosing a New Bullet from the Bullet Library

Word gives you a gallery of preset bullet styles to choose from and a virtually unlimited supply of bullet options you can pull from symbol typefaces, graphics libraries, and more. To choose a new bullet character for a list, follow these steps:

1. Select the list items with the bullets you want to change or position your cursor where you want to add a list.

2. On the Home tab, click the arrow next to Bullets to display the Bullet gallery, as shown in Figure 14-13.

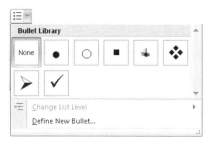

Figure 14-13 The Bullet gallery enables you to select another symbol or picture for a bullet list.

3. Browse the gallery and select another symbol or picture to use as a bullet.

A quick way to access the Bullet gallery is to select your list, right-click, point at Bullets, and then select a new bullet from the gallery.

Selecting a Bullet Character Outside the Bullet Gallery

If the bullets in the Bullet gallery do not meet your needs, you can select a new bullet from the Bullet gallery by clicking Define New Bullet. The Define Bullet dialog box appears. The Symbol and Picture buttons enable you to access additional bullets, and the Font button enables you to modify the font formatting of your bullet. Figure 14-14 shows the Define New Bullet dialog box.

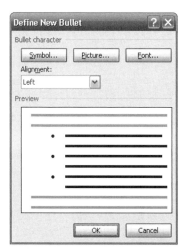

Figure 14-14 The Define New Bullet dialog box gives you the means to change the font and character you use for bullets. You can also change bullet position here.

Changing the Bullet Font

When you click Font in the Define New Bullet dialog box, the Font dialog box appears, as shown in Figure 14-15. Here you can select a typeface and change font settings for bullet characters.

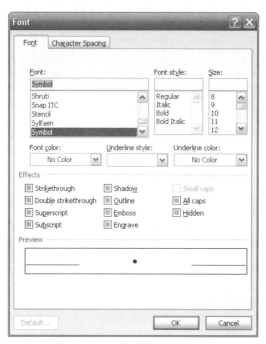

Figure 14-15 The Font dialog box enables you to change a bullet character's typeface, style, color, and text effects.

Changing a Bullet Symbol

When you customize bullets, you can click Symbol in the Define New Bullet dialog box to display the Symbol dialog box, as shown in Figure 14-16. The Symbol dialog box displays available characters for selected fonts. Use the Symbol dialog box to change font selections by choosing a font in the Font list box. After you find a character you want to use, simply click the character and then click OK.

For more information about working with the Symbol dialog box, see Chapter 6, "Mastering Document Fundamentals."

Notice that you can see the numeric character code in either decimal or hexadecimal format for each character you select in the Symbol dialog box. This enables you to be sure you've used the same bullet throughout this document and in other documents that need a consistent style.

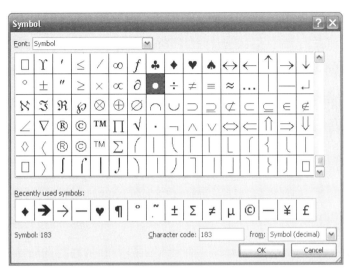

Figure 14-16 Click the symbol you want to select as a new bullet character. If you need to be consistent with lists in other documents, make note of the character code of the item you select.

You can resize the Symbol dialog box to view additional rows and columns of symbols at a time. To maximize or restore the dialog box, double-click the title bar.

Using a Picture Bullet

We live in an age of pictures—television and the Web have raised the bar on what we expect in terms of aesthetic presentation of information. One way you can subtly add imagery to your documents is to use picture bullets. Used judiciously, picture bullets in your documents can effectively liven up a document by adding color and interest to text.

What is a picture bullet? Simply, it's a graphic image that's small enough to use as a bullet character. Word offers a range of bullet styles and shapes, including animated bullets that you can use online. To display the Picture Bullet dialog box and see the available offerings, click the arrow next to Bullet on the Home tab, click Define New Bullet, and then click Picture. The Picture Bullet dialog box appears, as shown in Figure 14-17.

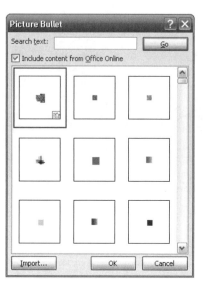

Figure 14-17 Picture bullet options appear in a dialog box that includes a Search Text option.

To select a picture bullet, you simply click the one you want and click OK. Word adds the picture bullet to the Bullet gallery.

If you don't see a picture bullet that you want to use in the Picture Bullet dialog box, enter text in the Search Text box and click Go. Word will search clip art and online files. Online bullet options appear with an image of the world in the lower left corner of the preview picture. Further, animated bullets (bullets that have small movements, size changes, or color changes when the bullet is viewed online on a Web page) appear with a star in the lower right corner of a preview picture, as you can see in the first button preview shown in Figure 14-17.

Improving Numbered Lists

Like bulleted lists, numbered lists enable you to make your own choices about the look and format of the numerals used. Many procedures you use to customize bulleted lists can also be used to fine-tune numbered lists. Most notably, in numbered lists, you can make modifications by specifying a font, selecting the number style you want, and choosing the number and text position of the items in your list.

Choosing a Numbering Scheme

The style of your numbers can add character to numbered lists. Depending on the nature of your publication, you might use simple traditional characters or larger, colorful characters. Begin by selecting the numbered list you want to change, or position your cursor in an empty paragraph in which you want to start your list, and on the Home tab, click the arrow next to Numbering, and then click a numbering format. Figure 14-18 shows the Numbering gallery.

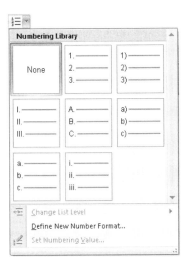

Figure 14-18 The Numbering gallery displays preset numbering styles that you can use when you create numbered lists.

Modifying the Numbering Style

If you aren't particularly happy with the available numbering styles, you can define a new number format. To create a new number format, display the Numbering gallery and then click Define New Number Format. The Define New Number Format dialog box appears, providing formatting options for numbered lists (as shown in Figure 14-19).

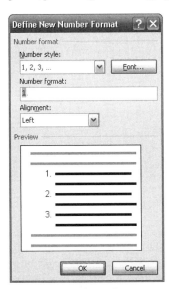

Figure 14-19 The Define New Number Format dialog box gives you the means to create a new number format and change number position.

To select a new number style, click the Number Style list to see the available style choices. You can determine at which number you want the list to start by clicking in the Start At text box and then typing the number for the starting point. If you prefer, you can use the up or down arrows on the Start At text box to increase or decrease the number by one.

> **Note**
>
> When you use Numbering, you are using a single style called List Paragraph. If you are using complex numbering or using multiple unique lists in a document, then create a new list style instead. The Define New List Style command is found on the Home tab in the Paragraph group, at the bottom of the Multilevel List gallery.
>
> This method will create a style for each new list and provide more control over editing the list and applying the correct list to the related paragraphs. For more information on creating list styles, see the section titled "Creating a New List Style" later in this chapter on page 397.

Continuing Numbering

Some of your numbered list items might be separated by elements such as charts, explanatory paragraphs, or sidebars. When you click the Numbering button, if Word doesn't continue with the next numbered step in your process, you can continue numbers in an existing numbered list in a couple of ways:

- Click the AutoCorrect Options button and then click Continue Numbering. (If available.)

- Display the Numbering gallery and then click Set Numbering Value. In the Set Numbering Value dialog box, shown in Figure 14-20, select Continue From Previous List. (This option is also available when you right-click a list item.)

Figure 14-20 The Set Numbering Value dialog box enables you to continue from a previous list and also to skip numbering.

- Right-click the first incorrect number in a numbered list and then click Continue Numbering.

Restarting Numbering

Restarting numbered lists is similar to continuing numbered lists, as described in the section titled "Continuing Numbering" earlier in this chapter on page 392. The main difference is that you'll want to choose the Restart Numbering option instead of the Continue Numbering option. To restart a numbered list with the number 1, take any of the following actions:

- Click the AutoCorrect Options button and then click Restart Numbering. (If available.)

- Display the Numbering gallery and then click Set Numbering Value. In the dialog box, select Start New List and type **1** (one) in the Set Value To text box. (This option is also available when you right-click a list item.)

- In a numbered list, right-click the number that you want to change to the number 1, and click Restart At 1.

If you want to restart a list with a number other than 1 (but you don't want to continue the preceding list), select Set Numbering Value from the Numbering gallery. Enter a number in the Start Value To text box and then click OK.

Converting a Bulleted List to a Numbered List (or Vice Versa)

You can easily convert bulleted lists to numbered lists and vice versa. To do so, simply select the list and then click either the Bullets button or the Numbering button on the Home tab. After you convert a list, you can tweak the list's appearance and settings while the list is selected by using the methods previously provided.

TROUBLESHOOTING

My numbered list will not continue from the previous list.

If you attempt to continue numbering from a previous list, and each time you select Continue Numbering the list still starts at 1, the underlying problem is that a new list has been defined in the document. This can occur if you modify the indents by using the ruler or Paragraph dialog box, or if you change to another list in the Numbering gallery.

To resolve this issue, select the last correctly numbered list item, be sure to include the paragraph mark in your selection since it holds the number format, and on the Home tab, in the Clipboard group, click the Format Painter to copy the correct list format. Then select the incorrectly numbered list item and be sure to include the paragraph mark in your selection. The correct number format should be applied.

To permanently resolve the issue, or if you need to change the list indents or adjust the formatting of the list, create a list style, described in the section titled "Creating a New List Style" later in this chapter on page 397. Use this new list style instead.

Chapter 14

Changing List Indents

Use the Adjust List Indents dialog box to modify the number position, text indent, or change the character that follows a number or bullet. To access the dialog box, right-click a list item and click Adjust List Indents. Figure 14-21 displays the Adjust List Indents dialog box.

Figure 14-21 The Adjust List Indents dialog box enables you to modify the number position, indent, and change the character following a number or bullet.

The Adjust List Indents dialog box includes the following options:

- **Number Position** Changes the position of the number or bullet's indent from the left margin

- **Text Indent** Changes the amount of space between the number or bullet and the beginning of the text

- **Follow Number With** Changes the default Tab character following the number to a space or nothing

- **Add Tab Stop At** If using a Tab character following the bullet or number, adds a manual tab stop at the selected position

---

CAUTION

When you change list indents by using the Adjust List Indents dialog box or using the indent methods described previously in this chapter, such as using the ruler or Paragraph dialog box, you apply direct formatting on top of the list, which can result in list instabilities. Consider creating a list style instead of using direct formatting, which is discussed in the section titled "Creating a New List Style" later in this chapter on page 397.

For more on the impact of using direct formatting in general, see Chapter 15.

Creating and Using Multilevel Lists

Multilevel lists, called Outline Numbering in previous versions of Word, provide the ability to define nine numbering levels. You access the Multilevel List gallery by using the same methods as you do to access the Bullets and Numbering galleries in the Paragraph group's Home tab. The Multilevel List gallery is shown in Figure 14-22.

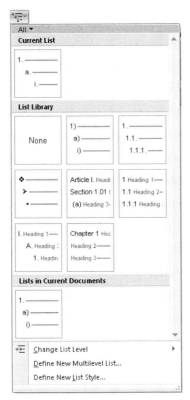

Figure 14-22 The Multilevel List gallery provides the Current List, lists from the List Library, and lists in the Current Document.

You create a multilevel list using the same methods as you would bullets or numbering, as described in the section titled "Creating a Quick List" earlier in this chapter on page 384. The only difference is you use multiple list levels, as opposed to a single list level. When using a multilevel list, you can change the list level by using any of the following methods:

- To promote a list level, press Enter. Continuing to press Enter will promote the list item to the highest level, at which point the list will end. Note that this behavior is new in Word 2007.

- Press Tab to demote the list level, Shift+Tab to promote the list level.

> **Note**
>
> To use Tab and Shift+Tab, the option Set Left And First Indent With Tabs And Backspace must be selected in the AutoCorrect dialog box on the AutoFormat As You Type tab. To display the AutoCorrect dialog box, display Word Options, click Proofing, and then click AutoCorrect Options.

- On the Home tab in the Paragraph group, click Increase Indent to demote the list level, or Decrease Indent to promote the list level.

- Right-click the list item and click Increase Indent to demote the list level, or Decrease Indent to promote the list level.

- Click Multilevel List and at the bottom of the gallery, point at Change List Level and then click the correct list level from the list of choices.

The Multilevel List gallery includes two options for creating a new multilevel list: Define New Multilevel List and Define New List Style. The Define New Multilevel List command is for creating a list that you won't ever change. The Define New List Style command essentially provides "packaging" for a multilevel list that can be easily modified and shared with other documents. Thus, the best practice is to define a new list style as opposed to defining a new multilevel list.

Another reason for this practice is that when you define a new multilevel list, you are actually defining a new list template in the document that cannot be modified. If you need to modify your list, as most do, then a new multilevel list, or list template, will need to be created. Too many list templates can result in general instability in your lists and errors such as "Too many list templates." In such a situation, the only way repair the document or manage and delete list templates is to use Microsoft Visual Basic for Applications (VBA).

> **Note**
>
> How to use VBA to manage and delete list templates is beyond the scope of this book.

Finally, when you create a new list style, you have more control over the list. For example, you can apply the correct list to related list items; format the list style, such as modifying indents; and delete unneeded list styles from your document.

The following sections provide additional information on working with list styles.

Creating a New List Style

To create a new list style, on the Home tab, click the arrow next to Multilevel List. At the bottom of the gallery, click Define New List Style. The Define New List Style dialog box will display as shown here.

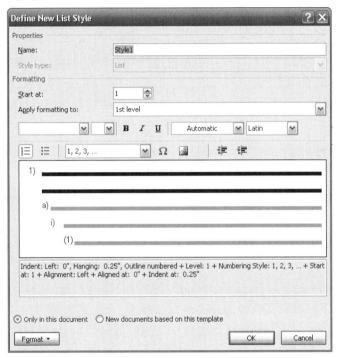

To complete your new list style, follow these steps:

1. In the Name text box, type a name for your style.

2. For a simple list, use the formatting options provided in the Define New List Style dialog box. For example, select a number format or bullet for each level of your list. For a more complex list, or to adjust the list indents, click the Format button at the bottom of the dialog box and then click Numbering. The Modify Multilevel List dialog box is shown here.

Chapter 14

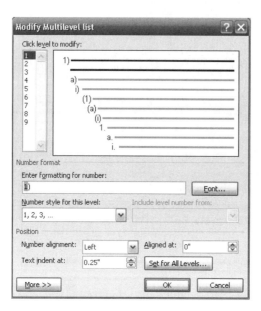

3. In Click Level To Modify, verify level 1 is selected and then set the following options in the order provided here (the order provided is based on the best method to follow, not the order the options appear in the dialog box):

- **Number** Select a Number Style from the Number Style For This Level list. If creating a multilevel list style using bullets, scroll to the bottom of the list to view bullet and picture options.

- **Enter Formatting For Number** Modify the character preceding or following the previously selected number or bullet. For example, replace a parenthesis with a period, or add text preceding the number, such as *Chapter* or *Heading*.

CAUTION

If you modify the shaded value (the number or character selected by using the Number Style For This Level list), the value will not dynamically update.

- **Font** Click the Font button to change the font formatting for the list number or character.

- **Include Level Number From** This option is enabled for levels 2 through 9. It provides the ability to include the number from the previous level, such as 2a), a format that is often used in technical documents.

> **Note**
>
> To use legal style numbering, such as 2.1.1, click More and select the Legal Style Numbering option. The Number list will be disabled, and each level will use legal style numbering. In the Include Level Number From list, select each level of numbering you want to include. For example, for Level 3, select Level 1 and then select Level 2.
>
> If you want periods to appear between the numbers, type them in the Enter Formatting For Number text box after you select each level from the Include Level Number From list.

- ○ **Position** Change the Number Alignment, if necessary. In the Aligned At text box, type a value for the space between the left margin and the number (Left Indent). In the Text Indent At text box, type a value for the space between the number and list text (Hanging Indent).

> **Tip**
>
> To set consistent spacing for each list level so that the next level begins below the text position of the previous level, click Set For All Levels and modify the settings accordingly. A standard offset is 0.25 inches, or 0.64 centimeters, between list levels.

4. Select the next list level and modify the formatting options using the recommended order provided in step 3. Repeat for any additional list levels.

5. When you are finished defining your list style, click OK to close the Multilevel List Style dialog box. Then click OK to close the Define New List Style dialog box and create your new list style.

After you have created your list style, you can use it as you would any other list in the Multilevel List gallery. Your new list style will appear in the section titled List Styles, as shown here.

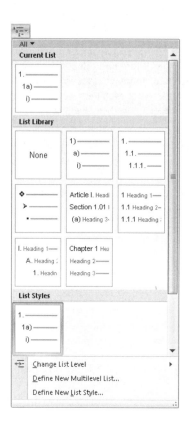

Modifying a List Style

You modify a list style much the same way as you create a new list style. The only difference is your starting point. Display the Multilevel List gallery, locate your list style, right-click the gallery item, and then click Modify. The Modify Style dialog box contains the same options as the Define New List Style dialog box described in the previous section.

If you have several list styles, hover your mouse over the list style that you want to modify, and the name of your style will display in a ScreenTip, as shown here.

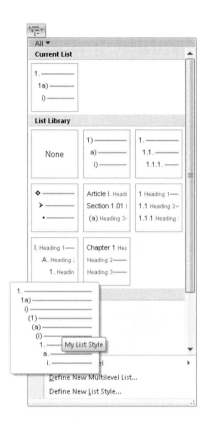

Note that although a list style is a style, it will not display in the Styles task pane. For more information on viewing and managing styles, see Chapter 15.

What's Next?

This chapter covered formatting paragraphs, including alignment, paragraph spacing, pagination formatting, hyphenation, drop caps, and lists in documents. The next chapter covers how to package formatting for ease of reuse and modification by increasing your formatting power with styles.

Using Styles to Increase Your Formatting Power

Styles are the foundation of document formatting. A *style* is a named set of formatting attributes that you can apply to characters, paragraphs, lists, and tables. When you use styles, you can quickly apply multiple formatting settings to specified text. In addition, styles enable you to modify the look of a document easily by changing a style (or styles) instead of manually reformatting components throughout your document.

If you're one who thinks you've never used styles before, indeed you have. Every new document based on the Normal template uses the Normal style by default; built-in templates and those from Microsoft Office Online (www.office.microsoft.com) also incorporate various styles.

There are those who believe that styles should only be used for complex and long documents. However, if you've ever struggled with document formatting, such as discovering that your formats have mysteriously changed in the middle of a document or suddenly finding yourself once again typing in Times New Roman, 12 points after you have selected the entire document content and changed the font to Arial 11 points more times than you can count and you're ready to throw your computer out the window, then this chapter is for you!

For those who already understand the concept of styles, then you'll be pleased to discover that the new Office Open XML file formats have exposed more capabilities than ever before and that style functionality has been greatly improved in Microsoft Office Word 2007. Some notable additions are the ability to define default formats by using Document Defaults, the Style Manager that enables you to restrict specific styles, the Style Inspector that allows you to determine the origination of formats, and Quick Style Sets, which are a new type of formatting template for documents.

This chapter covers how to effectively implement styles along with the new features and style improvements found in Office Word 2007. The first portion of this chapter focuses on formatting and style concepts—the more you understand the role that styles play in document formatting, the greater your formatting power and the easier it is to use styles effectively.

Chapter Assumptions

Because styles encompass numerous Word features, this chapter assumes that you have approached this book in a sequential process and are familiar with formatting basics such as selecting text, adding font and paragraph attributes, Themes, and templates. If you are not familiar with these aspects, then first review Chapter 2, "Document Creation with Word 2007," Chapter 4, "Formatting Documents Using Templates," Chapter 6, "Mastering Document Fundamentals," and Chapter 14, "Aligning Information and Formatting Paragraphs and Lists" to get the most out of this chapter.

Formatting Fundamentals

The first concept to understand when using Word is that there are two basic types of formatting: direct formatting and indirect formatting. Direct formatting is when you directly apply formats to document content such as selecting text, changing the font, adding paragraph indents, and modifying line spacing. Indirect formatting is when you apply a style and the formatting attributes stored in the style, such as the font, paragraph indents, and line spacing, are applied to the selected text indirectly through the style.

The second concept to understand, which is equally important as the first, is that Word is designed to implement styles and, as previously noted, they are the foundation of document formatting. Both of these concepts lead to the action taken by Word if there is ever a question about which type of formatting to maintain. Indirect formatting (or styles) always supersede direct formatting because styles are the formatting foundation, or "formatting glue," for document formats. If you have ever encountered uncontrollable formats, what you've actually encountered is the battle of direct versus indirect formatting—not gremlins or a buggy program. If you're still not convinced and want to see this battle in action, then the following steps provide an example, which for future reference in this chapter is called *Style Example 1*.

1. Create a new blank document (based on the Normal template).

2. Save the document as **Example Styles.docx** for additional examples used in this chapter.

3. On the first line, type **=rand(2,3)** and press Enter to add sample text (two paragraphs, each containing three sentences), in your document.

> **Note**
>
> The sample text, also found in many of the built-in templates, is a built-in function that uses AutoCorrect. If you do not see the sample text after typing =rand(2,3) and pressing Enter, then check your AutoCorrect settings (Alt+T+A) and make sure the Replace Text As You Type option is turned on.

4. Place your cursor in the first paragraph (no text should be selected), navigate to the Home tab, and in the Quick Styles gallery shown in Figure 15-1, click Heading 1 to apply the Heading 1 style to the first paragraph.

Figure 15-1 The Quick Styles gallery, found on the Home tab, contains commonly used styles.

5. Take note of the formats. If using the default styles, the Font is Cambria (Headings), the Font Size is 14 points, the Font Color is Blue (specifically Blue, Accent 1, Darker 25%), and the Bold enhancement is applied.

6. Select the second paragraph (formatted with the Normal style), and directly apply the formats previously noted, with the exception of the font color. That is, change the Font to Cambria (Headings), change the Font Size to 14 points, and add the Bold enhancement. (Or use the formats you previously noted if not using the default styles.)

7. Select both paragraphs, open the Font Color palette, and click Automatic. (If your font color is already Automatic, then use an alternate color.)

Both paragraphs should now display with identical font formatting as shown in Figure 15-2.

> **On the Insert tab, the galleries include items that are designed to coordinate with the overall look of your document. You can use these galleries to insert tables, headers, footers, lists, cover pages, and other document building blocks. When you create pictures, charts, or diagrams, they also coordinate with your current document look.¶**
> **You can easily change the formatting of selected text in the document text by choosing a look for the selected text from the Quick Styles gallery on the Home tab. You can also format text directly by using the other controls on the Home tab. Most controls offer a choice of using the look from the current theme or using a format that you specify directly.¶**

Figure 15-2 In the sample document, the first paragraph was formatted using the built-in Heading 1 style and the second with direct formatting.

8. Keep the paragraphs selected and press Ctrl+Spacebar to reset the formats to those of the underlying styles. (Essentially, this is what Word does in the event that the formats are questioned and only one type of formatting can remain.)

The result of Style Example 1 is that the indirect formats (or styles) are the victor over direct formats. The first paragraph appears almost unchanged, except the Automatic Font Color (direct formatting) has been removed and the blue font color, defined by the

Heading 1 style, has returned. The second paragraph has been stripped of all direct formatting and has reverted to its original formats, which are those of the Normal style, as shown in Figure 15-3.

On the Insert tab, the galleries include items that are designed to coordinate with the overall look of your document. You can use these galleries to insert tables, headers, footers, lists, cover pages, and other document building blocks. When you create pictures, charts, or diagrams, they also coordinate with your current document look.¶

You can easily change the formatting of selected text in the document text by choosing a look for the selected text from the Quick Styles gallery on the Home tab. You can also format text directly by using the other controls on the Home tab. Most controls offer a choice of using the look from the current theme or using a format that you specify directly.¶

Figure 15-3 In the sample document, the first paragraph maintains the formatting supplied by the Heading 1 style, while the second paragraph is stripped of all direct formatting.

If you've never taken advantage of styles before, this example might have shown you that styles are a quick and efficient way to apply numerous formats with one click of the mouse as opposed to five clicks—if you don't count the clicks for text selection. Additionally, one of the biggest advantages to using styles is the ability to change the style definition, or the formats defined in the style. Consequently, all of your document content that is associated with the style automatically updates to the new style definition—that is some incredible formatting power.

Style Fundamentals

As demonstrated in Style Example 1, you can apply multiple formats to text with a single click. The reason that formats were applied to the entire paragraph without the need to select it first is because a Paragraph style type was applied. Word has five primary types of styles for formatting specific content, which are described in the following list:

¶

- **Paragraph** Used for formatting a paragraph as a whole. All paragraph formats, such as alignment, line spacing, indents, tabs, paragraph spacing, borders, and shading, can be defined. Font, or character formats, can also be defined in a paragraph style, and those formats are considered the *Default Paragraph Font*.

> **Note**
>
> The Default Paragraph Font is used when a paragraph contains no direct font formatting and a character style is not applied.

a

- **Character** Font formatting, such as font, font size, bold, italic, underlining, font color, and proofing language, that can be applied to text *in addition* to the Default Paragraph Font defined in the paragraph style. For example, if you have a character style named Note that is defined with only the bold attribute, it takes on all font formatting defined in the paragraph style when applied to text and the only additional font formatting that is added is bold.

> **Note**
>
> Because the Bold format is considered a toggle format, if a character style defined with a Bold format is used in conjunction with a paragraph style that is also defined with the Bold format, the result of text formatted with the character style is not bold, which is an idiosyncrasy of toggle formats: two "on codes" result in an "off code." The result is similar to how a single light controlled by two light switches might work in your house or office. For a workaround to this issue, see Chapter 31, "Working with Macros and VBA."

¶a

- **Linked Style** A combination paragraph and character style. Font formats defined in the style can be used as a character style and applied to a portion of a paragraph, or it can be used as a paragraph style with both the font and paragraph formats applied to the entire paragraph. If you select text within a paragraph and apply a style but the entire paragraph is formatted, then you are using a paragraph style rather than a linked style. Note that the majority of built-in styles in Word 2007 are linked styles.

> **Note**
>
> Heading 1, for example, is actually a linked style and not a paragraph style. In Style Example 1, because the cursor was placed in the paragraph and no text was selected, Heading 1 acted as a paragraph style and the formats were applied to the entire paragraph. Had you selected a portion of the paragraph, then the font formats of the styles would have been applied to the selected text only.

- **List** Used for defining Multilevel Lists. Font formatting can be defined in the style, but the only paragraph formats that can be defined are paragraph indents, which are defined in the numbering format. See Chapter 14, "Aligning Information and Formatting Paragraphs and Lists," for more information on creating and modifying list styles.

- **Table** Used for defining table formatting. Paragraph and font formats can be defined along with Table Properties. Banding formats (alternating row or column colors) and specific table elements, such as the header row, total row, first column, last column, and so on, can be formatted individually.

TROUBLESHOOTING

How do "Char" styles originate and how do I remove them?

If you selected a portion of a paragraph in Microsoft Office Word 2002 and Microsoft Office Word 2003 and applied a paragraph style so as to use only the font formats defined in the style, then essentially you were using a type of linked style. However, in those versions, this capability was automatic and typically spawned the notorious "Char" styles. If you are not familiar with "Char" styles, these styles are given the same name as the paragraph style but have "Char" appended to the end. For example, "Heading 1 Char" is a fairly common style found in many documents created or edited in Office Word 2002 or Office Word 2003. (In versions prior to Word 2002, font formats were applied as direct formatting.) A single "Char" style wasn't a major issue; in fact, that was part of the design. It was the "Char Char" styles, such as "Heading 1 Char Char," that were spawned after applying a "Char" style to a text selection, as shown in the following image.

The Format Painter was the primary culprit behind the "Char Char" styles. After encountering five "Chars" appended to a style name in a document, to this day I use the Format Painter sparingly and can quickly tell how fond the author was of the Format Painter in previous versions by the number of spawned "Char" styles in the document. You can leave the "Char" styles as they are in a document, but if you have a document that contains an abundance of "Char" styles and would like to remove them, see the Inside Out tip titled "Clearing and Deleting Styles" later in this chapter on page 418 for a quick removal solution.

If this Troubleshooting tip has your head spinning in "Chars," thankfully this long-standing issue is rectified in Word 2007. The addition of the Linked Style type removes the automatic spawning of "Char" styles. Users can now specify whether a style must be used as a Paragraph style type, applied to the entire paragraph regardless of text selection, or a Linked style type, in which the font formatting of the style can be applied to text selected within a paragraph as a character style.

Styles are defined and stored with the document and wherever the document goes, the formatting travels with it. If a built-in style, such as Heading 1, is modified in a document, then by default those modifications are only stored in that document and the modification does not change the built-in style.

Word 2007 comes pre-equipped with 264 built-in styles that are available to your documents: 93 paragraph styles, 24 character styles, 4 list styles, and 143 table styles. For those who may be having a slight panic attack right now, rest assured that these styles aren't actually considered "in use" and these definitions are not stored in your document until you use them.

> **Note**
>
> When you create a new document based on the default Normal template, it includes the following defined styles: Normal, Headings 1-3, Default Paragraph Font, Table Normal, and No List. Other styles are available to the document, but they aren't actually defined in your document.

You can also create custom styles, and this chapter covers how to create new styles. Yet more than likely, you will find that one of those 264 styles will fit your formatting needs. If they don't, modifying a style is a matter of a few simple clicks of the mouse, as you will see in the next section involving the Quick Style gallery.

Understanding the Quick Style Gallery and Quick Style Sets

The Quick Style gallery is a new feature in Word 2007 and is intended to be used as a dynamic gallery of frequently used styles. You can add or remove styles shown in the Quick Style gallery as well as modify the formats used by the styles.

Quick Style Sets are, as the name implies, sets of Quick Styles stored as document templates (.dotx files) that you can use with any document. If you frequently used the Organizer to copy styles between documents, or templates, in previous versions of Word, then think of Quick Style Sets as a robust Organizer, or "style packager," that you can use to store various sets of your favorite styles.

In a sense, Quick Style Sets are a new type of template for Word 2007: a template that contains only formatting and no document content. As noted in Chapter 4, if your template needs consist of formatting only, then consider creating new Quick Style Sets instead of creating document templates.

This section covers the ease of applying and modifying styles and the role that Quick Style Sets play in document formatting.

Chapter 15

> **Note**
>
> You may have noticed that the term Quick Styles is used in other chapters. It is not used in reference to the Styles group found on the Home tab because the term Quick Styles is not limited to text styles. Quick Styles are galleries of predefined formats found throughout Word 2007, such as the Picture gallery (Picture Quick Styles), the Chart gallery (Chart Quick Styles), and the SmartArt gallery (SmartArt Quick Styles), to name a few. For a better understanding, if you reduce the width of your Word window small enough, the auto scale functionality of the Ribbon reduces these in-Ribbon galleries to a single button labeled Quick Styles.
>
> For the sake of clarity, the term Quick Styles in this chapter refers to the Quick Style gallery found on the Home tab.

Applying and Modifying Styles Using the Quick Style Gallery

As demonstrated in Style Example 1, using the Quick Style gallery to apply a style is simply a matter of placing your cursor in a paragraph or, depending on the style type, selecting a portion of a paragraph and clicking the desired style. But what if the desired style isn't quite what you are looking for? Perhaps you'd rather see Heading 1 formatted with the Automatic font color instead. To update a style using the Quick Style gallery, follow these simple steps:

1. Open Example Styles.docx, if necessary. Select the first paragraph (formatted with the Heading 1 style) and change the font color, such as to Red, to make your changes stand out.

    Keep the paragraph selected.

2. Navigate to the Home tab and, in the Quick Style gallery, right-click Heading 1. Click Update Heading 1 To Match Selection.

    Heading 1 should now be updated to match the formats found in the current paragraph.

That's all you need to do to redefine a style. If you want to verify your results, place your cursor in the second paragraph and click the Heading 1 style in the Quick Style gallery.

You might have noticed other options when you right-clicked the style, such as Select all # Instance(s); Rename, which allows you to rename the style; Remove From Quick Style Gallery, which removes the style from the gallery but does not remove the style from the document; and Modify, as shown in the following image.

The Modify option opens the Modify Style dialog box and provides additional options that are not available when updating a style using the Update Style Name To Match Selection method. Learn more about the Modify Style dialog box in the section titled "Creating and Modifying Styles" later in this chapter on page 421.

Switching and Modifying Quick Style Sets

Word 2007 includes 11 built-in Quick Style Sets, including a set for the default styles used in Word 2003, as shown in Figure 15-4.

Figure 15-4 Style Sets speed up the formatting process by providing a group of predesigned styles. To preview a style in an open document, simply point to a Style Set name.

Quick Style Sets can be exchanged with other Quick Style Sets, and they can be modi-fied for a document, or template, by using the steps provided in the previous section. To demonstrate exchanging Quick Style Sets, follow these steps:

1. Open Example Styles.docx if necessary, and apply the Normal style to the second paragraph.

2. On the Home tab, click Change Styles. Point at Style Sets, and hover your mouse over the Style Set list.

Note how Live Preview shows you how the formats of the Quick Styles Sets will look if used in your document.

3. Once you find a Style Set you like, click to exchange the Quick Styles with the new Style Set.

> **Note**
>
> To exchange document formatting in documents you already created using a Quick Style Set, styles in the document must use the same style names as those used in the new Quick Style Set.

If you find the results are a little garish, keep in mind that a heading paragraph, formatted with a Heading style, is typically a short paragraph consisting of only a few words. Feel free to modify the document content, such as creating a single paragraph out of the text that reads "On the Insert tab," and formatting the remaining text from the original paragraph with the Normal style or another style, such as Quote, which is shown in the following image with the Formal Quick Style Set.

ON THE INSERT TAB¶

The galleries include items that are designed to coordinate with the overall look of your document. You can use these galleries to insert tables, headers, footers, lists, cover pages, and other document building blocks. When you create pictures, charts, or diagrams, they also coordinate with your current document look.¶

You can easily change the formatting of selected text in the document text by choosing a look for the selected text from the Quick Styles gallery on the Home tab. You can also format text directly by using the other controls on the Home tab. Most controls offer a choice of using the look from the current theme or using a format that you specify directly.¶

> **Themes vs. Quick Style Sets**
>
> At first glance, applying Themes and Quick Style Sets might seem like a great way to set the stage for formatting conflicts. Actually, these two features work together to define document formatting for Theme-enabled documents, and it is the reason why Theme Colors and Theme Fonts are also accessible in the Change Styles options. To differentiate the roles, Themes control the Theme Fonts and Theme Colors in a document, while Quick Style Sets use Theme Fonts and Theme Colors in their style definitions. When you change the Theme, the fonts and colors used in the Quick Style Sets also change. For more information on Themes, see Chapter 2, "Document Creation with Word 2007" and Chapter 5, "Applying Themes for a Professional Look."

Custom Quick Style Sets

As previously mentioned, Quick Style Sets are stored in external document template (.dotx) files, and you can easily save the set of Quick Styles for any document as a Quick Style Set. For an example of how to create a new Quick Style Set, open Example Styles. docx and follow these steps:

1. Modify the formatting of the first paragraph (the one with Heading 1 style applied) to your choice of formats.

   Keep in mind that this is a heading style and that you typically want text format- ted with Heading 1 to stand out from the rest of the text in a document.

2. Once you have made your modifications, right-click Heading 1 in the Quick Styles gallery and click Update Heading 1 To Match Selection.

> **Note**
>
> If you want Theme-enabled Quick Style Sets, then use fonts from the Theme Fonts area of the Font list (use (Headings) or (Body) depending on the type of style you are modify- ing or creating) and colors from the Theme Colors area in the Font Color palette.

3. Apply Heading 2 to the first paragraph, make your desired formatting changes, right-click Heading 2 in the Quick Styles gallery, and click Update Heading 2 to Match Selection. Repeat this step as necessary for other Quick Styles you want to modify.

4. If you do not want to include a style in your Quick Style Set, right-click the style and click Remove From Quick Style Gallery.

   Note that this does not delete the style, but only removes it from the gallery.

5. Once you make all of your changes, click Change Styles, point to Style Set, and click Save As Quick Style Set at the bottom of the list. The Save Quick Style Set dialog box displays.

CAUTION

> In addition to saving the styles listed in the Quick Style Gallery, the Document Defaults are also saved in a Quick Style Set and should be set accordingly, or you may encounter undesired results in other styles when using your custom Quick Style Set in other docu- ments. For more on Document Defaults, see the section titled "Managing Styles" later in this chapter on page 431.

Chapter 15

6. In the Save As Quick Style dialog box, do not change the Save In folder. Type a name for your new Quick Style Set in the File Name text box, such as **Example Quick Style Set**, and click Save.

Your Quick Style Set is saved in the QuickStyles folder and is now assessable in the list of Style Sets for all documents, as shown in the following image.

7. Test your new Quick Style Set by creating a new document, and change the Quick Style Set accordingly.

> **Note**
>
> Any template, or document, placed in the QuickStyles folder that contains Quick Styles is available in the list of Style Sets. The QuickStyles folder will be in one of the following locations depending on your operating system:
>
> Windows Vista: C:\Users*user name*\AppData\Roaming\Microsoft
>
> Windows XP: C:\Documents and Settings*user name*\Application Data\Microsoft

To delete a custom Quick Style Set, simply delete the Quick Style Set file from the QuickStyles folder. Built-in Quick Style Sets, which are found in the installation path for the Microsoft Office 2007 system, can also be modified and deleted.

To learn more about customizing Quick Style Sets, such as defining the style sort order or blocking Quick Style Set switching in specific documents or templates, see the section titled "Managing Styles" later in this chapter on page 431.

INSIDE OUT   **Resetting Quick Styles**

When you modify styles that are part of the Quick Style Set or change Quick Style Sets, you have the option to reset the styles. The options for resetting can be found at the bottom of the Quick Style Set list. These two options, Reset To Quick Styles From Template and Reset Document Quick Styles, might appear to provide the same functionality; however, there is a distinct difference between these options.

Reset Document Quick Styles is only available if you change Quick Style Sets or modify styles in the Quick Style gallery. When this option is used, the Quick Styles revert to the formatting of the Quick Style Set saved with the last version of the document. If you are experimenting with Quick Styles, you can always return to the formatting defined in the Quick Styles when the document was first opened. Note that once the document is saved and closed, any changes you made to Quick Styles become the new document Quick Styles. Additionally, this option only applies to those styles that are part of the Quick Style gallery and does not reset any other styles in the document.

Reset To Quick Styles From *Template* (if the document template is not the Normal template, then the command reads Reset To Quick Styles From *Template Name* Template) resets the Quick Styles to those in the attached document template. This option is similar to using the Automatically Update Document Styles option found in the Templates And Add-ins dialog box, previously discussed in Chapter 4. However, it only applies to styles in the Quick Style gallery and not to all document styles. If you need to update all styles in a document, use the Automatically Update Document Styles option instead.

To set a Quick Style Set as your default set of styles for all new documents based on the Normal template, use the Set As Default command under Change Styles.

If the command reads Set Default for *Template Name* Template, then the defaults are set for all documents based on the template indicated in the text of the command.

Making Styles Work for You

If you are wondering about the other 248 built-in styles not shown by default in the Quick Style gallery, this section of the chapter covers how you can access them.

Along with the Quick Style gallery, there are two additional tools—the Styles task pane, or *pane*, and the Apply Styles pane—that you can use to access styles, as well as another style tool designed specifically for the Quick Access Toolbar, which is discussed in the Inside Out tip titled "Where is the Old Styles Combo Box?" later in this section on page 416. In general, they provide the same functionality, and you can use them either in combination or use only the tool that meets your needs. The following list describes the Styles pane and Apply Styles pane and how to access them:

- **Styles Pane** Primary tool for applying and modifying styles. Provides a list of styles and access to style management tools such as the New Style dialog box, Style Inspector, and Manage Styles dialog box. To access the Styles pane, click the dialog launcher in the Styles group on the Home tab or press Alt+Ctrl+Shift+S to toggle its view.

- **Apply Styles Pane** Smaller than the Styles pane, it uses a combo box to access styles. It is intended to be used as a small floating pane, but can be docked. To access the Apply Styles pane, click the More button on the Quick Styles gallery and then click Apply Styles below the gallery, or press Ctrl+Shift+S to display the Apply Styles pane shown in the following image.

> **Note**
>
> The keyboard shortcut, Ctrl+Shift+S, moves your cursor to the Apply Styles pane while pane is displayed. This enables a keyboard method for applying styles by typing the style name, or the first few letters if the AutoComplete Style Names option is turn on, and pressing Enter.

To apply a style using any of these tools, simply place your cursor in a paragraph, select a portion of a paragraph, or select multiple paragraphs and click the style to apply it.

INSIDE OUT   Where is the Old Styles Combo Box?

If you recognized the Ctrl+Shift+S keyboard shortcut from previous versions of Word but didn't see the old familiar Styles combo found previously on the Formatting toolbar, rest assured that you can still use the Styles combo box in Word 2007. Originally, the Apply Styles pane was to be the replacement control, but it wasn't quite the same. Namely, many Word veterans felt it took up too much room and, during the beta, they voiced their concerns. Microsoft listened to the feedback and created a Styles combo box that can be added to the Quick Access Toolbar—the ability to hold Shift and then click the list arrow to toggle the display of all styles was included as well. To add the Styles combo box, click the More button at the end of the Quick Access Toolbar and then click More Commands. From the Choose From list, click Commands Not In The Ribbon, locate Style as shown in the following image, and click Add to add it to your Quick Access Toolbar.

Keep in mind that commands added to the Quick Access Toolbar are automatically assigned keyboard accelerators. To view the KeyTip for your Styles combo, press the Alt key
and note the KeyTip so you can access the Styles combo using the keyboard by pressing
Alt and the number (or number and letter depending on the number of buttons you
have on your Quick Access toolbar) displayed in the KeyTip, if desired.

Mastering the Styles Pane

The Styles And Formatting task pane made its appearance in Word 2002 and, although
renamed to Styles in Word 2007, it continues to serve as your central hub for style management. To open the Styles pane, click the dialog launcher in the Styles group on the
Home tab, or press Alt+Ctrl+Shift+S. Two examples of the Styles pane, with and without
the formatting preview, are shown in Figure 15-5.

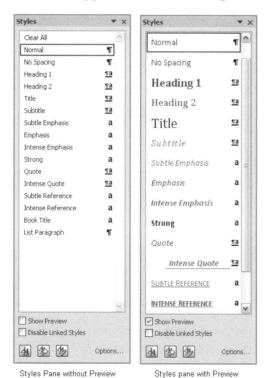

Figure 15-5 The Styles pane is shown with the default view on the left and the Show Preview option selected on the right.

When you create a new document based on the Normal template in Word 2007, the Styles pane shows the same styles found in the Quick Style gallery by default. You can display all styles by using the Options link at the bottom of the Styles pane.

Table and list styles do not display in the Styles pane. Instead, list styles can be accessed using Multilevel List on the Home tab in the Paragraph group, and Table styles can be accessed in the Table Styles gallery on the contextual Design tab that is displayed when a table is active. However, both the Apply Styles pane and Styles combo box can list all 264 styles, including table and list styles.

The Styles pane contains the following elements:

- **Styles list** The Styles list shows the name of the style followed by a symbol that identifies the style type—paragraph (¶), character (a), and linked (¶a). If no symbol appears next to a list item, the item represents direct formatting (not shown by default). For any style in the Style list, you can hover the pointer over the style to view a summary of the style's settings (style definition) and access additional options by clicking the arrow that appears to the left (or right-click the style), which includes options that are similar to those you see when you right-click a style in the Quick Style gallery such as Update Style Name To Match Selection, Select All # Instance(s), Modify, and Add To Quick Style Gallery. It also includes the ability to delete a style and clear the formatting from text that uses the style. For in-depth information on these options, see the following Inside Out tip titled "Clearing and Deleting Styles."

INSIDE OUT   Clearing and Deleting Styles

When you delete a style, if the style is currently used in the document, text formatted with the deleted style reverts to the Normal style and text formatted with a character style reverts to direct formatting. If the style is based on another style, the option reads Revert To *Style Name* and reverts to the style identified. However, styles that are linked to additional functionality in Word, such as the Heading styles and the Normal style, cannot be deleted.

Additionally, when you delete a built-in style, it's removed from the document but not necessarily deleted. It remains in the style list and is available for future use; however, if it was previously modified, it reverts to its default settings.

The Clear Formatting Of # Instances option, found when you click the arrow to the left of a style, or right-click a style, in the Styles pane, is similar to deleting a style. Text reverts to the Normal style, but all font formatting is cleared and the style itself remains unchanged. Note that you can also use the Clear Formatting option, found on the Home tab in the Font group, and the Clear All option in the Styles pane to accomplish the same result on selected text.

TROUBLESHOOTING

I can't use the Select All or Clear All options in the Styles pane

If you find that the Select All or Clear Formatting options are disabled when you click the arrow to the left of a style in the Styles pane and the style is in use—even if the disabled text indicates it isn't—this typically occurs because the Keep Track Of Formatting option is not selected in the Word Options dialog box. To locate this option, display Word Options, click Advanced, and The Keep Track Of Formatting option can be found in the Editing Options area.

- **Show Preview** You can view style formats in the Styles list to help you find styles visually. Figure 15-5 shows the Styles pane with the Show Preview option setting selected and without the Show Preview option setting selected.

- **New Style** Displays the Create New Style From Formatting dialog box, where you can create a new style. Additional details on new styles can be found in the section titled "Creating and Modifying Styles" later in this chapter on page 421.

- **Style Inspector** Opens the Style Inspector dialog box, which helps you to identify the style and formatting applied to paragraphs and text. Using the Style Inspector, you can open the Reveal Formatting task pane as well as identify and clear styles and formatting, discussed in the section titled "Inspecting Styles" later in this chapter on page 426.

- **Manage Styles** Opens the Manage Styles dialog box, which enables you to modify, create, and import/export styles; specify the names and order of the styles that show in the Styles pane and Apply Styles list by default; and restrict availability of styles and the ability to change style sets or Themes. For more information, see the section titled "Style Management Tools" later in this chapter on page 426.

- **Options** Opens the Style Pane Options dialog box, shown in Figure 15-6. Options enables you to specify which styles are displayed, such as Recommended, In Use, In Current Document, or All Styles, and how they are sorted. You can also enable the display of direct formatting in the Styles list and Styles combo box. As previously noted, direct formatting does not include a style type symbol to the left of the name.

Chapter 15

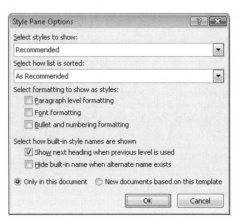

Figure 15-6 The Style Pane Options dialog box enables you to set display options for styles.

> **Note**
>
> The Hide Alternate Name If Built-In Name Exists option is used when an alias, or another name, is assigned to a style. They are created by typing a comma after the style name when creating, modifying, or renaming a style and then typing the alias. If you see a style name such as Heading 1, H1, H1 is the alias. The primary purpose of an alias is to enable quick navigation to the style when using the keyboard method to apply styles using either the Apply Styles pane or Styles combo box.

INSIDE OUT Selecting and Changing All Instances of a Style

After you apply styles to your text, you're ready to take advantage of the groundwork you've laid. You can easily conduct formatting tasks by working with styles instead of your content. For instance, when you use styles, you can select all instances of a style whenever the need arises. Being able to select all instances of a style speeds up a number of tasks related to consistent formatting or similar elements. For example, you might want to select all instances of styled text because you want to replace one style with another. You might want to delete all text that appears in a particular style (such as all paragraphs formatted as Notes To Self within a working document), or you might want to copy all similarly styled elements to a new document (such as all headlines from a newsletter to create a promotional piece). Regardless of your reasons, the Select All # Instances of *Style Name*, found by right-clicking a style in the Quick Style gallery or on the options displayed when clicking the arrow to the left of a style on the Styles pane, can make short work of what could otherwise be cumbersome tasks.

Creating and Modifying Styles

Up to this point in the chapter, we've looked at existing styles. You could most likely create the majority of your documents using the built-in styles. Doing so ensures that your documents look consistent, your formatting time is reduced, and your documents are able to interact with other Word functionality, such as switching Quick Style Sets, and tools that rely on styles such as a Table of Contents, the Document Map, and Outline view, to name a few. But there might come a time when you can't find an existing style to fit your needs, or you might need to modify a style beyond simply updating it to match the formatting.

Many complex documents, such as the manuscript used to create this book, may use a set of styles to format specific document components. For example, there are three primary styles used for an Inside Out tip: a style for the title, a style for the text in the tip, and a style to denote the end of the tip. These types of situations call for creating custom styles. This section covers creating new styles along with how to modify styles by using the Modify Style dialog box.

 One of the easiest ways to create a style is to format existing text and then define a style based on the formatted text. To successfully create a style using this technique, select and format text within your document (remember to consider font characteristics as well as paragraph settings) and then click the New Style button in the Styles pane to display the Create New Style From Formatting dialog box as shown in Figure 15-7.

Figure 15-7 The Create New Style From Formatting dialog box enables you to configure a variety of properties when you create a new style. Although the dialog box's options are similar for the paragraph, character, and linked styles, the dialog box's options change slightly when creating table and list styles.

> **Note**
>
> To familiarize yourself with the options for creating paragraph and list styles, review Chapter 14 and Chapter 11, "Organizing Concepts in Tables."

The Create New Style From Formatting dialog box offers options specific to the type of style you're creating (character, paragraph, linked [paragraph and character], table, or list), as well as access to formatting options found throughout Word. You'll find that the options in the Formatting area change depending on the type of style you are creating, and the Format button at the bottom provides access to the various dialog boxes if you are looking for a specific formatting option that isn't available in the main dialog box. Depending on the style type, some dialog boxes are inaccessible if the formats are not supported. If you need to review the style types and supported formatting, see the section titled "Style Fundamentals" earlier in this chapter on page 406.

After you customize your formats in a document and display the Create New Style From Formatting dialog box, finish creating your new style by following these steps:

1. In the dialog box, type a name for your new style in the Name box.

    Think carefully when you consider names to associate with styles—the more descriptive your style names are, the easier it is for you (and others) to identify each style's purpose and apply the proper style within documents.

2. In the Style Type list box, specify whether your style is a paragraph, character, linked (paragraph and character), table, or list style. Most styles are paragraph or linked styles.

3. Specify a style on which to base your new style. (See the section titled "Additional Style Options" on page 424 for more information on this option.)

4. Set the style for the following paragraph. (See the section titled "Additional Style Options" on page 424 for more information on this option.)

5. In the Formatting area, configure any additional properties for your style using the Font and Size options as well as color selection, alignment, line spacing, above and below spacing, and indents.

6. If necessary, click Format to access additional formatting options, as shown in Figure 15-8.

Figure 15-8 The Format button enables you to access dialog boxes that provide more de-tailed formatting options.

7. When you finish configuring formatting options, click OK.

> **Tip**
>
> To quickly create a new style based on your formatting and add it to the Quick Style gallery, right-click the text, point to Styles, and then click Save Selection As New Quick Style. Alternatively, click the More button on the Quick Style gallery and then click Save Selection As New Quick Style.

The newly created style appears in the Styles pane as well as in the Quick Styles gallery. You can use and modify your new styles just as if they were built-in styles. The next few sections address some of the additional configuration options found in the Create New Style From Formatting dialog box, such as the Style Based On and Style For Following Paragraph options.

Modifying Existing Styles

Modifying a style is just as easy as creating a style. The main difference between creating and modifying styles is that you use the Modify Style dialog box instead of the Create New Style From Formatting dialog box. The following list provides the most common methods used for accessing the Modify Style dialog box:

- **Apply Styles dialog box** Select a style in the Style Name list and click Modify.

- **Quick Styles gallery** Right-click the style and choose Modify. If you simply want to change a style's name, right-click a style and click Rename to open the Rename Style dialog box.

- **Styles pane** Hover the pointer over a style name, click the arrow, and choose Modify, or right-click a style name and click Modify.

The Modify Style dialog box looks very similar to its counterpart, the Create New Style From Formatting dialog box. It contains the same options and enables you to configure most of the same settings that are available when you create a new style.

Additional Style Options

The additional options in the Create New Style From Formatting dialog box can be quite powerful in document creation if used correctly. Some of the options need little explanation, such as Add To Quick Style List, which adds your style to the Quick Style gallery. Other options, such as whether the new or modified style should be added to all documents based on the document's template or limited to only the current document, Style Based On, Style For The Following Paragraph, and Automatically Update, need a little more explanation and are covered in this section.

Basing Styles on Existing Styles

By default, the styles you create in the Create New Styles From Formatting dialog box are based on whichever style was in use when you accessed the dialog box. A good way to understand a based-on style is to think of it as a parent style. When you base a style on another style, it means that your style uses all of the settings of the based-on style plus whatever modifications you make to the style unless you explicitly define the settings. This provides you with the capability to link or "chain" styles together.

For example, if you create a new style, base it on Heading 1, and your new style is defined with only the Center paragraph alignment format, then your new style inherits any changes made to Heading 1 but always maintains the Center format—even if Heading 1 uses the Left alignment format. Although this enables consistency in related styles, this option can also create a mess if you're not careful. It's for this reason that many people use Normal or (No Style) as their based-on style. If you want more insight into the difference between basing a style on the Normal style or (No Style), see the section titled "The Relationship Between Document Defaults, the Normal Style, and (No Style)" later in this chapter on page 434.

> **Note**
>
> When a style is based on another style, the Delete *Style Name* option in the Styles pane reads Revert To *Style Name*. When the Revert command is used, the style is deleted and all paragraphs formatted with the style revert to the base style as opposed to the Normal style.

Specifying Styles for Following Paragraphs

Some styles are predictable—you can predict which style elements are likely to precede or follow them 99 percent of the time. For example, most of the headings in your documents are probably followed by Normal text, or perhaps your documents use a figure number element that is almost always followed or preceded by a figure caption. You can take advantage of style predictability and save yourself many unnecessary formatting steps by configuring settings for paragraphs that follow specific elements.

When you specify a style for a paragraph that automatically follows text that has a particular style, you specify that you want to apply that style after you press Enter at the end of the current style. You can easily specify a style for a subsequent paragraph as you're creating a new style. To do so, select a style in the Style For Following Paragraph list box in the Create New Style From Formatting dialog box.

If you don't specify a subsequent paragraph style, Word continues to use the current style for subsequent paragraphs until you choose another style.

Allowing Styles to Automatically Update

The Automatically Update option can be one of the most dangerous options in the dialog box if used incorrectly or the most beneficial if used correctly. When you allow a style to automatically update, every formatting change you make to text to which the style is applied automatically changes the style definition, and all text formatted with the style updates before your eyes. While this sounds like a marvelous idea and one that could help tremendously with formatting tasks, consider applying the bold format to a portion of a paragraph and finding other paragraphs in your document are also bold. Better yet, if another group of styles is using that style as their based-on style, a good portion of your document could end up bold as well—except, of course, those words that are already bold. They will no longer be bold because bold is a toggle format and, as previously noted in the section titled "Style Fundamentals," two bold formats result in a not-bold format. (You might encounter similar results if you do not use a little thought when setting the Style Based On option.)

Even though the Automatically Update option is more stable in Word 2007 when it comes to adding some direct formatting to a portion of a paragraph and you're less likely to encounter such a dire change (it was fairly common in previous versions), it's still wise to use this option only for text that should always be formatted identically. For example, some features in Word, such as Table of Contents, use this option in the TOC styles that are used to format each level of a Table of Contents because those formats should always be identical.

Modifying the Document Template

By default, when you create a new style in Word, it is only added to the active document. If you modify a built-in style, that modification applies only to the existing document. But you have the option to add the style, or modifications, to the template attached to the active document. You can easily add a new style to a template by selecting the New Documents Based On This Template option in the Create New Style From Formatting dialog box or the Modify Style dialog box before you click OK.

Keep in mind that when you add a style to a template, you add the style to the template that's attached to the current document. As you might imagine, because Normal.dotm is the default template in Word, the Normal template is used for a great number of documents. If the style you are adding is not a style you commonly use, then consider creating either a Quick Style Set or, depending on your needs, a custom template instead, as described in Chapter 4.

Chapter 15

> **Note**
>
> If you add or modify a style to the document template, you are prompted to save changes when closing the file. However, if the document template is the Normal template, you are only prompted to save changes to the Normal template when you exit Word if the Prompt Before Saving Normal Template option is turned on in Word Options in the Advanced area.
>
> If you inadvertently add a style to a template, including the Normal template, you must open the template to delete the style or use the Import/Export button in the Manage Styles dialog box to display the Organizer and use it to delete the style. For more information on the Organizer, see Chapter 4.

Style Management Tools

You'll often want to inspect formatting by using the Style Inspector and the Reveal Formatting task pane, as well as another new exciting and long-awaited feature for styles called Manage Styles, which provides the ability to manage them.

Inspecting Styles

To open the Style Inspector, click the Style Inspector button in the Styles pane (press Ctrl+Shift+Alt+S to open the Styles pane). You can keep the Styles Inspector open even if you close the Styles pane or change views. Figure 15-9 shows the Style Inspector.

Figure 15-9 The Style Inspector helps you verify that styles are properly applied to paragraphs and text to clear formatting when necessary.

The Style Inspector distinguishes Paragraph Formatting and Text Level Formatting along with any additional direct formats that may be applied and provides four buttons for clearing formats. Each button uses the same icon, but they each serve a different purpose as described in the following list:

- **Reset To Normal Paragraph Style** Resets the paragraph to the Normal style, but leaves any character styles or direct font formatting.

- **Clear Paragraph Formatting (Ctrl+Q)** Clears any direct paragraph formats listed in the Plus area, such as an indent that is not defined in the style.

- **Clear Character Style** Clears a character style and resets font formatting to the Default Paragraph Font, but leaves any direct font formatting.

- **Clear Character Formatting (Ctrl+Spacebar)** Clears any direct font formatting listed in the Plus area, such as a font that is not defined in the style.

> **Tip**
>
> To quickly scan styles that are applied to a document, configure your Draft or Outline view to display the Style Area, which will list the style that is currently applied to the left of the paragraph. To view the Style Area, display Word Options and, in the Advanced area, navigate to the Display options. In the Style Area Width text box, type a value in your preferred unit of measure, such as 1 inch or 2.54 centimeters.
>
> Note that you must be using the Draft and Outline view to see the Style Area.

Reveal Formatting Task Pane

Occasionally, you might find that you need a deeper inspection of the formatting applied to a selection. The Reveal Formatting pane can be displayed using the Reveal Formatting button on the Style Inspector or by placing your cursor in the text you want to further inspect and pressing Shift+F1. The Reveal Formatting pane is shown in Figure 15-10.

Chapter 15

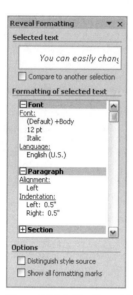

Figure 15-10 The Reveal Formatting pane lists the format settings for the text at the insertion point.

The Reveal Formatting pane lists all of the format specifications for the selected text. The format items are grouped into three basic categories:

- **Font** This group includes format settings that apply to the characters used in the document, including the font type and size, as well as the proofing language for the selected text.

- **Paragraph** This group contains format settings for aspects of the paragraph such as the selected paragraph style, text alignment, indentation settings, and paragraph spacing (before and after spacing, as well as line spacing).

- **Section** This group includes the format settings you use to control larger portions of the document including overall margin settings, page layout choices, and paper selections.

> **Note**
>
> Depending on the selected text, other areas display in the Reveal Formatting pane. For example, a table includes Table and Cell areas, and a numbered or bulleted list has a Bullets and Numbering area.

You can make formatting changes to the text at the insertion point right from the Reveal Formatting pane by simply clicking the blue underlined link to open the relevant dialog box.

Comparing to Other Text Formats

Another fantastic time-saving option available to you in the Reveal Formatting pane is the ability to compare and contrast similar text styles with subtle differences. Have you ever studied a heading and wondered why it doesn't look quite right compared with another heading in your document? Stop trying to visually note the differences and use Reveal Formatting to compare the formatting differences for you, as shown in the following graphic.

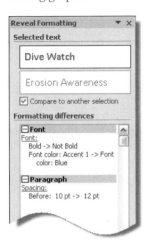

First, select your comparison text in a document, click Compare To Another Selection, and then make another selection. The Reveal Formatting pane shows every formatting difference between the selections. To modify the formats, click the blue underlined links in the task pane to open the relevant dialog box.

> **Tip**
>
> To access additional options for the compared text, click the arrow to the left of the compared text. Options include Select All Text With Similar Formatting, Apply Formatting Of Original Selection, and Clear Formatting.

Tracking Inconsistent Formatting

Another way to keep an eye on styles while you work is to turn on the option to track inconsistent formatting. When this option is turned on, a blue wavy line appears under text that uses direct formatting similar to a style used in your document. If this option were turned on for Style Example 1, the second paragraph would be identified as inconsistent formatting with a wavy blue line because the formatting was similar to the Heading 1 style. Similarly, if some italic formatting is directly applied while other italic formatting in your document is applied by using the Emphasis style, the italic formatting applied directly is identified with the blue wavy underline as shown in the following image.

Our fundraising has reached new heights, which enables us
to maintain a high-level of aid for our recovery programs
related to the *tsunami*, *hurricanes*, *oil fires*, and other
recent disasters.

To control whether this feature is turned on or off, you must configure Word Options. To do this, click the Microsoft Office Button, click Word Options and click Advanced. In the Editing Options area, select Keep Track Of Formatting (if necessary; this option is selected by default), select Mark Formatting Inconsistencies, and then click OK.

> **Note**
>
> The new contextual spelling feature also uses a blue wavy line to identify possible contextual spelling errors. For more on this feature, see Chapter 9, "Refining with Research Services and Reference Tools."

INSIDE OUT   Where Did that Style Come from?

One final offering in the Reveal Formatting pane that's worth a mention: You can find the source of a particular style by selecting the Distinguish Style Source check box at the bottom of the Reveal Formatting pane.

Selecting this check box causes Word to display the style from which the new style was created. For example, if a Note style applied to a segment of text in your document was created based on your Body Text style, the task pane shows you that information. That's helpful to know if you're planning to change the Body Text style at some point—you'll be able to see at a glance which other items in your document will be affected by the change.

Managing Styles

In previous versions of Word, there were few capabilities to manage styles. Namely, if you wanted to limit a document—or documents based on a specific template—to a specific set of styles, you needed to use the Document Protection features. Now, in Word 2007, the Manage Style dialog box enables you to limit formatting to styles, as in previous versions, and hide styles from the Styles pane and Apply Styles dialog box, as well as disable some style functions, such as Quick Style Set switching and Theme switching. To access the Manage Styles dialog box, on the Styles pane, click Manage Styles to open the dialog box. The four tabs in the dialog box are described in the following list:

- **Edit** The Edit tab, shown in the following graphic, enables modification of all styles, even those that are not currently displayed in the Styles pane, and allows for the creation of new styles. Additionally, the Sort Order option includes the ability to list styles By Type and Based On style.

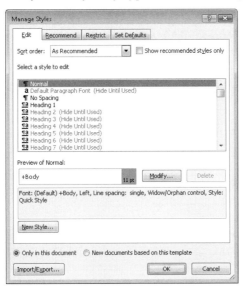

> **Note**
>
> The Import/Export button opens the Organizer, which allows you to copy styles between documents and templates, rename, and delete styles. For more information on using the Organizer to copy styles and between templates and documents, see Chapter 4.

- **Recommend**   The Recommend tab, shown in the following graphic, enables the creation of a Recommended list of styles that are used when displaying Recommended styles in the Styles pane. This tab allows you to specify the sort order of Recommended styles, hide styles from view until they are used, or always hide the styles. Those assigned with the same priority will sort alphabetically.

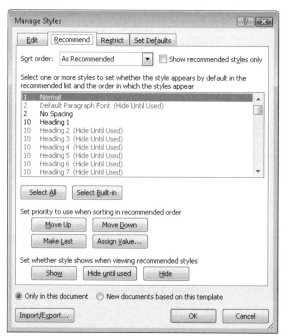

- **Restrict**   The Restrict tab, shown in the following image, enables you to restrict specific styles as well as block Theme switching and Quick Style Set switching. For example, if a document must be limited to Headings 1–3, then you can restrict all other heading styles. The Limit Formatting To Permitted Styles option restricts formatting to only those styles that are marked as restricted and disables direct formatting, which includes font formatting such as Bold, Italic, and Underline; a character style must be used instead. This option can also be password protected and is the same as using the Limit Formatting Styles To A Selection Of Styles option found on the Restrict Formatting And Editing pane, which can be displayed from the Review tab and Protect Document button.

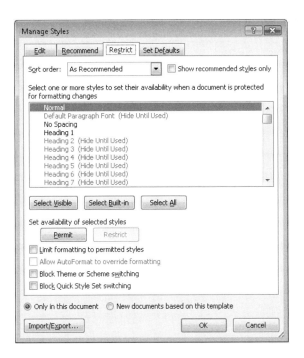

> **Note**
>
> In the option labeled Block Theme Or Scheme Switching, both terms refer to Themes. There isn't a separate Scheme functionality.

- **Set Defaults** The settings on the Set Defaults tab, shown in the following image, control the Document Defaults for font and paragraph formatting in a document. If you do not explicitly define a format in a style, the Document Defaults are used. For example, assume that you create a new style and do not change the default font. If you later change the font for the Document Defaults, your style also uses the newly defined font. Additionally, when you save a Quick Style Set, the current Document Defaults are also saved and defined as the Document Defaults for the Quick Style Set. For more information about this feature, see the following section titled "The Relationship Between Document Defaults, the Normal Style, and (No Style)."

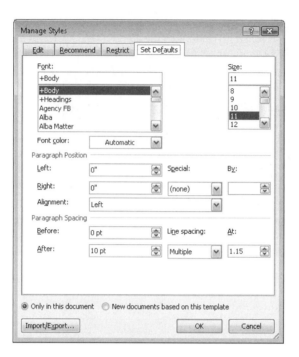

> **Tip**
>
> Additional font and paragraph formats can be set for the Document Defaults that are not displayed on the Set Defaults tab. To set additional font defaults, click the dialog launcher in the Font group on the Home tab to display the Font dialog box. To set additional paragraph defaults, click the dialog launcher in the Paragraph group on the Home tab to display the Paragraph dialog box.
>
> For either dialog box, set your desired formats, click the Default button at the bottom of the dialog box, and confirm the changes when prompted.

The Relationship Between Document Defaults, the Normal Style, and (No Style)

In previous versions of Word, the Document Defaults were hard-wired into the application and could not be changed. Now, in Word 2007, the switch to Office Open XML Formats enabled one of the biggest advancements in styles: the Document Defaults are now stored in documents (and templates) and can be modified easily. Understanding the role that Document Defaults play is crucial in creating well-behaved documents. It can help you determine what you should use for your based-on style and perhaps help you avoid certain style nuances that can occur if your styles are not set correctly.

An interesting style aspect that many Word veterans might never have realized is if you do not modify the Normal style in a document or if the formats for the Normal style match those of the Document Defaults, the Normal style isn't actually defined—it's an "empty" style and the Document Defaults are used instead. That being the case, in Word 2007, if you do not modify your Normal style and if you base your styles on the Normal style, essentially you are using the Document Defaults, and changes made to the Document Defaults are reflected in the Normal style.

The exposure of Document Defaults also changes the behavior of using (No Style) as your base style from previous versions. Like the Normal style, (No Style) also looks to the Document Defaults to obtain base formats. If your formats are not explicitly defined in your style, then those from the Document Defaults are used.

For example, assume that you base a style on (No Style) and do not use a font that is different from the font defined in the Document Defaults. If you later change the font in the Document Defaults, that change is also reflected in the style. It may be interesting to note that the behavior of (No Style) hasn't actually changed from previous versions; we simply did not have access to the Document Defaults and were unable to make formatting modifications.

TROUBLESHOOTING

My table Style will not accept my preferred font size

A longstanding issue when creating table styles is the inability to set a specific font size for the table style. Various scenarios might occur, but one example is if the font size of the Normal style is 12 points, you cannot set a font size of 10 points in the table style. Another example is if the font size of the Normal style is greater than 12 points, then you cannot specify a font size in the table style. In both examples, the font size for the Normal style is used instead.

The underlying reason for the table style issues is the modification of the Normal style. As explained in the previous section, "The Relationship Between Document Defaults, the Normal Style, and (No Style)," if the Normal style is the same as the Document Defaults, then the Normal style is empty and the Document Defaults are used. If the Normal style is not empty and a font size is defined, then the font size defined in the Normal style takes precedence over the table style.

Even if you may not completely grasp the underlying rationale—it took working through several scenarios to fully understand this myself—the solution to this issue is simple. All you need to do is modify the formats for the Normal style so that they match those of the Document Defaults. Then modify the Document Defaults and use it as your formatting base instead of the Normal style. If the Normal style is left unchanged, then the longstanding issues involving the Table Style type, as well as some issues involving the List Style type, are circumvented.

Additionally, if you encounter these issues in some documents but not others, this may help to explain why these events occur. Note that the resolution is the same even if the documents were created in a previous version of Word.

Chapter 15

At this point, you may be wondering whether you should ever modify the Normal style if you are using it as your based-on style. This answer depends on the complexity of your document. If it is a simple letter, memo, or small report, then modifying the Normal style should not be an issue. However, you may find it easier to leave the Normal style unmodified, use it as your based-on style, and then set the base formats using the Document Defaults. If your document, or template, maximizes the power of styles, then it's recommended that the Normal style go untouched and you should modify the Document Defaults instead.

Of course, you could create a style solely for the purpose of a based-on style in an attempt to avoid using the Normal style or (No Style). However, in my more than 15 years of experience using Word, I have found that the more I try to avoid using Word as it was designed, the more work I ultimately put into my documents.

Keyboard Shortcuts for Styles

One style modification that comes in handy when working with styles is to assign keyboard shortcuts to commonly used styles. If you use the same few styles throughout a document, you might find it tiresome to repeatedly click to apply styles. In those cases, you save time and mouse clicks if you use a built-in shortcut or create a keyboard shortcut that you can press whenever you need a particular style. Table 15-1 lists commonly used keyboard shortcuts for a few built-in styles.

Table 15-1 Keyboard Shortcuts for Built-in Styles

Style	Keyboard shortcut
Normal	Ctrl+Shift+N
Heading 1	Ctrl+Alt+1
Heading 2	Ctrl+Alt+2
Heading 3	Ctrl+Alt+3
Demote Heading Level	Alt+Shift+Right Arrow
Promote Heading Level	Alt+Shift+Left Arrow

To create your own keyboard shortcut, follow these steps:

1. Open the Modify Style dialog box for the style to which you wish to assign a keyboard shortcut by either right-clicking a style in the Quick Style Gallery and clicking Modify or using the Modify command available in the Style options in the Styles pane.

   You can also click the New Style button in the Styles pane to display the Create New Style From Formatting dialog box if creating a new style.

2. Click the Format button and then click Shortcut Key. The Customize Keyboard dialog box appears, as shown in Figure 15-11.

Figure 15-11 You can use the Customize Keyboard dialog box to create keyboard shortcuts for styles.

3. Press the keyboard shortcut you want to use. If the combination is already in use, the dialog box indicates which feature uses the keyboard shortcut. If the combination is available, the Currently Assigned To label (displayed below the Current Keys list after the keys are pressed) indicates that the keyboard command is unassigned, as shown in Figure 15-11.

> **Note**
>
> If the keyboard shortcut is currently assigned and is noted below the Current Keys list after the keys are pressed, the custom keyboard shortcut overrides the built-in keyboard shortcut if you click the Assign button in the Customize Keyboard dialog box.

4. In the Save Changes In list box, specify whether you want to save the keyboard shortcut in the global Normal template, in another template, or in the active document only (thereby not adding the shortcut to any template).

> **Note**
>
> If you save a keyboard shortcut in a template, make sure you also have the New Documents Based On This Template option selected in the Modify Or Create Style dialog box. Otherwise, you could inadvertently create a keyboard shortcut in the template that does include the style.

Chapter 15

5. Click Assign, Close, OK to close the Modify Style dialog box.

6. Test your keyboard shortcut and confirm the results you were expecting.

To remove the keyboard shortcut, follow the same steps for adding a shortcut to open the Customize Keyboard dialog box. In the Customize Keyboard dialog box, select the shortcut in the Current Keys area, use the Save Changes In list to specify where to implement the removal, and then click Remove.

Some Final Thoughts on Styles

After reading this chapter, you learned that styles can be as simple as applying multiple formats with a single click of the mouse or that they can take on a more complex nature when creating your own styles and adding various available options. You may be wondering whether you should use styles exclusively in your documents and never use direct formatting. Many style advocates will tell you to always use styles and never use direct formatting; however, how you implement styles in a document should be approached on a document-by-document basis.

If the document will undergo numerous edits, then the document should be formatted using styles or you might encounter the battle of direct formatting vs. indirect formatting, described at the beginning of this chapter. A little fore-planning will save you time in the long run.

If the document is a simple letter or memo that you will type up, send off, and store for future reference and it will take longer to format the document using styles than to type it, then use the method that works best for you—use all direct formatting or use a combination of updating built-in styles along with some direct formatting.

The key to using styles to increase your formatting power is implementing the method that ultimately involves less work for you in your document creation endeavors.

What's Next?

This chapter covered the ease of using styles to control font and paragraph formatting in documents along with the available tools you can use to manage styles and inspect text formatting. The next chapter covers another document-formatting aspect—the desktop publishing functionality included in Word that enables you to control the placement of text using text boxes and shapes.

Formatting Layouts Using Backgrounds, Watermarks, and Text Boxes

When you create documents using a word processor, such as Microsoft Office Word 2007, you probably take for granted how text flows seamlessly from margin to margin and page to page. Office Word 2007 is equipped with new features that take you beyond basic word processing and more into the realm of what many consider desktop publishing. For example, instead of filling a page with text, you might want to position and format blocks of text precisely within your document or place text in the left or right margin. Word 2007 includes a nice collection of desktop publishing tools that can serve most of your everyday desktop publishing needs without the need to turn to a high-end desktop publishing application.

To get an idea of desktop publishing capabilities in Word or to obtain a starting point for a newsletter or similar document, browse through the Newsletter templates in the Microsoft Office Online section in the New Document dialog box shown below.

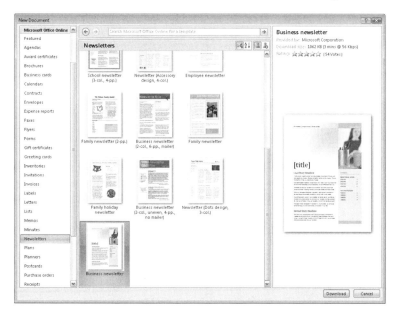

> **Note**
>
> Many of the templates found in the Microsoft Office Online section were created using the previous file format, so they are functional in several versions of Word. To take advantage of new features, click the Microsoft Office Button and then click Convert to upgrade the document to new functionality.

Specifically, Word lets you control text layout by using text boxes and shapes formatted to serve as text containers. Further, you can create rich documents by including backgrounds and watermarks. Themes, covered in Chapter 5, "Applying Themes for a Professional Look," provide a uniform color scheme, font set, and effects for your document creations. In this chapter, you'll learn how to use common desktop publishing tools to create high-impact, persuasive documents.

Layout and Design Fundamentals

When you decide to publish information, you probably focus on the words and pictures you will use to convey your message. After all, your content is the whole point! Word 2007 provides more tools than ever to aid you in adding and designing content. Yet interwoven throughout any project, you must keep in mind three fundamentals—alignment, balance, and white space (your ABWs!)—all of which relate to readability.

This chapter addresses two layout components—backgrounds and text containers—that clearly add professional polish to documents when used properly, but also offer easy avenues to design disaster. When working with backgrounds and text containers, think of giving your readers' eyes a rest—just like you need space to physically walk around a room, your readers' eyes need space to move around a page. To aid the creation of effective white space, align document elements to create expected paths and ensure that backgrounds don't create unnecessarily hard-to-read situations. Furthermore, while you think about the people who will be visiting your "room," also think about the purpose of your room (you don't want to end up with your bed in your bath!). If you're designing a document for a prestigious art gallery that has a lot of physical space, simulate that feel in your document by providing your readers with extra space. If you're designing a publication for an upcoming charity auction, you'll probably want to use less white space but alter text alignment to promote activity, action, and movement as you lead your audience through your information.

To help illustrate on a very simple level, Figure 16-1 demonstrates how making some basic layout choices to Coral Reef's Annual Report (shown on the left) can greatly enhance the page's readability, as shown on the right. Although both pages use a white background to simplify printing, breaking up the text by adding a single text box along with changing the size and shape of the image enables the addition of more white space and a larger font size. Additionally, the body text alignment is changed to Justify, the Bold text enhancement is removed, and 1.5 points of space is added between the characters of the headings to add additional space—it only takes a few subtle changes to create a more impactful document that is easier to read.

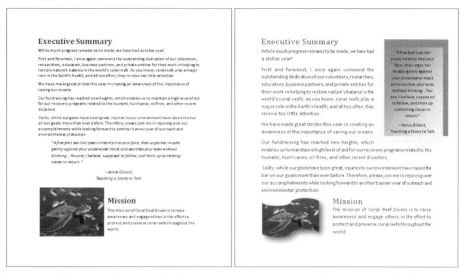

Figure 16-1 When you lay out text that will be printed or presented online, remember that your audience will be reading your document. Guide them by aligning elements, adding white space, and avoiding overpowering backgrounds.

Using Backgrounds and Watermarks

One quick and often effective way to add information and visual impact to your documents is to add backgrounds and watermarks (or both) to online and printed documents. Backgrounds are generally used to create backdrops for Web pages, online documents, and e-mail messages and aren't usually the best choice for long documents or documents that will be printed in large quantities. In Word, you can view backgrounds in all views except Normal view and Outline view. If you want to create a more print-friendly background, you should consider creating a watermark. A watermark is faded text or a pale picture that appears behind document text. By default, it is placed in the header and footer layer of a document so it appears on all pages. Watermarks are often used to add visual appeal to a document or to identify a document's status, such as "Draft" or "Confidential." You can see watermarks in Print Layout view, Print Preview, or on printed documents. In this section of the chapter, you'll learn how to create, control, and delete backgrounds and watermarks on your Word documents.

Creating Backgrounds and Watermarks

You can create custom backgrounds and watermarks for online pages as well as printed documents. When you create a background for a document, you can use color gradients, patterns, pictures, solid colors, or textures that repeat, or tile, to fill the page. When you create a watermark, you can use a light-colored picture (usually gray) or light-colored text to appear behind your document's contents. If you use text, you can choose from built-in phrases or enter your own.

Chapter 16

Adding Backgrounds to Online Pages

To add a color background to a page (such as an online document), click the Page Layout tab, click Page Color, and then perform any of the following actions:

- Click a color on the color palette to add a background color.

- Click More Colors to access additional colors that you can apply to your background.

> **Tip**
>
> If your desired colors are in the Standard or More colors, it's recommended that you first customize the Theme Colors to make efficient color choices based on uniform and complementing colors using the Theme Color section of the color palette.

- Click Fill Effects to access the Gradient, Texture, Pattern, and Picture tabs in the Fill Effects dialog box, which enable you to create custom backgrounds.

For more information about using fill effects, see Chapter 13, "Adding Visual Impact with Pictures, Drawings, and WordArt."

After you select a color or create a fill effect, Word automatically applies the background to the current document. You can see the background in all views except the Normal and Outline views. By default, if you print the document, the background won't be printed. To print a document with its background configuration, you must configure Word Options before you print, as follows:

1. Click the Microsoft Office Button and then click Word Options.

2. In the Display area in the Printing Options, select the Background Colors And Images check box and then click OK.

> **Note**
>
> You can quickly check whether Word is configured to print background colors and images by viewing a document that contains background formatting in Print Preview mode.

Adding Watermarks to Printed Documents

To add a watermark to a printed document, on the Page Layout tab in the Page Background group, click Watermark to view the Watermark gallery as shown in Figure 16-2. Then click a Watermark Building Block from the gallery to add it to the header and footer layer of the document. To add the watermark to the current page only, right-click the Watermark Building Block and then click Insert At Current Document Position.

Figure 16-2 The Watermark gallery includes Confidential, Disclaimers, and Urgent categories of built-in watermarks.

> **Note**
>
> You may need to scroll through the Watermark gallery to view the Disclaimers and Urgent categories.

Creating Custom Watermarks

You can also create a custom watermark using a picture or text by clicking Custom Watermark at the bottom of the Watermark gallery and configuring your settings in the Printed Watermark dialog box, shown in Figure 16-3, such as adding a picture watermark or customizing your own text.

Figure 16-3 You can use the Printed Watermark dialog box to add picture and text watermarks to your documents.

INSIDE OUT The Watermark Gallery vs. Custom Watermarks

The behavior of watermarks added using the Printed Watermark dialog box and those added using the Watermark gallery varies when it comes to documents that contain multiple sections, a different first page header, or different odd and even pages. When you use the Watermark gallery, the watermark is inserted into the active header and footer range, whereas using the Printed Watermark dialog box places the watermark in all header and footer ranges in the document. If you encounter this issue, see the Inside Out Tip titled "Additional Watermark Modifications" later in this chapter for instructions on manually editing a watermark.

If your document contains multiple unlinked sections, a different first page header, or different odd and even pages and you want your watermark to appear on all pages, when using the Watermark gallery to insert a watermark, make sure you check all header and footer stories and insert the watermark if necessary. For more information on sections and varying headers and footers, see Chapter 3, "Mastering Page Setup and Pagination."

You can insert a custom picture or text watermark by configuring the settings in the Printed Watermark dialog box, as described here:

- **Picture Watermark** To insert a picture watermark, click the Picture Watermark option and then click the Select Picture button to choose a picture for the watermark. You can use color or grayscale pictures for watermarks. The Scale option lets you specify a size for the watermark picture. In most cases, you should select the Washout check box (which is selected by default) so that the watermark doesn't interfere with your document's readability.

- **Text Watermark** To insert a text watermark, click the Text Watermark option and then type custom text in the Text box or choose from text in the Text list. Next, configure the Text, Font, Size, Color, and Layout settings. You can display the watermark text diagonally or horizontally. In most cases, you should select the Semitransparent check box so that the watermark doesn't interfere with your document's readability.

TROUBLESHOOTING

My watermark prints every other letter

Your watermark might display correctly in Print Preview or Print Layout view, but only print every other letter. To correct this issue, on the Page Layout tab, click Watermark and then click Custom Watermark. In the Printed Watermark dialog box, clear the Semitransparent option. The underlying cause of this issue is that your printer does not fully understand the Semitransparent option. If you need to use this option, then obtain an updated printer driver from the manufacturer's Web site, which might resolve the issue.

Once you configure your picture or text watermark settings, click Apply to preview the watermark without closing the dialog box to enable you to make additional modifications. If you like the results, click Close. (Click OK to apply the watermark and close the dialog box without previewing the changes first.) Figure 16-4 displays a document (in Print Preview) that has a Confidential watermark.

Figure 16-4 You can add standard or custom watermarks to documents that will be printed.

INSIDE OUT   Additional Watermark Modifications

When you add a watermark using the Watermark gallery or the Printed Watermark dialog box, the watermark is placed in the header and footer layer of the document as previously noted. If you need to make additional modifications beyond what is provided by the gallery or dialog box, such as change the color of a watermark inserted using the Watermarks gallery or move a watermark to another position, right-click the top or bottom edge of a page and click Edit Header or Edit Footer, respectively.

Next, on the contextual Header & Footer Tools in the Options group, turn off Show Document Text to make it easier to select and move or modify the watermark. After your watermark is selected, the contextual WordArt Tools are displayed if it is a text watermark. If the watermark is a picture, the contextual Picture Tools are displayed. If you need additional instructions for your desired modifications, see Chapter 13. To delete a watermark, simply select it and press Delete. If Delete does not appear to function, alternatively, right-click the watermark and click Cut.

Additionally, if you want to keep your customizations for reuse, add your customized watermark to the Watermark gallery by turning it into a new Building Block. Simply select the modified watermark and press Alt+F3 to display the Create New Building Block dialog box. Type a name for your new Building Block, make sure you add it to the Watermarks gallery, and fill in the additional options, such as assigning a Category so that it appears in the specified section of the gallery. For more information on Building Blocks, see Chapter 8, "Working with Building Blocks and Other Text Tools."

Changing and Removing Backgrounds and Watermarks

Once you add backgrounds and watermarks to online pages and documents that will be printed, you're free to change your mind at any time. You can easily change or remove backgrounds and watermarks that you have added to documents.

The following list provides instructions for changing or removing backgrounds or watermarks:

- **Change a background** Click the Page Layout tab, click Page Color, and then select new background settings.

- **Change a watermark** Click the Page Layout tab, click Watermark, and then click another Watermark Building Block in the gallery or click Custom Watermark.

- **Remove a background** Click the Page Layout tab, click Page Color, and then click No Color.

- **Remove a watermark** Click the Page Layout tab, click Watermark, and click Remove Watermark.

> **Note**
>
> If you are unable to remove a watermark using the Remove Watermark command, see the Inside Out Tip titled "Additional Watermark Modifications" earlier in this chapter for instructions on manually editing watermarks.

Controlling Text Placement with Text Boxes and Shapes

When you use Word, you might occasionally find that you need control over your text layout beyond setting margins, formatting paragraphs, and creating columns. At those times, you might benefit from entering your information into shapes that can contain text by using *text containers* or *text boxes*. Text boxes and shapes are free-floating objects (independent of the regular document) that you can use to enclose information. You can then format these objects the same way you format drawings by using their associated contextual tools.

For more information about working with shapes and other drawing tools, see Chapter 13.

When placing text in Word, you can use either text boxes or shapes that are formatted to contain text. Generally, you want to use text boxes when positioning several blocks of text on a page or when flowing a continuing story from one area in your document to another. For example, you might create a newsletter in which a story starts on the cover page but concludes on another page later in the newsletter.

In addition to creating interesting page layouts and continuing a story from one text block to another (also referred to as flowing text in linked text boxes), you might also want to use text boxes to accomplish the following tasks:

- Format text boxes using Text Box Tools

- Rotate or flip text

- Change text orientation

- Group text blocks and change their alignment or distribution as a group

This part of the chapter describes how you can manipulate and control text using text boxes and shapes as text containers. (Once a shape contains text, it is converted to a text box.) Keep in mind that when you're working with text boxes, you must work in Print Layout view. In Print Layout view, the text boxes appear on the screen as you work. Figure 16-5 displays a text box (formatted as a shape) on the left as well as two text boxes inserted using the Text Box gallery—all in Print Layout view.

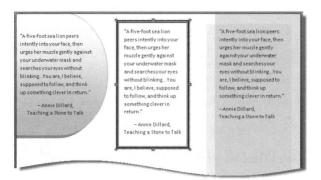

Figure 16-5 Text boxes bring attention to your information and separate related text from other document content.

As you can see, the active text box is shown surrounded by a frame-like border built from dashed lines and sizing handles. This border appears whenever you click a text box, and it serves a number of purposes, including enabling you to move and resize the text box as well as access text box properties.

Adding Text Boxes

Word 2007 makes adding text boxes a simple task with the Text Box gallery, found on the Insert tab in the Text group. An example of the Text Box gallery is shown in Figure 16-6.

Figure 16-6 The Text Box gallery provides preformatted, Theme-enabled text boxes.

The Text Box gallery includes various text box styles—from simple text boxes that can be moved and positioned anywhere on a page, called a pull quote (the middle text box in Figure 16-5), to those that are automatically placed on the edge of the page, called a sidebar (the text box on the right in Figure 16-5).

You can also use the Draw Text Box command, found at the bottom of the Text Box gallery, to manually draw and insert text boxes. However, if you need more than a standard text box, you may find that starting with a text box from the gallery and making minor formatting modifications, such as changing it to another shape, achieves faster results.

> **Note**
>
> To start with a Shape as a text container, use the Shapes gallery found on the Insert tab. To add text, right-click the shape and click Add Text, which converts the shape to a text box. You will see contextual Text Box Tools when the shape is activated instead of contextual Drawing Tools, which do not contain the additional text options described in this chapter.

As you create text boxes in your document, you can move and resize them in the same manner you move and resize drawing objects—by dragging them by their edges and sizing handles. To move a text box, point to the border, watch for the Move mouse pointer (multi-directional arrows), then click and drag the text box to another location. To resize a text box, you can drag the sizing handles, or the small blue boxes and circles shown in Figure 16-7, to change the text box's width and height.

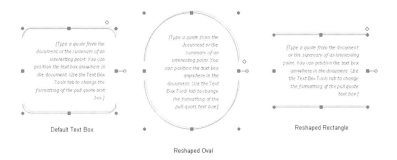

Figure 16-7 Use the blue boxes and circles surrounding text boxes to reshape text into more interesting configurations.

> **Note**
>
> The blue circles on each corner enable you to resize the shape proportionally; the blue boxes resize only the height or width.

If the text box is formatted as a shape, it can be rotated by dragging the green circle (only the shape rotates, the text stays horizontal). Some shapes can be reshaped by dragging the yellow diamond. In Figure 16-7, the middle text box was reshaped as an oval by dragging the yellow diamond inward toward the center of the text, and the right text box was reshaped as a rectangle by dragging the yellow diamond upward away from the text.

> **Note**
>
> To place existing text into a text box, select the text, click the Insert tab, display the Text Box gallery, and then click Draw Text Box at the bottom. The selected text is automatically inserted into a standard text box. Note that this method does not apply to using shapes.

Inserting Text into Text Boxes

After you create text boxes, you are ready to add text and formatting. You can insert text into containers in a few predictable ways such as typing, pasting copied information, and dragging content into the text box. If you are creating a newsletter-style document that will consist of multiple linked text boxes, see the Inside Out tip titled "Linked Text Boxes: Room to Edit" later in the chapter for a tip on creating the content in another document and inserting the content into the text boxes.

In addition to inserting text, you can insert graphics, tables, fields, and Content Controls into text boxes. Among the items that you cannot include in text boxes are the following:

- Columns
- Drop caps
- Footnotes
- Page and column breaks

- Comments
- Endnotes
- Indexes
- Tables of Figures

To include these elements in a text container, you must convert your text box into a frame as described in the following inside Out tip titled "What Happened to Frames?"

INSIDE OUT   **What Happened to Frames?**

Frames are still available in Word 2007, but they have been relocated to the Developer tab. (If you don't see the Developer tab, click the Microsoft Office Button, and then click Word Options. In the Popular area, select the Show Developer Tab In The Ribbon option.)

Text boxes are more flexible and powerful than frames, so you should use text boxes instead of frames whenever possible. However, text boxes do not contain a frame's unique quality to reside on the text layer of the document. If you need to place an element into a text box that must be in the text layer, then a frame must be used instead of a text box.

To add a frame, on the Developer tab in the Controls group, click Legacy Tools, click Frame, and then draw a frame in your document. Alternatively, select the text or element to be framed and then click the Frame command.

When converting a text box into a frame, if the text box is on a drawing canvas, drag the text box off the canvas. If the content of the text box is linked to another text box or boxes, you must break the link(s) and then proceed through the following steps. (See the section titled "Linking Text Boxes to Flow Text" later in this chapter on page 455 for more information on breaking text box links.)

1. Click the text box to active it. On the Format tab in the Text Box Styles group, click the dialog launcher. In the Format Text Box dialog box, click the Text Box tab.

> **Tip**
>
> Alternatively, right-click the text box (or the edge of the text box if it contains data) and click Format Text Box.

2. Click the Convert To Frame button. A message box appears, warning that you are about to change the text box to a frame and that some drawing formatting might be lost. Click OK.

Once the text box is converted to a frame, the contextual Text Box Tools are no longer available. To access frame options, right-click the edge of the frame and click Format Frame.

Unlike converting a text box to a frame, you cannot convert a frame to a text box in the same way. Instead, you must remove the frame and then create a text box. Although you can accomplish this in various ways, one of the easiest methods is to move content out of the frame and then select the content. On the Insert tab, display the Text Box gallery, and then click Draw Text Box.

Formatting Text Boxes

By default, when you create a text box as opposed to inserting a text box from the Text Box gallery, it appears as a white (not transparent) box surrounded by thin (0.75 point) black lines. Fortunately, text boxes don't have to be limited to plain white rectangles strategically placed around your document. You can format text boxes in the same manner that you format other drawing objects. For example, by using the formatting options found on the contextual Text Box Tools, you can apply fill and line colors by using the Shape Fill and Shape Outline tools, apply Text Box Quick Styles, change the text box to another shape, and add a shadow and 3-D effects. To format text boxes using the Format tab (shown in the following image), select the text box you want to format and then click the appropriate tool.

> **Note**
> To quickly activate and display the contextual Text Box Tools, double-click the edge of a text box.

In addition to the formatting tools on the Format tab, you can format text boxes using the Format Text Box dialog box. Namely, you can control the position of text inside text boxes, and you can have Word automatically resize a text box to accommodate the complete text of a story.

Controlling Text in Text Boxes

You can control the distance between the text and the edges of its bounding text box by adjusting the internal margin of the text box, as described in the following steps:

1. Click the text box to active it. Navigate to the Format tab and, in the Text Box Styles group, click the dialog launcher to display the Format Text Box dialog box.

2. Click the Text Box tab, as shown in Figure 16-8.

Figure 16-8 You can control the spacing around text in text boxes by configuring the internal margin settings in the Format Text Box dialog box.

3. In the Internal Margin area, increase or decrease the left, right, top, and bottom margin measurements to control the distance between the text and the selected object's edges. Click OK to apply the settings.

In addition to controlling internal margins, you can change the direction of text inside text boxes. To do so, click in a text box and then, on the Format tab in the Text group, click Text Direction. You can continue to click the button to cycle through the available text direction options: vertically, starting from the top or the base, and the original horizontal text direction.

> **Note**
>
> When you change the text direction in a linked text box, you change the text direction in all linked text boxes in the story. In other words, you can't change the text direction in a single text box if it's part of a linked series of text boxes. For more information about linked text boxes, see the section titled "Linking Text Boxes to Flow Text" later in this chapter on page 455.

Changing Text Box Shapes

 The beauty of using shapes is that you can change your mind regarding which shape you want to use at any time. Changing the shape of a text box is similar to changing shapes that don't contain text. To do so, ensure that you're working in Print Layout view and then follow these simple steps:

1. Click the text box you want to modify. To select multiple text boxes, press and hold Shift while clicking each text box.

2. On the Format tab, click Change Shape, and then select another shape from the gallery.

All selected text boxes take on the new shape but retain all other format settings, such as color and internal margins.

INSIDE OUT   Set tight text wrapping around text in text boxes

When a text box is placed in a paragraph and the line color for a text box has been removed, the text surrounding the text box continues to wrap to the boundaries of the text box, as opposed to wrapping to the text inside of the text box. In some instances, you might want to modify this behavior and wrap text around the text shown in the document instead of the invisible boundaries of the text box. In order to achieve the desired results, you can use the new Tight Wrap options for text box, found in the Paragraph dialog box on the Line And Page Breaks tab, shown in the following image:

Chapter 16

The Tight Wrap options apply to paragraphs that wrap around a text box, rather than the text inside of the text box. The following figure shows a text box with and without the Tight Wrap options.

Without Tight Wrap

With Tight Wrap

To effectively use the Tight Wrap options, follow these steps:

1. Click a text box to active it.

2. On the Format tab in the Text Box Styles group, click the dialog launcher. In the Format Text Box dialog box, set the following options:

   ❏ On the Colors And Lines tab, set both Fill Color and Line Color to No Color

   ❏ On the Layout tab, set the Text Wrapping Style to Tight

   ❏ On the Text Box tab, set the Vertical Alignment to Center

3. On the Home tab in the Paragraph group, click the dialog launcher. In the Paragraph dialog box, set the following options:

❑   On the Indents And Spacing tab, set the Alignment to Center

❑   On the Line And Page Breaks tab, set Tight Wrap to All

Depending on the text box placement and the amount of text in the text box, you may need to modify the Internal Margins for the text box, (found on the Text Box tab in the Format Text Box dialog box), and experiment with the other Tight Wrap options, such as First And Last Lines, First Line Only, or Last Line Only, in order to obtain the best text wrapping results for your specific text box.

Resizing Text Boxes Automatically to Show All Content

You can automatically resize a text box that contains text, graphics, and objects so that it is as long or as short as necessary to display all content inserted within it. You can use this option only with nonlinked (stand-alone) text containers because linked text containers are designed to flow text to the next linked container if content is longer than the current container's boundaries. To automatically size a nonlinked text container to accommodate inserted text, graphics, and objects, follow these steps:

1. Click the text box to active it. On the Format tab in the Text Box Styles group, click the dialog launcher.

2. In the Format Text Box dialog box, click the Text Box tab.

3. Select the Resize AutoShape To Fit Text check box and then click OK.

The text box automatically stretches or shrinks to accommodate the text.

Linking Text Boxes to Flow Text

If you've ever created a newsletter or brochure, you know how tricky it can be to fill text areas and manage jumps from one page to another properly. In Word, you can simplify these types of tasks by linking text boxes. When you link text boxes, you indicate that any text you insert into one text box will automatically flow into the next text box when the first text box cannot accommodate all of the inserted text. After you insert text into linked text boxes, you can edit the text to make your story longer or shorter. Word automatically reflows the text throughout the series of linked text boxes.

> **Note**
>
> The maximum number of linked text boxes allowable in one document is 31, which means that you can have up to 32 linked text containers in one document.

Chapter 16

When you want to link text boxes or shapes, you need to keep the following limitations in mind:

- Linked text boxes must be contained in a single document (note that they cannot be located in different subdocuments of a master document).

- A text box cannot already be linked to another series or story.

Before you flow text into a series of linked text boxes, you should be sure that you've made most of the changes to your text. You can then draw the text boxes you want to link and into which you'll import your story. When your text is ready and your text boxes are drawn, follow these steps to link the text boxes and insert the text:

1. In Print Layout view, click the first text box or shape into which you want to insert text.

2. On the Format tab, click Create Link (or right-click the text box border and then click Create Text Box Link). The pointer changes to an upright pitcher.

3. Move the pointer to the text box to which you want to link the first text box. When you move the upright pitcher pointer over a text box that can receive the link, the pitcher tilts and turns into a pouring pitcher. Click the second text box to link it to the first text box.

4. To link a third text box, click the text box that you just linked to the first text box, click Create Link, and then click the third text box.

   You can create a chain of linked text boxes using this method.

> **Note**
>
> If you click Create Link and then decide not to link to another box, press Esc to cancel the linking process.

5. Once you link your text boxes, click in the first text box and insert text by typing or pasting content.

For an efficient method to use for lengthy content, see the following Inside Out tip titled "Linked Text Boxes: Room to Edit."

> **Note**
>
> If you have a complete story that's ready to flow into text boxes, you can insert the story into the text boxes while you link them. To do this, insert your story into the first text box and then link to the next text box as described in Steps 1–3. When you use this approach, the text flows into the text boxes while you link them.

INSIDE OUT   **Linked Text Boxes: Room to Edit**

If the document you are creating is more of a newsletter-style document that will contain a series of linked text boxes, then consider typing and editing the text content in another Word document so you can format and fine-tune tasks in a larger editing area. After your text boxes are created and linked, you can insert the content of the document and populate the linked text boxes. To insert the file content, select the first linked text box and navigate to the Insert tab. Click the arrow next to Object, click the Text From File command, select your document, and then click Insert to insert the contents.

Moving Between Linked Text Boxes

After you link text boxes, you can easily jump from one text box to another. To do so, select a text box that's part of a linked series of text boxes. Right-click the edge of the text box, and then click Next Text Box to move to the next linked text box or click Previous Text Box to move to the previous text box. You can also move to the next text box by positioning your insertion point at the end of text in a filled text box and then pressing the right arrow key. You can also jump to the preceding text box by positioning your insertion point at the beginning of the text in a text box and then pressing the left arrow key.

Note

If you often need to move forward and backward among linked text boxes, you might want to add the Next Text Box and Previous Text Box buttons to the Quick Access Toolbar from Commands Not In The Ribbon. For more information about customizing the Quick Access Toolbar, see Appendix B, "Customizing Word and Enhancing Accessibility."

Copying or Moving Linked Text Boxes

You can copy or move a story (including text boxes and their contents) to another document or another location in the same document. If your story consists of multiple linked text boxes that aren't contained on a single drawing canvas, you must select all of the linked text boxes in the story before you can copy the story and text boxes. If the story's linked text boxes are on a single drawing canvas, you can select and copy any text box in the series of linked text boxes to copy the entire story and the selected text box to another location. Or, you can select all of the text boxes on the drawing canvas to copy the story and all of the associated text boxes.

> **Note**
>
> To create a drawing canvas, on the Insert Tab, click Shapes, and then click New Drawing Canvas. To automatically insert a drawing canvas by default when you insert a text box or shape, display Word Options. In the Advanced area, select Automatically Create Drawing Canvas When Inserting AutoShapes.

When you copy one or a few linked text boxes (but not an entire story) that are not on a drawing canvas, you copy only the selected text box or boxes without the content. When you copy a single text box that is part of an entire story that appears in text boxes on a single drawing canvas, you copy the entire story along with the selected text box. This means that when you paste the text box, you will probably need to resize it to see the entire story or will need to add text boxes and link them to the newly inserted text box.

If you want to copy an entire story along with all of the text boxes containing the story, you need to select all of the text boxes before copying them, as described in the following procedure:

1. In Print Layout view, select a text box in the story by clicking the edge of the text box.

> **Note**
>
> You must select the edge of a text box if you want to copy the text box. If you click inside the text box and then click Copy on the Home tab, or press Ctrl+C, Word does not copy anything.
>
> If you want to copy multiple text boxes, you can click anywhere in the text box while you press Shift and click to select additional text boxes.

2. Press Shift and then click the text boxes you want to copy or move.

3. On the Clipboard group of the Home tab, click Copy or Cut (or press Ctrl+C or Ctrl+X).

4. Click where you want to reposition the text boxes. On the Clipboard group of the Home tab, click Paste (or press Ctrl+V).

To copy or move content that appears within a text box without copying or moving the text box, select just the text or content in the same way that you select standard text and content and then copy or move it in the same way you normally copy or move content in Word documents. To select and copy all text in a linked story, click in the story, press Ctrl+A, and either copy and paste or drag the text to the desired location. You can select all of the text in a story by using Ctrl+A regardless of whether the story's text boxes are on a drawing canvas.

INSIDE OUT   Obtaining Word Count Statistics for Text Box Content

In Word 2007, you can include text within text boxes in your document's word count statistic—this ability was not available in earlier versions of Word. To control whether to include text inside text boxes in word count statistics, click Words in the status bar. The Word Count dialog box opens. Use the Include Textboxes, Footnotes And Endnotes check box to count or exclude text inside of text boxes in your word count statistics.

Breaking Text Box Links

You can break links between text boxes just as easily as you create them. When you break a link, you remove only the link between the selected text box and the text box that follows it in the series—you don't remove all of the links in a linked series. Essentially, when you break a link, you divide a story into two series of linked text boxes or segments. By default, the first series of linked text boxes contains the story, and linked text boxes in the second series are empty.

To break a link between text boxes, follow these steps:

1. In Print Layout view, click the edge of the text box from which you want the text to stop flowing. The selected text box becomes the last text box in the first linked series of text boxes.

2. On the Text Box Tools tab, click Break Link (or right-click the text box border and then click Break Forward Link).

At this point, text stops flowing in the last text box before the broken link, and the second series of linked text boxes are empty. If the text doesn't fit in the first series of linked text boxes after you break a link, you can create and link additional text boxes or enlarge existing text boxes to provide enough room to display the text.

Note

You can cut a text box in the middle of a linked series of text boxes without deleting any parts of your story. To do so, simply right-click the edge of a text box and then click Cut. When you cut a linked text box, the story readjusts and flows the text into the next text box.

Deleting Linked Text Boxes Without Losing Text

To delete a text box, you simply select a text box and press Delete or right-click the text box border and click Cut. Performing this action on a nonlinked text box deletes both the text box and its contents. In contrast, when you delete a text box that's part of a linked series of text boxes, the text from the deleted text box automatically flows into the remaining linked text boxes. If the remaining text boxes aren't large enough to properly display the story in its entirety, you must resize the remaining text boxes, create additional text boxes, or edit your story to fit in the existing text boxes. Keep in mind that Word doesn't notify you when text overflows the boundaries of the final text box, so you should always be extra diligent about checking the flow of stories and making sure that no text is hidden.

> **Note**
>
> To avoid deleting an entire story when you delete a stand-alone, nonlinked text box, click in the text box, press Ctrl+A to select the story, and then either drag or copy the selected story into your document before you delete the text box.

Configuring Word 2007 Layout Options

In addition to readily available page layout and component layout options, Word 2007 provides a large collection of option settings in Word Options that will be saved with the document. You'll find references to Word Options throughout this text. If you can't find a layout option that you're looking for, consider visiting the Layout Options included in Word Options, which is part of the Compatibility Options. To access the Layout Options, click the Microsoft Office Button, click Word Options, and click Advanced. Next, scroll to the bottom of the Advanced screen and expand the Layout Options. You'll find a list of options similar to the one shown in Figure 16-9. Scan through the options to see whether any settings might meet your current or future needs. Note that none of the Layout Options are selected by default.

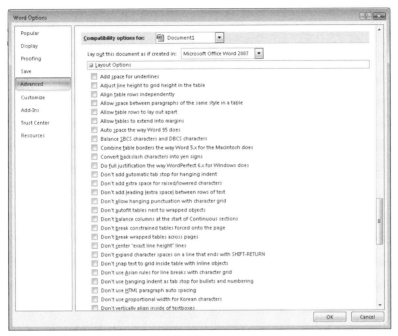

Figure 16-9 Word includes a long list of Layout Options that you can use on an as-needed basis. Reviewing the list helps you become aware of capabilities you might need now or in the future.

For a description of the Compatibility Options, visit the Microsoft Knowledge Base and search for article 288792, or type the following in the address bar of your Web browser: *http://support.microsoft.com/kb/288792.*

What's Next?

This chapter covered some of the desktop publishing tools that can serve most of your everyday desktop publishing needs in Word. The next chapter takes you a step further into adding a professional polish—how to use the borders and shading features to bring even more attention and impact to your documents.

Commanding Attention with Borders and Shading

One of the major enhancements in Microsoft Office Word 2007 is the addition of many professional and easy-to-use design features that make creating attractive documents simple. Sometimes producing a basic document on a clean white page is the best approach for communicating a message as clearly as possible. But at other times, you might want to shine a spotlight on a particular passage of text, a table, or an object on your page. Borders and shading can add a special look to important elements, helping them stand out.

The following are a few examples of ways in which you might want to use borders and shading:

- Create a border around a table.

- Use shading to set a heading as white text in an aqua background.

- Create a shaded sidebar for a section of text that accompanies an article.

- Add a border around a table of contents so that readers can find it easily.

Adding a Simple Border

The easiest way to add a plain border to an item in your document is to select the item and then click the Home tab. In the Paragraph group, click the arrow to the right of the Borders button, and a list of border options appears, as shown in Figure 17-1. Click Outside Border to enclose the selected text in a border (or choose another Border option if you prefer). Your most recent selection also becomes the option shown on the face of the button on the assumption that you might want to use it again soon.

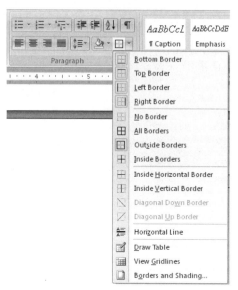

Figure 17-1 Clicking the Borders arrow in the Paragraph group displays a list of border choices.

> **Note**
>
> Keep in mind that the Borders button is a toggle button. This means that with a click of the button, you can add borders at the cursor position if they aren't present or remove borders if they are present.

INSIDE OUT   Clear borders quickly with No Border

Although you can use the toggle effect of the Borders button to remove border lines, you might want to clear all existing borders before applying new settings. To clear existing borders, highlight the section you want to modify, click No Border in the Borders gallery, and then, while the section is still selected, click the border style you want to use.

Creating Enhanced Borders

A simple one-line border may do the trick when you are interested in only a box that sets off items from surrounding text. If you want to use the border as a design element on your page, you can use the Borders And Shading dialog box to tailor the selections to create a more sophisticated effect. The Borders And Shading dialog box gives you the option of choosing from a variety of looks for your border (including 3-D and shadow effects). You can also change the style, color, and width of the lines you use or create a partial border by selecting only the line segments you want to display.

To create a customized border, begin by placing the insertion point in the paragraph where you want the border to start or by selecting the data around which you want to create the border. For example, if you want to add a border around a paragraph that lists your corporate Web site and contact information, highlight that paragraph and then display the Borders And Shading dialog box in one of two ways:

- Click the Page Layout tab and then select the Page Borders tool in the Page Background group. In the Borders And Shading dialog box, click the Borders tab.

- Click the Borders arrow (in the Paragraph group of the Home tab) and select Borders And Shading (the last option on the list).

  The Borders And Shading dialog box appears, as shown in Figure 17-2.

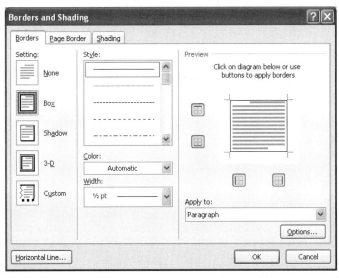

Figure 17-2 The Borders And Shading dialog box enables you to specify border types and border placement as well as line styles, colors, and widths.

Office Word 2007 offers some basic border settings that you can use, although you can create an almost unlimited number of combinations by adjusting the style, color, width, line, and shading settings. The Borders And Shading dialog box provides three tabs:

Borders, Page Border, and Shading. The following list presents a quick overview of what each tab enables you to do:

- The Borders tab contains options for choosing the border style, color, and width, as well as options for choosing partial borders (for example, you can choose to which edges of the selection you want to assign a border).

- The Page Border tab includes the same options you find on the Border tab, with one addition. The Art list at the bottom of the center panel enables you to add special border art to the pages in your document.

- The Shading tab enables you to put a background color or pattern behind selected text.

Choosing Border Options

The Setting options will likely be your first major choice when using the Borders And Shading dialog box. These options control the overall look of the border itself. Setting options vary depending on whether you're working in a table or with standard text. If you're working with standard text, you can choose from the following Setting options:

- **None** Shows no border around selected text and objects; this is the default

- **Box** Encloses the selection in a simple line box

- **Shadow** Outlines the selection with a box and adds a drop shadow below and to the right of the selection

- **3-D** Creates a three-dimensional effect for the selected border, making it appear to "stand out" from the page

- **Custom** Enables you to configure the Preview area so you can choose and customize the line segments you want to include in your border

If you're working with a table or selected cells, you can choose among the following Setting options:

- **None** Shows no border around the table or selected cells

- **Box** Encloses the table or selected cells in a simple line box without internal lines

- **All** Outlines the entire table or selected cells, including borders between cells; this is the default

- **Grid** Outlines a table or selected cells with a heavier exterior border and lighter interior borders

- **Custom** Enables you to configure the Preview area so that you can choose and customize the line segments you want to include in your border

> **Note**
>
> You can mix and match border types to achieve the effect you want. For example, you can add borders to part of a table and hide borders in other parts to create the appearance of lines for text on forms that users will fill out. You can further combine border options, such as color and line widths, to make borders visually appealing.

To apply one of the Setting options shown in the Borders And Shading dialog box, click in the paragraph, table, image, or other element that you want to format, or select text or cells. Then display the Borders And Shading dialog box and click the Setting selection in the Borders tab. If you don't want to make any additional customizations, you can simply click OK to return to your document. The border is added to the current text, table, or selected object. If the cursor is positioned in a new blank paragraph before you display the Borders And Shading dialog box, the border appears around the insertion point and expands as you type, including added paragraphs, images, tables, and other elements. To end the expansion of the border, either click outside the formatted area or press Enter at the end of the formatted area, and then format the new blank paragraph marker by using the No Border setting on the Borders button.

> **Note**
>
> If you add a border and decide that you don't like it, you can do away with it immediately by clicking Undo in the Quick Access Toolbar at the top of the Word window or by pressing Ctrl+Z. You can also click the Borders tool in the Paragraph group and select No Border to clear the border lines.

TROUBLESHOOTING

The changes I made to the borders in my table disappeared

If you change the border or shading of a table and discover that the changes you specified weren't made when you close the Borders And Shading dialog box, it could be because the table's formatting marks weren't selected properly before you applied formatting options. To avoid this problem, click Show/Hide in the Paragraph group on the Home tab to display all of the formatting characters in your document before you apply formatting. Then select the table, making sure to include the end-of-row marks at the ends of the rows. Next right-click the table, choose Borders And Shading to display the Borders And Shading dialog box, and then enter your settings. Because the table formatting marks are included, the changes should stick after you close the Borders And Shading dialog box.

Selecting Line Styles for Borders

Word provides 24 line styles that you can use to create border effects. From simple, straight lines to dotted, double, and triple lines, you can create a variety of looks by changing line styles. Figure 17-3 shows a few examples of borders created with different line styles.

Coral Reef Divers went through an extensive financial review during our strategic planning program during the summer of 2006. We found that due to climactic conditions, volunteer availability, and the nature of the projects we've undertaken in under-represented areas, our operating expenses are fairly evenly divided among our international sites. As would be expected, our site operating costs are highest in the U.S., where our worldwide administrative offices are housed.

Each international office includes one full-time paid staff member, one part-time paid staff member, and at least three volunteers (who are recognized throughout the year in various ways). At the present time, we pay rent for facilities in only three countries; the rest of our sites are donated by partnering NGOs, benefactors, or universities.

"The colors of the sea are only the indirect signs of the presence or absence of conditions needed to support the surface life; other zones, invisible to the eye, are the ones that largely determine where marine creatures may live." --Rachel Carson, *The Sea Around Us*

Figure 17-3 The line style you choose has a dramatic effect on the overall look of a border.

To choose a line style for a border, display the Borders And Shading dialog box and select a line style in the Style list on the Borders tab. The Preview area shows the effect of your choices. Set any other border choices you want and then click OK. The document is updated with your changes.

TROUBLESHOOTING

There's not enough contrast in my double line

If you create a double line and can't see enough contrast between lines of different weights, you can play around with the line widths to achieve a better contrast. Start by clicking in or selecting the area with the border. Then display the Borders And Shading dialog box by clicking the Borders button and choosing Borders And Shading at the bottom of the gallery. On the Width list, choose a new line width setting. In the Preview area in the dialog box, click the line you want to change.

Choosing Color

When you first start adding lines and borders to your publication, Word uses the Automatic color by default, which is black if using the standard Windows color scheme. However, you have all of the colors of Word at your disposal, so you can get as colorful as your needs and presentation medium allow. To specify border colors, follow these steps:

1. Click in or select the elements you want to format with border colors.

    If the content already has a border and you only want to color the existing lines, you can retain the current border and simply apply a color setting to the existing border settings.

2. Click the Home tab.

3. In the Paragraph group, click Borders And Shading. Choose Borders And Shading at the bottom of the list to display the Borders And Shading dialog box.

4. On the Borders tab, select a Setting option and line style if you're creating a new border.

    If you're working with an existing border, you can make changes as desired.

5. Click the Color arrow. The color palette appears, as shown in Figure 17-4.

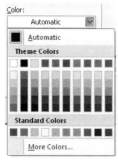

Figure 17-4 You can use the color palette to select a color for lines and shading.

6. Click the color you want to use from the color palette or, if you don't see the color you were hoping for, click More Colors.

   The Colors dialog box appears so that you can find the color you're looking for. Click the color you want. If you're creating a new border, the color setting is reflected in the Preview area immediately. If you're adjusting the color setting for an existing border, you need to click each line in the Preview area to apply the color setting. In this way, you can control the line color for each border line.

7. Click OK. The color settings are applied in your document.

Note

The Color palette is divided into two areas. The Theme Colors area provides colors from the document theme, and the Standard Colors area offers primary colors. More Colors displays the Colors dialog box so that you can choose from a wide range of colors or create your own custom color. If you choose a color that is not included in the Theme Colors section, it won't be changed automatically if you later choose a different theme for the document. To make sure that colors can be automatically swapped whenever you choose a new theme, select Theme Colors only.

When You Need to Match Colors Exactly

Suppose that you're using Word 2007 to create a Web page or document that must conform to last year's annual report, right down to the color scheme. When you need to match colors, choosing accurate border colors can become an especially important issue. For times like these, you can use the Custom tab in the Colors dialog box to enter the exact RGB (Red, Green, and Blue) or HSL (Hue, Saturation, and Luminance) color percentages for custom colors. To configure the Custom tab in the Colors dialog box for borders, perform the following steps:

1. Click the border where you want to change the color.

2. Select the Page Layout tab. From the Page Background group, choose Page Borders.

3. On the Borders tab in the Borders And Shading dialog box, click the Color down arrow.

4. Click More Colors on the color palette.

5. In the Colors dialog box, click the Custom tab.

6. On the Color Model list, choose RGB, HSL, or another available color scheme.

7. Enter values in the Red, Green, and Blue text boxes (available if you select the RGB color model), or enter values in the Hue, Sat, and Lum text boxes (available for the HSL color model).

8. Click OK to close the Colors dialog box.

9. Finish configuring your border settings. In the Borders And Shading dialog box, click OK to apply the custom color.

INSIDE OUT   **How do I choose the best colors for borders?**

The easiest way to choose colors for any section of your document is to choose a theme that controls the fonts, colors, and effects used throughout the entire piece. If you don't want to use an existing theme or customize a theme to include the elements you prefer, the question of choosing effective colors for your borders remains.

The trick to selecting effective colors for a document's text, images, table borders, lines, shading, and other components is to work with a color scheme that consists of three or four main colors that complement the document's design and provide appropriate contrast. After you identify a color scheme, you can play with the colors a little to add interest. For instance, if headings are dark blue, you might consider using the same blue or a slightly lighter shade of the same blue for borders and lines. In addition, document design often benefits from a consistent use of color across the board for similar design elements. For instance, in a magazine or newsletter, all sidebars might be placed in a green box while quotations appear in yellow boxes. That way, when readers see green, they know they're about to read a sidebar. When they see yellow, they recognize that they're reading a quotation. Color used wisely can greatly increase the readability and visual appeal of a publication.

You can simplify the task of selecting colors that work well together by using one of the predesigned Word Themes as you create your document. When you use a Word Theme, the colors displayed in the Theme Colors area of the Color palette help you choose colors that are already used consistently in the document color scheme.

Controlling Border Width

When you create a simple border, the default line width is $^1/_2$ point, which is a simple, thin line. If you want to create a more dramatic effect—whether you leave the line black or add color—you can change the width of the line. To change line width, display the Borders And Shading dialog box, click the Width arrow, and then click the width you want. Available point sizes include $^1/_4$, $^1/_2$, $^3/_4$, 1, $1^1/_2$, $2^1/_4$, 3, $4^1/_2$, and 6.

Note

You can use line widths to create a special effect for partial borders. For example, to add a wide line above and below content, select the area you want to enclose between the lines, display the Borders And Shading dialog box, and then click the Custom Setting option. Select a line style, click the Width arrow, and then choose a larger point size, such as 3 point. In the Preview area, click the top horizontal edge of the preview page. A line is added to the top border. Next, click the bottom horizontal edge of the preview page, and then click OK. Word adds the thick line border above and below the selected area.

Creating Partial Borders

Not every paragraph, table, or object you enclose in a border needs four lines encircling it. You might want to add two lines, such as along the top and right side of a paragraph, to help set it apart from an article that appears beside it. You might use only a top and bottom rule to contain your table of contents. Or you might use a single line to set off a quotation from the main text in a report or mark the start of a new section.

Creating a partial border is a simple matter. You use the Custom Setting option and the Preview area of the Borders And Shading dialog box to accomplish this task. Here are the steps:

1. Click in a table or paragraph, or select the information around which you want to create the border.

2. On the Home tab in the Paragraph group, click the Borders button.

3. On the Borders tab, click the Custom Setting option. Specify the border's line style, color, and width.

4. In the Preview area, click each edge of the preview paragraph to indicate where border lines should appear, or click the buttons that correspond to the edge or edges that should have a border line.

> **Note**
> You can toggle border lines on and off by clicking the borders in the Preview area's sample page or by clicking the Preview buttons surrounding the sample page.

Applying a Page Border

Many of the techniques you use to add a border to a section, table, or object in a document can be used to add borders to entire pages as well. Figure 17-5 displays a document with a page border. You can create standard page borders or use Art Border. This section shows you how.

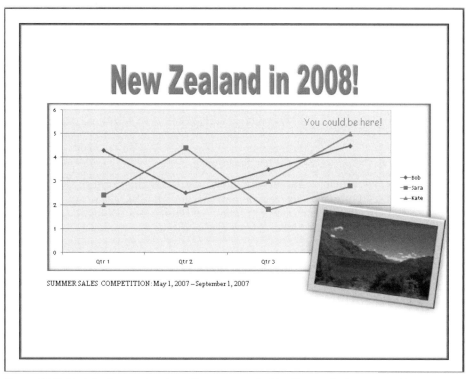

Figure 17-5 By default, page border settings are applied to all pages in the current document.

Creating a Page Border

When you add a page border, you start the process by displaying the Borders And Shading dialog box. Click the Page Border tab. The main visual difference between the Borders tab and the Page Border tab is the addition of the Art list (which is covered in the next section of this chapter). On the Page Border tab, after you make all of your border choices, the border is applied to an entire page, section, or document. The following procedure describes the process:

1. Click in a page or section that will have a border.

2. On the Home tab in the Paragraph group, click the Borders button.

3. In the Borders And Shading dialog box, click the Page Border tab.

Chapter 17

4. Click a page border setting (Box, Shadow, 3-D, or Custom).

5. From the Style list, select a line style.

6. On the Color list, select a color if desired.

7. Click the Width arrow and then choose the line width you want.

   The Style, Color, and Width settings are reflected in the Preview area.

8. If desired, use the Preview image to select which edges of the page will have a page border.

9. On the Apply To list, specify where the border should apply.

   Available options are Whole Document, This Section, This Section – First Page Only, and This Section – All Except First Page. By default, Whole Document is selected on the Apply To list, and the border is added to all pages in the current document.

10. Click OK to close the dialog box and apply the page border settings to the current document.

> **Note**
>
> To apply a page border to a single page (other than the first page) or to a few pages in a long document, you must first set off the page or pages by creating a section. To learn more about creating and working with sections, see Chapter 21, "Formatting Columns and Sections for Advanced Text Control."

INSIDE OUT How do I change the border on the first page only?

When you add a page border, Word applies the border to all of the pages in your document. What if you want to skip the border on the first page or apply the border only to the first page? You can do either of these things easily by using the Apply To setting on the Page Border tab in the Borders And Shading dialog box. To suppress the display of the border for the first page, click the Page Border tab in the Borders And Shading dialog box, click the Apply To arrow, and then select This Section – All Except First Page. To apply the border to the first page only, choose This Section – First Page Only in the Apply To list on the Page Border tab.

Adding an Artistic Border

The Art Page Border feature, known in earlier versions of Microsoft Office as BorderArt, enables you to add an artistic touch to entire pages in your document. Special graphics are placed in patterns—either in black and white or in color—and used as borders for a page, group of pages, or selected sides of pages. To apply an artistic page border, follow these steps:

1. Click in the document to which you want to add the border.

2. On the Home tab in the Paragraph group, click the Borders button to display the Borders And Shading dialog box.

3. Click the Page Border tab.

4. Click the Art arrow and then scroll through the art borders. Select an Art option.

   The Preview area displays your change. To control which borders will contain graphics, you can click the borders in the Preview Page area to add and remove the images.

5. On the Apply To list, choose which pages should include the border.

   You can include the border on the Whole Document, This Section, This Section – First Page Only, or This Section – All Except First Page.

6. Click OK. The border is added to the document according to the settings you configured in the Borders And Shading dialog box.

Artistic borders can be colorful and vibrant, but they can also be a bit much for some professional documents. For that reason, you should use art borders sparingly and use discretion to determine their appropriateness on a case-by-case basis.

Adding Borders to Sections and Paragraphs

Whether you're interested in applying borders to a single word, paragraph, image, section, or page, you can do it easily by using the Apply To list in the Borders And Shading dialog box. The tab you choose at the top of the dialog box—Borders or Page Border—depends on the element you want to enclose in a border.

- If you want to create a border around a section in your document, click the Page Border tab. On the Apply To list, you can find what you need to specify section bordering options.

- If you want to add a border around a paragraph, text, table, image, selected table cell, or other element in your document, click the Borders tab. The Apply To options in that tab offer choices specific to the item you chose.

Chapter 17

INSIDE OUT   My border covers up part of a photo in my document

If the page or section border that you've added overlaps an image placed in your document, you can fix this (and create a great effect at the same time) by moving the border behind the image. To do so, display the Borders And Shading dialog box (click Borders in the Paragraph group of the Home tab) click Page Border, and then click Options. In the Options section, clear the check box for Always Display In Front.

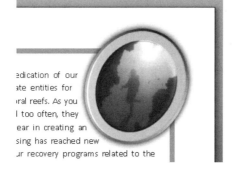

edication of our
ate entities for
ral reefs. As you
l too often, they
ear in creating an
sing has reached new
ur recovery programs related to the

Bordering Sections

You might want to create a border around a section when you have specific information to highlight or when you want to set a section apart from the flow of the text. To create a section border, start by placing the insertion point in the section you want to surround with a border. Display the Borders And Shading dialog box (click Borders in the Paragraph group of the Home tab) and then click the Page Border tab. Next configure the border effects, including the Setting option and line style, color, and width. Click the Apply To arrow and select your choice: Whole Document, This Section, This Section – First Page Only, or This Section – All Except First Page. Click OK to create the border.

If you want to see how the border looks for the entire section, click the Microsoft Office Button, then point to Print, and click Print Preview. By using the Two Pages option (in the Zoom group) in Print Preview, you can see the effect of your border selection on more than one page in your document. Click Close Print Preview on the Print Preview tab to return to the document window.

INSIDE OUT   **Use border settings to add blank lines**

Here's a great way to add horizontal lines for write-in spaces in your documents. Press Enter to insert a number of blank lines in your document in the area where you want to create horizontal lines. Then select the blank lines, click the arrow on the Borders button, and then click the Inside Horizontal Border option. Evenly spaced lines are added automatically, extending from the left to the right margin.

Adjusting Border Spacing

Word makes a few assumptions about the way borders appear in documents. By default, Word applies a small margin to borders applied to a paragraph and a larger margin to borders for sections and pages. When you add a border to a paragraph, Word adds a 1-point margin to the top and bottom and a 4-point margin along the left and right edges of the border. When you add a page or section border, Word adds 24-point margins measured from the edge of the page all the way around.

To access border options that enable you to adjust spacing between borders and content, display the Borders And Shading dialog box (click Borders And Shading in the Paragraph group on the Home tab). In the Borders And Shading dialog box, click the Borders tab if you're changing the options for a paragraph border, or click the Page Border tab if you're working with a document or section border. Each of these choices displays different selections in the Border And Shading Options dialog box.

If the Borders tab is displayed when you click Options in the lower right corner of the dialog box, the Border And Shading Options dialog box appears, as shown in Figure 17-6. If the Page Borders tab is selected, you will see the dialog box shown in Figure 17-7.

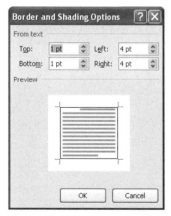

Figure 17-6 You control border margins and make choices about border alignment in the Border And Shading Options dialog box.

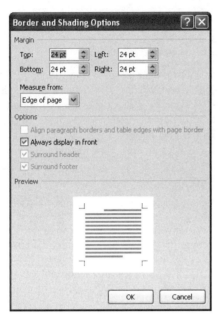

Figure 17-7 Click the Page Borders tab to display the options available for spacing the border of an entire page.

To make changes to the border margins, click in the box you want to change and type a new value, or use the up and down arrows to increase or decrease the value shown.

For page borders, Word automatically measures the margin from the edge of the page, but you can change the setting so that the measurement reflects spacing between text and the surrounding border. To make this change, click the Measure From arrow and choose Text. When working with the Borders tab, the Border And Shading Options dialog box only allows you to configure the space between the border and text.

Other options in the Border And Shading Options dialog box are available only if you're working with a page or section border. By default, Word includes any headers and footers inside the bordered area and, also by default, enables the Always Display In Front check box, which causes the border to be in front of any text or graphic objects that might overlap it. If you have other borders or tables within the bordered section, the Align Paragraph Borders And Table Edges With Page Border check box is also available to you. If you want Word to align all of these borders, select this check box.

After you finished choosing border options, click OK to close the dialog box and then click OK a second time to return to your document.

> **Note**
> If you select a table before you display the Borders And Shading dialog box, your options on the Apply To list display Text, Paragraph, Table, and Cell.

TROUBLESHOOTING

My border isn't printing correctly

If your page border doesn't print along one edge of the page or is positioned too close to an edge, check the border's margin options. To do this, display the Page Border tab of the Borders And Shading dialog box and then click Options. In the Margin area, check your settings. If you set up your border to be measured from Edge of Page, the space between the text and the border might be pushing the border into the nonprintable area. (Most printers do not print in the 0.5-inch area around the perimeter of the page.) Choose the Measure From arrow and select Text. Adjust the margins if necessary and do a test print to see whether this corrects the problem.

Inserting Graphical Horizontal Lines

Word provides a collection of graphical horizontal lines that you can insert in documents to help set off a section, call attention to a special element in text, or set off a sidebar or special section. To add a graphical horizontal line to a document, follow these steps:

1. Place the insertion point where you want to add the line.

2. Display the Borders And Shading dialog box and select the Border or Page Border tab.

3. Click the Horizontal Line button in the lower left corner of the dialog box to display the Horizontal Line dialog box, as shown in Figure 17-8.

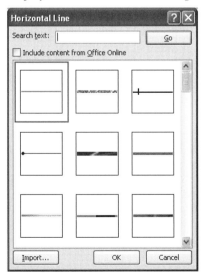

Figure 17-8 The Horizontal Line dialog box displays predesigned graphical lines that you can insert in your document.

Chapter 17

4. Scroll through the selections and click a line style to add the line.

After you place a horizontal line in a document, you can select, copy, paste, resize, move, and color it as you would other graphical items. To change the format of the line, right-click it, choose Format Horizontal Line, and select the settings you want to change. Furthermore, you can insert additional instances of the line by choosing the Horizontal Line option from the Borders button menu.

> **Tip**
>
> You can create your own graphical lines in Word or another program (such as Microsoft Paint or Microsoft Office PowerPoint 2007) and then add the customized line to your Horizontal Line gallery. To import a custom line, display the Borders And Shading dialog box and click Horizontal Line. In the Horizontal Line dialog box, click Import. Navigate to the file you want to use, click it, and click Add. The line is added to the gallery and remains selected, ready for you to use.

Adding Borders to Pictures

The process involved in adding borders to pictures takes you down a slightly different path. Instead of using the Borders And Shading dialog box, which is available when working with text sections, paragraphs, or entire pages, adding a border to a picture involves changing the formatting settings for that particular object in your document. Here's how it's done:

1. Click the picture or chart to which you want to add the border. The contextual Picture Tools appears above the Ribbon.

2. In the Picture Styles group, click Picture Border. The Picture Border list appears, as shown in Figure 17-9.

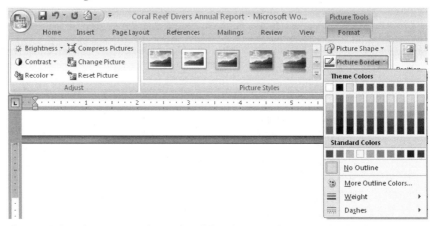

Figure 17-9 In the Picture Styles group of the Picture Tools contextual tab, choose Picture Border to add a border to an image in your document.

3. Click the color you want in the Theme Colors area of the gallery.

   It's a good idea to stay with the Theme Colors so that they coordinate with the colors in the rest of your document.

4. Use the Weight and Dashes settings to choose the width and style of the line used for the picture border.

   Remember that you can point to a selection to preview it before selecting it.

Note

You can also spruce up the images in your documents by adding drop shadows, applying 3-D settings, rotating images, and much more. For more about working with pictures in your Word documents, see Chapter 13, "Adding Visual Impact with Pictures, Drawings, and WordArt."

Adding Table Borders

Word includes an entire set of border options when working with tables. The tools are easy to use—and fun to apply. For in-depth coverage of creating and working with tables, be sure to check out Chapter 11, "Organizing Concepts in Tables." This section provides the basic steps for adding borders and shades to your tables.

As you know, Word includes a great gallery of table styles that you can apply to your tables. The table styles that are available to you depend on the Theme selected for the document. (For more information about themes in Word 2007, see Chapter 5, "Applying Themes for a Professional Look.") The table styles that display might supply all of the borders you'll ever need. However, if you want to add to the table style effect by adding an outside border or if you want to change the borders used in the style, knowing how to customize your table borders comes in handy.

In the Borders And Shading dialog box, you can choose the border setting, style, color, and width as you learned earlier in this chapter. If you want to experiment with custom lines and mix and match line styles in your table border, you can work with the tools on the Design tab that appear when you select the table to display the Table Tools contextual tab. The following procedure shows you how to do it:

1. Begin by selecting the table element to which you want to apply the border.

   You might select the entire table or simply a column, row, or selection of cells. To select a specific cell, simply click it to position the cursor in that location.

2. On the contextual Table Tools, click Design.

3. In the Draw Borders group, click the Line Style arrow to choose the line style you want for the border, as shown in Figure 17-10.

Chapter 17

Figure 17-10 Choose the line style and weight before you add a border to table elements.

4. Click the Line Weight arrow to choose the weight (or thickness) you want for the border.

5. In the Table Styles group, click the Borders arrow to display the list of Border options you saw earlier in this chapter.

6. Click your selection to apply the border to the selected table elements.

> **Note**
>
> If you like the border style you created for a table you've been working with, you can save the style and reuse it. Click the More button in the Table Styles gallery (available when you choose Design on the contextual Table Tools). Choose New Table Style from the bottom of the gallery. Enter a name for the new style and click OK to save it.

Applying Shading Behind Content

You might occasionally want more than a border to make something in your document stand out. Adding shading can help call attention to passages of text that you want to highlight. For example, you might add a shade to highlight a special quotation, draw the reader's eye to an important summary, or as a way to make items pop out on the page. When you add a shade to text, you can control the color, transparency, and pattern used to create the shaded effect.

Applying Shades to Tables and Paragraphs

Word includes many ready-made table styles that include various shading possibilities. You can use one of the preset table styles by selecting the table and then choosing the style you like from the Table Style gallery (available when you choose Design on the contextual Table Tools). Chapter 11 includes detailed information on using table styles to format your tables.

When you want to apply custom shading to text, paragraphs, table cells, tables, or headings, you can use the Shading tab in the Borders And Shading dialog box. You can also choose the Shading button in the Paragraph group of the Home tab (when you've selected text) or the Shading button on the Design tab on the contextual Table Tools (when you have selected a table). To apply shading effects, follow these steps:

1. Select the item you want to shade.

2. Display the Borders And Shading dialog box.

3. Click the Shading tab. The Shading tab contains various options that you can use to add and modify shades.

> **Note**
>
> The borders and shading features of Word work independently, which means that if you add shading without adding a border, the item appears with only the shade behind it— no outer border is added automatically. To add a border to a shaded item, select it and then display the Borders And Shading dialog box. Choose border settings on the Borders tab and then click OK to apply the border to the shaded selection.

1. In the Fill area, click the color you want to apply.

    If you don't see the color you want, you can click More Colors to open the Colors dialog box and choose from another selection. Alternatively, you can click the Custom tab in the Colors dialog box to enter the RGB or HSL values for a custom color.

2. In the Patterns area, click the Style arrow to display your choices for the density or pattern of the color you select. Choose a lower percentage for a lighter shade.

    The Preview area shows the effect of each selection. Check carefully to make sure that the pattern doesn't make your text more difficult to read.

3. Click OK to apply the shading settings.

To remove shading, select the shaded content and then perform one of the following actions:

- Highlight the shaded area, and click the Shading arrow in the Paragraph group on the Home tab. Choose No Color.

- Display the Borders And Shading dialog box, click the Shading tab, choose No Color in the Fill area, and then click OK.

- Remove the pattern by displaying the Borders And Shading dialog box, clicking the Shading tab, and clicking the Style arrow in the Patterns area. Click Clear to remove the pattern and then click OK.

Shading Considerations

As with the caveat given earlier about art borders, remember that a little shading goes a long way. Done thoughtfully and with readers' needs in mind, shading can be effective in calling attention to certain elements and helping special design objects stand out on the page (especially in a complex document). Yet overusing shading or using the wrong mix of colors and patterns can make your document or Web page harder for people to read, which means they'll turn the page or click away from your site—and you'll lose your audience.

To use shading effectively, consider the following guidelines:

- **Use shading on a need-to-use basis.** Don't sprinkle shades all the way through your document at random. Give a shade a reason, such as, "Every time we mention a new board member, we'll provide a brief biography in a shaded sidebar."

- **Choose intensities carefully.** A shade that looks light on the screen might be much darker in print. Always look at your document in print form whenever possible, even for online content. You never know when a reader will decide to print an online page for later reference.

- **Check your color choices.** If you doubt your color choices, use the Theme Colors area of the color palette. Apply your color based on the element you are formatting, such as text or background, and let the document Theme handle the contrasts for you.

- **Test your contrasts.** When you add a colored shade behind text, be sure to increase the contrast between the color of the shade and the color of the text. If you choose a dark blue background, black text won't show up clearly. If you choose a dark background, select a light (white or yellow) text.

- **Do test prints on a printer that produces comparable output.** If you're printing colored shades, be sure to print a test page on a color printer.

- **If you're creating a Web page, use Web-safe colors for your shades.** Most Web browsers today can support the standard colors used in the Windows palette. If you choose customized colors, however, some browsers might not display the color accurately. Test the display of the page with different browsers to check the colors you select. To see a listing of Web-safe colors and their RGB values, visit *www.creationguide.com/colorchart.html*.

> ### Adding Ready-Made Quick Parts
>
> When working in a Word 2007 document, the new Quick Parts enable you to apply ready-made formats to sections of your document. For example, you can add a shaded text box that's already been formatted for your document.
>
> To add a Quick Part to your document, click the Insert tab and choose Quick Parts in the Text group. Choose Building Blocks Organizer from the list that appears. In the Building Blocks Organizer dialog box, scroll down to Text Box selections and click different selections to preview them. When you find one you want, click OK to add it to your document. You can then click in the text box to replace the placeholder text with your own.

What's Next?

This chapter rounded out Part IV of this book, which focused on adding professional polish to your documents by demonstrating how to add borders and shading to your paragraphs, sections, pages, pictures, and tables. The next chapter introduces the concept of creating and working collaboratively on shared documents—techniques that come in handy in our now-global workplace.

PART 5

Collaborative Projects: Shared Documents, Revisions, Security

CHAPTER 18

Sharing Documents and Collaborating Online

We live in a connected world. To stay up to speed, you need to be able to stay in touch with coworkers and get quick updates on your projects. Most likely, you are used to staying in touch with the flow of information throughout the workday—and, if you're like many of us, into your evenings at home.

Luckily, today the options for connecting to the information you need—via cell phones, PDAs, or laptops—are almost unlimited You can schedule meetings on your Pocket PC while your daughter finishes her piano lesson; you can download the files you need for a presentation while you sit at a stoplight. The local sandwich shop isn't just a quiet place to go to "get away from it all" anymore—now it's a place to visit your team's Microsoft Windows SharePoint Services site, answer e-mail, or finish your review of the team's report for the next board meeting.

This chapter spotlights the enhanced collaboration features in Microsoft Office Word 2007 and shows you how to collaborate—from the coffee shop or the board room—by sharing your Office Word 2007 documents in a variety of ways. In this chapter, you'll find two different approaches to sharing documents. First, this chapter introduces the document sharing features included in Word 2007 that use Microsoft Windows SharePoint Services to enable you to create shared workspaces. Then, the chapter provides ways you can share documents without using a shared workspace—by posting your files directly to a network server; or sharing them via instant messaging, e-mail, or fax.

Sharing Documents in Word

Word 2007 includes a number of features that make collaboration easier—and more secure—than ever. Whether you're sending a file as an XPS or Portable Document Format (PDF) attachment, posting it on a document server or SharePoint site, or sending the file as an Internet fax, when you click the Microsoft Office Button, you'll find commands to help you accomplish your objectives:

- If you want to send your document as an e-mail message or as an attachment to a message in either PDF or XPS format, you'll find the options you want by pointing to Send (see Figure 18-1). This is also where you'll go if you want to send an Internet fax.

Note

If you don't have the option of e-mailing your document as a PDF or XPS attachment, you need to download the Save as PDF or XPS add-in for Word 2007. See Appendix C on the companion CD for details.

Figure 18-1 The Send options enable you to send a document as an e-mail message, as an attachment, or as a fax.

- If you want to post the document to a document server or create a document workspace by using Windows SharePoint Services, click Publish to see your choices (see Figure 18-2).

Figure 18-2 Use the Publish options to save the document to a document server or to create a document workspace by using Windows SharePoint Services 3.0.

In addition to these sharing techniques, you might want to collaborate with team members using any (or all!) of the following methods:

- Sending files back and forth while you're instant messaging with group members
- Posting updated files directly to network server space
- Creating shared files and folders others on your team can access
- Creating and sharing workgroup templates
- Sharing information via fax and e-mail
- Creating a dynamic shared workspace with Microsoft Office Groove 2007

Throughout this chapter, you'll learn more about using these features. The world is getting smaller by the minute! The techniques in this chapter show you how to increase your effectiveness and share-ability in Word.

Creating and Using Shared Workspaces

When you are working collaboratively on a document, keeping all team members up to speed can be a challenge. You need to be able to know that others in the group are getting their tasks done on time; you need to be able to review each others' versions of the growing document; you need to be able to standardize rules, formats, and decisions about images, diagrams, and more.

Word includes a shared workspace feature where you can create a real space where team members can work together on the document. In a shared document workspace, you can:

- Create document libraries to check files in and out and make sure versions are always up to date.

- Post events and announcements about upcoming meetings, chats, and more.

- Assign and follow up on tasks that different team members are responsible for.

- Reach team members directly through e-mail or instant message (IM).

- Add research material, background content, or resource links relevant to the project.

How Will You Create and Use a Document Workspace?

How will you first begin working with shared documents? Here are a few possible scenarios:

- You are at a departmental meeting when the department chair selects you to write the first draft of the document you're all responsible for. This means you'll create the document in Word and then turn it into a shared document so others can review and comment on the draft. (The next section shows you how to do this.)

- You are a member of a team and receive an e-mail message telling you that a copy of the first draft of the team document has been posted in the Document Workspace. How will you get to it?

- You are a member of the team and you receive an e-mail message with a shared file as an attachment. You can open the file as normal, make your changes, save the file, and then click Reply to send the revised file back to the teammate who sent it to you. In addition to sending the document back, the action also saves a copy of the document on the team site and ensures that each person works on the most recent version of the file.

The sections that follow take a closer look at each of these aspects of working on a team and sharing documents. In addition to basic how-to's for viewing, sharing, and managing shared documents, you'll also learn how to customize and use the team Web site to keep your entire team moving in the right direction.

Before we move into the step-by-step procedures, however, you should have a little background information about Windows SharePoint Services 3.0, which is required for you to create and manage a shared document workspace. The next section explores the relationship between Windows SharePoint Services and Word 2007.

Windows SharePoint Server 3.0 and Word 2007

As you'll learn later in this chapter, being able to create, use, and manage a shared workspace is a great benefit for teams that are scattered all over the globe. When you create a shared workspace—which is a highly customizable Web space where you can create document libraries, resource lists, and links; post schedules; assign tasks; and much more—you can stay in touch with your team no matter where team members may be traveling or what type of device they may use to check the status of your shared project.

The person who creates the shared workspace must have the necessary access and permissions to create a workspace on a server running Windows SharePoint Services 3.0 (which is a component of Windows Server 2003). If your organization is not running this software, these features will be unavailable to you

Users who participate on the team do not have to have Windows SharePoint Services or Windows Server 2003, however; this is required only for the site at which the workspace is created. Team members can log on to the site automatically by opening the Word document that is linked to the document workspace or by logging in using any Web browser.

Word 2003 first forged the way for the relationships with SharePoint Services, making the shared workspace feature available for the first time. In Word 2007, the shared workspace features have been greatly enhanced, in large part due to these new features in Windows SharePoint Services 3.0:

- Now you can send documents by e-mail to a SharePoint site. Add content, events, and documents by e-mailing them to your team site. You can set up your lists and libraries to accept e-mail, which then enables you to post directly to the site without ever opening your browser.

- Update your lists from your cell phone or PDA. Now SharePoint Services includes mobile support, which means you can view task assignments and receive alerts when content, tasks, documents, or events are added to or removed from the site.

- Create and maintain a blog on the SharePoint site. A blog enables you to add on-going information, giving daily (or more than once a day) updates to share the latest information with your team. You can easily add a blog to your shared team site and enable permissions so that additional team members can post to the blog as well.

- Create and grow a wiki on your SharePoint document workspace to bring a whole new dynamic to your team collaboration, management, and information gathering.

Chapter 18

INSIDE OUT   What's a wiki?

A wiki is a collaborative Web site on which visitors (or in this case, team members) can add, edit, or remove text. Wikipedia.com is one example of an on-going wiki.

- Polling improvements. Now you can use conditional features to further customize the polling you do. You can also create more polls and use better layout controls to design the poll. A new feature enables participants to save their responses half-way through and return to the poll later.

- Receive updates from your shared site via RSS (Really Simple Syndication). This feature is especially helpful if you are part of several team sites. Instead of logging on to each site to see what's changed (or relying on your e-mail alerts to deliver each modification individually), you can have all changes from all sites delivered to your mobile device or computer via RSS feeds.

If you're unsure whether your organization has the capability to create document work-spaces in Word 2007, ask your system administrator. To find out more about Windows SharePoint Services 3.0 and Windows SharePoint Server 2007, go to the SharePoint Services Web site, at *office.microsoft.com/sharepoint*.

Sharing a Document

After writing, revising, and editing your draft of the new departmental report, you think you're ready to distribute it to others on your team. You've reviewed it as well as you can—used the spelling checker, the grammar checker, and the Document Inspec-tor—and now you're ready to send your draft out for feedback. This is where you begin using the shared documents features that Word provides. You have more than one choice when you're ready to share a document:

- You can save the document to a document server your company already has set up (to use this option, you must have the uniform resource locator (URL) of the document server and the necessary permissions to post to it).

- You can create a document workspace for the document (to take advantage of this feature, you need Windows SharePoint Services 3.0).

- You can e-mail the document as a shared attachment to another person (or people).

Any of these approaches ends at the same place: a new team Web site on a shared server at a location you specify.

Saving the Document to a Document Server

If your company, organization, or department uses Windows Server 2003, you can save your document directly to the server by using the Publish command. This option simply places a copy of the document on the document server space; it does not create a document workspace where team members can log in and interact in various ways (that technique is the subject of the next section).

To save the document to your document server, follow these steps:

1. Click the Microsoft Office Button and point to Publish. Then click Document Management Server.

2. The Save As dialog box appears, displaying the accounts you've created in My Network Places (see Figure 18-3).

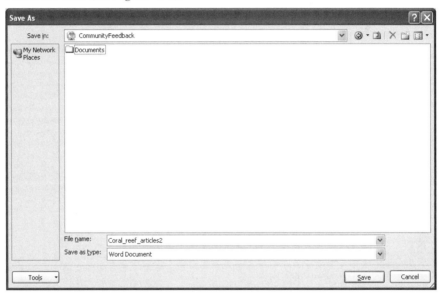

Figure 18-3 The accounts you've set up in My Network Places appear in the Save As dialog box.

3. Click the network place that's appropriate for the file and navigate to the folder you want.

4. Click Save to save the file to the document server.

> **Tip**
> If you haven't set up a network place yet, you can click the New Folder tool in the top right corner of the Save As dialog box to launch the My Network Places Wizard. Follow the prompts to set up access to the network space you want to use.

Chapter 18

Creating a Document Workspace

If you've just finished a draft of a document, and you want to create a shared workspace so others can review the file, click the Microsoft Office Button, point to Publish, and then click Create Document Workspace. The Document Management task pane appears, as shown in Figure 18-4.

Figure 18-4 Start the process of creating the document workspace in the Document Management task pane.

In the Location For New Workspace box, type the URL for the workspace you want to create. Then click Create to begin the process. If you have previously visited a Share-Point Services site or typed a Web address for your shared space, Word inserts that address automatically and displays the Connect box so that you can enter your user name and password. If you haven't already entered an address, you are prompted to provide it. (Check with your system administrator or Internet service provider [ISP] for the address of the server space you can use.)

> **Note**
>
> Providing the address for the server space is necessary only if you are the one creating the shared workspace. If you are simply working with documents on a shared site (see the sections, "An Overview of the Document Management Task Pane" and "Sharing Word Documents via E-Mail" for more information), the space has already been created, and you won't need to enter this information.

When the site is created, your name appears on the Members tab (as shown in Figure 18-5), and the name of the site appears at the top of the task pane.

Figure 18-5 The Document Management task pane displays information about the shared site.

An Overview of the Document Management Task Pane

Once you've created a shared workspace, the Document Management task pane changes to provide information about the document and the site where it is stored. Figure 18-6 provides an overview of the elements in the task pane. Table 18-1 lists the tabs in the Document Workspace task pane that can provide you with more information.

Figure 18-6 Elements in the Document Management task pane give you information about your collaborative project.

Table 18-1 Shared Workspace Tabs

Tab	Description
Status	Alerts you if the document needs to be updated, files have been checked in or out, or other changes have been made
Members	Lists current members on the team site and displays options for adding members and sending e-mail to them
Tasks	Lists all tasks assigned to each team member who has permission to work in the workspace
Documents	Shows all documents currently stored in the shared workspace
Links	Lists links that team members have provided as resources for the team
Document Information	Gives pertinent information about the document that currently appears

Working with the Document Workspace

At the top of the Document Management task pane, you see that you have the option of going to the team site that was just created. Position the pointer over the link, and an arrow appears. Click it to display a list of choices, as shown here:

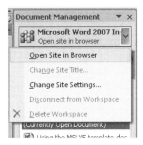

You can perform a number of site management tasks by using this list for now, however, click Open Site In Browser to go to the Web site.

Your new shared workspace will include the following elements:

- **Quick Launch** Serves as the navigation bar for your team Web site.

- **Announcements** Here, you might want to post information about upcoming meetings, new resources, or after-work gatherings. Click the Add New Announcement link to add your information.

- **Shared Documents** This is where your shared documents will be listed. You can view, edit, check out, and discuss documents by clicking the items displayed here.

- **Tasks** When you assign tasks to various team members—one person is gathering the images for the report, another is getting the financial information from the accounting department—click Add New Task and then add the information here.

- **Members** Shows all the members of your team and gives you the Add New Member link to expand your roster.

- **Links** Provides a common place for you to list helpful Web sites that can be used as resources for those working on your team.

Navigating the Site

The Quick Launch area helps you navigate to various pages on the new team site. The Documents link takes you to a page that lists all shared documents stored on the site. Clicking Pictures enables you to create a library of images, movie clips, and diagrams you will be using in your team project. The Lists link takes you to a page where you can make changes to the lists SharePoint Team Services enable you to collect information for.

> **Note**
>
> All the data items you enter in the Document Workspace—announcements, contacts, events, links, and tasks—are stored in list form. You can use the Lists view to modify the information that is shown, add information, and export list data to other Microsoft Office applications.

The General Discussion link enables you to create a message thread similar to those in newsgroups so that you can review and comment on the developing team project. Finally, the Surveys link takes you to a page that enables you to create online surveys to gather team opinions and reactions to topics related to the project.

Adding Information on the Site

As you can see, you can add information items on the shared workspace site, or you can add tasks, members, and other items by working with the Document Management task pane in Word. Because the focus of this chapter is really sharing documents from within Word, we're going to return to the Document Management task pane for most of the examples in this chapter. However, it's worth noting that there are a few actions that you'll want to perform on the site itself. On the team Web site, you will probably want to do the following:

- **Add announcements about upcoming team meetings** Click Add New Announcement to enter the information you want the team to know (as shown in Figure 18-7). Click the Choose Date From Calendar button to set the expiration date for the announcement.

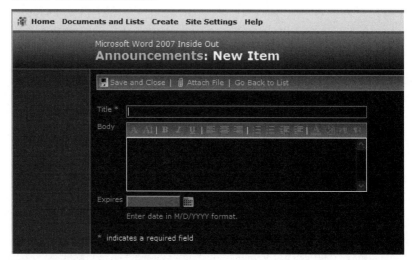

Figure 18-7 Use announcements to let team members know about changes to the site or upcoming events.

- **Create events to post upcoming deadlines or important meetings** To create an event, click Events in the Quick Launch area. Here, you can enter the beginning and ending time, the location, and a description of the event. Additionally, you can create recurring appointments that continue indefinitely or are scheduled to end on a specific date (as shown in Figure 18-8).

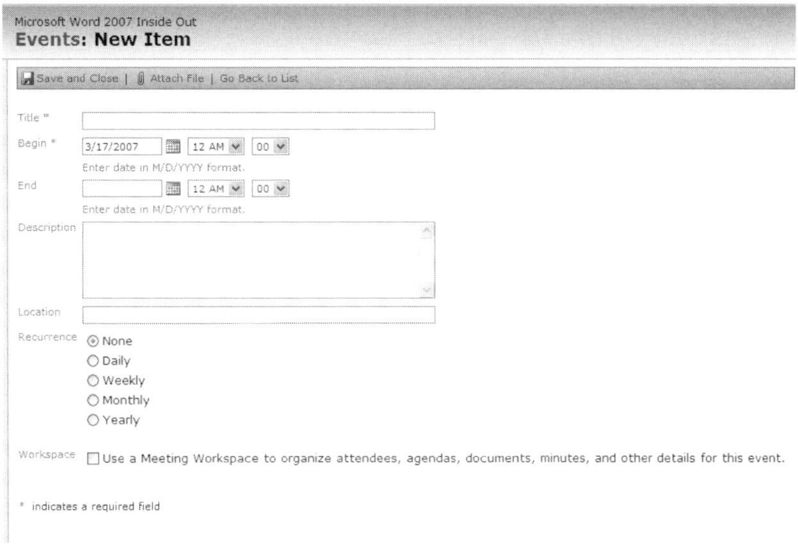

Figure 18-8 You can create events for the team and schedule face-to-face or virtual meetings online.

- **Have discussions about the project** On the team site, you can create a newsgroup-style discussion about issues related to your project. Click General Discussion in the Quick Launch area to go to the General Discussion page, where you can enter new postings and reply to other postings.

This is only a quick overview of some of the features you may want to try on the shared workspace site. The site is easy to use and modify—you'll want to spend some time exploring and experimenting to create just the right setup for your team.

Choosing Document Management Settings

You can choose a number of settings to control the way in which Word works with your document workspace. Start the process by clicking the Microsoft Office Button and clicking Word Options. Choose Advanced and then scroll down and click the Service Options button. The Service Options dialog box displays a range of options for updates and alerts for both the Document Management task pane and the shared workspace (see Figure 18-9).

Chapter 18

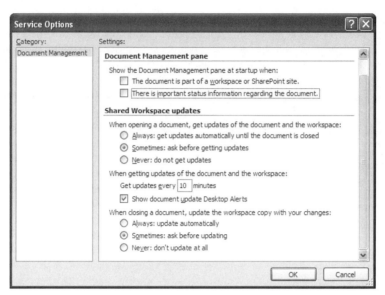

Figure 18-9 Use the Service Options dialog box to determine how your documents are updated when you are working with shared workspaces.

Click the options you want to change; also choose when (and how often) you want Word to check for changes on the site. After you've set the options the way you want them, click OK to save your changes. Click OK to close the Word Options dialog box.

Working in the Document Management Task Pane

Now that you know how to create a shared workspace and understand the site you've created online, you're ready to return to Word and use the features in the Document Management task pane. This is where the benefits of these collaboration features really shine—you can manage, review, access, edit, and update your team documents, all right from within Word. This process is really no more difficult than working with any other document. This section of the chapter takes you through the major tasks you'll want to perform on shared documents.

Adding Team Members

One of the first things you'll want to do is add team members for your shared project. Open the Document Management task pane when the shared document is open in the Word window by clicking the Microsoft Office Button, pointing to Servers (this option appears only when you're working with shared documents), and clicking Document Management Information. When the Document Management task pane appears, click the Members tab. This tab of the Document Management task pane lists all active members, shows you whether they are online, gives you a link to add new members, and offers the option of sending e-mail to all members at once, as shown in Figure 18-10.

Figure 18-10 The Members tab enables you to add, organize, and contact members.

To add a new member, click the Add New Member link at the bottom of the task pane. In the Add New Members dialog box, type the names or e-mail addresses of others on your team.

In the Choose Site Group section, you make selections that determine what kind of permissions you grant to the users you are adding. The four site groups and their permission levels are as follows:

- **Reader** Gives members read-only privileges

- **Contributor** Enables members to read and add postings on the site

- **Web Designer** Lets members read, post, and modify items on the site

- **Administrator** Includes full access; members of this group can read, post, modify, and add or delete users and pages

Chapter 18

> **Note**
>
> The site group you select will be applied to all users you list in the Choose Members box in the Add New Members dialog box. This means that if you want to assign different users to different site groups, you'll need to add the members in batches.

Click Next. The member names and e-mail addresses appear in the next display. Enter a display name for each member, if you like, verify the addresses, and then click Finish. A message tells you that the members have been added and asks whether you'd like to send an e-mail message to the new participants.

When you click OK, Word displays the e-mail message that will be sent to new team members. You can add your own message as needed and then click Send to deliver the message.

Adding Tasks

Delegation is a major part of getting any collaborative project done. Who does what is important, because everyone's work depends on everyone else. You can assign and review task assignments in the Document Management task pane. Here's how:

1. In the Document Management task pane, click the Task tab and then click Add New Task at the bottom of the task pane.

2. In the Task dialog box, shown in Figure 18-11, enter a title for the task. Then complete the Status, Priority, and Assigned To fields.

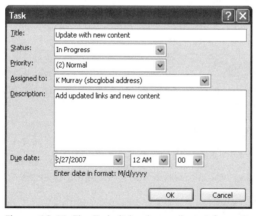

Figure 18-11 The Task dialog box collects information about the who, what, and when of any task that needs to be done.

3. If necessary, add a description to provide instructions about the task. Then enter a due date by selecting it from the calendar (click the arrow) or by typing it in the form m/d/yyyy.

4. Click OK to add the task.

After the task is added, you can view it at any time by clicking the Task tab. When you click the arrow to the left of the task, a list of task options appears. You'll use these options to update the status of your tasks or to remove tasks from the list.

INSIDE OUT   Setting alerts

One of the great features of SharePoint Team Services and the Document Management task pane is that they can automatically keep you in touch with any changes made on the team site or in your shared documents. At the bottom of the Task tab in the Document Management task pane, Click Alert Me About Tasks to go to the New Alert page of the team Web site. Here, you can set up a notification system so that you receive e-mail messages whenever tasks are completed or items are added, updated, or removed. This keeps you up to date with the most recent happenings on the site and in your project, which helps everybody stay together.

In addition, you can display pop-up information about a task (including any text that was entered in the Description field) by simply hovering the mouse pointer over it (see Figure 18-12).

Figure 18-12 Get full information about a task by positioning the mouse pointer over it.

Working with Documents

Once you have enrolled the members and assigned the tasks, you can get down to the real business of working with your collaborative document. The Documents tab in the Document Management task pane gives you everything you need to view, update, and work with the shared document. To see your options for working with a document, click the Documents tab and then click the arrow to the left of the document. A list of document choices appears, as shown in Figure 18-13.

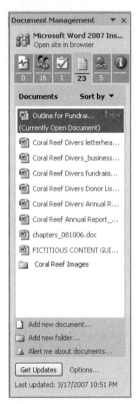

Figure 18-13 You can get information about the current document and update changes by using the Documents tab.

Each time you open a shared document, a prompt asks you whether you want to check for updates on the shared workspace site. If you click Get Updates, Word compares the open document with the most recent version on the site. If the uploaded document is more current than the one you're opening, Word displays the Document Updates task pane so that you can compare and merge any necessary changes.

We've just touched on the basics of working with shared documents in the Document Management task pane. The three basic tasks discussed here—adding new members, assigning tasks, and working with documents—are those that you are likely to use most as you begin to work with shared documents.

Collaborating with Office Groove 2007

Microsoft Office Groove 2007 is a new collaboration tool—available in Microsoft Office Ultimate 2007 and Microsoft Office Enterprise 2007—that helps you bring small teams together in a virtual workspace to get your projects done easily and efficiently. Groove works on your computer and it requires no special server configurations. In addition, the files you work on collaboratively are stored on team members' computers (and then updated when members log on), so all participants have access to files whether they are online or offline.

Groove really shines for collaborative projects, offering instant chat features, shared calendars, discussion groups, file sharing, alerts, whiteboards for group presentations, and more. And Groove syncs easily both with your individual computer (you can work on projects offline and then update files when you log in) and with SharePoint, enabling you to update lists and download information seamlessly.

Groove is ideal for creating, managing, and sharing libraries of Word documents related to a specific project or workgroup. To find out more about Groove, visit the Groove Web site at office.microsoft.com/en-us/groove/FX100487641033.aspx.

Online Collaboration with Word 2007

In this era of telecommuting, long-distance associations, and on-the-move lifestyles, online communication plays a much larger role in collaboration than it has in the past. Online communication gives people a convenient way to work together by sharing documents and ideas in near real time across networks, regardless of where participants are located. To help make online communication possible, the Microsoft Office system offers a number of online collaboration features.

The online collaboration features in Word work with other Microsoft Office applications to expand the Internet and network options available to you from within Word. For example, Word works with Microsoft Office Outlook to enable you to create and send e-mail messages; Word works with Windows Live Messenger to enable you to send and receive instant messages; and Word works with Microsoft Office Document Imaging (MODI) to create TIFF files and fax documents. In the remainder of this chapter, you'll learn about a few of the most common online collaboration tools accessible from within Word.

Using Instant Messaging While Working in Word

If you have joined the IM crowd, you know how helpful it can be to get a question answered instantly by simply typing a quick instant message and sending it to a coworker who is currently online. Not only can you trade a quick message or emoticon; you can also share files, visit Web pages together, and invite others into the IM conversation or to a telephone or video call. In addition to these online shared experiences, you can use Windows Live Messenging to send a Word document to a Windows Live contact.

You can send instant messages to contacts who are online while you work on your Word document. You can also send instant messages when you make changes to shared documents or workspaces.

If Person Name Smart Tags are enabled in your Word options, you can tell whether your contacts are online whenever you see their names within a document. Suppose, for example, that the draft of the document you are working on displays the name of each team member at the beginning of the sections they authored. When you see a Smart Tag or the telltale purple dotted lines beneath text (which you can hover the pointer over to display the Smart Tag), you can click the Smart Tag to access various communications options, such as sending an e-mail message, scheduling a meeting, or inserting the contact's address. To send a message to a contact, click the Smart Tag button and choose a message option from the list. Then type your message and click Send.

> **Note**
> Person Name Smart Tags become available after you complete a sentence by inserting closing punctuation (such as a period) or after you press Enter, whichever action comes first.

To enable Person Name Smart Tags, follow these steps:

1. Click the Microsoft Office Button and click Word Options.

2. Click Proofing. On the Proofing page click AutoCorrect Options.

3. Select the Smart Tags tab.

4. In the Recognizers list, select the Person Name (Outlook E-Mail Recipients) check box and then select the Person Name (English) check box if you're using the English-language version of Word (see Figure 18-14).

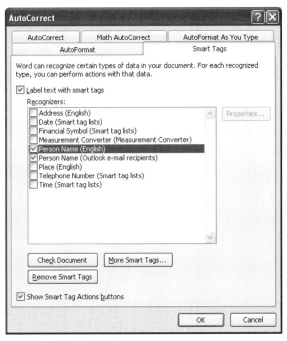

Figure 18-14 After you enable Smart Tags for names, you can send an instant message from within your Word document.

5. Click OK to save the Smart Tag settings and click OK a second time to close the Word Options dialog box.

INSIDE OUT   Contact names aren't showing up

One caveat to using Person Name Smart Tags is that a contact's name and e-mail address information must be entered in your Office Outlook address book or your instant messaging application (such as Windows Messenger or Windows Live Messenger), or the contact must be someone to whom you've previously sent an e-mail or instant message from Outlook or an instant messaging application. Although Smart Tags appear for any text that appears to be a name, Word can insert proper addressing information into messaging applications only if a contact's addressing information is properly configured on your system or network.

Working with My Network Places

In the true spirit of Web and desktop integration, you can use Word to create, copy, save, and manage folders and files that reside on a network, the Web, File Transfer Protocol (FTP) servers, or in a shared workspace. After you create shortcuts to online folders (and if you have the proper permissions), you can work with online files and folders as though they were on your local computer. Of course, taking advantage of working with networks and the Web implies that you are connected to a network or have a connection to the Internet. The first order of business when you're working with online documents involves configuring your system so that you can access network places and FTP sites.

Creating a Network Place

Although you can access documents and folders in existing Network Places from within Word, you need to set up links to new network places by using the Add Network Place Wizard.

To create a network place in Windows 2000 or later, follow these steps:

1. Click Start, My Network Places.

2. In the My Network Places task pane, click Add A Network Place.

3. Follow the steps on the Add Network Place Wizard pages to create a link to the network place.

After you add a network place, you can access documents and folders on the network place from within Word.

Linking to FTP Sites

In the same way that you access other network places, you can add FTP sites to your list of Internet sites if you have access to a network or the Internet. You can also add FTP sites to your list of network places while you're working in Word. To create shortcuts to FTP sites, follow these steps:

1. Click the Microsoft Office Button and click Open.

2. Click the Look In arrow and then choose Add/Modify FTP Locations from the bottom of the list. The Add/Modify FTP Locations dialog box appears (see Figure 18-15).

3. In the Name Of FTP Site box, enter the name or IP address of the FTP site (for example, **ftp.coralreefdivers.com**).

4. Click either Anonymous or User to specify whether you want to log on anonymously or provide a user name. If you must supply a user name, type the user name in the User box and then type a password (if necessary) in the Password box.

Figure 18-15 FTP provides a fast, secure, and simple way to upload large files to shared server space.

5. When you finish configuring the Add/Modify FTP Locations dialog box, click Add to add the new FTP location and then click OK to close the dialog box.

After you create an FTP link, you can use it to access your FTP site by clicking My Network Places on the left side of the Open dialog box and double-clicking the FTP link list box. To delete the link to an FTP site, right-click the link and then choose Delete.

Accessing Resources Stored in Network Locations

You access network locations in the same way you access local files and folders—you simply navigate to the online file and folder locations in the Open dialog box and then create a local shortcut to the document, if desired. To open an online folder or file by using the Open dialog box, follow these steps:

1. Click the Microsoft Office Button and choose Open.

2. Click the Look In arrow, click My Network Places or FTP Locations (or click My Network Places on the Places bar) and then double-click the location you want to access.

Navigate to the file you want to open, select it, and click Open to begin working with the file.

Saving Documents to a Network Location

In addition to opening files from network locations, you'll probably want to save files to online locations. The process of saving files to online locations is similar to saving files locally. To save a newly created file to an online location, follow these steps:

1. Click the Microsoft Office Button and click Save As.

2. In the Save As dialog box, click My Network Places.

3. Double-click the shortcut to the network location where you want to save the document and then double-click any subfolders you want to access as well.

4. In the File Name box, type a name for the file (or retain the current name) and then click Save.

Note

If you open a document from a network location, you can save your changes to the online document by by pressing Ctrl+S. To save the document locally, you must first use the Save As command to save the document to a location on your computer.

Using Workgroup Templates

A convenient way to keep a group supplied with the most up-to-date templates is to store common templates centrally on a network server. (These shared templates are generally referred to as *workgroup templates*.) By doing this, you can ensure that everyone working on similar projects can access the same versions of templates at any time. A central repository for workgroup templates also saves everyone the headache of distributing and obtaining individual copies of the latest templates and can greatly help to standardize documents across the board.

You create workgroup templates in the same way you create other templates. You then designate a folder as the workgroup template container and make sure that everyone's computer is configured to point to that file. Generally speaking, you'll want to make workgroup templates read-only files so that no one accidentally changes the template information. If you want to ensure that only certain people can access the files, you might want to assign passwords to the templates or make the network share read-only.

For more information about creating templates, see Chapter 4 "Formatting Documents Using Templates." For information about making documents read-only and password-protected, see Chapter 20, "Addressing Document Protection and Security Issues."

To specify the location of workgroup templates on an individual computer, follow these steps:

1. Click the Microsoft Office Button and click Word Options.

2. Click Advanced.

3. Scroll down to the General settings. Click File Locations.

4. In the File Types list, select Workgroup Templates, as shown in Figure 18-16.

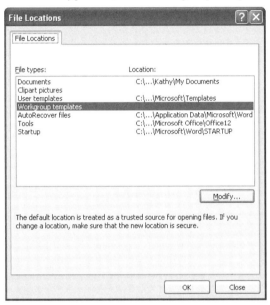

Figure 18-16 Click File Locations on the Advanced page of the Word Options dialog box to specify locations for a number of file types, including workgroup templates.

5. Click Modify to open the Modify Location dialog box.

6. Create a new folder or navigate to and select the folder that contains the workgroup templates, click OK to close the Modify Location dialog box, and then click OK to close the Word Options dialog box.

To access templates stored in the workgroup templates folder, users can click the My Templates link in Templates list in the New Document window. The templates appear on the My Templates tab. If workgroup templates are stored in a subfolder in the workgroup templates folder, the New dialog box includes a tab with the same name as the subfolder, and the templates stored within the subfolder appear on that tab (see Figure 18-17).

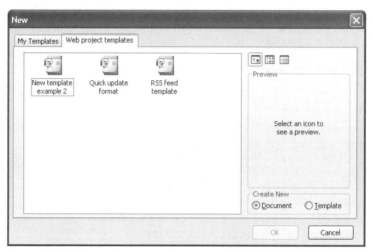

Figure 18-17 The workgroup templates are available in the New dialog box.

Store workgroup templates in a Web folder

You can't indicate an Internet location for your workgroup templates on the File Locations tab in the Options dialog box—the workgroup templates folder must be stored in a location on your computer or network. If you want to store templates in a Web folder, you should create a My Network Places link to the Web folder. You can then access the folder by clicking the On My Web Sites link in the New Document task pane.

Sharing Word Documents via E-Mail

Perhaps the easiest way to share a Word document is to e-mail it to other people on your team. Your teammates can then review the document, make a few changes, and send it back (or simply send you an e-mail message, saying "Perfect!").

Securely Sending Documents via E-Mail

If others won't need to make changes in the document, and you want to send it in the most secure form possible, consider downloading and installing the free Save As PDF Or XPS add-in utility by clicking the link provided in the Save As list (available when you click the Microsoft Office Button and point to Save As) or by downloading it from the Microsoft Downloads site (www.microsoft.com/downloads). After you install the utility, Word adds two commands to the choices that appear when you click the Microsoft Office Button and point to Send: E-mail As PDF Attachment and E-mail As XPS Attachment.

PDF and XPS formats save your document in a paginated, noneditable format that you can share with others for review. For more about working with PDF and XPS formats, see Chapter 20.

When you want to send your Word document directly to others on your team, follow these steps:

1. Start with your Word document open on the screen.

2. Click the Microsoft Office Button and point to Send.

3. Click E-mail. Word opens a new message window and includes your file as an attachment (see Figure 18-18).

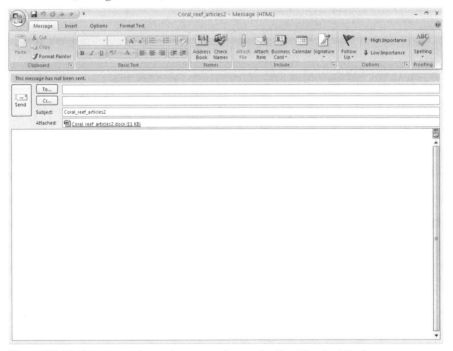

Figure 18-18 You can send your document via e-mail without leaving Word.

You will notice that the new message window Word opens looks similar to the Outlook 2007 new message window. You can specify the recipient information and send as usual. The rest of this section explores some of the Word e-mail features you may want to use when you are sharing documents with your colleagues.

Setting E-Mail Priority

Depending on the nature of the document you're sharing with others, you might want to mark e-mail messages as urgent or not-at-all urgent (also known as *high-priority* and *low-priority messages*). Marking your messages lets recipients know at a glance whether they should give special attention to a message.

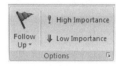

To set e-mail priority for a message, click either High Importance or Low Importance in the Options command set of the Message tab. Clicking High Importance adds a red exclamation point to the message so that when it arrives in the recipient's Inbox, the exclamation point clearly visible. Clicking Low Importance adds a blue down-arrow to the message, letting the recipient know that the message is not an urgent matter.

Flagging a Message for Follow-Up

You can add flags to e-mail messages to indicate that some sort of follow-up action needs to be taken after the message is read. When you add a flag to a message, the recipient sees the flag in Outlook when the message arrives in the Inbox. You use the Follow Up command in the Options command set to add a flag to a message. When you click Follow Up, a list of options appears so that you can choose when the follow-up action is to take place.

Requesting Receipts

We've all had the experience of sending a particularly important document by e-mail and then eagerly awaiting to hear what the recipient thought of the draft. By using the Receipts feature when you e-mail Word documents, you can make sure that you know when the document has been received and read.

Click the Options tab in the message window and choose either Request Delivery Receipt or Request Read Receipt (or both) in the Tracking command set. When you select Request Delivery Receipt, an e-mail message is sent to you automatically when the message is delivered to the recipient. When you click Request Read Receipt, you are notified by e-mail when the file has been opened.

Delaying Delivery

If you want to make sure that your recipients receive the document to review at a specific time—perhaps at the start of a fundraising drive, or with the public release of software—you can delay the document you use Word's e-mail feature to deliver. Click the Options tab in the message window and click Delay Delivery in the More Options command set. The Message Options dialog box appears so that you can specify when you want the message to go out (see Figure 18-19).

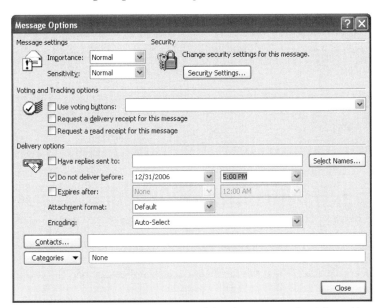

Figure 18-19 Specify when you want a delayed message to be delivered by setting options in the Message Options dialog box.

In the Delivery Options area of the Message Options dialog box, click the Do Not Deliver Before arrow and choose the date you want the message to be delivered. Next, click the time field and choose the appropriate time from the list. Click Close to save your settings, and the message will be delivered after the date and time you specified.

Include Voting Buttons

Another interesting e-mail feature that may be helpful when you're working on collaborative documents is the voting function. When you send your document attached to a message from Word, you can use Voting buttons to give recipients a say in whether you keep this document as your final report or go back for another draft.

To use the voting feature, display the message as usual and then click the Options tab. In the Tracking command set, click Use Voting Buttons. A list of voting options appears, as shown in Figure 18-20. Click the voting type you want to include and then send the message as usual.

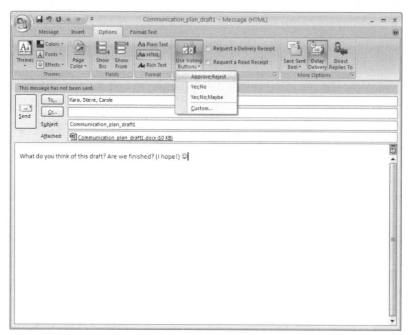

Figure 18-20 Choose the type of voting options you want to include and then send the message.

When the message arrives in the recipient's Inbox (in Outlook), a prompt tells the user Click Here To Vote. When the recipient clicks the message bar, the voting options appear (see Figure 18-21).

Communication_plan_draft1

Katherine

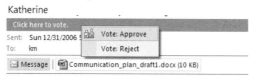

What do you think of this draft? Are we finished? (I hope!) ☺

Figure 18-21 Recipients can easily vote when they receive the message in Outlook.

Using Word to Send Faxes

Faxing is yet another fast, convenient way to get information from your office or home computer to other people around the country or around the world. Word enables you to use an online fax service to send your document via fax.

Creating a Fax

Word includes a number of fax templates you can use by clicking the Microsoft Office Button and choosing New. When the New Document window opens, select Faxes in the Templates list on the left side of the window. A collection of fax samples appears, as you see in Figure 18-22. Click one you want to see, and it is previewed in the panel on the right side of the window. Click Download to open the fax template you want to use. Word downloads it to your Word window, and you can click and replace the placeholder text with your own information.

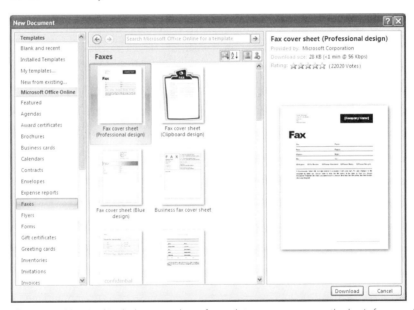

Figure 18-22 Word includes a number of templates you can use as the basis for your fax.

Using a Fax Service

If you don't have a fax modem installed on your computer, or you'd like to take advantage of features provided with online faxing, you can sign up to use an Internet fax service. Word now works seamlessly with Internet fax services, and you'll find that you have quite a bit of control over faxes you send using this method.

To sign up with a fax service, click the Microsoft Office Button and point to Send. Click Internet Fax. When you choose this option for the first time, you'll see a message box that states that you must sign up with a fax service provider before you can use a fax service to send faxes. Click OK to go to the Fax Services page of Microsoft Office Online, where you'll find a selection of available fax services.

After you select and sign up with an Internet fax service provider, you can fax a Word document by performing the following steps:

1. Open Outlook so that it is working in the background (Word uses Outlook to send the fax).

2. Open the document you want to fax. Add a fax cover page, if necessary.

3. Click the Microsoft Office Button and point to Send. Choose Internet Fax.

4. Follow the prompts to enter the recipient information and send the fax. You will receive a confirmation message when the fax has been successfully sent.

> **Note**
>
> If Outlook is installed but not open when you send a fax, the fax will be placed in Outlook's Outbox, and your fax will be sent the next time mail is sent from Outlook. If you want to send your fax immediately, ensure that Outlook is open before you send the fax.

INSIDE OUT   I can't use the Internet fax service to send a fax

When you use an Internet fax service to send a fax, you basically convert your document into a TIFF file and attach it to an e-mail message, which is then sent to the recipient's fax machine or fax modem. The body of the e-mail message contains the cover sheet, and the attached TIFF file is the fax document. By default, to use an Internet fax service, you must have both Outlook and Word installed and configured on your system. If your fax isn't being sent, or if you're not sure whether your fax was sent, you can perform the following checks:

- Verify that Outlook sent your fax. To do this, open Outlook and then look in the Sent Items folder. Your fax will appear as an e-mail message with an attachment. If your fax message is waiting in the Outbox folder, click Send/Receive to send the fax.

- Check the Outlook Inbox to see whether you received a message from your Internet fax service provider that states whether your fax transmission succeeded or failed. Generally, Internet fax services send confirmation messages to your Outlook inbox whenever you attempt to send a fax.

- Ensure that the Microsoft Office Document Image Writer print driver is installed in your Printers And Faxes folder. If it is missing, you can install it using Microsoft Office Setup. To do so, click Start, Control Panel, Add Or Remove Programs, Microsoft Office. Then click the Change button. Select Add Or Remove Features, click Continue, expand Office Tools, expand Microsoft Office Document Imaging, click Microsoft Office Document Image Writer, click Run From My Computer, click Update, and then click OK after the update completes.

- Ensure that your Internet fax service is properly activated. If you're unsure, visit your Internet fax service provider's online help pages or contact their support group. Usually, after you sign up with an Internet fax service provider, you'll receive a welcome e-mail message verifying your status, user information, and login parameters.

Tip

Usethe Mail Merge Wizard to send multiple faxes that you create. Start by opening the document you want to fax. Then choose Tools, Letters And Mailings, Mail Merge. The Mail Merge task pane opens. When the Mail Merge Wizard asks you to specify a print option, choose your fax application in the Name list in the Print dialog box. For more information about creating and working with mail-merged documents, see Chapter 28, "Performing Mail Merges."

What's Next?

This chapter has taken you on a whirlwind tour of the many different methods you can use to share your Word documents with others. The next chapter continues the theme of collaboration by showing you how to make the most of the markup and reviewing tools in Word.

As you probably know, many finished documents (including this book!) reflect the efforts of a group of people who worked together to create a polished product. For example, you might be involved with a single document that was written by an author, modified by an editor, commented on by a technical reviewer, and inspected and approved by a project manager. Such team collaboration can be simplified tremendously by using the markup tools available in Microsoft Office Word 2007. The following is a list of some of the notable enhancements to the markup features:

- **Inline revisions** Revisions can now be displayed inline in Print Layout view as opposed to limiting inline revisions to Draft view.

- **Moved revisions** Content that is moved when you use cut and paste operations (or drag-and-drop functionality) is now identified as Moved as opposed to an insertion and deletion.

- **Reviewing Pane** Enhanced detailed summary of the number of insertions, deletions, moves, formatting, and comments; can now be displayed vertically.

- **Compare and Combine** Enhanced options for specifying the types of changes you want to compare or merge, such as formatting and white space, along with displaying changes at the word or character level.

- **Table revisions** Expanded track change capabilities for tables when used in conjunction with Compare or Combine.

- **Tri-Pane Review panel** Used in conjunction with the Compare and the Combine features. The Tri-Pane Review panel displays the original document, the revised document, and a combined version of both documents.

Benefits of an Organized Revision Process

Revising documents can be a messy and confusing business—sometimes, it can even get downright frustrating when ideas and well-formed language are lost forever amidst an array of modifications and reviewers. Fortunately, with the revision tools provided by Office Word 2007, the revision process doesn't need to be painful—in fact, the process can be an enjoyable, educational endeavor when approached properly.

Over the years, the revision tools included in Word have been carving a name for themselves in businesses, educational institutions, and personal arenas. Using markup tools, coworkers can collaborate on publications without losing ideas along the way, educators can require students to track and show changes while the class works through the writing process, and you can keep an eye on personal document changes, such as changes to legal agreements or contracts in negotiation. Of course, like all tools, the effectiveness of markup and revision tools stems from knowing how to use them.

In Word, numerous people can review the same document and incorporate changes and comments with other people's changes and comments. After participants add their modifications to a document, others in the group can insert responses directly into the document. Throughout the process, Word can dutifully track and color-code everyone's comments and changes as long as you configure the markup features properly.

To help streamline the configuration and use of markup tools, Word now conveniently groups proofing, commenting, tracking, comparing, and document protection tools on the Review tab. This chapter thoroughly covers the markup features and reviewing options so that you can maximize your revision efforts when working with various versions of documents, either on your own or with others.

Familiarizing Yourself with Markup Tools

Although you can track changes for your own purposes, the true strength of revision tools becomes clear when you collaborate with others. When you collaborate on a document, you can use Word to track and merge people's changes and comments, highlight information to draw attention to selected text and graphics, and add ink and voice comments. Specifically, Word provides the following reviewing and markup tools:

- **Comments** Enable you to annotate a document with suggestions and queries without actually changing the document. In Word 2007, you can add text, ink, and voice comments to documents. Comments are identified by comment markers in the text, which can be displayed as balloons in the margin or as ScreenTips along with commenter's initials, as described in the section titled "Adding and Managing Comments Effectively" later in this chapter on page 532.

- **Track Changes feature** Records editing changes including deletions, added content, and formatting changes made to a document. Word can track and color-code changes from multiple reviewers, and the changes can later be evaluated and accepted or rejected on a case-by-case or global basis. For more information about the Track Changes feature, see the section titled "Tracking Changes" later in this chapter on page 534.

- **Compare (Legal Blackline) and Combine** Compare is used for comparing the differences between two documents, and all revisions are attributed to a single author. Combine is used for merging two or more documents along with identifying who changed what in the document. For more on these features, see the section titled "Comparing or Combining Documents" later in this chapter on page 554.

- **Ink support for Tablet PCs** Enables you to draw and write on documents directly by using a stylus or other drawing device. Using ink on a Tablet PC is discussed in the section titled "Inserting Voice and Handwritten Comments" later in this chapter on page 533.

- **Protect Document options** Enable you to restrict formatting and editing capabilities for reviewers, as mentioned in the section titled "Protecting a Document for Comments or Revisions" later in this chapter on page 551 and described in Chapter 20, "Addressing Document Protection and Security Issues."

- **Voice comment** Enables you to insert Voice comments into a document, as described in the section titled "Inserting Voice and Handwritten Comments" later in this chapter on page 533.

This chapter shows you how to make the most of these collaboration features. You'll find that many key collaboration features can be accessed from the Review tab, shown in Figure 19-1.

Figure 19-1 The Review tab provides tools that you can use to work with comments, tracked changes, proofing, document comparison, and document protection.

> **Note**
>
> If using Microsoft Office Ultimate 2007, Microsoft Office Professional Plus 2007, and Office Enterprise 2007, those that support Information Rights Management, the Protect Document command also shows an arrow.

As you can see in Figure 19-1, the Review tab is an expanded, easier-to-use version of the Reviewing toolbar found in Microsoft Office Word 2003. Other than the added features—such as the inclusion of the proofing and document protection tools—and the provision of two separate functionalities for Comparing (legal blackline) or Combining (merging revisions) along with enhanced functionality, a few tools were relocated. The Highlight command moved to the Home tab and is now accessible on the new Mini Toolbar, and the Insert Ink and Insert Voice commands are available as customizations to your Quick Access Toolbar. Table 19-1 describes the main markup features found on the Review tab.

Table 19-1 **Markup Features on the Review Tab**

Button	Name	Description
	New Comment	Inserts a new comment balloon that you can use to enter a text comment
	Delete Comment	Deletes a selected comment, deletes only shown comments (when selected reviewer comments are shown or hidden), or deletes all comments at once
	Previous Comment	Jumps to the previous comment in the current document relative to the insertion point
	Next Comment	Jumps to the next comment in the current document relative to the insertion point
	Track Changes	Controls whether the Track Changes feature is turned off or on and provides access to Tracking options and user name settings
	Balloons	Controls whether revisions and comments display in balloons or inline with text and enables displaying comments and formatting in balloons
	Display For Review	Controls how Word displays revisions and comments in the current document; available options are Final Showing Markup, Final, Original Showing Markup, and Original
	Show Markup	Provides options that enable you to show or hide Comments, Ink Annotations, Insertions And Deletions, Formatting, and Reviewers
	Reviewing Pane	Shows or hides the Reviewing Pane, which displays the complete text of tracked changes and comments; can be opened in vertical or horizontal position
	Accept And Move To Next	Accepts a selected tracked change in the document and moves to the next, accepts a change without moving to the next change, accepts all changes shown (when selected reviewer revisions are shown or hidden), or accepts all changes in the document at once
	Reject And Move To Next	Rejects a change (which returns the text to its original state) and moves to the next change, rejects a change without moving to the next change, rejects all changes shown (when selected reviewer revisions are shown or hidden), or rejects all changes in the document at once

Button	Name	Description
	Previous Change	Jumps to the previous tracked change or comment in the current document relative to the insertion point
	Next Change	Jumps to the next tracked change or comment in the current document relative to the insertion point
	Compare	Provides access to the Compare (legal blackline) and the Combine (merge revisions) functions
	Show Source Documents	New Tri-Pane Review panel; used in conjunction with Compare or Combine; hides source documents and displays Combined or Compared document only, displays Original and Combined or Compared documents, displays Revised and Combined or Compared documents, displays Original, Revised, and Combined or Compared documents
	Protect Document	Enables document protection for Comments only or Tracked Changes

Now that you've had a quick introduction to the primary markup tools, you are ready to look at the finer details. This chapter begins with configuring your settings for adding comments and tracking changes.

Configuring Reviewer Settings

Before you start inserting comments and tracked changes, you need to tell Word how to identify the marks you create. In other words, you need to configure your user name in Word. In fact, each person collaborating on the document must properly configure his or her user name to maximize the reviewing features. To set your user name information, you simply configure the Word Options settings. Word 2007 speeds up the process of accessing the settings by providing a command on the Review tab, as described here:

1. On the Review tab, click the arrow below Track Changes, and then click Change User Name. The Popular area in Word Options appears.

   The User Name settings are located below the heading Personalize Your Copy Of Microsoft Office.

2. In the User Name text box, type the name you want to use to identify your comments and then enter your initials in the Initials text box, as shown in Figure 19-2.

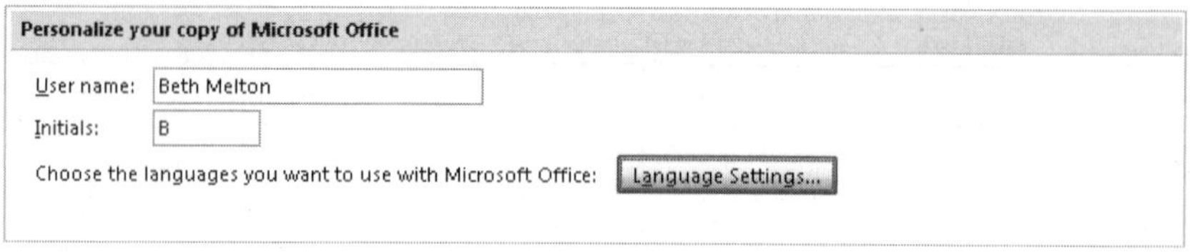

Figure 19-2 Word uses the User Name and Initials entered in Word Options to identify comments and tracked changes in documents.

3. Click OK to close Word Options.

Keep in mind that the information you enter in Word Options is used by all of the programs in the 2007 Microsoft Office system. Any changes you make to these settings affect future documents in other Microsoft Office programs as well. Fortunately, this is not as dire as it sounds. For example, if you're temporarily using someone else's machine to review a document, you can change the user name in Word Options before you work without affecting existing documents. Then, when you are finished working with the document on that machine, you can return to Word Options to restore the original user information.

Configuring Colors Associated with Reviewers

By default, Word automatically uses a different color for each reviewer's comments and tracked changes in a document. If you prefer all comments and tracked changes to be displayed in a single color, you can change the default setting by clicking the Review tab, clicking the arrow below Track Changes, and then clicking Change Tracking Options. The Track Changes Options dialog box opens, as shown in Figure 19-3.

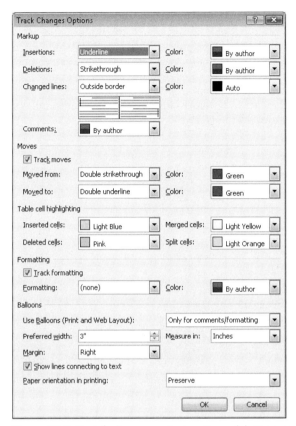

Figure 19-3 By default, comments, insertions, deletions, and formatting changes are displayed in a different color for each reviewer.

Using the Track Changes Options dialog box, you can specify a color for all comments, insertions, deletions, and formatting changes by selecting a color on the Color lists. By default, By Author is selected for Insertions, Deletions, and Comments, which means that Word automatically assigns a different color to each person who inserts comments or tracked changes. Keep in mind that this setting doesn't always color-code each person's changes with the same color every time. Instead, the By Author option simply guarantees that every person's marks appear in a distinct color—each person's color will most likely change each time Word is restarted and the document is reopened. For more information about configuring additional options shown in the Track Changes Options dialog box, see the section titled "Adjusting the Appearance of Tracked Changes" later in this chapter on page 537.

If you're viewing a document that's color-coded for a number of reviewers, you can quickly see which colors are currently assigned to which reviewers. To do so, click Show Markup on the Review tab and then point at Reviewers. You'll see a list of reviewer names accompanied by color-coded check boxes, as shown in Figure 19-4. (Of course, you can't see the color-coding in this book, but you can get an idea of how the color-coding system works.) In addition to seeing the reviewer color assignments, you can use the Reviewer options (found on the Review tab under Show Markup) to specify whose comments and tracked changes are displayed in the current document by selecting and clearing the check boxes next to reviewers' names. When you clear a check box while in Print Layout, Full Screen Reading, or Web Layout view, that reviewer's comment and tracked change balloons are hidden, and text inserted by the reviewer appears as regular body text. To redisplay a reviewer's comments and changes, reselect the reviewer's check box.

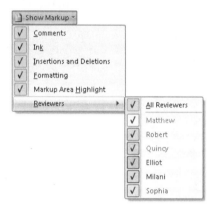

Figure 19-4 You can use the Reviewer option to quickly see the colors currently assigned to reviewers and to control whose comments and changes are displayed in the current document.

Viewing Comments and Revisions

Comments and revisions can be displayed in balloons and in the Reviewing Pane if you're working in Print Layout, Full Screen Reading, or Web Layout view. The Reviewing Pane can be opened in a horizontal or vertical position relative to the document's workspace. You can access the Reviewing Pane in Print Layout, Web Layout, Outline, and Draft views. If the Reviewing Pane is open and you switch to the Full Screen Reading view, the Reviewing Pane closes and balloons are then used to show comments along with revisions.

> **CAUTION**
>
> It's recommended that you use Outline view for viewing comments and revisions only. At the time of this writing, revisions made in Outline view are a bit buggy. For example, some modifications, such as moving content that contains revisions, cause all insertions to be accepted and deletions to be rejected within the content that is moved.

When balloons display information, they appear next to your document's contents in either the left or right margin and the commented content in the document is highlighted. Figure 19-5 presents a sample document in Print Layout view, with comment balloons in the right vertical position and the Reviewing Pane visible in the left vertical position.

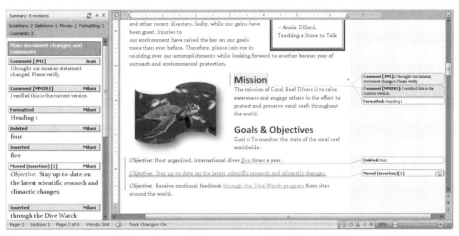

Figure 19-5 You can display color-coded comments and revisions in balloons or in the Reviewing Pane. In both views, each comment includes the initials of the person who created the comment and a numeric identifier.

In addition to balloons, Word 2007 implements a number of visual cues when displaying comments and revisions. For example, notice in Figure 19-5 that in both the balloons and the Reviewing Pane (in the shaded heading), the word *Comment* identifies the information as a comment. Deletions, formatting changes, and moves display in balloons and the Reviewing Pane, and insertions display in the document and Reviewing Pane. Balloons and headings in the Reviewing Pane can be color-coded to associate them with particular users, and each heading in the Reviewing Pane displays the user name of the person who inserted the comment or made the revision. In addition, comments include the reviewer's initials and are automatically numbered sequentially throughout the document. When viewing comments in balloons, the content associated with comments is highlighted in the document to help visually link commented areas to corresponding comments. The highlighting of each instance of commented content matches the corresponding comment's balloon color, which simplifies identifying who created which comments. The combination of user initials, comment numbering, and color-coded content highlight makes identifying and referring to comments much easier than in earlier versions of Word (prior to Microsoft Office Word 2002).

> **Note**
>
> The highlight used in the document for comments and revisions is not the same as the Text Highlight Color found on the Home tab in the Font group. When comments and revisions are removed, the highlight on the text is also removed. Many reviewers use the Highlight tool to annotate content in the document; however, text highlighted by using the Text Highlight Color command must be manually removed. For more information on using the Highlight tool, see Chapter 6, "Mastering Document Fundamentals."

Adding and Managing Comments Effectively

Comments enable those who collaborate on documents to ask questions, provide suggestions, insert notes, and generally annotate a document's contents without directly inserting any information into the body of the document. As previously noted, when you work with a document that contains comments, you can display the comments in the Reviewing Pane while viewing the document in all views (with the exception of Full Screen Reading view) or in margin balloons.

Inserting Standard Comments

After you configure your user name information and specify how to color comments, you are ready to insert comments into documents. Inserting a comment is a straightforward process. You can insert your comment at the insertion point, or you can select content that you want to associate with your comment. If you insert a comment at the insertion point, Word indicates the existence of your comment in the text by highlighting the nearest word, adding a comment reference (only visible in Print Layout View when showing revisions inline), and placing comment indicators around the word (see Figure 19-5 for an example). If you select content to be associated with a comment, Word marks the selected content in the same way by highlighting the content, adding a comment reference, and placing comment indicators around the selected content.

To insert a comment, on the Reviewing tab, click New Comment or press Ctrl+Alt+M.

When you work in Print Layout, Full Screen Reading, or Web Layout view, an empty balloon opens by default when you insert a comment. If you work in Outline or Draft view or in Print Layout View with balloons hidden, the Reviewing Pane opens.

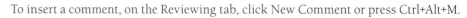

> **Note**
>
> After you enter a comment in a balloon, you can press Esc to return the insertion point to the main body text.

Comments can be edited just as you would edit standard text. If a comment is long and its contents aren't entirely displayed in a balloon, click the ellipsis in the balloon to open the Reviewing Pane. If the Reviewing Pane isn't visible, you can toggle it on by clicking Reviewing Pane on the Review tab.

> **Tip**
> To close the Reviewing Pane by using the keyboard, press Alt+Shift+C.

INSIDE OUT   Editing text in the Reviewing Pane

As in previous versions, you are still unable to select text and press Backspace to delete it in the Reviewing Pane. Therefore, to delete text while working in the Reviewing Pane, you need to either select the text and use the Delete key or position your cursor at the text you want to delete and then use the Backspace or Delete key to delete the information one letter at a time. Note that you can press Ctrl+Backspace or Ctrl+Delete to delete entire words at one time.

Inserting Voice and Handwritten Comments

If you are using a Tablet PC, you can include *voice comments* and *handwritten comments* with documents. Basically, voice comments are sound objects added inside comment balloons. Before you can add a voice comment, you need to add the Insert Voice button, found under Commands Not In The Ribbon, to the Quick Access Toolbar. See Appendix B, "Customizing Word and Enhancing Accessibility," to learn how to customize the Quick Access Toolbar. To create ink comments, simply click the New Comment button on the Review tab and write your comment in the comment bubble.

INSIDE OUT   Saving a document with comments as a Web page

You can save a document that contains comments and other marked-up text as a Web page. When you do this, Word retains the comments and tracked changes in the text, although all reviewers' comments and changes are displayed in the same color and without initials or names. To save a reviewed document as a Web page, click the Microsoft Office Button, point to Save As, and then click Other Formats. In the Save As dialog box, make sure that the Save As Type box displays Web Page and click Save.

Keep in mind that the online display of comments and tracked changes in your document depends on your browser. In Microsoft Internet Explorer 4 and later, comments appear as dynamic ScreenTips, as shown below in Internet Explorer 7.

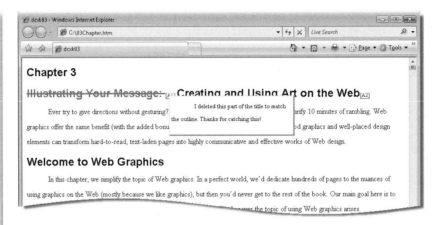

Also, revised text appears in a color other than black with underlining and strikethrough formatting (but remember, color-coding based on reviewers' user names and user identification elements are lost), similar to how you see markup changes in Word when a single color is selected to show markup. In browsers earlier than Internet Explorer 4 as well as in Netscape Navigator 4 and later, comments appear as footnotes beneath the main Web page instead of as dynamic ScreenTips.

Tracking Changes

Adding comments to documents is invaluable when reviewers need to annotate and query text, but you need another set of features when you want reviewers to conduct line-by-line edits to help smooth a document's text and layout. When your document is ready for detailed editing in a team setting, you want to turn to the Track Changes feature.

> **Note**
>
> If you've been using Word for a few versions now, you might still consider the Track Changes feature as the Revision feature, which was the name of this feature in Microsoft Office Word 95 and earlier, and many still refer to insertions and deletions in a document as *Revision Marks*.

When you turn on the Track Changes feature, Word records the deletions, insertions, and formatting changes made by each reviewer who modifies the document. By default, Word displays each reviewer's changes in a different color so that you can easily identify the sources of changes within your document. When you work with a document that has been modified by reviewers, you can use the Display For Review list on the Review tab to display the changed document in four views, as described here:

- **Final Showing Markup** The default display view. Displays the final document showing deletions, comments, formatting changes, and moved content. Insertions are displayed in the document, and deletions are displayed in balloons by default.

- **Final** Hides the tracked changes and shows how the document would appear if you accepted all the changes. Comments are also suppressed in this view.

- **Original Showing Markup** Displays the original document and shows deletions, comments, formatting changes, and moved content. Insertions are shown in balloons, and deleted content is displayed in the document.

- **Original** Hides the tracked changes and shows the original, unchanged document so that you can see how the document would look if you rejected all changes. Comments are also suppressed in this view.

Being able to display your document in these various ways can help as you add, accept, and reject tracked changes. Before we discuss the details of working with tracked changes, you should note that Word doesn't track some changes when you modify a document, including changes you make involving the following list:

- Background colors

- Embedded fonts

- Some types of mail merge information, such as whether a file is a main document or data file

- Some table modifications

You probably won't find that these limitations interfere with tasks involving tracked changes, but you should be aware of the exceptions just in case. In addition, you might sometimes see a message box warning that an action will not be marked as a change—such as modifying a table. In these cases, you have the option of clicking OK to proceed or Cancel to avoid making a change that won't be tracked.

Tracking Changes While You Edit

When you track changes in a document, you can opt to display or hide the tracking marks while you work. Generally, it's easier to hide tracked changes if you're editing and writing text, and it's better to view tracking marks when you're reviewing a document's changes. When Word tracks changes, it automatically records insertions or deletions in balloons (depending on your view, as described in the preceding section), which you can view in Print Layout, Full Screen Reading, or Web Layout view. Word marks tracked changes in a document as follows:

- **Added text** Appears in the reviewer's color with underlining.

- **Deleted text** Displayed in the reviewer's color in a balloon. If the inline option is chosen, deleted text shows in the content area with a strikethrough line indicating the deletion.

- **Moved text** New in Word 2007, text moved within a document is automatically marked in green, by default, with double-underlines below the moved text. In addition, the balloons for moved text include a Go button in the lower right corner that you can click to move from the original location to the new location and vice versa.

> **Note**
>
> Moved text is unavailable when using Compatibility Mode.

- **Text added and then deleted by the reviewer** Displayed as if the text had never been added. No marks appear in a document in places where a reviewer adds information and then deletes the added information. (Rest assured your typographical errors will not be tracked!)

In addition to these actions, Word automatically inserts a vertical line, called *a changed line,* along the left margin to indicate that a change has been made. This line appears wherever text or formatting changes are made while the Track Changes feature is turned on. Finally, the Reviewing Pane automatically generates a summary of changes including the number of insertions, deletions, moves, formatting changes, and comments as well as a grand total.

In Figure 19-5, the document is displayed in Final Showing Markup view, which shows inserted text in line; deleted, formatted, and moved text in balloons; and both parts associated with moved text in the Reviewing Pane. Notice the changed line in the left margin, which specifies that the text next to the line has been modified in some way. For more information about configuring changed lines, see the section titled "Customizing the Appearance of Changed Lines" later in this chapter on page 539.

Also notice in Figure 19-5 that the status bar displays *Track Changes: On.* To view this information in your status bar, right-click the status bar and click Track Changes on the Customize Status Bar menu. After you add Track Changes to your status bar, you can control whether the Track Changes feature is turned on or off simply by clicking Track Changes in the status bar.

Track
Changes ▾

You turn track changes on or off in a document by using one of the following methods:

- On the Reviewing tab, click the top half of the Track Changes button (if you click the bottom half, you display options for Track Changes).

- Press Ctrl+Shift+E.

- If you added Track Changes to your status bar, click Track Changes.

When Track Changes is turned on, Word tracks your changes regardless of whether your view reflects the tracked changes as marked-up text. You can always tell whether changes are being tracked by looking at the Track Changes button on the status bar because the button indicates On or Off depending on your current working mode.

> **Note**
>
> You can control who can make tracked changes to your document by using the Restrict Formatting And Editing task pane, as described in the section titled "Protecting a Document for Comments or Revisions" later in this chapter.

Adjusting the Appearance of Tracked Changes

You can change how Word identifies deleted, inserted, and reformatted information when the Track Changes feature is turned on. You use the Track Changes Options dialog box (shown earlier in this chapter in Figure 19-3) to configure formatting settings, as follows:

- **Format** The drop-down lists next to the specific type of revision enable you to show insertions, deletions, and reformatting without any special formatting (shown as normal text) or to display the insertions, deletions, and reformatting with additional formatting such as boldface, italic, underline, or strikethrough. By default, when not shown in balloons, inserted text appears with an underline, deleted text appears with a strikethrough, and reformatting does not display with additional formatting.

- **Color** Use the Color boxes next to the tracking options to specify whether you want Word to assign author colors automatically. The By Author default setting is frequently used to show markup, comments, and formatting revisions in team projects because this enables reviewers to visually determine who made the revision simply by viewing the color.

> **Note**
>
> The settings you configure for displaying tracked changes are global and apply to all documents you open in Word that have Track Changes marks in them.

> **Note**
>
> You cannot create custom colors for any of the settings in the Track Changes Options dialog box.

In addition to formatting inserted and reformatted information, you can also track moved text and some table revisions in Word 2007, as described in the following section.

Tracking Moved Text and Inline Shapes

New to Word 2007, you can track moved text and inline shapes. When you cut and paste or drag and drop a complete sentence, paragraph, group of paragraphs, or inline shape, Word marks the revision as *moved* content instead of *deleted* and *inserted* content and indicates whether the data was moved up or moved down. By showing text as moved, reviewers can see that information has been relocated as opposed to appearing as newly added data. In previous versions, determining whether moved content, which was marked as an insertion, contained additional modifications was next to impossible.

> **Note**
>
> If moved content is not a complete sentence, paragraph, or group of paragraphs and if it is moved inside of another sentence, it may be displayed as a deletion and insertion rather than moved content because the revision could result in erroneous content.

By default, Word formats moved text indicators in green with a double strikethrough in the moved content and a double underline below the content in its new location. To control the Track Moves settings, open the Track Changes Options dialog box (as described in the preceding section), check the Track Moves check box to toggle the feature on or off, and then select settings in the Moved From, Moved To, and Color lists if desired.

> **Note**
>
> Moves options are not available when using Compatibility Mode.

Showing Revisions in Tables

In Word 2007, you can now track many changes made to tables. When you make revisions to tables in earlier versions of Word, you often receive a dialog box warning that your changes will not be marked. You can still see this message box on occasion in Word 2007—such as when you delete a column in a table—but many table changes can now be tracked and highlighted. When using track changes on a document, only table row insertions and deletions are tracked, as in previous versions of Word. Inserted columns may be categorized as a Formatted Table change. The added table revision functionality is only available when you use the Combine or Compare feature to review revisions made to a document.

When using Compare or Combine, Word 2007 can highlight table cells that are inserted, deleted, merged, or split during the revision process. By default, Word highlights each type of change by using a different color. You can choose custom colors if you prefer, including using the By Author option. To access the table revision settings, display the Track Changes Options dialog box and then configure the color options in the Table Cell Highlighting area. For more information on using Compare or Combine, see "Comparing or Combining Documents" later in this chapter.

Customizing the Appearance of Changed Lines

Regardless of your selections for formatting inserted, deleted, moved, and reformatted information, you can still use changed lines to indicate in a general way where changes have occurred in a document. As shown in Figure 19-5, Word automatically inserts a black vertical line, called a *changed line*, in the margin next to text that contains tracked changes. You can specify where changed lines are displayed on the page (along the right, left, or outside borders) and the color in which they are displayed. By default, changed lines are set to Auto, which is typically black. To configure how changed lines are displayed, open the Track Changes Options dialog box and modify the Changed Lines options in the Markup section.

After you configure the changed lines settings, all documents you open that contain tracked changes will use the newly configured settings. In addition, any currently opened documents that contain tracked changes will be reformatted automatically to reflect the new settings.

> **Note**
>
> In Draft view, all changed lines appear on the left regardless of the setting you configure in the Markup section in the Track Changes Options dialog box. The changed lines color setting applies in all views.

Configuring Balloon and Reviewing Pane Options

When you work with comment and track change balloons, you can control a variety of balloon options. Specifically, you can format balloon and Reviewing Pane label text (which is the text displayed on Reviewing Pane bars above each comment or tracked change), specify when balloons are to be displayed, adjust balloon width and placement, and specify whether lines should connect balloons to text.

Balloon and Reviewing Pane Styles

You can modify the font styles of balloon and Reviewing Pane text and labels in the same manner you modify other styles in Word documents—by using the Styles task pane. To modify the Balloon Text style that controls the balloon labels (such as Comment, Inserted, Deleted, and Formatted) and to change the Comment Text style (the text typed by reviewers), follow these steps:

1. On the Home tab, click the Styles dialog launcher (or press Ctrl+Alt+Shift+S) to open the Styles task pane.

2. In the Styles pane, click the Manage Styles button.

3. On the Edit tab in the Sort Order list, select Alphabetical, select Balloon Text, and then click Modify.

4. In the Modify Style dialog box, select any options you want.

   Choose whether you want to make the changes to the current document only or add the formatting to the document's template (either Normal.dotm or another attached template), and then click OK.

5. In the Manage Styles dialog box, select Comment Text and click Modify.

6. In the Modify Style dialog box, select any options you want.

   Choose whether you want to make the changes to the current document only or add the formatting to the document's template, and then click OK twice to close both dialog boxes.

You can also modify comment text by selecting the text or label in an existing comment in the Reviewing Pane or balloon, applying format settings, and then updating the style to match the selected text. For more information about working with styles, see Chapter 15, "Using Styles to Increase Your Formatting Power."

When you modify the Comment Text style, you change the appearance of the text only (not the labels) in the comment balloons and comment entries in the Reviewing Pane. You do not modify the inserted or deleted text displayed in tracked-change balloons or labels for Reviewing Pane entries.

Showing and Hiding Balloons

If you prefer to work with the Reviewing Pane and not with balloons, you can turn off balloons. If you prefer, you can use balloons only to show comments and formatting changes. To control balloon display in Print Layout, Full Screen Reading, and Web Layout views, on the Review tab, click Balloons, or you can configure the Use Balloons option in the Change Tracking Options dialog box. The following describes the options found under Balloons on the Review tab.

- **Show Revisions In Balloons** Shows all changes in balloons (equivalent of Always in the Track Changes Options dialog box).

- **Show All Revisions Inline** Turns off balloons (equivalent of Never in the Track Changes Options dialog box).

- **Show Only Comments And Formatting In Balloons** Shows comments and formatting changes in balloons and shows inserted and deleted text inline (equivalent of Only For Comments/Formatting in the Track Changes Options dialog box).

Regardless of whether you hide or show balloons, comments are displayed as Screen-Tips when you position your mouse pointer over a comment indicator.

> **Note**
>
> You can specify whether the lines used to connect balloons to text are displayed or hidden by selecting or clearing the Show Lines Connecting To Text check box on the Track Changes Options dialog box. When you clear this check box, balloons are displayed in the margin without a connector line when they aren't selected. When you select a comment, the comment is displayed with a solid line that connects the balloon to the comment indicator in the text.

Adjusting Balloon Size and Location for Online Viewing

If you are new to balloons, you might find that they take some getting used to even if you've used comments and tracking tools in the Reviewing Pane. To help you customize balloons to suit your working style, Microsoft provides a few options that you can use to control the width and position of balloons when you choose to view them. In fact, you can control balloon width and location for online viewing as well as for printing purposes. This section addresses configuring the online presentation of balloons. For more information about configuring balloons for printing, see the section titled "Printing Comments and Tracked Changes" later in this chapter on page 543.

To set the balloon width and specify whether balloons are displayed in the right or left margin, you must configure the Track Changes Options dialog box, as follows.

1. On the Review tab, click the Track Changes arrow and then click Change Tracking Options.

2. In the Track Changes Options dialog box, make sure that the Use Balloons (Print And Web Layout) list box is set to Always or Only For Comments/Formatting.

3. Click the Measure In arrow and select whether you want to measure balloons by using your preferred unit of measure (such as inches or centimeters) or percentage of the page.

> **For more information about the Measure In options, see the Inside Out tip titled "Sizing Balloons—Measurement vs. Percentage" in the following sidebar.**

4. In the Preferred Width box, enter a percentage or measurement (such as inches or centimeters) for the width of the balloons.

5. In the Margin box, click the Left or Right option to specify on which side of the document text you want balloons to appear.

6. Click OK to apply the balloon settings.

Unfortunately, you can't preview how your balloon settings are displayed from within the Track Changes Options dialog box. Your best plan when configuring balloons is to try a few settings and see which setting works best for you on your monitor.

INSIDE OUT   Sizing balloons—Measurement vs. Percentage

When you size balloons, Word configures them without compromising the document's content area. This is accomplished by expanding the view of your document and not by reducing the document's content area. To clarify, let's look at the two Measurement In options.

Note

The unit of measure shown in the Measure In list is dependent on your preferred measurement setting controlled by the Show Measurement In Units Of option found in Word Options in the Advanced section.

When you use the unit of measure, you provide a set size in which your balloons appear in your document's margin. For example, if you specify 2 inches or 5.08 centimeters, your page's view expands so that balloons are displayed within an area that's 2 inches (or 5.08 centimeters) wide, starting from the document's margin.

Similarly, if you size balloons using the Percent option, the balloons are displayed as a percentage of the page's size without compromising the document's content area. For example, if you specify balloons to be 100 percent, the balloons are sized equal to 100 percent of the page, and the width of your view is expanded accordingly (doubled, in this case).

You can easily see how balloons are displayed relative to the current document by modifying the balloon size and then viewing your document in Print Preview mode.

Printing Comments and Tracked Changes

As previously mentioned, you can control how comments are displayed on the screen as well as in print. The section titled "Configuring Balloon and Reviewing Pane Options" earlier in this chapter on page 539 addresses how to control the display of comments in balloons and in the Reviewing Pane. This section discusses the ways in which you can print tracked changes and comments. When you print a document containing comments and tracked changes, you can configure print settings in two areas: the Track Changes Options dialog box and the Print dialog box. Let's look first at the Track Changes Options dialog box.

In the Balloons area of the Track Changes Options dialog box (accessed by clicking the arrow below Track Changes on the Review tab), you can specify how Word should adjust paper orientation to accommodate balloons. You can select any of the following settings on the Paper Orientation list:

- **Auto** Specifies that Word can determine the best orientation for your document automatically based on your margin settings and balloon width settings.

- **Preserve** Prints the document with the orientation specified in the Page Setup dialog box. This is the default setting.

- **Force Landscape** Prints balloons and the document in landscape format to allow the most room for the display of balloons.

After you choose how you want Word to handle page orientation issues when you print documents with comment balloons, you're ready to configure the Print dialog box.

In the Print dialog box (click the Microsoft Office Button, then click Print), you can specify whether to print the document showing markup (the default setting when comments and tracked changes are displayed) or you can opt to print simply a list of the markup changes made in a document. If you want to print a document's changes, you typically want to print the document showing changes instead of printing only a list of changes. Depending on the length of the document and number of revisions, when you print a list of changes, the list can become long and confusing.

To efficiently print tracked changes and comments in a document, follow these steps:

1. Display your document in Print Layout view.

2. Display the tracked changes in the manner you want them to be printed by using the Show Markup list on the Review tab.

   In addition, you can select specific reviewer's tracked changes and comments by clicking Reviewers (under Show Markup) and specifying which reviewers' revisions and comments should be displayed and subsequently printed.

> **Tip**
>
> The easiest way to print a document with only its comments is to print the document with comment balloons in the margin and hide the other types of margin balloons (including balloons that show insertions, deletions, and formatting changes).

3. Click the Microsoft Office Button and then click Print, or press Ctrl+P to open the Print dialog box.

4. In the Print dialog box, make sure that the Print What box shows Document Showing Markup, and then click OK.

The document is printed with balloons in the margin and Word reduces the view of the page to accommodate them. This doesn't affect your document's layout parameters—it's just a temporary modification for printing purposes when you're printing balloons along with a document.

> **Note**
>
> When you print a document with markup, the Markup Area Highlight shading (the light gray shading behind balloons onscreen) is not printed.

Reviewing Comments and Tracked Changes

Assume that your document has made its rounds, and now it's up to you to review the tracked changes and comments in the document. You can review all tracked changes and comments at the same time, or you can suppress the view of comments or tracked changes and review them individually. Regardless of which method you choose, the process is the same and can be accomplished by using these steps:

1. On the Review tab, make sure that either Final Showing Markup or Original Showing Markup is selected on the Display For Review list.

2. Click Show Markup on the Review tab and make sure all options are turned on, such as Comments, Ink, Insertions And Deletions, and Formatting, to view all changes and comments.

   Or you can turn on only those options that you want to review.

> **Note**
>
> The Markup Area Highlight option in Show Markup controls whether the Markup Area (where the balloons display) appears shaded. By default, Markup Area Highlight is selected and the Markup Area appears light gray.

At this point, you can review the tracked changes and comments manually by scrolling through your document or the Reviewing Pane. If you prefer to use the navigation commands on the Review tab to navigate between comments only, use the Previous and Next commands in the Comments group. To navigate between both comments and tracked changes, use the Previous and Next commands in the Changes group.

> **Note**
>
> You can navigate between comments only by using the Select Browse Object feature (press Ctrl+Alt+Home), which enables you to navigate between comments using Ctrl+Page Up (Previous) and Ctrl+Page Down (Next) in any view.
>
> You can also use the Go To tab in the Find And Replace dialog box (press Ctrl+G). On the Go To tab, you can select Comment on the Go To What list. Then choose to view all reviewers' comments or a selected reviewer's comments by selecting Any Reviewer or a specific name in the Enter Reviewer's Name list. For more information about using the Browse Object feature and the Go To tab, see Chapter 6.

Depending on the current view, the behavior of either set of Next and Previous commands may vary. The views and variations in behavior are described as follows:

- **Draft view** Revisions are shown inline; comments can be displayed in the Reviewing Pane, or you can view the comment by positioning your cursor over the comment marker and reading the ScreenTip text. When you click either set of Previous or Next commands, the Reviewing Pane opens when a comment is encountered (if it isn't open already).

- **Full Screen Reading view without balloons** Revisions are shown inline; comment indicators are shown, but the Reviewing Pane doesn't open. You can view the comment by positioning your cursor over the comment marker and reading the ScreenTip text. (Previous and Next commands are not available in this view.)

- **Outline view** Revisions are shown inline; comments can be viewed as ScreenTip text or in the Reviewing Pane. When you click either set of Previous or Next commands, the Reviewing Pane opens when a comment is encountered (if it isn't open already), and the view changes to Draft view automatically.

- **Print Layout, Full Screen Reading, or Web Layout view with balloons** The active balloon is indicated by a dark outline, darker shading, and solid connector line. As previously noted, Previous and Next commands are not available in Full Screen Reading Layout. You can press the Alt+Up arrow or Alt+Down arrow to move up or down among balloons on a single page. (The Alt+Up and Alt+Down keyboard commands also work in Print Layout and Web Layout views.)

- **Print Layout or Web Layout view without balloons** Revisions are shown inline; comments can be viewed in the Reviewing Pane. When you click either set of Previous or Next commands, the Reviewing Pane opens when a comment is encountered (if it isn't open already).

When you view balloons, you might notice that some have an ellipsis in the lower right corner. This symbol indicates that the entire text doesn't fit in the balloon. To view the remainder of the text, click the ellipsis to open the Reviewing Pane, which displays the entire revision or comment.

Responding to Comments

Naturally, as you read through comments, you might want to respond to them. You can do so in the following ways:

- Type directly in a comment, in which case your response won't be color-coded according to your user name. In this scenario, you may want to include your name or initials so others know who is making the additional comment.

- Click in the comment you want to respond to and then click New Comment on the Reviewing toolbar, or press Ctrl+Alt+M. A new balloon opens directly below the balloon you're responding to, or a blank entry opens in the Reviewing Pane with the format Comment[initials#R#] in the header. The first number is the number of the comment, and the R# indicates that the comment is a response to the comment number indicated. To add your response, simply add your comment.

> **Note**
>
> To quickly see when a comment was inserted and who created it, you can hover the mouse pointer over the comment balloon. When you do this, a ScreenTip appears that displays the comment's creation date and time as well as the user name of the person who created the comment. If you're working in the Reviewing Pane, each Reviewing Pane bar displays the user name and insertion date and time automatically.

Deleting Comments

Generally, comments serve a temporary purpose—reviewers insert comments, someone addresses the comments, and then the comments are removed before the document's final publication (either online or in print). If you work with comments, you need to know how to delete them so that you won't unintentionally include them in your final publication. As you might expect, you can delete comments in several ways. Namely, you can delete a single comment, delete comments from a specific reviewer (or reviewers), or delete all comments by using the following techniques:

- **Delete a single comment.** Right-click a comment balloon and then click Delete Comment on the shortcut menu. Or select a comment balloon, and in the Comments group on the Review tab, click Delete.

- **Delete comments from a specific reviewer.** First clear the check boxes for all reviewers by clicking Show Markup on the Review tab and clicking Reviewers, All Reviewers. Next display only the comments you want to delete by clicking Show Markup, clicking Reviewers, and then selecting the check box next to the reviewer's name whose comments you want to delete. (You can repeat this process to select additional reviewers as well.) To delete the displayed comments, in the Comments group on the Review tab, click the arrow below Delete and then click Delete All Comments Shown.

- **Delete all comments in the document.** Make sure that all reviewers' comments are displayed. (This is the default setting, but if all reviewers' comments aren't displayed, click Show Markup on the Review tab and click Reviewers, All Reviewers.) In the Comments group on the Review tab, click the arrow below Delete and then click Delete All Comments In Document.

CAUTION

Keep in mind that when you delete all comments at once by clicking the Delete All Comments In Document option, you delete all comments in the document regardless of whether they are visible on the screen.

You can also delete comments one at a time from within the Reviewing Pane. To do so, right-click a comment in the Reviewing Pane and click Delete Comment on the shortcut menu, or click in a comment and click Delete on the Review tab.

Accepting and Rejecting Proposed Edits

After a document has gone through the review cycle and you receive a file containing a number of tracked changes, you can keep or discard the edits by accepting or rejecting the changes. You can address each edit on a case-by-case basis (generally, this is the recommended practice), or you can accept multiple changes at once. In either case, you can reject and accept proposed changes by using the appropriate buttons on the Review tab or by right-clicking changes or balloons and clicking options on the shortcut menu.

Figure 19-6 shows the shortcut menu that you see when you right-click moved text. Notice the new Follow Move option, which enables you to jump to the origin or destination of moved text in relation to the text you right-click. (If you right-click deleted text, you receive the same menu without the Follow Move option; if you right-click inserted text, the Accept Deletion and Reject Deletion options change to Accept Insertion and Reject Insertion.) The next few sections describe ways you can accept and reject changes.

✂	Cu_t
📋	_Copy
📋	P_aste
⟋	Acce_pt Change
⟍	_Reject Change
	_Follow Move
📝	_Track Changes
🔗	_Hyperlink...

Figure 19-6 You can right-click tracked changes to access options enabling you to resolve proposed changes, including the option to jump to the origin or destination of moved text.

> **Note**
>
> Before you start accepting and rejecting tracked changes and deleting comments, consider saving a version of the document with all of the tracked changes and comments intact. In that way, you'll have a copy on hand if you want to return to the marked-up version of the document.

Addressing Tracked Changes One at a Time

The key to accessing the changes you want to review is to configure your view properly before you start navigating among changes and making editorial decisions. When you're ready to resolve tracked changes, you should configure the following settings:

- **Show document markup** Show your document in either Final Showing Markup or Original Showing Markup in the Display For Review list in the Tracking group on the Review tab.

- **Specify the type(s) of changes to display** Use the Show Markup options on the Review tab to specify which types of changes you want to review. If you want to view revisions only, then make sure Comments is not selected.

- **Display selected user revisions and comments** Click Show Markup on the Review tab, click Reviewers to open the list of reviewers, and then choose which reviewers' markup changes you want to resolve. You can resolve all changes at one time (by selecting the All Reviewers option), or you can select any combination of listed reviewers.

Note

Unfortunately, the list of Reviewers closes automatically after each change you make to the list. Therefore, if you want to view the revisions and comments of only a few reviewers from a long list, first clear the All Reviewers check box (instead of clearing each name's check box one at a time). Then, click the names of those who made the changes you want to review. The goal is to configure the list with as few clicks as possible to avoid having to reopen the list repeatedly.

INSIDE OUT   Optimizing a document's readability when some reviewer marks are hidden

When you turn off the display of a reviewer's tracked changes, the text deleted by the reviewer appears restored and text inserted by the reviewer appears as regular text. As you can imagine, this can result in some strange mixtures of restored and added text. If some text looks particularly confusing, display all reviewers' marks or change the display of revisions to Final before you enter additional (and possibly unnecessary) revisions.

- **Specify how balloons should display** Click Balloons on the Review tab and then click to show revisions in balloons, all revisions inline, or only comments and formatting in balloons.

- **Show or hide the Reviewing Pane** Decide whether you want the Reviewing Pane to be open while you work as well as whether it should appear along the bottom or left side of your window.

After you display the changes you want to work with, you can move from tracked change to tracked change by using the Previous and Next buttons on the Review tab in the Changes group (if Comments are displayed, the Previous and Next commands in the Changes group will navigate between both tracked changes and Comments). You can also view and click edits in the Reviewing Pane, or you can scroll through the document and address edits in a less linear manner. Regardless of how you arrive at a tracked change, you can handle it in any of the following ways:

- Right-click a change (in the document body, in the Reviewing Pane, or in a balloon) and choose to accept or reject the change by using the shortcut menu.

- Click in a change and then click the Accept or Reject button on the Review tab to accept or reject the change and move to the next revision. Or, click the Accept or Reject arrow and click Accept Change or Reject change to accept or reject the change without moving to the next revision.

After you accept or reject a change, Word displays the revised text as standard text. If you change your mind about a change, you can undo your action by clicking Undo on the Quick Access Toolbar or pressing Ctrl+Z.

Accepting or Rejecting All Tracked Changes at Once

At times, you might want to accept or reject all changes in a document. For example, maybe you've gone through the document carefully, reading and changing the document in Final view. When you're satisfied with the document, you want to simply accept all changes instead of resolving each change individually. You can do so by executing a single command.

To accept or reject all changes in a document, use the Accept All Changes In Document or Reject All Changes In Document commands. To access these commands, click the arrow below Accept or Reject on the Review tab and click the appropriate command, as shown in Figure 19-7.

Figure 19-7 You can accept or reject all changes or only those changes by a particular reviewer by using the Accept and Reject options, which are accessible from the Review tab.

In addition to accepting or rejecting all changes in a document, you can show a subset of reviewers' changes and accept or reject only those changes. To control which changes are displayed in your document, click Show Markup on the Review tab, click Reviewers, and then select which reviewers' changes you want to display and resolve. After you configure your display, click the Accept or Reject arrow, and then click the Accept All Changes Shown or Reject All Changes Shown option.

> Tip
>
> Between resolving tracked changes individually and globally accepting or rejecting all changes in a document lays the realm of accepting and rejecting edits contained in selected text. In other words, you can resolve editing issues on a piecemeal basis. For example, you might want to select a paragraph or two that you've reviewed. To do so, select text, and then click Accept or Reject on the Review tab to accept or reject the tracked changes contained in the selected text.

INSIDE OUT   Comments, revisions, and the Document Inspector

You can remove all comments and revisions by using the Document Inspector. To do so, click the Microsoft Office Button, point at Prepare, and then click Inspect Document. Ensure that the Comments, Revisions, Versions, And Annotations check box is selected, and then click Inspect. If the Document Inspector finds any leftover comments or revisions, you can click Remove All to accept all revision marks and delete all comments.

Keep in mind that when you use the Remove All option in the Document Inspector to delete all revisions and comments, you cannot use the Undo command to retrieve the revisions and comments. If you suddenly realize you do not want to remove the revisions and comments after you click Remove All, your only recourse is to close the document without saving changes. Therefore, always save your documents before you run the Document Inspector!

> **Note**
>
> If you forget to save your document before running the Document Inspector, you will be prompted accordingly.

For more information about using the Document Inspector, see Chapter 18, "Sharing Documents and Collaborating Online."

Protecting a Document for Comments or Revisions

You can protect a document for comments only or tracked changes during the review phases of a project. To do this, on the Reviewing tab, click Protect Document to display the Restrict Formatting And Editing task pane, shown in Figure 19-8. By using the Editing Restrictions feature, you can ensure that the only modifications reviewers can make to your document are to add comments or that any revisions made will be tracked.

> **Note**
>
> If using Microsoft Office Ultimate 2007, Microsoft Office Professional Plus 2007, or Microsoft Office Enterprise 2007—which are those that support Information Rights Management (IRM)—click Protect Document and then click Restrict Access to access the Restrict Formatting And Editing task pane.

Figure 19-8 The Restrict Formatting And Editing task pane enables you to limit reviewers' actions to only certain types of changes, such as inserting comments.

To arrange this setup, follow these steps:

1. In the Restrict Formatting And Editing task pane, click the Allow Only This Type Of Editing In The Document check box, and then select Tracked Changes or Comments from the list below the option.

2. Specify any groups or users (click More Users) who are exceptions to the editing restriction.

INSIDE OUT   The Scoop on Exceptions

If you protect a document for Comments or Read-only, you can add exceptions to specific parts of the document and allow users to freely edit the content. Exceptions can work in conjunction with IRM, which is discussed in Chapter 20.

Exceptions can be set using one of the following methods:

- **Everyone** Allows anyone to make modifications without restriction in the areas marked by the exception.

- **Users** Allows only select users to make modifications without restriction in the areas marked by the exception. Users can be added using one of these three methods:

- **Domain** Authenticates the user by their domain credentials by using the *DOMAIN\UserName* format that is retrieved by the operating system. Works with IRM and password-protected files.

- **Local machine** Authenticates the user by the *UserName* used to log on to the computer. Works with IRM or password-protected files.

- **E-mail Address** Authenticates the user by their e-mail address; however, this works in conjunction with IRM only and does not work with password-protected files.

- **Groups** If you add exceptions for two or more users in the same area of the document, then a group is created automatically for ease in reuse.

  - If using IRM, you can use standard levels of permission, such as all users with Full Control or all users with Edit rights.

Click Yes, Start Enforcing Protection. The Start Enforcing Protection dialog box opens.

3. If desired, type a password in the password boxes and click OK. If you specify a password, the password must be entered to stop the document protection.

    If you choose not to assign a password in step 4, reviewers can then click the Stop Protection button in the Restrict Formatting And Editing task pane and be able to unlock the document and edit your document freely. In other words, this document protection plan is actually more of a deterrent than a fail-safe protection, but many times a deterrent is all you really need.

    For more information about protecting documents and allowing particular groups or individuals to edit parts of a document, see the Inside Out tip titled "The Scoop on Exceptions" earlier in this section as well as Chapter 20.

TROUBLESHOOTING

I forgot the document protection password

Because the Protect Document options are intended to be used in a collaborative environment and not used as a means for document security, if you forget the password for a protected document, you can gain access to the document content by circumventing the password protection. To do so, create a new document. On the Insert tab in the select Text group, click the Object arrow and select Text From File. Navigate to the location of the protected document, select the document, and click Insert to insert the file contents and bypass the password.

Fortunately, when you use this method on a document that contains tracked changes and comments, the newly created document retains all the reviewers' marks and color-coded settings.

Comparing or Combining Documents

At times, you might want to expedite a reviewing process by sending separate copies of an original document to reviewers. Then, when reviewers return the documents, you can combine the changes into one document. At other times, you might want to compare two versions of a document and simply look at the differences between the two documents or take advantage of the new revision features for tables.

> **Tip**
>
> Assume that you have a document that contains tracked changes. If you want to see changes made to tables using the new Table revision functionality but no longer have the original document, create a copy of the document and reject all changes. This produces an original copy of the document that you can use with either the Compare or Combine features.

Although Compare and Combine appear to provide the same functionality, there is a distinct difference between them: *Compare* is used when comparing the differences between two documents, and *Combine* is used when comparing two or more documents as well as identifying who changed what in the document.

Compare and Combine were available in previous versions of Word under a single command, Compare and Merge Documents. Legal Blackline (Compare) was an option in the Merge Changes dialog box. In Word 2007, the Compare and Combine commands are distinct and contain more flexibility. You can specify the types of changes you want to compare, such as formatting and white space, along with displaying changes at the word or character level. The Combine and Compare features can be found on the Reviewing tab in the Compare group.

> **Note**
>
> A character-level change occurs when a change is made to a few characters of a word, such as when only the case of the first letter is changed. At the word level, the entire word is shown as a revision; at the character level, only the letter is shown as a revision.

The following section of the chapter describes comparing and combining documents after changes have been made to a document.

Comparing Two Versions of a Document (Legal Blackline)

Ideally, when you use Compare, the original and the revised document don't contain tracked changes. If either document contains tracked changes, Word treats the documents as though the changes have been accepted and doesn't display them in the comparison document. Additionally, all revisions in the comparison document are attributed to a single author, and you can see what changes have been made to the original document regardless of whether track changes were turned on when modifications were being made. The changes made in the revised document are shown in the original as tracked changes. To compare two versions of one document and view the differences, follow these steps:

1. On the Review tab, click Compare, and then from the list, click Compare. The Compare Documents dialog box opens.

2. In the Original Document area, click the Folder icon to navigate to and select the original document, or select the document from the drop-down list.

3. In the Revised Document area, click the Folder icon to navigate to and select the revised document, or select the document from the drop-down list.

4. Click More to show the Compare Documents options. Verify that New Document is selected in the Show Changes In area (you can also choose to show changes in the original or revised document), as shown in Figure 19-9.

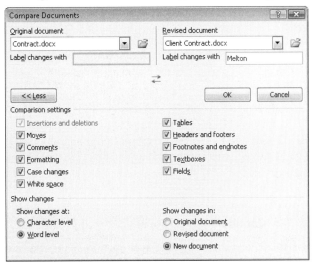

Figure 19-9 The Compare Documents dialog box enables you to choose two documents to compare—an original and a revised version.

5. Click OK. The original and revised documents remain unaltered and a new Compared Document is created and shown automatically.

Chapter 19

> **Note**
>
> If either (or both) of the documents being compared has tracked changes, you'll see a message box stating that Word will compare the documents as if the tracked changes have been accepted. Click Yes to continue the comparing procedure.

6. To view all three versions of the document at once, click Show Source Documents on the Review tab, and then click Show Both. In this view, the original, revised, and compared documents are displayed in the new Tri-Pane Review Panel, as shown in Figure 19-10.

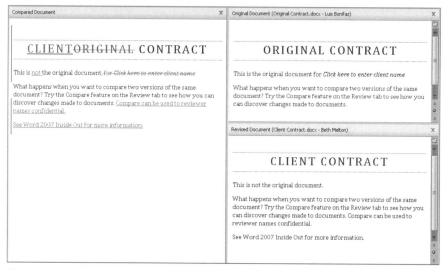

Figure 19-10 The new Tri-Pane Review Panel displays the original, revised, and comparison results on the screen at the same time.

The new Compared Document displays the changed text in an unnamed document file. You need to save and name the file if you want to store it for future use.

INSIDE OUT   Confidential Revisions

The Compare function can also be used as a tool to keep reviewer names, dates, and times of revisions confidential. If you no longer have an original copy of a document containing tracked changes, simply create a copy of the document, reject all changes, and use it as the original. Display the Compare dialog box and select the original and the revised documents. In the Revised area in the Label Changes With text box, type another name, such as Reviewer. This method does not allow you to change the dates and times of revisions, but all revision dates and times reflect the system date and time that the Compare function was used. Note that this doesn't apply to Comments that may be contained in the documents.

Combining Revisions from Multiple Authors

In contrast, you use Combine to combine, or merge, two or more documents. All modifications made to the original or revised documents become tracked changes. Unlike the Compare feature, if the revised document contains tracked changes, these changes appear as tracked changes in the combined document. All authors are identified and their revisions are combined into one document. To use the Combine function, use the following steps:

1. On the Review tab, click Compare, and then click Combine. The Combine Documents dialog box opens, which looks similar to the Compare Documents dialog box shown in Figure 19-9.

2. In the Original Document area, click the Folder icon to navigate to and select the original document, or select the document from the drop-down list.

3. In the Revised Document area, click the Folder icon to navigate to and select the revised document (or select the document from the drop-down list) and then click OK. Figure 19-11 depicts a sample combination in which Original Contract.docx is combined with Modified Contract.docx, which results in the Combined Document.

Figure 19-11 The Original Contract.docx is combined with Modified Contract.docx, which creates a third document, Combined Document, containing the merged changes.

> **Note**
>
> If you do not see the Tri-Pane Review panel, on the Review tab, click Show Source Documents and then click Show Both.

To combine additional documents, combine the resulting Combined Document with another document containing changes.

Note

At times, you might want to compare two documents side-by-side without merging them. In those cases, you should adjust your view without using the Compare or Combine features. To learn how to use the View Side By Side feature, see Chapter 6.

TROUBLESHOOTING

What happened to the File Versions feature?

In previous versions of Word, you could save versions of your document and store the information within the document file. Word 2007 does not offer the capability to save versions of your local documents. You can, however, view the version history of documents stored in a Document Library. To do so, open a file stored in a Document Library and then click the Microsoft Office Button, Server, View Version History, as shown in the following graphic.

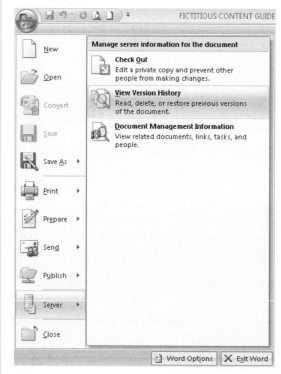

For more information about saving and viewing versions of documents stored in the Document Library, see Chapter 18.

What's Next?

This chapter provided in-depth information on how you can use Word to add comments, track changes, and combine or compare multiple versions of a document. It also included information on how to protect documents so only comments can be added or if revisions are made they will be marked as tracked changes. If the protection aspect of Word intrigues you then the next chapter covers protecting documents, such as successfully protecting document content from being printed or copied, saving documents using the PDF and XPS add-in, along with information on how to protect yourself from macro viruses and malicious code.

Addressing Document Protection and Security Issues

The world has changed since Microsoft Office 2003 was released several years ago. Today working with teammates across the country or around the globe is common. People check e-mail from sidewalk cafes and airports; they review and share documents from multiple places at multiple points in their day.

With this kind of mobile, flexible workforce—with data flying every which way, all around, all the time—how can you make sure your documents are secure? If you are working on materials announcing a new product release, how can you be sure that the new spec sheet you need the designer to review isn't being read by someone who intercepted the file? How do you protect your files so that only the right person sees them, and only the people you grant permission to can make changes to the format or content of the document?

This chapter is all about the ways in which Microsoft Office Word 2007 can help you secure your files. Document security in Office Word 2007 comes in a number of forms. Most people know the importance of employing security measures at the network level, but you can also provide data integrity by securing your information at the document level. For example, you can perform the following document security tasks in Word.

- Control who can open, modify, distribute, and print your documents

- Specify the types of changes others can make to your documents

- Remove personal and hidden information

- Save the document in a nonmodifiable fixed format so others can view and print, but not change, the file

- Identify yourself as the author of a document (by using digital signatures)

- Protect yourself and others from macro viruses

It's likely that you'll use a number of these features together to provide the best measure of protection for your Word documents. The next section gives you a quick overview of the security features in Word.

Protection Features in Word

Word is designed to meet the reality that our workplace has changed—the global, mobile, and wireless workforce now has security concerns that standalone, desktop PC users did not have. Many of today's users need to be able to access documents in a variety of versions and share them with people all over the world, at a moment's notice. Securing sensitive documents has become more important than ever.

When you click the Microsoft Office Button and point to Prepare you'll find the following features to give you what you need to safeguard your documents:.

- **Inspect Document** When you click Inspect Document, the Document Inspector launches, enabling you to have Word review your document and point out any sensitive or personal information you might not want to share.

- **Encrypt Document** Clicking Encrypt Document lets you encrypt (which includes setting a password) your document before sending it to others.

- **Restrict Permission** Restrict Permission enables you to limit the functionality of a document while still allowing others to view it, and, if they have the necessary permissions, work with it. For example, you might want to set options that block the print or copy commands so that others cannot print copies of your document or copy and paste sections into other files.

> **Note**
>
> The Restrict Permission feature is available only in 2007 Microsoft Office Ultimate, available through retail outlets, or 2007 Microsoft Office Professional Plus and 2007 Microsoft Office Enterprise, both available through volume licensing.

- **Add A Digital Signature** Add a Digital Signature enables you to authenticate your document for others by adding a digital signature directly in the document file.

- **Mark As Final** Mark as Final saves the document in its final form, as read-only, so others receiving the file will only be able to view and print the file.

In addition to the options available in the Prepare menu, Word enables you to safeguard your documents in the following ways as well:

- **The Word 2007 Trust Center** You'll find the Word 2007 Trust Center by clicking the Microsoft Office Button, choosing Word Options, and clicking Trust Center. The Word 2007 Trust Center enables you to disable macros in your Word documents, choose whether Microsoft ActiveX controls are enabled in documents you receive, and create a list of Trusted Publishers.

- **PDF and XPS formats** Support for saving your documents in PDF and XPS is available as a downloadable add-in utility, and the options will appear as choices when you point to Save As (display this by clicking the Microsoft Office Button) after you've installed the utility. PDF and XPS formats give you the means to save your formatted and finished Word documents in a platform-independent format others can view but not change.

> Tip
>
> If you haven't installed the PDF and XPS utility, Word will display a link in place of the command that enables you to download and install the tool.

Encrypting Documents

Another way to restrict which users can open or modify a document is to encrypt the document and use password protection. Encrypting a document encodes it so that it will be unreadable to those who don't have the password to unencrypt it. When you encrypt the file, users must enter a password before they can open or change the document. Standard passwords in Word are case-sensitive. They can be up to 15 characters long, and they can contain any combination of letters, numerals, spaces, and symbols.

Here's how to encrypt your document.

1. Open the document you want to protect.

2. Click the Microsoft Office Button and point to Prepare. The Prepare menu appears, shown in Figure 20-1.

Chapter 20

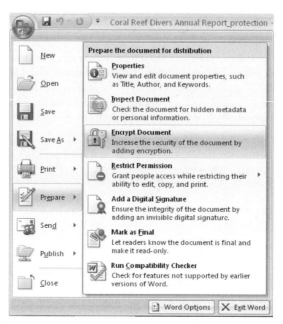

Figure 20-1 Click the Microsoft Office Button and point to Prepare to display security options in Word.

3. Click Encrypt Document. The Encrypt Document dialog box appears, as shown in Figure 20-2.

Figure 20-2 The Encrypt Document dialog box enables you to add a password to protect your document

4. Type the password for your document. After you click OK, Word will prompt you to reenter the password to verify it. After you click OK the second time, password protection and encryption features will be in effect.

CAUTION

It's important that you keep track of the password you assign to your encrypted document because Word has no way to recover it if it is misplaced or forgotten. You may want to keep a backup copy of the document somewhere that is available only to you—just in case.

5. After you assign a password to open a document, the Password dialog box will appear whenever a user attempts to open the document, as shown in Figure 20-3. To open the document, the user will have to enter the correct password and click OK. If a user doesn't know the password, he or she can click Cancel to abort the process.

Figure 20-3 The user must enter the correct password to access the encrypted file.

Removing Protection

You may decide somewhere along the line that you don't need the level of protection you've added to your document after all. If you want to remove permissions or cancel password protection, you can do it easily. Here's how to do it:

- To move permissions, click Change Permissions in the message bar (below the Ribbon). The Permission dialog box appears. Click the Restrict Permission To This Document check box to clear it. Click OK to save your changes, and permissions will no longer be in effect for the current document.

- To remove password protection, you must first gain access to the document by using the password. After you open a password-protected document, click the Microsoft Office Button, point to Prepare, and click Encrypt Document. In the Encrypt Document dialog box, delete the password. Click OK to save the setting, and the password will no longer be used for the document.

> **Note**
>
> In most cases, you'll lose your password protection if you save your document in a format other than document format. For example, if you save a Word document as a Web page or a PDF file, Word will let you know that password protection will be lost if you continue with the save operation.

Applying Formatting Restrictions

In Word, you can restrict the available styles and formatting capabilities in a document. When you restrict formatting, users are able to open the document, but they can't format text other than applying approved styles. Most of the character formatting tools on the Ribbon, along with other text formatting tools (such as formatting keyboard commands), are inaccessible when a document has formatting restrictions applied. You can control the styles that appear in the Styles gallery and block users' ability to choose different Quick Style sets in the document.

> **Note**
>
> Be aware that even if the document is protected with a password, the Protect Document functionality is intended to be used in a collaborative environment and offers only a limited means of security. For a higher level of security, use encryption, or save it as a PDF or XPS file.

To restrict formatting, click the Review tab on the Ribbon and click Protect Document (on the far right). The Restrict Formatting And Editing pane shown in Figure 20-4 appears along the right side of the Word window.

Figure 20-4 You can turn on formatting restrictions to stop users from applying character formatting or unapproved styles to document text.

To set up formatting restrictions in the Restrict Formatting And Editing pane, follow these steps.

1. Click the Limit Formatting To A Selection Of Styles check box and then click Settings. The Formatting Restrictions dialog box appears.

2. The Limit Formatting To A Selection Of Styles check box is already selected; go through the list and click any of the items you want to restrict users from changing in the document.

3. You can take the following actions.

- ❏ Manually select and unselect style check boxes to specify a group of styles that you want to allow users to access.

- ❏ Select All if you want all styles to be allowed.

- ❏ Click Recommended Minimum to limit styles to a recommended group of styles.

- ❏ Click None if you don't want users to have access to any styles.

4. In the Formatting area of the Formatting Restrictions dialog box, choose whether you want to allow AutoFormatting to be applied in spite of formatting restrictions. You can also elect to make it impossible for users to change the Theme or color scheme, or choose a different Quick Style set. Click the check box of any item you want to apply.

5. Click OK. If the document contains styles that you didn't select in step 3, a message box appears, stating that the document contains formatting or styles that aren't allowed and asking whether you would like to remove them. Click No to apply the formatting settings without changing the document's current formatting, or click Yes to remove the styles from the document. Keep in mind that if you click None in step 3 and then click Yes in the message box in this step, your document will be formatted in Normal style throughout. In most cases, you'll probably want to retain the current formatting in the document, so you should click No in the message box.

6. Back in the Restrict Formatting and Editing pane, click Yes, Start Enforcing Protection. The Start Enforcing Protection dialog box opens.

7. In the Start Enforcing Protection dialog box, enter a password in the Enter New Password (Optional) box and then reenter the password in the Reenter Password To Confirm box. If you don't want to use password protection, leave the password boxes empty. Click OK to complete the procedure.

After formatting restrictions are enforced, users won't be able to apply character formats or use styles that aren't included on the approved list of styles.

To turn off formatting restrictions, click Protect Document again, click Stop Protection at the bottom of the Restrict Formatting And Editing pane, enter a password if required, and click OK.

Chapter 20

> **Note**
> If you are using Microsoft Office Ultimate 2007, Office Professional Plus 2007, or Office Enterprise 2007, click Restrict Formatting and Editing after clicking Protect Document to access the Restrict Formatting And Editing pane.

Restricting Tracked Changes, Comments, and Forms

In addition to granting users access and modification rights to a document, and formatting control, you can control how users can manipulate information within a document. Specifically, you can choose any of the following options.

- **Tracked changes** The Tracked Changes option lets users change a document but highlights all changes made so that you can review them. When a document is protected for tracked changes, users can't turn off tracking, nor can they accept or reject changes.

- **Comments** When Comments is selected, users can insert comments, but they can't make any other changes to the contents of the document.

- **Filling in forms** The Filling In Forms option protects a document from any changes other than entries in form fields or unprotected areas.

- **No changes** You can prevent users from making any changes to a document by making the document read-only; alternatively, if you want to allow editing in some parts of the document but not in others, you can mark the document as read-only but allow some exceptions.

To configure any of these editing limitations, follow these steps.

1. Open the document you want to protect and then click Protect Document on the Review tab. The Restrict Formatting And Editing pane opens, as shown previously in Figure 20-4.

2. Click the Allow Only This Type Of Editing In The Document check box in the Editing Restrictions section.

3. Click the arrow and then choose Tracked Changes, Comments, Filling In Forms, or No Changes (Read Only), depending on how you want to protect the document.

4. If you selected Comments or No Changes, you have an additional step. If you want to specify that some users will be able to edit specified areas in the document, use the Groups list to select the users to whom you want to grant access. If you want to add users to the list, click More Users and enter their names, separated by semicolons, in the Add Users dialog box.

5. Click Yes, Start Enforcing Protection.

6. If you want to apply a password, type a password in the Enter New Password (Optional) box, type the password again in the Reenter Password To Confirm box, and click OK. If you don't include a password, users will be able to unprotect your document by clicking Stop Protection in the Protect Document task pane. If you do assign a password, users will have to enter the password before they can unprotect the document.

After you restrict editing in the document, users will be limited by the settings you've configured. You can turn off document protection by clicking Protect Document on the Review tab and clicking Stop Protection in the Restrict Formatting and Editing pane. If you assigned a password, you'll need to enter the password to unprotect the document.

Chapter 20

Removing Personal Information and Hidden Data

One easy security measure you can take when sharing documents with others is to re-move information you don't intend others to see. For example, you can remove personal information so that people who view your document won't be able to see the names of reviewers, the author of the document, and so forth. If your document contains other hidden information, you'll want to eliminate that information as well. If you don't de-lete hidden information, other people who view your document might see information you'd rather they didn't, especially if they save your Word document in another file format (because information hidden in a Word document doesn't remain hidden when a Word document is saved in another format and viewed in another application). This section shows you how to remove unnecessary personal information from documents before you share the documents with others.

In addition to removing personal information, be sure to remove hidden text and accept or reject any tracked changes before you pass your document to others. For more information about accepting and rejecting tracked changes, see Chapter 19, "Revising Documents Using Markup Tools."

Removing Personal Information

In Word, you can easily remove the following types of personal information.

- File properties, such as author name, manager name, company name, and last saved by information

- Names associated with comments and revisions (Word will change reviewers' names to *Author* automatically)

- Routing slips

- E-mail message header generated when you click the E-Mail button

To remove these informational tidbits, run the Document Inspector, available in the Prepare menu. Here are the steps.

1. With your file open, click the Microsoft Office Button and point to Prepare.

2. Click Inspect Document.

3. The Document Inspector dialog box appears, as you see in Figure 20-5. All items are selected. This means that all the listed checks will be performed automatically. If you want to skip any of the items in the list, click it to deselect it.

Figure 20-5 The Document Inspector searches the document for sensitive, personal, or hidden information and prompts you to remove it.

4. Click Inspect to evaluate the document. The results show you what the Document Inspector found. If hidden items were discovered, the Inspector alerts you and provides a Remove All button for each inspection type so that you can delete the unwanted information.

5. Click Remove All to clear the unwanted items.

6. Click Reinspect to run the Document Inspector again.

7. When the inspection reveals no more hidden information, click Close to complete the process and return to your document.

Preparing PDF and XPS Files

For years, Word users have been asking for PDF support for their Word documents. And in Word 2007, the feature has finally arrived—sort of. You may have heard that when Microsoft Office 2007 was in Beta 1 (the first round of prerelease testing for the developing product), Word included a Save As PDF feature. But during the course of the beta, Microsoft and Adobe were unable to come to complete agreement on how the inclusion of the feature would be handled. So right after Beta 2 was released (in May 2006), Microsoft moved the feature from being a hard-wired part of Word to being a downloadable utility you can get (for free) from Microsoft's Downloads page.

Chapter 20

Download the PDF and XPS Utility

Downloading the PDF and XPS utility will just take a few moments of your time, and Microsoft has made it very easy for you to do. When you click the Microsoft Office Button and point to Save As, you will see the link you can use for downloading the PDF and XPS add-in. Simply click the link and follow the instructions on the screen.

> **Note**
>
> The add-in is also available on the Microsoft Downloads web site (*www.microsoft.com/downloads*)

The next time you click the Microsoft Office Button and point to Save As, you'll see PDF Or XPS listed so you can easily save the files you create in either of these secure formats. For more about how PDF and XPS files work—and what they can mean to the security of your documents—read on.

Understanding PDF and XPS

PDF (Portable Document Format file) files are saved in a fixed layout, meaning that although readers can view, print, and share files, they cannot modify the format or content. Users must have a special PDF reader to read PDF files. The most popular PDF reader is Acrobat Reader, a free downloadable utility from Adobe Systems (*www.adobe.com*). Because PDF preserves the format of the final document, this format is often used for submitting final files to commercial printers, to post documents online, and to save and share work that includes highly detailed and colorful graphics.

XPS (XML Paper Specification) is a fixed-layout format that has been developed by Microsoft. The format is actually a page-definition format that creates the page electronically in a way that can be read by people, programs, and PCs. Similar to PDF, XPS file format enables users to view, print, and share files but limits others from making changes in the file itself. One additional benefit XPS offers is the ability to include "live links," which enable users to click and follow hyperlinks in the document.

To learn more about the XPS format, visit the XPS Web site at *www.microsoft.com/whdc/xps/*.

Saving Your Document as PDF and XPS

Once you've downloaded and installed the Save as PDF or XPS utility, the actual process for saving the file is simple. Here's how to do it.

1. Open the document you want to save as PDF or XPS.

2. Click the Microsoft Office Button, point to Print, and choose Print Preview.

3. Ensure that you've made all content and formatting changes you want to make to the document.

4. Click the Microsoft Office Button and point to Save As (see Figure 20-6). Then click PDF Or XPS. The Publish As PDF Or XPS dialog box appears.

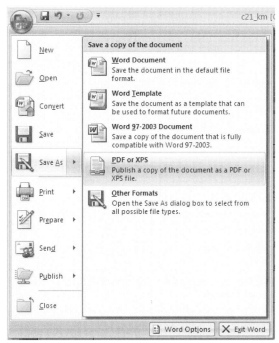

Figure 20-6 Point to Save As and click PDF Or XPS to access the Publish As PDF or XPS dialog box.

5. Navigate to the folder in which you want to store the file. Then click in the File Name box and type a name for the file.

6. Click Save As Type to choose either PDF or XPS Document.

7. If you want to view the file after saving it, click the Open File After Publishing check box.

8. In the Optimize For area, choose whether you want to save the file in Standard or Minimum size.

9. Click the Options button to display choices about the page ranges included in the file and the type of information saved with the file (see Figure 20-7).

Figure 20-7 Choose Options to enter your preferences for the range of pages and information to be included in the PDF or XPS file.

After you click OK, the utility saves the file in the format you specified. If you selected the Open After Publishing check box and you have a PDF or XPS reader installed on your computer, the file will open automatically so that you can see your file the way others reading the file will view it.

Signing Your Documents with Digital Signatures and Stamps

Word enables you to digitally sign your documents so that others know the file is authentic—and you can add stamp signature lines as well. Word supports digital certificates that are provided by third-party vendors (a link to Office Marketplace is built into the program so that you can evaluate different services easily) as well as digital certificates that you create yourself.

- When a document is prepared using a third-party digital signature service, the document is authenticated and people who receive your files can be certain they have been authenticated.

- When you create a digital certificate yourself, the item is not authenticated, but it does provide a useful service. A document you digitally sign says to the user that they are receiving a document that has not been modified since you created it. (A digital signature becomes invalid if the document is revised after it is signed.)

Chapter 20

> **Note**
>
> Microsoft Office Excel 2007, Word 2007, and Microsoft Office PowerPoint 2007 all support digital signatures.

Getting a Digital ID

To get your own digital ID, start by clicking the Microsoft Office Button, pointing to Prepare, and clicking Add A Digital Signature. If you don't have a signature of your own, a message box appears explaining the limits and availability of digital signatures and providing a button you can click to see the signature services that are available from third-party services on Office Marketplace. Click OK, and the Get A Digital ID dialog box appears (see Figure 20-8).

Figure 20-8 You can opt to get a digital ID from a vendor or create your own in the Get A Digital ID dialog box.

If you select the first option, Office Marketplace opens, providing links to a variety of digital ID services (see Figure 20-9). Click the ones about which you want to find out more. (Note: Some of the services provide free trials.)

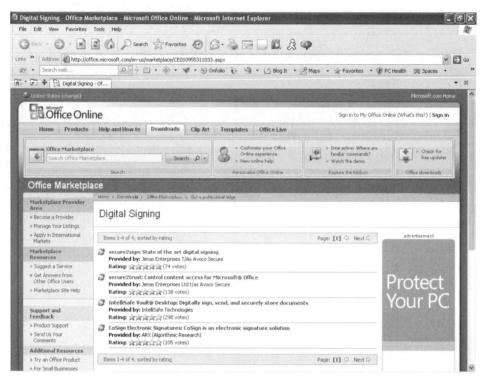

Figure 20-9 Office Marketplace provides links to a number of third-party vendors offering digital signature services.

Working with Certificate Authorities and Security Administrators

When you obtain a digital certificate from a certification authority, you must submit an application to the authority and pay a fee (which is usually an annual rate based on the type of security you want to obtain). When you receive your digital certificate, the certification authority provides instructions for installation. Similarly, if you work with an in-house security administrator, you'll need to follow your organization's policies regarding how digital certificates are distributed and how digital signatures are added to your macros and files.

For more on signing macros with a digital signature, see Chapter 31, "Working with Macros and VBA."

Creating a Digital ID

When you choose Create Your Own Digital ID in the Get A Digital ID dialog box and click OK, the Create A Digital ID dialog box is displayed (see Figure 20-10). You can fill in your information and click Create to create your own digital certificate. Remember, however, that this type of certification is unauthenticated, so it doesn't provide much security assurance to others outside your local area network. It can assure those receiving your files that they have the most recent version of your original work, however.

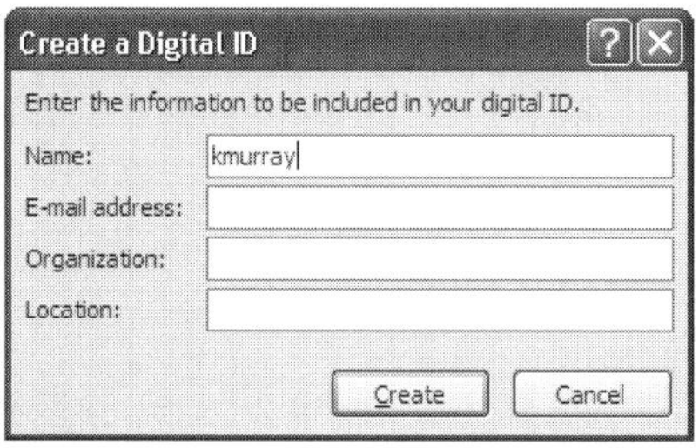

Figure 20-10 You can create your own digital ID for use on your computer and local area network.

Complete the information and click OK. The Sign dialog box appears, providing an area for you to enter the reason you are signing the document (see Figure 20-11). Additionally, you can verify that you are the person shown to be signing the document (if others use your computer, be sure to verify that the correct digital ID appears in the Signing As: line). Click Sign to add your digital signature to the document.

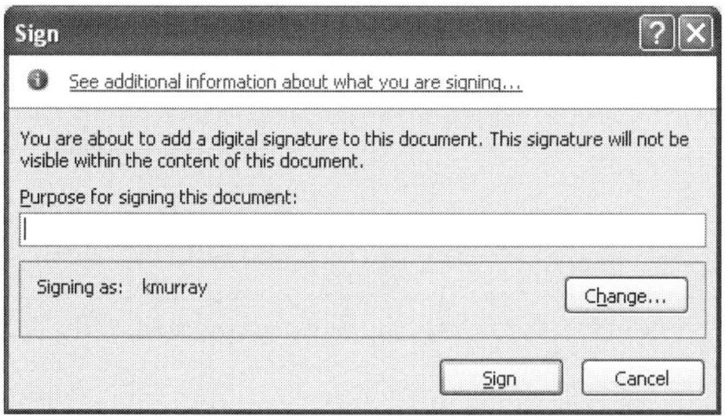

Figure 20-11 The Sign dialog box enables you to enter your purpose for signing and complete the process.

The Signature Confirmation dialog box lets you know that your signature has been saved with the document. If the document is changed after this point, the signature will no longer be valid and you will need to re-sign the document.

At this point, you've successfully created an unauthenticated digital certificate that you can use to sign your documents.

Attaching a Digital Signature to a File

After you create or obtain a digital certificate, you can authenticate your files by digitally signing them. Basically, digitally signing a file means that you've attached your digital certificate to the document. In the last section, you saw how Word automatically applies the newly created digital ID to the currently open document. If you want to attach your digital signature to another file, follow these steps.

1. Open the document you want to digitally sign and then click the Microsoft Office Button.

2. Point to Prepare and click Add A Digital Signature. Click OK in the message box that appears.

3. The Sign dialog box is displayed. Type the purpose for signing the document and verify that the *Signing As:* value is correct.

4. Click Sign to attach your signature to the document.

INSIDE OUT   How can I tell that a document has been digitally signed?

When a digital signature has been added to a document, a small red symbol appears in the status bar of your Word document. When you position the mouse pointer over the symbol, the ToolTip displays "This document contains signatures." To display information about the signatures, click the symbol once. Signatures are displayed in the Signatures pane along the right side of the Word window.

Adding a Stamp

The stamp signature is a new feature in Word 2007 that enables you to use an image, or if you have an inking feature, such as on a Tablet PC—a hand-written signature, as a stamp on your Word documents. (Note that this feature is also available for Excel workbooks.)

You will need a digital ID to add a stamp signature to your documents. The process involves two parts: First you create the stamp signature line in the document, and then you add the image you want to use for the stamp and digitally sign it. (Note that depending on how you will be using the document, you may be creating it and sending it to another person, who then signs the signature line and returns it to you.)

To add the stamp signature line to the document, click the Insert tab and click the Signature Line arrow in the Text group. Select Stamp Signature Line. The Signature Setup dialog box appears so that you can enter the signer's information and add any instructions you want the signer to see before signing. Click OK to save your changes.

To sign the stamp signature line, double-click it. The Sign dialog box appears. Click Select Image to display a dialog box in which you can select the image you want to use as your digital signature. Navigate to the file and click Select. Then simply click Sign and the stamp signature is added to the document.

Viewing Signatures

When a document has been digitally signed, the View Signatures option becomes available in the Prepare menu when you click the Microsoft Office Button. When you click View Signatures, the Signatures pane appears along the right side of the signed document by default. You can view information about a signature by pointing to the signature name and clicking the arrow. A context menu appears (see Figure 20-12).

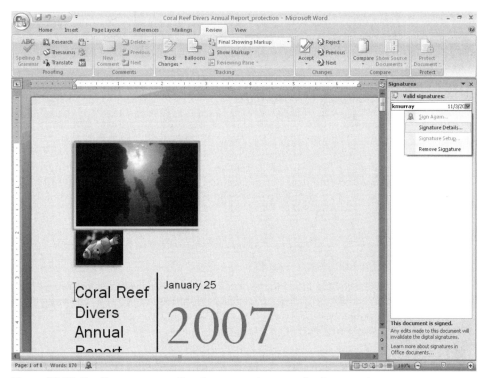

Figure 20-12 The Signatures pane lists the current signatures for the open document.

Click Signature Details to see more information about the signature. Clicking the View button will give you additional information about the creation of the digital certificate (see Figure 20-13).

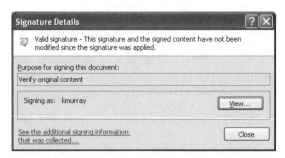

Figure 20-13 The Signature Details window provides information about the purpose of the signature and the identity of the signer.

Removing a Signature

After you add a certificate to a document, you can remove it at any time. To do so, display the Signatures list by clicking the Microsoft Office Button, pointing to Prepare, and clicking View Signatures. Click the arrow of the signature you want to remove and select Remove Signature. The Remove Signature box appears, asking you to confirm that you want to complete the operation. Click Yes to delete the signature. Note, however, that this action simply removes the signature from the current document—it doesn't delete the certificate.

> ### Checking for the Red X
>
> When you are checking the certificates associated with files you receive, be on the lookout for the red X. A digital certificate displayed with a red X may mean the certificate is unauthenticated or cannot be verified. A red X can also indicate the following security issues associated with a certificate.
>
> - The signed file has been tampered with.
> - The certificate was not issued by a trusted certification authority.
> - The certificate was issued without verification (such as a free certificate authority trial download).
> - The certificate was invalid when it was used to sign the file or macros.
>
> When you see a certificate with a red X, proceed with caution. This is a clear sign that something about the certificate is amiss.

Working with the Trust Center

Each of the Microsoft Office applications includes the new Microsoft Office Trust Center, a special area within the program options that enable you to control settings related to security and privacy. Some Trust Center settings you enter in one application flow through to other applications as well.

To display the Word Trust Center, follow these steps.

1. Click the Microsoft Office Button.

2. Click Word Options in the bottom right corner. The Word Options dialog box appears.

3. Click Trust Center in the navigation pane on the left side of the dialog box. Then click the Trust Center Settings button. The Trust Center opens, as you see in Figure 20-14.

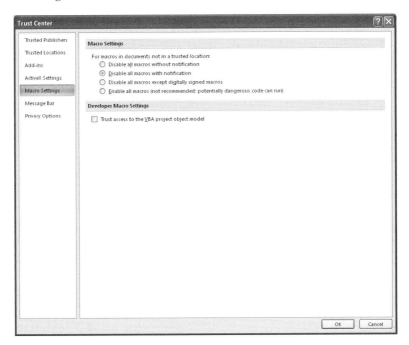

Figure 20-14 Use the Trust Center to set security and privacy options while you work with Word.

The Trust Center includes seven different categories, each tailored to a specific area of security or privacy. Here's a quick run-down of what you'll find in the various groups.

- **Trusted Publishers** Displays a list of the digital certificates you've accepted from other individuals or companies. When you open a document that includes a macro, the Message Bar appears alerting you to that fact. If the document is from a trusted source, and if a digital signature has been added, you can choose to add that publisher to your Trusted Publishers list.

- **Trusted Locations** Shows the locations that you have accepted as safe sources for files you open. You can add new locations, change locations, or remove locations by working with the options on the Trusted Locations screen. Note that the Workgroup Templates folder (found in Word Options/Advanced and File Locations at the bottom) is also considered a trusted location and it does not automatically appear in this list.

- **Add-ins** Enables you to determine whether you will require the authentication of add-ins (meaning they must be signed by someone in your Trusted Publisher's list before you approve their installation) or whether you choose to disable all add-ins.

- **ActiveX Settings** Gives you the choice of what to do with ActiveX controls that do not come from a trusted source. Your options range from totally disallowing ActiveX controls to running them after being prompted to openly running all ActiveX controls (which is not recommended for security reasons).

- **Macro Settings** Offers selections for working with macros that are not authenticated or from a trusted location. You can disallow them, disable macros with notification, allow only macros with digital signatures, or enable all macros unconditionally (again, not recommended).

- **Message Bar** Enables you to choose whether you want the message bar to display information when content has been blocked.

- **Privacy Options** Includes several different groups of settings that help you control how much information is shared about your computer use and individual documents. Additionally, you can set your preferences for the Research and Translate tools in Word.

Simply choose the settings that best fit the way you want your version of Word to operate and then click OK to save your settings. The settings you select in the Trust Center are global settings, in effect for the entire application. You can at any time return to the Trust Center to check or remove Trusted Publishers, change Trusted Locations, or modify any of the settings you've previously entered.

Viewing and Removing Trusted Sources

When you open a file that includes digitally signed macros (and the signer isn't included on your Trusted Publishers list, as described in this section), you'll be asked whether you want to trust all macros from the signer. If you click Yes, the signer will be added to your list of trusted publishers. Before you add a signer, you should carefully review the publisher's certificate (watch for the red X). You should especially review the certificate's Issued To, Issued By, and Valid From fields. After you add a signer to your Trusted Publishers list, in the future, Word will automatically enable macros signed by the publisher. As you add new trusted sources, they'll be added to the Trusted Publishers list.

If you later decide that you'd like to remove a signer from your Trusted Publishers list, you can do so at any time, as follows.

1. Display the Trust Center by clicking the Microsoft Office Button, clicking Word Options, clicking Trust Center, and choosing Trust Center Settings.

2. Click Trusted Publishers in the navigation bar in the Trust Center window.

3. Select the publisher you want to remove, click Remove, and then click OK.

Microsoft digitally signs all add-ins and templates (if they contain macros) that you download from Office Online. After you add Microsoft to your list of trusted publishers for one of these installed files, all subsequent interactions with these files will not generate messages.

Marking a File as Final

Have you ever finished a document and then sent it out to team members or managers, only to get a marked up copy back with someone's last-minute changes? Word now includes the Mark As Final feature to enable you to mark a finished file as final.

When you are finished with a document, double-check it and then click the Microsoft Office Button. Point to Prepare and click Mark As Final. A message box tells you that the document will be marked as final and then saved. Click OK to continue.

After the file is saved, many of the commands on the Ribbon become unavailable because you can no longer modify the file in any way. In addition, a Marked As Final symbol appears in the document's status bar to let you know that the document has been finalized.

> **Note**
>
> When you use Mark As Final without additional security functionality, such as a digital signature, users can disable the Mark As Final command, edit the document, and turn on Mark as Final again. The only indication that changes have been made is the Save Date. To ensure that the document is secure, be sure to use an additional feature such digital signatures.

Setting Permission Levels

Depending on the suite of Office 2007 you are using, you may also be able to control a variety of permission levels so that those viewing and working with your document can have only the access you specify. This feature is known as IRM (Information Rights Management) functionality, and it is included in Microsoft Office Ultimate 2007, Office Professional Plus 2007, and Office Enterprise 2007.

When you have IRM functionality, Word enables you to restrict permission to documents and document content so that only those who you want to have access to your files can open them. By setting permissions, you can control whether documents can be forwarded, printed, or accessed after a specified number of days. You can specify the following three access levels for Word documents.

- **Read** Enables specified users to read a document but not edit, print, or copy the content.

- **Change** Enables specified users to read, edit, and save changes to a document but not print the document.

- **Full Control** Gives specified users full authoring permissions and the freedom to do anything with a document. (Document authors always have full control.)

To set access levels for specified users, use the Permission dialog box, as shown in Figure 20-15. To open the Permission dialog box, click the Microsoft Office Button. Then point to Prepare and click Restricted Access. After the Permission dialog box appears, select the Restrict Permission To This Document check box to make the Read and Change boxes available.

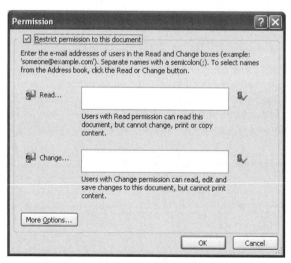

Figure 20-15 You use the Permission dialog box to grant Read or Change access to users by entering their e-mail addresses in the Read or Change boxes.

Customizing Permissions

Along with access levels, you can set additional permissions and settings using the Permission dialog box. To access the additional permissions and settings options, click More Options in the Permission dialog box. You can also change a user's access level in the More Options dialog box by clicking the Access Level setting next to the user's e-mail address and selecting a new access level. Additional permissions and settings that you can set for each user include the following:

- **This Document Expires On** Enables you to set an expiration date for the document, after which the document will be unavailable to selected users.

- **Print Content** Enables you to grant printing capabilities to users with Read or Change access levels.

- **Allow Users With Read Access To Copy Content** Enables you to allow users with Read access to copy the entire or partial document.

- **Access Content Programmatically** Enables you to allow users to use certain Word program features in the document, such as Smart Tags.

- **Users Can Request Additional Permissions From** Enables you to specify an address that users can send requests to change their permission status.

- **Require A Connection To Verify A User's Permission** Enables you to require that users connect to the Internet to verify their credentials each time they access the document.

- **Set Defaults** Enables you to set the current settings as the default for documents with restricted permissions.

Applying Permissions to Documents

To apply permissions to a document, follow these steps.

1. Open the document you want to protect.

2. Click the Microsoft Office Button and point to Prepare.

3. Click Restrict Permission.

4. In the Permission dialog box, select the Restrict Permission To This Document check box.

5. Click the Change or Read label (hovering the mouse pointer over the label will change the label to a button) to access your address book or enter e-mail addresses in the Read or Change boxes of the users who can access the document. If you're entering more than one e-mail address, separate the addresses with a semicolon. If desired, click More Options to further configure user permissions.

6. Click OK to save your settings.

When you open the document in the future, the message bar shows that the document now has restricted access (see Figure 20-16). You can click Change Permission to display the Permissions dialog box so that you can change the settings currently in effect for the document if necessary.

Figure 20-16 The message bar, just below the Ribbon, lets you know that restrictions have been applied to the current document.

What's Next?

This chapter has introduced you to the far-reaching security and privacy features in Word 2007. The next chapter starts Part VII of the book by showing you how to set up and format columns and sections in complex documents.

PART 6

Complex Documents: Sections, Master Documents, and References

Formatting Columns and Sections for Advanced Text Control

Depending on the types of documents you create, you may rely heavily on the ability of Microsoft Office Word 2007 to create columns and sections. When you combine these two elements, you can control how the text flows in various parts of the same document. You can create single or multiple columns, even or uneven columns, and columns with line dividers or with blank spaces (gutters) in between. This chapter explores the use of both columns and sections in Office Word 2007 and helps you create interesting formats for your newsletters, reports, and more.

The Nature of Complex Documents

What makes a long document complex? If you've ever put together a large project, you know how many things you have to plan for before you can reach the goals you set. Planning for complex documents includes dealing with the following issues.

- **Getting a clear vision of the project** If the document you're in charge of preparing is an elaborate annual report, a training manual, a corporate policy statement, or something similar that requires the input of many people, most likely everyone involved will have an opinion about the way it should look and what it should contain. Establishing early on what message you want to communicate in the document, what you want to leave the reader thinking at the end, and what kind of impression you want to make will be critical to ending up at the right place—and on speaking terms with the entire team.

- **Organizing the vision and assigning tasks** Once you have an idea of where you're headed, you need to determine the scope of the project. How many pages? How many colors? Who will do what? These are all important questions that need to be answered right up front when you're working with a large and potentially very expensive project.

- **Evaluating costs, setting a budget, and determining deadlines** Putting the facts on the vision isn't an easy step. Especially if you are preparing this document with the help of a committee or team, you need to carefully weigh the cost, time, and effort requirements. Seemingly small considerations—such as paper weight, page size, and colors used—can make a huge difference in the costs of the project.

- **Staying in touch with the document team** If you have assigned different sections of a document to different people on the team, how do you ensure each person is on track to make his or her goal? Communicating is important, as is ensuring that everyone is on the same page—literally—by working with the same style, Theme, or XML schema.

- **Creating and compiling content** Think about what a nightmare footnotes and endnotes could be when you have 15 different people creating their own parts of an individual document. Luckily, Word 2007 simplifies working with references, and the Compare and Combine features (in the Compare group in the Review tab) make pulling it all together easier than ever.

- **Formatting the document with the end in mind** As you envision the type of document you and your team are creating, design will play a big part of your considerations. If you are creating something that matches other publications your company has produced, you will already have a set of design specifications to use. If you are creating something new that isn't tied to other formatting considerations, you will need to consider the type of design your audience will respond to. It's a big job—and each person will have his or her own opinion. You can use templates, Themes, and Quick Styles in Word to simplify the process of developing a look that hits the mark.

- **Editing and reviewing the first draft** Depending on the number of people on your team and the number of review cycles your document will go through, reviewing and editing your document may require you to send various sections in various directions. Be sure to leave time in your schedule so that others have the time they need to review and respond to the sections you send.

- **Incorporating changes and proofreading** When you receive the reviewed and edited sections back from various members of your team, you need to merge the various sections back into a master document. Then it's up to you to review and accept (or reject) the various changes proposed by team members. You'll also want to run the spelling and grammar checker, and double-check any citations, before you finalize the document.

- **Preparing for final production** The choices you make about the final production of your document will depend on your budget, your audience, and the overall goals of your publication. A four-color, commercial printing process will cost more than something you print on your desktop printer, obviously, but some projects (usually complex ones) just can't be finished any other way. Word includes a number of features to help you prepare to finalize your document. One important feature is Inspect Document (available when you click the Microsoft Office button and point to Prepare), which enables you to search for and remove any hidden or personal information left in the file.

- **Finishing and distributing the document** The final step in preparing your complex document is to save it in the final format you choose (whether that's PDF, XPS, or as a final (read-only) document). You can then send the document to others on your team, publish it to the Web, or print and distribute as needed.

Creating a Cover Page

Long or complex documents need cover pages to provide the reader with information about the publication. For example, your 40-page business plan may be a work of genius, but if prospective business investors can't find your contact information, the plan isn't going to do you much good. A long, involved document with text, charts, illustrations, and diagrams needs some kind of introduction—and a cover page gives readers a professional welcome to the document they'll be spending their time reading.

Word makes it easy for you to create professional cover pages with just a few clicks of the mouse. To add a cover page to your document, follow these steps.

1. Open the document to which you want to add the cover page.

2. Click the Insert tab.

3. Click Cover Page in the Pages group. The Cover Page gallery opens, as you see in Figure 21-1.

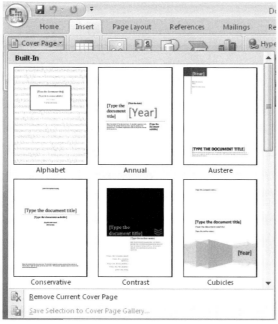

Figure 21-1 You can add a predesigned cover page to give readers a professional introduction to your long document.

4. Scroll through the list and click the cover page style you like. The cover page is applied to the document.

5. Click in the text box and type the information you want to add to the page (see Figure 21-2).

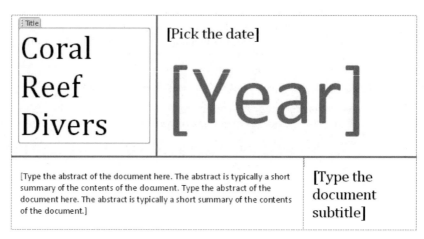

Figure 21-2 Click in a text box on the cover page and replace the placeholder text with your own information.

6. Press Ctrl+S to save the document.

INSIDE OUT   **Creating your own cover page**

You can easily create your own custom cover page and then save it to the Cover Page gallery by clicking the Insert tab, choosing Cover Page, and clicking Save Selection To Cover Page Gallery, at the bottom of the Cover Page Gallery. In the Create New Building Block dialog box, type a name for the cover page and add a description, if desired. Click OK to save the cover page to the gallery. The next time you click Cover Page on the Insert tab, you will see your custom cover page in the gallery of available styles.

Planning Your Document

If the design of your document is up to you, it's a good idea to start out not at the computer keyboard but at the drawing board, literally sketching out how you want your pages to look. Will you use two columns or three? Do you want the columns to have equal widths, or will one be narrow and the other two wide? Thinking carefully about your document's final appearance will go a long way toward helping you create it the way you want.

Word gives you the capability to create up to 13 columns, but in all but the rarest circumstances (such as a simple word or number list), you won't use 13 columns–the width of each column would be a scant 0.5 inch! Most traditional documents use one, two, or three columns. In some instances, you might use four, but even those columns will provide little room for more than a few small words on a line.

As you prepare your document design, consider these questions.

- How many columns do you want? Table 21-1 lists the column widths Word uses by default for a table with one to six columns on an 8.5-by-11-inch portrait page with the Equal Column Width option selected.

- Will you include graphics around which your columns need to flow?

- How much space do you want to leave between columns?

- Do you want your columns to be of equal widths or varied widths?

- Will you include a table of contents column that might require more space than a traditional text column?

- Do you want the column settings to extend the full length of the page, or do you want to include a section at the top or bottom of the page that is only a single column?

Table 21-1 Default Column Widths in Word

Number of columns	Width of each column (inches)	Width of each column (centimeters)
1	6.5 inches	16.51 cm
2	3 inches with 0.5-inch spacing	7.62 cm
3	1.83 inches with 0.5-inch spacing	4.66 cm
4	1.25 inches with 0.5-inch spacing	3.17 cm
5	.9 inches with 0.5-inch spacing	2.29 cm
6	0.67 inches with 0.5-inch spacing	1.69 cm

Chapter 21

Working with Predesigned Columns

If you know you're going to create a multicolumn document, it's best to start off by looking through the Word templates. Word gives you access to a huge collection of template styles so that you can find a ready-made column arrangement that fits your needs.

You can get a closer look at the templates by following these steps.

1. Click the Microsoft Office Button. Click New. The New Document dialog box appears.

2. If you have templates saved on your computer, you can click Installed Templates or My Templates in the Templates area. If this is your first time working with a multicolumn template, in the Microsoft Office Online section of the New Document dialog box, click a template type you'd like to see. (Note: You must be connected to the Internet to access templates on Microsoft Office Online.) Some templates, such as Brochures, Newsletters, and the Oriel style of Reports, offer columns.

3. Click the template you want to use and then click Download, as shown in Figure 21-3. (If the template is resident on your computer, you will see an Open button instead of Download.)

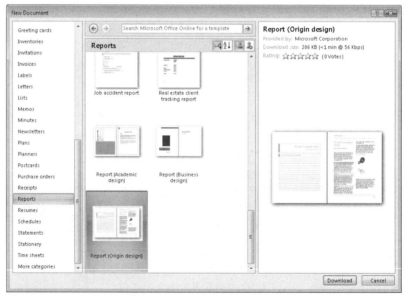

Figure 21-3 You can begin working with columns by using Word's predesigned templates.

Creating a Multi-Column Document

There are several ways to format your document in multiple columns. If you want to create columns on the fly (as opposed to working with a predesigned template), click the Columns button in the Page Setup group in the Page Layout tab. If you have certain specifications—for example, exact column measurements, a spacing requirement of a certain size, or more than four columns—use the Columns dialog box to choose those settings.

> **Tip**
>
> Be sure to display your document in Print Layout view before you begin working with columns. In Draft view, Web Layout view, and Outline view you can't see columns as they will appear in print. To choose Print Layout view, click the Print Layout icon in the View controls in the lower right corner of the Word window.

Using the Columns Button

The easiest way to create a multicolumn document is to click Columns in the Page Setup group on the Page Layout tab. When you click the button, the choice of one to three columns is presented, as shown in Figure 21-4. In addition to the choice of one to three columns, you can click a column style (narrow column on the left or right) by using the choices available when you choose Columns. Click the column setting you want, and Word will automatically update the layout in your document.

> **Tip**
>
> If you want to create columns for only a portion of a document, select the text to which you want to apply the column format before you click the Columns button.

Figure 21-4 The Columns gallery enables you to select up to three columns from the Standard toolbar.

Choosing Column Specs in the Columns Dialog Box

If you have certain column specifications that you need to enter—for example, you're creating a follow-up report using a style your department has adopted as its report format of choice—you can create and work with columns by using the Columns dialog box. Follow these steps.

1. Click the Page Layout tab and click Columns in the Page Setup group. The Columns gallery appears.

2. Click More Columns at the bottom of the Columns gallery. The Columns dialog box is displayed.

3. Click the column format you want to use. The Preview section shows you the format you've selected, as shown in Figure 21-5.

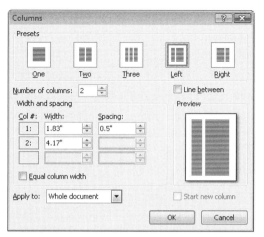

Figure 21-5 You can enter more specific column settings in the Columns dialog box.

4. Click OK to apply your formatting.

By default, Word assumes that you want your columns to be created equally (unless you choose either the Left or Right preset selection) and that you don't want a line to be placed between the columns you create. If you want to add a line between columns, select the Line Between check box, and Word will add the necessary rule.

Creating Columns for Part of a Document

The column settings that you choose will extend by default from the current cursor position through the end of the document (or the end of the current section). But Word also makes it easy for you to vary the way columns are used in your document. You might want, for example, to open your document with a paragraph or two in single-column format and then break up the rest of the document into three columns, as shown in Figure 21-6.

> **Note**
>
> If you add one or more section breaks to your document, you'll find that This Section becomes one of your choices in the Apply To box in the Columns dialog box. It also becomes the default choice by Word as to where to apply the columns.

Chapter 21

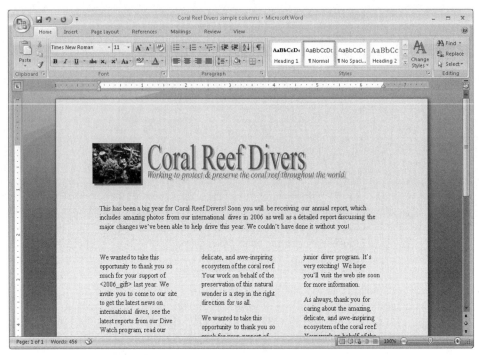

Figure 21-6 You can mix single-column and multicolumn formats in the same document.

To create a mixed format, follow these steps.

1. Type the opening paragraph, leaving the document set to single-column format.

2. Click to position the pointer where you want to create columns. Click the Page Layout tab and click Columns in the Page Setup group.

3. Click More Columns to display the Columns dialog box.

4. Choose the number of columns you want and enter any spacing specifications as needed.

5. Select the Line Between check box if you want a line to be displayed between columns.

6. Click the Apply To arrow and choose This Point Forward. Click OK. The Columns dialog box closes and you're returned to the document.

Creating Unequal Column Widths

Although Word sets a number of options for you in the Columns dialog box, you can change those options to create columns that suit your document specifications. By choosing the Left or Right preset format, you can tell Word to create columns of unequal width. When you choose the Left preset format, the column to the left will be smaller than the one to the right. When you choose the Right preset, the right column will be the smaller one.

To customize column widths using the Columns dialog box, follow these steps.

1. Choose Columns/More Columns in the Page Setup group of the Page Layout tab to display the Columns dialog box.

2. Click in the Number Of Columns box and type the number of columns you want to create.

3. Clear the check box to the left of Equal Column Width. The Width settings will become available so that you can customize the settings, as shown in Figure 21-7.

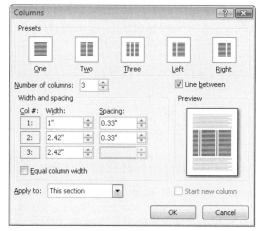

Figure 21-7 Use the Columns dialog box to specify the width and spacing for unequal columns.

4. Modify the Width and Spacing settings for your columns to get the effect you want. The Preview section shows the result of your choices.

5. Click OK to save your choices and return to the document.

Changing Column Width on the Ruler

You can also change the width of columns by dragging the column margins on the ruler at the top of your work area. If you want to keep the spacing the same between columns, position the pointer at the center of the spacing bar. When the pointer changes to a double-headed arrow, move the spacing bar in the direction you want to change the column. For example, to make the left column narrower, drag the spacing bar to the left. To make the left column wider, drag the spacing bar to the right. (See Figure 21-8.)

Chapter 21

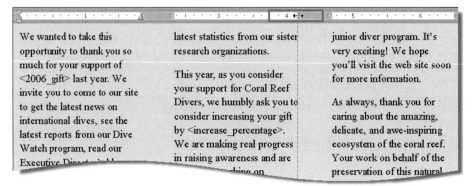

Figure 21-8 You can easily change the width of a column by dragging the spacing bar on the ruler.

You can also increase or decrease the amount of spacing between columns by dragging the edge of the spacing bar to the right or left. For example, to extend the spacing into the right column, drag the right edge of the spacing bar to the right. The size of the right column is reduced by the same amount of space you added to the spacing bar. Note that if Equal Column Widths is checked in the Columns dialog box, all columns will be resized when you click and drag one column edge.

INSIDE OUT   Using the ruler to meet precise column measurements

You can display and control accurate sizing of your columns when you're resizing them by using the ruler. Press and hold Alt while you drag the edge of the spacing bar in the ruler. The measurements of the column appear in the ruler, helping you know when the column you're working with is just the size you want.

Flowing Text into a Column Layout

Everything in Word should be as simple as putting text into a column layout. When you're turning a single-column document into a multiple-column document, Word does all the work for you. You simply display the Columns dialog box, choose the number of columns you want, specify any width and spacing settings, choose whether you want a line divider, and click OK. Word then formats the document as you selected, whether you already have a document full of text or an empty page.

If you're entering text into columns as you go, no text will appear in the second column until the first column has been filled. That is, if you intend to have only headings in the left column and flow your text into the right column of a two-column format, you'll need to fill the left column with line spaces between headings until you get to the end of the column and Word wraps back up to the top of the right column. In the example shown in Figure 21-9, you can see the paragraph marks showing the line spacing inserted to cause the text to flow to the next column.

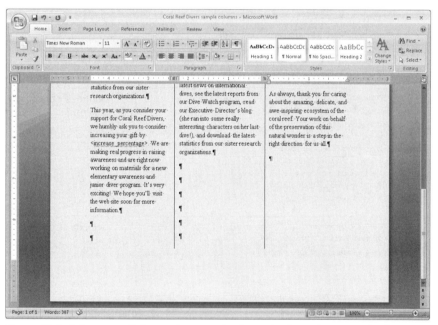

Figure 21-9 Before text will flow to the second column, the first column must be filled.

Note

There *is* a far more efficient way to do this, if your left column is going to be blank except for perhaps a heading at the top. When you know you've entered all you want in a column, you should add a column break instead of using empty paragraphs to achieve your desired results. You'll learn how to do this in the section titled "Inserting Column Breaks" later in this chapter.

Choosing Text Alignment

The way your text looks—and how readable your readers think it is—has a lot to do with the alignment you choose for the text. Traditional document alignment is often left-aligned, in which the text is aligned along the left margin of the page only. Other alignments include centered, which is often used for headings, and right-aligned, which aligns text along the right margin and is rarely used for traditional documents. Another alignment, fully-aligned text, aligns text along both the left and right margins, adding spaces between words to spread out the text enough to make the both-edge alignment possible. Table 21-2 gives you a look at alignment differences.

Table 21-2 Text Alignment Differences

Example	Alignment type	Usual Use
As always, thank you for caring about the amazing, delicate, and awe-inspiring ecosystem of the coral reef. Your work on behalf of the preservation of this natural wonder is a step in the right direction for us all.	Left	For traditional body text, headlines, captions, and more
As always, thank you for caring about the amazing, delicate, and awe-inspiring ecosystem of the coral reef. Your work on behalf of the preservation of this natural wonder is a step in the right direction for us all.	Centered	For headlines, special text effects, captions, callouts
As always, thank you for caring about the amazing, delicate, and awe-inspiring ecosystem of the coral reef. Your work on behalf of the preservation of this natural wonder is a step in the right direction for us all.	Right	For specialty text designs, table text, captions
As always, thank you for caring about the amazing, delicate, and awe-inspiring ecosystem of the coral reef. Your work on behalf of the preservation of this natural wonder is a step in the right direction for us all.	Full	For text in columns, some special text elements, quotations

Users often prefer left-aligned text for just about everything. However, some people like using fully aligned text for documents with multiple columns. In some cases, formats work well with the left column right-aligned, lining up along the leftmost edge of the right column, which is fully aligned.

Beginning a New Column Layout

Longer documents often require a number of different general layouts. For example, the introduction and summary of your report might read better in a single-column format. When you begin to talk about the specifications of your new product line however you might go to a multicolumn format that shows photos of your products on the left and descriptions on the right. You may also want to incorporate graphs and tables in the body of those columns.

How can you easily switch between column layouts without disturbing the way text flows in your document? The easiest way to change to a multicolumn format is to place the insertion point where you want to start the new column layout and then follow these steps.

1. Click the Page Layout tab and choose Columns in the Page Setup group.

2. Click the More Columns option in the Columns gallery.

3. In the Columns dialog box, select the number of columns you want to include and then add width and spacing settings, if necessary. Select the Line Between check box if you want a line separating the columns.

4. In the Apply To box, click the arrow and choose This Point Forward.

5. Select the Start New Column check box.

6. Click OK to return to the document. Word moves to the top of the next column, and your column settings are in effect.

Inserting Column Breaks

When you've entered everything you want in a specific column and you're ready to flow text to the next column, you can add a column break to force the flow. To add a column break, follow these steps.

1. Place the insertion point where you want to insert the column break.

2. Choose the Page Layout tab and click Breaks. The Breaks gallery appears, as shown in Figure 21-10.

Chapter 21

Figure 21-10 You can force a column break to begin entering text at the top of the next column.

3. In the Page Breaks section, click Column.

4. Click OK. You are returned to the document, and Word adds a Column break at the insertion point. The text in the column past that point will be wrapped to the top of the next column.

Removing Column Breaks

In Word, you can delete columns as easily as you add them. They can be removed simply by removing a character—just position the insertion point immediately following a break and press Backspace (or select the break itself and press Delete). The column break is removed and the text is flowed back into the previous column.

Working in Sections

Because Word includes features that give you a variety of formats and controls for long documents, you need a way to limit the changes made to individual portions of your document. That's what sections are all about. By using sections, you can control a change from a single-column format to multiple columns and back again. You can create layouts that look different on odd and even pages. You can modify the margins of a section and then revert to the regular document formatting when the section is completed.

Creating a Section

Starting a section is as easy as starting a column. You can begin a new section anywhere—in the middle of a page or at the beginning of a new one. To start a new section, follow these steps.

1. Place the insertion point where you want to start the new section.

2. Click the Page Layout tab and click Breaks. The Breaks gallery appears.

3. Click one of the section break types (further described in Table 21-3) and click OK. The section is created, and the text flows accordingly.

Chapter 21

Tip

If you prefer to use a dialog box to set up your sections, you can click the dialog launcher in the Page Setup group to display the Page Setup dialog box. Then click the Layout tab. The first group of settings on the Layout tab in the Page Setup dialog box deals with sections. You can choose Continuous, New Column, New Page, Even Page, or Odd Page in the Section Start list, just as you can in the Breaks gallery. As always, you can change any of your selections at any time, and making changes in the Breaks gallery later will carry through to the settings you entered in the Page Setup dialog box.

Table 21-3 **A Quick Look at Section Types**

Section type	Description	Use
Page	Inserts a page break at the cursor position and creates a new page	You want to begin a new page in the document
Column	Inserts a column break so the text at the cursor position is moved to the top of the new column	You want to control the placement of text among columns
Text Wrapping	Enables you to control text flow around objects in your document	You want to set off special text, titles, or captions
Next Page	Creates a new section at the top of the next page	You want to start a new section with different formatting specifications on the next page in the document
Continuous	Creates a new section beginning at the document insertion point	You want to begin a new section in the middle of the current page
Even Page	Creates a new section beginning on an even page; if the current page is an even page, an odd page is inserted and left blank	You want to create a new section with a format used uniquely for even pages
Odd Page	Creates a new section beginning on an odd page; if the current page is an odd page, an even page is inserted and left blank	You want to create a section for odd pages only

Removing Section Breaks

You can remove the section breaks in your Word document in the same way you delete column breaks—simply select them and press Delete. Once you delete a section break, the document settings that were in effect before the break are applied to that section.

You can display the formatting marks in your document by clicking the Home tab and clicking the Show/Hide button in the Paragraph group. The paragraph, spacing, and section markers are visible, as shown in Figure 21-11. Simply click the section break you want to delete and press the Delete key.

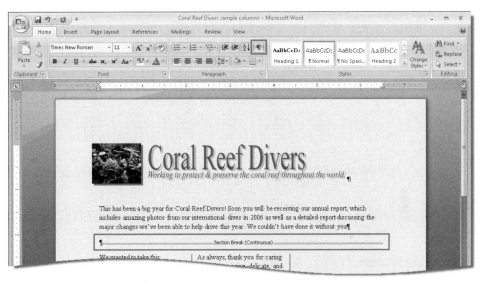

Figure 21-11 You can show formatting marks to see the section marker before you delete it.

Saving Formats as Your Own Templates

A reminder: Whenever you go to any significant trouble to create your own format, especially if there's a chance you'll use the format again, consider saving the format you've created as a template you can use again as the basis for other documents.

To create a template from a document you've made, follow these steps:

1. Click the Microsoft Office Button.
2. Point to Save As and click Word Template.
3. Type a name for the template in the File Name box.
4. Click Save to save the template file.

Using Line Numbers

Depending on the nature of your document, you may want to add line numbers to your document so that teammates who are reviewing the document—and perhaps discussing it in a teleconference call—can be sure they are all in the same place. Word gives you a number of options for displaying line numbers in your document.

Begin by clicking the Page Layout tab and choosing the Line Numbers button. A list of options is displayed, as you see in Figure 21-12.

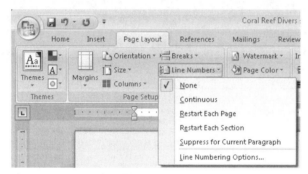

Figure 21-12 Word enables you to add line numbers to your long document for easy reference.

Choose Continuous if you want the line numbering to continue consecutively throughout your document. If you are more concerned with reviewing page by page or section by section, you may want to choose Restart Each Page or Restart Each Section, respectively. If you want to hide the numbering for the paragraph at the cursor position, click Suppress For Current Paragraph.

Display additional line numbering choices by clicking Line Numbering Options at the bottom of the Line Numbers list. The Page Setup dialog box appears, with the Layout tab selected. Click the Line Numbers button at the bottom of the dialog box to display the Line Numbers dialog box (see Figure 21-13).

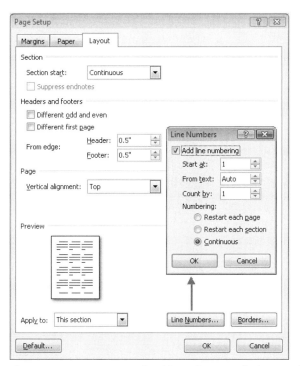

Figure 21-13 You can specify additional settings for line numbering in the Line Numbers dialog box.

In the Line Numbers dialog box, choose from the following settings:

- In the Start At box, enter the number you want to use to begin the numbering.

- In the From Text box, indicate the amount of space you want between the text margin and the line numbers.

- In the Count By box, choose the increment by which you want the line numbers to increase.

- In the Numbering area, choose whether you want to number lines continuously, restart with each page, or restart with each section. (These options are also available in the Line Numbers list on the Page Layout tab.)

Click OK to save your settings and then click OK again to close the Page Setup dialog box. The line numbers are added to your document.

Chapter 21

Deleting Line Numbers

You may want to use line numbering only when you are creating, reviewing, and editing your document. In that case, when you're getting close to final preparations for your document, you can remove line numbers by clicking the Page Layout tab and choosing Line Numbering in the Page Setup group. Choose None to remove the line numbers.

What's Next?

This chapter focused on various ways in which you might create and work with columns and sections in your long document. The next chapter shows you how to work with master documents and subdocuments to manage collaborative and complex projects.

Creating and Controlling Master Documents

In today's global workplace, being able to create collaborative documents is an impor-tant part of accomplishing everyday tasks. Just a few years ago, it would have been considered a rare thing to have one person doing a section of report at her desk in Germany, another checking the financial narrative by using his PDA at a sidewalk café in Singapore, and another designing the document template in a cubicle at an Indiana office building.

Today, flexibility and collaboration are two keys to an expanding, effective workforce. The master document feature in Microsoft Office Word 2007 enables you to maximize the benefits each of these keys can offer.

Particularly when you work on longer documents, consistency and continuity become important. You need to make sure that all the parts of your document use the same styles, treat tables and figures the same way, and have consistent headers and footers. You need to be able to check the overall organization of your document, making sure that the topics flow logically, and that you've arranged them in the best possible order.

This is fairly easy to do in a normal document when you're working with 10, 20, or even 30 pages. But what about those book-length projects for which various team members are taking a chapter or two, somebody else is plugging in the charts, and yet another person is checking the citations and references? It's in this type of situation that the master and subdocument features in Office Word 2007 really shine. By using these features, you can divide a large document into pieces—for example, giving a chapter to each team member—and then integrate them back into one piece; you can have both the benefit of working with a team to get a major project done and the confidence that the consistency and continuity of your document are intact.

When Master Documents Make Sense

At its most basic level, a master document holds several separate files together. You might create a master document to handle the following projects:

- A book-length manuscript in which each team member writes and edits one chapter.

- A grant proposal in which different committee members are responsible for different pieces (for example, your executive director is writing the executive summary, your financial officer is providing the budget, and your development committee chairperson is writing the objective and evaluation sections).

- Your international company's annual report, which is a compilation of a number of different sections, including the introduction, the program descriptions, the donor thank-you section, sections from each office site, and letters from clients served. Each person on your publications team could research and write a different piece of the report.

- A technical manual that's a collaborative effort between your IT department and a technical illustrator. After each chapter is written, you can send it as a subdocument to the illustrator, who can create and place the illustrations and then return the subdocument to be integrated into the master.

> **Master documents and subdocuments create a great opportunity for you to use Word's team review and collaboration features. For more about tracking, comparing, and integrating changes in a collaborative document, see Chapter 18, "Sharing Documents and Collaborating Online."**

No matter what type of project you're working on—whether you're working with a team or doing it all yourself—you can use master documents to complete the following tasks:

- Keep track of disparate sections and open and print them all rather than working with individual files

- Display and collapse subdocuments to switch between views easily

- Coordinate pieces of a project that are distributed to other team members

- Review and easily reorganize a long document

- Control styles, margins, and other formats throughout a long document

- Work with a long document as a whole for operations such as printing, checking spelling, and using the Find and Find And Replace features

Getting Started with a Master Document

In Chapter 10, "Outlining Documents for Clarity and Structure," you worked in Outline view to create, check, and change the basic organization of your document. The idea behind master documents builds on this basic philosophy and takes it to a more sophisticated level. By working with the big picture of your document, you can easily see how your sections or chapters compare, what needs to be moved, and which pieces you want to assign to other team members. The best place for this big picture approach is Outline view. That's where you'll do your work with master documents and subdocuments.

Displaying Master Document and Subdocument Tools

When you first change to Outline view, either by clicking the View tab and choosing Outline in the Document Views group or by clicking the Outline button in the view tools in the lower right corner of the Word window, Outline view appears (see Figure 22-1). The Master Document group contains the items you'll use to begin a master document. When you click Show Document, additional tools become available in the Master Document group (see Figure 22-2). Table 22-1 introduces you to the Master Document tools.

Facilities

- Each international office includes one full-time paid staff member, one part-time paid staff member, and at least three volunteers (who are recognized in various ways throughout the year). At the present time, we pay rent for facilities in only three countries; the rest of our sites are donated by partnering NGOs, benefactors, and universities.

Where in the World Are We?

- The following table shows you the full scope of services and programs Coral Reef Divers is now offering throughout the world. As you can see, we provide a variety of programs for people of all ages and experience levels.

	International Offices, San Diego, CA	Seas of the Middle East, Oman	Indian Ocean, Madagascar	East Asia, Thailand
Offices	3	2	1	2
Dive Training	Yes	Yes	Yes	Yes
Volunteers	Yes	Yes	Yes	Yes
Dive Watch	Yes	Yes	No	Yes
Eco-Friendly Tourism	Not Yet	Not Yet	Yes	Yes
School Presentations	Yes	No	No	Yes
Erosion Awareness	No	No	Yes	Yes

Figure 22-1 Start in Outline view when you want to create master documents and subdocuments.

Figure 22-2 When you click Show Document, additional tools become available.

Table 22-1 Master Document Tools

Tool	Description
Show Document	Switches the display to master document view so that you can see subdocument icons
Collapse Subdocuments	Limits the display of subdocument sections to their heading levels
Create	Creates a subdocument of the current selection
Insert	Inserts an existing document as a subdocument
Unlink	Removes the subdocument designation and returns the selection to being a normal part of the master document
Merge	Puts two or more selected subdocuments together
Split	Divides a subdocument into two subdocuments
Lock Document	Secures the subdocument so that no further changes can be made

What's in a Master Document?

Master documents can include text, graphics, charts—anything you put in your documents. One of the best things about working with master documents and subdocuments is the ability to build documents from segments and vice versa. Once you set up your master document to include subdocuments, you'll see a number of items in Outline view, as shown in Figure 22-3:

- **Subdocument icons** Once you create a subdocument from a selection in a document, Word displays the subdocument with an icon in outline form.

- **Document text** When the master document is fully expanded, you can see everything in your document, all the way to text level.

- **Subordinate headings** The subdocument headings enable you to see at a glance how your document is organized. You can also easily determine how to assign the various portions to other team members.

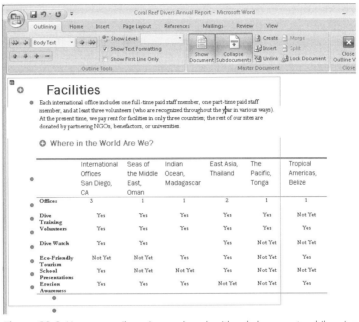

Figure 22-3 You can easily review and work with subdocuments while using Outline view.

Preparing Master Documents and Subdocuments

You can see the benefits of working with master documents and subdocuments—especially if you're managing a large project. As with anything else that requires the cooperation of a number of people, it's best to start with a plan. Take some time to consider all the different aspects of your document and plan the types of assignments you want to make before you get started. Be sure to create a table or listing of various assignments that will enable you to track the different parts of your document.

> **Tip**
>
> You might want to use the Table Of Contents (TOC) feature to automatically generate a table of contents that you can use as an assignment list. If you have a large project with many different pieces (and as many team members), you'll need to track the list so that you know who has which piece. For more about using the TOC feature, see Chapter 24, "Generating First-Class Tables of Contents and Reference Tables."

Creating a Master Document

You have two different options for creating a master document—and both procedures are simple ones:

- You can start with an existing document and turn it into a master document by creating subdocuments within it.

- You can create a master document from scratch, creating the outline headings and subdocuments as you go.

Starting with an Existing Document

If you have a document you want to use as a master document, start by opening the file you want to use. Click the Microsoft Office Button, click Open, navigate to and select the file you want, and then click Open. Change to Outline view by clicking the Outline view button in the lower right corner of the Word window. The document appears in Outline view, as shown in Figure 22-4.

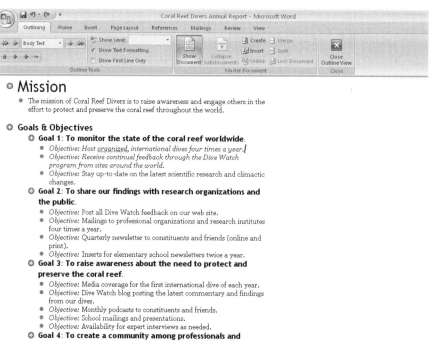

Figure 22-4 Outline view enables you to see easily the sections you want to mark as subdocuments.

The heading styles you've assigned to the text in your document become the headings in the master document outline. You divide the master by selecting the portion you want to mark as a subdocument; Word inserts a link in place of the actual text in the master and then saves the text as a subdocument. In the section titled "Creating

Subdocuments," later in this chapter, you'll learn how to select sections and create the subdocuments you need.

TROUBLESHOOTING

My document headings don't appear in Outline View

When you change to Outline View, you might find that your headings don't look like headings anymore. If you created your own styles and didn't base them on the Heading 1 or Heading 2 styles in Word, or you simply entered the headings using the Normal style, Word won't recognize your headings.

To fix this easily, click the Promote button in the Outline Tools group to raise the text to Level 1, which also assigns the Heading 1 style. You can easily modify your custom styles and base them on the Heading 1 style so that you can get the look you want and still be able to work with Outline vView and Master Documents mode. For more on setting up and working with styles, see Chapter 15, "Using Styles to Increase Your Formatting Power."

Starting from Scratch

You can create a master document right from the beginning of your project. Once you have a concept and thoughts for a beginning outline, you can create the outline in Outline View and then make the assignments for your subdocuments as needed. Here are the steps for starting a new master document from scratch:

1. Start a new document and then change to Outline view by clicking the Outline tool in the lower right portion of your Word window.

2. Enter the headings for the document title and subdocument titles. Word automatically creates the headings with the default style Heading 1. Make sure each heading you intend to turn into a subdocument is assigned the Heading 1 style. This is the style Word will use in dividing the master document into subdocuments.

Chapter 22

Tip

If you think you might like to keep a copy of your outline before it's been divided into subdocuments, click the Microsoft Office Button and choose Save As to save a backup copy of the outline file. Although you can easily remove subdocument divisions and integrate subdocuments into the master later, that's a big hassle if you simply want an original version of the outline to work with.

3. Enter the headings and assign them the heading levels you want by using Outline Tools on the Outlining tab.

4. When you have your outline the way you want it, save the file, type a name for the file, and then clicking Save.

Creating Subdocuments

Once you have the basic outline in place, you can determine how you want to divide the master document. Create a subdocument by following these steps:

1. First, make sure that all headings and subheadings you want to include in the subdocument are displayed. Click the Show Level drop-down arrow in the Outline Tools group on the Outlining tab and select All Levels.

2. Click the symbol to the left of the heading for the text you want to use for the subdocument. For example, if you want to create a subdocument out of the "Goals & Objectives" section in Figure 22-5, click the plus (+) symbol, and the entire topic is selected.

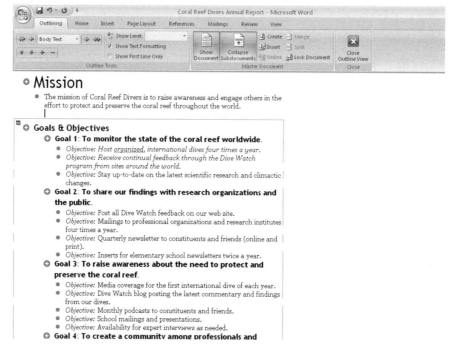

Figure 22-5 Be sure to display and select all text you want to include in your subdocument before clicking the Create Subdocument button.

3. Click Create in the Master Document group. The topic is marked as a subdocument, as Figure 22-6 shows.

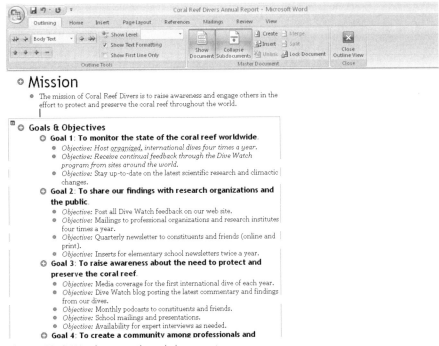

Figure 22-6 Word creates the subdocument.

4. Save the document. Word saves the subdocument as a separate file in the same folder by default but you can change this. The Heading 1 text at the beginning of the file is used as the file name.

Importing Data for Subdocuments

You can also create subdocuments by inserting other files into your master document. In this case, you might have a partial outline you're working with, or you might start a new file for your master and then open existing files into it. Regardless of how you get the document pieces together, begin with your master document open on the screen. Display the document in Outline view. Place the insertion point where you want to add the subdocument and then click Insert in the Master Document group. This opens the Insert Subdocument dialog box, shown in Figure 22-7.

Navigate to the file you want to import, select it, and then click Open. The subdocument is added to the master document at the insertion point. Add or create other subdocuments as needed. When you're finished creating subdocuments, save the file. Word saves the master document and the subdocuments in the folder you specify.

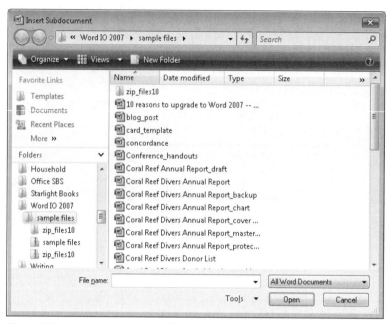

Figure 22-7 Importing an existing file into a master document to use as a subdocument saves you data entry and organizing time.

Navigating to and from the Master Document

The basic idea behind master documents is that you can have one large file in which all pieces are represented, but for convenience and expediency's sake, each of the pieces can be worked on by different people at the same time. As you begin to work with and edit the text of your document, you'll need to know how to navigate among the files to make the changes you want to make.

Working with the Master Document

After you create a master document and subdocuments within it, Word changes the way it saves the file information. No longer is everything stored within the single document. Now the master document contains links to the subdocuments, and when you expand and work with the subdocuments within the master, you are really, through links, working in the individual subdocument files themselves.

After you save and close your master document, reopen it and notice the change. As Figure 22-8 shows, the "Goals & Objectives" section saved as a subdocument now appears as a link in the master document.

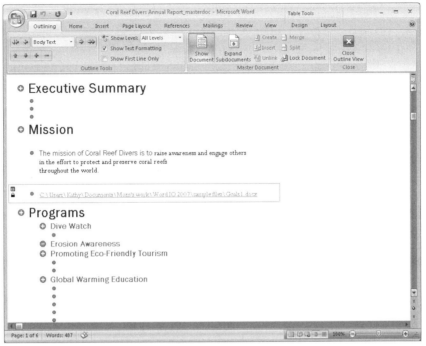

Figure 22-8 After you save, close, and then reopen the master document, Word displays links to the subdocuments in place of the subdocument text.

Following Links to Subdocuments

To move to the subdocument, simply press Ctrl and click the link. The subdocument file opens in a new Word window on your screen. You can now edit the file as needed.

TROUBLESHOOTING

Word can't find my subdocument files

If you later reorganize your files and move subdocuments from one place to another—even if you are moving them within the same directory to new subfolders—Word will display the message "cannot open the specified file." To re-establish links between your master document and subdocuments, first delete the broken subdocument link and then use Insert in the Master Document group on the Outlining tab to relink the document from its new location.

Expanding and Collapsing Subdocuments

You can collapse an outline in order to move and reorganize the document easily. As you learned when working in Outline view, however, you can collapse and expand only text that's been formatted with the built-in heading styles or preset outline levels. To expand and display the subdocuments in the master document, begin by clicking at the beginning of the document. (Change to Outline view, if necessary.) Click Expand Subdocuments in the Master Document group on the Outlining tab. All subdocuments in your master document are displayed. The subdocument icon and any subordinate text and graphics also appear.

> **Tip**
>
> When you expand subdocuments in the master document, you can change to Print Layout view to see how the sections will look in print form. You can make formatting changes, check spelling, and use Find and Replace to your heart's content while you're in Print Layout view so that you can see how the format is affected. Then return to Outline view to finish working with the master document and to move sections, if needed.

Once you've expanded the subdocuments in the master, the Expand Subdocuments button changes to Collapse Subdocuments so that you can again suppress the display of the subdocuments. You'll want to do this before you reorder subdocuments in your master document. To collapse the master display, click anywhere in the document and select Collapse Subdocuments. The master goes back to its links-only display.

> **Note**
>
> If you want to collapse only the heading levels within a subdocument, use the normal Collapse button on the Outline Tools command tab of the Outlining tab to control that display.

Editing Master Documents and Subdocuments

Master documents and subdocuments are two different kinds of files, each storing different things, so you'll make different editing changes in each of them. Table 22-2 gives you an idea of the editing tasks you'll want to perform in each of the document types.

Table 22-2 Editing Master Documents and Subdocuments

Editing Task	Master Document	Subdocument
Text editing and correction	X	X
Applying heading levels	X	
Changing topic order	X	
Checking spelling	X	
Global formatting	X	
Local formatting of individual elements	X	X
Changing margins and page setup	X	
Adding headers and footers	X	
Adding borders and shading to specific objects		X
Adding new content to specific sections	X	

Making Master Changes

The types of changes you'll make to your master document include those that will affect the entire publication. For example, you'll add styles to a template in the master document so that all the styles can be consistent among the various pieces of the publication. You'll also change margins, specify column settings, and do things like run the spelling checker and print while you have everything together in your master document.

You'll also add headers and footers to your master document so that you can ensure consistent treatment throughout all your subdocuments. If you leave it up to the various team members to add headers and footers and change global formatting settings in their own subdocuments, those changes will be overridden when the subdocument is merged into the master document.

Entering Subdocument Changes

The most basic changes will have to happen in the subdocuments, especially if you are assigning subdocuments to different team members to write, edit, proofread, and review. Line-by-line editing, word choice, and object work (such as the addition of tables, graphics, and text boxes) all are best done in the subdocument file.

Each person working on a subdocument can make changes as needed and then save the file . When the master document is opened and the document is expanded, all changes made in the various subdocuments will be reflected in the master. The person working with the master can then change global formatting options, check spelling, add headers and footers, and print the document as needed.

TROUBLESHOOTING

Different styles appear in the master document and subdocuments

If you notice that the headings in your master document and subdocuments look differ-ent, check the template you've applied to the documents. To do this, click the Microsoft Office Button. Then choose Word Options and click Add-Ins. Click the Manage arrow and choose Templates from the list that appears. Then click Go. The Templates And Add-Ins dialog box appears. In the Document Template section, review each file to make sure that both the master and the subdocument have the same template selected and that the Automatically Update Document Styles check box is selected. If necessary, attach a different template by clicking Attach and, in the Attach Template dialog box, navigating to the template file you want. Make your selection and click Open. Then click OK to close the Templates And Add-Ins dialog box and return to the document.

Locking Subdocuments

Word provides a subdocument locking feature that enables you to protect documents so that no further changes can be made to them. This is particularly helpful if you're working as part of a team and want to make sure another team member doesn't modify a file after it's been finalized.

To lock a subdocument, simply click the subdocument icon and click Lock Document in the Master Document group. A small lock symbol appears beneath the subdocument icon to the left of the subdocument text, as shown in Figure 22-9.

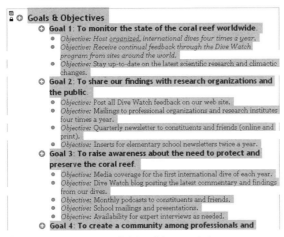

Figure 22-9 Once you finish editing a subdocument, you can lock it against further changes by clicking Lock Document in the Master Document group.

Rearranging a Master Document

One of the greatest benefits of working in a master document is the ease with which you can rearrange subdocuments. Start by opening your master document and reviewing the order of the listed subdocuments. Click Expand Subdocuments to show all the headings and text of the subdocuments within the master. Review the selected section and make sure you've selected the information you want to move; then click the Collapse Subdocuments to return the subdocument to the link that represents it.

Click and drag the subdocument to the new location. A heavy indicator line moves with the pointer, showing you the placement of the subdocument.

When the indicator line is positioned where you want to insert the subdocument, release the mouse button. The subdocument is then moved to that position.

> **Tip**
>
> Be sure to place the indicator line outside another subdocument boundary before you release the mouse button. Otherwise, Word will create a "nested" subdocument, placing the subdocument you just moved inside another subdocument. If this was not your intention, drag the subdocument icon to a new location outside an existing subdocument area or press Ctrl+Z to undo your action and start again. For best results when moving subdocuments, work in Collapsed mode.

> **Tip**
>
> You can select multiple subdocuments by pressing and holding Shift while clicking the subdocument icons if they are contiguous. If you want to select noncontiguous subdocuments, press and hold Ctrl while selecting the subdocuments you want to move.

Merging Subdocuments

Although splitting documents into subdocuments for organizing, editing, and enhancement purposes is a useful function, sometimes you want to combine subdocuments after you've worked with them independently. To merge two subdocuments, follow these steps:

1. Open the master document with links to the subdocument files.

2. Click Expand Subdocuments to display the contents of the subdocument files.

3. Make sure that the subdocuments you want to combine are next to one another. Rearrange the subdocuments if necessary.

4. Select both subdocuments by clicking their subdocument icons. (Press and hold Shift while you select the second subdocument.)

5. Click Merge in the Master Document group. The second subdocument is combined with the first.

> **Note**
>
> When Word combines subdocuments, the first file "takes on" the new data, and everything is saved into that file.

Separating Subdocuments

If you create a new topic or want to divide a subdocument into two, simply create a new heading at the point where you want to make the break (or raise an existing heading to a Heading 1 level) and then click Split in the Master Document group of the Outlining tab. The subdocument is divided at the insertion point.

Converting Subdocuments

Depending on the nature of the document you're creating, you might want to convert all the subdocuments back to a single document. This is an easy process. Start with the master document open and display the document in Outline view. Select the first sub-document you want to convert and then press and hold Shift while clicking subsequent subdocuments.

When you've selected all the subdocuments you want to convert, click Unlink in the Master Document group of the Outlining tab. The subdocument icons and boundaries are removed, and the subdocuments become part of the master document—once again, you have a single document. Save your file by clicking the Microsoft Office Button and choosing Save, or by pressing Ctrl+S.

Printing a Master Document

When you're ready to print your master document, begin by opening the master document and expanding the document display to the level you want to print. First click Expand Subdocuments in the Master Document group of the Outlining tab to show the headings of all subdocuments. Then use the Expand tool in Outline Tools to expand the text level as desired. Finally, change to Print Layout view by clicking Print Layout in the View tools in the lower right corner of the Word window.

Click the Microsoft Office Button and choose Print, select any necessary print options, and then click Print. The entire master document, including the subdocument text, is printed.

> **Tip**
>
> Take a look at the document as it will appear in print by clicking the Microsoft Office Button and pointing to Print. In the Print submenu, choose Print Preview. You can select Two Pages view if you want to page quickly through the document to get a sense of the overall look applied to the combined subdocuments in the master document. Click Close Print Preview to return to the Print Layout view and make any necessary changes before printing.

Chapter 22

TROUBLESHOOTING

The master document is incomplete when printed

If you find that some sections are missing when you print your master document, return to Outline view and scroll through the document to make sure all sections have been expanded. Anything left collapsed will not be printed, so make sure that you expand the entire document, if that's your intention, before choosing Print.

Managing Master Documents

As you can see, working with master documents and subdocuments is a great way to manage complex files of any size, but especially large ones. The only downside to master documents is the sometimes complicated task of keeping your files straight. Some procedures you take for granted with ordinary files—such as saving, opening, renaming, and moving—take a little more thought when it comes to working with master documents. Here are some tips for managing your master documents.

Saving Subdocument Files

Word saves the master document and all subdocuments when you click the Microsoft Office Button and choose Save or press Ctrl+S. The master document is saved under the name you entered the first time you saved the file, and Word names all the subdocuments automatically, using the first words of the first heading as the file name. If you have several headings with the same title, Word adds numbers to the file names, such as "Lesson Plan1," "Lesson Plan2," and so on.

If you want to save a master document to a new location, click the Microsoft Office Button and click Save As. Remember to create a new folder for the new master document and files. Then you'll need to select each subdocument and use Save As to save it to the new folder. Otherwise, the next time you open your master document, you'll see an error message telling you that the subdocument cannot be found. Click Close to save the file and return to the document.

Renaming Subdocuments

If you want to rename a subdocument, start in the master document and select the subdocument you want to rename. Click the Microsoft Office Button and click Save As. When the Save As dialog box appears, enter the new name for the file and then click Save. Because you renamed the subdocument file from within the master document, the link will be updated and preserved within the master document.

Selecting Subdocuments

One of the tricks to accurately dividing a document into subdocuments is displaying and selecting the text you want to include. Make sure that you expand the selection fully and review it before clicking Create; otherwise, Word might not include all the text you want in the new subdocument.

> **Note**
>
> If you don't get the whole subdocument the first time, click Unlink to merge the text back into the master document. Then select all the text for the subdocument and click Create.

What's Next?

This chapter showed you how to divide master documents into subdocuments and manage the subdocuments you create, an important feature when you are working collaboratively and need to be able to assign parts of your document to various team members. The next chapter continues the discussion of complex documents by showing you how to create a table of contents for your long documents.

Chapter 22

When you use a variety of sources to prepare a complex document, compiling, organizing, and adding all the references can be a big job. You have magazines and books piled high on your desk, report pages are folded open so you can type in the quotations you want to include, and which citation style is the right one to use? It's hard to remember if you don't create these kinds of documents very often.

Luckily, Microsoft Office Word 2007 includes a number of flexible reference features that help you cut down on the amount of time and effort you'll invest in adding reference notes to your document. When you add citations from books, articles, reports, presentations, or online sources, Source Manager in Office Word 2007 helps you enter and organize the citations you need so that they appear consistently—in the style you want—throughout your document. Additionally, adding footnotes, endnotes, and cross-references is much easier with the help of the groups on the References tab. This chapter shows you how to use the Word 2007 referencing features to add accurate references that are easy to update in a variety of ways.

> **Note**
>
> This chapter shows you how to insert reference items in your document. See Chapter 24, "Generating First-Class Tables of Contents and Reference Tables," for details on using the references you mark to compile tables.

References in Word 2007

The References tab in the Word 2007 Ribbon conveniently brings together all the commands you need to add footnotes, citations, and more to your document. The References tab, shown in Figure 23-1, includes the following groups:

Figure 23-1 The References tab includes all the tools you need to add and manage references in your document.

The Table of Contents group includes the commands you'll use to mark items in the document as entries for your table of contents, as well as compile and insert a table based on those entries and update the table after you change it.

- The Footnotes group enables you to insert footnotes and endnotes in your document. Additionally, you can hide the notes from view if you choose.

- The Citations & Bibliography group enables you to select a style to be used in the current document, add citations, select a bibliography style, and manage the sources you've used in the document.

- The Captions group enables you to add captions to diagrams and illustrations in your document. You can also create and update a table of figures and add cross-references to give your readers additional resources to refer to.

- The Index group includes everything you need to mark index entries and compile and update the index.

- The Table of Authorities includes the commands for marking legal cases and statutes within a document. After you mark the citations, you can insert and update a table of authorities to display all the authorities references in the document.

In addition to using the References tab to easily insert references, you can also apply styles to the citations, footnotes, and references so they appear in the format you want. The Bibliography command in the Citations & Bibliography group includes a gallery of styles you can apply to the bibliography you create.

Know Your References

Here's a quick list of the various items you can create using the commands on the References tab:

- **Footnotes** You add, edit, and manage footnotes by using the Footnotes group. A footnote is a note displayed at the bottom of the printed or displayed page that adds to the information in the text. For example, you might add a footnote citing a resource for a quotation or providing some background information about a statistic you've included.

- **Endnotes** You add an endnote by clicking Insert Endnote in the Footnotes group. An endnote is a note placed at the end of a chapter, article, report, or essay. Similar to a footnote, the item might provide additional information, a resource citation, or a Web link for further study.

- **Citations** You use the Citations & Bibliography group when you want to refer to print or electronic documents as sources in your work. A citation is typically a quoted or referenced selection from a source and it may or may not reference specific page ranges. When you use Insert Citation to create a reference, Word enables you to choose from a source list you've already created. This helps you keep references consistent throughout the document and add them easily to your document as you write.

- **Sources** A source can be almost anything--book, article, conference presentation, Web site, audio recording, TV show or report --that you are using as a source of information for the document you are creating. You add and manage your sources by clicking Manage Sources in the Citations & Bibliography group.

- **Bibliography** After you have inserted all the references you need in your document, you can easily create a bibliography by choosing Bibliography in the Citations & Bibliography group. A bibliography provides a listing of all cited sources. (For more information, see the section titled "Generating a Bibliography" later in this chapter, on page 640.)

Other items on the References tab are beyond the scope of this chapter. See Chapter 24, "Generating First-Class Tables of Contents and Reference Tables," for details about creating a table of contents; Chapter 25, "Creating Effective Indexes," for indexing; and Chapter 13, "Adding Visual Impact with Pictures, Drawings, and WordArt," to learn about adding captions to the pictures and diagrams in your document.

Referencing in Style

One of the first choices you'll make as you prepare to add references to your document involves selecting the bibliography style you want to use. The bibliography style controls the way in which citations are listed (for example, name first or title first) and which information items are included in the reference.

To choose the style for your document, follow these steps:

1. Click the References tab.

2. Click the arrow in the Style setting in the Citations & Bibliography group. A list of styles appears, as shown in Figure 23-2.

Figure 23-2 Choose a bibliography style to determine the way in which your references will be displayed.

3. Select the style you want to use. The most common styles are APA, Chicago, and MLA. The Turabian style is often used in academic settings.

When you add sources to your document, the style you select determines the types of information you enter for each source. You'll learn more about this in the next section.

Adding and Managing Sources

To add a source, follow these steps:

1. Click the References tab and select Manage Sources in the Citations & Bibliography group.

2. In the Source Manager dialog box, click New.

3. In the Create Source dialog box, click the Type Of Source arrow and choose the type of item you're referencing (see Figure 23-3). The fields shown in the dialog box may change depending on the type of item you select. For example, when you choose Article In A Periodical, Periodical Title, Month, Day, and Pages fields are added to the list.

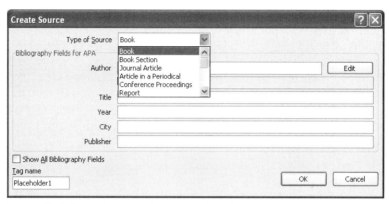

Figure 23-3 Select the type of source you're referencing.

3.   Notice that the style you selected is shown above the reference fields. For example, in Figure 23-4, APA is the selected style, and Article In A Periodical is the type of source. Click in a field and type your information. Press Tab to move to the next field.

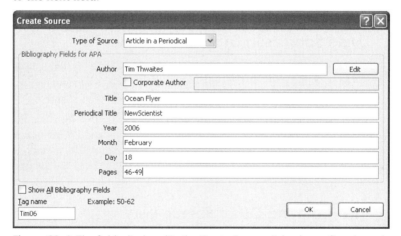

Figure 23-4 The fields displayed in the Create Source dialog box reflect the style selected and the type of source.

4.   Click OK to save the source information. The Create Source dialog box closes, and the item is displayed in both the Master List and the Current List in the Source Manager, as shown in Figure 23-5.

Chapter 23

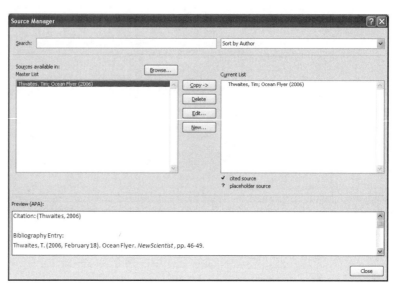

Figure 23-5 The new source is added to the Source Manager dialog box.

Using Sources in Other Documents

The sources you added to the Source Manager will be available to other documents you create in Word 2007. Whenever you click the References tab and select Manage Sources, you will see all the sources you compiled in the Master List in the Source Manager.

To add sources from the Master List to the Current List for the document, display the Source Manager, click the source you want to use, and click Copy. Add the sources you want to the Current List and click Close to close the Source Manager. Those sources will now be available when you choose Insert Citation from the Citations & Bibliography group.

Incorporating Other Source Lists

If you are collaborating on a document, you may need to share your resources with others—or work with the sources others have compiled. You can add other source lists to your Master List by following these steps:

1. Display the Source Manager by clicking the References tab and clicking Manage Sources.

2. In the Source Manager, click Browse.

3. The Open Source List dialog box appears, with the Bibliography folder selected. If necessary, navigate to the folder containing the source list you want to add to the current document.

4. Select the file and click OK to add the sources to the Master List.

Inserting a Citation

Now that you've selected the style and added the sources you will be referencing in your document, inserting a citation is simple:

1. Click where you want to add the citation.

2. Click the References tab and click Insert Citation in the Citations & Bibliography group.

3. A list of available sources appears, as shown in Figure 23-6. Click the source you want to add. The reference is inserted at the cursor position.

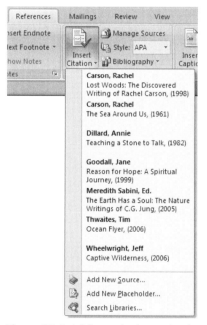

Figure 23-6 Adding a citation to the document is as simple clicking Insert Citation.

Editing a Citation

After you insert a citation, you may decide that you want to change the way the item is referenced or modify the information in the citation. To edit the citation, right-click it and choose Edit Citation. The small Edit Citation dialog box appears, Here you can enter different values for the citation fields or suppress their display (see Figure 23-7). Type the new information and click OK to save your changes.

> **Note**
>
> If you are working with Track Changes on, right-clicking displays the Accept/Reject Changes options. If you are using Track Changes and want to edit a citation, click the arrow on the bounding box around the citation to open the correct menu.

"That is part of the fascination of the ocean. But most of all, the sea is a place of mystery. One by one, the mysteries of yesterday have been solved. But the solution seems always to bring with it another, perhaps a deeper mystery. I doubt that the last, final mysteries of the sea will ever be resolved. In fact, I cherish a very unscientific hope that they will not be." (Carson, Lost Woods: The Discovered Writing of Rachel Carson, 1998)

Figure 23-7 You can edit citations by right-clicking them in the document and changing values in the Edit Citation dialog box.

Modifying Sources

When you need to change information in the source reference itself, right-click the citation in the document and choose Edit Source. (If Track Changes is enabled, click the arrow that appears when you point to the citation to display your options.) In the Edit Source dialog box, make the necessary changes and click OK to save the edits. The citations in the document are changed to reflect the modifications.

Adding a Placeholder

If you are working on the draft of your document and find that you don't have all the sources you need, don't worry—you can insert placeholders for the citations and then add the data when you have it. For example, suppose that you are writing an article for your organization's newsletter and want to reference a research study on volunteers and Internet use that you recently read in a professional journal. Instead of interrupting your writing and looking for the source, you can insert a placeholder where you want to incorporate the information. Here's how:

1.   Click where you want to add the placeholder.

2.   Click the References tab.

3. Click the Insert Citation arrow and choose Add A New Placeholder. The Placeholder Name dialog box appears so that you can enter a name for the placeholder. Type the name and click OK.

> **Tip**
>
> When you're entering a placeholder name, use only letters, numbers, and the underscore character. Punctuation and spaces aren't accepted in placeholder names.

Replacing Placeholder Information

When you're ready to replace the placeholder information with real citation data, begin by clicking the References tab. Click Manage Sources to display the Source Manager dialog box. In the Current List, placeholders are preceded by a question mark. Click the placeholder you want to change and click the Edit button. The Edit Source dialog box appears, as shown in Figure 23-8.

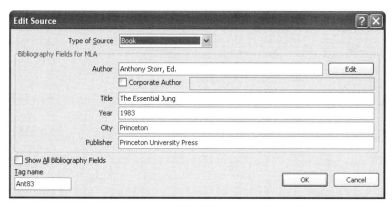

Figure 23-8 Replace placeholder information with citation data by using the Edit Source dialog box.

Enter the citation information in the Edit Source dialog box and click OK to save your changes. The citation is automatically updated in the document, and the source is added to the Master List in the Source Manager.

> **Note**
>
> You can change the style used to display the resources in your document at any time. Simply click the Bibliography Style arrow in the Citations & Bibliography group, and choose the new style. Both the citation references and the bibliography are changed in your document.

Generating a Bibliography

A good bibliography is a great service, providing your readers with full references they can use to find more information on the topics introduced in your document. After you add citations to your document, you can easily create a professional bibliography by using the Bibliography command in the Citations & Bibliography group.

Begin by positioning the cursor at the point in the document where you want to insert the bibliography. Then click the Bibliography command. A gallery of bibliography styles opens, offering you the option of creating a bibliography or a works cited list (see Figure 23-9). Click the style you want or click Insert Bibliography. The bibliography is then inserted in your document.

Figure 23-9 Choose a bibliography or a works cited list, or choose to insert a bibliography without a heading.

You can also create and save your own style of bibliography to the Bibliography gallery. Create a listing of sources and add the heading you want to use. Then select the list and heading and click Bibliography in the Citations & Bibliography group. In the Bibliography gallery, click Save Selection To Bibliography Gallery. The next time you open the gallery to display bibliography options, your new style will appear.

Adding Footnotes and Endnotes

Another way of referring to sources in your documents involves adding footnotes and endnotes. In some views, footnotes appear in an area at the bottom of your page, with a separator line and a note reference mark to identify the note. (See Figure 23-10 for an example.) A matching note reference mark appears in the text at the place you create the footnote. By default, the reference marks are numbers, but you can change the referencing style to letters, symbols, or other characters of your choosing.

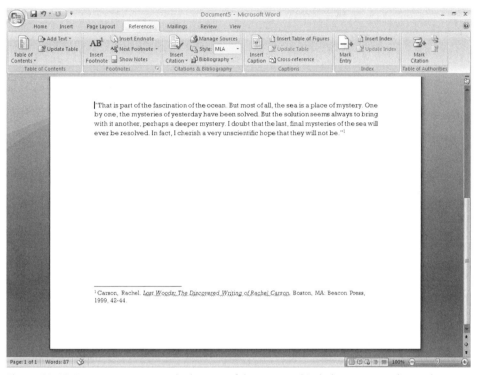

Figure 23-10 Footnotes appear at the bottom of the page and include a separator line and a note reference mark.

Endnotes are similar to footnotes, except they're placed at the end of a document. Only one separator line separates the text and the endnotes.

> **Note**
>
> You can enter footnotes of any length, but because the notes are displayed in a small typeface, and they take up room on the document page, it's best to use endnotes when you want to include notes with a lot of commentary.

Inserting Footnotes and Endnotes

When you're ready to insert a footnote or endnote in your document, follow these steps:

1. Click where you want to add the footnote or endnote.

2. Click the References tab.

Chapter 23

3. In the Footnotes group, click either the Insert Footnote or Insert Endnote command. The reference marker is added (to the bottom of the current page, for a footnote, or on the last page of the document, for an endnote). Default values are used to determine the reference marker, the format, and the numbering sequence of the notes.

4. Type the text for the note. Save your document by pressing Ctrl+S after you have added the notes.

Customizing Footnotes and Endnotes

You can modify a number of footnote and endnote settings to customize the way the notes appear. For example, you might want to use letters instead of numbers as the reference marks; or perhaps you would like to insert a symbol to indicate a footnote or endnote instead of using traditional numbers or letters.

Another change you might want to make involves the sequencing of the notes. If you are working on a collaborative document and have divided a master document into subdocuments for assignment to different team members, you might want to start the footnote numbering at a number other than 1. You can do this by changing the Start At value in the Footnote And Endnote dialog box (see Figure 23-11).

Figure 23-11 The Footnote And Endnote dialog box enables you to customize the default settings for footnotes and endnotes.

Display the Footnote And Endnote dialog box by clicking the dialog launcher (the small arrow) in the lower right corner of the Footnotes group on the References tab. Then follow these steps to customize the default settings:

1. In the Location section of the Footnote And Endnote dialog box, click either the Footnotes or Endnotes option.

2. In the Format section, click the Number Format arrow and then choose the numbering scheme you want to use for the note reference marks that identify your footnotes or endnotes (depending on which item you selected). You'll find all the traditional choices—numeric, alphabetic, and roman numerals—plus something different: a collection of special symbols. You can choose your own special symbol by clicking Symbol and choosing the symbol you want to use from the displayed gallery in the Symbol dialog box.

3. If you want to start the footnote or endnote with a number other than 1, click in the Start At box and then type the number you want.

4. To indicate that you want footnote and endnote numbering to restart at the beginning of each new section, choose Restart Each Section in the Numbering box.

5. Finally, if you have divided your document into sections, you can change the default value in the Apply Changes option. Click the arrow to display your choices—you can leave the default setting of Whole Document or choose This Setting.

6. Click Insert to add the note with your customized settings.

Viewing and Editing Footnotes and Endnotes

You can view your footnotes and endnotes in every view Word 2007 offers. Some views give you a more complete look than others, but in every view you can get to the information you need about the references in your document.

When you add a footnote or endnote to your document, a small reference mark is inserted in the text to let your readers know that more information is provided elsewhere—either at the bottom of the page or the end of the document.

Word 2007 includes five different views: Print Layout, Full Screen Reading, Web Layout, Outline, and Draft views. In each of the views, you can review a footnote or endnote by positioning the cursor over the reference mark in the text. A small ScreenTip appears, displaying the note in its entirety (see Figure 23-12).

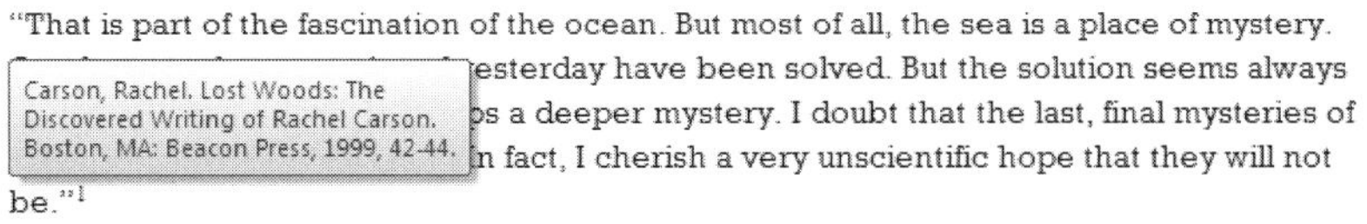

"That is part of the fascination of the ocean. But most of all, the sea is a place of mystery.

> Carson, Rachel. Lost Woods: The
> Discovered Writing of Rachel Carson.
> Boston, MA: Beacon Press, 1999, 42-44.

esterday have been solved. But the solution seems always ps a deeper mystery. I doubt that the last, final mysteries of n fact, I cherish a very unscientific hope that they will not be."[1]

Figure 23-12 A ScreenTip displays the footnote or endnote when you position the pointer over the reference marker.

The complete footnote and endnote references—the notes that appear at the bottom of the page or the end of the document, respectively—footnotes are visible only in Print Layout and Full Screen Reading view by default. If you want to display and perhaps edit a footnote while working in Web Layout, Outline, or Draft view, simply double-click the

Chapter 23

reference marker. This opens the Footnotes pane at the bottom of the Word window (see Figure 23-13).

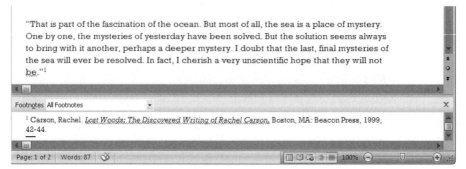

Figure 23-13 When you're working in Web Layout, Outline, or Draft view, you can view footnotes in a pane at the bottom of the Word window.

You can modify the footnotes or endnotes by clicking in the note and making any necessary text and formatting changes. When you're finished, press Ctrl+S to save the document and click the Footnotes pane close box in the top right corner of the pane.

TROUBLESHOOTING

My footnotes disappear on my Web page

If you created a document, complete with footnotes and endnotes, and then saved it as a Web page, your footnotes haven't disappeared completely—they've simply been moved to the end of the Web document. The footnote reference marks are turned into hyperlinks so that you can access the footnotes easily from within the page. Just click the hyperlinked reference mark, and you'll move directly to the footnote. To return to the previous page, click your browser's Back button.

Moving Footnotes and Endnotes

If you want to move a footnote or endnote from one position to another, select and drag the footnote or endnote marker in the text to the new location. If you want to move the mark to a location that's too far away to drag, you can cut and paste the mark by using Ctrl+X to cut and Ctrl+V to paste.

Note

If the position to which you move the footnote precedes another footnote, Word changes the numbering automatically.

Copying Footnotes and Endnotes

If you have a footnote or endnote you plan to use more than once, you can copy a note reference mark instead of typing a duplicate entry. Simply select the note reference mark and then press and hold Ctrl while dragging the mark to the new place in the document.

Deleting Footnotes and Endnotes

When you want to remove a footnote or endnote from your document, go to the place in the document where the note reference mark appears and delete it. Simply removing the text in the Footnotes or Endnotes pane doesn't remove the note itself—Word will still keep the note reference mark in place and reserve the space at the bottom or end of your document for the note.

TROUBLESHOOTING

Deleted footnotes won't go away

If you've deleted a footnote or endnote, but it keeps reappearing, chances are that a portion of formatting for the note has been left behind. To find the culprit character, click the Show/Hide command in the Paragraph group of the Home tab. All the paragraph marks will appear, and you can move to the footnote area and delete the stray paragraph mark. The reference in the text will then be deleted.

Creating a New Separator Line

The separator line Word uses to show where the document text ends and the footnote text begins is a fairly nondescript line that extends a short distance across the page. If you want to change the separator line—perhaps to add color or choose a different line style or thickness—use the Borders And Shading dialog box to make the change. To do this, follow these steps:

1. View the document in Draft view

2. Double-click the footnote or endnote reference mark in your document. The Footnotes or Endnotes pane opens at the bottom of the Word window.

3. Click the Footnotes arrow and then select Footnote Separator in the Footnotes list.

4. Delete the existing separator line by clicking it and then pressing Delete.

5. Click the Home tab and click the Border command arrow in the Paragraph group.

6. Click Borders and Shading at the bottom of the gallery. The Borders And Shading dialog box appears.

Chapter 23

7. Click the Borders tab.

8. In the Style list, select the border style you want.

9. Click the bottom and side segments in the Preview section to remove them, leaving only the top line.

10. Click OK to add the new separator line to the document.

TROUBLESHOOTING

My footnote is split across two pages

Sometimes getting footnotes to print just where you'd intended can be a bit tricky. You might wind up with too many additional blank lines on the page after the footnote, or you could find that your footnote has been divided, with one line appearing on the first page and a second line printing on the next page.

If you find that part of your footnote has moved to the next page, look at the margin settings for the page. The text on the page, the margins, and the footnote length all play a role in the amount of space reserved for your footnote area. Click the Page Layout tab and then click the Margins down-arrow. Note the space allowed for the margins. Try clicking Custom Margins and reducing the bottom margin setting to allow more room for the footnote. Then click OK to return to the document.

Note

If you do customize the margins of your page in order to adjust the amount of space allowed for footnotes, be sure to preview your page and do a test print before printing your final document.

For best results, try to keep your footnotes short—one or two lines if possible. If you need to insert a long footnote, consider converting it to an endnote so that it can be placed at the end of the document.

Using Cross-References

When you're working on a long document in which you want to refer to other parts of the document, you can use cross-references to help readers find the information they seek. Word lets you add cross-references to a number of different elements in your document—including captions, headings, footnotes and endnotes, and bookmarks you've created.

> **Tip**
>
> You can create cross-references only within the current document. You might create a reference at the beginning of a long report, for example, that points readers to a table in a later section that lists statistics related to a new study. You can't create a cross-reference to a table in another document, however.

If you're working with master documents and subdocuments, be sure to maximize the master document by clicking Expand Subdocuments in the Master Documents group of the Outlining tab. This makes all text accessible before you enter cross-references.

Creating a Cross-Reference

When you're ready to create a cross-reference, start by placing the insertion point where you want the cross-reference to appear in your document. Then follow these steps:

1. Add the text that refers to the cross-reference (for example, you might use a phrase such as "To review the results of our survey, see").

2. Click the Reference tab and click Cross-Reference in the Captions group. The Cross-Reference dialog box appears, as shown in Figure 23-14.

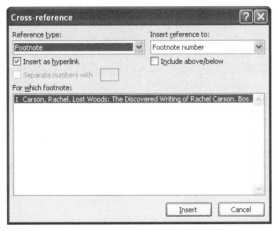

Figure 23-14 Cross-references enable you to point readers to different elements in your document.

3. Click the Reference Type arrow and then make your selection. You can choose from the following document elements:

   ❑ **Numbered Item** Lists all the text entries beginning with a number

   ❑ **Heading** Shows all headings based on Word's outline levels or Heading 1, 2, or 3 styles

   ❑ **Bookmark** Displays all the bookmarks currently listed in the document

- ❑ **Footnote** Shows all the footnotes inserted in the document
- ❑ **Endnote** Lists the endnotes you have created
- ❑ **Equation** Shows any equations you've inserted in the document
- ❑ **Figure** Lists all figure references
- ❑ **Table** Shows all available tables in the document

4. Click the Insert Reference To arrow and then choose the element you want Word to insert in the document. This item will be inserted at the insertion point.

5. Select the item to which you want to refer by clicking it in the For Which list box.

6. Click Insert, and Word adds the cross-reference to your document as you directed.

7. Click Close to return to your document.

INSIDE OUT　Create links for a Web page

If you plan to save your document as a Web page or make it available as an electronic file, you can have Word turn your cross-references into hyperlinks so that readers can easily move from one page to another. To create links for cross-references, select the cross-reference you've created and then display the Cross-Reference dialog box by clicking the References tab and then clicking Cross-Reference in the Captions group. In the Cross-Reference dialog box, click the Insert As Hyperlink check box and then click Insert. The inserted cross-reference is created as a link to the other location in the document. Modifying, Moving, and Updating Cross-References

You can edit and delete the text that introduces a cross-reference the same way you would modify any other text in your document. If you want to modify the item to which a reference refers, you need to make a different kind of change. Here are the steps:

1. Select the item inserted as the cross-reference (for example, you might select *Table 1-1*).

2. Display the Cross-Reference dialog box by clicking the References tab and choosing Cross-Reference in the Captions group.

3. In the For Which list in the Cross-Reference dialog box, click the new item to which you want the cross-reference to refer.

4. Click Insert and then click Close to close the Cross-Reference dialog box.

INSIDE OUT   Make a reference relative

By selecting the Include Above/Below check box in the Cross-Reference dialog box, you can have Word create a relative reference to a cross-reference you enter. Create your cross-reference as usual. Then, in the Insert Reference To list box, after selecting the item you want inserted, select the Include Above/Below check box. If the insertion point is on the same page as the section or item referenced, Word will insert "above" or "below," based on the position of the reference.If you want to move a cross-reference, simply select the reference in your document and then cut and paste it as you would normally. Once you have the reference in the location you want, press F9. Word updates the reference and makes the connection to the new location. If you want to update all references in a document, select the entire document before pressing F9.

Note

When you want to delete a cross-reference, simply select the reference and then delete it as you would any other text.

TROUBLESHOOTING

Cross-referencing in my document produces an error message

If you go through the steps to create a cross-reference and instead of the reference you expect, you get an error message saying, "Error! Reference source not found," check to make sure that the information you're referring to hasn't been removed from your document. If the item is still in your document, but the reference still displays an error message, try fixing the problem by selecting the cross-reference and pressing F9 to update the reference. If the problem is caused by a broken link or a moved reference, the item should now be displayed properly.

Chapter 23

What's Next?

The next chapter continues the topic of working with references in your document by showing you how to create reference tables—tables of contents, tables of figures, and tables of authorities.

Generating First-Class Tables of Contents and Reference Tables

Including a good table of contents (TOC) in your document is a great way to ensure rave reviews from the peers, customers, and supervisors who read your document. If you want people to get your point, so the old adage goes, make it easy for them to find it. A table of contents gives readers a road map through your document, helping them know what to expect and find what they need in the most efficient way. Other reference tables, such as the table of figures and table of authorities described in this chapter, can give your readers additional resources for locating important elements in your document that they may need to reference in critical moments (like when a board member asks a pointed question about a chart they've included in the annual report).

> **Note**
>
> Often readers will review a table of contents—or the index—of a document or book before deciding whether to read it. They are wondering (1) Is this worth my time? (2) Will I find what I need in here? and (3) Is this document relevant to me? If you want people to read what you've prepared, create a good table of contents to show them how your document fits what they're looking for. The clearer your table of contents, the better your readers will like it.

This chapter introduces you to creating all these reference tables in Microsoft Office Word 2007. You'll learn to create, edit, customize, and update your table of contents and add entries for the special reference tables that make it easy to locate figures, citations, and more in your long documents.

Creating Effective Reference Tables

Headings are the real secret to creating a helpful table of contents. If you've written clear, understandable headings, your readers will know where to turn for the information they want.

The next consideration is the way in which you format these headings—if you don't use styles Office Word 2007 recognizes, the program won't collect the headings the way you want. To create the TOC you want, keep these guidelines in mind.

- Use Word's built-in heading styles—or create your own custom styles based on them When you're working in Outline view or working with master documents, use Word's built-in heading styles—Heading 1, Heading 2, and Heading 3. Additionally, you are probably familiar with the various outline levels—1 through 9—you can assign in Outline view. When you use Word to create a table of contents, Word uses the built-in heading styles by default. You can teach Word how to use the outline levels or your own custom styles, but it takes a few more steps than creating a simple point-and-click TOC.

- Make your headings clear and concise The best headings are short—between four and ten words—and communicate the subject clearly. The headings for your document will vary, of course, depending on content, but if your objective is to help readers find what they want quickly, you'll be closer to meeting your goal if you keep your headings short, sweet, and smart.

- Avoid confusing headings If the tone of your document is conversationally hip, you might be tempted to throw in little humorous sayings or quips as headings throughout your text. As a wise editor once asked, "Would readers understand what this heading means if they opened the book at this page?" If helping readers understand your message is your main goal, avoid phrases that might confuse them.

You can include literally any text in your document as part of the TOC by selecting entries manually. For more information on manual table of contents entries, see the section titled "Adding TOC Entries Manually," later in this chapter.

Creating a Table of Contents

Once you've checked your headings to make sure they're clear and concise and that you've assigned a heading style Word will recognize, you can generate the table of contents. You can use two different procedures to do this. The easiest way is to choose a TOC style from the gallery and let Word do the rest. Or, if you prefer, you can use the Table Of Contents dialog box to customize the look of the table in a way that fits your needs. This section takes you through each of these techniques.

Using a TOC Style

If you want to use one of Word's ready-made templates to create a table of contents, follow these steps.

1. Place the insertion point where you want to add the table of contents.

2. Click the References tab on the Ribbon.

3. Click the Table Of Contents command in the Table Of Contents group. A gallery of TOC styles opens, as shown in Figure 24-1.

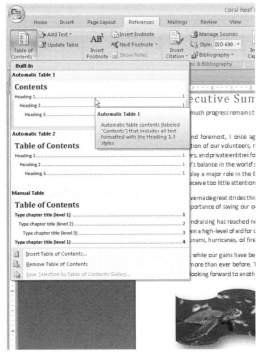

Figure 24-1 The Table Of Contents gallery displays a number of styles you can use to create your TOC.

4. Click the table style you want to create. Word compiles the TOC and places it at the cursor position, using the headings as formatted in your document (see Figure 24-2).

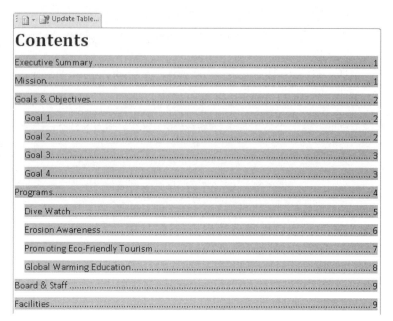

Figure 24-2 You can choose a TOC style from the gallery to use preset formats for the TOC in your document.

Word automatically adds the word Contents at the top of the table of contents and adds right-aligned page numbers and dot leaders (the dots spanning the space from the end of the text to the beginning of the page numbers). First-level headings are aligned with the left margin, while second-level headings are indented one tab to show their subordination.

When you click the table of contents (as shown in Figure 24-2), the table highlights and contextual commands appear above the selected table. (You'll learn more about these commands later in the chapter, in the section titled "Editing and Updating a TOC."

Creating a Customized TOC

If you want to create a table of contents that meets certain specifications, you can use the Table Of Contents dialog box to make your selections. Start the process by clicking the References tab and then click the Table Of Contents command in the Table Of Contents group. Next, click Insert Table Of Contents at the bottom of the Table Of Contents gallery. The Table Of Contents dialog box appears (see Figure 24-3). At the left side of the dialog box, you can see the way in which the default settings will be applied to your table of contents. As you can see, in the Print Preview region, each level of heading is indented one tab, tab leaders are used, and numbers are aligned along the right margin. In the Web Preview region on the right, no leaders are used, no page numbers are used, and each heading is actually a hyperlink. When users click a link in the TOC, they will be taken to the corresponding section in the Web document.

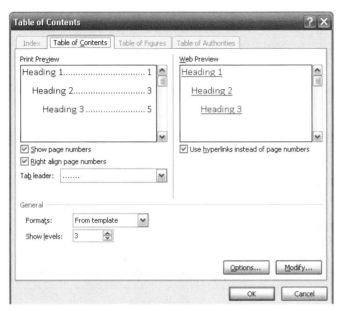

Figure 24-3 You can customize the settings for the table of contents by using the Table of Contents dialog box.

Using the various settings in the Table Of Contents dialog box, you can customize your table of contents in the following ways:

- Position the page numbers immediately following the headings by clicking the Right Align Page Numbers check box to clear it.

- Remove the page numbers altogether by clearing the Show Page Numbers check box.

- Change the tab leader by clicking the Tab Leader arrow and choosing a different line setting.

- Choose a different format set for the heading styles by clicking the Formats arrow and choosing a different set (see Figure 24-4). For more information on working with formats, see the section titled "Choosing a Format," later in this chapter.

Chapter 24

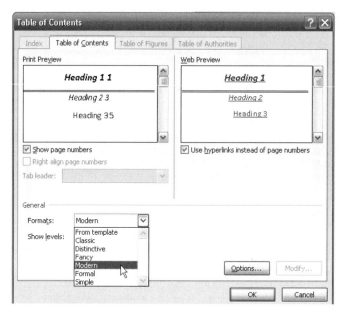

Figure 24-4 Choose a different format to change the heading styles used in the TOC.

- Change the number of levels that are displayed in your table of contents by clicking the upward-pointing arrow (to increase) or the downward-pointing arrow (to decrease) the value in the Show Levels field.

- If you're preparing a Web document and want a traditional TOC to appear instead of links, you can click the Use Hyperlinks Instead Of Page Numbers check box to clear it. This causes page numbers and tab leaders to be displayed in the Web document.

> **Note**
>
> The Options and Modify buttons in the Table Of Contents dialog box display options that enable you to choose the headings and styles that are used in your table of contents. For more about customizing the styles of your TOC, see the section titled "Changing TOC Styles," later in this chapter.

After you select the settings you want to use for your TOC, click OK to save your selections and return to the document. The table of contents is inserted at the cursor position.

Adding TOC Entries Manually

You aren't limited to using headings in your table of contents. You can select any word or phrase in your document for inclusion in the TOC by following these steps.

1. Select the text you want to use in the TOC.

2. Press Alt+Shift+O. The Mark Table Of Contents Entry dialog box appears, as shown in Figure 24-5. The entry you selected appears in the Entry box.

Figure 24-5 Enter TOC entries manually in the Mark Table Of Contents Entry dialog box.

3. If you use more than one TOC in a document, click the Table Identifier arrow to assign this entry to a TOC. (This step is unnecessary if you're creating only one TOC at a time.)

4. In the Level box, enter the level at which you want the entry to be listed. The first-level entry is the default.

5. Click Mark to add the entry. Word adds the table of contents field code to the entry.

6. For subsequent entries, select the text you want to use in your document, click in the Entry box (which causes the word to be added to the box), and then click Mark.

7. When you're finished adding entries, click Close.

Next, to generate the table of contents to include the manual TOC entries, follow these steps.

1. Place the insertion point where you want to insert the TOC.

2. Display the Table Of Contents dialog box by clicking the References tab, clicking Table Of Contents, and choosing Insert Table Of Contents from the gallery.

3. Click Options on the Table Of Contents tab.

4. In the Table Of Contents Options dialog box, select the Table Entry Fields check box. This adds the TOC entries to the table of contents. (To find out more about the Table Of Contents Options dialog box, see the section titled "Customizing a TOC," later in this chapter.)

5. Click OK twice to close the dialog boxes. Word adds the new TOC at the insertion point.

Chapter 24

INSIDE OUT
Display only your manual entries

If you want your table of contents to include only the entries you've added manually, display the Table Of Contents dialog box by choosing Insert Table Of Contents from the Table Of Contents gallery. Click the Options button in the lower right corner of the dialog box. In the Table Of Contents Options dialog box, clear both the Styles and Outline Levels check boxes. Click OK to save your settings and then click OK a second time to return to the document. Press F9 to update the TOC, and only your manual entries should appear.

Choosing a Format

The simple table of contents format gives you a standard TOC with right-aligned page numbers, dot leaders, and left-aligned headings. You can choose from a number of specially designed TOC formats so that your table of contents fits the style of your publication.

You can choose a format for your table of contents when you first generate it. When you choose Insert Table Of Contents from the Table Of Contents gallery, the Table Of Contents dialog box appears. Click the Formats arrow in the Table Of Contents tab. The formats shown there—From Template, Classic, Distinctive, Fancy, Modern, Formal, and Simple—offer different combinations of text styles for your TOC. Click one to view the style is shown in the Print Preview and Web Preview windows. When you find the one you want, click OK. The table of contents is created and formats are assigned as you selected.

> **Note**
>
> If you want to change the format of a table of contents you've already created, select the table before you display the Table Of Contents dialog box. Select the Formats arrow and then choose the style you want. Finally, click OK. Word displays a message box asking whether you want to replace the selected TOC. Click OK to replace the selected TOC, and then Word updates the TOC with the new format.

TROUBLESHOOTING

Headings are missing in my TOC

After you generate a table of contents for your Word document, review the document and check your headings carefully. If any headings are missing in the TOC, determine whether you've added the headings in text boxes or shapes.

Word creates your table of contents by gathering all the headings and table of contents entry fields. If you've added text in objects you've added to the document, the entries might not be found automatically. To add these items to the TOC, just select the text items, copy them, and paste them on the text layer. Finally, press F9 to update the TOC.

Editing and Updating a TOC

As you work with your document, you might move sections around and add and edit headings and text. That means that when you make a heading change, your TOC is out of date because it won't reflect your most recent changes. You can update the table of contents in two different ways.

- Press F9

- Click Update Table in the contextual tab that appears at the top of the TOC when it is selected (see Figure 24-6)

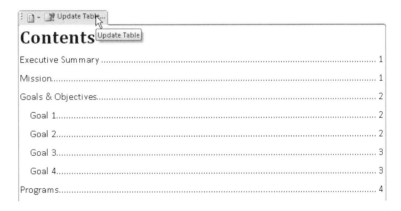

Figure 24-6 Contextual commands appear when you select the TOC in your document.

Word searches the document and updates the TOC to reflect any changes you've made to headings.

Chapter 24

> **Note**
>
> You can use the contextual TOC commands to choose a different style for your TOC as well. Select the table of contents and click the Table Of Contents arrow (just to the left of the Update Table command). The Table Of Contents gallery appears so that you can choose a different TOC style.

CAUTION

> To remove a TOC, use the Remove Table Of Contents, found at the bottom of the Table Of Contents gallery instead of deleting the TOC field. When you manually delete a TOC, hidden bookmarks are left in the document and could later cause incorrect references in the TOC or if too many bookmarks have been added it can result in document corruption.

Preparing a TOC for the Web

When you generate a table of contents for your document, a Web Preview appears next to the TOC Print Preview in the Table Of Contents tab in the Table Of Contents dialog box. Try out a Web TOC in your document by placing the insertion point where you want to add the TOC and clicking Insert Table Of Contents in the Table Of Contents gallery. In the Table Of Contents dialog box, make sure the Use Hyperlinks Instead Of Page Numbers check box is selected and then click OK. The TOC is added at the insertion point. To see the TOC in Web format, choose View, Web Layout. The TOC appears as a table of active hyperlinks, as shown in Figure 24-7, each of which takes you to the corresponding document section.

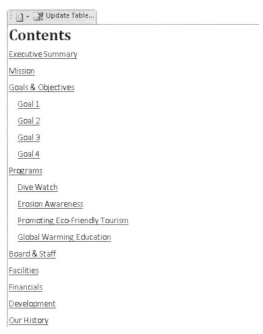

Figure 24-7 When you display Web Layout view, you'll see hyperlinks in your Web TOC.

Customizing a TOC

You can make additional changes to your table of contents by customizing both the elements you include in the TOC and the styles you use to include them. Figure 24-8 shows the Table Of Contents Options dialog box and the features available to you. To display these options, choose Insert Table Of Contents from the Table Of Contents gallery and click Options.

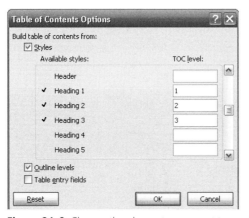

Figure 24-8 Choose the elements you want to use in the Table Of Contents Options dialog box.

Matching Entry Styles to TOC Levels

Part of making sure the right entries show up in your table of contents in the right way involves ensuring they are mapped to the right TOC levels. The Table Of Contents Options dialog box is where you make that happen. For example, Headings 1, 2, and 3 are assigned to TOC levels 1, 2, and 3. This indicates that Heading 1 is shown as level 1, meaning it will be aligned with the left margin of your document. Level 2 appears indented one tab, and level 3 is indented two tabs from the left margin. You can set additional levels as well if your document requires that level of detail in the TOC.

To add styles to the TOC, scroll down through the list to find other styles in your document—either styles you've created or existing styles—and then enter a TOC level in the text boxes on the right. The styles you select are included in the TOC when it's generated, appearing according to the level you specified. Click OK to save your changes and then click Yes when prompted about whether you want to replace the existing table of contents with the updated table.

Changing TOC Styles

When you are working with styles in the Table Of Contents Options dialog box, the styles that are available are taken from the template being used to format your document. If you've selected From Template in the Formats list in the Table Of Contents dialog box, the Modify button is enabled. When you click Modify, the Style dialog box appears, and you're given the choice of adding, deleting, or changing the styles used in the table of contents. When you click Modify in the Style dialog box, the Modify Style dialog box appears so that you can make font and formatting changes to the selected style (see Figure 24-9).

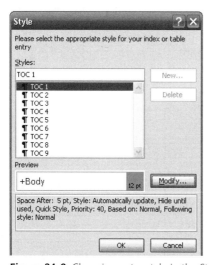

Figure 24-9 Changing entry style in the Style dialog box.

Select the item you want to change in the Styles list. The specifications used to create the look appear in the description box at the bottom of the dialog box. Preview shows you how that particular item is formatted. Click Modify to make changes to the style.

In the Modify Style dialog box, you can make all kinds of modifications to the style of the table of contents. You've seen this dialog box before—it's the same one you use to change styles throughout the rest of your document. Make any necessary changes and click OK to save the new settings. Click OK in the Style dialog box to save the changes to the style. Finally, click OK once more to return to your document and update the TOC by pressing F9.

For a refresher on creating new style effects in the Modify Style dialog box, see Chapter 15, "Using Styles to Increase Your Formatting Power."

> **Note**
> If you want to undo your selections and reset the options to their default settings, click Reset in the Table Of Contents Options dialog box.

Incorporating Other Reference Tables

TOCs aren't the only reference tables you'll use as you work with long documents. If you use illustrations, tables, diagrams, or equations, you'll like having the choice of numbering and labeling those elements automatically. If you work with legal briefings and citations, the ability to create a table of authorities will save you considerable time and trouble.

Building a Table of Figures

When you have Word generate a table of figures to use as a reference tool in your document, Word searches for and collects the figure captions in your document. This means that you need to set up your captions before you generate the table.

Adding Captions

First things first. Start by adding labels to the items you want to include in your table of figures. You can add captions while you work by using Word's AutoCaption feature. Here are the steps to follow.

1. Click the References tab and click Insert Caption in the Captions group. The Caption dialog box appears, as you see in Figure 24-10. This is where you enter the text for the caption and choose the way you want the caption labeled and numbered.

Figure 24-10 Enter the settings for your captions in the Caption dialog box.

   2. Click the AutoCaption button. In the AutoCaption dialog box, select the file type of the object you want to create captions for, as shown in Figure 24-11.

Figure 24-11 AutoCaption enables you to add labels and numbers to your figures automatically.

   3. In the Options area, click the Use Label arrow and choose whether you want the captions to be added to equations, figures, or tables.

   4. Click the Position arrow and indicate whether you want the caption to appear above or below the item.

   5. Click OK to have Word search for and update the elements in your document.

Controlling Figure Numbering

To add figure numbering to your captions, start in the Caption dialog box. Select the element to which you want to add the numbering (or update your other caption choices) and then click the Numbering button. The Caption Numbering dialog box appears, as shown in Figure 24-12.

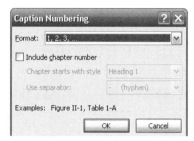

Figure 24-12 The Caption Numbering dialog box enables you to choose the format and style of the numbering sequence.

Begin by choosing the format you want to use for the numbering sequence. You can choose the traditional 1, 2, 3 or A, B, C, or you can choose roman numerals in the Format list box. If you want to include chapter numbers (which Word picks up from the text), select the Include Chapter Number check box. Next, specify the first heading style in the chapter (this shows Word where to begin looking) and then select a separator character from the Use Separator list box (Word will place this between the chapter number and the figure number in the caption). Click OK to save the settings. When you add your next figure, the caption number will be applied automatically.

Generating a Table of Figures

After you've added captions to your illustrations, you can use those captions to create a table of the figures in your document. A table of figures is a helpful reference in long documents that include important charts, diagrams, or other illustrations readers will want to find quickly. Follow these steps to generate a table of figures.

1. Click in your document at the point you want to create the table of figures.

2. Click the References tab and click Insert Table of Figures in the Captions group. The Table Of Figures dialog box appears. The default selections for the table are displayed in the preview boxes, as shown in Figure 24-13.

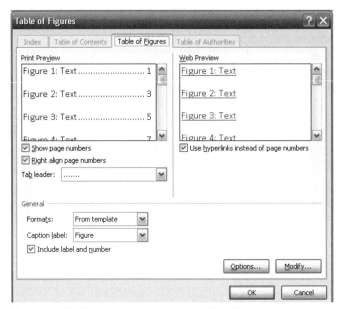

Figure 24-13 The preview boxes in the Table Of Figures dialog box show the default selections.

3. Change the settings as needed and then click OK to create the table. The table of figures is placed in the document at the insertion point.

Building a Table of Authorities

A table of authorities is a more specialized table reference that helps you track, compile, and display citations in your document. You'll use this feature most often for legal documents that reference cases, rules, treaties, and other documents. Before you can create a table of citations, obviously, you need to have placed those citations within the body of the document.

Adding Citations Manually

In Chapter 23, "Configuring References," you learned how to use citations to create effective bibliographies. Because you need to have entered citations before you can create a table of them, we'll include a brief summary here. Here are the steps for adding a citation to your document.

1. Select the citation in the document.

2. Press Alt+Shift+I. The Mark Citation dialog box appears with the selected citation displayed in the Selected Text box, as shown in Figure 24-14.

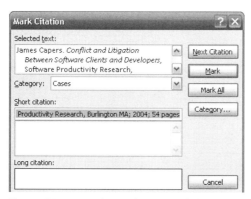

Figure 24-14 Use the Mark Citation dialog box to include citations in your table of authorities.

3. Click the Category arrow and then choose the type of citation you're creating.

4. Edit the citation, if needed, in the Short Citation box.

5. Click Mark. Word adds the necessary codes to your document to identify the citation for inclusion in the table of authorities.

6. If you want to continue adding citations, click Next Citation.

7. Click Close to close the dialog box when you're finished adding citations.

> Note
>
> You can also add citations directly into the Table Of Authorities dialog box. Click the References tab and select the Insert Table Of Authorities command in the Table Of Authorities group. Click Mark Citation to display the Mark Citation dialog box. Enter your citation as needed and then click Mark to complete the entry.

Generating the Table of Authorities

After you've entered the citations you want to reference, you can start the process of creating a table of authorities by following these steps.

1. Click the References tab and choose Insert Table Of Authorities in the Table Of Authorities group. The Table Of Authorities dialog box appears, as Figure 24-15 shows.

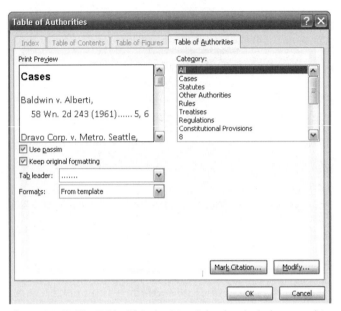

Figure 24-15 The Table Of Authorities dialog box includes everything you need for entering and formatting the table.

2. Choose your category from the list on the right.

3. Choose the formatting and styles you want and then click OK to create the table of authorities.

> **Note**
>
> If you've created multiple tables in your document, be sure to update each table independently. To update, click in the table and then press F9.

What's Next?

This chapter has provided you with the techniques for creating reference items that will be helpful to your readers when they are navigating through a long or complex document. The next chapter focuses on another important reference item: creating an effective index.

CHAPTER 25

Creating Effective Indexes

You may have lots of good ideas, a solid financial plan, and inspiring stories in your long, complex document, but if you don't give readers an easy way to find the information they're looking for, much of your work may go unnoticed. A good index gives your readers a doorway into the topics—large and small—you present in your document.

In this chapter, you'll learn how to create indexes for your Microsoft Office Word 2007 documents. Whether you create entries one by one or use a table to automate index entries, you'll find the process fairly intuitive and fast.

Anatomy of an Index

An index is one of those things that you may not notice until you discover that it's missing. Suppose that you are researching the statistics on Web advertising in 2006. Your own startup business will rely on advertising for a revenue stream, and this is an important item to include in a business plan that you hope will attract investors. You have a number of reports the chief executive officer (CEO) passed along to you about the state of the Web in 2006, but none of them includes an index that enables you to easily find the advertising statistics you need. Now you'll need to spend the afternoon skimming the reports to find the data you need.

An index entry may include the following items:

- A primary topic (for example, Advertising)
- A subtopic (such as Web)
- Page numbers (inserted automatically by the indexing tool)
- Cross-references (for example, *See also Banner advertising*)

Figure 25-1 shows a draft of an index as it was first generated in Office Word 2007. As you can see, simple elements include the primary topics and subtopics, page numbers, and a cross-reference.

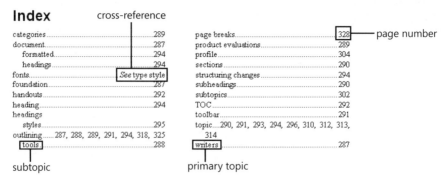

Figure 25-1 You can easily create an index with various levels of entries and cross-references.

What Makes a Good Index?

Think of the various indexes you've used in the past—no doubt some were better than others. Some left out the main topics you were looking for, or they seemed disorganized. And some documents may not have had an index at all, which can be really frustrating when you're looking for something specific.

There's a recipe for creating a good index, so if you've never created one before, take heart. Here are some things you should be sure to check in the indexes you create:

- **Usability** An index is first and foremost a reader service. Make sure that you've included all major topics, and that you've thought through the alternative ways readers might be looking for those topics. Include topics, subtopics, and references to other topics for related information (for example, *See* Parenting teens).

- **Readability** Using terms your readers will recognize—whether or not they're familiar with the content of your document—is important. If you're unsure about the various ways a reader might reference a certain topic, ask others how they would look it up so that you know what kinds of phrasing would be helpful. Talk to others on your team or in your department to make sure you've used words and phrases that will be easily understood.

- **Cross-references** Cross-references in an index refer readers to other topics that provide more information. In Figure 25-1, the *fonts* entry shows a cross-reference.

- **Logical structure** One mistake new indexers often make is to include every important-sounding word they think would be helpful. You'll help your readers find what they are looking for if you think through your index carefully. Which topics are most important? How many different ways might a reader refer to them? What are the words that will be searched for most often?

- **Multiple entries** Listing a topic in more than one way helps readers find what they're looking for. For example, someone wanting to know how to choose a background color for a heading might look under *document*, *headings*, *color*, or *background* to find that particular topic.

Note

After you identify key words and phrases for your index, create a list and send it to others in your department, asking for input, additions, and suggestions. Doing this type of phrase testing for your index before you create it can save you editing time later.

Note

One place you can get clues for important index terms is your table of contents. Which words and phrases are used in your headings? Definitely include those terms in your index and look for plenty of opportunities to create subentries from the topics within those sections.

Indexing with Word

Creating indexes in Word is an interactive process that is partly hands-on and partly automatic. You create a Word index in three basic stages:

1. Mark the index entries in your document.

2. Position the cursor at the point in the document where you want to place the index (typically this is the end of the document).

3. Use the Insert Index command to compile the index from the entries you entered.

Tip

If there are terms you're sure to include in your index, you can add them to a concordance file. Word will use the file to quickly mark the index entries you want. For more about creating a concordance file, see the section titled "AutoMarking Entries with a Concordance File" later in this chapter, on page 680.

Creating Index Entries

The first step in creating your index is to indicate which words and phrases you want to include in the index. Word makes it easy for you to enter index entries as you go—and once you display the Mark Index Entry dialog box, you can mark additional entries, add subentries, and add cross-references and page ranges.

Marking Index Entries

Marking an index entry is the process of selecting a word or phrase you want to use in the index. You can create an index entry in two different ways:

- If you want to begin with text that is already in the document, select and use existing text.

- If you want to add an entry that is not based on an existing word or phrase in your document, click to place the insertion point in the paragraph where you want to add the index entry.

To add index entries, follow these steps:

1. Select the text you want to include in the index and click Mark entry (in the Index group of the References tab). The Mark Index Entry dialog box appears, as shown in Figure 25-2.

Figure 25-2 You use the Mark Index Entry dialog box to enter index entries and subentries.

2. The selected text appears in the Main Entry box. If necessary, edit the text that appears. (If you placed the insertion point rather than selecting text, in the Main Entry box, type the entry you want.)

3. Click Mark to mark the entry. Repeat this process to include additional entries.

4. When you are finished adding entries, click Close to save your changes and return to the document.

> **Tip**
>
> Edit the entry in the Mark Index Entry dialog box to make it as clear as possible. For example, instead of a phrase that appears in your document, *such as served in the state legislature*, you might enter *legislature*, or *government service*.

Creating Subentries

A subentry is a secondary topic you use to narrow the search on a specific topic. For example, if your report is about a new HR training program your company offers, one main index entry and the related subentries might look like this:

Human resources

Creating a personnel file, 21

Updating personnel data, 24

Personnel evaluations, 26

Training program for, 30

A subentry provides readers with additional references they can look up. It also adds depth and functionality to your index as a whole, and it makes reading the index easier.

Here's a quick way to enter subentries if you want to avoid repeated clicks in the dialog box: Just type the main entry and the subentry in the Mark Index Entry dialog box, separating the entries with a colon. You can use this technique to create up to seven levels of subentries, although an index that complex would probably confuse most readers! For best results, stick to one or perhaps two subentry levels, depending on the complexity of your document.

> **Tip**
>
> If you find yourself entering too many subentries for a particular topic, you might want to create another main entry to divide the list. If your main entry is followed by a whole column of subentries, your readers might get lost in the list and not remember the main entry heading.

Selecting Repeated Entries

When you're putting together a quick index and want to reference all occurrences of a particular word or phrase, you can do that easily using the Mark Index Entry dialog box. Start by selecting the text you want to index and then display the Mark Index Entry dialog box using either method previously provided. Change the Main Entry text to show the entry you want and then enter a subentry, if you want to include one. Finally, click Mark All. Word searches for the word or phrase throughout the document and applies an index entry to every occurrence.

> **Note**
>
> One of the limitations of Mark All is that the program marks every occurrence as it appears. This means that not only will you have the same index entry for each item (which doesn't give you the flexibility of creating multiple references to the same topic), but also that Word will find only the words or phrases that exactly match the text you've entered. For example, if you enter **composer**, *composers* will be found, but not *composing* or *composition*. So if you feel it's important to reference multiple forms of a particular word, be sure to create index entries for each one to ensure that they are all included in the finished index.

INSIDE OUT   Indexing long entries

If the entry you are adding actually spans several pages, instead of inserting an entry on every page, you can create a bookmark and then reference that bookmark in your index. Start by highlighting the text passage you want to index. Then click the Insert tab and click Bookmark in the Links group. Enter a name for the bookmark and then click Add. Next, click the References tab and click Mark Entry in the Index group. In the Mark Index Entry dialog box, click Page Range in the Options area. Click the Bookmark arrow and choose the bookmark you just created. Click Mark to add the bookmark entry to your index.

Formatting Entries

As you add index entries, you can specify formatting for the characters and page numbers, thus cutting down on time spent editing and formatting after you create the index. Here are the steps to apply formatting to your index entries:

1. Select the text for the index entry.

2. Display the Mark Index Entry dialog box.

3. Edit the text in the Main Entry box as needed.

4. In the Main Entry box, select the text you want to format.

5. Press Ctrl+B to apply bold, Ctrl+I for italic, or Ctrl+U for underline styles. You can also right-click the entry, choose Font, and select additional formatting settings for the entry.

6. Complete the entry as desired and then click Mark to create the entry.

By selecting or clearing the check boxes in the Page Number Format section of the Mark Index Entry dialog box, you can also control the format of the page numbers Word adds to the index. You might want to use bold or italic to highlight certain entries. For example, a bold page number might indicate the most in-depth coverage of an item, and an italic page number might include biographical information or reference another work.

Adding Cross-References

Not all your entries will provide page number references. Some might instead point readers to other topics in your index. A cross-reference gives readers a pointer to an entry (or group of entries) for related information. To create a cross-reference in your index, follow these steps:

1. Select the text for the index entry or position the insertion point in the document.

2. Display the Mark Index Entry dialog box.

3. Enter the Main Entry text, if needed.

4. Click the Cross-Reference option.

5. After the word *See*, type the index entry you want to refer readers to. For example, you might create cross-references that look like this:

Training sessions. *See* Retreat sessions.

Specifying Page Ranges

By default, Word assigns the index entry the number of the current page. If you select and create an entry on page 3, for example, Word shows that page number with the index entry. If you want to indicate a span of pages so that you can give your readers the full range of pages on which a specific topic is covered, you can do so by using bookmarks you've already created.

If you haven't created bookmarks to mark places in your document and want to find out how, see Chapter 7, "Honing Document Navigation Skills." To use a bookmark to indicate a page range in your index, follow these steps:

1. Display the Mark Index Entry dialog box.

2. Enter the text you want in the Main Entry and Subentry boxes, if needed.

3. Click the Page Range option.

4. Click the Bookmark arrow to display the list of bookmarks in the current document. Then click the bookmark you want to use.

5. Click Mark to add the entry.

When you create the index later, Word will insert an en dash (a long dash) between the page numbers in the range. A page range entry looks like this:

Human resources, 21–29

Generating an Index

Once you've marked all the entries you want to include in your index, you're ready for Word to compile the index and place it in your document. When Word compiles the index, it gathers all the entries you've marked, assigns page numbers as you've specified, and alphabetizes the entries. Finally, after you click OK, Word places the index at the insertion point.

INSIDE OUT Review your document

Although you can update an index easily by pressing F9 (which enables you to go back and edit your index entries if you choose), you'll lose any additional formatting you've added to the index after it is compiled. For example, if you've added alphabetical headings (- A -, - B -, and so forth), when you select the index and press F9, the headings will disappear. So it's worth your time, *before* Word compiles the index, to go back through the document and review your index entries to make sure you haven't missed anything important. Page through the document to review important headings, sections, and captions for inclusion in your index. Start the process of creating the index by placing the insertion point where you want to create the index and then clicking the References tab. Choose Insert Index in the Index group. The Index dialog box appears, with the Index tab selected, as shown in Figure 25-3. In this dialog box, you are able to choose the format for both text entries , page numbers, tabs and leader characters.

Chapter 25

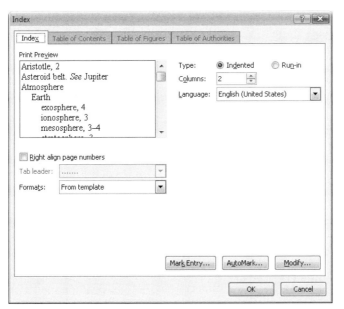

Figure 25-3 The Index tab provides the options and commands you need to create the index.

> **Note**
> Notice the Mark Entry button on the Index tab of the Index dialog box. If you begin making your formatting choices for the index and suddenly remember a topic you want to include in the index, you can click Mark Entry to open the Mark Index Entry dialog box. Doing this action closes the Index dialog box.

Choosing the Index Format

One of the most important choices you'll make in the Index dialog box involves the format for the compiled index. How do you want the index to look? When you click the Formats arrow, Word gives you the following choices:

- **From Template** The default; leaves out alphabetical headings that separate sections in the index

- **Classic** Centers the alphabetic headings over the index column

- **Fancy** Encloses the heading in a shadowed box

- **Modern** Italicizes the heading and places a rule above it
- **Bulleted** Formats the heading as a block letter and centers it over the index column
- **Formal** Right-aligns page numbers, adds dot leaders, italicizes the heading, and indents the heading from the left margin
- **Simple** Removes all alphabetic headings and special formats

Choosing each of these options produces a different index format, which is displayed in the Print Preview region of the dialog box. To make your choice, click the Formats arrow and then click the selection you want.

If you later decide to change the default alignment of the numbering or choose a different leader character, those changes will override the settings belonging to the different formats.

> **Tip**
>
> Experiment with the different formats for your index before selecting the one you want by clicking the choices in the Formats list on the Index tab in the Index dialog box. When you choose a format style, the Print Preview region of the dialog box shows your selection so that you can see the formatting effect of each style.

Choosing Alignment

After you create your index, you might want to make changes to the alignment and tab leaders that the format applied. You can change these settings so that page numbers are aligned along the right edge of the index column, and tab leaders are added to help lead the reader to the related page number. To change the alignment of page numbers in your index, follow these steps:

1. Click the References tab and choose Insert Index on the Index tab to display the Index dialog box.

2. Click the Indented option if necessary and then select the Right Align Page Numbers check box.

3. Click the Tab Leader arrow and select the type of leader you want.

4. Click OK to create the index, and the page numbers are formatted as you selected.

Changing the Way Entries Are Displayed

Another choice in the Index dialog box enables you to choose whether you want index subentries to be run in with the index main entries or indented below them. Simply click your choice, and Word will format the index accordingly.

When you choose Indented, your index subentries are indented beneath the main entries, like this:

Human resources

    Creating a personnel file, 21

When you choose Run-In, the subentries are placed on the same line with the main entries, like this:

Human resources: Creating a personnel file, 21; Updating personnel data, 24

TROUBLESHOOTING

Error messages appear in my index

You've marked your index entries and created the index by clicking Insert Index on the Index tab of the References tab. But after Word places the index in your document, you notice that error messages appear instead of the page numbers. The most likely cause is that you created the index in a subdocument rather than in the master document of your publication.

To resolve the problem, close the current document by clicking the Microsoft Office Button and clicking Close. Then open the master document. (For more information on working with master documents, see Chapter 22, "Creating and Controlling Master Documents.") Expand all subdocuments and then press F9 to update your index. The page numbers should be displayed correctly.

Changing Index Columns

Depending on the length of your document and the index you're creating, you might want to format your index in multiple columns. By default, Word compiles your index in two columns, but you might want to change this setting if you have a short index that will occupy only a partial column, or if you want to run text in the column beside the index you create.

You can create up to four columns on each page of the index. To make a change, display the Index dialog box and click the Columns up arrow or down arrow to increase or decrease the number of columns you want.

TROUBLESHOOTING

My index columns don't line up

You've finished marking all the entries in your long document. You click the References tab, choose Insert Index, and select the format you want. You elect to create an indented index that's displayed in three columns. After reviewing your choices, you click OK to have Word compile the index. But when you see the index on the screen, you notice that the middle column seems out of alignment with the other two. What's going on?

Although Word automatically creates a section break both before and after your index, it's possible that an extra line space is preceding the first line in the second column. Click the Home tab and click the Show/Hide button in the Paragraph group to display hidden paragraph marks in your document. Then review the top and bottom entries in each column. If you see an unwanted paragraph mark, select it and press Delete to remove it. Then press F9 to have Word update your index and balance the columns.

Updating an Index

You can update an index at any time by clicking anywhere within it and pressing F9. This means that after you look at the compiled index, you can go back into the document and add entries you missed. The index is updated, and the choices you made in the Index dialog box are preserved.

> **Note**
>
> If you've made any formatting changes, such as selecting a different format style or changing from Indented to Run-In style, Word asks whether you want to replace the existing index with the new one. If you haven't made any editing changes in the current index—or you're willing to re-enter the changes you've made—select Yes. Word replaces the existing index with the new, updated one, and you'll need to re-enter those edits. If you select Cancel, the operation is canceled, and your changes are not made.

AutoMarking Entries with a Concordance File

A concordance file is a simple table you create to track and enter index entries easily. The table you create is a two-column table. In the first column, you enter the text you want Word to mark as the entry. And in the second column, you enter the index entry you want to use. Here are the steps to create a concordance file:

1. Create a table in a new document by clicking the Insert tab, choosing Table in the Tables group, and creating a two-column table.

2. In the first column, enter the words or phrases you want Word to mark for the entry.

> **Note**
>
> The entries in the first column are case sensitive. To create case insensitive entries, use all lowercase characters. Note that AutoCorrect may capitalize the first letter of each word automatically. If this behavior occurs, display the AutoCorrect Options (hover your mouse over the automatic change) and then click Stop Auto-Capitalizing First Letter Of Table Cells.

3. In the second column, type the index entry for the text in the first column. Be sure to type each entry in a separate cell.

4. Save and close the concordance file.

5. Open the file you want to index.

6. Click the References tab and choose Insert Index to display the Index dialog box.

7. Click the AutoMark button to display the Open Index AutoMark File dialog box (see Figure 25-4).

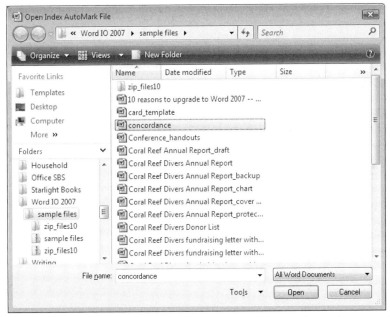

Figure 25-4 Use the Open Index AutoMark File dialog box to choose the concordance file for your index.

8. Navigate to and select the concordance file and then click Open. Word automatically searches your document and locates each entry with the words you specified in the concordance file. (Word marks only the first occurrence of an entry in any one paragraph.)

> **Tip**
>
> Indexing in Word is a fairly straightforward process, but it's a good idea to practice working with the indexing features before you use them on a real document.

INSIDE OUT   Creating a lean and effective concordance file

You think you're saving lots of time and trouble by creating a concordance file that lists topics you want to be sure to include in your index. After you finish creating and saving the list, you create the index, but you wind up with all kinds of unnecessary entries. For example, in your publication on contemporary music, you wanted to index references to *jazz*, but when your index is compiled, you see that the word *jazz* appeared in your publication in many different places and contexts. As a result, your index has many more references than you need.

A workaround for compiling huge indexes full of unnecessary AutoMarked entries is to create the majority of the index entries manually, using the Mark Index Entry dialog box (which you display by pressing Alt+Shift+X). Then use the concordance file and AutoMark in the Index dialog box to add to your basic index entries, including only key words or phrases that are used in the sections to which you want to refer your readers.

What's Next?

This chapter wraps up the discussion of working with complex documents in Word. The next chapter starts Part 8, "Publishing: Word to the World," by exploring the tasks and options involved in previewing and printing your documents.

Printing with Precision

The phenomenal surge of personal computing introduced the concept of a modern "paperless" society, but years later, the world has yet to fully realize that ideal—as plenty of buried desks and bulging file cabinets can attest—and there's speculation that the surge also brought more paper usage overall. Yet the trends suggest that we're still slowly heading toward a paperless (or at least a less paper-filled) society as more and more people read blogs rather than newspapers, and Yahoo! says approximately 62 billion e-mail messages are sent per day. For the most part, people continue to rely heavily on printed matter in many capacities.

When you work in Microsoft Office Word 2007, you'll probably need to print information frequently. In most cases, printing a document requires you simply to click the Microsoft Office Button and then click Print—not a complex task. However, as a more experienced Office Word 2007 user, you might want a higher level of control over your print jobs—especially if you want to do more than simply print single copies of entire documents. For example, you might want to print selected sections of a document, print more than one copy of a document, print several document pages per printed page, print a series of related documents, or print a summary of the styles used in the document, Building Block entries, or a summary of tracked changes in a document. Fortunately, the printing options included in Word give you this additional control (and more) over printing—and that's what this chapter is all about.

Print vs. Digital

While the worlds of digital and printed content overlap and merge, content developers face more decisions than ever regarding design choices. When you create documents in Word, you have numerous graphic design options, but you need to design with your goal in mind—are you creating a print product, digital publication, or content that will be used for both? As with all printing, your design choices are driven by a wide range of factors. You need to consider practicalities such as costs, profit, editing capabilities, time constraints, resources, ability to reach a desired audience (and knowing the audience's capabilities to receive electronic or printed material), publication standards, and more. In addition, you need to make some graphic design choices based on your end product.

When you design online content, some of the benefits are that you can use colorful backgrounds and creative layout elements (without worrying about printing costs), interactive features (such as hyperlinks), and, fundamentally, as many "pages" as you need to get your message across. With that said, online content is limited by the fonts you can use, quality of images, and writing style (online content should be concise and easy to scan), to just name a few constraints. As you might imagine, printed content also has benefits and drawbacks. Two of the main benefits of printed material are that you can precisely control the page layout of printed content and your audience doesn't need to log on to access your publication.

Often, material is adapted for use in both print and online content. When you are faced with this dual-purpose task, consider setting up some common processes and rules to ensure that your content best serves each desired purpose. For instance:

- Use Web fonts in all online materials, but feel free to use custom fonts for your printed material. Many marketing departments create consistency among materials by pre-establishing two "required" sets of fonts—one set for online content and another set for printed works. An easy way to accommodate both sets is to create Quick Style Sets for each type, as discussed in Chapter 15, "Using Styles to Increase Your Formatting Power."

- Include color blocks in online materials (such as for backgrounds or navigation bars), but omit large color areas from most printed materials. Word helps in this department by including an option to not print background colors and images by default, and the added benefit of Themes, discussed in Chapter 5, "Applying Themes for a Professional Look," aids in quick color switching.

- Show hyperlinks online, but verify that all links in printed materials show the actual Web address instead of the linked text.

Of course, you won't always be in charge of the content you work with—you might need to print online content or print colorful pages in black and white, for example. In this chapter, all of the primary print options are covered so you'll be able to control your print jobs, regardless of whether you are printing online content or designing content to be printed.

Previewing Before Printing

One of the most important aspects to keep in mind when preparing your document for printing is that Word is always in contact with your current printer. Word uses the driver for the current printer for various tasks, such as to obtain the available fonts that are displayed on the Font list and for document pagination. When you view a document in Print Layout view, you are seeing the document as it will look when printed. For this reason, if you plan on printing a document, you should make sure the printer you intend to use is set as the current printer prior to setting printing options or making any layout adjustments in your document. To change to a different printer, click the Microsoft Office Button and click Print to display the Print dialog box. When you select another printer from the Name list, the Cancel button changes to Close. To accept the changes without printing, click the Close button. After you make this change, you may see slight pagination changes in your document.

Because pagination may change when you use another printer, another important aspect to keep in mind is that attempts to control pagination using manual page breaks typically fail and result in empty or partially empty pages when another printer driver is used to print or view the document. For additional information on how to control document pagination, see the Inside Out tip titled "When to Use Pagination Formatting Instead of Manual Page Breaks" in Chapter 3, "Mastering Page Setup and Pagination."

> **Tip**
>
> If you intend to print your document on a printer that is not available, such as when you are working at home and you intend to print the document at your office, you can still install the correct printer driver and use it for document preparation even if the printer is not physically available.

Even though Print Layout view displays your document as it will look when printed, you should make a habit of using the Print Preview feature. Like a painter stepping back from the canvas, you can use Print Preview to take a big-picture look at a page or series of pages before you commit the information to hard copy. In Print Preview, you can examine entire pages at once, checking for obvious page setup errors and oddities and even applying minor fixes to correct some of the errors you discover. For example, using Print Preview, you can quickly see when an image box overlays text (or vice versa), when a single line runs onto the next page, or when indented text is misaligned.

Getting Comfortable in Print Preview

Print Preview gives you a chance to view your document from a variety of perspectives before you print. By default, when you activate Print Preview, the current page is shown. To activate Print Preview, open your document in Word and then use one of the following techniques:

- Click the Microsoft Office Button, point at Print, and then click Print Preview.

- Click the Print Preview on the Quick Access Toolbar.

> **Note**
>
> To add Print Preview to your Quick Access Toolbar, right-click the Print Preview command and click Add To Quick Access Toolbar.

- Press Ctrl+F2 (or Ctrl+Alt+I).

Figure 26-1 shows a document in Print Preview. The Print Preview tools are described in Table 26-1.

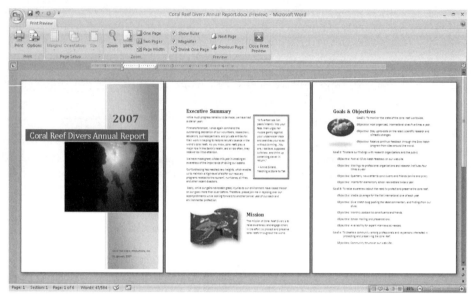

Figure 26-1 Previewing documents can help you troubleshoot page layout issues before you print.

Table 26-1 Print Preview Tools

Name	Icon	Description
Print		Opens the Print dialog box.
Options		Opens Word Options to the Display section, which includes basic Print options.
Margins		Opens the Margins gallery, which you can use to set standard or custom margins. To set margins manually, click Custom Margins to access the Margins settings in the Page Setup dialog box.
Orientation		Provides options for Portrait (vertical) and Landscape (horizontal) page layout options.

Name	Icon	Description
Size		Opens the Paper Sizes gallery, which you can use to set standard paper sizes, including Letter, A4, envelopes, and many other options, for sections in your document or the whole document. You can click the More Paper Sizes option to access the Paper settings in the Page Setup dialog box.
Zoom		Opens the Zoom dialog box. You can also access the Zoom dialog box by clicking the Zoom Level, such as 100%, in the Status Bar.
100%		Sets the page view to 100% of the normal size.
One Page	One Page	Displays a single page in Print Preview.
Two Pages	Two Pages	Displays two pages in Print Preview.
Page Width	Page Width	Sets the page view so that the width of the document fills the current window size.
Show Ruler	☑ Show Ruler	Toggles rulers on and off in the same way that the View Ruler button located at the top of the right scroll bar controls the rulers. Rulers enable you to modify margins and indents and set tabs from within Print Preview.
Magnifier	☑ Magnifier	When the check box is checked, you can click the document to enlarge or reduce the view. When the check box is cleared, you can edit the document.
Shrink One Page	Shrink One Page	Reduces the number of pages in the current document by one if possible by reducing the font size.
Next Page	Next Page	Jumps to the next page or groups of pages if you are viewing more than one page at a time.
Previous Page	Previous Page	Jumps to the previous page or groups of pages if you are viewing more than one page at a time.
Close Print Preview		Exits Print Preview and returns to the same page, cursor location, and view that appeared before you activated Print Preview.

To exit Print Preview, you can use the Close button on the Print Preview tab or any of the methods you used to switch to Print Preview. For example, you can click the Print Preview command again to toggle off the view. You can also press Esc or switch to another view using the View buttons (located to the left of the Zoom Level on right side of the Status bar by default).

Chapter 26

When you exit Print Preview, Word returns the insertion point to the position in which it was located before you selected Print Preview.

Zooming In on the Details

Using the Zoom tools on the Print Preview tab or the View tab in other views, you can examine your documents by zooming in to see details and zooming out to evaluate the flow of content on multiple pages. You can select a specific section, page, or group of pages on which to focus.

One of the notable additions to Word 2007 is the Zoom Slider, found to the right of the Status bar.

> **Note**
>
> If you do not see the Zoom Slider or the Zoom Level, right-click the customizable Status bar and click Zoom Slider or Zoom, respectively.

You can change your view by sliding the indicator marker or clicking the minus (−) and plus (+) signs at each end of the spectrum to decrease or increase the current view by 10 percent per click. Using the slider, you can view your document from 10 percent to 500 percent of its normal size. Furthermore, as you change the percentage, Word automatically shows the number of pages that fit within the view in the workspace by default (for example, if you view a multipage document formatted for standard 8.5-by-11-inch paper at 30 percent, you will probably see three pages onscreen simultaneously). You can use the Zoom Slider and Zoom Level in this manner in both Print Preview and Print Layout view. Figure 26-2 shows 90 A5 pages in Print Preview.

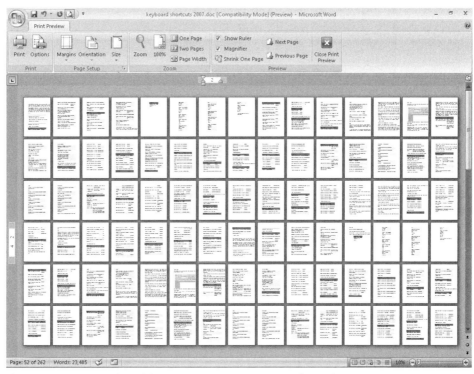

Figure 26-2 Zoom tools enable you to preview many pages of your document at varying percentages.

Note

In other views, such as Draft and Outline, the Zoom methods still increase and decrease the display of the document, but you do not see the representation of the individual pages as shown in Figure 26-2.

Note that the Zoom Slider and Zoom Level are not available in Full Screen Reading view.

You can use the Zoom dialog box, shown in Figure 26-3, to further modify your view. To open the Zoom dialog box, click Zoom in the Print Preview window or click the Zoom Level, such as 100%, in the Status bar. A few useful options in the Zoom dialog box are the Many Pages option, used to specify how many pages to show, and the Whole Page option, which sets the zoom to the width of the document's text.

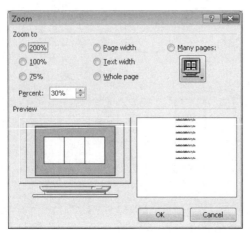

Figure 26-3 The Zoom dialog box enables you to configure exact viewing details in Print Preview.

INSIDE OUT   What Happened to Full Screen View?

Full Screen, found in previous versions of Word under the View menu, was replaced with Full Screen Reading view. As you might have discovered, Full Screen Reading view does not represent how pages appear when the document is printed. Instead, Full Screen Reading view optimizes the view of a document for online reading. To display how pages will print while using Full Screen Reading view, click View Options and then click Show Printed Page. (For more information about the Full Screen Reading view, see Chapter 7, "Honing Document Navigation Skills.")

Additionally, Full Screen Reading view shows the full page or multiple pages on the screen, as opposed to filling the screen with a page. If you want to emulate the old Full Screen view, in Print Preview, click Page Width on the Print Preview tab, and then double-click the Print Preview tab to minimize the Ribbon. Unlike the old Full Screen view, you still see the Title bar, Quick Access Toolbar, and Status bar, but this setup maximizes the view of your document.

Editing in Print Preview

As you zoom in, out, and around in Print Preview, you'll occasionally see details you want to adjust. If you exit Print Preview to fix the problems, you'll be returned to your original location, which means that you might have to search all over for the areas you identified in Print Preview. Fortunately, you don't have to leave Print Preview to make minor editing adjustments. If you need to edit some text, condense a document slightly, or adjust alignment, you can do so in Print Preview using the techniques described here.

- **Editing text in Print Preview** You can modify text in Print Preview by deleting, adding, cutting, copying, pasting, moving, and formatting text and other document components in much the same way that you edit documents in other views. First, click the page you want to edit, and then zoom in on the page if necessary. Clear the Magnifier check box (if necessary) to change the pointer to an insertion point. Keep in mind that you don't have to edit in 100% view; you can edit in any view size. At 100% (and larger), you can edit text in detail; at smaller sizes with several pages on the screen, you can easily drag elements, such as an image, from page to page.

INSIDE OUT   Displaying a Print Preview Page in Another View

When you exit Print Preview, your insertion point returns to where it was located before you selected Print Preview. In some instances, you might prefer to go directly to the page you were viewing in Print Preview. Unfortunately, Word doesn't provide an option to display the current page in Print Preview in other views—you're forced to return from whence you came. A quick workaround to this little impediment is to click the page to activate it and then click the Page Number in the Status bar (or press Ctrl+G) to display the Go To dialog box. Type the current page number, leave the dialog box open (it is modeless, so you can still use the application), click once to activate the Word window, click the Close Print Preview button on the Preview tab, and then click the Go To button in the Go To dialog box to navigate to the page.

- **Condensing text to shorten a document by one page** You can use the Shrink One Page tool to tighten up a document. This method works best for documents that are just a tad too long. To do so, click Shrink One Page on the Print Preview tab. Word attempts to reduce your document by at least one page by decreasing the font size in half-point increments. Be forewarned that you might not like the changes Word makes if you use Shrink One Page multiple times (for instance, fonts can be reduced up to five point sizes, and you might need to use a magnifying glass to actually read the document) and, in some cases, Word presents a message box stating that it is unable to shrink the document. To undo shrinking, use the Undo feature. For other methods you can use to reduce or increase the page count, see the Inside Out tip titled "'Fitting' Text" later in this chapter.

> **Note**
>
> The Shrink One Page feature does not remove manual page breaks. If you think text should be able to fit on the page but you encounter the message stating that Word is unable to shrink the document, check for manual page breaks in your document. To view manual page breaks, on the Home tab in the Paragraph group, click the Show/Hide button, or press Ctrl+Shift+* (asterisk on numeric keypad does not work) to toggle the view of formatting marks.

- **Adjusting margins, indents, and tabs** You can click the Show Ruler check box on the Print Preview tab or click the View Ruler button above the right scroll bar to toggle rulers on and off in Print Preview. When the rulers appear, you can drag the margin indicators, indent markers, or manual tabs to adjust them. If you're displaying multiple pages, the rulers display above and to the left of the page that's currently selected. You can also adjust margins using the Margins gallery, as shown in Figure 26-4. Also notice in Figure 26-4 that the Print Preview button is added to the Quick Access Toolbar and the rulers correspond to the currently selected page—the fourth page in the second row (page 49 in the document, as you can see in the Status bar).

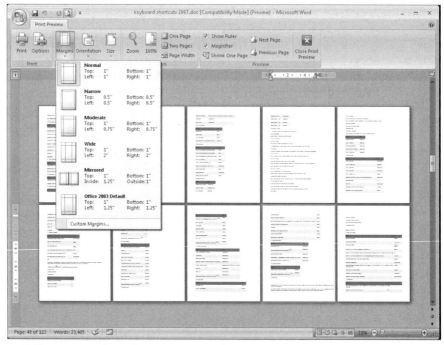

Figure 26-4 You can adjust margins, indents, and tabs while in Print Preview by using the vertical and horizontal rulers as well as the Margins gallery.

For more information about controlling margins and using rulers to adjust, indents, and tabs, see Chapter 3 and Chapter 14, "Aligning Information and Formatting Paragraphs and Lists."

> **Note**
>
> When rulers are visible, you can quickly display the Page Setup dialog box, which enables you to change a document's margins, page orientation, and other page setup options. To display the Page Setup dialog box, double-click the ruler. (If you double-click within the white portion of the top ruler, you might accidentally set unwanted tabs instead; should this occur, drag it off of the ruler to remove it). Similarly, you can also click Custom Margins at the bottom of the Margins gallery to open the Page Setup dialog box.

INSIDE OUT   "Fitting" Text

If you need to fit text to a specific number of pages or to a specific page, you can use several methods to accomplish this task. Reducing the font size or changing the page margins are typically the first methods that come to mind, but there are times when these methods cannot be used. The following list provides a few common alternatives to using the Shrink One Page option, manually reducing the font size, or modifying the page margins.

- **Spacing Before/After Paragraphs** If you use formatted space between paragraphs as opposed to empty paragraphs, you can adjust the spacing before or after paragraphs. Space between paragraphs rarely needs to be 10 or 12 points, and you can type any amount, even as small as one-tenth of a point. You can also type other units of measure after the value and they will be converted to points. Use cm for centimeters, *in* for inches, and *li* for line. For example, *.6 li* is converted to 7.2 points. The Spacing Before and Spacing After options can be found in the Paragraph dialog box on the Indents And Spacing tab in the Spacing area. To display the Paragraph dialog box, click the dialog launcher in the Paragraph group on the Home tab.

- **Set Exact Line Height** Line spacing, or the amount of space between the lines of a paragraph, is typically more space than necessary. Setting line spacing to an exact line height can reduce the space between lines and allows more text to fit on a page. The line height you need depends on the font size, and it might take some experimentation to find the best height so that the text is still easy to read. To adjust the line spacing, on the Home tab, click the dialog launcher in the Paragraph group. In the Spacing area, change Line Spacing to Exactly and start by making the adjustments in 1-point increments using the At text box. Note that you can also use increments of one-tenth of a point by typing directly in the At text box.

- **Condense Character Spacing** Condensing the amount of space between characters is a common method used to reduce page count, and the results are hardly noticeable. Condensing your text by even one-tenth of a point makes an impact on page count. To condense spacing between characters, on the Home tab, click the dialog launcher in the Font group to display the Font dialog box. Click the Character Spacing tab, change the Spacing option to Condensed, and modify the points in the By text box.

These methods can be used in combination, or you might find that a single method resolves the issue. While the methods presented are for reducing page count, the same methods can be used to increase page count should the need arise. Additionally, depending on the document, you should modify the document styles or Document Defaults instead of using direct formatting, as described in Chapter 15.

Printing Quickly and Efficiently

After you've approved your document's appearance using Print Preview, you're ready to print. By far, the easiest and most common printing task is printing an entire document. If you want to send the entire document to the current printer, use Quick Print (formerly the Print button on the Standard toolbar), found by clicking the Microsoft Office Button and pointing at Print.

> **Tip**
>
> To determine your current printer, hover your mouse over Quick Print and it displays in the ScreenTip, provided that ScreenTips is turned on in Word Options in the Popular area.

For faster printing, you might want to add Quick Print to your Quick Access Toolbar. To do so, click the More button at the end and then click Quick Print.

You can also print a Word document without opening the file or the Print dialog box by right-clicking a file or group of files in the Open dialog box and then clicking Print from the shortcut menu. Note that you will likely encounter a message box stating that the command cannot be performed because a dialog box is open. After you click OK to close the message and you then close the Open dialog box, the document or documents are sent to the printer.

> **Note**
>
> At the time of this writing, there is a known issue with using Quick Print in Outline view. If all levels of the document are not displayed, the outline of the document does not print correctly—the headings are overlaid on top of the document text. To print a document outline using Outline view, use the Print dialog box instead.

TROUBLESHOOTING

An extra blank page prints when I print

If an extra blank page prints at the end of your print job, there might be an extra paragraph return or two inserted at the end of your document. To delete the empty paragraphs, display hidden characters in your document (click the Show/Hide button in the Paragraph group on the Home tab, or press Ctrl+Shift+*) and then delete the extra paragraph markers. After you delete the extra paragraph markers, you can verify that the extra blank page has been removed by viewing your document in Print Preview.

If the extra paragraph mark is after a table, then this paragraph mark cannot be deleted. The workaround for this issue is to select the paragraph mark and change the font size to 1 point. You also need to remove any spacing before or after the paragraph and make sure it is formatted with single line spacing.

To print from Word, you must have a printer and printer driver installed. If you're in charge of configuring your own printer, use the Printers category in Control Panel, or check your printer manufacturer's Web page for updated drivers to download if you run into Word 2007 compatibility issues. For additional assistance, visit the Microsoft Knowledge Base at *http://support.microsoft.com* and search for all articles for your specific printer in the Word 2007 or 2007 Office Suites product categories.

Canceling a Print Job

On occasion, you might decide at the last moment to cancel a print job. The way you cancel a print job depends on whether background printing is turned on. By default, Word activates background printing, which means that you can continue working while you print a document. To change this setting, display Word Options and click Advanced. Then scroll to the Print area and clear the Print In Background check box. To halt printing from within Word while your computer is sending a document to the printer, follow one of these two procedures:

- If background printing is disabled, click Cancel or press Esc.

- If background printing is enabled, click the Cancel button in the Status bar while the document is being sent to the printer. If you're printing a short document, the Cancel button might not be visible long enough for you to cancel the printing task.

TROUBLESHOOTING

The wrong font appears in my document on the screen or when printed

In some cases, a font that you're using might not show up in your document. Instead, Word substitutes another font for the unavailable font. You can control which font is used as the substitute font by performing the following steps:

1. Click the Microsoft Office Button, click Word Options, and click Advanced. Scroll to the Show Document Content options and click the Font Substitution button.

If your document doesn't require font substitution (because all fonts used in the document are available), Word displays a message stating that no font substitution is necessary. If your document does require font substitution, the Font Substitution dialog box opens, as shown in the following image.

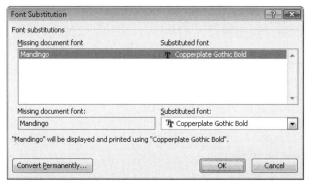

2. Under Font Substitutions, click the missing font name under Missing Document Font and then click a substitute font in the Substituted Font box.

3. Click the Convert Permanently button to permanently convert all of the missing fonts in the current document to their current substitute fonts, which means that the document now uses the substitute fonts and if the document is opened on another computer, the substitute fonts are used instead of the original fonts. Once the missing fonts are converted to the substitute fonts, they cannot be converted back.

Similarly, some fonts might show up on the screen but print differently from the way they are displayed. In these cases, Word might be printing a draft copy (display Word Options, click Advanced, and scroll down to view the Print options) or the font you're using might not be available in your printer. To fix a missing printer font, you should change the offending font to a TrueType font or another font that's supported by your printer.

Using the Print Dialog Box

As an experienced user, you probably need to perform printing tasks that are more complex than merely printing single copies of entire documents, and there may be times when you do not want to use Quick Print and send the entire document to the current printer. For example, you might need to change the printer or print only specific pages. For these tasks, you need to use the Print dialog box, shown in Figure 26-5. You can access the Print dialog box by clicking the Microsoft Office Button and then clicking Print or by pressing Ctrl+P. (If viewing your document in Print Preview, click the Print button on the Print Preview tab.) In this part of the chapter, you'll learn how to customize and control many of the printing settings that Word offers.

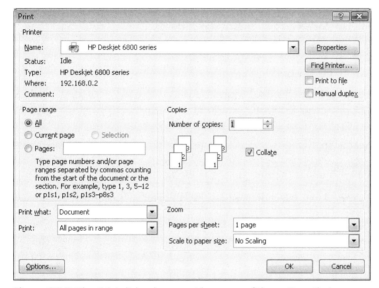

Figure 26-5 The Print dialog box provides many of the options that you can use to control your print jobs.

Printing More than One Copy of a Single Document

To print multiple copies of a document, display the Print dialog box and then select or type a value in the Number Of Copies box. By default, Word collates multiple copies of a print job. (Notice that the Collate check box is selected in the Copies area in the Print dialog box.) When collating is enabled, Word sends one copy of your print job to the printer with the collating instructions. In the long run, this method is probably easier for an end user. But depending on the printer, it might take longer to process if the document is printed, and then the next copy is printed, and so forth, and it can cause bottlenecks in a print queue if the document contains many large graphics or extensive formatting. If you prefer, you can clear the Collate check box. On some laser printers, printing without collating might speed the process and avoid bottlenecks in the print queue because the printer won't have to reprocess information for each copy of a page.

> **Note**
>
> The Print To File option creates a .prn file that can be created using a Printer Command Language (PCL) or PostScript (PS) printer driver. Primarily, these files are used for creating PDF or TIF files. To actually print a .prn file, you need to type a print command at a Command Prompt, such as COPY /B *Filename.prn \\ComputerName\PrinterShareName*.

Printing Ranges

In many cases, you'll want to print a selection of pages instead of an entire document. For example, you might want to select and print a few paragraphs of text, print two or three noncontiguous sections within a long report, or print the cover letter attached to your updated résumé. To print specific pages and sections within a document, use the following options in the Page Range area of the Print dialog box:

- **All** Prints the entire document; the default selection.

- **Current Page** Prints the page currently displayed on the screen (even if you have scrolled away from the page containing the cursor) or the selected page in Print Preview (if multiple pages are shown).

- **Selection** Prints selected text starting at the top of the printed page. To use this option, text must be selected in the document prior to displaying the Print dialog box. Note that the selection must be a contiguous text selection.

  To review text selection methods, see Chapter 2, "Document Creation with Word 2007."

- **Pages** Prints only the pages, page ranges, and sections you specify. Use commas for individual pages and hyphens for a range of pages. For example, enter **1-5,9,15-18** to print pages 1 through 5, page 9, and pages 15 through 18. If your document contains sections, you must specify which pages and sections to print. Precede the page number with *p* and use *s* for section. For example, type **s2,s4** to print all of sections 2 and 4; type **p3s4-p6s5** to print from page 3, section 4 to page 6, section 5.

> **Tip**
>
> Word uses the formatted page number, as opposed to the physical page number (Page X Of Y shown in the Status bar), for printing. To quickly determine the formatted page number and section number, note the Page and Section in your Status bar and enter the values as you see them in the Print dialog box. If you do not see the Page and Section, right-click the customizable Status bar, click Formatted Page, and then click Section to add them to your Status bar.

For more information about defining and using sections, see Chapter 3 and Chapter 21, "Formatting Columns and Sections for Advanced Text Control."

INSIDE OUT   **Printing Odd and Even Pages to Simulate Duplex Printing**

If you want to print using both sides of each sheet of paper but don't have a *duplex print-er* (a printer that can automatically print on both sides of a sheet), use the Manual Duplex option in the Print dialog box. If this option is selected, Word prints all of the pages that appear on one side of the paper and then prompts you to turn the stack over and feed the pages into the printer again.

Another alternative is to use the Odd Pages and Even Pages print options in the Print dialog box. To accomplish this, you can print all of the odd pages first, turn the printed pages over, reinsert the paper into your printer's paper tray, and then print the even pag-es. You'll probably have to experiment with your printer tray to ensure that you insert the paper properly. To assist in this task, take a few sheets of paper and annotate them with Top, Bottom, Odd, and Even and print only the same number of pages so you can get a better idea of how your printer prints without using a lot of paper.

Bear in mind that printing in this way can eventually cause printers to jam as a result of the ink from the already printed pages building up as they pass through your printer. If you do a lot of two-sided printing, you should probably invest in a printer that is de-signed to handle it.

Printing Document Elements

As you know, documents consist of much more than just the content that appears on a page. Documents can include document properties, styles, tracked changes, and com-ments as well as other elements available to the document, such as Building Blocks and keyboard shortcut assignments. In some cases, you might want to print these items instead of the actual document. The Print dialog box enables you to print common ele-ments by selecting them on the Print What list. Using this technique, you can print the following:

- **Document** Prints the entire document; the default setting.

- **Document Properties** Prints information stored in the File Properties such as the file name, location, template, title, author, creation date, last saved date, num-ber of words, and so forth. You can view a file's properties without printing the information in the Open and Save As dialog boxes if using Windows Vista or by opening the document, clicking the Microsoft Office Button, pointing at Prepare, and then clicking Properties (note that you cannot view document properties when you are in Print Preview). To view advanced properties, click the Document Properties arrow in the Document Properties pane and click Advanced Proper-ties. The Document Properties pane, Properties dialog box, and Save As dialog box are shown in Figure 26-6.

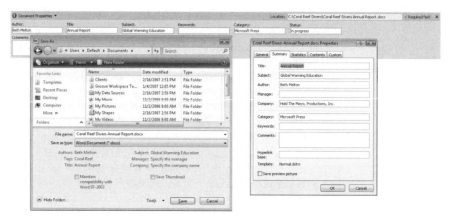

Figure 26-6 The Print dialog box enables you to print in list format the information stored in the Document Properties pane and advanced properties dialog box.

- **Document Showing Markup** Prints the document and all of the tracked changes made in the text. You can see how a document containing tracked changes will be printed by previewing the document in Print Preview, as shown in Figure 26-7. Keep in mind that if you have turned on tracking so that all revisions appear in your document, when you send that document to print, the Document Showing Markup print option is selected in the Print dialog box by default. To avoid printing markup when the feature is turned on, show the document in Final view in Word before you print.

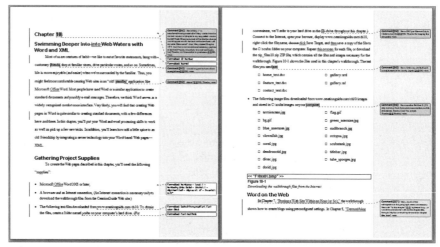

Figure 26-7 A document printed with markup shows all tracked changes and comments along with the document's contents, similar to how a marked-up document appears in Print Preview.

For information about using tracked changes, see Chapter 19, "Revising Documents Using Markup Tools."

- **List Of Markup** Prints a summary of each tracked change made in a document on a separate line below a color-coded heading. The color coding is based on who made each change, and the text of each color-coded heading indicates the page number, action (deleted, inserted, or comment), name of the user who made the change, and date and time of the modification. This printout provides a very detailed list of changes. If the document contains more than a few changes or comments, this print job could take a few minutes to queue and even longer to print. This option can create fairly large print files, so use this option with caution.

- **Styles** Creates an alphabetical list of styles defined in the current document. Each list entry includes the style definition such as formatting attributes, style for the following paragraph, based on style, style type, and so forth.

    For more information about creating and using styles, see Chapter 15.

- **Building Block Entries** Prints a complete alphabetical list of the Building Block entries available to the document that are stored in Building Blocks.dotx, any global templates, or the current document template.

    For more information about Building Blocks, see Chapter 8, "Putting Text Tools to Work."

- **Key Assignments** Prints an alphabetical list of custom shortcut keys created for standard Word commands and other functions, such as macros and styles. If no custom shortcut keys or macros are included in the document, the printout includes the document location and the text Global Key Assignments to indicate that only the global shortcuts are in effect for the document.

    For more information about working with macros, see Chapter 31.

TROUBLESHOOTING

Printing a markup list for a page range doesn't work

Unfortunately, you can't print a markup list for a range of pages—you must print either a complete list of all changes made to an entire document or none at all. Luckily, if you're flexible, you can work around this limitation. The easiest approach is to forget about the list and instead print a range of pages using the Document Showing Markup option. You'll be able to see the tracked changes and comments in this view—it just won't be printed in list format (and in many cases, the changes make more sense when you see them in a document instead of listed one after another). Of course, in some instances, you might really need to print a list of markups for a range of pages. Don't worry—there's still hope. One way you can accomplish this is to copy the portion of the document containing the tracked changes to a new document and print the list of markup for the new document instead.

Printing Several Pages per Sheet

In Word, you can print more than one document page on a single sheet of paper. This feature, introduced in Word 2000, helps you to better see a document's layout and can be used to present information in a visually concise manner. You'll find that printing several pages per sheet is similar to previewing multiple pages in Print Preview. (The difference is that the printed pages generally provide a clearer view of the pages' contents.) When you print multiple pages on a single sheet of paper, Word shrinks the pages to the appropriate size for printing purposes. To set up this arrangement, follow these steps:

1. Click the Microsoft Office Button, and then click Print (or press Ctrl+P) to open the Print dialog box.

2. In the Zoom area of the Print dialog box, on the Pages Per Sheet list, select the number of pages per sheet you want to print. You can print up to 16 pages per sheet.

> **Note**
>
> You must use the values in the Pages Per Sheet list to specify the number of pages to be printed—you can't type a value. In addition, the feature is available only when the Document or Document Showing Markup option is selected in the Print What list.

Scaling Printed Documents

Just as you can reduce and enlarge copies when you use a photocopier, you can reduce and enlarge your print output in Word by using the Scale To Paper Size option. Scaling documents can come in handy when you are printing on nonstandard paper sizes or when you want to shrink your output slightly to ensure that information isn't cut off at the margins.

The key to scaling documents is to use the Scale To Paper Size list, which is located in the Zoom area in the Print dialog box. The Scale To Paper Size list includes a variety of sizing options including Letter, Legal, Executive, A4, various envelope sizes, index cards, photo sizes, banners, and so forth. To view the list of options, click the Scale To Paper Size list. By default, the No Scaling option is selected.

Using the Print dialog box to scale a document scales your document for the current printing session only. It doesn't resize or alter the document's contents, unlike the Shrink To Fit feature in Print Preview, which modifies the formatting in your document.

Setting Other Printing Options

In addition to the options available in the Print dialog box, Word offers a number of other printing options, some of which are discussed earlier in this chapter. Two sets of primary printing options are found in Word Options. Common print options are found in the Display area, and others can be found in the Advanced area, as shown in the following image.

Print

- ☑ Use draft quality
- ☑ Print in background ⓘ
- ☐ Print pages in reverse order
- ☐ Print XML tags
- ☐ Print field codes instead of their values
- ☐ Print on front of the sheet for duplex printing
- ☐ Print on back of the sheet for duplex printing
- ☑ Scale content for A4 or 8.5 x 11" paper sizes

Default tray: Use printer settings   ▾

Advanced Section

Printing options

- ☑ Print drawings created in Word ⓘ
- ☐ Print background colors and images
- ☐ Print document properties
- ☐ Print hidden text
- ☐ Update fields before printing
- ☐ Update linked data before printing

Display Section

Chapter 26

Some noteworthy printing options are also found in the Compatibility Options as well. Table 26-2 provides the location of each option along with a detailed summary.

Tip

To view the effect of the majority of printing options on a document prior to printing, view the document in Print Preview.

Table 27-2 **Additional Printing Options in Word Options**

Option	Description
Printing Options in the Display Section	
Print Drawings Created In Word	Prints drawing objects, such as shapes and text boxes, and floating objects, such as images and embedded objects. If this option is turned off, white space is used in place of inline drawing objects, floating objects are suppressed, and inline objects, such as an embedded Excel workbook, are printed.
Print Background Colors And Images	Prints page colors and other effects, such as images added using the Page Color command on the Page Layout tab.
Print Document Properties	Prints the document properties on a separate page whenever you print the document.
Print Hidden Text	Prints text formatted as hidden text even if it is not currently displayed in the document.
Update Fields Before Printing	Updates all fields, such as cross references, Tables of Contents, calculations, and so on, in a document before printing. This option also updates most fields when switching to Print Preview.
Update Linked Data Before Printing	Updates data linked from other documents, such as a linked and embedded Excel workbook, before printing.
Printing Options in the Advanced Section	
Use Draft Quality	Prints a document with minimal formatting if your printer supports draft-quality output.
Print In Background	Enables you to continue working while print tasks are being processed (although you might notice a slight slowing in response times as you work).
Print Pages In Reverse Order	Prints a document in reverse order, beginning with the document's last page.
Print XML Tags	Prints the XML tags embedded in the content of a document marked with XML tags provided by the attached schema.
Print Field Codes Instead Of Their Values	Prints the field code, such as {DATE} or {TIME}, in place of the value of the field.
Print On The Front Of The Sheet For Duplex Printing	Prints the front of each sheet when printing on a printer that does not have duplex capability. Pages print in reverse order so that when you flip the stack to print on the back, the pages print in the proper order.
Print On The Back Of The Sheet For Duplex Printing	Prints the back of each sheet when printing on a printer that does not have duplex capability. Pages print in ascending order so that they correspond to a stack of pages that are printed on the front in reverse order.

Option	Description
Scale Content For A4 Or 8.5 x 11" Paper Sizes	Enables automatic switching between standard 8.5-by-11-inch paper and the narrower, slightly longer A4 paper size used in most countries. This option is selected by default.
Default Tray	Specifies which printer tray should be used by default. For more information about selecting paper sources, see Chapter 3.
Print Postscript Over Text	Prints PostScript code (such as watermarks or overprinted text) when a document contains PRINT fields.
Print Only Data From A Form	Prints only the text entered into a document using form fields relative to their placement in the document. Used for printing on pre-printed forms.
Compatibility Options **(Located at the bottom of the Advanced area in the Layout Options)**	
Print Body Text Before Header/ Footer	Prints the main text layer before the Header/Footer layer, which allows for the process of PostScript codes in the text layer. This functionality is the reverse of the default order.
Print Colors As Black On Non-color Printers	Prints all colors as black, instead of using grayscale, when using a noncolor printer.
Use Printer Metrics To Lay Out Document	Word uses built-in metrics to lay out the document, as opposed to information from the printer driver. This option allows your document to look the same on the screen no matter what printer driver is installed; however, it still prints using information provided by the printer driver.

Chapter 26

Printing Individual Labels and Envelopes

On occasion, you might want to print a single envelope or an individual sheet of labels instead of a document. If you have several envelopes or labels to print, you might want to consider using Mail Merge instead. When you want to print a simple envelope or set of labels, click the Mailings tab and then click either Envelopes or Labels to open the Envelopes And Labels dialog box, as shown in Figure 26-8.

For information about conducting mail merges, see Chapter 28, "Performing Mail Merges."

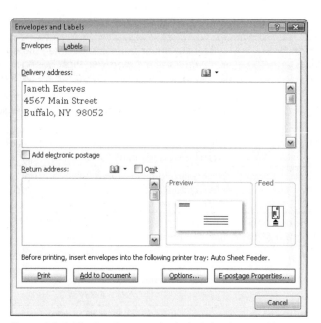

Figure 26-8 The Envelopes And Labels dialog box enables you to complete simple envelope and label print jobs.

If you're working with an open document that has an address block, such as for a letter, the address is shown automatically in the Envelopes And Labels dialog box, as shown in Figure 26-8.

> **Tip**
>
> If the address block is not automatically displayed in the Envelopes And Labels dialog box or if you have multiple address blocks, select the address block prior to displaying the Envelopes And Labels dialog box.

The Envelopes tab includes a number of quick options that you can set before printing an envelope. Here's an overview:

- **Print** Starts the print process, so make sure to set your other options and load the printer before clicking this button.

- **Add To Document** Adds the envelope to the current document so that the envelope and document can be printed together.

- **Options** Displays the Envelope Options dialog box so that you can choose the envelope size, font, and printer feed specifications. You can also click the Preview envelope image or the Feed preview image to access the Envelope Options dialog box.

- **E-Postage Properties** Enables you to work with an e-postage account if you've previously set up an electronic postage add-in from the Web.

- **Cancel** Closes the Envelopes And Labels dialog box without saving settings.

To print an envelope, simply follow these steps:

1. On the Mailings tab, click Envelopes.

2. If necessary, type the recipient address in the Delivery Address box or click Insert Address next to the Delivery Address label. If you click Insert Address (above the Delivery Address text box), choose a profile (such as Outlook) and select the recipient in the Select Name dialog box.

3. Type a return address in the Return Address box or click Insert Address next to the Return Address label, and then select the return address you want to use. Or, if you prefer not to include a return address, click the Omit check box.

4. If you want to choose a nonstandard size envelope or change the font used in the address blocks, click Options or click image in the Preview area to display the Envelope Options dialog box. Select the envelope size and font you want to use and click OK.

Chapter 26

> **Tip**
>
> To change the font for individual lines or portions of the address, select the text you wish to format, right-click the selected text, and click Font to display the Font dialog box.

5. If you've subscribed to an e-postage service and want to add electronic postage to the envelope, click E-Postage Properties to set postage options. Select the Add Electronic Postage check box to enable the feature for the current envelope.

6. Make sure your printer is ready and the envelope is inserted as shown in the Feed area of the dialog box.

7. Click Print. If you want Word to save the created envelope with the document, click Add To Document.

Creating Labels

Instead of printing directly on envelopes, you might want to print mailing labels. Word provides an easy way for you to print labels in a wide range of shapes and sizes. If you want to print a single label or a few labels—not enough to warrant using mail merge—you can use the Labels tab in the Envelopes And Labels dialog box to print labels quickly. The options on the Labels tab enable you to enter the label information, choose the way you want the label printed (a single label or a whole page of labels), and make selections about the label size and e-postage. Here's how to print labels:

1. On the Mailings tab, click Labels. The Envelopes And Labels dialog box opens with the Labels tab displayed, as shown in Figure 26-9.

Figure 26-9 The Labels tab in the Envelopes And Labels dialog box enables you to process simple label printing jobs.

2. By default, Word prints a full page of labels. If you want to print only one, click the Single Label option in the Print area.

3. The selected label is shown in the Label area. If you want to select a different label, click the graphic in the Label area or click Options to make a new selection. (Both actions open the Label Options dialog box). Click OK after you select your label size and feed setting.

4. When you finish entering your choices, make sure your printer is loaded correctly and click Print, or click New Document to create a full page of labels in a new document.

> **Tip**
>
> To create a document with blank labels, leave the Address text box blank, select the Full Page Of Same Label option, and then click New Document.
>
> This method also enables you to type several addresses and print them on a sheet of labels instead of printing individual labels one at a time in the Envelopes And Labels dialog box. If you've already used labels on the sheet, simply start your first address in the column and row that corresponds to the next available label. Note that depending on the way your printer feeds a sheet and the type of labels you are using, feeding a label sheet multiple times could result in a printer jam.

For more information about printing envelopes and labels using mail merge, see Chapter 28.

Chapter 26

What's Next?

This chapter covered the art of printing Word documents from simply sending the entire document to the printer to optimizing the printed document by implementing various printing options. The next chapter covers a new function that has been added to Word 2007—the ability to create a new blog entry and post it, all from within Word.

Blogging from Word 2007

For many people, blogging has become a big part of the way they share their experiences with the world. A blog (short for weblog) gives individuals the power of publishing without relying on media outlet channels or traditional print publications. Everyone with something to say has the ability to say it on the Web. All they need is the necessary server space and the right software to post the blog content online.

In the 2007 Microsoft Office system, Word has become that software. Now bloggers can create blog posts from within Microsoft Office Word 2007 with a few simple clicks of the mouse. This chapter shows you how you can create blog posts with Office Word 2007 and post them to the blogging account you've created.

A Brief Blogging Introduction

If you're new to blogging, you may be wondering what all the excitement is about. Blogging started in the mid-1990s, but most of the phenomenal growth in the "blogosphere" has taken place since 2000. Bloggers come from all walks of life, all age groups, and all perspectives—and that's what makes blogging such a force in the world today.

Blogging is personal (or corporate) web publishing that can be done almost instantly—but it's also more than that. What sets blogs apart from other documents on the Web is their fast-changing nature and the fact that they are all about the links—links to other blogs, to resource sites, to communities, to media, and more. Links are created when others reference your blog in their own posts (and vice versa). Trackbacks enable people reading blogs to move from one to the next to the next. Bloggers are able to publish the latest news and can, within minutes, reach a worldwide audience, thanks to all the other bloggers who are searching for and linking to posts on that same topic.

Some people blog for pleasure, to stay in touch with family and friends, or simply to share their interests and outlook with the world. Others blog with purpose, to comment on political, corporate, or societal ideas and events, or to highlight stories that the mainstream media misses (or won't cover, such as the Stephen Colbert performance at the White House Press Corp dinner in early 2006).

Bloggers told it like it was during and after the destruction caused by Hurricane Katrina, they report on the Iraq war, they help expose corrupt politicians and companies, and they provide a voice—sometimes a very loud and far-reaching voice—that broadcasts a part of the cultural debate that may not be well-represented elsewhere.

The first blogging tools were a bit clunky and required users to learn HTML to post. As a result, most of the early bloggers were experts in technology. As blogging caught on, the tools became more user-friendly, enabling those without any programming experience to simply add their writing and photos to a page without a lot of hassle or technical know-how.

Blogging sites such as Blogger and LiveJournal have had a lot to do with the ever-expanding popularity of blogging. Utilities such as Blogroll.com (a free utility that bloggers use to show links to their own favorite blogs) helped expand the links. Social networking sites, such as MySpace, Friendster, and Windows Live Spaces, enable bloggers to add their words and pictures and also connect to their friends' spaces and build their own communities.

Today more than more than 60 million blogs are on the Internet—and huge numbers of new blogs are started every day. Many blogging tools are available online—Windows Live Spaces, Blogger, and LiveJournal are just a few. People blog for all sorts of reasons and write about all kinds of topics. Some blogs show mainly photos; others include audio recordings and video recordings; some people blog about movies, books, trivia, and more; others are part of a company strategy for marketing communications.

You might wonder what blogging has to do with professional or corporate communications. Depending on the type of business you have, to a greater or lesser extent, your communication with your customers is important. Letting them know what you're doing by writing about your new products, showing key new features, or introducing them to staff members can help the customer feel he or she "knows" your company.

Many companies today are encouraging their employees to blog about their projects (within nondisclosure guidelines) to help give potential customers a behind-the-scenes look at corporate life and mission. Microsoft is one of those companies with a large group of corporate bloggers—in fact, during the beta testing of Microsoft Office 2007, various Microsoft Office 2007 program managers blogged for many months before the release. Interested users could go to the blogs to find posts on the latest new features in their favorite applications, as well as information on the user interface, the Open XML Format, the XPS specification, and much more.

Microsoft Office Blogs

Some of the Microsoft Office 2007 program managers have been publishing great, insightful, and helpful blogs for many months. If you want to see some of the background of the Microsoft Office 2007 release and learn more about some of your favorite features, check out the following blogs:

- Jensen Harris, Office UI PM blog: blogs.msdn.com/jensenh/
- Excel team blog: blogs.msdn.com/excel/
- Word team blog: blogs.msdn.com/microsoft_office_word/
- Outlook blog: blogs.msdn.com/michael_affronti/
- Access blog: blogs.msdn.com/access/

Be sure to also take a look at the Windows Vista blog (www.microsoft.com/windows-vista), which includes the latest news about Microsoft's new operating system.

Starting a New Blog Post

Basically, creating a blog post is the same as creating any document—you click and type your text as you want it to appear. Follow these steps to start a new blog post:

1. Click the Microsoft Office Button. Then click New.

2. In the New Document window, click New Blog Post (see Figure 27-1).

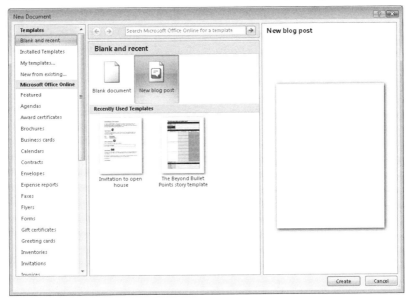

Figure 27-1 Choose New Blog Post in the New Document window to start the process of creating a blog entry.

3. The Blog Post window opens, and a popup dialog box asks you to register your blog account. If you already have a blog account with one of the blogging service provides (such as Windows Live Spaces, Blogger, or other services, as shown in Figure 27-2), you can select the service to enter the information for that account.

Figure 27-2 Word asks you to register your blog account so that the program will know where to send your blog entry when you're finished.

4. For now, click Register Later (you will register your account later in this chapter) and you are returned to the Blog Post window as shown in Figure 27-3.

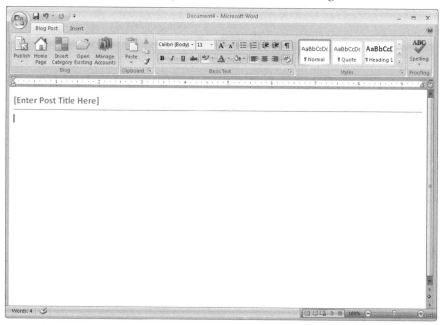

Figure 27-3 The Blog Post window includes tools used just for blogging.

The Blog Post window includes two command tabs: Blog Post and Insert. When Blog Post is selected, as it is in Figure 27-3, the groups provide you with the tools you need for working with your blog, working with the clipboard, entering basic text, applying styles, and proofing your entry. The Insert tab is available only if your blogging service enables you to include photos.

Entering Text

To begin entering text for your post, click in the [Enter Post Title Here] prompt and type the title for your blog entry (see Figure 27-4).

Figure 27-4 Click the prompt and type your own post title.

Click below the line to begin entering the text for the body of your post. After you type the entry, click the Spelling tool to run the spelling checker. If you choose, you can change the typeface, size, color, or alignment of the text as you would modify the formatting of a traditional document.

If you want to change the style of the text, click the More button in the lower right corner of the Styles gallery. The Styles gallery opens so that you can review and select the type of text style you want to apply to the post text.

Inserting a Web Link

As mentioned earlier, blogs wouldn't be blogs without the links—they would be static Web pages. To add a hyperlink to your blog post, follow these steps:

1. Highlight the section to which you want to add the link.

2. Click the Insert tab. The Ribbon changes to include groups for Tables, Illustrations, Links, Text, and Symbols (see Figure 27-5).

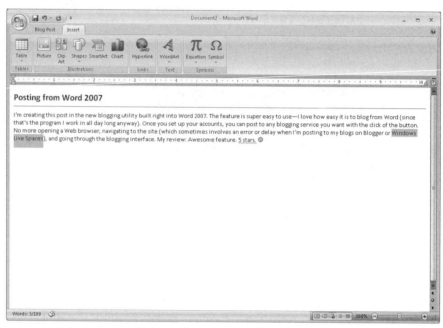

Figure 27-5 Add a link by clicking the Insert tab and choosing Hyperlink.

3. Click Hyperlinks. The Insert Hyperlink dialog box appears.

4. In the Address box, type the URL to which you want to link the selected text.

5. Click OK to save the link. The text will appear underlined in a blue font, indicating that it is now a hyperlink. If you want to ensure that you typed the link correctly, position the pointer over the link. The URL will appear in a pop-up box above the link so that you can double-check the link.

Adding a Category to Your Post

Categorizing your blog post helps search engines locate what you're blogging about and also gives your regular readers a way to find all posts related to a specific topic. To add a category to your post, click the Insert Category tool in the Blog group of the Blog Post tab. The Category field appears above the body text of your post. Click the arrow to see the list of categories (see Figure 27-6). Click the one you want to apply to the post you created.

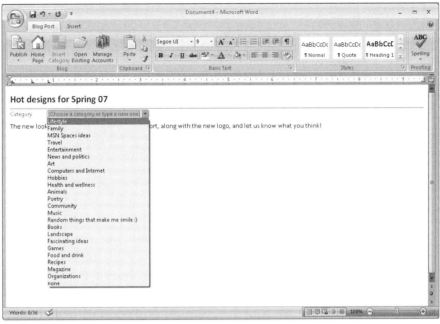

Figure 27-6 You can add categories to your post to help readers—and search engines—find it easily.

> **Note**
>
> The categories that appear depend on the categories created to work with your blog program. Some programs provide ready-made categories; others enable you to set up and use categories of your own.

What Will You Blog About?

The content of your blog will depend largely on your purpose. If you're just blogging for fun, to keep family apprised of all the happenings in your part of the world, or to share your interest or expertise in a particular topic, the posts will probably include stories, events, photos, and more. If you are blogging to build your expertise in a particular area, you may want to include all the latest news stories on your area of interest. If you are hoping to inspire others to join your nonprofit organization in serving others, you might include stories of those who have been helped by your organization in the past. If you

want to get the word out about your candidacy, share your passion for movies, or share your philosophy with the rest of the world, you may include links, stories, photos, resources, and engaging bits of information in the areas you want to highlight.

Here are some questions to consider as you plan the content for your blog:

- Who is your "typical reader"? Getting a clear picture of that person—and that person's expectations—can help you connect with your reader right from the start.

- What age is he or she? Knowing the general demographics of your typical reader will be helpful. Chances are that, because blogging is a kind of "real voice" medium, you may connect most easily with those close to your own age level. But many people have a knack for speaking to everyone at once. Know the interests, energy level, and passions of the audience you are addressing.

- What is he or she most interested in? Is your reader fascinated with technology, passionate about the environment, concerned about the political climate, or focusing on her newborn? Thinking about what your reader may be fascinated by right now will help you develop a sense for what others will find interesting on your blog.

- What do I want the person to do after reading my blog? If you want the person to come back, subscribe to your newsletter, try your product, sign up for your mailing list, or write to their congressperson, be sure you say so directly somewhere in the body of your blog.

- Are there any limitations on your subject matter? If you are writing a corporate blog, there may be definite guidelines for the type of content you can include. Additionally, you need to consider the fact that public blogs can be read by virtually everyone, which means you may have children as well as adults reading what you write (including your mother and grandmother!). Think through any limitations—and any ramifications of your posting—before you post.

Adding a Picture to Your Post

Most blog posts include a heading and supporting text. Some blog posts include photos as well. You can add photos to your Word blog post by following these steps:

1. Click to position the pointer at the place you want to add the picture.

2. Click the Insert tab and then click Picture in the Illustrations group.

3. In the Insert Picture dialog box, navigate to the folder storing the picture you want to include. Select the picture and click Insert (see Figure 27-7).

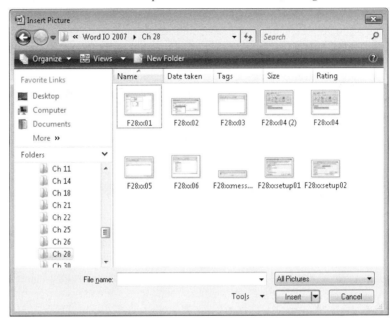

Figure 27-7 Choose the picture you want to include in your post by selecting it in the Insert Picture dialog box.

Once you add the picture to the post, the contextual Picture Tools appear in the Ribbon (see Figure 27-8). You can use the tools to do any (or all) of the following things:

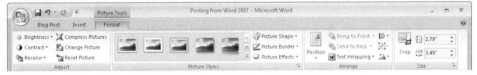

Figure 27-8 The contextual Picture Tools give you what you need to modify, enhance, size, and position the image in your blog post.

- **Resize the image.** The picture is inserted at the cursor position at a default size. You can resize the image by clicking any one of the handles around the outer edge of the object and dragging to resize it. You can also use the options in the Size group to crop the image or resize it to meet precise measurement requirements.

- **Edit the image.** Word includes a number of picture adjustment tools you can use to improve the look of the image. While the image is selected in the document, choose any of the tools in the Adjust group of the contextual Picture Tools to modify the image before posting.

- **Add special effects to the image.** The Picture Styles group enables you to apply one of the preset picture styles (including border settings, shape, and shadowing features) to the image. You can create a drop-shadow for the image; apply 3-D effects; change the shape, color, or thickness of the border; and more.

- **Control text placement.** When the image is added to the post, the text automatically moves to the bottom of the image. You can change the way the text flows around the picture by using the commands in the Arrange group. The Position command enables you to control where in the post the image appears; the Text Wrapping command gives you choices about how the text flows around the text.

Want To Know More About Blogging?

To learn more about blogging basics, check out the following resources:

- "Get Started Blogging," by Katherine Murray and Mike Torres, from Share Your Story: Blogging with MSN Spaces. Online at *www.microsoft.com/athome/intouch/ startblogging.mspx*.

- "Blog Basics: Learn How to Keep an Online Journal," by Mara Gulens. Online at *www.microsoft.com/athome/intouch/onlinejournal.mspx*.

- "Blog," Wikipedia entry. Online at *wikipedia.org/Weblog*.

Configuring Your Blog Account

When you're ready to publish your blog post, click the Blog Post tab and click Publish in the Blog group. If you haven't yet set up your blog account (or if you clicked Register Later in the Blog Post window, as mentioned earlier in this chapter), you will be asked to enter the information for your blog account or sign up for a new one.

Click Manage Accounts in the Blog group to start the process of setting up your new blog account. In the Blog Account window, click New. The New Blog Post window appears. Begin by clicking the Blog arrow and choosing your service from the list. Here's a quick introduction to each of the items on the list:

- **Windows Live Spaces** Windows Live Spaces is a free blogging and social networking service that enables you to blog, post photos, and connect with friends and family online. Go to spaces.live.com to find out more.

- **Blogger** Blogger is one of the largest and oldest blogging services available. Now part of Google, Blogger offers free blogging services without ads. Go to *www.blogger.com* for more information.

- **SharePoint Blog** To use this feature, you must have access to a company server running Windows SharePoint Services. Ask your system administrator for more information on whether your local server runs Windows SharePoint Services and to find out whether you have the permissions you need to post a blog to that server.

- **Community Server** Community Server is an online community-building program that is free for personal use but has varying licenses for commercial use.
  Community Server includes both blogging and forum posting features. For more
  information, go to *communityserver.org/i/overview.aspx*.

- **Other** This simply indicates that you have a service provider different from those
  shown in the list. If you have a different provider, click the My Providers Isn't
  Listed link.

Make your choice and click Next. The New Account Window appears, asking for information about the blog. If you selected Windows Live Spaces, the New Windows Live
Spaces Account dialog box appears, as shown in Figure 27-9. If you selected a Blogger
account, the New Blogger Account window asks you to enter your user name and password.

Figure 27-9 Setting up an account in the New Windows Live Spaces Account dialog box.

Type your space name and enter the secret word (for instructions on how to set this up
for your Windows Live Spaces account, see the following sidebar). Click the Remember
Secret Word check box if you want Windows Live Spaces to save your secret word and
apply it automatically whenever you post. These settings set up the access to your blog.

Now you need to set up the picture options so that you'll be able to include photos,
graphics, pictures, diagrams, and charts in your posts. Click the Picture Options button
to display the Picture Options dialog box (see Figure 27-10). Here you'll choose the way
in which your pictures will be hosted. Click the Picture Provider arrow and choose My
Own Server if you have server space in which your images can be housed. If you have
your own server space, click that option and enter the upload URL and source URL.
Then click OK twice to return to your post.

Figure 27-10 You can choose Picture Options to control the way images are uploaded to your blog.

Preparing Your Windows Live Spaces Blog

Before you can post from Word directly to your Windows Live Spaces blog, you have to turn on e-mail publishing in the blog. To do this, follow these steps:

1. Log in to your space. In Edit mode, click Options.

2. Click E-mail Publishing in the Options panel on the left side of the window.

3. Click the Turn On E-mail Publishing check box to turn on the feature.

4. Enter the e-mail address you will use for remote posting.

5. Type a secret word that will serve as a password to let Windows Live Spaces know you have permission to post remotely to the space.

6. Choose whether you want to save the entries as drafts until you can review and post them in Windows Live Spaces or you want to automatically post the received entry to the space.

7. Click Save to save your settings in Windows Live Spaces.

What's Next?

This chapter introduced you to the new blogging utility that is built into Word 2007. The next chapter offers another way of sharing your documents by showing you how to prepare and send mailings in Word.

Performing Mail Merges

Unless you work in the marketing department of a large company, chances are that you have to use mail merge only once in a while. Figuring out which fields go where, what you want to say, and how it all fits together can be confusing, frustrating, and time-consuming. In the past, a successful mail merge required considerable trial and error (not to mention pages of wasted labels and printer paper).

Microsoft Office Word 2007 has greatly simplified the mail merge process and—through the changes in the user interface—has brought all the commands you need to the Ribbon in just the order you need them. Whether your merge projects are large or small, the process is easier than ever to follow.

This chapter introduces you to the mail merge features in Office Word 2007 and shows you how to master the techniques for individual merge projects. You can capitalize on the work you've done by applying the "create it once, use it many times" techniques mail merge offers.

Mail Merge Overview

Using the mail merge feature in Word, you can create letters, faxes, e-mail messages, envelopes, labels, and directories once and use them many times. The merge process is basically the same for all document types. All the commands you need are on the Mailings tab on the Ribbon, arranged in the order you need them (see Figure 28-1). Here's a quick rundown of the steps involved in the mail merge process.

1. Select the document type you want to create by choosing Envelopes or Labels in the Create group or by clicking Start Mail Merge in the Start Mail Merge group. In this step, you tell Word whether you want to create a letter, e-mail message, envelope, labels, or directory.

2. Select the recipients by choosing Select Recipients in the Start Mail Merge group. In this step, you can type a new list, choose your data list from an existing file, or select your Outlook Contacts list.

3. Write your letter (or e-mail message) and then add the necessary merge fields by using the commands in the Write & Insert Fields group.

4. Preview the merge operation and make any last minute changes by selecting commands in the Preview Results group.

5. Merge the document and the data source and print or send the results by using the Finish & Merge command in the Finish group.

Figure 28-1 The Mailings tab contains the commands you will use to create your mailing project.

The next several sections explain more about each of these steps.

INSIDE OUT   Where is the Mail Merge Wizard?

The Mailings tab is convenient because it provides you with all the commands you'll use for completing a mail merge project. You can see all the commands at once and simply click the one you need. But if you prefer to follow a more directed process for your project, you can use the Mail Merge Wizard that is also available in Word 2003. To start the Mail Merge Wizard, click the Mailings tab and then click the Start Mail Merge button. The last command on the list of options that appears is Step By Step Mail Merge Wizard. Click this command to launch the wizard in a task pane on the right side of the Word window. Follow the prompts in the wizard to complete your project.

Know Your Merge Terms

The following terms might be new to you if you are learning about mail merge for the first time.

- **Main document** The letter, e-mail, envelope, or label into which the data will be merged

- **Source file** Also known as the source list or recipients list, the file from which the merge data is taken

- **Merge fields** Identifiers inserted in the text that indicate to Word the position and type of data you want inserted at that point in the document

- **Address block** Includes name and address information

- **Greeting line** Adds the opening salutation, along with the name(s) of the recipient(s) you select

Starting the Mail Merge Project

A little forethought is in order when you are organizing a big mailing project. Depending on the size and type of the mailing, you may begin working on the project weeks—or months!—in advance of your mailing date. Here are some examples of mailing projects, ranging from small to large.

- A quick thank you letter to people who recently visited your open house

- A fundraising letter that thanks donors for their contributions last year and asks them to make a pledge for this year

- A personalized e-mail newsletter sharing your latest company news and inviting others (through Web links) back to your site

- A prospectus mailed to a particular client, designed to include the client's personal, business, and purchasing data

> **Note**
>
> When you're planning the process, be sure to leave a little extra time for merging. The 2007 release of Word does simplify mail merge, but most of us, to one degree or another, have to relearn the process each time we do it. Leave yourself an extra hour or two (at minimum) to set up your merge fields, do a test merge, and finalize the document.

Selecting the Document Type

Your first choice in the mail merge process involves selecting the type of document you want to create. Will you be sending a direct mail letter, an e-mail message, or a fax? Perhaps you want to start with envelopes and labels, or create a directory to store listings of data such as customer names and addresses, product information, and personnel contact data. The Start Mail Merge command tab includes the tools you'll use for the first part of preparing your mailing project. Click Start Mail Merge to display the options showing the type of merge document you can create (see Figure 28-2). When you click Letters, E-Mail Messages, or Directory, Word displays the type of document you are creating.

Chapter 28

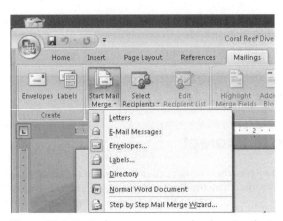

Figure 28-2 Begin the merge process by choosing the type of merge document you want to create.

If you want to simply open a blank Word document, choose Normal Word Document. Additionally, if you prefer to use the Mail Merge Wizard that is also available in Word 2003, click Step by Step Mail Merge Wizard. This wizard appears in a task pane on the right side of the window and takes you through the steps involved in the merge process.

> **Note**
>
> Choosing Envelopes or Labels in the Start Mail Merge options displays the Envelope Options or Label Options dialog box so that you can enter the information to print either of these items. For more about preparing envelopes and labels, see the section titled "Printing Envelopes and Labels," later in this chapter.

Starting Out with the Main Document

The main document is the document that holds the text that doesn't change—in other words, the boilerplate text that will appear on all the sales letters you send out or all your past due notices (or, for a happier example, all the birth announcements you send via e-mail). Word gives you a number of choices for the way in which you select your main document. You can do any of the following.

- Use the current document
- Start from a template
- Start from an existing document

Using the Current Document

If you elect to use the current document as the main document for your merge operation, you can simply type the text for the document as you want it to appear. You can omit the address information and the greeting at this point, because Word provides the means to do that automatically when you add the merge fields to your document. Figure 28-3 shows an example of a form letter used in a merge print.

One consideration, however: If you're creating an e-mail message you want to broadcast in a merge operation, remember that many graphic images and special text formats can create larger files and possibly require more time for downloading. For the convenience of your readers, consider going light on the graphical enhancements if you're creating an e-mail message.

Figure 28-3 The main document stores the boilerplate text you'll use for the body of the message.

Starting from a Template

If you don't want to work with the current document, you can choose a template instead. Word gives you access to a number of mail merge templates you can start with and then modify to fit the document you want to send. To do this, perform the following steps.

1. Click the Microsoft Office Button.

2. Choose New to display the New Document dialog box.

3. Click in the Search Microsoft Office Online For A Template box at the top of the dialog box and type merge template. Word searches Microsoft Office Online for templates that include merge fields and displays the results in the Search Results area (see Figure 28-4). You'll find everything from postcards and brochures to labels and reports.

Figure 28-4 You can easily search for merge templates that fit the type of project you're creating.

4. Click a template you'd like to see, and the item is displayed in the preview panel on the right side of the dialog box.

5. When you find the template you want to use, select it and click Download.

6. The Microsoft Office Genuine Advantage dialog box appears the first time you download any of the Office 2007 templates (see Figure 28-5). The Genuine Advantage program is a new security measure that ensures you are using an authentic copy of Microsoft Office 2007. Click the Do Not Show This Message Again check box. Even though the validation will occur when you download templates in the future, the message won't show up again. When you click Continue, your software is validated and the template is downloaded to your computer.

7. Press Ctrl+S to display the Save As dialog box, enter a name for the document, and click Save. Now you can begin filling in your own information and tailoring the document for your merge project.

Figure 28-5 The Microsoft Office Genuine Advantage program validates your software before downloading a template.

Starting from an Existing Document

If you've used a letter in the past that was particularly effective, or if you want to save time by converting some of your marketing copy to an e-mail mailing, you can simply open that document and use it as the main document for your mailing. A main document can include text, images, borders, colors, shades, tables, and more—anything a traditional Word document can contain.

> **Tip**
>
> If you used a form letter in a past mail merge operation, you can always use it again, even if it was created in an earlier version of Word. Simply open the existing document, click the Microsoft Office Button, and then click Convert. This converts the legacy file into Word 2007 format. Now you can add and modify information and fields as needed.

> **Tip**
>
> If you want to send a simple merge document but don't want to invest the time in creating a document from scratch, you can open an existing merge document and simply modify it with your own text.

Choosing Your Recipients

The next step in the mail merge process involves choosing the recipients of your mailing. To do this, use the Select Recipients command in the Start Mail Merge group to select your recipient list (you may have seen the recipient list called the data source or source list in previous Word versions). Here your choices are to use an existing list, choose Outlook Contacts, or type a new list (see Figure 28-6).

Chapter 28

Figure 28-6 Selecting recipients involves selecting the contact information of the people who will receive your mailing.

Creating a New List

Sometimes the fastest way to do something is to simply type it in yourself. If you have only a few recipients for the mailing you're preparing, you may want to use the Type A New List option to enter the names and addresses and save the information with the document. You might use Type A New List, for example, when you are creating a merge template for the minutes of your monthly board meeting. You can enter the names, street addresses, and e-mail addresses for the board members once and then save and use the file for all the board meeting minutes throughout the year.

Here's how to create the new list.

1. Click the Mailings tab and click Select Recipients in the Start Mail Merge group. Select Type New List from the options.

2. In the New Address List dialog box, type the information for the first recipient, you can press Tab to move the selection from field to field (see Figure 28-7).

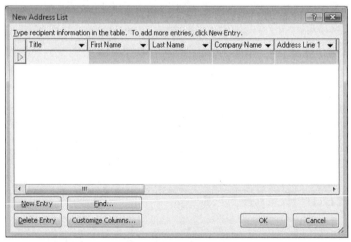

Figure 28-7 Type information for the recipient list in the New Address List dialog box.

3. To start a new recipient entry, click New Entry. The selection moves to the next row in the new address list.

4. Continue entering the information for each recipient and then click OK when you're done.

After you click OK, the Save Address List dialog box appears, with My Data Sources selected as the current folder, as shown in Figure 28-8. Enter a name for the file and then click Save.

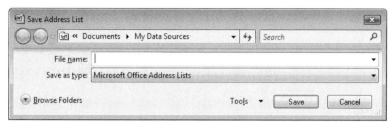

Figure 28-8 Microsoft Office Address List files are stored by default in the My Data Sources folder, where they can be accessed by all Office applications.

Customizing Address List Items

If you want to change the items listed in the New Address List dialog box, click Customize Columns. The Customize Address List dialog box appears. You can make the following changes to the Field Names list.

- To add a field name, click Add. The Add Field dialog box appears. Type the name for the field you want to create and click OK.

- To delete a field and all the field information, select the field, click Delete, and then click Yes in the confirmation message box.

- To rename a field, select it and click Rename. Then enter a new name for the field and click OK.

- To move a field, select it and click either Move Up or Move Down to change its position in the list.

When you're finished making modifications to the field list, click OK to return to the New Address List dialog box. Add or edit your data as needed and then click Close to return to the document.

Using an Existing Recipient List

To select a list you've already created, click Use Existing List in the Select Recipients list. The Select Data Source dialog box appears so that you can choose a data list you've already created. Navigate to the folder containing the file you want and then click Open. If the file includes more than one data table, the Select Table dialog box will appear so that you can choose the one you want (see Figure 28-9).

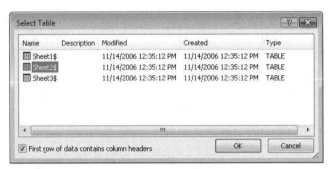

Figure 28-9 If more than one table is used in your data source, Word will prompt you to choose the table containing the data you want to use.

Choosing Outlook Contacts

Perhaps the most seamless way of integrating up-to-date contact information with your main document for mailings and e-mail broadcasts is to use your contact manager, Outlook. Because contacts in Outlook are kept up-to-date as you work, with smart tags that enable you to insert and update contact data as you work, your Outlook contact information might be more current and complete than static data lists. E-mail addresses are added automatically from messages you receive and send, which means data is gathered for you while you go through your daily routine. Of course, the most complete data records—for example, client information that includes name, address, home and office phones, e-mail address, Web pages, and spouse names and birth dates—are available only because you entered them. This means that the degree to which Outlook can actually help you will depend on how consistently you've entered contact information.

To select your Outlook Contacts list, simply click Select From Outlook Contacts in the Select Recipients list. The Select Contacts dialog box appears, as shown in Figure 28-10. Click the contacts list you want to use and then click OK. The entries in your Contacts list appear in the Mail Merge Recipient dialog box.

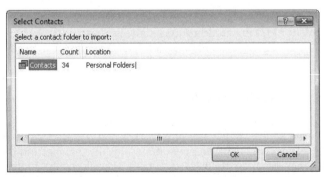

Figure 28-10 You can easily import your Outlook Contacts for use in your Word mail merge operations.

> **Tip**
>
> To start your merge from Outlook, for example to create individual e-mails for a mass mailing, in Outlook display your Contacts and then from the Tools menu, click Mail Merge. In the Mail Merge Contacts dialog box, select you options, such as Only Selected Contacts, then select your Document File and Document Type. After you click OK, your merge document will automatically display in Word.Use the steps provided in the following sections to complete your merge.

Choosing and Sorting Recipient Information

Now that Word knows where to find the information you want to use in the merge operation, you can narrow things down further by clicking Edit Recipient List in the Start Mail Merge group of the Mailings tab. Use the Mail Merge Recipients dialog box to choose, sort, and edit the information in your data source file (see Figure 28-11). If you plan to make changes, such as updating the address of a particular client, changing a company name, or deleting customer information you no longer use, you can use the commands in this dialog box to carry out those tasks. Table 28-1 lists the various ways you can work with merge data.

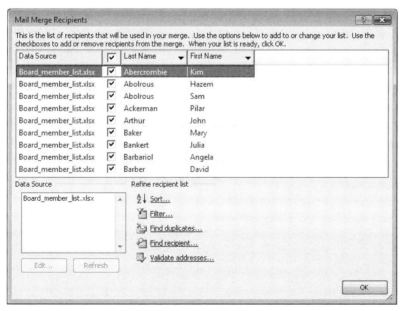

Figure 28-11 The Mail Merge Recipients dialog box enables you to select the recipients for your mailing and to edit information as needed.

Table 28-1 Working with Merge Data

Action	Result
Clear the check mark in the selection column to deselect the recipient row.	Removes a recipient from the merge operation.
Select the check box in the selection column.	Adds a recipient to the merge operation.
Click the arrow in the heading of the column by which you want to sort (for example, Last Name).	Reorders recipient records based on a particular field (if the listing was A to Z, clicking the heading will arrange the list Z to A).
Click a Data Source entry and click Edit. When the address list dialog box appears, click New Entry and enter the new recipient data. Click Close to close the dialog box.	Adds a new recipient to the list.
Click Sort.	Displays the Filter And Sort dialog box so that you can choose the field(s) by which you want to sort the information.
Click Filter.	Displays the Filter Records tab of the Filter And Sort dialog box so that you can enter the fields and values by which you want to filter the data used.
Click Find Duplicates.	Locates and displays any duplicates in your data list and enables you to deselect them to leave them out of the merge operation.
Click Find Recipient.	Displays the Find Entry dialog box so that you can search for a specific word or phrase in your data list.
Click the Validate Addresses link.	Checks the data validity for your address data if you have a validation program installed.

Filtering Your Recipient List

Most of the items in the Mail Merge Recipients list are straightforward, but one needs a bit more explanation. If you want to filter the information in your current recipient list, use the Filter command in the Mail Merge Recipients dialog box. When you click Filter, the Filter And Sort dialog box appears, as shown in Figure 28-12. To filter the records and create a specific subset (for example, all recipients who live in Denver, Colorado), click the Field arrow and choose the field you want to use as the first filter (in this example, State).

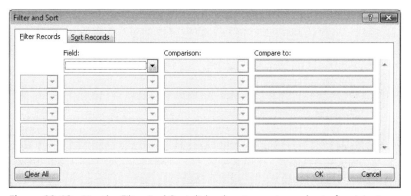

Figure 28-12   Use the Filter And Sort dialog box to create a subset of recipients you want to use in the merge.

Click the Comparison arrow to display the list of choices to assist you in filtering the data. Choose from among the 10 different items (in this example, Equal To). Then, in the Compare To field, type the value you are looking for (which here is CO). Figure 28-13 shows the filtering criteria used to locate all recipients in the database with a home location of Denver, Colorado.

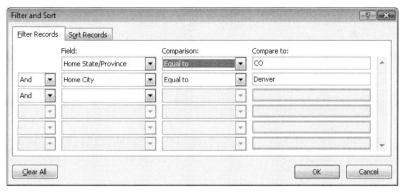

Figure 28-13   Enter the filtering criteria in the Field, Comparison, and Compare To fields.

When you click OK, the recipient list in the Mail Merge Recipients dialog box changes to reflect only the subset of data returned as a result of the filtering. Click OK to return to the merge document.

Adding Merge Fields

So now you've selected the document you want to use and you've identified the people to whom you want to send it. The next group in the Mailings tab involves adding the placeholders in the document where the data will be inserted for the individual recipients. The Write & Insert Fields group includes the following merge fields you can insert in your document.

- **Address Block** Displays the Insert Address Block dialog box so that you can add the name, street address, city, state, and postal code at the insertion point.

- **Greeting Line** Displays the Greeting Line dialog box, enabling you to select the salutation you want to use as well as the format for the recipient name.

- **Insert Merge Field** Displays options listing the fields available in the recipient list you've selected for the document so that you can add specific fields in your document as needed.

- **Rules** Offers a number of conditional controls that enable you to add programming capability to your merge form. For example, when you click choose Next Record If from the Rules list, the Insert Word Field: Next Record If dialog box appears so that you can enter the conditions under which you want the merge process to move on to the next record (see Figure 28-14). You might use this, for example, if you are sending a thank you fundraising letter to donors who contributed more than $1,000 to your campaign last year. By using the Next Record If control, you can tell Word to skip the records in which the donated amount was less than $1,000.

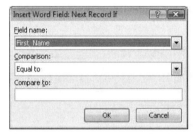

Figure 28-14 The Insert Word Field: Next Record If dialog box enables you to tell Word when to move on to the next record during the merge process.

- **Match Fields** Enables you to match up the fields in your recipient list to the fields in your database. See the section titled "Matching Fields with Your Database," later in this chapter, for details.

- **Update Labels** Updates changes you've made in the recipient list and the labels you're creating. (This command is available only when you select Labels as the document type you're using for the merge process.)

Inserting an Address Block

The Address Block includes the collection of data you're likely to use most often. The block includes the recipient name, street address, city, state, and postal code. You can also include the company name and the country and region in the address if you choose. To add the Address Block to your main document, follow these steps.

1. Place the insertion point where you want to insert the Address Block.

2. Click the Insert Address Block command in the Write & Insert Fields group of the Mailings tab. The Insert Address Block dialog box appears, as shown in Figure 28-15.

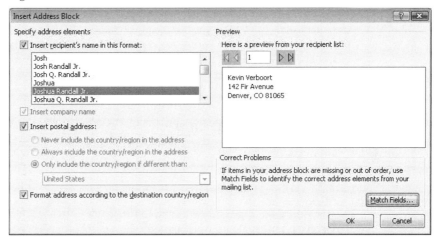

Figure 28-15 In the Insert Address Block dialog box, specify the address format you want to use.

3. Scroll through the Insert Recipient's Name In This Format list to choose the format you want to use for the recipient name. Then select the style you want to use.

4. If you want to omit the company name from the Address Block, clear the Insert Company Name check box. (Note, though, that this option is available only if your recipient list includes a Company field.)

5. To hide the postal information in the Address Block, clear the Insert Postal Address check box. The Preview section shows your current selections.

6. You can advance through the recipient data by clicking the Next button above the preview window.

7. If you don't see the fields you want to include, click the Match Fields button to match up the data names in your recipient list with the field names used in the merge operation. (For specifics, see the section titled "Matching Fields with Your Database," later in this chapter.)

8. Click OK to close the dialog box. Word inserts the following code at the insertion point.

```
´´AddressBlockᵃᵃ
```

Chapter 28

> **Tip**
>
> You can let Word take some of the guesswork out of sending international mail. How do they format postal codes in Denmark? On which line should you put the primary and secondary addresses? When you use the Insert Address Block feature in the mail merge process, be sure to click the Format Address According To The Destination Country/Region check box to let Word take care of those and other details for you.

Choosing a Greeting Line

The Greeting Line merge field enables you to say hello in the language and format you want. To add a greeting line, follow these steps.

1. Place the insertion point in the document where you want to add a greeting line.

2. Click the Greeting Line command in the Write & Insert Fields group. The Insert Greeting Line dialog box appears, as shown in Figure 28-16.

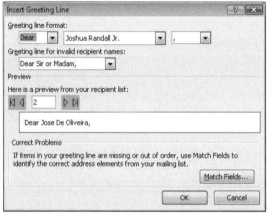

Figure 28-16 Use the Insert Greeting Line dialog box to choose the salutation and name format for your greeting.

3. For those recipients that show an empty or invalid name entry, you have the option of adding a generic phrase. Choose either Dear Sir Or Madam, To Whom It May Concern, or type your own phrase in the text box.

4. Similar to the Address Block entry, you can preview the greetings by using your recipient list data. Then use Match Fields to correct any problems in the way information is being displayed.

5. Click OK to close the dialog box and insert the greeting line. Word inserts the following code at the insertion point.

    ```
    <<GreetingLine>>
    ```

Inserting Merge Fields

Word offers a number of preset merge fields you can insert by pointing and clicking. You can further personalize your main document by adding address or database fields. To display the additional merge fields you can use in your document, click Insert Merge Field in the Write & Insert Fields group. The Insert Merge Field dialog box appears, as shown in Figure 28-17.

Figure 28-17 The Insert Merge Field dialog box enables you to insert either Address Fields or Database Fields.

If you want to use fields available in your Address Book, click the Address Fields option. You'll see quite a list of offerings, from basic contact information to spouse's name to nickname. When you click the Database Fields option, you'll see traditional database fields, including Title, First Name, Last Name, Company Name, Address Line 1, Address Line 2, City, State, ZIP Code, Country, Home Phone, Work Phone, and E-Mail Address.

To insert one of the additional merge fields, follow these steps.

1. Place the insertion point where you want to add the field.

2. Display the Insert Merge Field dialog box by clicking the Insert Merge Field command in the Write & Insert Fields group.

3. Click Address Fields or Database Fields.

4. Click the field you want to add and then click Insert.

5. When you're finished, click Close to return to your main document.

Figure 28-18 shows a form letter after two merge fields have been added. Highlight Merge Fields was used to highlight the fields so they would be easy to spot on the page.

Chapter 28

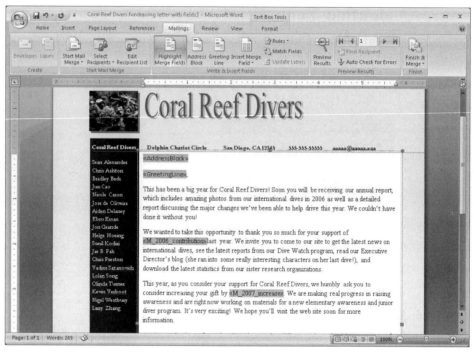

Figure 28-18 You can add database and address fields in the body of your document as needed.

TROUBLESHOOTING

I'm having trouble getting my merge fields to line up

When you're adding merge fields to your document, hidden spaces can change the alignment of your fields. To fix the problem, turn on paragraph marks by clicking the Home tab and then clicking Show/Hide in the Paragraph group. Displaying paragraph marks shows all paragraph marks, spaces, and tab characters so that you can better control the placement of merge fields in your document.

Matching Fields with Your Database

Word enables you to use data you've entered and organized in other programs—such as Access, Excel, other database programs, or compatible e-mail utilities—to serve as the source for your mail merge. If the fields you've created in your database don't match the fields in the address list, don't worry—you can use the Match Fields tool to equate the fields so data automatically flows into the right places.

You can display the Match Fields dialog box in several different ways.

- Click the Match Fields button in the Write & Insert Fields group of the Mailings tab.

- Click the Match Fields button in the Insert Address Block dialog box.

- Click the Match Fields button in the Greeting Line dialog box.

Tell Word how to match fields by clicking the arrow of the field you want to match. For example, in the example shown in Figure 28-19, the field name Word is looking for is Address 1, but in the database, the address is called Home Street. Click the Address 1 arrow and choose Home Street from the list.

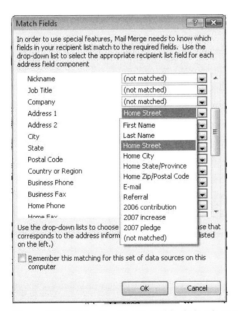

Figure 28-19 Use the Match Fields dialog box to tell Word how to correctly import the data you've created in other programs.

Continue to match up other fields as needed. After you make your matches, click OK to close the dialog box and return to the document.

> ### Mail Merge Quick Tips
>
> Here are a few tips to help your merge projects go smoothly.
>
> - Keep a listing of your data fields on hand so that you can draft your merge documents to use your available data most effectively.
>
> - Save merge documents as templates you can use regularly to cut down on the time spent on your merge operation.
>
> - Do a test print of envelopes, labels, and letters on inexpensive printer paper (as opposed to special stationery, labels, or company envelopes) to make sure the placement of the fields is correct.
>
> - When printing envelopes and labels, print an extra set if you regularly send mailings to the same group.
>
> - If you update your data list, reattach the most current version of the data file to the document by choosing Use Existing List in the Start Mail Merge group and reselecting the name of the data file.

Adding Word Fields

Along with the merge fields you are given in the Mail Merge Wizard, you have another set of fields at your disposal. Word fields enable you to personalize your document, message, or form even further. You might want to add a Word field, for example, that skips a record based on the data in a particular field.

To add a Word field to your main document, follow these steps.

1. Place the insertion point in your document where you want to add the field.

2. Click the Rules button in the Write & Insert Fields group of the Mailings tab. A menu appears, listing the Word field choices. Click your choice, and Word prompts you to add additional information. Table 28-2 gives you an overview of the Word fields available in mail merge operations.

Table 28-2 Word Fields for Mail Merge

Field	Description	Options
Ask	Adds a customized dialog box that asks for more information during a merge	You can use a predefined bookmark or add a new one to mark the placement of the Ask field
Fill-In	Prompts user for additional information	You can choose to have Word ask for information with each merged record or only once, at the beginning of the process
If...Then...Else	Creates conditional text segments that insert one phrase in one situation and another phrase in another	You can control the fields you want to compare as well as the qualifier (Equal To, Not Equal To, Less Than, Greater Than, Less Than Or Equal, Greater Than Or Equal, Is Blank, Is Not Blank)
Merge Record #	Adds the number of the current record to the merged document	Place the insertion point where you want the number to appear; no dialog box is displayed
Merge Sequence #	Inserts numbering for all documents in the merge	Place the insertion point where you want the number to appear; no dialog box is displayed
Next Record	Includes data from the next record in the current record	You can include several records at once; however, to list many records, create a directory
Next Record If	Includes data from the next record if a certain condition is met	You can include record data if a field contains a value you seek
Set Bookmark	Adds a bookmark and attached text in every merged document	You can use existing bookmarks or add new ones to accommodate the merge
Skip Record If	Omits records depending on a specific condition	You can choose the fields to compare and the qualifier (Equal To, Not Equal To, Less Than, Greater Than, Less Than Or Equal, Greater Than Or Equal, Is Blank, Is Not Blank)

Chapter 28

Previewing the Merge

The next step in the merge process involves reviewing the data merged into your document. The Preview Results group contains the commands you need. Click Preview Results to start the process. The first document is displayed by default with your first recipient's data in the Word window (shown in Figure 28-20). You can page through the recipients by clicking the previous (<<) or next (>>) button in the wizard task pane.

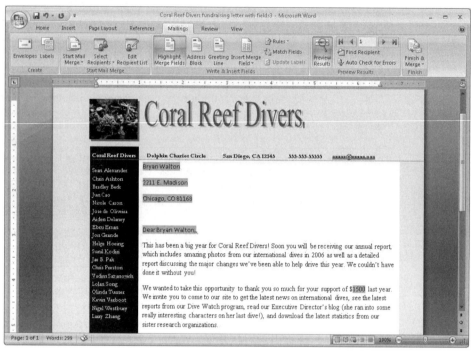

Figure 28-20 The merge data is shown automatically in your main document during Preview.

Finding a Specific Entry

If you want to locate a particular recipient in your list, click Find Recipient in the Preview Results group. The Find Entry dialog box appears so that you can type in the Find box the data you'd like to locate. Specify the field you want to search, if necessary, and then click Find Next. Word locates the text you indicated in the merge document.

Checking for Errors

If you're preparing a merge operation with hundreds or even thousands of records, it's an especially good idea to run a test before you perform the actual merge. Word gives you an easy way to run a quick check for errors. Simply click the Auto Check For Errors button in the Preview Results group. The Checking And Reporting Errors dialog box appears (shown in Figure 28-21). You can test your merge in three different ways: You can simulate the merge and save the errors in a new document; you can go ahead and run the merge operation, but have Word stop and alert you when an error is found; or you can complete the merge without pausing for errors and have Word report the errors in a new document.

Figure 28-21 Select an error-checking method in the Checking And Reporting Errors dialog box.

The difference between these options is that one runs a "practice test" that reports on errors it finds but does not make changes in the document. The second option, the default, performs the merge but alerts you immediately whenever an error is found. If this is the first time you've used the mail merge utility in Word, it's a good idea to test it out using the simulation until you feel comfortable proceeding with the real thing. The third option enables you to go ahead and print, but it collects any errors in a separate document so that you can review them after the merge is complete.

Merging the Documents

The final step in the mail merge process involves printing, sending, or saving your document with the data intact. The actual merge is a bit anticlimactic. To finalize the merge, you simply click Finish & Merge in the Finish group on the Mailings tab. Three choices appear: Edit Individual Documents, Print Documents, and Send E-Mail Messages. The first option saves the merge operation as individual files, the second sends the documents to the printer, and the third prepares and sends e-mail messages with your merge information included.

Merge to a New Document

When you click Edit Individual Documents in the Finish group, the Merge To New Document dialog box opens, and you can choose whether you want to merge all records, the current record only, or a range of records you specify. Make your choices and then click OK to complete the merge.

Choosing Merge Print Options

To prepare your merge documents for printing, click Print Documents in the Finish group. The Merge To Printer dialog box appears, and you can choose from the following options:

- All Prints all records in the current document

- Current Record Prints only the displayed record

- From And To Enables you to set a range—from record 2 to 5, for example—so that you can select only those records you want to print

TROUBLESHOOTING

Instead of values, fields are printed in my mail merge document

You went through all the steps in the merge process, checked the merge for errors, and selected the merge process you wanted. Everything looked fine. But when you printed the merged documents, you saw the merge field names instead of the values in the document. What's going on?

It might be that the Print Field Codes Instead Of Their Values check box has been selected in your Word options, which by default causes fields, rather than the values they store, to be displayed. To check this option and change it if necessary, click the Microsoft Office Button and click Word Options at the bottom. In the Word Options dialog box, click the Advanced category in the left panel. Scroll down to the Print options and clear the Print Field Codes Instead Of Their Values check box by clicking it. Click OK to close the dialog box and return to the document.

Merge to E-Mail

If you choose Send E-Mail Messages in the Finish group of the Mailings tab, the Merge To E-Mail dialog box appears. Before you send the messages, you can specify whether you want to send the e-mail in HTML or text format or send the message as an attachment. You can also choose the field you want to use in the To line (this is helpful if you have more than one e-mail address in a recipient list) and add a Subject line to describe the content to the recipient.

After you enter these choices, select which records you want to send in the Send Records area. Similar to the printing options, you can choose All, Current Record, or enter a range of records you want to use. Click OK when you're ready to send.

Creating a Directory

All the merge operations in this chapter thus far have enabled you to take multiple data items and plug them into documents you can replicate easily. There will be times, however, when you will want a complete listing of the records in your source file. You might, for example, want to keep a listing of all the people you sent a catalog mailing to in fall 2006. To create a directory of records from your data source, you can use the Directory document type. Here are the steps.

1. Click the Mailings tab and, in the Start Mail Merge group, choose Directory.

2. In the Select Document Type section, click Directory.

3. Using the Select Recipients command in the Start Mail Merge group, choose whether you want to type a new list, use an existing list, or select Outlook Contacts.

4. If necessary, click Edit Recipient List and filter, sort, or edit the data to be used in the directory.

5. Next, in the Write & Insert Fields group, click the fields you want to insert (most likely you'll want only Address Block). If you want to add additional fields, click the Insert Merge Field command and make your choices.

6. Click Preview Results to see how the directory entry will look. Don't worry that only one record is shown in the document window to preview; you'll see an entire list when the merge is completed.

7. Click Edit Individual Documents in the Finish & Merge command in the Finish group. Choose All to include all records in the merge. Click OK. The merge is completed and the directory is displayed in your document window. You can now save the directory file and use it for future merge operations.

> **Tip**
>
> You can quickly add a two-column format to your directory by clicking the Page Layout tab and clicking Columns in the Page Setup group. In the Columns list, choose the number of columns you want to use. The document is instantly reformatted to reflect your selection. Remember to save your changes by pressing Ctrl+S.

Printing Envelopes and Labels

In some cases, you might want to print only a single envelope or an individual sheet of labels. In such a situation, working with the data source and inserting fields in a document isn't necessary—no merge is needed. When you want to print a simple envelope, click Start Mail Merge on the Mailings tab and choose Envelopes. The Envelopes Options dialog box appears, as shown in Figure 28-22.

Chapter 28

Figure 28-22 The Envelopes Options dialog box enables you to create and print individual envelopes.

> **Note**
>
> If you're working with an open document that has an Address Block inserted (or a default address you've entered yourself), the selected address is the one that will be used.

To print an envelope, simply follow these steps.

1. Select the recipient address and then display the Envelope Options dialog box.

2. Click the Envelope Size arrow and choose the size of the envelope you will be printing.

3. Click in the Delivery Address area and click Font to select the font you want to use. Use the From Left and From Top controls to set the amount of space between the printed address and the edge of the envelope.

4. Set the font and spacing settings for the return address as well. The Preview area shows you how your envelope will look when printed.

5. Click the Printing Options tab to determine the way in which you should position the envelope in the printer.

6. Click OK. Word saves your information, and your envelope is displayed in the Word window as you specified.

Creating Labels

Instead of printing directly on envelopes, you might want to print mailing labels. Word makes it easy for you to print labels in a wide range of shapes and sizes. If you want to print single (or a few) labels and don't want to use mail merge to do it, you can use the Label Options dialog box to create labels quickly. Here's how.

1. Start by selecting the data you want to use to create the labels.

2. Click the Mailings tab and choose Labels from the Start Mail Merge command list. The Label Options dialog box appears.

3. The options here enable you to enter the vendor of the labels and choose the way the labels are arranged on the page.

4. Click the Details button if you want to change the page size or enter a different dimension for the label.

5. Click OK to save your changes.

> **Tip**
>
> If you have a number of labels that you want to print quickly, it's best to use the Mail Merge Wizard to lead you through the steps for printing labels. To start the wizard, click the Mailings tab and then click Start Mail Merge in the Start Mail Merge group. Choose Step by Step Mail Merge Wizard. Choose Labels in the Select Document Type area and follow the prompts on the screen.

TROUBLESHOOTING

I can't feed envelopes from a loaded tray

If you've loaded envelopes in a paper tray and Word keeps prompting you to feed your envelopes to the printer manually, make sure that you've selected the correct paper feed choices. To check the settings, display the Label Options dialog box by clicking Start Mail Merge and choosing Labels. In the Tray field, choose the name of the tray in which you loaded the labels. Click OK to save your changes.

What's Next?

This chapter took you through the process of creating a variety of mail merge projects with Word so that you can share your documents with donors, teammates, board members, and prospective customers all over the world. The next chapter moves a bit deeper into the customizable document realm by showing you how to add Word 2007 content controls to your Word documents.

Chapter 28

Customizing Documents with Content Controls

In the previous chapter, you learned to use Microsoft Office Word 2007 to create, compile, and print (or e-mail) your mail merge projects. The commands available on the Mailings tab in the Office Word 2007 Ribbon enable you to easily add controls to the document so that you can insert data automatically at appropriate points in your document. This chapter shows you an exciting—and super simple—way to customize and automate your Word documents by using Word 2007 Content Controls. The new Content Controls enable you to easily add user-selected items to your document, resulting in customized documents that track automatically with your business processes.

Let's consider an example. Suppose that you are working on an annual report for Coral Reef Divers. If all the people who needed to review the document before it is finalized worked in the same office, you might create a cover sheet that includes a table where each member of the document review team could initial and date their review. That way you'd know when each person on the team reviewed the document so that you could begin working on the final draft. But because your organization includes sites in a variety of locations around the world, including a paper cover sheet for signing off isn't practical. You can add simple Word 2007 Content Controls to the top of the document to take care of this task in a matter of minutes.

> **Tip**
>
> This book just touches on the capabilities that Content Controls and other high-end Word 2007 customization techniques offer. For more information on specialized and advanced techniques in Word 2007, see *Advanced Microsoft Office Documents 2007 Edition Inside Out* by Stephanie Krieger (Microsoft Press, 2007).

Understanding the Word 2007 Content Controls

Previous versions of Word included a collection of form controls used to add form fields to documents. This enabled you, for example, to create an invoice document, a travel expense report, or a registration form that a user could fill out electronically and submit. The data then was saved with the document and could then be used in other data applications. The form controls available in previous versions are still available in Word 2007—now they are referred to as Legacy Form controls.

The new Content Controls in Word 2007 are something totally new, friendly, easy-to-add and modify. Content Controls do what you'd imagine them to do—give users control over the type of content displayed in a document, populating specific selections based on the choices users make in alignment with business practices. Coral Reef document reviewers can click a Content Control item at the top of the annual report, choose their name from the list, select the date, and choose their site before they save and close the document. Content controls are XML-based, which means that the data and the presentation of the data can be stored separately.

When might you use Content Controls in your Word 2007 documents? Here are a few ideas:

- You are creating a training document with a short quiz at the end to evaluate if organization volunteers have learned key elements of your program.

- You want to add a routing system to standardized documents that automatically shows the user who to send their report to once it is finished.

- You need to standardize the documents used across your organization to stream-line the way information is collected, shared, and used in your business processes

> **Note**
> Content Controls will work only in your Word 2007 documents. Because they are based on XML, Content Controls can be saved only in the new Office Open XML File Format.

Integrating Data and Processes with Content Controls

The Content Controls in your Word 2007 documents pack even more punch when they are used with the XML functionality in Word. For example, Coral Reef Divers offers a variety of training programs for beginning, intermediate, and advanced divers. You can create a document new divers fill out when they register for classes. When a user selects the Content Control that displays the list of experience levels and clicks a selection, the appropriate training program and instructor are automatically selected. When the document is saved, the XML information is updated, and the new diver is assigned to the appropriate instructor.

If Coral Reef later hires a new instructor or adds classes, the selections in the Content Controls on the document continue to reflect the XML data used to populate the document. In this way, information flows back and forth—from the document to the XML store and back again into the document, giving both you and your applications access to the most recent information in a seamless way.

XML Mapping in Word 2007

The example given in the preceding paragraph—connecting selections with a larger data store through the use of Content Controls—is what's known as *XML mapping*, another new feature in Word 2007. Put simply, XML mapping creates and maintains a connection between the application and your business logic in order to provide the most current data to both sites. Creating XML mapping solutions can be fairly straightforward or very complex—the key objective is to maintain the connection in such a way that the two-way communication of information (from the document into the business application or data store and vice versa) is kept up-to-date. This allows for any data changes to be reflected immediately in the documents and forms that are bound to that data, and it also ensures that when any data changes made in the document or on the form (for example, if a user adds an item to a list), the data in the XML store is automatically changed to reflect the addition.

Creating the Document

When you create the document you want to use with Content Controls, you can start with a Word template (most templates include Content Controls of some kind), modify an existing document, or create a new document from scratch.

You can choose to add the Content Controls first and then drag them to any point in the document where you want them to appear, or you can create the body of the document—with its Theme, styles, and illustrations, as appropriate—and then add the Content Controls last. Either way, the process is straightforward.

Displaying the Developer Tab

Your first step in creating a document that includes Content Controls involves displaying the Developer tab. The Developer tab is hidden by default because its function is specialized. To display the Developer tab, follow these steps:

1. Click the Microsoft Office Button and click Word Options.

2. On the Popular tab, click Show Developer Tab In The Ribbon.

Chapter 29

The Developer tab appears on the far right side of the Ribbon, as you see in Figure 29-1. The tab includes five different groups:

Figure 29-1 The Developer tab includes the tools to add Content Controls to your documents.

- The Code group includes the tools you'll use to record macros, and write and edit Microsoft Visual Basic for Applications code.

- The Controls group contains the Content Controls you add to the document in order to gather information from users. The Controls group enables you to add a number of different control types (including Legacy Controls and ActiveX controls), change to Design Mode, modify control properties, and group controls.

- The XML group includes tools for displaying the XML structure of the current document, adding an XML schema, attaching transforms, and adding expansion packs.

- The Protect group offers only one tool—Protect Document—which displays the Restrict Formatting And Editing task pane so that you can control the permissions others have to modify your document.

- The Templates group includes a single tool—Document Template—which enables you to add templates, schemas, and other add-ins to the current document.

Word Content Controls vs. InfoPath Forms—Which Is for You?

You can add Content Controls on your Word documents to take care of all kinds of data collection needs. Whether you create an invoice, a data list, a travel log, or an expense listing, you can as add the Content Controls to your Word document and update the document as needed.

Some suites of the 2007 Microsoft Office System include a program called Microsoft Office InfoPath 2007. This application is a sophisticated form-generation program that enables users to create custom forms and share them in a variety of ways. Office Info-Path 2007 is intended for users and businesses that rely heavily on form technologies to carry out their day-to-day work. You can add an InfoPath form to an e-mail message you create in Microsoft Office Outlook 2007 or convert one of your Word documents into an InfoPath form. InfoPath also offers centralized management of the forms you create, which is helpful if forms are a big part of your work. If you use Content Controls only occasionally, the Content Control features Word provides are probably enough for your needs. On the other hand, if your requirements call for more sophisticated form management, check out Microsoft Office InfoPath 2007 by going to *http://office.microsoft.com/en-us/infopath/default.aspx*.

Adding and Formatting Static Text

The beauty of Content Controls is that they are so easy to use, the process feels just like creating an ordinary document. The Content Controls simply add to the functionality of the document by enabling you to use it for more than a flat, read-it-once-and-put-it-away purpose. Now you can read the document, respond to questions or information items, or add to the information by selecting your choices within the body of the document. In this way, a simple document becomes "smart." Here are a few examples of ways you can transform a traditional document into a document that makes use of Content Controls:

- In a document that helps prepare your volunteers or staff members for travel, you might want to use the first page as an information-gathering section that enables the user to enter information items such as Name, Address, Phone, and more. Additionally, you'll record travel and passport information (see Figure 29-2). On the next page, you may want to include a how-to guide to travel reporting, country-specific site-seeing tips, or information about customs in the area.

- In a document you're preparing that describes your plan for an upcoming project, you will include the purpose for the project, an overall description, as well as a list of team members and contact info, and areas on the form for the various tasks and stages in the project. The list of team members and their contact items, as well as the assigned tasks, can all be placed in Content Controls, so the information for the team members is continually updated and in sync with your organization's data.

- In the patient records in your small medical office, you have a number of items that would appear on a traditional form—such as name, birth date, address information, and social security number—but you also want to include your privacy policy and other information related to your practice in the file. In this way the traditional form and document become one, easy to update, track, and secure.

Chapter 29

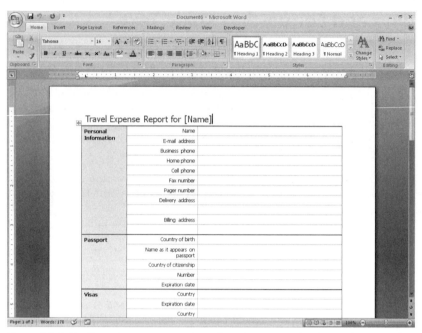

Figure 29-2 You'll need to enter a number of text items on a simple travel expense form so users know where to enter information.

You may want to simplify the form's formatting by choosing a theme and then assigning specific Quick Styles to the various elements. You can also add Quick Parts, objects, photos, and more to spruce up the form any way you'd like. If you have designed letterhead for your company and want the form to resemble your other business documents, you can use the letterhead as the basis for your form. Figure 29-3 shows several formatting enhancements that have been added to the travel expense form.

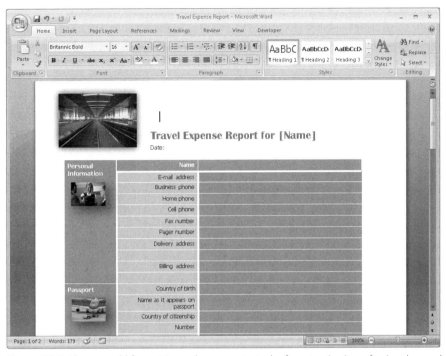

Figure 29-3 You can add formatting enhancements to the form to give it professional appeal.

Adding Content Controls

As mentioned earlier, Content Controls are so simple and flexible that you can add them at any point during the creation of your document. If you want to add them as you type, go ahead—you can just drag them to the point in the document you want them to be used. If you decide later that you want to move the control in a new spot, just drag it there. All things should be so simple.

Here's a quick list of some of the ways in which you might want to use Content Controls in your documents:

- Enter simple text in a comment box.

- Choose from among a series of options in a list.

- Select one of several pictures to cast votes for their favorite new logo design.

- Add their own information in addition to the list items presented.

- Select a date they choose from a visual calendar.

- Format the text they enter on the form.

You'll find everything you need to add those items to your form in the Controls group in the Developer tab. Table 29-1 gives you an introduction to the various commands, and the sections that follow provide more detail on each control type.

Table 29-1 Word 2007 Content Controls

Command	Name	Description
Aa	Rich Text	Enables users to enter text with most types of formatting, as well as tables and images
Aa	Text	Accepts plain text or text with simple formatting only
	Picture	Enables you to add a picture to the form
	Combo Box	Creates a text list in which the user can edit list items
	Drop-Down List	Lets you create a list in which the items are non-editable
	Date Picker	Adds a calendar object so users can select the date
	Building Block Gallery	Enables you to make specific Building Blocks and galleries available to users
	Legacy Tools	Displays a palette of tools that includes Legacy Forms (form controls available with previous versions of Word, such as text box, check box, or drop-form form fields) and ActiveX Controls
Design Mode	Design Mode	Displays the document in Design Mode so that you can arrange and edit Content Controls in the document
Properties	Properties	Opens a dialog box containing options you can change for the selected control
Group ▾	Group	Enables you to group a region of a form

> **Tip**
> It's helpful to have an idea of the types of Content Control you want to add to your document before you add them. You may want to sketch out the document on a piece of paper or use an existing document as a guide.

Control Types in Word 2007

If you've worked with forms in a previous version of Word, you know that you can add three basic types of fields, or controls—Text, Drop-Down Lists, and check boxes. The Content Controls in Word 2007 are a different animal entirely—and dramatically easier to use. They enable you to seamlessly connect your data with your business processes—and there are more of them to work with. But the legacy controls are still there, so if you really like using those check boxes, don't worry—you can still add them (for more information, see the section titled "Adding Legacy Controls," later in this chapter on page 775 for more information). In addition to the familiar control types previously listed, Word 2007 also includes a Rich Text control, a Picture control, a Combo Box control, a Date Picker, and a Building Block Gallery control.

Rich Text Control

The Rich Text control enables you to add an item to your document that the user can then format as real text. For example, suppose that you want users to have the ability to change the format of the text they enter in a control. When you add a Rich Text control to the form, the Mini Toolbar appears whenever the user enters and then selects text (see Figure 29-4).

Figure 29-4 A Rich Text control enables users to format text after they enter it.

Rich Text controls also accept larger amounts of text (multiple paragraphs) and can include tables and graphics. When you need to provide the flexibility of gathering information in a variety of forms and formats, Rich Text controls will give you what you need.

Text Control

The Text control command inserts a simple Text control at the cursor position. When might you want to use a Text control? This control is useful for all kinds of things—you can record comments, names, addresses, volunteer projects, campaigns, staff member names, and more. Text controls can accept a minimal amount of formatting; basically, any text your users need to enter that doesn't require special formatting capabilities can be entered in a Text control. In Figure 29-5, the First Name, Last Name, and Address fields are all Text controls.

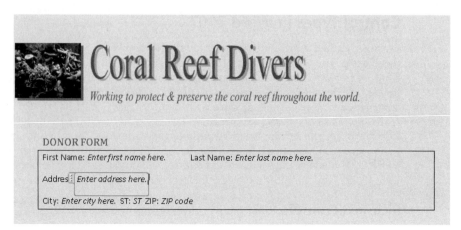

Figure 29-5 Text controls enable users to enter plain text—no formatting required.

Picture Content Control

A Picture control comes in handy when you want to add special images in a document. For example, the travel document for Coral Reef Divers includes a section for passport information. A volunteer reading and adding her own info to the travel document can insert her passport photo directly into the document so management can be sure they always have the most current data on file (see Figure 29-6).

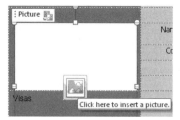

Figure 29-6 The Picture Content Control gives users the option of adding images directly into the document.

Combo Box Control

Use a Combo Box control when you want to give users a range of choices from which they can select, while also giving them the option of entering a new item not represented on the list. For example, in the control shown in Figure 29-7, volunteers with Coral Reef Divers can choose the Frequent Flyer program they use from the list. Or, if they don't see their program on the list, they can click in the text box and type the one relevant to their information.

Figure 29-7 Combo boxes give users a choice and also enable them to enter their own information.

Drop-Down List

A Drop-Down List control enables you to create a list from which users can select an answer. Unlike the combo box, which enables users to add their own entries, a drop-down list is locks users into only the answers you provide. The sample drop-down list in Figure 29-8 shows the regional offices for Coral Reef Divers. When a volunteer fills out a travel expense report, she chooses the country in which she served during her volunteer assignment.

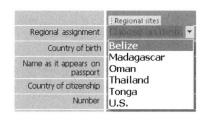

Figure 29-8 A drop-down list provides users with a range of choices.

Date Picker

The Date Picker control makes it easy for users to select the date relevant to the information they are entering. When they click the control, a small calendar appears, displaying the current month (see Figure 29-9). Users can display different months by clicking the left or right arrows in the Date Picker title bar. To select a date, they simply click the day they want (or click Today to enter the current date).

Figure 29-9 The Date Picker control displays a graphical calendar users can use to insert a date in the document.

Chapter 29

> **Tip**
>
> The date picker doesn't provide a way to show a range of dates, so if you want to include information about a span of time (to record the amount of time spent on a volunteer assignment, for example), create Start Date and End Date fields to record the beginning and the completion of the project.

Building Block Gallery

The Building Block Gallery control offers you a more specialized type of control for your documents. By using this control, you give those working with your document the ability to insert Building Block you specify. For example, using this control, users could insert an AutoText Building Block, an equation, special tables, or other customized Quick Parts that you've created and saved to the Building Blocks Gallery. Users can also choose custom galleries you have added to the document template.

When might you want to do this? In the Coral Reef Divers example, the person using the document can enter her hotel room preferences using this type of Content Control. If you have saved a number of text entries in AutoText, such as "No thanks," or "Non-smoking please," you can use the Building Blocks Gallery control to add the AutoText Building Block set to the control. The user can then choose the AutoText she wants to insert by clicking the AutoText control and choosing the text item from the gallery (see Figure 29-10).

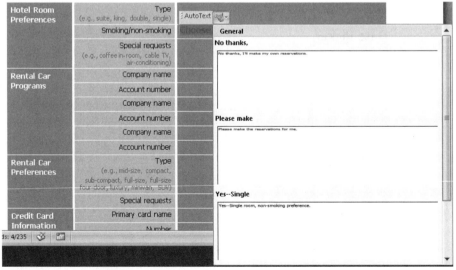

Figure 29-10 You can add a Building Blocks Gallery control to enable users to choose predesigned elements to insert in the document.

Adding a Control

Now that you know what to expect from the various controls, you can begin adding them to your document. When you are ready to add a control, the process is simple. No matter which type of control you are adding, the process is the same. Follow these steps:

1. Click at the point in the document where you want to add the Content Control.

2. Click the Developer tab and click the control in the Controls group that you want to add to your form. For example, to add a Combo Box control to your form, click the Combo Box control.

3. Word adds a Combo Box control to your form and inserts the text *Choose an item* (see Figure 29-11).

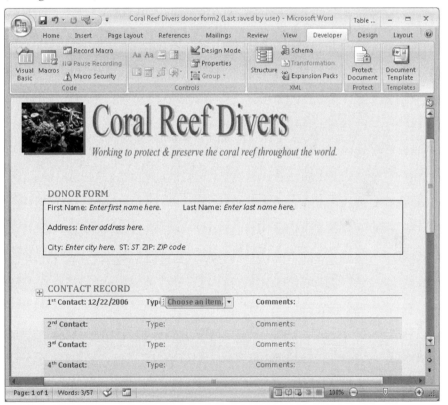

Figure 29-11 Adding a control is as simple as positioning the insertion point and clicking the control you want.

When the user clicks the arrow to the right of the prompt text, a drop-down list appears, but only the prompt text appears in the list. You add the items for the list by working with the control's properties (which is the subject of the next section).

Chapter 29

Changing Content Control Properties

After you've created a Content Control, you can tailor it to include the information you want users to enter. You will change control properties when you want to do one of the following:

- Add a title to the field

- Specify a tag so that you can locate the field easily

- Choose a formatting style to apply to the displayed text

- Control whether the field contents can be edited or not

- Choose the format of the content

- Select a locale and calendar type (Date Picker control only)

- Determine how to store the date if the control has an XML mapping (Date Picker control only)

- Indicate whether you want Word to allow multiple paragraphs (Text field only)

- Add and arrange items in a list (Combo Box and Drop-Down List only)

- Assign Document Building Block Properties, such as a gallery and category, to populate a list of choices (Building Block Gallery control only)

To display the properties for a control you've added to the document, simply click the control and then click Properties in the Controls group (or right-click the control). The Content Control Properties dialog box appears so that you can customize the settings for that particular control.

Each control type has its own set of options. For example, when you add a Combo Box Content Control and then choose Properties, you see the dialog box shown in Figure 29-12. When you display the properties for a Text Content Control, the dialog box shown in Figure 29-13 is displayed.

Figure 29-12 When you add a Combo Box Content Control, you add list items in the Properties dialog box.

Figure 29-13 The Content Control Properties dialog box for a Text Content Control includes Plain Text Properties .

Adding Titles and Tags

Adding a title to a control on your form can help give users a little more information about the type of data you want them to enter. When you add a control title, the title appears on a tab above the control when the user clicks it.

Chapter 29

To add a title to a control, select the control and click Properties in the Controls group. In the Content Control Properties dialog box, click in the Title text box and type the control title you want to use. Click OK to save the change.

You can also add tags in the Content Control Properties dialog box. When you add a tag, the control is enclosed in a set of tags that helps you locate, sort, and easily work with that data. Add a tag by clicking in the Tag box in the Content Control Properties dialog box. Type the tag name and click OK. By default, the tag is not visible on the form. To see the tags, click Design Mode in the Controls group to display the tags. Figure 29-14 shows both the control title and tags displayed in Design Mode.

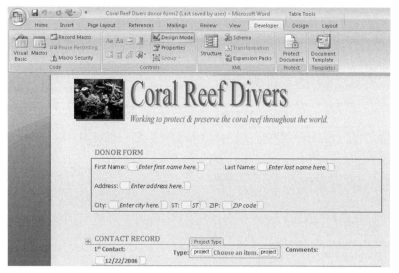

Figure 29-14 You can display the tags used to mark each Content Control by clicking Design Mode in the Controls group.

> **Tip**
> When a Content Control is mapped to a data store the tags will appear orange in Design Mode. Content Controls that are not mapped will have blue tags in Design Mode.

Styling Your Control

Word enables you to control the way the text in your control looks by providing style options. You can use an existing style for the control items or create a new style for the look of the text. The great thing about this is that you can automate the formats you use regularly in forms text. You can create a style you like and then choose it each time you create a control so that all your controls have a similar look.

To choose an existing style for your Content Control, follow these steps:

1. Click the control you want to change.

2. Click Properties in the Controls group of the Developer tab.

3. Click the Use A Style To Format Contents check box. The Style selection becomes available.

4. Click the Style arrow to display the available styles (see Figure 29-15).

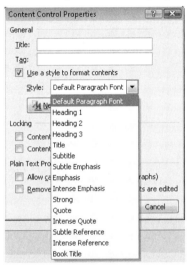

Figure 29-15 You can apply an existing style to document control text.

5. Click the style you want to use for the control text, and then click OK.

If you want to create your own style for the text users will see on in the document, follow these steps:

1. Click the control you want to change and display the Content Control Properties dialog box by clicking Properties in the Controls group.

2. Click the Use A Style To Format Contents check box.

3. Click the New Style button. The Create New Style From Formatting dialog box appears.

4. Type a name for the style in the Name box, and then select a Style Type and Style Based On settings if necessary.

5. Click the Formatting arrow and choose the font you want from the displayed list.

6. Apply additional formatting settings, such as size, style, font color, or alignment, and more, using the controls in the Formatting area of the dialog box. The preview window shows you how the style will look in your document.

Chapter 29

7. Click OK to save the new style. Click OK a second time to apply the settings to your control and return to the document.

For more information on styles, see Chapter 15, "Using Styles to Increase Your Formatting Power."

Locking Controls

By default, no locking features are in effect for the Content Controls you create, meaning that for controls where editing is allowed (Rich Text controls and Combo Box controls), users may be able to edit the control itself as well as the control's content. Word 2007 offers you two different kinds of locking capability for the controls on your document. You can opt to lock the Content Control so that it cannot be deleted, or you can lock the contents so that they cannot be edited. When would you use these different options?

- Select Content Control Cannot Be Deleted when you want to make sure that the user of your document will not be able to intentionally or unintentionally delete the document control.

- Click Contents Cannot Be Edited when you want to limit users from modifying the content displayed in the Content Control. For example, you might want to lock a text control to prohibit users from changing content that has already been added to the control.

You can also use the Contents Cannot Be Edited option to force a particular selection on a document. For example, in the Coral Reef Divers example, the Type field includes a Drop-Down List control that enables users to select one of three choices: Winter Project, Fall Project, or Year-Long Project. If you have all the volunteers you need for the Fall Project and Year-Long project, you can select the Winter Project option and then click the Contents Cannot Be Edited check box. This locks the selected item in place so that users cannot choose a different item in that particular control. When you reopen the Fall and Year-Long programs, you can display the control's properties and deselect the Contents Cannot Be Edited check box in the Content Control Properties dialog box so that users once again have a range of choices.

Adding Content to Lists

This last setting in the Content Control Properties dialog box may be one you'll want to use first. When you create a Combo Box control or a Drop-Down List control, the whole idea is to give document users a range of choices from which to choose. But when you initially create the control, only prompt text appears—which isn't going to get you very far! To add the items to the lists, follow these steps:

1. Select the Combo Box or Drop-Down List control to which you want to add list items.

2. Display the Content Control Properties dialog box by clicking Properties in the Controls group.

3. In the Drop-Down List Of Properties area, click Add. The Add Choice dialog box appears (see Figure 29-16).

Figure 29-16 The Add Choice dialog box enables you to add both a Display Name and a Value for your list items.

4. Type the text you want to appear in the list and click OK. The item is added to the list. Repeat step 3 and this step until you've entered all the items you want to appear in the list.

5. Arrange the items in the list the way you want them to appear in the control by using the Move Up and Move Down buttons in the Content Control Properties dialog box. Additionally, you can edit an item by selecting it in the list and clicking Modify. Or, you can delete an item by clicking it and choosing Remove.

6. Click OK to save your changes.

Try out the list by clicking the arrow to the right of the control on the document. The list should appear in the order you specified.

> **Note**
>
> The Combo Box control enables users to add their own items in to the text list. The latest added item is automatically displayed at the top of the list if the control is mapped to a data store.

Mapping Controls to XML

When you click Design Mode on the Developer tab, the tags that are displayed indicate the start and end of Content Controls and help you see what's going on in your document, but they don't automatically provide XML functionality for the data you are displaying or capturing. To map the data to the XML data store, follow these steps:

1. Right-click the Content Control to display the Controls context menu.

2. Point to Apply XML Element. A list of XML tags available in the current document appears. (Note that you must have an XML schema attached to the document before these tags will appear. See Chapter 30 for more information on attaching a custom XML schema in Word 2007.)

3. Click the XML element you want to apply to the Content Control.

Now the information displayed through or gathered by that Content Control is mapped directly to the XML data, and the latest information will be reflected by that control.

Chapter 29

Using Content Controls

Designing a document with Content Controls is the first part of the story; using the controls is the second part. Working with a document that includes Content Controls is so simple it feels just like working with any traditional document (which is one of the main points of Content Controls!). To use Content Controls in a document, follow these steps:

1. Click the Microsoft Office Button and choose New. The New Document task pane opens.

2. Click Open. Choose the document or template you want to use for the current document.

3. Create, modify, and format your document normally.

4. Each time you encounter a Content Control, click in the control and then type the requested information (or choose it from the displayed list).

5. Save your document as you normally would.

For More on Content Controls

This chapter only scratches the surface on Content Controls, but if you really get excited about this new functionality in Word 2007 (and many people are), check out Matt Scott's Word 2007 Content Control Kit. This is a free, custom-designed tool that works outside of Word 2007, enabling you to map all the Content Controls in your Word document to XML. Using this tool, you can add, edit, or delete custom XML in your document, as well as change Content Control properties. Here's the link to the tool: *http://www.codeplex.com/dbe.*

Additionally, Andrew Coats from MSDN has posted an online tutorial showing how to use the Word 2007 Content Control Kit. You'll find that tutorial by following this link: *http://blogs.msdn.com/acoat/archive/2007/03/01/linking-word-2007-content-controls-to-custom-xml.aspx.*

Protecting Documents

When you're working specifically with forms, the Protect Document tool is an important item on the Developer tab. You'll use this type of protection when you want to safeguard all information in the document, allowing users to enter data only as you've specified it in the individual Content Controls.

When you protect a form, you lock the controls in place so that no further changes can be made to formats or specifications. This also protects other items on the form—titles, help text, photos, and more. Of course, users will still to be able to use the lists as intended and enter text in text and legacy fields. To protect a document that includes Content Controls, follow these steps:

1. Click the Protect Document command in the Protect group.

> **Note**
>
> If you are using Microsoft Office Ultimate 2007, Office Professional Plus 2007, or Office Enterprise 2007, click Restrict Formatting and Editing after clicking Protect Document to access the Restrict Formatting And Editing pane.

2. Click the Allow Only This Type Of Editing in the Document check box.

3. Click the list arrow and choose Filling In Forms (see Figure 29-17).

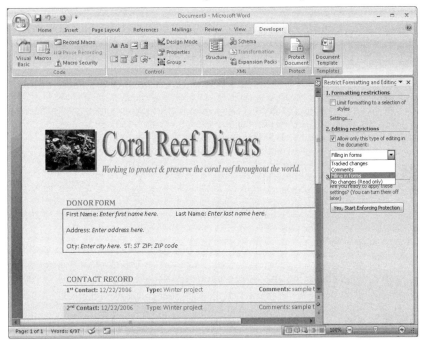

Figure 29-17 You can protect the form but allow users to fill in form fields as needed.

4. Click Yes, Start Enforcing Protection to protect the form.

5. The Start Enforcing Protection dialog box appears, offering you the chance to enter a password for the form. If you want to add a password, type it in both text boxes in the dialog box. If not, leave the text boxes blank.

6. Click OK to put the protection settings in effect.

TROUBLESHOOTING

My Building Block Gallery Content Controls are disabled or I cannot Paste in a Content Control

If your document is protected for Filling In Forms you might find Building Block Content Controls are disabled and you are unable to use Paste in a Rich Text control, Plain Text control, or a Combo Box control.

The following provides two workarounds for this issue:

- Use a selective protection method described in the following Inside Out tip titled, "Nested Content Controls and Selective Document Protection."
- Use the No Changes (Read Only) protection option and mark each Content Control as an exception.

INSIDE OUT   Nested Content Controls and Selective Document Protection

If you find the Protect Document method of document protection is too restrictive you can protect portions of your document using nested Content Controls. The general procedure is to place static text and Content Controls used for data entry in a Rich Text control. Then for the Rich Text control, enable both Locking options, Content Control Cannot Be Edited and Content Control Cannot Be Deleted. The result is only the nested Content Controls can be edited and the static text cannot be modified or deleted. Here are the specific steps:

1. For each Content Control you want to protect, display the Content Control Properties and verify the Locking option Content Control Cannot Be Deleted is selected.

2. Select the Content Controls and all static text that you want to protect.

3. On the Developer tab, click the Rich Text Content Control. A Rich Text control should be placed around the selected data.

4. Select the newly added Rich Text control and then click Properties.

5. Select both Locking options, Content Control Cannot Be Edited and Content Control Cannot Be Deleted and then click OK.

If you need to edit the static text or Content Controls after you enable the Locking options for the Rich Text control, simply click the Design button and make your modifications.

See this book's companion CD for a sample document, named "Sample Content Controls.dotx," that uses this selective protection method.

Adding Legacy Controls

Legacy controls are available in Word 2007, but unless you have a specific reason for using them (for example, one of your remote offices is still using a previous version of Word), the new Content Controls in Word 2007 are a better choice. You can add the following legacy controls in Word 2007:

- The legacy Text control is a basic text input tool. When you add a legacy text control, Word 2007 inserts the {FORMTEXT} field at the cursor position in the document.

Note

The field codes that Word inserts automatically can't be modified. To change the settings for the inserted field type, double-click the field.

- The Check Box control enables you to create a list consisting of multiple check boxes. The {FORMCHECKBOX} field is inserted at the cursor position.
- The Drop- Down control enables you to provide a list of choices for the user in a legacy document. {FORMDROPDOWN} is added at the cursor position.

Tip

If you want to see which code Word is inserting in your document when you add legacy controls, simply press Alt+F9. The display changes to show the field codes. When you're ready to return to the original display, press Alt+F9 again. Be sure to protect the form once again before you begin using it. Although this is not required for Content Controls, form fields will not work properly until the form is protected.

Adding ActiveX Controls

For special situations, you might want to use an ActiveX control to carry out actions when your user selects an item on your form. You might use an ActiveX control, for example, to run a macro that automates a task. ActiveX controls can add flexibility and power to your forms, but you need to be careful using them. Because of the type of objects they are, ActiveX controls can potentially access your local files and even be used to modify your registry. As such, you need to be careful to use ActiveX controls in a secure environment to ensure that hackers don't find a doorway into your network through an unsecured ActiveX control.

ActiveX Controls and the Trust Center

The new Microsoft Trust Center, built into Microsoft Office 2007, is one line of defense against those who might want to tamper with ActiveX controls. The Trust Center automatically reviews any document when you open it, looking for macros from sources not on your Trusted Publishers list, as well as ActiveX controls. To review the ActiveX settings currently in effect on your system, follow these steps:

1. Click the Microsoft Office Button and click Word Options.

2. Click Trust Center and then click the Trust Center Settings button.

3. Choose ActiveX Settings. The range of settings for ActiveX controls is displayed in the Trust Center window.

4. Review the settings and click the one that works best for your application.

5. Click OK to save any changes.

> **Note**
>
> If you include ActiveX controls on your form and plan to deploy the form so that it can be used on other computers, be sure to include some explanatory text to tell readers how to change their ActiveX settings. This way you will be able to ensure the controls of your form work properly on other systems.

Adding an ActiveX Control

To use ActiveX controls, you should be comfortable with Microsoft Visual Basic for Applications (VBA). To add an ActiveX control to your form, follow these steps:

1. Open the template to which you want to add the control.

2. Click the Protect Form button on the Forms toolbar to unprotect the form.

3. Place the insertion point where you want to add the control.

4. Click the Legacy Tools command in the Controls group of the Developer tab.

5. Click the ActiveX control button on the Legacy Tools gallery that you want in the document. Word adds the control to your form and changes the display to Design Mode.

Changing Control Properties

You can change the way an ActiveX control appears by modifying the control's properties. Display Design Mode, and then right-click the control to display the shortcut menu, and then choose Properties. The Properties dialog box appears, as shown in Figure 29-18.

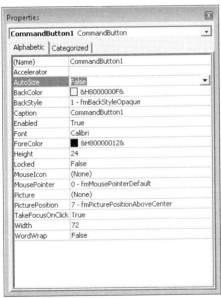

Figure 29-18 Change the way a control looks by making changes in the Properties dialog box.

Chapter 29

Click the Categorized tab to see the various properties organized by category. If you want to make a change— for example, you might change the font—double-click the setting in the right column. When you double-click the font selection, for example, the Font dialog box appears so that you can make the necessary changes. and then click OK.

Programming a Control

Although an in-depth discussion of using VBA to program an ActiveX control is beyond the scope of this chapter, you can easily access the code window for programming your control. To access the code window, follow these steps:

1. Right-click the ActiveX control.

2. Click View Code. Word displays the Visual Basic Editor.

3. Enter the code for the control's event procedure.

4. Click File, Close And Return To Microsoft Word to exit the editor and return to your document. Alternatively, you can simply press Alt+Q.

What's Next?

This chapter introduced you to the new Content Controls in Word 2007 and walked you through the simple process of adding Content Controls to your Word documents. The next chapter builds on this one by introducing you to the XML features in Word 2007.

CHAPTER 30

Working with XML

XML—Then and Now 780

The Benefits of XML in Word 2007 781

Introduction to XML 790

Working with Custom XML in Word 2007 793

What's Next? 803

In the last chapter, you learned how you can use the new content controls in Microsoft Office Word 2007 to easily make use of data in your document in a way that makes sense for you. No more huge cumbersome forms to design or struggle with. This chapter builds on that kind of "easy-data-in, easy-data-out" benefit XML offers. Whether you have amassed a huge collection of XML data and now want to create documents that provide some kind of presentation for that data (for example, creating a listing of articles your organization has published) or you want to know more about how the XML format enables you to make global changes in multiple documents, this chapter takes you into the inner workings of XML in Office Word 2007.

So get ready for something completely different. The Ecma Office Open XML format, which controls the way in which your Word files are stored, is one of the top stories in the Microsoft Office 2007 release. Instead of the familiar .doc format (which saved the file in a binary format), the native file format for Word 2007, Excel 2007, and PowerPoint 2007 files is now Office Open XML. For most situations, this big change (and it is a really big change—you'll find out why in the section, 'The Benefits of XML in Word 2007") may be completely transparent to you as an end user and creator of Word documents. But if you are responsible for creating and deploying templates for your workgroup or organization, developing content solutions for clients, or designing documents that interact with your company databases or Web sites, you will find that Office Open XML in Word 2007 simplifies, secures, and streamlines your work.

Office Open XML Is Approved as an International Standard

On December 7, 2006, the General Assembly of Ecma International approved Office Open XML as an Ecma standard. Ecma is an international non-profit organization comprised of technology professionals, vendors, and users working to establish standards for the industry. Here's a clip from the press release posted on Ecma International's Web site (*www.ecma-international.org/news/PressReleases/PR_TC45_Dec2006.htm*):

"The work to standardize Open XML has been carried out by Ecma International as part of an open, cross-industry collaboration via Technical Committee 45 (Ecma TC45), which includes representatives from Apple, Barclays Capital, BP, The British Library, Essilor, Intel, Microsoft, NextPage, Novell, Statoil, Toshiba, and the United States Library of Congress."

779

XML—Then and Now

When XML was given such visibility in Word 2003, many users were uncertain about what they'd do with it. XML (which stands for Extensible Markup Language) had been around since 1998, but for the most part, it had been used only by people who were comfortable with the technologies and programming languages for the World Wide Web. XML functionality had been available in a limited way in earlier versions of Word, but Word 2003 took a big step forward in making XML a real, usable format that extended the flexibility of content for document authoring, sharing, and reuse. With the XML tools in Word 2003, users had the option of saving documents as XML files and can attach and work with XML schemas relevant to the industries in which they work. Developers designed what's known as smart documents to create interactive documents that collected information, prompted users with context-sensitive help, and more. The XML features in Word 2003 acted as a kind of bridge, giving you the ability to apply XML tags to your data and extend the functionality of your documents.

Something New on the Way

As the Word developers began to research the ways in which people wanted to use XML in their Word documents, a number of important qualifications began to emerge. Among those key considerations, two important points—for two different types of Word users—stood out:

- Users needed to be able to work with their documents normally—cutting and pasting content blocks, changing formats, inserting objects—without worrying about "breaking" the XML schema

- Developers needed to be able to design, create, and deploy smart documents with features that couldn't be affected by the way in which the user modified the document

The XML data store and XML mapping features speak to these primary considerations by separating the data from the way in which it is presented. This simplifies document creation and editing for the end user (you can just work with a Word doc as you always have), while giving template developers the ability to design and populate documents with XML data in such a way that the underlying structure of the document is not changed by the way in which the user works with it.

Word 2007 XML

XML in Word 2007 is totally different from the way Word 2003 handled XML. Now XML is the native format for all documents you create and save. Because every document you create is real XML, there's no tagging to be done (unless you want to attach a custom schema after the fact and need to manually tag specific data items in the document), there's no converting or transforming to worry about. It all happens seamlessly, and transparently, as a natural part of saving a document.

Each Word document you create and save in the Word 2007 default format stores the document so that it is actually a collection of component files. The text, images, and styles are all saved in different files that are compressed in a ZIP file. The data is stored in what's known as the XML data store, separate from the document presentation, which includes themes, styles, and more. When you modify the way your document looks, you are changing only the presentation of the data—not the data itself. This is an important distinction for XML applications because the fact that the data is indepen-dent of format enables you to easily use (or present) that data in an almost unlimited number of ways.

When you open and close files—even if you use Windows Explorer to do that—the docu-ment will look like a single file, ending with the .docx extension. In reality, that file is a ZIP file (a file that is created when a number of files are compressed together). Even though you open the document as a normal, singular file, Word is actually opening the whole set of files behind- the- scenes. This way of storing and managing files makes your files dramatically smaller, easier to work with, and safer than ever before.

This new file packaging approach in Open XML uses what is called the Open Packag-ing Convention to break out the elements and resources involved in creating the XML file. This enables the elements to be saved in their native format (for example, a photo can be saved and accessed as a JPG file) and gives you more control over the items and relationships that comprise the XML file.

This improves the "reusability factor" of your documents, making it easy for you to use the content from your annual report in a brochure for new volunteers, an agenda for a workshop, or as the main text on your Web site's home page. Additionally, if multiple documents reference content in one of the source files—such as your organization's mis-sion statement—you can change the mission statement in the documents that use that file by simply making a change in source file.

The way the Word 2007 document is stored significantly reduces the size of the file (which also means it loads faster) and makes it easier to recover part or all of a file that includes a damaged element. Suppose, for example, that a diagram used in one of your documents is producing an error. In previous versions of Word, this error would keep the entire file from opening. But in Word 2007, because the file is actually saved in its component parts, with graphics data separate from text data, the rest of the document can open normally and the damage is limited to only the affected component.

The Benefits of XML in Word 2007

The world of document authoring has been changing rapidly over the past several years. With the advent of online publishing, we are consuming content at an ever-in-creasing rate. Web pages need to be updated regularly, if not daily; electronic newslet-ters go out monthly or perhaps weekly; letters, e-mail messages, electronic brochures, and more are created quickly, disseminated electronically, and updated almost as soon as they are finished.

Chances are that whoever the readers of your document may be—students, parents, customers, volunteers, constituents, or subscribers—they now expect fast communication, quick updates, and relevant and current information in your reports, on your Web page, and in the brochures and documents you send them. They may expect to be able to fill out forms, register for events, and send customized information to you by using interactive electronic forms. Depending on the nature of your organization, this may put a heavy demand on your document needs.

Office Open XML in Word 2007 can help you meet this demand by organizing and preparing your content so that it can be used in a variety of ways with very little additional work from you. Even better, you can bind the information you collect to your back-end business processes (known as data binding) so that the data you collect flows naturally into the database or Microsoft Windows SharePoint Services site you have designed to store and manage it.

> **Tip**
>
> Chapter 29, "Customizing Documents with Content Controls," explores the new Content Controls in Word, showing you how easily you can create documents that gather the information you need from the people who read and use your files.

Faster, Smaller Files

Previously, in Word 2003, the .doc files were saved by default in binary format, the traditional system of bits and bytes that make up your computer's files. Word 2003 did enable you to prepare and save files as XML, but it required that you use the Save As command to do so. With the Office Open XML format native in Word 2007, the files are saved in XML by default, thus significantly reducing the file size of the stored data. Office Open XML files use ZIP compression technology so that each of the components within the file is compressed, and then the entire file is compressed. This compression is handled transparently, however; there is nothing you need to do to reduce the size of your Word files—it's all taken care of for you.

> **Note**
>
> The image files used your Word 2007 documents are not compressed, which means that you don't need to be concerned about a possible loss of image quality.

Better Data Recovery

Not only are the files in Word 2007 smaller, but they are saved in a modular format that stores the various file components separately—images, content, and embedded code are all stored independently. This helps to maximize the amount of data you can recover when a component in the file is damaged; for example, if an image in your document has been corrupted, the remaining elements in the file can load normally, even though one portion of the file is damaged. If your document were saved in binary format, the entire file would be unusable.

Reusable Content

One aspect of XML's flexibility is the way it separates form from function. Because the Open Packaging Convention saves the actual data separately from the styles, images, and other resources, you can easily use the XML data in other XML applications. For example, you might use the same set of XML data as content for a brochure, a catalog, and event announcements.

Suppose you're writing a marketing flyer about a new volunteer workshop your nonprofit organization is offering. When you save the document, the text content is stored in one XML file; the images you use are stored in another; and the links you include are in yet another. You can easily use the text content in other documents—perhaps in a catalog, a Web page, or an annual report. This enables you not only to save keystrokes but also to reduce the margin for error—instead of having different people write different types of content about one workshop, you can have someone do it once, and then allow everyone to use the finalized content. This creates a consistent message (everybody says the same thing about the workshop, which is a great help toward consistent communication) and frees time others would spend rewriting the same text. Later, if you need to go back and make a change in the text, you can make a simple change and know that it is replicated through all files that use that content part.

> **Note**
>
> The Building Block functionality in Word 2007 is built on this modular XML concept. When you create a Building Block of content in Word 2007—perhaps legal information about your company, your mission statement, a copyright statement, or other boilerplate text—the content is saved as XML data and inserted, along with its format specifications, when you choose it from Quick Parts in the Text group of the Insert tab.

Chapter 30

Map Your Data to Business Processes

The Content Controls available in Word 2007 enable you to make the most of XML by adding features to gather data and integrate it into your business processes. For example, suppose that your department uses a SharePoint site to track and manage performance reviews. Using Content Controls in Word, you can collect information that posts directly to the SharePoint site, where other team members with the necessary permissions can access and work with it directly. Chapter 29 is all about adding Content Controls to your Word 2007 documents.

> **Tip**
> To view a video prepared by the Word 2007 team detailing the process of creating a Word template and fitting it with Content Controls that work seamlessly with SharePoint sites, visit http://channel9.msdn.com/showscreencast.aspx?postid=273005.

Make Your Own Rules

If you are working with specialized content needs, you can attach a customized XSD (XML Schema Definition) to your Word 2007 document. This means that you can create your own rules for naming and storing your data—and you can also share schemas with others in your office, company, or industry.

> **Note**
> Creating a schema is a fairly complicated task—certain rules govern the development of "well-formed" code—but it's not as daunting as you might think. If you'd like to know more about XML and learn to develop your own schemas for your customized XML use, see XML Step by Step, Second Edition (Microsoft Press, 2002), by Michael J. Young.

An Inside Look at a Word 2007 XML Document

Each Word 2007 document you create is actually a small collection of files, although it looks like a single file when you're viewing it in the Word window. To get a better sense of the way in which XML is used in Word 2007, you can unpack a Word 2007 document and take a look at the individual elements that make up the file. If you want to follow along, you'll need these applications in addition to Word 2007:

- A compression utility, like WinZip
- An XML editor or other text editor, like Windows NotePad

Begin by opening any document you've created in Word 2007. If possible, choose something in which you've inserted a picture and some text. Suppose, for example, you are working with a Word 2007 document that resembles the one shown in Figure 30-1. Save and close the file normally.

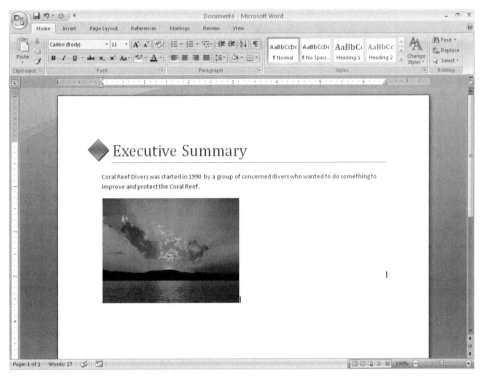

Figure 30-1 A simple Word 2007 document with a heading, text, and a picture.

Next, launch the utility you use to zip files, such as WinZip. Open the Word 2007 file you want to view. (Note that the icon will not appear as a ZIP file in the file list, so you'll need to choose All Files in the Files Of Type box in order to be able to see the Word 2007 document.) When you open the Word 2007 document, depending on the complexity of the file you've opened, you will see a number of different files, as shown in Figure 30-2.

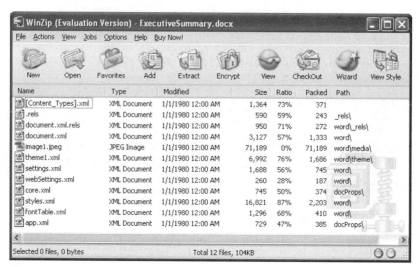

Figure 30-2 You can see the packaged files that comprise your Word 2007 document by viewing them in a compression utility.

The compression utility shows that a number of different files actually go into displaying the document you see in your Word window. Here's a quick overview of some of the key files you see represented in Figure 30-2:

- The file with [Content_Types].xml determines the file types used in the Word 2007 document and associates file types with their respective content.

- The file with the .rels extension sets up the relationships among the elements in the packaged file.

- The document.xml.rels file establishes the relationship within the document to the different elements in the file.

- The document.xml file contains the XML code that provides content and relationships used to build the displayed Word file.

- The image file used in the Word document is image1.jpg.

Additionally, you see files that contain settings for themes, fonts, Web settings, and more. For this example, we'll focus on the primary files shown at the top of the file list.

Right-click one of the files you'd like to see and choose Open With from the options that appear. Choose the option that enables you to view the contents of the file (see Figure 30-3).

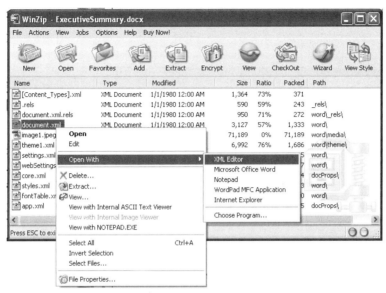

Figure 30-3 Right-click the file you want to see and choose the program you want to use from the displayed list.

When the file opens, it will look something like the XML document shown in Figure 30-4. You can easily read through the code and identify elements that are part of your Word document. In this case, "Executive Summary" is the heading of the XML document file being viewed. Scroll through the document to get a sense of the way in which the content is handled. When you're finished reviewing the file, click the Close box for the file.

```
          </w:pict>
        </w:r>
 -    <w:r>
          <w:t>Executive Summary</w:t>
        </w:r>
      </w:p>
 -  <w:p w:rsidR="00FA3A83" w:rsidRDefault="00FA3A83" w:rsidP="00FA3A83">
 -    <w:r>
          <w:t>Coral Reef Divers was started in 1990 by a group of concerned divers who wanted to do something to improve
            and protect the Coral Reef.</w:t>
        </w:r>
      </w:p>
 -  <w:p w:rsidR="0068681C" w:rsidRDefault="00FA3A83">
 -    <w:r>
 -      <w:rPr>
            <w:noProof />
          </w:rPr>
 -      <w:drawing>
 -        <wp:inline distT="0" distB="0" distL="0" distR="0">
              <wp:extent cx="2847975" cy="2135981" />
              <wp:effectExtent l="19050" t="0" r="9525" b="0" />
              <wp:docPr id="1" name="Picture 0" descr="Sunset.jpg" />
 -          <wp:cNvGraphicFramePr>
                <a:graphicFrameLocks xmlns:a="http://schemas.openxmlformats.org/drawingml/2006/main"
                  noChangeAspect="1" />
              </wp:cNvGraphicFramePr>
 -          <a:graphic xmlns:a="http://schemas.openxmlformats.org/drawingml/2006/main">
 -            <a:graphicData uri="http://schemas.openxmlformats.org/drawingml/2006/picture">
 -              <pic:pic xmlns:pic="http://schemas.openxmlformats.org/drawingml/2006/picture">
 -                <pic:nvPicPr>
                      <pic:cNvPr id="0" name="Sunset.jpg" />
```

Figure 30-4 You can find and review the data in an XML document by simply reading through the file.

Understanding Relationships in Word 2007 XML

The Open Packaging Convention that is used to save your Word 2007 document in its component parts is a great way to ensure document reliability, reusability, and compactness. But this compartmentalization creates a need for a way to tie it all together. You still need to interact with the file as though it were a single file. The Open Packaging Convention takes care of this through the use of relationships.

Each document package includes a *.rels* file that specifies the way in which the various components relate to each other, to the overall package, and to any external resources referenced in the document. For example, a relationship establishes the connection between a logo and the document in which it's used. You can view the relationship one part has to another by opening the .rels file. For each part type, you will see three elements:

- The relationship ID (rID#)

- The relationship type

- The relationship target

By reviewing the relationships among the component parts of the Word document, you can easily see all the resources that are used, analyze the different parts, and remove unnecessary or potentially threatening items. Figure 30-5 shows the .rels file for the sample Word 2007 document. You can see that the file opens with the <Relationships> tag and ends with </Relationships>. Various relationships are identified with values such as "rID3". This file names the relationships within the file, and other component files in the package reference the relationships by this ID name rather than spelling out the actual relationship in the file (which allows for smaller file sizes).

```
<?xml version="1.0" encoding="UTF-8" standalone="yes" ?>
- <Relationships xmlns="http://schemas.openxmlformats.org/package/2006/relationships">
    <Relationship Id="rId3"
      Type="http://schemas.openxmlformats.org/officeDocument/2006/relationships/extended
      -properties" Target="docProps/app.xml" />
    <Relationship Id="rId2"
      Type="http://schemas.openxmlformats.org/package/2006/relationships/metadata/core-
      properties" Target="docProps/core.xml" />
    <Relationship Id="rId1"
      Type="http://schemas.openxmlformats.org/officeDocument/2006/relationships/officeDocument
      Target="word/document.xml" />
  </Relationships>
```

Figure 30-5 The .rels file establishes the relationships among the various components in the document package.

> **Tip**
>
> The new file structure of Word 2007 documents enables developers to build and troubleshoot document solutions independent of Microsoft Office 2007. They can review, search, modify, and deploy the XML code as needed to adjust, add to, or enhance existing documents—all without writing any code or even working in the Word 2007 application!

Managing Content in Word 2007

Most organizations, school, and businesses have discovered the simple secret of copy-and-paste: You can easily reuse information you've already prepared by selecting it, copying it, and pasting it in a new document. The problem with copying and pasting is that it's easy to make a mistake (you might leave off a few words, select too much information, or accidentally incorporate typos), and then you have to deal with formatting issues when you paste the content into the new file. Copying and -pasting can be time-consuming and cumbersome.

This simple document-to-document approach doesn't help much when you are responsible for working with hundreds of documents in a particular agency, and you need to change one thing in every file. For example, suppose that the name, photo, and e-mail address of your executive director is included on every piece of outgoing correspondence your organization distributes. This means e-mail messages, mailed letters, articles, newsletters, your annual reports, your Web pages, and all public service announcements include that information. When your organization hires a new executive director, all the documents need to be updated. You could take a few days and go through and make all these changes by hand, but if you're using Word 2007, the Open XML format enables a developer to simply make the change by modifying the XML document in the package to reflect the new information.

Another way Open XML helps you manage content effectively in large operations is through the use of Building Blocks. For example, Coral Reef Divers is an international organization with a number of sites around the world. Although the organization offers a number of different programs, not all programs are offered at every site. You can create Building Blocks in Word 2007 to create a library of content items that can be inserted into documents manually, when a user wants to add the official program description to a document he or she is creating, or programmatically, by developing a solution in which a specific Building Block is inserted in a document automatically.

Chapter 8, "Working with Building Blocks and Other Text Tools," shows you how to make the most of Building Blocks and other Word 2007 text tools.

Chapter 30

Introduction to XML

Because Open XML is the native file format for your Word 2007 files, you don't need to do anything out of the ordinary in order to save the file as XML. The XML tools you'll use to attach an XML schema or style sheet and tag the data items in your file are simple and straightforward. When you unzip a Word 2007 document and look at the document.xml file, you will see XML data that can be read by the human eye—although the tags around it may not make much sense—but more importantly, can be read by all other XML applications.

In some cases, you may want to attach your own custom schema with data items specific to your industry or document needs. For that reason, we've included some basic XML information to help you understand a little more about what XML is, and how it enables you to extend the functionality of your documents.

XML Glossary

The following list introduces you to some of the common terms you may see used in articles and on Web sites related to XML:

- **XML data**   The XML file is the raw XML data stored independently of the format for presenting it.

- **XML datastore**   The data file that stores the data separately from any format applied to it.

- **XML mapping**   The process by which the XML data and the way in which it is presented (letter, brochure, report) are linked.

- **Well-formed**   A "well-formed" XML document is one that adheres to the constraints defined by either the DTD (Document Type Definition) or the XML schema.

- **Element**   A unit of data—which could be anything from a single character to pages in length—defined in an XML document, enclosed with start and end tags. For example, in <TITLE>Microsoft Office Word 2007 Inside Out</TITLE>, TITLE is the element name.

- **XML schema**   A definition of the data elements allowed in the XML document. The XML schema is a superset of the DTD. You may also see the acronym XSD used to refer to an XML schema definition.

- **DTD (Document Type Definition)**   Similar to an XML schema, a DTD is a definition of the data elements allowed in the XML document. A DTD is similar to an XML schema but is more highly structured.

- **Cascading Style Sheets (CSS)**   A collection of formatting instructions that control the display of the document. Style sheets can be in a separate file and linked to the document or can be embedded in the document itself.

- **XSLT (XSL Transformations)**   XSLT is used to convert XML documents into various document formats, most commonly HTML.

XML Defined

Some people refer to XML as a markup language because, after all, that's what its name implies (that is, Extensible Markup Language). But XML is more than a language of tags; XML actually lets you create a type of markup language that is specific to your data needs. XML has quickly become a "common denominator" for the easy exchange of application-independent, flexible data.

Depending on how you use XML, you may use specific rules to create your own tags and style sheets; the individual tags describe the content and meaning of the data rather than its display format, which HTML controls. This means that you can in effect create your own markup language (in the XML schema you create and attach) that is specific to the needs of your business or organization. XML provides the means for you to create your own way of classifying and storing your content.

For example, if you are working with a real estate document, you might attach your agency's customized XML schema so that you can identify key items in the form you're working on. For example, you might use the following tags to identify important data in a purchase offer on a new home:

<SELLER>

<PURCHASER>

<OFFER>

When you select and tag information as XML in Word 2007, the content you selected is marked with an open and closed XML tag (for example, <SELLER>Insert Name</SELLER>).

For more information on creating customized, interactive documents, see Chapter 29, "Customizing Documents with Content Controls."

> ### Note
>
> XML tags are case-sensitive by default. If you're creating an XML document that contains data to be used by various business systems, before creating your document, be sure to verify how the systems expect to operate with your tags.

Because XML enables you to name the content of the data, you can use that same class information as easily in a database as you can in a spreadsheet, a word processing document, a report, or an e-mail. Using an XML schema, which defines the rules for naming the XML data, and an XSLT, which is the template that will provide the format for the final document, you can make XML data usable in many different forms in all sorts of contexts, from one end of your organization to another.

By comparison, HTML (Hypertext Markup Language) is a tagging system that controls the way information is formatted, not the content of the data itself. A heading, for example, might have an <H1> or <H2> tag to designate the size of the heading; the <FONT> tag is used to specify the type family, size, color, and style of the text. But the HTML tags can't describe the content of the heading, and it's the content—the actual data itself—that can be used in other documents, such as databases, spreadsheets, or reports, and so forth. The XML tags name the content of the data—not the formatting.

Note

What is an "open standard"? A technology based on an open standard is open for use and development by the public; there are no licensing fees or proprietary standards owned by a specific company or organization. Office Open XML is made available as an open and royalty-free license.

XML in Industry

A number of industry-wide schemas exist to help standardize content storage in specific professional arenas. To find out more about the use of XML standards in your industry, check out the Organization for the Advancement of Structured Information Standards (OASIS), an international XML interoperability consortium. This group hosts the site XML.org (http://www.xml.org/, which), provides links with information about and examples of XML development in each of the following industry groups:

- Defense
- e-Government
- Financial services
- Healthcare
- Human resources
- Insurance
- Localization
- Printing and publishing
- Retail
- Security
- Tax/Accounting
- Other Industries

Working with Custom XML in Word 2007

The popularity of XML as a data-exchange format has grown dramatically over the last couple of years, and it is going to increase. Because XML is straight-forward, humanly readable, and uniform, XML data is easy to read, create, and reuse in an unlimited number of forms.

The XML capability in Word 2007 gives you the flexibility to easily and simply include and work with data in your documents in variety of ways. If you want to make use of XML data already available in your business or organization (for example, suppose that Coral Reef Divers has just received a large XML file of donor records from one of its international sites), you can bring that into your Word 2007 documents and create correspondence, reports, specialized donor kits, and more, all using the same data. Additionally, you might bring data into an existing document (for example, using a content control to identify your department and employee identification before sending a reviewed document back to a team member). You can also attach a custom schema developed by your business or organization to apply the custom XML tags to existing documents, thus enabling you to save the data independent of its format and use it in many other ways.

> **Note**
>
> The way in which your organization or business uses XML data and presentation will be unique to the business processes that work for you. To find out more about the concepts of XML mapping and simple ways to use readily available data in your Word documents, see Chapter 29, "Customizing Documents with Content Controls" to discover how to add content controls to expand the functionality of your documents—and your data. The rest of this chapter focuses on using the tools included within Word 2007 that enable you to add your own custom XML schemas to Word documents and prepare those documents for use in a virtually unlimited number of ways.

Displaying Word 2007 XML Tools

The first thing you need to do in order to work with the XML features in Word 2007 is display the Developer tab. The Developer tab adds the XML tools to the Ribbon so that you can add content controls, attach a custom schema, and more. Here's how to add the Developer tab:

1. Click the Microsoft Office Button and choose Word Options.

2. On the Popular tab, click in the Show Developer Tab in the Ribbon check box. This adds the Developer tab to the Ribbon, providing you with a set of XML tools you will use as you work with XML in your Word documents (see Figure 30-6).

Figure 30-6 Display the Developer tab to locate the XML group.

Each of the tools in the XML group enables you to work with a different element of an XML document. Table 30-1 gives you more information about the tools in the XML group.

Table 30-1 XML Tools

Name	Description
Structure	Displays the XML Structure task pane so that you can work with the XML elements in your document
Schema	Opens the Templates And Add-Ins dialog box with the XML Schema selected so that you can add a schema and set XML options
Transformation	Enables you to add an extensible style sheet (XSLT) to your document
Expansion Packs	Enables you to add an XML expansion pack to the current document

> **Note**
>
> An XML expansion pack is a group of files used in smart documents. The XML expansion pack manifest describes all the files and components used in the smart document and tells Microsoft Office 2007 how to work with the various elements. For more about working with expansion packs in Word 2007, go to http://msdn2.microsoft.com/en-us/library/aa193903(office.11).aspx.

Attaching a Custom XML Schema

As mentioned earlier in this chapter, your work with XML in Word may be completely transparent. You may never need to look at the XML that underlies the document you work with in the Word window. But if your organization or industry uses a specific XML schema to define common data elements, you can easily attach the schema to your Word documents. To attach a schema to your Word document, follow these steps:

1. Open the document you want to use.

2. Click the Developer tab and click Schema in the XML group. The Templates And Add-Ins dialog box appears, with the XML Schema tab selected (see Figure 30-7).

The Checked Schemas Are Currently Attached list shows all schemas available for use in the open document.

3. Click the schema you want to use and click OK.

Figure 30-7 The XML Schema tab in the Templates And Add-Ins dialog box enables you to add and work with XML schemas.

After you add a schema to the document, the XML Structure task pane appears on the right side of the Word window (see Figure 30-8). You will use the XML Structure task pane to tag the content items in your document. At first, the message "No XML elements have been applied to this document" appears at the top of the task pane. When you begin applying the elements, this view will change, as you'll see in the section, titled "Tagging Word Content," later in this chapter on page 798.

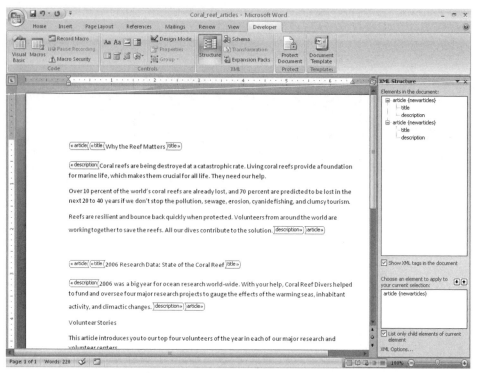

Figure 30-8 You use the XML Structure task pane to tag the content for reuse in your Word document.

Tip

If you have an XML data file you want to use in Word, but you don't have a schema to attach to the document, you will still be able to read and use the data in the file. When you open the file in Word, Word automatically displays the XML data and tags in the document. The XML Document task pane appears, providing any available views you can able to apply to the data.

Adding a Schema to the List

The first time you attach a schema, the list will be blank. You can use the Add Schema button in the Templates And Add-Ins dialog box to tell Word where to find the new schema. Here are the steps:

1. In the Templates And Add-Ins dialog box, click Add Schema. The Add Schema dialog box appears, where you can navigate to and select the schema you want to use.

2. Click the schema, and then click Open.

3. In the Schema Settings dialog box, in the URI field, enter a name for the schema and then click OK. The schema is added to the list.

4. Click the check box of the schema you want to use and then click OK to apply the schema to the current document.

> **Note**
>
> This section assumes that you have a schema to work with. If you have not been supplied an XML schema by your administrator or workgroup leader, you can search online for sample schemas to use or follow along with the XML examples in the book *XML Step by Step*, Second Edition, as mentioned earlier in this chapter. The book includes a CD with numerous XML sample data files, schemas, and transforms you can use to learn more about XML.

Working with the Schema Library

If you work with a number of XML schemas and XSLT (Extensible Stylesheet Language Transformation) files to control the structure and format of your XML documents, the Schema Library comes in handy for organizing, managing, and working with the various files you need. Display the Schema Library by following these steps:

1. Click the Developer tab.

2. Click Schema.

3. In the Templates And Add-Ins dialog box, click Schema Library. The Schema Library appears, as shown in Figure 30-9.

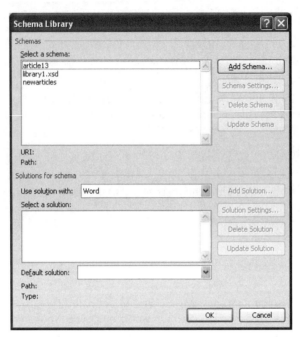

Figure 30-9 You can add, manage, and control options for schemas and transforms in the Schema Library dialog box.

The top portion of the Schema Library lists the XML schemas you've attached to the current document. The bottom portion of the dialog box enables you to add XSLT transforms, also called *solutions,* to the document. To add a solution, click Add Solution, navigate to the folder in which the transform is found, and then choose the XSLT transform from the list that appears. Click OK to add the transform and return to the Schema Library.

Tagging Word Content

As you prepare your data for reuse, much of your work with XML will rely on working with tags—the small code identifiers you attach to data to name the content. The tags available for use in a particular document depend on the schema attached to it—the schema contains the definitions for the tags, much as a style sheet defines the styles that are allowed in a document formatted for the Web.

After you add the schema to your document, the XML Structure task pane contains the tools you'll use to apply the tags to your document. Here's the simple process for adding tags:

1. Highlight the content you want to tag.

2. Click an XML element in the XML Structure task pane. The first time you do this, a message box asks you whether you want to apply the element to the entire document or to the selection. Click the selection that fits your needs. The opening

and closing tags for that element are added to the selected content. The tags that are available will depend on the level of the tag you are applying. Because XML tags are nested, tags on a subordinate level appear in the Choose An Element list in the XML Structure task pane only when the higher-level tag is selected. For example, in Figure 30-8, the ARTICLE tag is displayed. When you click that tag to apply it, the three tags nested within the article tag—TITLE, DESCRIPTION, and AUTHOR—become available for selection (see Figure 30-10).

Figure 30-10 When you choose an element in the XML Structure task pane, nested elements within that element become available.

Adding Tag Attributes

XML attributes are special characteristics of an element that enable you to further categorize your data. For example, suppose that the articles in the previous figure may include two different types of information: OVERVIEW and TUTORIAL. To help further classify the type of information in the document, you can assign OVERVIEW and TUTORIAL attributes to the DESCRIPTION element. To add an attribute, perform the following steps:

1. Right-click the XML element in the XML Structure task pane, and then click Attributes in the list, as shown here:

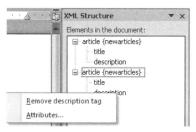

2. The Attributes dialog box appears. Click the attribute you want to use, enter an attribute value in the Value text box, click Add, and then click OK.

3. The new attribute is added to the list of available attributes. Now, select the one you want and then click OK to add it to the XML element you selected.

Chapter 30

Displaying Tags

After you attach a schema and apply tags to the data in your document, you can easily show and hide XML tags while you work by pressing Ctrl+Shift+X. If you prefer, when the XML Structure task pane is visible, you can click the Show XML Tags In The Document check box to remove the check mark and hide the tags.

In addition, to make finding the tag you want easier, you can choose which tags appear in the selection box at the bottom of the task pane by clicking the List Only Child Elements Of Current Element check box.

Removing XML Tags

If you make a mistake entering a tag in your document, and you want to remove it, simply right-click the tag you want to remove, and then choose Remove Tag. The data is still in your document, but both the opening and closing tags are deleted.

Setting XML Options

As you get more comfortable working with XML, you may want to modify some of the options to further control the way your XML files are saved, validated, and displayed. To display the XML Options dialog box, click the XML Options link at the bottom of the XML Structure task pane or click the XML Options button on the XML Schema tab of the Templates And Add-Ins dialog box. The XML Options dialog box appears, as shown in Figure 30-11.

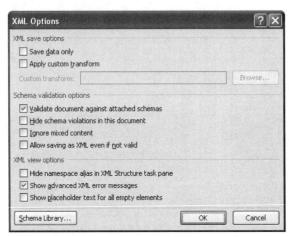

Figure 30-11 XML options enable you to control the way XML files are saved and to make choices about validation and display.

Saving XML

When you save your XML document, you have the option of saving only XML data or saving the data and the format together. In the XML Options dialog box, you can make one of these settings the default choice for saving the current document. If you click the Save Data Only check box, the current XML document will be saved as data only.

When you click the Apply Custom Transform check box, the Custom Transform field becomes available so that you can click Browse, and then choose the transform file you want to attach to the document.

Dealing with Schema Violations

If the tags you've added to your document—or the content they describe—create something that doesn't fit the schema you've attached, Word will let you know that you have a validation error. *Validation* is the process of checking the tags against the schema to make sure the code is properly formed. If Word finds a problem, it lets you know by displaying a purple wavy line along the left margin of the text.

In addition to the purple indicator, a small error icon appears in the XML Structure task pane next to the tag that is in error. To see a description of the problem, position the mouse pointer over the tag. A description of the problem appears, as shown in Figure 30-12.

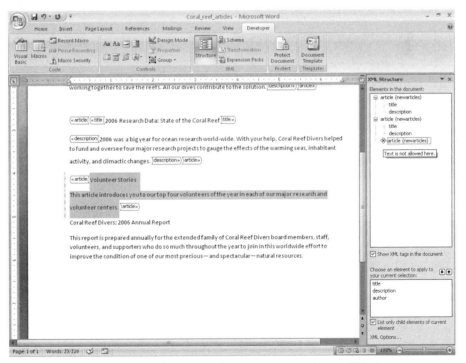

Figure 30-12 Word provides a description when an error occurs in your XML document.

The schema validation options in the XML Options dialog box enable you to control how—and whether—Word checks your code for validation (this option is also available in the Templates And Add-Ins dialog box, where you first attach the schema). By default, the document will be validated against attached schemas. You can choose to hide errors in the current document, ignore mixed content, or even save the file as XML, errors and all. (You might want to do this, for example, if you have an error you can't figure out, and you want to give the file to an XML guru for further investigation.)

View Options for XML

The XML view options in the XML Options dialog box enable you to provide additional information about the XML elements you're working with. By default, the *namespace alias* (the name you assign to the schema or solution when you attach it) appears in the XML Structure task pane, and you can hide it by selecting the Hide Namespace Alias In XML Structure Task Pane check box. If you want to get additional information on the XML validation error messages you receive, select the Show Advanced XML Error Messages check box. Finally, if you want to see where empty elements occur in your document, select the last option, Show Placeholder Text for All Empty Elements.

If you are just learning how to use XML, you'll find that selecting the Show Advanced XML Error Messages feature will help you learn more quickly from your mistakes. The error messages that appear provide much more information about what's going on. For example, compare Figure 30-13 with the earlier, more limited error message shown in Figure 30-12.

Figure 30-13 When the Show Advanced XML Error Messages option is checked, Word provides more explanation of validation problems.

> ### Sharing Files with Previous Versions of Word
>
> You've seen this earlier in the book, but we want to repeat it here because it's relevant to our discussion of Word 2007 formats. Because Office Open XML is a completely different format from the binary .doc format used in Word 2003, users working with versions of Word prior to 2007 need a conversion utility (available from Microsoft free of charge) to open and work with Word 2007 documents. Users can download the utility from the Microsoft Downloads site (http://www.microsoft.com/downloads).
>
> Word 2007 users can also click the Microsoft Office Button and use the Save As command to save files in Word 97-2003 format if necessary. Note, however, that saving a file in 97-2003 format will reduce the functionality of the new program features and erase the benefit of the XML native format.

What's Next?

This chapter introduced the new Office Open XML format, and showed you the major benefits of Open XML, and touched on how to attach your own custom XML schemas for specialized content. The next chapter rounds out this part of the book with advanced coverage of Word 2007 macros and Microsoft Visual Basic tools.

Chapter 30

Working with Macros and VBA

A *macro* is a set of instructions written in the Microsoft Visual Basic for Applications (VBA) programming language. This definition alone may make many users think macros, or VBA, is out of their grasp and a feature of Microsoft Office Word 2007 that is targeted for developers. After all, doesn't one need to be a programmer to implement this type of functionality? Absolutely not. Macros can be as simple as recording a specific set of steps in the application, and Office Word 2007 will write the instructions—or *code*—for you. As a matter of fact, you don't even need to look at the macro code to create and use macros in your everyday tasks, such as those in the following list:

- Speed up routine editing and formatting, such as using Find and Replace to clean up data copied from another source that contains manual line breaks and multiple paragraph marks.

- Automate a complex series of tasks—for example, inserting a table with a specific size, table style, and certain table options, such as including a total row and banded columns.

- Make an option in a dialog box more accessible, such as turning on and off the display of text boundaries.

- To work around various limitations in Word, such as inserting a static date (one that does not update to the current system date) with a single click or keyboard shortcut.

- Combine several repetitive tasks, such as switching to a specific document view, modifying the Zoom Level, and setting other view options.

If the idea of speeding up cumbersome tasks, such as those just listed, with a simple click of a button or keyboard shortcut is appealing, then read on—you do not need any previous programming knowledge to benefit from this chapter. You do need to be familiar with the content contained in this book, or at least be familiar with those areas in which you want to automate specific tasks.

This chapter covers the basic fundamentals of macros by showing you how to automate several of the tasks previously listed. We'll start with using the Macro Reorder to create a few macros, cover some simple editing tasks, and take a look at sharing macros with others, either your own or those that you obtain from someone else.

> **Note**
>
> Full exploration of macros and VBA is beyond the scope of this chapter—entire books are dedicated to this subject. Those who want to learn more will find a list of recommendations in the section titled "What's Next" at the end of the chapter on page 836.

A Bit About VBA and Macros

When you start working with macros, you should become familiar with a few concepts and some terminology, even if you do not intend to go beyond recording macros and simple editing. For starters, Visual Basic for Applications, or VBA, is a subset of Microsoft Visual Basic. The primary distinction between the two is VBA is dependent on a host application, such as Word, and if you share macros created in Word with other users, they must have Word installed to use them.

A macro is actually a VBA procedure, and the terms are used interchangeably. A *procedure* is a series of statements, or actions, that are grouped together to form one specific set of instructions that is associated with a specific name, or what is referred to as a macro.

Macros can be saved in macro-enabled documents or templates. When a document or template contains macros, they are contained in a specific portion of the file called a *VBA Project* (also known as a project). A VBA Project stores objects, such as a *module*, and a module stores macros. If this seems confusing, consider how documents are stored: They are stored on a specific drive (VBA Project), they are placed in a folder (module), and they are assigned a name (macro).

When you create a template that contains macros, documents that are attached to the template are able to use macros stored in the template, and you can access the template's VBA Project through the document. This means you can modify and create new macros in the attached template without actually opening the template in Word. However, like most features, the default behavior can be changed, and you can disable the editing capability, discussed in the section titled "Protecting Your Macros" later in this chapter on page 831.

With some of the basics out of the way, let's move on to learning more about how easy it is to automate repetitive tasks in Word, starting with saving macro-enabled files.

Saving Macro-Enabled Documents and Templates

 The switch to Office Open XML File Formats changed how documents and templates containing macros are saved. A document containing macros must be saved using the Word Macro-Enabled Document (.docm) file type. Templates containing macros must be saved using the Word Macro-Enabled Template (.dotm) file type. If you save a document or template using the macro free file types, Word Documents (.docx) or Word Templates (.dotx), any macros contained in the files will be removed. Should you inadvertently try to use a macro-free file type to save a document or template that contains macros, a message box (shown in Figure 31-1) will display, stating the VBA Project cannot be saved in a macro-free document.

Figure 31-1 If you use a macro-free file type to save a document or template containing macros, a message box will display and notify you that another file type must be selected.

CAUTION

If you answer Yes to confirm you want to save the file using a macro-free file type, the VBA Project will be discarded when you close the file. However, prior to closing, if you modify the VBA Project, such as editing or recording a new macro, which you will learn how to do in this chapter, you can recover the macros by using a macro-enabled file type to save the document or template.

To save a document or template containing macros, follow these steps:

1. Click the Microsoft Office Button and then click Save As.

2. In the Save As dialog box, display the Save As Type list and select either Word Macro-Enabled Document or Word Macro-Enabled Template.

3. Provide a File Name and Save In location, and click Save.

New macros and changes to existing macros are automatically saved when the document or template is saved.

> **Note**
>
> If you are saving a file in an older file format, such as a Word 97-2003 Document (.doc) or Word 97-2003 Template (.dot), there is no distinction between macro-enabled and macro-free files, and macros are saved in the file when using these file types.
>
> Additionally, when you save a macro-enabled file the macros are not converted to XML, they are saved in a binary format. For those interested in knowing more about the document parts that comprise an Office Open XML file, macros are stored in a document part named vbaProject.bin.

Recording a Macro

As mentioned earlier, a macro can be as simple as recording steps, or actions, you already perform in Word—you don't even need to learn a programming language. You can also use the Macro Recorder to record the bulk of your macro and later edit it in the Visual Basic Editor. This section of the chapter eases you into the realm of macros, starting with how to plan a macro, considerations you should take into account, and using the Macro Recorder to record a macro.

> **Note**
>
> Examples of the macros used in this chapter can be found in MyFirstMacros.docm in the sample files on this book's CD.

Setup and Planning

Before you start working with macros, you'll want to first turn on the display of the Developer tab on the Ribbon, shown in Figure 31-2. The Developer tab contains options for recording and running macros in the Code group. If you do not already have the Developer tab displayed, follow these steps:

1. Click the Microsoft Office Button and then click Word Options.

2. In the Popular section, select Show Developer Tab In The Ribbon.

3. Click OK to close Word Options.

Figure 31-2 The Developer tab contains access to advanced features, such as macros, and it is not displayed by default.

You also need to check your Macro Security settings and make sure you are able to allow your macros to run after they are created. To check Macro Security, follow these steps:

1. Click the Microsoft Office Button, click Word Options, and then click Trust Center.

2. Click the Trust Center Settings button and then click Macros Settings. Your macro security options will display as shown here.

3. Select the option Disable All Macros With Notification if necessary. (You can use any option except Disable All Macros Without Notification, but Disable All Macros With Notification is the recommended setting.)

4. Select the Message Bar section and verify the option Show The Message Bar In All Applications When Content Has Been Blocked is selected.

5. Click OK to close the Trust Center Settings and then click OK to accept your changes and close Word Options.

If you have not disabled the Message Bar and your Macro Security settings are set to Disable All Macros With Notification, when you open a document or template that contains macros (or open or create a document based on a template that contains macros) macros are initially disabled, the Message Bar will display, as shown in Figure 31-3, and provide the option to enable macros.

Figure 31-3 The Message Bar will alert you when you open a document or template with macros, or if the attached document template contains macros.

To enable the macros, click the Options button. In the Microsoft Office Security Options dialog box, select Enable This Content and click OK.

> **Note**
>
> If you want to disable macros, you should still display the Microsoft Office Security Options dialog box and select Help Protect Me From Unknown Content (Recommended), as opposed to closing the Message Bar.
>
> Some macros have been known to cause the Message Bar to redisplay when opening or creating new documents even if the document or template you are opening or creating does not actually contain macros.

For more information on Macro Security, see Chapter 20, "Addressing Document Protection and Security Issues."

Prior to recording a macro, consider the following:

- First, practice the steps that you will record. The macro recorder is similar to a video recorder, and every action will be recorded, including switching document views and moving your insertion point—even your mistakes are recorded. For macros that will involve several steps, consider jotting down a few notes to help you remember the correct sequence of steps.

- When you are recording, the mouse cannot be used to select text or move the cursor—you will need to use the keyboard instead. You can review navigation and text selection methods in Chapter 2, "Document Creation with Word 2007."

- If you are creating a macro for a specific template, and the macro will navigate to specific locations in documents based on the template, then consider adding Bookmarks in the template. Then in your macro you can use Go To (F5) to navigate to the correct location. For more on using Bookmarks, see Chapter 7, "Honing Document Navigation Skills."

For our first simple macro example, which will insert the current system date as a static date in your document, if you've ever inserted a date by using the Date And Time dialog box, more than likely practice is not necessary. To use the Macro Recorder and record a new macro, follow these steps:

1. Create a new document and use the Word Macro-Enabled Document file type (as described in the preceding section) to save it in My Documents as **MyFirstMacros.docm**.

2. Navigate to the Developer tab and in the Code group, click Record Macro. This will display the Record Macro dialog box, shown in Figure 31-4.

Figure 31-4 The Record Macro dialog box provides all of the options for creating a macro, including assigning the macro to a button or keyboard shortcut.

3. In the Macro Name text box, type a name for your macro, such as **InsertTodaysDate**.

> **Note**
>
> Naming a macro is similar to naming a document, and you should use descriptive names. Macro names are limited to 80 characters when using the Record Macro dialog box, they must start with a letter, they can include letters and numbers, and they can't include most special characters or spaces. However, the underscore character can be used to represent a space.
>
> If you give your macro the same name as an existing macro, you will be prompted to replace the existing macro. You can click Yes to replace the macro, click No to return to the Record Macro dialog box and modify the name, or click Cancel to cancel the macro recording.
>
> Additionally, if your macro uses the same name as a built-in command, your macro will replace the built-in functionality. For more on viewing built-in Word commands, or replacing them with your own macro, see the Inside Out tip titled "Viewing Word Commands" later in this chapter on page 830.

4. In the Store Macro In list, select MyFirstMacros.docm. (If you save the macros in Normal.dotm, they will be available to all documents. However, it's recommended you initially save your macros in a separate document during the learning stages.)

5. Provide a description for your macro, if desired, and click OK to begin recording. Your mouse pointer displays with a cassette tab, shown to the left of this paragraph, and the Record Macro button on the Developer tab will change to Stop Recording (you'll use this button when you are finished recording your macro).

Chapter 31

> **Tip**
>
> While you are recording a macro, you can click the Pause Recording button to perform any steps you do not want to record in your macro. When you are finished, click the Pause Recording button again to continue recording.

6. Navigate to the Insert tab and in the Text group, click Date & Time to display the Date & Time dialog box.

7. Select your preferred date format, clear the Update Automatically option if necessary, and click OK. Do not add any additional steps unless you want your macro to contain other actions. For example, if you want to start a new paragraph after inserting the date, press Enter.

8. Navigate to the Developer tab and click Stop Recording in the Code group.

9. To test your macro, delete the previously inserted date, on the Developer tab in the Code group, click Macros (or press Alt+F8), in the Macros dialog box, click InsertTodaysDate, and then click Run. The current system date should be inserted in your document at your insertion point.

> **Tip**
>
> For a one-click method to start and stop recording a macro, right-click the customizable status bar and click Macro Recording. Then, to access the Record Macro dialog box, click the Record Macro button on the status bar. Like the Record Macro button on the Developer tab, the Record Macro button will change to Stop Recording when you are recording a macro.

You may be wondering how navigating to the Developer tab, clicking the Macros button, selecting the macro from the list, and clicking Run can save time. You are correct in thinking it's not necessarily any faster than inserting a date by using the Date & Time dialog box. For simple macros, the time-saving steps occur when you add the macro to your Quick Access Toolbar or assign it to a keyboard shortcut. Accomplishing both of these tasks is covered in the next section.

Running Macros

As you may have found in the previous section, using the Macros dialog box is not the most efficient way to run your macros. Ideally, running a macro should be as simple as clicking a button or pressing a keyboard shortcut. This section of the chapter covers how to add a macro to your Quick Access Toolbar, how to assign a keyboard shortcut to your macro, and how to use specifically named macros that will automatically run without being assigned to a button or keyboard shortcut.

> **Note**
>
> Macros can also be added to the Ribbon. However, doing so requires some XML knowledge, and this capability isn't found within the Word application. For more information on customizing the Ribbon, see "Introducing the Office (2007) Open XML File Formats" on the Resources tab of this book's companion CD.

Adding a Macro to the Quick Access Toolbar

As you may know from reading previous chapters, the Quick Access Toolbar can be easily customized with commands that are not on the Ribbon or with commands you prefer to have visible at all times. The Quick Access Toolbar can also be used as a one-click method for running macros. To add the previously created macro to your Quick Access Toolbar, follow these steps:

1. Open MyFirstMacros.docm, if it's not already open.

2. Click the More button at the end of the Quick Access Toolbar and then click More Commands to open Word Options with the Customize section displayed.

3. In the Choose Commands From list, select Macros. Your macro named InsertTodaysDate will appear as Project.NewMacros.InsertTodaysDate in the list of commands, as shown in Figure 31-5.

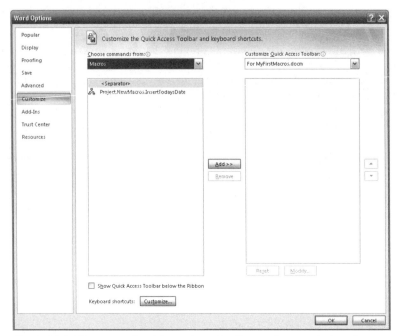

Figure 31-5 When you select Macros from the Choose Commands From list, your macros will be displayed so that you can add them to your Quick Access Toolbar.

Note

The name of the macro, Project.NewMacros.InsertTodaysDate, provides the location where the macro is stored, as previously discussed in the section titled "A Bit About VBA and Macros" earlier in this chapter on page 806. *Project* is the name of the VBA Project, *NewMacros* is the name of the module (which is automatically created when you use the Macro Recorder), and *InsertTodaysDate* is the name of the macro.

4. In the Customize Quick Access Toolbar list, select For MyFirstMacros.docm. You should store your Quick Access Toolbar customizations in the same location as your macro. Use For All Documents (Default) if the macro is stored in your Normal template.

Note

The list of current Quick Access Toolbar commands will disappear after you select For MyFirstMacros.docm from the Customize Quick Access Toolbar list. When you customize the Quick Access Toolbar for a specific document, or template, the customizations will merge with the commands listed under For All Documents (Default) when the document, template, or a document attached to the template is opened.

5. Select the macro, if isn't already selected, and then click Add to add it to your Quick Access Toolbar.

6. Click the Modify button to open the Modify Button dialog box, shown here.

7. Select a symbol, or icon, for your macro, such as the Clock. Then to modify the ScreenTip, change the Display Name for your macro. For example, type **Insert the current date**.

8. Click OK to accept the changes in the Modify Button dialog box and click OK to accept the Quick Access Toolbar customizations. Your custom macro button should appear on your Quick Access Toolbar, as shown here.

When you close MyFirstMacros.docm, the custom macro button will be removed from the Quick Access Toolbar. To use the macros in MyFirstMacros.docm for any document, it can be used as a global template. For more on working with templates, see Chapter 4, "Formatting Documents Using Templates."

INSIDE OUT   When is a macro actually warranted?

In past versions of Word, macros are created for every repetitive task, such as inserting frequently used text, graphics, tables, and formatting text and paragraph. Now, with all of the new features Word has to offer, alternate methods for reusing data are available. At the beginning of this chapter, the list of tasks that you could create a macro for provided the example of inserting a table with a specific size, table style, and certain table options. Depending on your needs, a macro is not the only way to accomplish this task. If you need precisely formatted content, such as a graphic, table, or frequently used text, consider creating a Building Block instead. For example, a specifically formatted table can turned into a Building Block and be placed in the Quick Tables gallery, as shown here.

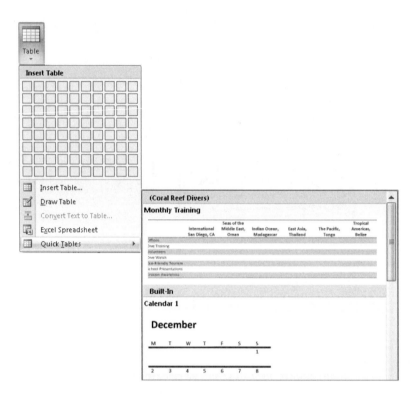

A Building Block provides more flexibility than a macro does, especially when it comes to modifications. To modify a macro, you need to either record the macro again or manually edit the code. To modify a Building Block, you can insert the Building Block, make your modifications, and then redefine the Building Block with your modified content.

If you want to add a single Building Block to your Quick Access Toolbar, use a combination of Building Blocks and macros. Create a Building Block for the content to be inserted in a document and record a macro for inserting the Building Block.

If you want to create a keyboard shortcut for a Building Block, a macro isn't necessary. Building Blocks are available in the Customize Keyboard dialog box, which is described in the next section, under the AutoText category.

If the purpose of your macro is for text or paragraph formatting, consider using a style instead of a macro. As with Building Blocks, formatting can be easily redefined in the style without having to record the macro again or manually edit the code.

Keep in mind that the key to undertaking any task is to first determine the easiest route and then to use the most efficient tool for the job.

For more information on creating Building Blocks, see Chapter 8, "Working with Building Blocks and Other Text Tools." For more on creating and using styles, see Chapter 15, "Using Styles to Increase Your Formatting Power."

Assigning a Keyboard Shortcut to a Macro

In addition to adding your macros to your Quick Access Toolbar, you can assign keyboard shortcuts to your macros. The initial steps are similar to the steps used to add a macro to your Quick Access Toolbar. You open MyFirstMacros.docm—if it isn't already open—display Word Options and the Customize section, then follow these steps:

1. In the Customize section in Word Options, click the Customize button at the bottom, next to the Customize Keyboard label, to display the Customize Keyboard dialog box, shown in Figure 31-6.

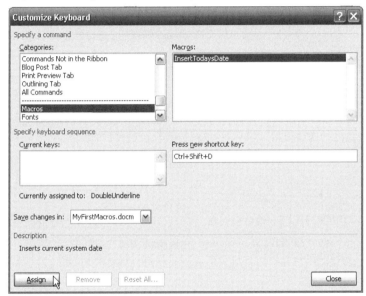

Figure 31-6 The Customize Keyboard dialog box enables you to create keyboard shortcuts for your macros.

2. In the Categories section, scroll to the bottom of the list and select Macros.

3. Click the Save Changes In list and select MyFirstMacros.docm. InsertTodaysDate should now be visible in the Macros list, as shown in Figure 31-6.

4. Place your cursor in the Press New Shortcut Key text box and press your desired keyboard shortcut on the keyboard, such as Ctrl+Shift+D. Note that Ctrl+Shift+D is a built-in keyboard shortcut and is assigned to Double Underline. If you use this keyboard shortcut to add double underline, select an alternate keyboard shortcut for your new macro and press those keys on the keyboard instead.

Note

If the keyboard shortcut is currently assigned, a situation that is noted below the Current Keys list after the keys are pressed, the custom keyboard shortcut will override the built-in keyboard shortcut.

5. Click Assign and click OK to assign the keyboard shortcut. Then close the Customize Keyboard dialog box and click OK to close Word Options.

Tip

After you are familiar with steps for adding a macro to your Quick Access Toolbar, or assigning a keyboard shortcut to a macro, you can select one of these options when you start recording a new macro. In the Record Macro dialog box, shown in Figure 31-4, click the Button option to add the macro to your Quick Access Toolbar or click the Keyboard button to assign a keyboard shortcut.

TROUBLESHOOTING

My macro cannot be found or is disabled

If you try to run a macro and encounter the message saying your macro cannot be found or has been disabled because of your Macro Security settings, the first thing to check is your Macro Security settings, which are described in the section titled "Setup and Planning" earlier in this chapter on page 808.

If you're still having trouble after you have verified that your Macro Security settings enable you to run macros, and if you are trying to run the macro from your Quick Access Toolbar or a keyboard shortcut, try running the macro by using the Macros dialog box, found on the Developer tab in the Code group (or press Alt+F8). If the macro does not appear in the list, your macro is missing. Either you do not have the document or template in which the macro is stored open, or the macro was inadvertently deleted. If you can successfully run the macro from the Macros dialog box, try recreating the keyboard shortcut or the button on your Quick Access Toolbar.

Running a Macro Automatically

Most macros require you to click a button or use a keyboard shortcut to run the macro. However, a few macros will run automatically when a specific event occurs, such as when Word starts; when you open, close, or create a document; and when you exit Word.

A macro must be stored in your Normal template for it to run automatically for any document that is created, opened, or closed. And it must use a macro name listed in Table 31-1, which also describes the events associated with the macros.

Table 31-1 List of Automatic Macros

Auto macro name	Description
AutoExec	Runs when Word starts
AutoOpen	Runs each time a document is opened
AutoNew	Run each time a document is created
AutoClose	Runs each time a document is closed
AutoExit	Runs when Word exits

> **Note**
>
> You can use other events, called Document-Level Events, to cause a macro to run automatically. However, they are out of the scope of this chapter.

For our automatic macro example, we'll take a look at another task listed at the beginning of this chapter—combining several repetitive tasks, such as switching to a specific document view and modifying the Zoom Level.

Word users often need to open documents in a certain view and at a specified Zoom Level. In recent versions, if you create a new document based on the Normal template, Word uses the current view settings and Zoom Level, as opposed to older versions that use the settings stored in the Normal template. But you still can't open documents in certain views and at specified Zoom Levels when you're accessing previously created documents. However, a simple macro, and the power of VBA, will enable you to specify which view, Zoom Level, and any other viewing options you need. And these settings will be applied to every document you open automatically using a macro named AutoOpen. To create the macro, use the following steps:

1. On the Developer tab, click Record Macro.

2. In the Macro Name text box, type **AutoOpen**. From the Store Macro In list, select All Documents (Normal.dotm), if it isn't already selected, as shown here.

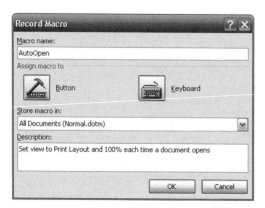

3. Click OK to start recording. In the View options (on your status bar), click your desired view. Even if it's the view you are currently using, the action will still be recorded.

4. Click Zoom Level to open the Zoom dialog box and select your desired Zoom settings. (Changes made using the Zoom Slider are not recorded.)

5. Make any other desired changes to your view and then click Stop Recording.

6. Test your macro by opening a document.

To fully test your macro, create a new document, switch to another view, change your view settings, and make another editing change, such as typing a space in the empty document and then pressing Backspace to delete the space. Then, save the document, close it, and reopen it.

> **Note**
> Altering your view or Zoom settings is not enough to trigger a change to the document. An action must appear in your Undo list to actually save changes to your view.

Alternatively, you can verify your recorded macro by viewing the recorded code in the Visual Basic Editor, which is covered in the next section.

TROUBLESHOOTING

The Macro Recorder did not record all of my actions

When you use the Macro Recorder, you might find all of your actions are not recorded, such as when you use the Zoom Slider to alter your view or select various options in a dialog box, such as the Open, Print, or Save As dialog box.

In general, Word can record the result of your choices in a dialog box but not the steps used to obtain the result. And if the steps are not part of the end result, they will not be recorded. In some instances, unfortunately, there is no valid reason you are unable to record specific actions. Each version of Word adds more capabilities to the Macro Recorder. For example, in Word 2007, when you use the Macro Recorder to record a change to an option in Word Options, only the option you changed is actually recorded—that alone is a significant and welcome change from previous versions. But some areas still need to be tweaked.

However, just because you are unable to record an action, doesn't mean it's impossible to accomplish your goal. For these situations, you may need to find an alternate method, such as using the Zoom dialog box instead of the Zoom Slider, or manually editing the macro and making the necessary additions. For the latter, VBA knowledge is required, but the more you learn about Word and VBA the easier it will become.

Editing Macros

Depending on the macro you record, sometimes you may need to edit and refine the results of the recorded macro. The beauty of VBA is that the syntax is fairly easy to read and comprehend. If you are interested in learning more about macros, viewing recorded code is a good place to start. For our editing example, we'll take a look at another task discussed at the beginning of this chapter—making an option in a dialog box more accessible. This example will clear the Show Picture Placeholders option, which speeds scrolling through a document that contains a large number of inline images in Print Layout view, and we'll make a simple edit to the macro so that each time you run it, the option will toggle on or off depending on its current state. To get started, follow these steps:

1. Open MyFirstMacros.docm, navigate to the Developer tab, and click Record Macro.

2. In the Macro Name text box, type **TogglePicturePlaceholders**. From the Store Macro In list, select MyFirstMacros.docm, add a description if desired, and click OK to start recording.

3. Click the Microsoft Office Button, click Word Options, and then click Advanced. Clear the option, Show Picture Placeholders, which is located under the Show Document Content heading. Then click OK to accept the change and close Word Options. (If the option is already cleared, select it; all we need is to have a change recorded.)

4. On the Developer tab, click Stop Recording and then click Macros. Select TogglePicturePlaceholders in the list of macros and then click Edit. The Visual Basic Editor will open, and you will see both recorded macros, as shown in Figure 31-7.

```
Sub InsertTodaysDate()
'
'  InsertTodaysDate Macro
'  Inserts current system date
'
    Selection.InsertDateTime DateTimeFormat:="MMMM d, yyyy", InsertAsField:= _
        False, DateLanguage:=wdEnglishUS, CalendarType:=wdCalendarWestern, _
        InsertAsFullWidth:=False
End Sub
Sub TogglePicturePlaceholders()
'
'  TogglePicturePlaceholders Macro
'
'
    ActiveWindow.View.ShowPicturePlaceHolders = True
End Sub
```

Figure 31-7 The InsertTodaysDate and TogglePicturePlaceholders macros shown in the Visual Basic Editor.

Prior to editing, let's take a closer look at the macro we just recorded. (We'll take a closer look at the Visual Basic Editor in the next section.)

- Each macro, or *procedure*, begins with the statement Sub, which stands for subroutine, and ends with End Sub. The text in between these lines is the code that is executed when you run the macro.

> **Note**
>
> Another set of paired statements you'll see in recorded macros is With and End With. This structure groups related statements together, such as a group of options in a dialog box, and like Sub and End Sub, the group begins with the statement With and ends with the statement End With.

- The green text, preceded by an apostrophe, is called Comment Text. As the name implies, this text is used for notes and documentation purposes and is skipped when the macro runs. You can safely delete these lines, and if you add an apostrophe anywhere in the macro, the text that follows will be treated as Comment Text.

- ShowPicturePlaceholders is set to a True/False (Boolean) value, as are all check boxes. True means the check box is selected, and False means the check box is cleared.

As mentioned earlier in this chapter, you do not need to know VBA to follow the syntax. Take the statement in the TogglePicturePlaceholders macro, for example. In the active window, the view option—Show Picture Placeholders—is selected, or turned on.

Because the Show Picture Placeholders option is a True/False (Boolean) value, to use the macro to toggle the view of Picture Placeholders, all we need to do is set Show Picture Placeholders to the reverse of its current value. To make the edit, follow these steps:

1. Locate the TogglePicturePlaceholders macro. It should appear similar to the code here.

```
Sub TogglePicturePlaceholders()
'
' TogglePicturePlaceholders Macro
'
'
    ActiveWindow.View.ShowPicturePlaceHolders = True
End Sub
```

2. Select `ActiveWindow.View.ShowPicturePlaceHolders` and copy it.

3. Replace `True` at the end of the line with `Not` and then paste the previously copied statement. The revised statement is shown here.

```
ActiveWindow.View.ShowPicturePlaceHolders = Not ActiveWindow.View.ShowPicturePlaceHolders
```

> **Note**
>
> When you reference only an option (in VBA this is called a *Property*), as opposed to changing the value of the option, the current value of the option is returned. The `Not` operator reverses the current value, and if the current value is `True`, the `Not` operator causes the value to change to `False`, and vice-versa.

1. From the File menu, click Close And Return To Microsoft Word.

2. Assign the macro to your Quick Access Toolbar by using the steps provided in the section titled "Adding a Macro to the Quick Access Toolbar" earlier in this chapter on page 813.

3. Verify you are using Print Layout view, insert an inline image (Text Wrapping is set to Inline With Text) in your document and try out your new macro. The macro should toggle between viewing empty placeholders and viewing the image in the document.

The Visual Basic Editor

The Visual Basic Editor is a powerful automation tool. As mentioned earlier, covering all aspects of VBA, and the Visual Basic Editor, is beyond the scope of this chapter because entire books are dedicated to this subject alone. This section will discuss the elements of the Visual Basic Editor, many of which are used in this chapter. A diagram of the Visual Basic Editor is provided in Figure 31-8, and Table 31-2 describes each element in the diagram.

Project Explorer

Procedure List

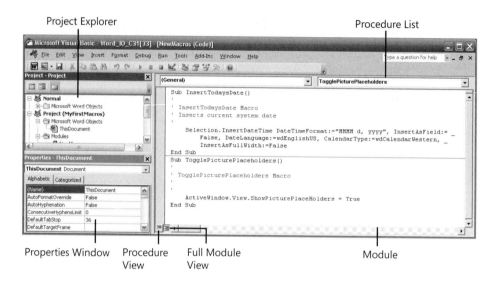

Properties Window   Procedure   Full Module   Module
                    View   View

Figure 31-8 The Visual Basic Editor is the central hub for all of your macro needs and can be used for creating, editing, and deleting macros.

Table 31-2 The Visual Basic Editor

Element or term	Description
Project Explorer	Provides access to all available VBA Projects including open documents, templates, Normal template, loaded global templates, and an attached document template. The name of the file that contains the project is enclosed in parentheses next to the name of the project. Double-click a VBA Project—or an object, such as a module—in the VBA Project to open it and view the contents. If the Project Explorer is closed, from the View menu, click Project Explorer or press Ctrl+R.
Properties Pane	Displays properties of the selected object in the Project Explorer. Can be used to change the name of a module or project. The Properties pane is primarily used for other types of objects available in VBA, such as a UserForm, which is also called a dialog box. If the Properties pane is closed, from the View menu, click Properties Window or press F4.
Module	Contains a collection of macros. Each macro in the module is visually separated by a horizontal line.
Procedure View	Displays only the active macro in the module.
Full Module View	Displays all macros in the module.
Procedure List	Enables quick navigation between macros in the module. To quickly jump to another macro, select the macro from the Procedure List. This option is useful if you have several lengthy macros, or if you are viewing the module in Procedure view.

Recording Built-in Dialog Box Options

In previous versions of Word, when you use the macro recorder to record an option in a dialog box, every single option is recorded—not just the option you changed. Thankfully, for the most part, every single option is no longer recorded when you access Word Options in Word 2007, but the problem still persists with other dialog boxes, such as the Font dialog box, the Paragraph dialog box, and other built-in dialog boxes. If you use the Macro Recorder to change an option in these dialog boxes, or if you access the dialog box and click OK, when you run the macro, the settings that were in use at the time the macro was recorded will also be applied. In these cases, you should edit the macro and leave only the option you wish to change. For example, here is what you record when you access the Font dialog box:

```
Sub FontDialogBox()

' FontDialogBox Macro

' Selected Bold in the Font dialog box


    With Selection.Font

        .Name = "+Body"

        .Size = 11

        .Bold = True

        .Italic = False

        .Underline = wdUnderlineNone

        .UnderlineColor = wdColorAutomatic

        .StrikeThrough = False

        .DoubleStrikeThrough = False

        .Outline = False

        .Emboss = False

        .Shadow = False

        .Hidden = False

        .SmallCaps = False

        .AllCaps = False

        .Color = wdColorAutomatic

        .Engrave = False
```

```
        .Superscript = False

        .Subscript = False

        .Spacing = 0

        .Scaling = 100

        .Position = 0

        .Kerning = 0

        .Animation = wdAnimationNone

    End With

End Sub
```

As you can see, every option in the dialog box is recorded. Note that even though the Animation option was removed from view in the Font dialog box it was also recorded and can still be used in a macro even if it isn't visually present in the Font dialog box.

When I recorded the macro, the only change I made was to the Bold format. That's the only format I want to change, and the statements for all other options need to be deleted. Here is a revised example:

```
Sub FontDialogBox()

' FontDialogBox Macro

' Selected Bold in the Font dialog box

' Recorded macro has been edited


    With Selection.Font

        .Bold = True

    End With


End Sub
```

In the revised macro, only the lines in between **With** and **End With** were deleted, with the exception of **.Bold = True**. As previously noted, a **With** structure uses a pair of statements to group related statements together. Both must be present, or an error will occur. An alternative revision would be to delete **With** and **End With** and use **Selection. Font.Bold=True** instead.

Chapter 31

INSIDE OUT   The idiosyncrasy of Toggle formats

You may be wondering why I used the Font dialog box instead of clicking Bold on the Home tab. The Bold button on the Home tab is actually a toggle format, as described in Chapter 15. When you record a toggle format, such as Bold, the recorded code isn't the same as what is recorded when you use the Font dialog box. It uses special value, called a *Constant* named wdToggle, as shown here:

```
Selection.Font.Bold = wdToggle
```

This is what causes the idiosyncrasy of toggle formats and is similar to the TogglePicture-Placeholders macro, in which the value of the option is reversed each time the macro runs. This being the case, if you want to use the Bold format, or another toggle format, in a macro and if you do not want the format to be toggled off if it is already applied to the text, you can edit the macro and make sure True is used instead of wdToggle. Or use False if you want to remove the Bold format.

Additional Macro Options

As you become more familiar with using macros, you might find you have macros that could use a more descriptive name, macros you no do not want (it's not unusual to have several failed macro recording attempts when you are in the learning stages), and macros that you want to use in other documents or templates. How to deal with each of these situations is covered in this section.

Renaming a Macro, Module, or Project

The easiest way to rename a macro, module, or project, is to use the Visual Basic Editor. Note that the previously provided rules for naming macros still apply—names must start with a letter, they cannot contain spaces or special characters, and an underscore can be used. An exception to the rules previously provided is the character limit. You can use up to 255 characters in the macro name if you are naming or renaming it in the Visual Basic Editor, and names for modules and VBA Projects are limited to 30 characters. Additionally, similar to documents, macros contained in the same module must have a unique name, and modules in the VBA Project must be uniquely named.

To rename a macro, simply change the name of the macro after the line that begins with **Sub**.

To rename the module or VBA Project, select the module or VBA Project in the Project Explorer. In the Properties pane, change the name in the (Name) text box as shown here.

CAUTION

If your macro is assigned to a button on your Quick Access Toolbar or a keyboard short-cut, changing the name of the macro, module, or VBA Project will disable the button or keyboard shortcut. You need to remove the disabled button from your Quick Access Toolbar and create it again. For a keyboard shortcut, you will need to reassign the key-board shortcut to the renamed macro.

TROUBLESHOOTING

I've encountered an "Ambiguous name detected" error

When you try to run a macro and encounter an error that states an Ambiguous Name is detected, you have two macros with the same name in your module.

To resolve the error, first note the name of the macro listed in the error message. Then, if the Visual Basic Editor does not automatically open and locate the macro for you, on the Developer tab, click Macros to open the Macros dialog box, select the macro in the list, and click Edit. The Visual Basic Editor will open with the macro displayed.

If you cannot find another macro with the same name, click the Procedure list, shown here, and you should see two macros with the same name.

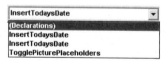

Click either macro in the list to navigate to the macro in the module. To correct the error, you need to rename one of the macros and provide a unique name. Or if it is a duplicate macro, delete one of the duplicates by using the steps provided in the next section.

Deleting and Exporting Macros and Modules

To delete a macro, you can use one of the following methods:

- Display the Macros dialog box, click Macros on the Developer tab or press Alt+F8, select the macro in the macros list, and click Delete.

- In the Visual Basic Editor, select the entire macro—starting with the line that begins Sub, through End Sub—and press Delete on the keyboard.

Deleting a macro does not remove the macro from your Quick Access Toolbar, and you need to manually remove the button. If you assigned a keyboard shortcut to the macro, no further action is required.

To delete a module, select the module in the Project Explorer. From the File menu, click Remove *ModuleName*. You will be prompted to export the module before removing it, as shown here.

If you click Yes, the Export File dialog box will display and enable you to provide a name and location for your exported module, as shown in Figure 31-9.

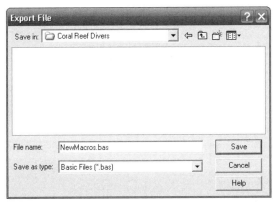

Figure 31-9 The Export File dialog box enables you to export your module and save it prior to deleting and removing the module from your VBA Project.

You can use standard file naming rules for your exported module because it will be saved as an external file. Note that the file uses a .bas file extension. However, it is nothing more than a text file, and you can use Notepad to open it and view the contents.

> **Tip**
>
> If you want to delete an entire VBA Project, save the document or template in a macro-free file format, such as Word Document (.docx) or Word Template (.dotx). Doing so will remove the entire VBA Project from the document or template. If you want to preserve the macros, export the modules from the VBA Project prior to saving the file in the macro-free file format.

Importing Macros and Modules

There may be a time you want to add your exported module back to the VBA Project, or import a module for use in another VBA Project. To import a previously exported module, in the Project Explorer, select the VBA Project you want to add the module to. Then, from the File menu, click Import File. The Import File dialog box will display (it is similar to the Export File dialog box, shown in Figure 31-9). To import the module, navigate to your saved module, select it, and then click Open. The module should now be added to your VBA Project.

If you want to use a single macro from the exported file, you can use Notepad to open the previously saved file, copy the macro, and paste it in any module. Alternatively, you can import the entire module and delete any macros you do not want to keep.

Another way to share macros between documents and templates is to open both files and then copy and paste the macros between the modules, just as you would copy and paste content between documents.

> **Note**
>
> You can also use the Organizer—available in the Macros dialog box on the Developer tab—to copy, rename, and delete modules. However, if you are comfortable using the Visual Basic Editor, you will find it is more flexible than the Organizer because the Organizer is limited to working only with modules and not individual macros. For more information on using the Organizer, see Chapter 4.

INSIDE OUT Viewing Word commands

If you give a macro the same name as a built-in Word command, your macro will run instead of the built-in command. To access the list of built-in Word commands, on the Developer tab, click Macros. Then in the Macros In list, select Word Commands, as shown here.

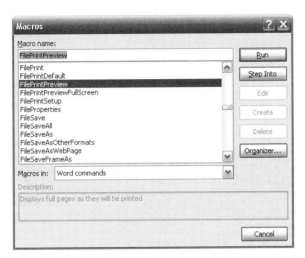

Many of the built-in Word commands are named according to how they are accessed in previous versions of Word. For example, if you are looking for Print Preview, use FilePrintPreview. (To quickly jump to a specific Word command, type the first few letters of the name in the Macro Name text box.)

If you find a Word command you wish to intercept, you can change the name of a previously recorded macro to match the name of the built-in Word command.

Alternatively, if you want to view the code used in the built-in Word command so that you can copy it and use it another macro, learn more about VBA, or append additional code, select the command from the Macros list, click the Macros In list, select your document or template, and then click Create.

Keep in mind, if you add a macro with the same name as a built-in command and are not planning to replace the built-in command with your macro, you need to delete the macro or modify the macro name. Otherwise, Word will use the macro in place of the built-in command. For more information on deleting macros, see the section titled "Deleting and Exporting Macros and Modules" earlier in this chapter on page 829.

Protecting Your Macros

You can protect your macros from alteration by assigning a password to your VBA Project. To do so, follow these steps:

1. Display the Visual Basic Editor (click the Visual Basic button on the Developer tab or press Alt+F11).

2. From the Tools menu, click *ProjectName* Properties.

3. Click the Protection tab, as shown below, and select Lock Project For Viewing.

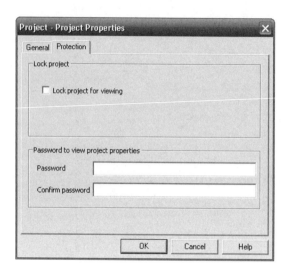

4. In the Password text box, type a password and then type it again in the
    Confirmation text box. (The Password and Confirmation are both required.)

Once your VBA Project is protected, you will be prompted to enter the password the
first time you access the VBA Project, such as when you double-click the VBA Project in
the Project Explorer to open it or use the Macros dialog box to edit or delete the macro
after the file has been closed and reopened.

As with passwords in general, keep in mind that if you lose the password, you won't be
able to access the VBA Project. Though some password cracking utilities are available,
there are no guarantees they will work, and their success depends on the password you
used to secure the VBA Project.

Digitally Signing Macros

Macros are digitally signed for a couple reasons. The primary reason is to provide
authentication for the macros when you share them with others. Another reason is to
enable a user to disable all macros except for those that are digitally signed for security
reasons. Even if you do not intend to digitally sign your macros, this section of the
chapter will still be beneficial to you. You may come into contact with macros that have
been digitally signed, and the more you know about digital signatures, the more informed decisions you will be able to make when it comes to macro security.

You can use two types of digital signatures to digitally sign macros: one that is obtained
from a third party, such as those offered on Office Marketplace (*www.office.microsoft.com
/marketplace*) or SelfCert, a digital signature utility that comes with Microsoft Office
2007 applications. The type of digital signature you should use depends on the purpose
of the digital signature—whether you are sharing your macros with others or they are
for your own personal use in documents and templates. This section describes the two
types of digital signatures you can use to sign macros and how to digitally sign your
macros after obtaining a digital signature.

Third-Party Digital Signature

If you are sharing your macro with others, you need to obtain a third-party digital signature for code signing. A digital signature for code signing is issued by a third party and is called a Certificate Authority (CA). This third party validates the identity of the applicant for the digital signature before it is assigned and later keeps track of the digital signature to determine if it has expired or been revoked.

To obtain a digital signature for code signing, visit Office Marketplace on the Internet or visit a specific Certificate Authority's Web site, such as VeriSign or Thawte.

Creating a Self-Signed Digital Signature

Using SelfCert enables you to create a digital signature yourself, and it is intended to be used for macros you use in your personal documents and templates. A SelfCert digital signature enables you to disable all macros except for those that are digitally signed. (For more on macro security settings, see Chapter 20.)

A digital signature created using SelfCert can be shared with others. However, it relies more on trust than true authentication. When SelfCert is used to create a digital signature, no authentication is required, and any name can be used for the digital signature. As you have likely surmised, anyone can easily create a digital signature using someone else's, or a corporation's, name. It's for this reason that an authenticated digital signature can be provided only by a Certificate Authority, as described in the preceding section.

CAUTION

If the other user does not have your digital signature when you use SelfCert.exe to digitally sign a VBA Project and later share your macros with others, they will be prevented from enabling the macros. For more information, see the Troubleshooting tip titled "I Can't Enable Macros" later in this section on page 835.

To create a digital signature using SelfCert, follow these steps:

1. Locate SelfCert.exe in the Office 2007 installation path, called the *Office Bin*, such as C:\Program Files\Microsoft Office\Office12. Alternatively, use Windows Search to locate the file.

2. Double-click Self-Cert.exe to display the Create Digital Certificate dialog box, shown in Figure 31-10.

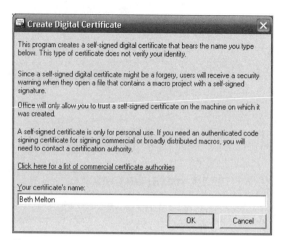

Figure 31-10 The Create Digital Signature dialog box enables you to create a digital signature for your personal use.

3. In the Your Certificate's Name text box, type a name for your digital certificate and click OK.

Your digital signature has been created, and you can now use it to sign your macros for personal use.

Digitally Signing a VBA Project

When you digitally sign your macros, you are actually providing a digital signature for the VBA Project, which as previously mentioned is the primary container for your macros. After you have obtained a digital signature or created one for your personal use, you can digitally sign your VBA Project as follows:

1. Open the document or template you want to sign.

2. On the Developer tab, click Visual Basic or press Alt+F11.

3. In Project Explorer, select your VBA Project and from the Tools menu, click Digital Signature to display the Digital Signature dialog box, shown here.

4. Click Choose, select your digital signature from the Select Certificate dialog box, and then click OK. The digital certificate name will display in the Digital Signature dialog box.

5. Click OK to digitally sign your VBA Project and close the Digital Signature dialog box.

> **Note**
>
> If you previously selected a digital signature, you do not have to click Choose and select the digital signature again. To use the current digital signature, click OK in the Digital Signature dialog box.

After your VBA Project has been digitally signed, depending on the type of digital signature you used, you may need to digitally sign the VBA Project again if you create new macros or modify previously created macros.

TROUBLESHOOTING

I can't enable macros

If you open a document or template—or if you create a new document based on a template—and you find you cannot enable the macros, first check your Macro Security settings, as described in the section titled "Setup and Planning" earlier in the chapter on page 808.

If your macro security settings are ok, then the likely cause of the problem is macros that were signed with a digital signature created using SelfCert. The error message you encounter will be similar to one of these images. (If the Visual Basic Editor is open, the message on the right will display immediately. The message on the left is displayed after you click Options in the Message Bar.)

Use one of the following methods to resolve this issue:

- If the digital signature is one you previously created or a digital signature you trust, you can install the digital signature on your system. Click the Show Signature Details link, click View Certificate, click Install Certificate, and then follow the steps in the Certificate Import Wizard.

- If you do not want to install the digital signature, you can remove it to enable the macros. Allow the macros to be disabled, display the Visual Basic Editor (Alt+F11), click Digital Signature on the Tools menu, and then click Remove. Save the file, close it, and reopen it. You will then be allowed to enable the macros.

Of the two methods provided, the second is recommended if the digital signature is not one you created. Once you install a digital certificate on your system, it is considered a System Root Certificate, which doesn't display in the Trusted Publisher dialog box in the Trust Center, and it could potentially be exploited. Note that Internet Explorer Options enable you to remove a previously installed digital certificate by viewing Certificates on the Content tab.

What's Next?

Now that you know the information in this chapter, you might be amazed at how much you can do using the Macro Recorder and a little knowledge about the Visual Basic Editor. If this chapter has whet your appetite for macro knowledge, several resources are available to help you learn more. Here are a few recommendations:

- *Advanced Microsoft Office Documents 2007 Edition Inside Out,* by Stephanie Krieger (Microsoft Press, 2007). This book includes a fantastic VBA primer. Previous programming knowledge is not required, and the content is easy to follow and comprehend.

- The Word MVP Site (*www.mvps.org/word*). This Web site contains answers to frequently asked Word questions and provides tutorials and articles for using VBA in Word.

- The Microsoft Developers Network (MSDN; *msdn2.microsoft.com/en-us/office /aa905482.aspx*). This Web site isn't strictly for developers; it includes topics for beginners, too. It also contains a wealth of sample code that you can copy and paste in your VBA Projects. Some samples can be used as-is, whereas others may need to be tweaked to fit your needs.

As you delve further into the world of automation and into the new territory of mastering Word 2007, here are a few final thoughts: Never stop learning, make it your goal to learn something new every day, and share what you have learned with others.

Index to Troubleshooting Topics

About the Authors

Kathy Murray Katherine Murray is the author of many books on technology, with a special emphasis on Microsoft Office. She's been working with the 2007 Microsoft Office System since it was little more than a gleam in the development team's eye. (Okay, truthfully, she started working with it in beta 1—but it was love at first Ribbon sighting.) In addition to her other computer books, Katherine wrote the in-the-box documentation for Microsoft Office Professional and Small Business Editions; and she designs, writes, and produces projects for clients using Microsoft Office Word 2007. She is also a regular contributor to a number of Microsoft sites and publishes a blog called BlogOffice (*www.revisionsplus.com/blogofficexp.html*), offering tips, updates, news, and resources related to a variety of Microsoft Office versions and events.

Katherine has been fascinated by computers since the early 1980s when she got her hands on one of the first IBM PCs to arrive in the city of Indianapolis. She still lives in the Midwest, close to her three children and new grandbaby, with two dogs, three cats, and a turtle. When she's not writing or playing with the baby, she enjoys many non-technical activities, including gardening, cooking, reading, listening to live jazz, and playing Trivial Pursuit with the kids.

Mary Milhollon Mary Millhollon is the founder and owner of Bughouse Productions, a creative multimedia venture based in Portland, OR, and a full-time Content Developer for the Institute of Computer Technology (*www.ict.org*), working extensively on worldwide training and curriculum for Intel® Education programs (*www.intel.com/education*). Mary is a "beyond full-time" technology and educational writer, developer, Microsoft Word, and Internet expert, consultant, Web designer, editor, instructor, and volunteer, working daily (and nightly) with a menagerie of technologies. She has over a baker's dozen years of professional publishing, design, and technology experience.

Mary's educational background is a blend of art, English, journalism, and computer science, which lends itself well to today's constantly morphing technologies. Her most recent technology-related publications and projects include *Easy Web Design*, 3rd edition (Microsoft Press), *2007 Microsoft Office System Inside Out* (Contributor, Microsoft Press), and EasyTech animation scriptwriting and production for Learning.com (*www.learning.com*). You can contact Mary via e-mail at mm@creationguide.com or visit *www.creationguide.com*.

Beth Melton Beth Melton has been a computer instructor and developer since January 1995. Along with developing custom Microsoft Office solutions for a wide range of clients and instructing computer classes for local area colleges, she writes regularly on the Microsoft Office applications for Web sites including Microsoft Office Online, Tech-Trax Online Magazine, The Word MVP Site, and the Microsoft Knowledge Base. She has been a Microsoft Office Most Valuable Professional since 2000 and is a Microsoft Office Specialist Master Instructor.

Beth began working with the 2007 Microsoft Office System in April 2005 as a participant in the Office 12 Technical Adoption Program (TAP) and began alpha testing in August 2005. She was a columnist for the 2007 Microsoft Office Preview site, an expert in the Ask The Experts Area during the Ready for a New Day Launch Tour 2007, and offers peer-to-peer support for the Microsoft Office applications in the Community Discussion Groups on Microsoft Office Online.

Prior to becoming immersed in technology, Beth served 15 years as a member of the Illinois Air National Guard in the 183rd Fighter Wing. Her primary duty was as an Aircraft Fuel Systems Mechanic on the F-4 Phantom and the F-16 Fighting Falcon. Her leisure time is spent with her husband and two sons.

Index

3-D (three-dimensional) effects, 346–349

A

ActiveX controls, 776–778
adding
  backgrounds, 441–442
  Building Blocks, 192–196
  charts, 300–302
  cross-references, 647–648
  custom dictionaries, 237–238
  custom templates. See creating custom templates
  custom Themes, 130–133
  digital IDs, 576–577
  document workspace, 496–497
  documents. See creating documents
  exclusion dictionaries, 240–241
  faxes, 519
  headers and footers, 83–88
  indexes. See indexes
  list styles, 397–401
  lists, 384–386
  master documents, 616–618
  outlines, 252
  sections, 605–606
  SmartArt diagrams, 292–294
  styles, 421–423
  subdocuments, 618–620
  table of contents (TOC), 652–654
  tables. See creating tables
  templates. See creating custom templates
  text boxes, 448–450
  watermarks, 441–445
alerts when sharing documents, 505
aligning content
  art objects, 349–351
  headers and footers, 86–87
  indexes, 678
  layouts. See layouts
  paragraphs, 360–364
  shapes. See shapes
  tabs, 370–375
  text alignment commands, 149–151
  text alignment differences, 602–603

  text boxes. See text boxes
  vertically between margins, 81
all caps format, 144–145
Apply Styles pane, 415–416
area charts, 299
art
  adding to documents, 323–330
  adding WordArt objects, 330
  aligning objects, 349–351
  Art Page Border feature, 475
  charts. See charts
  clip art, 324–327
  converting text into WordArt objects, 331
  cropping pictures, 335–336
  diagrams. See diagrams
  distributing vs. aligning objects, 351
  drawing grid, 90–91, 329–330, 362
  figures. See figures
  grouping objects, 351
  lines, 327–330
  modifying drawings, 339–349
  multiple images, 324
  New Drawing Canvas, 328
  object layering, 352
  outlines, 342–343
  overview, 323
  photos as page backgrounds, 324
  picture adjustment tools, 334–335
  picture borders, 333
  picture captions, 338–339
  picture effects, 333–334
  picture shapes, 332
  picture styles, 331–332
  position, 352
  resizing pictures, 337
  rotating pictures, 338
  shadows in shapes, 343–345
  shape custom colors, 343
  shape fills, 342–343
  shape styles, 340
  shape text, 341
  shapes, 327–330
  SmartArt. See SmartArt
  text wrapping, 353–354

Additional Resources for Home and Business

Breakthrough Windows Vista™: Find Your Favorite Features and Discover the Possibilities
Joli Ballew and Sally Slack
ISBN 9780735623620

Jump in for the topics or features that interest you most! This colorful guide brings Windows Vista to life—from setting up your new system; accessing the Windows Vista Sidebar; customizing it for your favorite gadgets; recording live television with Media Center; organizing photos, music, and videos; making movies; and more.

So That's How! 2007 Microsoft® Office System: Timesavers, Breakthroughs, & Everyday Genius
Evan Archilla and Tiffany Songvilay
ISBN 9780735622746

From vanquishing an overstuffed inbox to breezing through complex spreadsheets, discover smarter ways to do everyday things with Microsoft Office. Based on a popular course delivered to more than 70,000 students, this guide delivers the tips and revelations that help you work more effectively with Microsoft Office Outlook®, Excel®, Word, and other programs. Also includes 'webinars' on CD.

Look Both Ways: Help Protect Your Family on the Internet
Linda Criddle
ISBN 9780735623477

You look both ways before crossing the street. Now, learn the new rules of the road—and help protect yourself online with Internet child-safety authority Linda Criddle. Using real-life examples, Linda teaches the simple steps you and your family can take to help avoid Internet dangers—and still enjoy your time online.

The Microsoft Crabby Office Lady Tells It Like It Is: Secrets to Surviving Office Life
Annik Stahl
ISBN 9780735622722

From cubicle to corner office, learn the secrets for getting more done on the job—so you can really enjoy your time off the job! The Crabby Office Lady shares her no-nonsense advice for succeeding at work, as well as tricks for using Microsoft Office programs to help simplify your life. She'll give you the straight scoop—so pay attention!

Microsoft Office Excel 2007: Data Analysis and Business Modeling
Wayne L. Winston
ISBN 9780735623965

Beyond Bullet Points: Using Microsoft Office PowerPoint® 2007 to Create Presentations That Inform, Motivate, and Inspire
Cliff Atkinson
ISBN 9780735623873

Take Back Your Life! Using Microsoft Office Outlook 2007 to Get Organized and Stay Organized
Sally McGhee
ISBN 9780735623439

See more resources at **microsoft.com/mspress**
and **microsoft.com/learning**

Microsoft Press® products are available worldwide wherever quality computer books are sold. For more information, contact your bookseller, computer retailer, software reseller, or local Microsoft Sales Office, or visit our Web site at **microsoft.com/mspress**. To locate a source near you, or to order directly, call 1-800-MSPRESS in the United States. (In Canada, call **1-800-268-2222**.)

What do you think of this book?

We want to hear from you!

Do you have a few minutes to participate in a brief online survey?

Microsoft is interested in hearing your feedback so we can continually improve our books and learning resources for you.

To participate in our survey, please visit:

www.microsoft.com/learning/booksurvey/

...and enter this book's ISBN-10 number (appears above barcode on back cover*).
As a thank-you to survey participants in the United States and Canada, each month we'll randomly select five respondents to win one of five $100 gift certificates from a leading online merchant. At the conclusion of the survey, you can enter the drawing by providing your e-mail address, which will be used for prize notification only.

Thanks in advance for your input. Your opinion counts!

* Where to find the ISBN-10 on back cover

ISBN-13: 000-0-0000-0000-0
ISBN-10: 0-0000-0000-0

0 00000 000000

Example only. Each book has unique ISBN.

No purchase necessary. Void where prohibited. Open only to residents of the 50 United States (includes District of Columbia) and Canada (void in Quebec). For official rules and entry dates see:

www.microsoft.com/learning/booksurvey/